GOOD SMALL BUSINESS GUIDE

How to start and grow your own business

Second edition

A & C Black • London

First published in Great Britain 2003
Reprinted 2003, 2004
This second edition published 2005

A & C Black Publishers Ltd
38 Soho Square, London W1D 3HB

© Bloomsbury Publishing Plc 2003
© A & C Black Publishers Ltd 2005

British Library Cataloguing in Publication Data
A CIP record for this book is available from the British Library.

ISBN-10: 0–7136–7501–2
ISBN-13: 978–0–7136–7501–6

A & C Black uses paper produced with elemental chlorine-free pulp,
harvested from managed sustainable forests.

Design by Fiona Pike, Pike Design, Winchester
Typeset by RefineCatch Limited, Bungay, Suffolk
Printed in Great Britain by William Clowes Ltd, Beccles, Suffolk

CONTENTS

Marketing Your Idea

Working with Customers

Communicating with Your Customers

Growing Your Business

Working Online

Selling Online

Managing Yourself and Others

Retreating with Dignity

ESSENTIAL INFORMATION DIRECTORY

A Note to the User

This new edition of the *Good Small Business Guide* is aimed at anyone thinking of starting or growing a business in the United Kingdom. Designed for readers to dip into as and when they need practical help on a range of issues, the *Guide* contains advice on:

- planning
- setting up or acquiring a business
- getting to grips with the figures
- finding premises
- marketing your idea
- working with customers
- communicating with customers
- growing your business
- working and selling online
- managing yourself and others
- dignified retreats

All of the above topics are covered in over 160 easy-to-read actionlists, which appear in the following format:

Getting Started—an overview of the main points addressed in the actionlist
FAQs—a series of frequently asked questions on the topic
Making It Happen—fuss-free advice on how to achieve your goal
What to Avoid—tips on how to avoid common mistakes
Recommended Links—a selection of the very best websites to help you investigate the topic further

Not everyone who wants to set up their own company will necessarily have business experience, so this book explains all you need to know in jargon-free language. Its contents take you from the beginning of developing your idea right the way through to steps to help your business expand successfully. For more in-depth comment and advice on some key topics, look at the 'Focus On' series of actionlists, for example pp. 452–54). These articles have been written by some of the world's leading business writers, including Meredith Belbin and Al Ries, and bring together their considerable experience.

This book also contains the **Essential Information Directory** (pp. 486–554). This section covers 30 key topics of interest to anyone in business, and offers carefully chosen information on the most helpful books, organisations, and a wider selection of Internet sites.

The **Essential Information Directory** is also available free online to all subscribers to **www.ultimatebusinessresource.com**. All links are live, so you can click straight through to the site you're interested in. To subscribe, please go to:

www.ultimatebusinessresource.com/register, type in your e-mail address and key in your password: **smallbiz2**

Finally, turn to our 'Viewpoints' section in the centre of the book to read about the experiences of other people running and growing small businesses.

Contributors

Meredith Belbin is the author of several successful business books, including the European bestseller *Management Teams: Why They Succeed or Fail* (2nd ed, Butterworth-Heinemann, 2003) and *Team Roles at Work*. He has acted as a consultant to the European Commission and the OECD as well as many manufacturing companies and service organisations.

Patrick Forsyth runs Touchstone Training and Consultancy, an independent firm specialising in marketing, sales, and communication skills. He writes extensively on matters of marketing and management and is the author of a number of successful books, including *Marketing Stripped Bare* (Kogan Page, 2003.)

Tim Hindle is a former business features editor of *The Economist*. He is the author and editor of many books including *Guide to Management Ideas* (Profile Books, 2002) and *Essential Manager's Manual* (Dorling Kindersley, 1998; co-edited with Robert Heller).

Max Landsberg is the author of *The Tao of Coaching* and *The Tao of Motivation* (both rev eds, Profile Books, 2003).

Malcolm McDonald is Emeritus professor of marketing at Cranfield School of Management. He has written or co-written more than 30 books, including the best seller *Marketing Plans: How to Prepare Them, How to Use Them* (5th ed, Butterworth-Heinemann, 2002).

Al Ries and Laura Ries are the best-selling authors of *The 22 Immutable Laws of Branding* (Profile Business, 2000) and *The Origin of Brands* (Harper Business, 2005).

Philip Sadler is the former chief executive of Ashridge Management College, one of the world's leading business schools. He has also written several books, including *The Seamless Organization* (Kogan Page, 2000).

Introduction by Richard Reed

The best advice I can give anyone wanting to set up their own business is to stop reading this introduction. There is nothing I can tell you that is going to help your business more than putting this book down and ringing that potential supplier, finishing off the business plan, or improving your designs for a range of elasticated trousers for fat blokes. The success you have in your business will be in direct proportion to the amount of focus and energy you put into it. Every single second counts.

I am conscious of this fact as I sit here writing this paragraph. I should be at Fruit Towers (our head office) making our next smoothie recipe taste better or doing something for one of our customers. Or at least unblocking the toilet (the gents in unit 3 can be a bit temperamental). But that is my weakness, I am a complete sucker when it comes to a bit of free publicity.

But seeing as you're still here and the toilet remains blocked, allow me to pass on a few more thoughts regarding setting up your own business. The first of these is that you can definitely do it. Anyone can. Business is an inherently simple endeavour, and anyone who tells you otherwise hasn't experienced life when it gets complicated. If you have ever organised a wedding, a party, or moved house, you can run a business. Setting up a company is ultimately an exercise in project management; you have to get a group of people to do a series of things to a set of deadlines within a fixed cost. It's simple.

Obviously, though, to be successful at business you have to be exceptionally charismatic, attractive, rich, well educated and most of all be an incredible lover. Or so a lot of people make the mistake of thinking. Actually, to be good at business you have to just realise that everyone else is scared too, and the only difference between those that succeed and those that don't is that the successful think, 'I'm scared, but sod it, I'll give it a go anyway.'

None of this, of course, should be used to gloss over the fact that is essential you do your homework; find out everything you can about your consumers, market and competitors; don't stop until you have developed a product or service that is meaningfully better than the rest; and make sure that your business works financially—that you can sell things at a higher price than you buy them at. Weirdly, a lot of people miss this one, which is sort of fundamental, if you know what I mean.

But don't be afraid to start small. Every big business was small once. We're not exactly massive but we're doing OK, and we sold our first smoothies from a market stall at a music festival. We still had our regular jobs at the time and were nervous about giving them up. So we put up a big sign above our stall saying 'Should we give up our jobs to make these smoothies?' and put out a bin saying 'YES' and a bin saying 'NO'. We asked people to put their empty bottle in the appropriate bin, and at the end of the weekend the 'YES' bin was full so we went into work the next day and resigned. We've never looked back since.

And bear in mind, there is one thing that accounts for any successful company, and that is people. If you think about it, every single thing a company achieves is the result of a person doing or not doing something, of caring or not caring, or wanting to make something better or not bothering. It follows therefore that the more you surround yourself with brilliant, talented, motivated people, who share your values and goals, the more chance you have of creating success. So do everything you can to build the best possible team to help you.

The final thought I'd leave with you is that a business as well as being a commercial entity, will always be an agent of social change too. Everything you do, every bit of your business system, will have an impact on the world around you, be it the way you source your raw materials, the way you dispose of your waste products, the way you treat the people you come across. So I urge you to do what you can to try and make those impacts positive—to show that you can profit from having a business that takes its responsibilities seriously, treads lightly, and tries to leaves things a little bit better than it finds them. That may sound a bit trite, but that doesn't stop it from being a good thing to aim for.

Good luck.

Richard Reed
Co-founder, innocent drinks
www.innocentdrinks.co.uk

Foreword
Ten Myths About Small Businesses
by Tim Hindle

Few things are more exciting than starting a new business, and few things are more satisfying than making one work, so it is not surprising that so many people give it a go. There are more than two and a half million small businesses in Britain today. Lots of them are corner shops with no great ambitions to expand. But at least as many are run by people with seemingly impossible dreams.

Small businesses account for a big chunk of the economy. According to the Federation of Small Businesses, 12 million people in the United Kingdom work in small firms (ie, businesses with fewer than 50 employees). These same companies account for 50% of the private sector workforce in the country, and more than 50% of the GDP. They may be small individually, but they are quite large collectively.

Sadly, this huge body of businesses does not stay the same from one year to the next. There is a steady turnover: approximately 400,000 new companies open every year in Britain, and about the same number close down. In times of recession this balance changes. At the worst time in 1992, for instance, almost twice as many companies were closing down as were opening up. Even in the best of times, only about 50% of new businesses survive for more than four years; 10% disappear within 12 months, and very few make their owners seriously wealthy.

Making lots of money, however, is only part of the dream. There are many other reasons why people start new businesses, as you'll see in the Viewpoints section in the centre of the book.

High on the list is the idea of being your own boss, of pleasing yourself as to where and how you spend your working day. But here we come across one of the many myths about small businesses. The truth is that anyone starting their own company is unlikely to be able to dictate how they spend their working day. The founders of most small businesses are in a constant whirl of activity. Naturally busy when there is lots of business, they are even busier when there is none. For then they are eagerly looking around for new markets and for new customers. They can rarely relax, in good times as well as bad.

It may be worth looking at a few more of these myths. The rest of this book contains a wealth of sound advice on how to do what and when. However, on the principle that to be forewarned is to be forearmed, before you get stuck into the hows, whats, and whens, here are the rest of my top ten myths about running a small business:

Myth number two. You can make your fortune by the time you are 40 and then move on to what you really want to do—play golf or ride horses. For the vast majority of us, enough is never enough. Bill Gates founded Microsoft and made it into the biggest company in the world. But he has not yet let go of the reins.

The drive to get bigger and bigger in business is hard to resist. For a start, growth is an in-built assumption in 99.9% of all business plans. 'Small is beautiful', they say. But most small businessmen behave as if they think the famous title of E. F. Schumacher's book is propaganda put out by their bigger rivals to keep them in their place. If golf and horses are your true passions, then open a stables or a golf club. That way you can indulge in your passion both before and after your 40th birthday.

Myth number three. Everyone loves a small business entrepreneur and is out to help them. At best, this is a short-lived phenomenon; hot-blooded competition soon comes into play. Competitors will want to make life as hard as possible for you from the very beginning. As the animal kingdom shows us, the young and inexperienced are the most vulnerable. Moreover, every unemployable youth with the slightest trace of your DNA will claim the right to a job in your organisation, while Uncle Henry, 20 years on the board of MegaCorp PLC, will continue to exchange no more than a dozen words with you every Christmas.

Banks are much more helpful than they used to be. In the early 1980s, one budding entrepreneur was crisply told by his bank manager, 'We are not a charity'. Today the problem is finding a bank manager that has the time to talk to small businesses at all. Banks will try to encourage you to do business with them impersonally—over the Internet or the phone.

Myth number four. It takes a certain type to be a successful entrepreneur. This is, of course, not true. Successful entrepreneurs range from the Alexander the Great 'type' to the Jane Austen 'type'. There is no one type of personality best suited to starting a small business. I defy anyone to find a common trait in the people described in our case studies.

The only thing that can be said about successful entrepreneurs is that they rarely emerge from among the most academically brilliant pupils at school; very few successful small businesses have been started by people who got a first-class degree from Oxford or Cambridge. You don't need a Harvard MBA (or even a degree) to start a business. Richard Branson is an outstanding example of a successful entrepreneur who never went to a university.

Myth number five. I only need one big, well-known customer and I'm made. This has been known as the Marks & Spencer myth. But it is very dangerous to become too dependent on one customer—just imagine what happens if you lose them. What's more, someone the size of Marks & Spencer is likely to be so demanding on your limited resources that you are going to find it hard to cultivate other significant customers at the same time.

Moreover, as a general rule, the bigger the firm, the slower they pay. Big firms have systems that grind exceedingly slow. Despite recent legislation that gives businesses a statutory right to claim interest and compensation on overdue commercial debts, big firms well know that you are unlikely to sue if they are a bit late in their payment.

Myth number six. There is nothing more valuable than a satisfied customer. This needs some modification. Customers come in all shapes and sizes, and they can be a real pain in the neck. Horror stories abound. The travel industry, for example, has an unusually high number of small businesses, and small tour operators almost invariably receive demands from returning holidaymakers for a free holiday next year, 'because the spaghetti was cold/the bed was too narrow/the buses were late'. Some seem to have spent half their time on the beach composing their letters of complaint. There are customers who can never be satisfied. Identify them as fast as you can, then let them go.

Myth number seven. I can leave all the figures to my accountant. Be warned: if you're no good at maths, you need to find someone who is vaguely numerate to join you at an early stage. Small businesses need to be on top of their numbers all the time. The cash flow, the sales figures, the prices of competitors' products—they're changing all the time, and their latest lurch could presage disaster for your business. You need to turn your brain into a sort of living Excel spreadsheet. In any case, if things go wrong and the taxman starts getting excessively curious about your returns, it is no excuse to say that you left it all to your accountant because sums were never your strong point.

Myth number eight. You are going to share responsibilities across the board with a partner. If you think you are going to be Hewlett and Packard, forget it. For every one of them there's 50 partnerships that fall out before they're 12 months old. Don't assume your small business can manage with more than one boss. Do climbers reach the summit of Everest as members of an egalitarian co-operative? No, they don't. Be sure in yourself that you can carry on alone if you need to.

Myth number nine. Export or die. For a lot of businesses, it has been a case of 'export *and* die'. Exporting can be very difficult. The paperwork involved is often daunting, even within the EU. But, more importantly, if you're having difficulty getting domestic customers to pay on time, imagine what it's like trying to extract payment from a small customer in, say, Sicily. The average payment period for an Italian customer is 80 days—in the United Kingdom it's 43 days. (Incidentally, the best payers, statistically, are the Russians, where the average is 24 days. But before you catch the next plane to Moscow, remember that is only because there is very little trust among businessmen there—much of the Russian economy is run on a cash basis.)

Myth number ten. To start a successful new business you need cutting-edge technology or a big new idea. Not true. Look at the 2004 winner of the FSB's Small Business Champion of the Year Award. Noel Chadwick Ltd is a family-run butcher's shop and food emporium. And another point to note: the business is not based the throbbing south-east of England nor in Britain's version of silicon valley along the banks of the M4, but in Wigan, Lancashire.

This is not to say that the best small businesses hang around in the backwoods and ignore new technology altogether. There are plenty of software tools that can help make a one-man band seem like an orchestra. And the Internet is an encyclopedia and a DIY manual all at the same time. More than a third of UK small businesses say that they use the Internet daily as a source of business advice.

This book is similarly designed for dipping into daily and one section, the Essential Information Directory, is available online at *www.ultimatebusinessresource. com*. Go to the sections that cover issues you are having to face today or in the near future, and we hope that you will find there some help and some comfort.

The very best of luck to everyone who is trying to build a small business. It is not easy, as these myths have probably demonstrated, but it is extraordinarily invigorating—far more so than playing golf!

Tim Hindle

Assess Yourself

The fact that you're reading this now means that you must be pretty serious about setting up your own business. You've got an idea, you've done some research, and you've picked up this book in search of some sound advice about how to take it to the next level and beyond. Or perhaps you're already on your way and are looking to hone your entrepreneurial skills, plug any gaps in your knowledge, and shore up your business acumen with some expert guidance. Either way, you have already shown that you have one of the key attributes belonging to the entrepreneurial mindset: you are willing to question yourself to take stock of what you do know and then deal with what you don't. You are here because you want to know the answer to two big questions: 'can I do it?' and then, 'how do I do it?'.

Here are some more questions to guide you towards those answers. This quick quiz is designed to help you assess your strengths and weaknesses, and in so doing, point you to the pages within this book that will be most useful to you.

YOU

Would you describe yourself as an 'ideas person'?
a) Yes—I always have a list of ideas that I am thinking about.
b) I have the odd flash of inspiration, but don't tend to dwell on it.
c) Not really—I don't like to be distracted from the job in hand.

How often do you talk to friends and family about your new ideas?
a) Regularly.
b) From time to time, when something particularly interests me.
c) Never

How do you think your friends and family would react if you were to start your own business?
a) Positively—from the evidence of my past successes they will feel confident in my business abilities.
b) Apprehensively—I've talked about setting up on my own a lot but haven't ever done anything about it.
c) Negatively—I've never mentioned it before, so it will come as a complete surprise.

How persistent are you?
a) I'm ready to try many new approaches until I have a successful outcome.
b) I keep trying, but I do get discouraged.
c) I'm easily discouraged, and don't like to feel I'm 'pestering' people.

How do you enjoy working with people?
a) Very much—I like to get to know as many people as possible.
b) I enjoy spending time with certain people, but don't make an effort with everyone.
c) I prefer to work alone and concentrate on doing my job.

How do you feel about taking risks?
a) I thrive on risk-taking—I find it exciting and stimulating.
b) I will take the odd risk, but on the whole prefer to be confident about the outcome of my actions.
c) I dislike not knowing what will come of the choices I make—I don't take risks.

How many of the following attributes do you consider yourself to have: dedication, persistence, drive, stamina, intuition, courage, positive outlook, good communication skills, good 'people' skills, ambition, pragmatism, adaptability, financial savvy, energy, self-awareness?
a) 11–15
b) 6–10
c) 1–5

If you answered mostly **a**, you're already in an entrepreneurial mindset. The next stage is to take time working on your business idea and researching your target market. This book's **Refining and Protecting Your Idea** (pp. 18–38) section will help you do that.

If you answered mostly **b**, you're part of the way there. If you answered mostly **c**, you may not be sure that being your own boss is really for you. The **Planning** section (pp. 2–16) will give you some key pointers on evaluating your idea, yourself, and your current circumstances.

Whether you answered **a**, **b**, or **c**, read the **Viewpoints** between pp. 270–71 to find out how other entrepreneurs started their own businesses.

YOUR IDEA

Can you explain your business idea succinctly?
a) Yes, I can get the basics across in a sentence.
b) Yes. A paragraph should do it.
c) Not really. I need a five-page document to explain it.

How clear are you about your target market?
a) I've done a lot of research and I know exactly the group I am aiming at.
b) I have a fair idea of who will use my product/service.
c) Not very, but it's such a good idea I just know it will appeal to a lot of people.

How do you rate research?
a) Essential.
b) Useful.
c) An unnecessary extra cost.

Are you ready to take on board other people's comments?
a) Absolutely. It will be good to get some feedback and I'll adjust my plans accordingly.
b) I'll bear in mind any feedback, but I'd be reluctant to change to change my plans.
c) No. I don't want to compromise my idea.

Whatever your area of interest of area or expertise, thorough market research is essential when you're thinking about starting your own business. If you answered mostly **a**, you're aware of this already. The **Marketing Your Idea** section (pp. 208–223) will help you take your idea further.

If you answered mostly **b**, this section will be helpful to you too, but also look at pp. 11–13 in the **Planning** section (Coming Up with a Business Idea) to reinforce the importance of research. Read this too if you answered mostly **c**. Research in the early stages of your business is well worth the time and money you'll spend on it.

YOUR FINANCES

How do you handle your personal finances?
a) Well. I'm rarely in debt.
b) I take some risks, but I'm not often out of my depth.
c) I'm often in debt for prolonged periods.

How do you view your business or your business idea?
a) As a long-term source of income.
b) As an investment, to sell as soon as possible for a profit.
c) As a way of escaping my current job.

How well can you cope with financial matters?
a) I have quite a lot of experience and am confident when working with figures.
b) I have some experience, but some terms confuse me.
c) I don't know where to start.

Have you considered how you will cover yourself financially if things go wrong?
a) I have set aside a financial 'bumper' to allow for unforeseen expenses.
b) I have planned my expenditure and

income very carefully and do not
envisage any problems.
c) I'm banking on things not going wrong.

If you answered mostly **a**, you are already
financially aware and have realised that
you'll need some funds for a 'rainy day'.
The **Figuring It Out** section (pp. 108–205)
offers advice on a wide range of funding
issues, from understanding budgets to
applying for funding from various sources.

The **financial ratios** (pp. 163–205) will be
particularly helpful if you are going to be
doing the book-keeping for your business.

If you answered mostly **b** or **c**, you have
some financial knowledge but need a bit
more support. **Figuring It Out** will also be
helpful to you as it explains many key issues
without using jargon. **The Essential
Information Directory** (pp. 486–554) also
contains the best sources of help for you if
you want to research further.

YOU AND OTHERS

How do you react to advice or complaints?
a) I see negative feedback as an opportunity
to change plans and ideas for the better. I
believe in being proactive.
b) I do listen to and remember complaints
and advice, but don't tend to act
c) I prefer to follow my own plans, and don't
like others to interfere—no-one knows my
business like I do.

**How do you rate your people-management
skills?**
a) I think they're good. I can usually sense
how people are feeling and react
appropriately.
b) They're not too bad. I generally get on
well with most people, but I feel I lose touch
from time to time
c) They could be better. I often find it hard
to connect with others.

**You'll have many demands on your time
when you're setting up or growing your
business. How do organise what you need to
do?**
a) I'm prioritise tasks and build in extra time
if I can.
b) I get through everything in the end, but I
tend to underestimate how long things will
take.
c) I work all night if I have to.

**Pressure affects everyone who works,
whatever their job, but you're the boss it can
seem overwhelming at times. Can you deal
with pressure?**
a) Yes, I can recognise the signs and try to
keep things in perspective.
b) I thrive on stress, but my partner doesn't
so that can lead to extra tension.
c) Sometimes, but I find it hard to say 'no'.

Once your company is up and running,
you'll need to develop or gain management
skills to get the best from yourself and your
team if you employ others. Stress can also
put a strain on personal and business
relationships, which can make challenges
harder to deal with.

If you answered mostly **a**, you have a
good appreciation of what makes yourself
and others tick. The **Focus On . . .** articles
on pp. 449–454 of the **Managing Yourself
and Others** section will help you develop
the skills you have already.

If you answered mostly **b** or **c**, the
Managing Your Time (pp. 406–408),
Managing Pressure (pp. 409–411), and
Delegating (pp. 412–14) actionlists in this
section will help you manage your day
better.

If you answered **c** more than **b**, the
Essential Information Directory
(pp. 486–554) will offer you further support.

Acknowledgments

We would like to thank the following people for their help during the compilation of the first and second editions of this book:

Cobweb Information Ltd
Catherine Gough
Tim Hindle
Philip Holden,University of Greenwich
Martha Lane Fox and lastminute.com
Ian Linton
Hughie Naughton
Richard Reed and innocent ltd
Richard Scriven
Kate Stenner
Nicky Thompson

The following articles are © Cobweb Information Ltd 2005 (www.cobwebinfo.com):

A Guide to Business Regulations When Starting Up
A Guide to Health and Safety at Work
An Introduction to Intellectual Property
Applying for a Patent
Buying a Business Property
Choosing and Using an Architect
Complying with Fire Safety Regulations
Complying with the Copyright of Others
Coping in a Cashflow Crisis
Deciding to Move On
Delegating
Developing and Protecting an Invention
Employing People with Disabilities
Ergonomics at Work
Export Documentation
Exporting for the First Time
Exporting—Methods of Market Entry
Financing a New Business
Implementing Job Share Arrangements
Franchising Your Business
Setting Up Job Shares
Importing for the First Time
Insuring a Business

Benefiting from Apprenticeships
Obtaining Planning Permission
Planning Staff Needs
Registering a Trademark
Renting a Business Property
Running a Family Business
Selling by Mail Order
Setting Up a Business As a Non-profit Organisation
Setting Up a Business As a Private Limited Company
Setting Up a Franchise
Setting Up a Payroll
Starting a Business Under the Age of 18
Succession Planning
Taking the Decision to Diversify
Telemarketing
Understanding Building Regulations
Understanding the Minimum Wage
Understanding the Pros and Cons of Mail-Order
Using Copyright to Protect Your Work
Working Time Regulations 1998
Writing a Sales Letter

Business Information Sources © Chartered Management Institute 2005

ACTIONLISTS: PLANNING

Deciding Whether to Start a Business

GETTING STARTED

Setting up your own business can be very rewarding, but there are pressures involved. It's not enough just to have a good, viable idea: you also need to have the right skills and temperament to make the opportunity succeed. Starting your own business is also a risky thing to do, so you need to be aware of what problems to look out for as early as possible. This will help you decide if you are willing and able to take those risks, and will also help you to apply strategies that will reduce them.

Before you go any further, it's important to find out as much as you can about what sort of person you are. Be honest and objective, and discuss the project with friends, colleagues and relatives. Think about how you have dealt with past challenges, as an indication of your response to difficult new situations. This actionlist will help you to decide whether starting a business is the right thing for you to do.

FAQS

Do I have the right personality to start a business?

While the technical aspects of your business will require specific qualifications, skills, or experience, there are broader demands that are as important. These could include the ability to negotiate with suppliers, mediate between staff, be sociable with customers, be convincing with prospects, think clearly under pressure, take criticism, portray confidence, and use your time effectively.

There is no single type of self-employed person, but experience has shown that there are some characteristics which successful self-employed people often have in common. They tend to be logical, perceptive, organised, and responsible. They are usually extrovert and confident, and able to communicate and get their point across. They are also often sociable, with the ability to lead. Self-employed people are generally single-minded, but able to take advice. They are flexible and adaptable, quick to take opportunities, and ready to take risks. They tend to be tough-skinned, and able to handle failure. They are usually creative and imaginative, always coming up with new ideas for the business, and also hard working, committed, and determined. Finally, they are often individualists, who are not afraid to stand out from the crowd.

Are older people more successful at running a business?

There is no doubt that it helps to have some experience in the workplace, and it's even more useful to have it in the sector in which you want to start a business. Surveys reveal that many successful businesses have been started by people in their 30s who have some management experience. People over the age of 50 (sometimes called 'third-age entrepreneurs') are also responsible for many business start-ups and many think about a change of direction after taking early retirement. Having said that, a wide range of people have established their own businesses successfully and have much to offer. For example, young people have fewer domestic commitments, plenty of energy, new ideas, and the potential to develop and adapt to the challenges of self-employment.

What kinds of skills will I need?

You will almost certainly need technical skills. If you have qualifications relevant to your business activity this will obviously be helpful. Customers, and anyone lending your business money, will be more comfortable if you have the right qualifications. Additionally, certain businesses require exceptional ability, for example design skills, artistic skills, or technical skills.

Business skills are a huge advantage. It is

important to understand the principles of business and management, including marketing, strategic planning, accounts, personnel management, and so on. Ideally, you should aim to get some basic training in business administration before you start. If this is not possible (and many people do not have the time or money initially), then read as much as you can to fill the gaps in your knowledge. Leadership skills are important, too. If you expect the business to grow, you will inevitably have to employ people, and the ability to show leadership and to manage people will be critical.

All businesses require an element of selling, and you'll need to develop skills in this area if you do not already possess them. Initially it is important to persuade people to support you, and crucial to be able to win over potential customers. It is possible to learn basic selling techniques, but being outgoing and articulate is equally important. Your organisational skills will also be essential to the success of your business. To generate sufficient income, small businesses must be well organised and efficient. It is important that you can organise yourself and others, plan ahead, and manage your time. You also need to have the discipline to set and meet deadlines. Try to think laterally about how many of these skills you have, and don't be put off too easily. Starting a business is challenging, yes, but think about the skills you use in everyday life and how you could apply them to a different context. For example, if you are a woman with a family, or one who has juggled full- or part-time work with family life, think about how you have developed your time management skills, probably without even noticing it.

MAKING IT HAPPEN
Assess your abilities and resources

Starting your own business is a risky thing to do, so you should get to grips with the various risks as early as possible. This will help you decide if you are willing and able to take those risks. It will also help you to apply strategies that will reduce the risk.

You need to ask yourself several ques-tions. Do you have the financial resources, and can you afford to risk them? For example, you might take a secured loan based on the value of your home; what are your plans if the business fails and you are forced to sell your house? Do you have sufficient experience and technical skills to perform the core functions of your new business? Are you familiar enough with the market to be able to assess its needs and adapt to its changes? Do you have the tenacity and discipline to see through hard times when cash will be short and demands will be heavy (from customers, bankers, staff, and, crucially, your family)?

While you might not be able to answer all these questions completely, it really is important to find out as much as you can about what sort of person you are, and to do that you must be honest and objective. Discuss the project with friends, colleagues, and relations. Think about how you have dealt with past challenges, as an indication of your response to difficult new situations.

Look at your motives

Why *do* you want to start your own business? There are many good reasons, but there is often the danger of having unrealistic expectations. Here are some reasons that people often give, and some notes of caution:

- **independence.** Yes, it can be a pain working for someone else, but you still need to be disciplined and able to get on with others when you work for yourself.
- **greater job satisfaction.** Self-employment allows you to do the job in your own way, and it is very satisfying when your way is shown to work. You do, of course, also have to take responsibility for your way when it *doesn't* work, as is bound to happen at some point.
- **achievement and success.** There can be some cachet attached to the idea of running your own business, but make sure that you are not trying to prove that you're something you're not. If the venture failed, would you be able to deal with it?
- **more money.** While the thought of being better off financially is naturally attractive,

doing it for the money is not usually a good enough motive in itself, and greater wealth is by no means guaranteed. In particular, beware of starting a business when you have no other choice—you'll be putting yourself under even more pressure. If you do go down this route, though, try be pragmatic about what you can achieve as well as positive.

Assess your skills

Assessing your skills is a useful process as it will help you identify areas in which you need training. These in turn will contribute towards your chances of being successful in business. There are many sources of training available to small businesses, and several courses are run by local colleges and universities. The addresses of specialist training providers can be found in the *Yellow Pages* under 'Training Services'. Also bear in mind Trade Associations and Sector Skills Councils—they may run industry-specific courses.

Advice on, and assistance with, training is available from local Learning and Skills Councils (LSCs) in England, Education and Learning Wales (ELWa), Local Enterprise Companies (LECs) in Scotland (contact Highlands and Islands Enterprise, website address below, if you live in Northern Scotland) and the Department for Employment and Learning (DEL) in Northern Ireland. Many of these organisations will also be able to provide details of any loans and financial assistance available to help with training for small businesses, such as the Small Firms Training Loan run by the Department for Education and Skills.

Business Links (Business Gateways in Scotland, Business Eye in Wales, Invest Northern Ireland), Chambers of Commerce and Enterprise Agencies will often run business courses and provide information on training providers.

Be prepared for the pressures

The pressures of being self-employed are inescapable. You may have to work long hours, and there will be times when things get on top of you. You may well get into debt in order to finance the enterprise. You will need to maintain your faith in your business, often in the face of other people's doubts.

There will be some days when you feel lonely and isolated. If you employ people, you will need to be positive and show leadership all the time. There will be some days when you need to be tough and prepared to discipline difficult employees, or make difficult demands of your suppliers. You need to be polite and helpful, even when an awkward customer is giving you a hard time.

Many of those who successfully start their own business have the backing of their family. You will be under pressure, working long hours. Your family must be prepared for the impact this can have on family life. Also, you must be sure that your family can accommodate the risks that self-employment can bring, especially in terms of lower income in the initial stages, and maybe even the implications of the business failing. Take time to talk to all members of your family who might be affected by your choice to be your own boss.

WHAT TO AVOID
Assuming that being your own boss is easy

Everyone at some point has come across a boss who makes his or her life difficult, but don't assume that working for yourself will be all plain sailing. There are many benefits, to be sure, but you have to get used to the idea that the buck stops with you. Make sure you're ready take on that responsibility.

Doing it for the wrong reasons

As noted above, don't do it for the money alone. Weigh up the pros and cons of your idea and the impact that starting a business will have on all areas of your life. It will take a lot of effort, but you *can* do it—read on to find out how.

RECOMMENDED LINKS
Business Eye (Wales):
www.businesseye.org.uk
Business Gateway (Scotland):
www.bgateway.com

Business Link (England):
www.businesslink.gov.uk
Department for Education and Skills:
www.dfes.gov.uk
Highlands and Islands Enterprise:
www.hie.co.uk
Invest Northern Ireland:
www.investni.com
Learndirect:
www.learndirect.co.uk

Sector Skills Development Agency:
www.ssda.org.uk

SEE ALSO
**Assessing Your Entrepreneurial Profile:
Do You Have What It Takes? (p. 6)
Coming Up with a Business Idea (p. 11)
Entrepreneurs (p. 511)
Small and Growing Businesses (p. 486)
Understanding Business Models (p. 42)**

Assessing Your Entrepreneurial Profile: Do You Have What It Takes?

GETTING STARTED

Once you've started thinking about setting up a business, you need to consider your own role in it. Are you the right type of person to make a success of a new venture? There's a great deal of romance surrounding the notion of being an entrepreneur, but not everyone has the aptitude. And it's important to understand that there's nothing wrong with *not* being an entrepreneur. The world wouldn't function half as well if it were peopled solely with them.

There are, though, some general personality traits that are essential for entrepreneurs. If the following list seems to fit your personality, you may have what it takes:

- I am persistent, with a great deal of drive and stamina. I see problems as opportunities. I have a good intuitive sense and thrive on new ideas.
- I tend to rebel against authority. I want to be my own boss.
- I am positive, communicate well, and enjoy working with people.
- I have a strong need to succeed, financially and otherwise.
- I'm not afraid to make mistakes, and I learn from them.

FAQS

How can I be sure I've got what it takes?

Before leaving your job and dipping into your savings to start a business, you owe it to yourself to approach your entrepreneurial venture with some practicality. Take a more in-depth personality test and talk to small business advisers, who are often available at no cost through business associations. Also try to speak to people in business already as they'll be able to give you a no-holds-barred account of what day-to-day life is like as an entrepreneur.

How much money will I need?

Whether you want to buy an existing business, purchase a franchise, start your own company, or merely offer services to others from a home office, starting a business depends on first knowing the numbers. People in the same or similar businesses are a good source of information—use your ingenuity to find out what it cost them to get started, and where they got the funds to do so. Be tactful and don't pester someone with questions if it's clear that he or she doesn't want to disclose this information to you, though. Other sources include trade associations, franchise organisations, business articles in magazines and newspapers, Internet research, or business consultants.

Besides being an ideas person, what else do I need to be good at?

Success in a new enterprise depends on dedication and the consistent application of good business principles. Some of these principles include: being good with money; being good with people (investors, suppliers, employees, and so on); being a good promoter (marketing, sales, PR); and being good to yourself. Many entrepreneurs burn out before their businesses take hold. In this game, pacing yourself and your business is important.

MAKING IT HAPPEN

Check that you have the right idea

If you've got a great new idea and no competition in sight, you must be sure that the product or service will be of value to customers—at a price at which you can afford to sell it. There may be no competition for a very good reason. . . If your aim is to enter a field with established competitors, you have to know your own strengths and weaknesses, as well as those of your competition. Be sure that you can provide a better product or service for a competitive price. Finding out all these things is called 'market research', and you'll have to do a thorough job of it to succeed.

Develop a detailed, professional business plan

This is the key to building a successful business. Having a well-considered and systematic plan allows you to recognise problems as they arise in time to be able to take corrective action. The plan should be a living document, flexible over time to adapt to changes in the marketplace and your industry. It should include sections on every facet of your business—whether you're a sole proprietor or the executive director of a new manufacturing venture.

Get financial backing for your idea

Take your ideas and business plan to a variety of people, starting with friends and close supporters. Be prepared for critical feedback, and be flexible. Take the inevitable first few comments of 'no thanks' as opportunities to fine-tune the next presentation. One of the hallmarks of an entrepreneur is the ability to regroup, rethink, and reach a goal in another way.

Seeking publicity for your business is a way not only to notify potential customers but also to get the attention of possible investors. The more people who know about your idea, the better the chances that you'll attract the right investor.

Be willing to share a portion of the company with the right partners, but be wary of finance companies and investors who want full control, or the lion's share of the proceeds. You could also think about entering into a joint venture with another company, or position your company to attract start-up funds from government sources.

Practise your networking

Being entrepreneurial doesn't mean being a lone ranger. Being successful often depends on your ability to network with potential customers, suppliers, new investors, and even those in government who control certain aspects of the business environment.

Plan your marketing and PR

An integral part of your business plan involves a marketing plan—how you intend to create the demand for your product or service. While market research tells you the 'what' and 'where' of your opportunities, the marketing plan outlines the steps by which you will find potential customers and convince them to buy from you. Networking, advertising, and PR (public relations) are all forms of marketing and promotion.

Make sure you have the right financial and management support

Most entrepreneurs are better at ideas than at managing budgets, business operations, and employees. Anticipate that you'll need more capital than you reckoned on at the start, and don't be lavish with spending beyond the company's means. If you find yourself in a questionable position, make sure you have a network of trusted and experienced advisers to help you see the proper perspective and cover the things you are not naturally good at.

WHAT TO AVOID
Setting up equal partnerships

Entrepreneurs often share the start-up responsibilities with a partner or partners. However, sharing 50–50 or by thirds or quarters is a big mistake, because conflicts will inevitably arise and need someone in a controlling position to make a final decision. Choose (or employ) a CEO—someone with the experience and skills needed for success—and give that person a greater decision-making authority and a bigger salary, even if it is only bigger by a small margin.

Having inadequate people and planning

Entrepreneurs must become strong managers when the company gets going. Many businesses fail because the people in charge don't have the managerial qualities or strength to cope with the challenges. In addition, stress can put a strain on personal relationships and this can make the challenges harder to deal with. Personality assessments can determine if you're cut out for a managerial position, and managerial training can prepare you for your new role as an executive.

Without proper market research and a solid business plan, a business is more likely to fail. The more preparation you do, the better your chances of success.

Relying too heavily on one or two customers

Having too few customers makes your business vulnerable, because it ties your future to the decisions of other organisations. If their business falters, it puts your hard work and dedication at risk, through no fault of your own. The advice of personal financial consultants is appropriate here. Having lots of customers, even though none of them are gigantic, is healthier in the long run.

Causing cash-flow troubles through insufficient financing

While some people are successful at jump-starting their own enterprise with little or no outside investment, they do so by being fortunate, being modest in their spending, and by ploughing profits back into the business.

The majority of businesses, however, don't deliver the projected first-year sales volume. It's better to overestimate your need for capital resources at the beginning and to underestimate your projected sales figures. It's preferable to be pleasantly surprised at your success than to lose the business and your house because the money isn't there when it's needed.

When contemplating an expansion of your business, be wary of spiralling costs. If you're in a cyclical business, or one vulnerable to recession, be sure to be very calculating about your expenses—and develop 'Plan B' well before you need to implement it.

Failing to admit mistakes

Entrepreneurs are sometimes the last to admit that their idea hasn't the sparkle it once had. Having advisers that you trust is important—either on staff or on contract. Be willing to cut your losses and move on if your advisers all agree that you should. Doing so may save the company, if you can move quickly enough to capitalise on your mistakes, or shift the product or service to take advantage of other opportunities.

Underestimating the competition

Your competition won't stand still for long, once you've demonstrated their weakness in the marketplace with your product or service. Expect them to plug the hole quickly and even try to outflank you in the process. Your business and marketing plans should anticipate how to deal with new initiatives from your competition. If you conduct ongoing research, product and service evaluations, and marketing campaigns, you should always be one step ahead of the competition.

RECOMMENDED LINKS

The Entrepreneurship Programme:
www.entrepreneur.co.uk
iVillage.co.uk:
www.ivillage.co.uk/workcareer
UK Business Incubation:
www.ukbi.co.uk

SEE ALSO

Assessing Your Entrepreneurial Profile: Do You Have What It Takes? (p. 6)
Coming Up with a Business Idea (p. 11)
Deciding Whether to Start a Business (p. 2)
Entrepreneurs (p. 511)
Finding and Keeping Top Talent (p. 418)
Small and Growing Businesses (p. 486)

Identifying the Purpose of a Business

GETTING STARTED

Whether you're starting up or in business already, it's crucial to be clear about what your business does or will do, so that you can stay focused on the appropriate target market. Prospective lenders or investors in your business will look closely at this purpose when they assess whether you have the strategic direction for future success. You also need to be clear about why you are going into this business in the first place, and what you want out of it. Investors need to understand your motivation and your intentions, so that they can judge whether these match the plans that you set out for the development of the business. This actionlist aims to help you define both your own inspiration and the purpose of your business in order to bring clarity to your direction.

FAQS

Why am I in business and what do I want out of it?

Ask yourself this crucial question first of all, and then consider the other questions that arise in consequence. Will the business supplement your main income or replace it? Are you starting it as an investment, to sell as soon as you can? Is it to provide jobs for family members?

The answers to questions like these will have an impact on the business's aims, development, and strategies. For example, if you are starting a business as an investment opportunity, the focus of your planning will be leading up to your exit—the sale of the business. Your strategies must focus on building the business quickly and maximising its value to get the best selling price possible. On the other hand, if you are building up a business for a less-experienced family member, your plan will focus on a succession strategy. This might mean keeping the business small and easily manageable.

What exactly should my business do?

Be as specific as possible about the kind of business that you are starting. If you are going to open a restaurant, for example, will it be a family restaurant serving good quality, local food at competitive prices in a family-friendly environment? Or will it be more up-market, serving gourmet dishes to discerning customers?

Describe your business in terms of a mission statement that clearly summarises its purpose and is easily understood by you, your staff, your customers, and your potential investors. If you cannot describe your business in these terms, rethink your business idea; focus on your business's core activities and direction.

What is a business's vision?

A vision reflects what you care about most and represents what your business is trying to achieve. Defining purpose expresses what the business does, while the vision drives the business forward to its long-term aims. Vision is about having challenging but achievable goals within defined time scales. It is simply a statement of your desired competitive position within your best guess of the future environment. Realistic visions can be achieved and will improve staff morale, and once a vision is reached you can further expand your business aims.

A vision is created from the fundamental values of the employees and the purpose and awareness of the current environment of the business.

MAKING IT HAPPEN
Identify your customer

Product-driven businesses focus on making a product, then trying to get customers to buy it. A better starting point is to define the purpose of your business in response to customer needs—making your business market-driven. Define your business purpose in terms of your customers, and what you perceive their needs to be. For example, a fast food take-away selling healthy food might see its purpose as: 'Providing health-conscious eaters with quick, convenient, and tasty take-away meals and snacks all day'.

Make your purpose different

To succeed against competitors, your business needs to offer something different. Build this differentiation into your purpose, so that everything you do can be judged in terms of whether it supports the purpose or not. Potential investors want to see your business's unique selling proposition (USP), as this is the basis on which you will compete and on which customers will be attracted.

Write a mission statement

At its simplest, your business's mission is a statement of purpose that guides your activities. It is a summary of 'what you do'. The mission provides the guiding direction for developing strategy, searching out opportunities, and making resource allocation choices. It is built on your core values, so should be easily understood by staff, customers, and financial backers. You can often establish your mission in terms of the question: 'What business are we in?'

For example, the company Blooming Marvellous describes its mission as follows: 'To offer a refreshingly wide choice of stylish, practical and good value maternity wear and baby clothing, and the best in safe, innovative and stimulating nursery equipment.' As can be seen from this statement, it has carefully defined what it does, its specific products, and its market niche.

Decide what you want your business to be after two years

Start by considering what the working environment is going to be like in, say, two years' time. Ask yourself what opportunities and threats there might be, and summarise your vision into a single statement. For example: 'Octo aims to be respected as a leading design group working throughout Europe'. This business has chosen not to disclose publicly the timescale to which it is working, but it makes it clear it has a vision.

Try to envisage this so that you can start to move your business towards that point. For instance, you might work towards becoming a market leader, an innovator, a specialist, a good employer, a large concern, or a supplier of superior quality.

WHAT TO AVOID
Working without a clearly defined purpose

If you don't know exactly what the purpose of your business is, it is going to be very difficult to plan for the future, formulate objectives and goals, and design a strategy to achieve them. One of the good reasons for writing a business plan is that it will force you to clarify your purpose; without that clarity, it is difficult to define your markets and your marketing plans.

Taking on work outside your core business

It is always a temptation for service-based businesses to take on jobs that are not in their usual line of work. These can often end up taking longer and costing more than anticipated, with poor results for the customer and little likelihood of any repeat business for you. A well-worded business purpose, however, can help keep your mind focused on what your business aims to do and what it is best at doing. One useful book that may help you keep your mind on the job is *The On-Purpose Business: Doing More of What You Do Best More Profitably* by Kevin McCarthy, published in 2002 by Navpress Publishing Group.

RECOMMENDED LINKS
Business Eye (Wales):
www.businesseye.org.uk
Business Link (England):
www.businesslink.gov.uk
Invest Northern Ireland:
www.investni.com
Business Gateway (Scotland):
www.bgateway.com

SEE ALSO
Entrepreneurs (p. 511)

Coming Up with a Business Idea

GETTING STARTED

You've decided that you want to go into business, but you don't know what that business is going to be. You're looking for a great idea. The best advice is to begin by breaking down the bigger picture into more manageable pieces. First, look at your own skills and knowledge. Consider your present occupation, and whether you could you do your present job working for yourself rather than being employed by someone else. Successful businesses are frequently started by people with practical experience in the type of work that the new venture is entering. They go into business because they decide that they want more independence in their working lives.

It may be that you feel that the skills you have are already over-supplied. If this is the case, it's possible that there is no room in the marketplace for yet another joiner, furniture restorer, or undertaker. Or it may be that you simply do not want to carry on doing the same thing for yourself that you've done for others in the past. You perhaps then need to think of ways in which you could modify the skills and experience that you've acquired while working for somebody else.

Take a careful look at yourself; it could be that your personality or physique suggests a business idea. If you've persistence, charm, and good communication skills, for example, you might be a good salesperson. There are frequent openings for self-employed sales agents to sell other people's products. If you're good at dealing with people, you might be just the person to take up a retail franchise.

FAQS

How do I identify new ideas?

Try brainstorming with friends or relations to see if you can identify any totally new ideas. There are opportunities for entirely new products or services, such as energy conservation, providing better insulation in homes and factories. You may have an idea for a simple device which you think people might use. It might be worth commissioning a search at your local patent office to see if anyone has thought of the idea already.

Can I look at an existing idea in a new way?

Contrary to popular belief, there are few original ideas. Most successful businesses come from modifying, refining, or rethinking an existing business idea. Post-it® notes resulted from a glue product that went wrong. Perhaps more important is the fact that it might not have happened if the company had not deliberately set aside time when staff could think about innovative product ideas. Try thinking laterally about existing products or materials you know about.

What goods or services could I provide locally?

Think of the problems and difficulties you've experienced in getting things for your home, garden, or at work, or in your leisure activities. Analyse what the problems were which caused you most inconvenience, or cost you the most to put right. Think about times when you've urgently required a service, and then found that it was not available. Alternatively, you might be able to think of parts or products that were hard or impossible to obtain locally. Think about the things that you and your neighbours and friends most frequently complain about. Listen to people talking in the pub, at the gym, or in the supermarket checkout queue. Then ask yourself whether there is any way of providing a local service or product for any of these markets, and whether people would actually pay for it.

What goods or services could I provide to local companies?

Do some research among local companies. Find out whether there are any goods or services that they have difficulty in obtaining. A new industrial estate for example, may contain several small and medium-sized firms, none of which have their own staff canteen, but all of which need some kind of catering service. Perhaps a sandwich bar could be set up on the estate. There may be room in the market for a despatch service linking the estate with other industrial centres.

How do I find out about opportunities for tourism or leisure businesses in my area?

The type of tourism business you consider will depend on whether the area is urban or rural, whether it's a popular tourist region, and the demographics of the local population. For example, a business such as a teashop may thrive in an area with a high population of pensioners and a high influx of tourists. You may want to consider opening an outdoor activity centre in a rural area. Try talking to people working in the local sports centre or Tourist Board. They may have suggestions for market opportunities in the area.

How could I find out about selling goods made by other people?

Many new firms start off by selling goods that somebody else makes. A number of opportunities exist to distribute foreign goods in Britain. For example, the United States Department of Commerce publishes a regular magazine listing businesses looking for facilities and distributors (this is available from all US embassies and consulates). Chambers of Commerce have regular listings of businesses seeking partners willing to manufacture under licence, or to act as sole distributors.

What do large companies, local authorities, and other public bodies buy in from outside the area?

In many cases they will be buying goods from outside the region because there is no one to supply them locally. Similarly, local councils and organisations like the Area Health Authority and the Police Force are purchasers of equipment and services. Try contacting the purchasing officer of your local council to find out what large and frequent purchases they make. In order to help new suppliers, some companies produce briefing documents for small businesses explaining what they buy and their purchasing procedure.

Is there potential for import substitution in the area?

One stage further is to look at things which are currently being bought from abroad. Look around in shops and factories to see where the goods on sale, or being used, were made. HM Revenue & Customs keep lists of imported products. The single European market has opened up new opportunities abroad too. Do you have language skills? Have you worked abroad before? You could have enough useful knowledge of another country to enable you to act as an export agent.

MAKING IT HAPPEN
Turn your hobby into a business

You may have skills that you acquired as a hobby, but which could form the basis for a business. For example, if you like gardening, you might consider starting a garden design business. If you're good at cooking, you could think about starting a catering service for people entertaining at home.

Work from home

If you're a parent, and consequently at home a lot of the time, you could think about working from home (if space allows). It might be possible for you to set aside space to sew, knit, or perhaps make soft toys. Another option is to sell products for other people over the phone. There are also an increasing number of opportunities for people to do office work using a computer and modem. This can include anything from word processing letters and keeping accounts up to date, right through to freelance writing and consultancy.

Buy an existing business

Another option is to consider buying an existing business. However, if you do, make sure you find out why the owner is selling. Even if the seller is retiring, establish exactly why it wasn't worth his or her while to continue with the business. Look carefully at the business's accounts, and be sure that you understand them. Businesses for sale are usually advertised in the local paper, and could also be advertised in relevant trade magazines.

WHAT TO AVOID
Not giving it enough time

Don't expect an idea to come to you in a flash; sometimes ideas take time to develop. Also remember that the time you spend on planning will be time well spent when you finally do come up with a great idea.

Not doing enough research

If you fail to do any market research, you'll have far less chance of success. Research will definitely save you a great deal of time and money in the long run.

RECOMMENDED LINKS
Business Eye (Wales):
www.businesseye.org.uk
Business Link (England):
www.businesslink.gov.uk
Invest Northern Ireland:
www.investni.com
Business Gateway (Scotland):
www.bgateway.com

SEE ALSO
Assessing Your Entrepreneurial Profile: Do You Have What It Takes? (p. 6)
Deciding Whether to Start a Business (p. 2)
Developing and Protecting an Invention (p. 21)
Entrepreneurs (p. 511)
New Product Development (p. 530)
Profiling Your Target Market (p. 18)

Networking and Marketing Yourself

GETTING STARTED
Everyone can always benefit from networking and marketing themselves, but those setting up or running a small business can certainly benefit from getting themselves and their company known. Business is driven by relationships and marketing yourself requires you to build strong and meaningful relationships—many that will be long term. The following are questions to consider as you prepare to network and to market yourself:

- Why are you networking? What is your personal or professional goal?
- What are your strengths that will help you to market yourself?
- What organisations or events will be valuable places for networking?
- How much time do you want to spend on networking, and when will you do it?
- How will you know when you've been successful?

FAQS
Why should I bother to network and to market myself?
Research has shown that people who have a vast network of contacts, who are involved in professional and community activities outside their business, and who look for opportunities to be visible are more successful in their careers.

Isn't networking blatant self-promotion, and won't it look bad?
No. Networking is done for the good of your business, rather than for personal gain. If you are a successful networker, people are drawn to you because they know you are well connected and that you have good resources.

When is the best time to network?
Networking should become a way of life, a way of being. You should be networking all the time. As you build professional relationships, be constantly thinking: 'What can I offer this person?' 'How can I be of help?' The more you try to be of service to others, the more people will want to do things for you, and in the initial stages of a new business this will be a huge help.

 ## MAKING IT HAPPEN
Be clear about why you are networking and marketing yourself
There are many reasons for networking and for marketing oneself. When you are start-ing up or trying to grow a small business, these reasons may include gaining support for a major project, finding funding, or setting up a partnership with other local businesses. Although it is important to continually build relationships, it is much more effective to know from the outset why you are building these relationships and what you hope to accomplish. Everyone has limited time, and this will help you to decide how to prioritise your networking activities.

Make a list of your strong points
It is important to have a sense of who you are and what your strengths are when you are networking and marketing yourself. What are your special skills and abilities? What unique knowledge do you have? What experiences will other people find valuable? What characteristics and beliefs define who you are? Once you have made this list, make copies for your bathroom mirror, for your car dashboard, and for your wallet. Knowing your strengths helps you to remember that other people will value what you have to offer.

Never network from a position of weakness, but from a position of strength. This means having something of value to offer others, so that they don't see you as an annoyance. It's also a good idea to begin networking before you need anything from other people. Join or create a network to build relationships, and do what you can to help others or the organisation.

Make a list of organisations and events for networking

Identify professional organisations and events that may be helpful to you in your career or with your project. Look for special interest groups like those for 'entrepreneurial women' for example. Get involved. When you are at professional events, make sure that you attend social functions, that you join people for dinner, and that you seek out volunteer opportunities.

Create a contact list

Keeping in mind your reasons for networking, brainstorm all the people you know who might be of help to you. Prioritise the list according to who is most likely to be helpful. Think about people you have done favours for in the past who might not be of direct help, but who may know someone who can be. After you have spoken to each one, ask him or her, 'Who else do you know that can be of help to me?'

Create an action plan with a schedule

Take your list of organisations and events and your contact list, and put together an action plan for making connections. Schedule networking events in your diary, along with organisational meetings, conferences and so on. Using your contact list, set up a schedule for making a certain number of calls per day or per week.

Meet with people and attend events

Before you meet with someone or attend an event, review your list of strengths, and focus on your purpose for networking and marketing yourself. It helps to visualise or picture a successful outcome. Be friendly and professional, but most of all, be yourself. Spend time connecting with people on a personal level before asking for help or sharing your reason for networking. If you are meeting in person with someone on your contact list, always bring a gift—something they can remember you by.

Network on the Net

The Internet is a valuable place to make connections and to learn fruitful informa-

tion from colleagues. If you have a special interest or a special field, there is sure to be a newsgroup or threaded bulletin board on your topic. If not, start one by setting up a listserv at **www.topica.com**, or at similar sites.

Market yourself

The actions you take depend on why you are marketing yourself, but think of yourself as a brand; 'Brand You'. When marketers are marketing a product, they look for the 'unique selling proposition' (USP). A USP is something relevant and original that can be claimed for a particular product or service. The USP should be able to communicate: 'Buy our brand and get this unique benefit'. When marketing yourself, you need to define who your 'customers' are and what your Unique Selling Proposition is. Your list of strengths above should give you some clues, but the USP needs to be stated in a short phrase. People who are closest to you can often give you suggestions. It might be something like: 'I help people to realise their dreams', or 'My leadership brings out the best in others', or 'I solve problems quickly and simply'.

Once you know your USP, brainstorm ways that you can market yourself and your uniqueness. The key is to let people know what you have to offer. Write an article for the company newsletter or a professional newsletter related to your USP. Volunteer to give a talk. Design a project that uses your unique talents and propose it to the right people. Be visible.

Assess your progress towards networking goals

You may wish to keep a notebook of your action plans and your progress. It also helps to have someone as a sounding board. That person can be a friend, a partner, or a professional adviser. When we feel accountable for our actions to someone we trust, we are much more likely to follow through. It also helps to have someone who is willing to celebrate your successes and accomplishments with you.

Always say 'thank you'

As you network, many people will offer you information, opportunities, and valuable contacts. In your notebook, keep track of the favours that people have done for you and make sure that you write each one a short and simple thank-you letter. People are always more willing to help someone who has been appreciative in the past.

Be patient

Networking is a long-term activity. Steven Ginsburg of the *Washington Post* describes networking as 'building social capital'. You may not see results overnight, and at first should expect to give more than you get. But over time, your network will become one of your most valued assets.

WHAT TO AVOID
Not wanting to bother anyone

Remember that people love to help others. Don't take up too much of their time, and come well prepared. When you ask for someone's time, be specific. Say, 'I'd like 30 minutes of your time', and then stick to it. Don't outstay your welcome. Whenever you meet with someone, always be thinking, 'Is there something I can do to help this person?' Create a win-win situation.

Coming on too strong

Networking is not about selling something to someone who doesn't want it. You are looking for opportunities to create a mutual relationship, where there is give and take. In order for networking to be successful, you have to be interested in developing a long-term relationship. Remind yourself that your focus is on relationship building, not on immediate results.

Not coming on strongly enough

You put yourself in networking situations, but never talk about your needs or interests. This may be because you are not clear enough about why you are networking, or it could be that you are networking for reasons that are not particularly important to you. Go back to step one and clarify your purpose.

RECOMMENDED LINKS
City Women's Network:
www.citywomen.org
Networking People UK:
www.npuk.com

SEE ALSO
Assessing Your Entrepreneurial Profile: Do You Have What It Takes? (p. 6)

REFINING AND
PROTECTING YOUR IDEA

Profiling Your Target Market

GETTING STARTED

Before your business can realistically or effectively begin a marketing campaign, you'll need to be able to answer two vital questions: who is your target market, and what does your target market want or need that your business can provide?

Without detailed and precise answers to these questions you won't be able to define your marketing strategy, or put in place an effective sales and marketing plan. It's worth recalling the classic tale of two shoe sales representatives out exploring opportunities in a country in which their company had yet to establish a market. The first sales representative sent back an initial report saying, 'everyone goes barefoot in this country, no market here at all'. The second sales representative's report, however, was somewhat different: 'everyone goes barefoot, massive opportunity for us'. Who was right?

This illustrates the necessity for any business to understand accurately the needs of its target customers, in terms of knowing enough about them and gathering sufficient information about what they really want. Without this precise understanding your efforts to market your goods and services won't be effective.

FAQS

How do I identify my target customers?

Your first job when profiling a target market is to be able to identify precisely who your audience is. Can you accurately describe the characteristics of your ideal customers? Which clients currently spend the most with you? Why do they do this? If you don't know the answers, you need to find out.

You'll probably already have a good idea about the groups of people or types of businesses that you think you can sell your service to. For individual customers this might be people of a certain age, gender, socio-economic status, occupation, or a group with common or special interests such as sports or hobbies. For business customers these might be located in a specific area, or in a particular sector, or could have similarities in terms of the customer groups they sell to.

Your aim should be to concentrate your marketing on these groups of people, businesses, or existing customers who are most likely to buy your product or service. Doing this in the most profitable way takes experience, but once you have identified this target group of people or businesses, you'll have completed the first step in profiling your market and now have your list of target prospects—your ideal customers.

Is it about quality or quantity of prospects?

Having a precision-driven marketing approach—where you have a high-quality list of prospective clients or leads—will, pound-forpound of marketing spend, prove far more productive and profitable than an untargeted blanket approach to generate sales.

Quality of leads, based on your understanding, knowledge, and careful profiling of your customers and their needs, will massively increase your ability to convert them into sales.

MAKING IT HAPPEN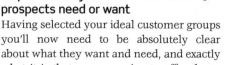

Pinpoint what your customers and prospects need or want

Having selected your ideal customer groups you'll now need to be absolutely clear about what they want and need, and exactly what it is that you are going to offer them. This understanding will enable you to develop the specific marketing message and proposition that will most effectively sell the benefits of your product or service to them.

If you get these messages wrong then it's almost certain that your marketing efforts will fail, as your customers will buy from your competitors instead. Your product, service, or business proposition will have missed the target completely.

Speak to target customers before developing your marketing strategy

Before you start to develop or choose your marketing strategy it's always worthwhile to speak first to a sample from your target audience. By doing this you'll be able to check that your profile of your intended market has been the right one, and test your assumptions about what you think they want and why they could buy from you.

You could do this by speaking directly to a group of people or you could undertake a survey in the form of a questionnaire which can be posted to a sample of target customers. Alternatively, you could talk to passers-by in a location that is frequented by your ideal customers.

Don't forget that you could also speak to your existing clients or, even better, clients of your competitors if that is possible.

Double-check that your marketing message is right for your target market

Once you have spoken to a sample of your target market and you are satisfied that you have confirmed your assumptions about their needs, you'll be in a position to create or adapt a marketing proposition to sell the benefits of your product or service to that audience. After you have established the basic proposition, consider carefully whether there is anything further that will make your marketing message even more appealing. Will these communications convince them that your service can provide the benefits that meet their exact needs?

Check that your list of prospects is as precise as possible

Your prospects list will only be of real use in your marketing campaign if it accurately reflects the profile of the audiences you are targeting. Have the consumers of your product or service been identified in terms of their geographic and demographic profile, their employment status, profession, special interests, membership of clubs, and so on? Have you compiled a list of your business

targets in terms of where they are located, their size, names of the main buyers, repeat purchase rate? Have you identified the best sales channels to enable you to reach these target customers?

Your sales efforts can only be as good as the list of prospects you have selected in your target markets, and that list must reflect the profile of the audience you are developing your marketing proposition to reach.

Be sure that you are giving them what they want

With a thorough understanding of the needs of your ideal customers, you should then strive to create an offering and proposition based on four criteria that will give them a product or service that is:

- exactly what they want from you
- precisely when they need it
- convenient for them
- at a price they can afford and are prepared to pay

If you are not convinced that your sales proposition meets all of these criteria, then you'll need to study the profile of your customers again and revise your offering.

WHAT TO AVOID
Failing to test

The most common mistakes made when targeting products and services towards specific users or customer groups are caused by not testing the assumptions you have made about your audience. You'll waste valuable time and marketing budget if you launch a campaign towards an audience when you have not accurately identified who those customers are, and cannot precisely define what they want, and why they could buy from you instead of your competitors.

Lack of focus

Do not buy into a list of unknown prospects, no matter how attractive it seems to get names of thousands of people you can blanket sell to in the short term.

Find out who they are, where they are located, and test your assumptions about what you believe they want. By testing, you can either confirm that your profiling was right, or you can adjust your offering until you get it right. Being precise will lead to more sales more quickly, and more profit over the longer term.

One book you might find helpful when learning to sharpen your focus is *The Discipline of Market Leaders: Choose Your Customers, Narrow your Focus, Dominate Your Market* by Michael Treacy and Fred Wiersema, published by Perseus Books and available on Amazon.com.

RECOMMENDED LINKS
Business Link:
www.businesslink.gov.uk
Chartered Institute of Marketing:
www.cim.co.uk
Internet marketing:
www.it-advice.org

SEE ALSO
Coming Up with a Business Idea (p. 11)
**Market Research and Competitor
   Intelligence (p. 526)**

Developing and Protecting an Invention

GETTING STARTED

A new invention is often the starting point for a successful business, but the journey from an idea or prototype to a product on a store shelf can be long and difficult. This actionlist looks at the steps involved in this journey, from the protection of the idea, to the financing and marketing of the final product.

FAQS

How can I tell if my invention will sell?

If your invention exists only as a sketch, simple model, or even just an idea, your first step is to express this in concrete form. This could be a proper set of manufacturing drawings or a scale model that can be shown and demonstrated to others while you fully research your idea and evaluate its commercial potential.

To succeed in the market, your product must solve a problem for the purchaser in an original and cost-effective way. Your research and evaluation phase has to achieve four main aims, each of which has spin-off benefits. You must prove that your product is original and demonstrably better than competing products, so that it can be protected with a patent. You must also show that it is marketable, in order to attract venture capital and interest retailers. You must demonstrate that your product can be made, and that the cost and quality of the component parts allow the product to be produced economically. Finally, you must ensure that your product offers a unique selling proposition (USP), and that the scope and cost of reaching the target market is affordable.

How do I prove that my product is original?

You have ownership rights to your original creation that allow you to exploit it commercially but, unlike copyright in a book, song, or work of art, these rights are not automatic and must be secured by registration. This means filing a patent claim for your new product. (Remember that it is the actual product that is protected, not the original idea.) You may need the services of a patent lawyer to assist with a search of previous patents and help you register your patent.

How do I show that my product is marketable?

You'll need to do plenty of market research to work out the value and potential of your product in the market. You could try this on your own. Alternatively, if you can afford it, get a market research agency to draw up survey questions from your input.

You'll need to do qualitative *and* quantitative research. Qualitative research should show you what people think of your idea or product—its visual appeal, its practicality, and its perceived acceptability. It should also show what people perceive your product as lacking, and what improvements they think need to be made. Other questions can be directed at finding suitable names, colours, shape, pack sizes, and an acceptable price range for the product. Remember that the comments and answers you get do not necessarily indicate how well your product will sell; this may depend upon other factors, such as competitive activity or unexpected fashion trends.

Quantitative research evaluates the sales potential of your product: how many people would buy it; how different pricing levels would affect projected sales; whether there would be demand for different versions of the product, and so on.

How do I demonstrate that my product can be made?

This may require the services of a professional designer or engineer to perform a component analysis, and to set optimum specifications and quality levels for every part of the product. Other aspects to be determined are the availability and price stability of raw materials, the labour costs and skill required, and the factory or workshop location.

Do I have a USP?

The unique selling proposition is what puts your product ahead of a competitive field, and is a key aspect of your marketing plan. The truly unique feature of your idea can make your product the most desirable in the marketplace, and become the lynchpin of a successful advertising campaign.

Having decided on your product's USP, you should draw up your marketing plan. The plan should include your thoughts on distribution. You need to decide whether the product is a consumer product, or for businesses. Think about whether it will be sold regionally, nationally, or internationally, through direct, retail, or wholesale methods. Also consider whether you will use your own transport to deliver it or use outside carriers.

Packaging is an important part of your marketing plan. Decide what you will call the product. Consider whether the packaging needs to be suitable for display purposes, whether the produce will be disposable or returnable, and whether packaging regulations might affect your product.

Two other important factors are advertising and promotion. Think about which media will be the most appropriate for advertising: newspapers, magazines, pamphlets, direct mail, the Internet, posters, radio, television, or point-of-sale material. Consider whether you could use exhibitions and trade fairs, and whether you have your own sales force or use agents.

Price is an important consideration, and you need to consider what sales volumes you can expect at different price levels, and how different volumes and prices would affect cash flow. You might need to think about making promotional offers.

Where can I go to for more information?

The Institute of Inventors is an inventors' club run by professional engineers. It helps private inventors to evaluate new ideas, gadgets, and inventions, as well as assisting with prototype drawings and development, patent specification, drawings and applications, and licensing of intellectual property.

The Institute of Patentees and Inventors campaigns on behalf of its members and inventors in general, and is recognised as an advocate for the invention process and the fair treatment of inventors. The Innovation Relay Centre Gateway is a European source for innovative technologies or new technology solutions, run for people wanting to market your innovation, looking for new technologies to exploit, or searching for an innovative solution to a technology need.

MAKING IT HAPPEN
Choose the next step

Once the research has shown a potential market for your product, you have several options available: you could choose to manufacture and market your invention yourself; you could outsource production, but distribute and market the product yourself; you could merge your production, sales, and marketing with an established partner; or you could license the rights to the invention for others to make and market it themselves.

If you go for any of the first three options, the deciding factor will be your own level of management expertise. If your planned business is small, you will need to decide whether you have sufficient skills in manufacture, marketing, and distribution, and the time to give each area the attention it needs. The last option of licensing to others may well be the preferable one if your real interest is in developing new ideas and innovations.

Develop your business plan

Your invention may have too much scope for you fully to exploit its potential on your own. Or you may feel that you do not have the depth of specialised knowledge and skills to develop all the individual aspects of a successful business plan—management, finance, manufacture, marketing, sales, and distribution—without professional aid, but do not wish to consider a partnership or merger at this stage. Additionally, your potential investors will more easily be persuaded to fund a well-structured business venture that presents an attractive and totally developed plan to them.

There are agencies that will help you develop your investment proposition to its full potential before presenting it to their investors. They can also provide management support for the start-up of your operation from their pool of proven specialist managers; skilled management is often a requirement imposed by investors to ensure the success of the business. Government business support agencies provide specialist help and advice for individuals and businesses with a good product idea, or who are seeking technical advice and financial support for product design and development. Initial consultations are usually free and other services may be offered at a subsidised cost. The four national business support networks are Business Link (England), Business Gateway (Scotland), Business Eye (Wales), and Invest Northern Ireland. Website addresses are given on pp. 4–5.

Raise capital
The three main options open to you are private equity, a business loan from a bank, and venture capital. In some cases, there may possibly be a government grant.

WHAT TO AVOID ✗
Talking too early about your invention
Do not describe your invention to anyone before filing a patent application. If you really need to discuss your invention with others before filing, always get them to sign a confidentiality agreement.

Not considering the options
Remember the objective is to maximise the revenue from your invention. Consider the option of simply licensing your design to others; this could save you a lot of expense.

RECOMMENDED LINKS
Innovation Relay Centres (Innovation in Practice link):
www.cordis.lu
Institute of Inventors:
http://members.ad.com/mikinvent
Institute of Patentees and Inventors:
www.invent.org.uk
Patent Office:
www.patent.gov.uk
World Intellectual Property Organization (WIPO):
www.wipo.org

SEE ALSO
Applying for a Patent (p. 27)
Coming Up with a Business Idea (p. 11)
Intellectual Property (p. 520)
Registering a Trade Mark (p. 37)

An Introduction to Intellectual Property

GETTING STARTED

Intellectual property (IP) enables people to own their creativity and innovation in the same way that they can own physical property. The owner of IP can control, and be rewarded for, its use. The four main types of IP are patents for inventions, trademarks for brand identity, designs for product appearance, and copyright for written material and artistic works. This actionlist gives an overview of each of these rights and briefly describes how to obtain them.

FAQS
What do I need to know?

Owners of intellectual property (IP) have the right to benefit from it, sell it, hire it, or license it out. IP is quite easy for other people to steal or use without permission, so IP law has been developed to define the rights of IP owners and provide them with the ability to protect their rights and defend them through legal action. Some of these rights apply automatically, while others require a registration process to become legally enforceable. It is almost always necessary to register before disclosing your IP concept to others, or your rights will not exist. The Patent Office is the government agency responsible for administering the UK IP rights system.

MAKING IT HAPPEN
Patents

A patent gives an inventor the right, for a limited period, to stop others from making, using, or selling an invention without his or her permission. Patent rights are specific to the country they are granted in. Patent rights last for up to 20 years in the United Kingdom.

See the actionlist 'Applying for a Patent' on p. 27 for full information on how to do what, and when.

Copyright

Copyright is an automatic right that protects the way an original idea is expressed in a piece of work, and is relevant to any business that produces original literature, drama, music, publications, films, videos, or broadcasts.

Copyright for artistic, dramatic, literary, and musical works originating within the European Union lasts for 70 years after the author's death. The owner can control how the work is exploited, including copying, adaptation, public performance, broadcasting, and public distribution, and can transfer ownership of copyright to someone else. Some unlicensed use of a copyright work is allowed under a concept known as Fair Dealing. This includes limited photocopying and quotation of extracts for teaching or review purposes.

Copyright comes into effect immediately, as soon as something is created and recorded in some way. Marking your work with the copyright symbol © followed by your name and the date is not legally required in the United Kingdom and most other countries but may help should there be any infringement proceedings. Providing evidence that you created the work at a particular time is also a useful precaution. A number of private companies operate unofficial registers, but you should check carefully what you will be paying for before engaging their services.

Design

There are two levels of design right, unregistered and registered. Unregistered design right is automatically owned by the designer (unless the design was commissioned). It provides protection for purely functional, three-dimensional designs, and only protects their shape and configuration. (Two-dimensional designs are covered by copyright.) Unregistered design right protects for a maximum period of 15 years, depending on when the product comes to market. It must be an original design to qualify; one that has not been used or sold before in its specific design sector. Recorded evidence may be required to prove the commencement date of the design right.

You can give your design increased legal protection by registering it through the Design Registry within the Patent Office. Design registration enables you to stop others from making, using, importing, or selling articles to which the design has been applied, for a period of five years. This can be extended at five-year intervals up to 25 years maximum from the date of filing. A renewal fee is required each time. To qualify for registration, your design must be novel, that is, materially different from any other previously published design. Registering a design is usually done through a patent agent, and involves submitting your design along with an application form and the specified filing fee.

Design registration protects the appearance of all, or part of an industrially produced product, in particular its outward shape, colours, texture, construction materials, and its ornamentation. A design must be registered under a particular category of manufactured product, for example, a clock or a coffee pot. A design does not need to have aesthetic qualities to be registered. Some designs can't be registered. Generally, these will be designs where copyright protection applies instead, such as sculptures or calendars.

European Community design regulation provides two additional rights: registered Community design right, similar to a UK registered design, which applies across the whole Community from a single application to the Office for Harmonization in the Internal Market (OHIM); and unregistered Community design right, which protects the same type of designs from copying for three years from first disclosure, without the need for registration.

Trade marks

A trade mark is a distinctive symbol that makes a business's goods and services immediately recognisable. The Trade Marks Act 1994 defines a trade mark as 'any sign that is capable of being represented graphically, capable of distinguishing goods or services of one undertaking from those of another undertaking'. Signs that can be represented graphically include a marking such as words, letters, and numerals, the shape of the goods or their packaging, and musical jingles (or even smells).

Registration of a mark is not compulsory, but by registering a trade mark, your business gets the right to prevent others from using an identical or confusingly similar mark on goods and services that are the same (or similar) to your own. Before making your application, search the Trade Mark Register at the Patent Office (also available on the Patent Office's website) for existing marks that might prevent your mark from being registered. Alternatively, on application, the Search and Advisory Service will ensure that a new mark fulfils the correct criteria. To make an application, a form must be completed and sent with the fee to the Trade Marks Registry. Applications can be made by an individual or by a trade mark agent.

Protection lasts for 10 years from the date of registration, and can be renewed every 10 years, for a fee. Once a mark has been registered, no changes can be made to the mark itself (except in a few circumstances), so it is important that the description submitted is clear and correct. A third party can request a mark's removal from the register if it has not been used for five years. The Madrid Protocol provides for international registration of trade marks through the World Intellectual Property Organization (WIPO). An application for registration can be made to the Office for Harmonization in the Internal Market. Registration prevents the use of identical or similar marks by other firms anywhere in the European Union.

Moral rights

The Copyright, Designs, and Patents Act 1988 gives additional protection to creative people through the introduction of moral rights. These include: the right of an author/director to be identified as such whenever a work is used by someone else;

the right of authors not to have their works altered in a way that may prejudice their reputation or honour; preventing false statements being made about the true authorship or directorship of works; and the right to privacy (a person who has commissioned photographs or film of themselves can control the number of copies made public).

WHAT TO AVOID
Not keeping records
Mark your products as protected, and keep records of the design and (if applicable) the registration process. This will strengthen any case should registration be challenged or design rights infringed.

Not taking out insurance
It is a good idea to take out insurance against the cost of bringing legal action for infringement of rights.

RECOMMENDED LINKS
British Copyright Council:
www.britishcopyright.org
Chartered Institute of Patent Agents:
www.cipa.org.uk
Design and Artists Copyright Society:
www.dacs.co.uk
European Patent Office:
www.european-patent-office.org
Institute of Trade Mark Attorneys:
www.itma.org.uk
Patent Office:
www.patent.gov.uk
Office for Harmonization in the Internal Market (Trade Marks and Designs):
www.oami.eu.int
World Intellectual Property Organization (Small and Medium-Sized Enterprises Division):
www.wipo.int/sme/en/index.html

SEE ALSO
Intellectual Property (p. 520)

Applying for a Patent

GETTING STARTED

Patents are granted by the Patent Office to inventors, giving them the right to prevent exploitation of their inventions by others. The full process of patenting a new invention is expensive and requires the services of a professional patent agent. You need to be very sure of the commercial viability of your idea before you go ahead with the full process.

You can obtain a useful period (one year) of protection at minimal cost just by filing an initial application. This has two advantages:

- it allows you to discuss the full details of your invention with others (for example, with possible financial backers or purchasers)
- it allows you time to investigate the marketability of your idea before committing yourself to the expense of the full process

This actionlist explains the steps to follow to lodge both an initial and a full patent application.

FAQS

What can be patented?

Your invention must meet four requirements before you can apply for a patent:

1. It must be new. This means that information about the invention must not have been previously published (even by you). So you are not allowed to make any public disclosure in any way at all before making your application to the Patent Office.
2. It must have an inventive step. It may not simply be an obvious modification of an existing piece of equipment or process.
3. It must be industrially applicable. This means your invention must be made or used in some kind of industry, in the form of a new machine, product, or manufacturing process.
4. It must not be on the excluded list. This list includes scientific theories and mathematical methods, animal and plant varieties, and works of art or literature.

What rights do I have as the patent holder?

You own your invention. Like any other form of property you own, you may sell it or rent it out. However, patents are territorial rights only. Protection is limited to the countries to which the patent application extends.

What is an 'initial application' and what protection does it give?

To obtain a patent you must first lodge an application at the Patent Office. They then allocate a patent application number to you. You may now say 'patent pending' or 'patent applied for' in relation to your invention. This gives you precedence over patent applications for similar inventions should they be lodged later by others.

Additionally, you are free to disclose publicly whatever information you have lodged at the Patent Office without affecting the validity of any subsequent patent that is granted to you. If 12 months have elapsed from the date when your documentation was received by the Patent Office and you have taken no further steps, this initial application is terminated. You may still file another new application at this stage to restart the patenting process, should you wish.

What should I do before making an application?

It's a good idea to research past and recent work in your area of technology on the Patent Office website (see below), where you can review more than 30 million patents from all countries. You should also perform a patent search to avoid wasting time and money trying to patent an existing invention. You can attempt this yourself on the Patent Office website, but it will be far more effective to use the services of a professional patent searcher.

The Patent Office's Search and Advisory Service can perform a commercial patent search. Try looking through several previous applications as well, to get a good idea of what a well-prepared patent application should contain.

MAKING IT HAPPEN
File an initial application
This is a very straightforward procedure and one you can easily complete yourself. Your only cost is the time taken to prepare a suitable description of your invention. If you feel uncomfortable about the do-it-yourself approach (perhaps you have a particularly complex invention to describe), you can use a professional patent agent, who will charge a fee based on the complexity of the application. Your application needs to include just two items:

1. A 'request for grant of a patent', made on Form 1/77. You get this form from the Patent Office and it contains comprehensive instructions. You must provide a brief title for the invention, your name and address, and details of any patent agents you have used. As your application is for an initial filing, you can bypass the sections dealing with earlier applications and declaration of priority.

2. Two copies of a written description ('specification') of your invention. Bear in mind the following when you write the description:
- The description of your invention has to be fully comprehensive.
- Always include all the features that may be incorporated, even if you are not yet sure about them. They can easily be deleted at a later time, whereas you are not allowed to add any additional technical details or improvements to your application after the filing date. Difficulties will occur afterwards if any critical features are not mentioned in the initial application.
- Describe the advantages of your invention

versus the disadvantages of previously known products or processes.
- State all the ways you can think of in which your invention can be used or applied.
- Give a more detailed description (as an example only) of one particular way in which your invention can be put into practice.
- Your written description should be able to stand alone in providing a clear summary of all aspects of your invention, but it is always a good idea to supplement it with drawings of any parts and equipment incorporated. Clearly-drawn freehand pencil sketches are fine for this purpose.
- Working models are neither required nor accepted by the Patent Office.

Steps to complete the full patent application
It normally takes between three and four years from the initial filing date to obtain a granted United Kingdom patent. During this period, certain procedures, including some extensive legal and technical requirements need to be completed, and a chartered patent agent normally carries out the procedures on your behalf. An agent would also be able to make sure that the next steps are carried out in good time. The patents system was deregulated to a certain extent in January 2005, but it's still best to move as quickly as you can. Patent agents' fees can be high, but by appointing a professional you can be assured that your patent is made as secure as possible.

Within 12 months
You have 12 months from the date of filing to develop your invention and look into its commercial viability. If you decide to pursue your application for a full patent, you will need to file further information by that time. This includes a set of 'claims', an abstract that will give a brief summary of the invention, and a request for a search (with a fee payable). The Patent Office will conduct a search of earlier patents and technical journals in the relevant technology, to determine whether the alleged invention is both novel and inventive as claimed.

Within 18 months

The application will be published 18 months after the first filing date (sooner if requested). This makes public notice that you are seeking certain rights in relation to your invention. From this day onwards, if anyone tries to copy your invention, damages can be sought for any infringement of the technology occurring—provided the patent is eventually granted.

Publishing the application before a patent is granted gives third parties the opportunity to read about your invention. Should they feel it is not worthy of being granted a patent, they can write to the Patent Office explaining why they think it is not a 'patentable' invention.

Within two years

You must request a detailed examination of your invention by filling in Form 10/77. This also has to be accompanied by the required fee.

Within about another 12 months, the Patent Office will carry out a detailed examination. The Examiners consider the citations found during the earlier search and any more which have come to light since. They may request you to disclaim any features in your application that are not novel or inventive or otherwise not meeting criteria for a patent. If they then agree that, after these exclusions, what remains of your invention is both novel and inventive, your patent will be granted. They will also give you a time limit within which to respond. Your application will be republished as granted and you will be issued with a certificate.

WHAT TO AVOID

Talking too early about your invention

Don't tell anyone about your invention before filing an application. If you really have to discuss your invention with others before filing, always use confidentiality agreements.

Not seeking the right advice

Basic advice from the Chartered Institute of Patent Agents (CIPA) is freely available at their clinics throughout the United Kingdom. Full details can be found on the CIPA website (see below). The CIPA website also provides a searchable directory of patent agents by geographical area. Before using the services of any agent, you should check their qualifications and reputation. If patents are key to your business, you may wish to make use of a patent watching service. This will report on the patent activities of your competitors, as well as all other activity in your field in foreign countries.

Worrying that the whole process is taking too long

There is a 'fast track' procedure available whereby the whole process from initial filing to grant can be achieved within 18 months. This will require a full patent specification from the outset, so you will have to be prepared to pay patent agent fees up front.

RECOMMENDED LINKS

Chartered Institute of Patent Agents:
www.cipa.org.uk
European Patent Office:
www.european-patent-office.org
Institute of Inventors:
www.newgadgets.freeserve.co.uk
Patent Office:
www.patent.gov.uk
Patent Office:
www.intellectual-property.gov.uk

SEE ALSO

Developing and Protecting an Invention (p. 21)
Intellectual Property (p. 520)

Using Copyright to Protect Your Work

GETTING STARTED

Copyright is an automatic right that protects the way an original idea is expressed in a piece of work. It is relevant to any business that produces original literature, drama, music, publications, films, videos, or broadcasts. There are no forms to fill in and no fees to pay, but copyright gives the creator or first owner of any original work the legal right to control how this material may be used.

This actionlist explains the principle of copyright and how you can use it to protect your original material. It also gives guidelines on what to do if you think your copyright is being infringed.

FAQS

What is the purpose of copyright?

Copyright helps creators to gain economic rewards for their efforts and encourages future creativity. It gives rights to creators of certain kinds of material to control the ways in which their material may be used. The rights broadly cover: copying and adapting the work; issuing, renting, and lending copies to the public; performing the work in public; or broadcasting the work. In many cases, the creator will also have the right to be identified on the work. The creator will decide how to exploit the work and how to enforce his or her copyright. He or she can also benefit by selling or agreeing a transfer of copyright to someone else. Without protection, it could be very easy for others to exploit material without paying the creator.

Who owns copyright?

In the case of a written, dramatic, musical, or other artistic work, the person who created the work is the first owner of the economic rights under copyright. This rule also applies to commissioned works. However, where a work is created during employment, the employer is the first owner of these rights, unless an agreement has been made between the employee and employer indicating otherwise.

Copyright, like physical property, can be bought or sold, inherited, or transferred to another person in another way, for example, as a gift. So some or all of the economic rights may later belong to someone other than the first owner.

What laws enforce copyright?

United Kingdom legislation is based on the Copyright, Designs and Patents Act 1988, which defines copyright as a property right which can be given away, licensed, or sold. There are several other major pieces of legislation that add to the scope and detail of the 1988 Act.

The Copyright (Computer Programs) Regulations 1992 extends the definition of literary work to include design material for programs, allows some back-up copying of licensed software, and provides for limited 'decompiling' of licensed programs to make them work with other programs. The Copyright and Rights in Database Regulations 1997 determines the circumstances for copyright protection to apply to databases.

The Duration of Copyright and Rights in Performances Regulations 1995 harmonises the copyright and related rights across member states of the European Union, and the Copyright and Related Rights Regulations 1996 implement European Union Directives on rental, lending, and other rights in the copyright field, and on copyright and related rights in relation to cable and satellite broadcasting.

An EC directive on Copyright and Related Rights in the Information Society came into force on 9 April 2001. The directive harmonises the rights for the use of copyright material in e-commerce (that is the rights of copying and electronic transmission) and will be transposed into UK law during 2003.

The Broadcasting Acts 1990 and 1996 made certain changes to the 1988 Act, particularly in introducing a statutory licence for broadcasting of sound recordings where the copyright owners license this use collectively.

What kind of work does copyright protect?
This includes original literary, dramatic, and artistic works, original music, and published editions of works (that is, the style and layout of a publication). Sound recordings on any medium—which can also include recordings of other copyright works, films, and videos—and broadcasts and cable programmes are also protected.

How does copyright apply to the Internet?
Under UK law, copyright material available over the Internet will generally be protected in the same way as material in other media. Generally, it is a good idea to mark each page you put on a website with the international © mark, followed by the name of the copyright owner and year of publication. You could also include information on your website about allowing others to reproduce your copyright material without permission.

Websites are accessible from all over the world. If material on your website is used without your permission, you would probably need to take action for copyright infringement in the location where the infringement occurs.

MAKING IT HAPPEN
Ensure copyright protection
There is no official register for copyright (unlike patents, registered designs, or trademarks). You don't actually need to take any action for your copyright to be protected. There are no application forms to fill in or fees to pay. Copyright comes into effect immediately, as soon as something is created and recorded in some way, for example, on paper, on film, as a sound recording, or on the Internet.

It is a good idea, however, to mark your work with the copyright symbol ©, followed by your name and the date, to warn

others against copying it. While this is not legally required in the United Kingdom and most other countries, marking in this way may help you during infringement proceedings. Take steps to provide evidence that you created the work at a particular time. For example, a copy of your work could be deposited with a bank or solicitor. Alternatively, send yourself a copy by special delivery, leaving the envelope unopened when you receive it.

A number of private companies operate unofficial registers, but check carefully what you will be paying for. Using one of these options does not prove that a work is original or created by you. However, it might be useful to be able to show that the work was in your possession at a particular date, for example if someone else claims that you have copied something of theirs that was actually created after your work.

'Fair dealing'
One of the exceptions to copyright protection is the concept of 'fair dealing'; this allows some unlicensed copying and other use without infringing copyright. Some copyright works may be used (photocopied, for example) to a limited extent, for research and private study, even if for commercial ends (except where work is a database). Making single copies of short extracts of a work or a single article from a journal may count as fair dealing. Copying by someone other than a researcher or student is not allowed if copies will be given to more than one person at the same time for the same purpose, for example, for a training session.

The economic impact of the use on the copyright owner is an important factor that the courts consider when deciding whether use is fair dealing.

License copyright
As a copyright owner, it is for you to decide whether and how to license use of your work. An exclusive licence could be granted, which enables the licensee to use the copyright work to the exclusion of all others, including you, the copyright owner. A

licence can be limited, for example, in duration, or in any other way. It is a contractual agreement between the copyright owner and user.

There are various organisations that can license certain uses of your work on your behalf, for example, the Performing Rights Society (**www.prs.co.uk**). Collective licensing means that a user may be offered a licence covering use of all the works covered by the collecting society.

Enforce your rights

Copyright is essentially a private right, so it is up to you how you decide to enforce it. It is sensible to try to resolve the matter with the party you think has infringed your copyright without resorting to official proceedings. If you are unable do this, you might have to go to court. Courts may grant a range of remedies, such as injunctions (to stop the other person making use of the material), damages for infringement, or orders to produce infringing goods. In some cases it may be necessary to demonstrate to the court that you have tried to solve the matter by mediation or arbitration if you wish the court to consider awarding you the best available remedy, including an award covering your costs. If you decide to go ahead with legal action you must get some professional advice, as this is a particularly complicated area of law. One of the many organisations that represents copyright owners may also be able to give you advice, or sometimes act on your behalf if you are a member.

Deliberate infringement of copyright can be considered a criminal offence. If it is on a large scale, for example pirate or counterfeit copies of compact discs, then you should inform either the police or your local trading standards department. They can decide whether action, including potential prosecution, is justified. If the police or trading standards decide not to take any action, you could still consider a private criminal prosecution if you believe there is a criminal offence, and you can still pursue a civil action against the alleged infringer.

Other ways of protecting your product

Copyright does not protect ideas. Although the work itself may be protected, the idea behind it is not. To protect an original idea, you will need to obtain a patent, which is a fairly complicated procedure. Names, titles, slogans, or phrases are also not protected by copyright; however, these could possibly be registered as a trade mark.

Copyright may protect the drawing from which an article is made, but it can not prevent the manufacture of purely industrial articles. However, articles that are replicated by an industrial process but which are of an aesthetically pleasing appearance may be protected by copyright where the article itself is an artistic work. This includes sculptures as well as works of artistic craftsmanship. Wherever it is possible to obtain a registered design for such articles, the copyright term will be reduced to match the term of protection for registered designs.

Protect your material overseas

Copyright material is protected in most other countries. The United Kingdom is a member of several international conventions in this field, including the Berne Convention for the Protection of Literary and Artistic Works, and the Universal Copyright Convention (UCC). Copyright material that is created by UK nationals or residents is protected in each member country of the conventions by the national law of that country. Most countries belong to at least one of the conventions, including all the Western European countries, the United States, and Russia. A full list of the conventions and their member countries may be obtained from the Copyright Directorate at the Patent Office.

In order to benefit from the automatic protection in other countries arising from the UCC you must mark your work with the international © symbol, followed by the name of the copyright owner and year of publication. Protection overseas can also arise from obligations in the agreement on Trade-Related Aspects of Intellectual Property Rights (TRIPS), which forms part of the World Trade Organisation (WTO) Agreement. Once again, this is automatic so you may also find your work is protected in WTO countries.

WHAT TO AVOID
Not keeping records
It is essential to keep records showing the date and author of any work produced in which copyright exists.

Failing to negotiate fair limits for copying needs
Check with trade associations or professional bodies to ensure that fair limits have been negotiated for typical copying needs within the type of business you are dealing with.

Not using the copyright symbol
Marking with a copyright symbol ©, followed by the copyright owner's name and year of publication is not required by UK law, but it can deter infringement. It may also be needed for protection overseas.

RECOMMENDED LINKS
Alliance Against IP Theft:
www.aacp.co.uk
British Copyright Council:
www.britishcopyright.org
Copyright Licensing Agency:
www.cla.co.uk
Federation Against Software Theft:
www.fast.org.uk
Patent Office:
www.patent.gov.uk

SEE ALSO
Complying with the Copyright of Others (p. 34)
Intellectual Property (p. 520)

Complying with the Copyright of Others

GETTING STARTED

If your business uses articles, literature, music, or other published work in producing goods or providing services, you may be at risk of contravening the copyright on that work. This actionlist outlines the types of published work that are protected by copyright, and gives guidance on how they may be used in compliance with copyright legislation. All small businesses need to be aware of these issues, as non-compliance can lead to a fine or even imprisonment.

FAQS

What kinds of material do you need permission to use?

Copyright protects various types of works. Any original literary works, for example, books, training materials, computer programs, song lyrics, newspaper articles, and some types of databases, are all protected by copyright. So, too, are original dramatic works, including dance or mime, and original music. Original artistic works, for example, paintings, engravings, photographs, sculptures, architectural designs, technical drawings, diagrams, maps, and logos are also protected, as are published editions of works (that is, the style and layout of a publication). Sound recordings on any medium, for example, tape or compact disc, are protected, and this can also include recordings of other copyright works. Finally, films and videos, and broadcasts and cable programmes also come under the protection of copyright. You will need to get permission from the owner of the copyright to use this material or any part of it unless it is subject to a copyright exception (see below).

When do you need permission?

In the majority of cases where you are intending to copy or use copyright material, you need to obtain permission from the copyright owner. If you are copying large amounts of material and/or making multiple copies, it is likely that you will need permission.

You must remember that buying or owning an original or a copy of a copyright work doesn't grant you permission to use it any way you wish. For example, buying a copy of a book, compact disc, video, or computer program does not necessarily give you the right to make copies (even for private use). Also, you will not necessarily have the right to play or show them in public. Other uses of copyright material, such as photocopying, scanning, or downloading from a CD-ROM or online database, all involve copying the work, so permission is generally needed.

However, there are certain exceptions to copyright. 'Fair dealing' is a concept that allows some unlicensed copying and other use without infringing copyright. Some copyright works may be copied (photocopied, for example) to a limited extent for research and private study without infringing copyright, even if this is for commercial ends. The exception to this is where the work you are copying is from a database. Making single copies of short extracts of a work or a single article from a journal may count as fair dealing, too.

Other copyright exceptions exist, for example, where a work is accidentally included in an artistic work, sound recording, film broadcast, or cable programme. You can find out more about copyright exceptions by visiting the Patent Office's intellectual property website (address given below).

Do I need permission to use material published on the Internet?

If you wish to put copyright material on the Internet, or distribute or download material that others have placed on the Internet, you should ensure that you have the permission of the copyright owners.

MAKING IT HAPPEN

Check that permission is required

Your first step is to approach the copyright owner to find out whether you need his or her permission to use the work. This can either be done directly, by going straight to the owner, or you can also make inquiries via one of the various copyright licensing bodies, if the owner belongs to one of them.

It is more usual to approach the copyright owner directly and ask for a licence to cover the use you require. The licence is a contract between you and the copyright owner and you can negotiate the terms and conditions, including the way the work is to be used and the cost of licence. There are no rules in copyright law governing what are acceptable terms and conditions.

Sometimes copyright owners are members of collective licensing bodies who can be approached for a licence. In particular, collective bodies exist for licensing the use of music and sound recordings, printed material, artistic works and characters, broadcast material, films, and television listings. More information about these licensing bodies is given below.

The main collective licensing bodies

One of the major issuers of copyright licences is the Copyright Licensing Agency (CLA). This is a non-profit making agency that licenses organisations for photocopying and scanning.

It licenses business, education, and government copying of extracts from books, journals, and periodicals. It also pays authors and publishers their share of fees. Licences include, for example, copying one book chapter or one article (under 30 pages) from a periodical, copying up to 5% of a law report, or making up to nine photocopies of extracts from books, journals, or periodicals. There are also licences for copies from published originals (not from faxed or photocopied books, journals, or periodicals) and the supply of copies to colleagues and those outside the organisation working together on related matters.

It is important to remember that copies made under the licence cannot be sold. If you need to exceed the limits of your licence, the CLA Rapid Clearance Service (CLARCS) generally allows you to pay for extra permissions.

The CLA's licensed works include all books, periodicals, and journals published in the United Kingdom and other countries where a reciprocal agreement exists. However, there are exceptions. These include works on the Excluded Works List (this list can be found on the CLA website, the address of which is given below), newspapers, maps, charts or books of tables, printed music (including words), public examination papers, workbooks, work cards or assignment sheets, in-house business publications, and works published overseas where there is no agreement.

There are many other licensing bodies. The Newspaper Licensing Agency (NLA), licenses the photocopying, faxing, and digital copying of all of the United Kingdom's national newspapers and many regional and international newspapers. It offers sole traders, companies, and any other body a one-stop-shop for a licence to copy, for internal management use. The British Library Document Supply Centre enables you to obtain copies of a huge range of published work. Customers pay for standard photocopying costs, as well as a copyright fee, which varies according to the individual publisher. This is then passed on to the CLA for distribution to copyright owners worldwide. The Performing Right Society (PRS) administers the performing right in the musical works of its members, who comprise composers, songwriters, and music publishers. It issues licences and distributes fees on behalf of music copyright holders. You will need a PRS licence if you plan to play or perform music in public (even if it is just a radio in a shop or factory). The Music Publishers' Association (United States) provides contact details of copyright owners if you wish to photocopy printed music, arrange music, or use music in a film or commercial. This will enable you to contact the copyright owner directly.

The Mechanical Copyright Protection

Society (MCPS) licenses the recording of copyright music. You will need to contact it if you want to record copyright musical works. The Phonographic Performance Ltd (PPL) issues licences for the public performance or broadcasting of sound recordings, and collects licence fees from broadcast and public performance users on behalf of the record companies. Generally, any business which plays recorded music should have a PPL licence. Video Performance Ltd is the UK collecting society that licenses music videos for broadcast, and issues licences for the public performance of video recordings.

If you, as a user or prospective user of copyright works that are licensed collectively, are dissatisfied with the terms or conditions of licences or licensing schemes operated by collective licensing bodies, you can apply to the Copyright Tribunal for independent adjudication on the matter.

WHAT TO AVOID
Not checking with the copyright owner
It is vital to check with the copyright owner before using copyright material. You may be liable for a fine or even imprisonment for infringing copyright work. The name of the copyright owner should be provided somewhere on the piece of work, but if you are unable to find it, contact the relevant licensing body for help.

Not seeking the right advice
The Copyright Directorate is an executive agency of the DTI providing information and advice on all intellectual property issues, and is part of the Patent Office. The government's intellectual property website (address given below) can provide you with detailed information about copyright and whether you will need to get copyright permission.

RECOMMENDED LINKS
The Copyright Licensing Agency Ltd:
www.cla.co.uk
Newspaper Licensing Agency:
www.nla.co.uk
British Library Document Supply Centre:
**www.bl.uk/services/document/
   dsc.html**
Performing Right Society:
www.prs.co.uk
Music Publishers Association:
www.mpaonline.org.uk
Mechanical Copyright Protection Society
   Ltd:
www.mcps.co.uk
Patent Office:
www.patent.gov.uk
Phonographic Performance Ltd:
www.ppluk.com

SEE ALSO
Intellectual Property (p. 520)
**Using Copyright to Protect Your Work
   (p. 30)**

Registering a Trade Mark

GETTING STARTED

A trade mark is a distinctive symbol that your business can use to make its goods and services immediately recognisable to consumers. It is a good way of differentiating your products and services from those of your competitors, and it implies a consistent level of quality or service. There are several restrictions on what can be registered and protected as a trade mark. This actionlist looks at what is involved in successfully registering a trade mark, both in the United Kingdom and abroad.

FAQS

What is a trade mark?

The idea of trade marks was developed in the late 1800s to help established businesses stop competitors stealing their sales and possibly damaging their reputation by imitating their products. A trade mark may be a brand name for a specific product or be representative of the business as a whole. Today, a successful brand name or company logo is a valuable asset to its owner.

The Trade Marks Act 1994 defines a registerable trade mark as 'any sign that is capable of being represented graphically, capable of distinguishing goods or services of one undertaking from those of another undertaking'. This Act also makes provision to harmonise UK law with that of the European Union.

A sign that can be represented graphically is a marking such as words, letters, and numerals; the shape of the goods or their packaging; and musical jingles (or even smells). There are other special types of trade marks. For example, Certification Trade Marks, which are used to show that items to which they apply possess specific characteristics (such as materials used, place of origin, or method of manufacture). The owners of Certification Trade Marks can obtain a monopoly on such marks provided that they do not trade in the goods/services themselves. The owners can also authorise others to use the mark in regard to its specific qualities. Collective Marks are marks for use by members of an organisation or association. The Trade Marks Act 1994 also provides for the registration and use of Collective Marks.

When is it important to register a trade mark?

Registration of a mark is not compulsory, but it does protect the use of the reputation that the mark represents. By registering a trade mark, your business gets the right to prevent others from using an identical or confusingly similar mark on goods and services that are the same (or similar) to your own.

If your mark is registered, your business can sue for infringement, with its certificate of registration as evidence of ownership. Without this, you would have to demonstrate that a reputation has been established with regard to that mark and that its use by others will damage this reputation.

When registering a trade mark, you will specify the class of goods and services that your business wants to protect; but the legislation allows you to protect the trade mark against confusion with a wider range of goods, including those that may not be similar to your own.

How can I protect a trade mark overseas?

Registration within the United Kingdom does not give automatic protection overseas, but several schemes allow international registration without having to undertake individual applications in each country. If you think that you may trade overseas, it is worth investigating existing countries' trade marks before investing in packaging and promotional literature that may have to be changed.

When a UK application has been filed, the date can be used to establish a priority date within countries party to the Paris Convention, provided this is taken up within six months. A UK application can also be used as the basis for an international application within the member countries of the Madrid Protocol, through the World Intellectual Property Organization (WIPO). This gives protection in the states that are members of the Madrid Protocol, by designating which states are to be covered.

You can apply for a European Union trade mark from the Office for Harmonization in the Internal Market (OHIM) in Spain. This gives protection in all 15 member states of the European Union, including the United Kingdom. Applications can be submitted directly to the OHIM or through the United Kingdom Patent Office. Applications are usually submitted directly to OHIM. If protection is required in only one or two states, it may be cheaper to make a direct application to the Trade Mark office in each country, as opposed to a European Union application.

What are the requirements for new trade marks?

The definition of what can be registered as a trade mark was widened in the Trade Marks Act 1994, but a number of conditions still apply. Getting it right first time will save you time and money.

A new trade mark must be distinct from all existing marks (including those of overseas registers that can claim protection in the United Kingdom) and from words and symbols that may be in use in the normal course of trade, or are customary in the current language. A mark containing geographical marks, or referring to the quality or character of the goods, can now be registered, but only if it has become distinctive and associated with that product through use.

A mark that arises exclusively from the nature of the goods, gives substantial value to the goods, or is necessary to obtain a technical result, cannot be registered. A mark must not be misleading or contrary to public morality, and marks containing representations such as the crown or heraldic

symbols are restricted. Registered trade marks should not consist of words or symbols in common usage, or which will unnecessarily restrict other traders' activities, because of the monopoly granted to the owner. The exception to this is if it can be shown that the mark has become established as distinguishable through use.

If a mark should be refused registration, Hearing Officers can advise on the amendments that will meet the requirements.

MAKING IT HAPPEN
The registration process

Before making your application, you can search the Trade Mark Register at the Patent Office (also available on the Patent Office's website) to see if any existing marks might prevent your mark from being registered. Alternatively, upon application, the Search and Advisory Service will ensure that a new mark fulfils the correct criteria.

To make an application, complete form TM3 and send it, with the fee, to the Trade Marks Registry. Currently the application fee stands at £200, for one class of goods or services, with a further £50 for each additional class under which protection is sought. Applications can be made by an individual or by a trade mark agent; a UK address must be given on the form for correspondence.

The Patent Office will examine the application within two months. Applicants then have up to six months to overcome any objections or put their application in order. Following this, the new mark will be published in the weekly *Trade Marks Journal*, to allow any objections by others to be raised, before it is entered onto the register.

Protection lasts for 10 years from the date of registration, and can be renewed every 10 years, for a fee. Once a mark has been registered, no changes can be made to the mark itself (except in a few circumstances), so it is important that the description submitted is clear and correct. It is the responsibility of the trade mark owners to uphold the rights afforded by the registration of their trade marks. Any infringements have to be pursued through the courts, inevitably involving specialised legal services and costs; these costs would normally be recoverable by the trade mark owner if the case against the infringement is successful. A third party can request a mark's removal from the register if it has not been used for five years.

If you have already applied to register a trade mark in a country which is party to the Paris Convention or the Madrid Protocol, you may be able to use the date of that application as the priority date of application for registration in the United Kingdom.

Domain names and trade marks
In recent years, use of the Internet as a trading medium has grown, resulting in a conflict between the allocation of domain names and trade marks. The Internet Corporation for Assigned Names and Numbers (ICANN) has partly resolved these issues through an administrative system for resolving domain name disputes involving trade marks. These measures have led to fewer cases of 'cybersquatting' of trade marks in the generic top-level domains. Further consultation is now under way to protect intellectual property at the level of the country code in top-level domains.

WHAT TO AVOID
Not carrying out thorough research
Before investing in registration, think about why you're doing it. This will help you determine how many classes of goods and services you wish to apply for, and whether you will require protection overseas, now or later. When designing product names and promotional literature, check what your competitors (or businesses in similar fields) have already registered; this will avoid possible complaints later.

Not being consistent in the use of your trade mark
Always display your trade mark in the form in which it was registered. The symbol ® should be used in conjunction with the trade mark in countries in which it is registered, and ™ where it is not.

Not enforcing your rights
Check what is being registered through the Office for Harmonization in the Internal Market, as those marks have rights throughout the European Union. Also check the *Community Trade Mark Bulletin* for applications. It is possible to subscribe to a professional watching service, so that either the trade mark holder or the client can be notified if a third party tries to register a trade mark, company name, or domain name which is confusingly similar to that of the client.

RECOMMENDED LINKS
Institute of Trade Mark Attorneys (ITMA):
www.itma.org.uk
Patent Office:
www.patent.gov.uk

SEE ALSO
Intellectual Property (p. 520)

SETTING UP OR
ACQUIRING A BUSINESS

Understanding Business Models

GETTING STARTED

There are three main types of legal status available to you when starting a business. These are sole trader, partnership, and limited company. You will need to take into account several considerations when deciding which of these will be best for your new business. For example, you will need to think about tax and administration implications, the image of the business, legal requirements, financial issues, and so on. This actionlist shows you how to decide which status is most suitable for your business, and raises some of the issues you may need to consider.

FAQS

When is sole trader status suitable?

The status of sole trader is convenient in situations where just one person will own the business, and will have final responsibility for its management and development. It is possible to employ other people if you are a sole trader, but ultimately the business is the individual, and there is no separate legal status.

There are various advantages to operating as a sole trader. You are not required to register the business with Companies House. This means that you can avoid the costs involved in registration, such as employing accountants or lawyers to carry out the registration process. There is also less paperwork to deal with, regarding legislation and tax, than for a limited company. The National Insurance contribution levels for sole traders are generally lower than those paid by limited companies. Also, the owner is entitled to all the profits made by the business. He or she is also able to keep overall control of the business.

When is partnership status suitable?

A partnership is a good vehicle to use when your business will involve two or more people owning a business together. Like a sole trader, a partnership has no separate legal identity, and does not need to register with Companies House.

There are several advantages to operating as a partnership. The structure of a partnership can be flexible, according to the deed of partnership. As with sole traders, there is less paperwork to deal with, regarding legis-

lation and tax, than for a limited company. However, unlike sole traders, management responsibilities, risks and losses are shared. Partners can often bring a variety of different skills and experience to the business. Also, involving more people means that more capital can be raised among them. Another advantage is that partnerships cannot be taken over by other businesses.

There are two other kinds of partnership, a limited partnership and a limited liability company. A limited partnership is a partnership which has at least one partner who is a general partner (that is to say, he or she has management rights and unlimited liability), and at least one limited partner. A limited partner, who may be an individual or a company, contributes a fixed amount (as capital or property) to the partnership, but is only liable for partnership debts or liabilities up to the amount they have contributed. A limited partnership must register its details with Companies House.

A limited liability partnership (LLP) has the flexibility and tax status of a partnership, but the benefits of limited liability. The liability of all of the partners is limited to their capital contribution to the LLP, so personal assets cannot be seized to settle debts. Limited liability partnerships are required to register with Companies House.

When is limited company status suitable?

The main advantage of limited company status is that the owners (shareholders) have limited liability for the debts of the business up to the value of their shareholding; they are not personally liable for company debts. This means that the liability of the owners of the business is limited to the initial cost of their shares.

The status of a limited company tends to raise the credibility of the business in the eyes of suppliers and customers, as it suggests that business is large and relatively established. This could be important if your business is competing in a market dominated by large companies, or where customers may feel less comfortable with small or new businesses.

There are many other advantages, including the following:

- finance can be raised by selling shares in the business
- employees are able to own a share in the business
- a limited company has a separate legal identity to that of its owners, and this allows the company to continue trading despite the death or resignation of a member
- the name of the company is protected effectively

What is a franchise?

A franchise is where a licence has been granted by one business (the franchisor) to another (the franchisee), allowing the franchisee to use the trademark and name of the franchisor, as well as its methods for marketing, managing, administration, and so on, within the business.

There are several advantages to franchising. The franchisee, by investing in a proven business format, can become the owner of a business with a well-known brand name, while at the same time overcoming some of the difficulties associated with a new business. The franchisee also receives help in finding and refurbishing premises. Help will be given in obtaining any planning permission and purchasing stock and equipment, as well as with staff training, marketing, and advertising. The franchisee is therefore able to concentrate on the day-to-day running of the business, without many of the pressures usually associated with self-employment. The franchisor will be able to provide

specialist managerial advice and guidance to help overcome any problems that a small business is likely to encounter, and the franchisee will benefit from the economies of scale of operating as part of a large organisation.

MAKING IT HAPPEN
Set up as a sole trader

As a sole trader, you can simply start trading; there is no requirement to register with Companies House, although there are certain rules about disclosure of ownership. It is important to remember, however, that during the first three months of trading you must contact your local HM Revenue & Customs (HMRC) office to register for income tax and National Insurance. If you don't, you may be liable for a fine.

Setting up as a partnership

If you decide to set up a partnership, each partner must tell HMRC that he or she is starting in business. All letterheads, business cards, and other relevant business stationery must be printed to display both trading names and personal names, if these are different. Partners should draw up a deed of partnership with a solicitor to set out clearly the terms and conditions of the partnership.

Set up as a limited company

A limited company must be registered with Companies House before trading commences. This requires certain documents, available from Companies House, to be completed and submitted with a registration fee of £20. An accountant or solicitor can help you to draw up and submit these documents. A private company must have at least one shareholder, one director, and a company secretary (who must be different from the sole director). If you are setting up a limited company, it is possible to buy existing or 'off-the-shelf' companies via a Company Registration Agent, accountant, or solicitor. All the paperwork will have already been prepared, and the company will be able to start trading almost immediately.

Set up a franchise

Before you make a decision, contact the British Franchise Association (BFA), and talk to existing franchisees, to find out more information about the franchise you are considering purchasing. If you decide to go ahead, and your application is accepted, you will probably find that a first interview with the franchisor is offered. This is valuable, as it gives both parties the opportunity to appraise one another. Provided both parties wish to continue, there will be a second interview to begin formalising the agreement. It is a good idea to take advice from a specialist professional adviser before signing any documents.

WHAT TO AVOID

Underestimating your liability

A sole trader has unlimited liability for the debts of the business, such as bank loans and amounts owing to creditors. This means that if your business fails, your personal savings and assets could be at risk.

In a partnership there is also unlimited liability, and each partner is personally responsible for the debts of the partnership. As a partner, therefore, your personal assets may be seized to pay off debts.

A limited company must comply with a wide range of complex and detailed legislation which is not applicable to sole traders and partnerships; this can add to the administrative and financial burden.

Underestimating the role of franchisors

Franchisors exert a fairly high degree of control over the franchise operation, so although the franchisee is legally independent, he or she will never be completely independent of the franchisor.

The franchise proving more expensive than originally thought

Franchises can be expensive investments. After the initial fee, there will be ongoing fees for the continuing support provided by the franchisor. Under the franchise agreement the franchisee may be obliged to buy supplies and equipment from the franchisor, which they may have been able to purchase cheaper elsewhere.

RECOMMENDED LINKS

British Franchise:
www.british-franchise.org
Companies House:
www.companieshouse.gov.uk
Companies Registry (Northern Ireland):
www.detini.gov.uk

SEE ALSO

Deciding Whether to Start a Business (p. 2)
Setting Up a Business as a Non-profit Organisation (p. 63)
Setting Up a Business as a Private Limited Company (p. 60)
Small and Growing Businesses (p. 486)

Running a Family Business

GETTING STARTED

Working with their family is an option that appeals to many small business owners. The main advantage of a family-run business is that the ownership structure is built on lasting relationships of trust and commitment. These are usually essential to the successful running of a small business, and are often more easily achieved between members of the same family. Conversely, this kind of business can hit problems if disputes erupt over the sharing of profits or the ownership of assets. Family ties can sometimes take precedence over the need to make objective, and sometimes painful, business decisions.

FAQS

Is there more than one type of family business?

As with any other type of small business, there are three principal forms in which a family business can operate: as a sole trader, a partnership, or a limited company. In the first example, a single family member would own the business but they would be able to employ relatives if required. A partnership could involve a husband and wife, a parent and child, or some similar combination, which would jointly own the assets of a business. You may decide to manage things on even terms or split responsibilities in some other way, but at the end of the day everybody would share equally in the profits or proceeds from selling the enterprise. The third option, which is also known as incorporation, requires the registration of a company, the appointment of directors and the issuing of shareholdings among the family members—and perhaps other investors—taking part. Family members may get involved in the practical running of the business, or they may choose simply to be shareholders and not necessarily do any work in the company.

What difficulties could a family business experience?

The informal relationships and culture of family life will stand in stark contrast to the formal demands of managing a business. A family unit may find it difficult to adjust to working together in a businesslike way. For example, if you work with members of your family, you'll need to be able to discuss and develop ideas effectively with them. This can be hard for some people to get used to and conflicts can build up: we all play 'roles' in our families and it may be hard, for example, for an elder sibling to get used to working for a younger brother or sister. You'll also need to be on guard against insular attitudes developing, a cultural resistance to change, and possibly inter-generational conflicts between older and younger family members.

Everyone involved should clearly understand that being in business requires a commitment in time, energy, and money. Your entire family's way of life may be affected, so don't be surprised by some resentments and frustrations along the way.

What strengths do family businesses have?

Combining your knowledge, skills, and experience gained from other walks of life can prove very rewarding. If you can find the right chemistry and balance of abilities between the different individuals involved, you'll be helping your business stand out from others and contributing towards its success. Many businesses gain their strength from family commitment and loyalty, resulting in high levels of trust, co-operation, and shared long-term goals. Getting the right mix of complementary temperaments and talents is important. Younger family members may, for instance, have a better grasp of technology and may be more comfortable with newer techniques for managing a business and adapting to change. Older members could bring with them the experience and authority that help build up good contacts and business relationships with suppliers and customers.

MAKING IT HAPPEN
Think about whether it's the right option for you and your family

Before embarking on your venture a number of factors could help to determine what kind of structure you should adopt. The deciding factors should include:

- Can you arrange and secure adequate finance?
- Are you creating a trading, manufacturing, or service business?
- Will you be able to generate profits quickly, or will you have to take some losses while you're establishing the business?
- Can you cope with the compliance requirements of a limited company?

It's vital to get good advice before putting together your business plan and you should spell out in detail the consequences of the decisions about the nature and structure of your enterprise to every family member involved. They should be aware of the legal and other implications of such things as directorships and share ownership, complying with tax, financial, and employment rules, buying or leasing premises, professional and employer's liability insurance, and the myriad other regulations that increasingly have an impact on businesses.

Make a realistic assessment of your strengths and weaknesses as well as the long-term opportunities and threats you could face. List such things as the different abilities, educational backgrounds, and technical knowledge of your family members and anyone else you are planning to employ in the business. Also think about:

- your target markets
- products and services
- who your main competitors will be
- technological and other changes are taking place in your chosen sector
- marketing and promotional techniques you'll be using

Remember to weigh risks against benefits. It's also essential to put in place from the outset monitoring and measuring systems that will allow you to track how well your business is performing and to review the progress it's making. This will help you to modify the targets and operating methods you'll be using to keep the business on course.

Investigate the relevant regulations

While most laws and regulations that apply to other kinds of businesses also affect a family business, there are some additional rules you'll need to be aware of:

- Employment legislation applies to family companies who 'employ' their directors, even if wages are not actually drawn.
- Copyright may have to be protected if a member dies. Patents, trade marks, and licences need to be reviewed to prevent infringements.
- Inheritance tax planning is essential if assets are held that can be used within the business.
- Capital gains tax planning is also important because transactions are often between connected persons for tax purposes. If a transaction is not conducted at arm's length and the price appears too low, HM Revenue & Customs can use the open market value (instead of the actual price) for tax purposes.
- If you sell goods at less than the true value or take goods from the business for personal use this must be accounted for in your financial records.
- Farm tenancies can contain rights of succession. Land and property owned by individuals but used in the business may create problems if there is a change of ownership or usage.

WHAT TO AVOID
Being unrealistic about how well you are doing

In a family business there may be a tendency to take an unrealistic view of what is going on and how well it's performing. For example, if your spouse or children are involved they'll often end up working long hours without extra pay, which can give a false sense of how you're doing. You should therefore assess the true value of the time and effort being put in, and if possible compare how well you're performing against similar businesses. If your business manages to survive only at the expense of family members who are receiving poor wages, you're not doing justice to them or operating your enterprise on a sound basis. If they should fall ill or quit the business, would you be able to find anyone else to do the job for the same rate of pay?

Overestimating family members' commitment

Don't be tempted to take too rosy a view of the commitment of family members. Those with less enthusiasm for the hard work involved, or who may be reluctant to take on some of the more mundane but necessary tasks, could end up causing you major problems.

Relying too much on one person

If you or one of your family has natural leadership qualities, and is likely to provide most of the drive behind the business, you might face a problem if that person retires or moves on to pastures new. Try to avoid over-dependency of this kind and build in greater adaptability. Aim to retrain members of the business as things develop, so you'll have the capacity to re-assign or replace individuals if necessary.

Responding ineffectively to disputes

In a family environment members can often have trouble defining what belongs to them and what is the property of the business. You need to put in place effective systems to monitor the finances of your business, and some form of mediation for handling disputes. Your bank manager or accountant can provide a dispassionate review in the event of any serious conflict over cash. There will be other kinds of disagreements for which you'll have to establish some method of arbitration if matters threaten to get out of hand.

RECOMMENDED LINKS

Centre for Family Enterprise, Glasgow
  Caledonian University:
www.familyenterprise.org
The Family Business Centre:
www.thefamilybusiness.co.uk
Stoy Centre for Family Business:
www.scfb.co.uk

Setting Up Your Franchise

GETTING STARTED

One of the most readily available ways of starting your own business is to buy a franchise. Compared to other forms of start-up, this is often a relatively risk-free method of getting established in business, because the development of the product or service has already been done for you by the source company (franchisor). One of the most important things for many people is that franchising gives them an opportunity to become their own boss within the protective framework of a larger organisation with a successful formula. When you buy a franchise, however, you should understand that your success or failure in the enterprise will be largely down to your own hard work and the business skills you learn. It shouldn't be seen as an easy option, because to become successful the operation of a franchise requires as much dedication and effort as any other kind of business.

Franchising offers both advantages and disadvantages over other types of business, and there are some basic steps that should be followed in setting up in this way.

FAQS

What is a franchise?

A franchise is basically an agreement between one business (the franchisor) and yourself (the franchisee) that enables you to use the trade name and trade mark, and supply the branded services or products, of the franchisor. You pay a fee in return for the granting of a franchise licence and you have to comply with any terms and conditions set by the franchisor in an agreement. Another definition of franchising, put forward by the European Franchise Federation, describes it as 'a system of marketing goods, products, or services, based on a close and ongoing collaboration between legally and financially separate and independent undertakings'. Typical franchise sectors are fast food chains, fitness centres, grocery and convenience stores.

What should I look for in a good franchise?

Perhaps the most important thing a good franchise opportunity should offer you is a product or service with a proven track record. You should, ideally, gain access to a recognised brand name. All the research and development effort on the service or product should have been carried out by the franchisor, who'll also be responsible for maintaining standards and guaranteeing quality control. Other benefits should include access to help, advice, and training, as well as participation in marketing and advertising activities that would be beyond your reach as a small business.

What is a franchise network?

This is an association of independently owned businesses selling a range of products or services developed by an umbrella organisation. They are linked together by the common brand identities and the support activities they share, such as marketing, advertising, and training.

What are the disadvantages of franchising?

There are certain things over which you may have no control as a franchisee. For example, you're unlikely to have any decisive say over the development and introduction of new products or services. The franchise agreement will normally require you to contribute to expenditure (up to an agreed amount) on marketing and advertising campaigns on behalf of the franchise network, and you may have little or no opportunity to influence the way that this is done. Furthermore, the appointment of other franchisees to the network, who you may feel are unsuitable or less competent than you, will be beyond your control (though the franchise agreement should give you exclusive rights over a defined geographic area). Any damage done to the reputation of the network could impact adversely on your business.

What costs should I expect?

Before you begin trading you'll have to pay a fee to the franchisor for granting the initial licence. This will normally be followed by an annual premium, called the management services fee, which is likely to be based on a percentage of your annual turnover. You'll be responsible for the professional fees of solicitors, accountants, and business consultants you appoint for negotiating the franchise agreement and setting up your enterprise. The normal overheads of your business will include such things as buying supplies and materials; staff wages; taxes and VAT; rent, rates, and maintenance of machinery and property; vehicle running costs; and any advertising and promotional material you produce under your own steam.

MAKING IT HAPPEN
Look for a suitable franchise

You should look for a franchise package that will include all the things necessary to enable you successfully to operate an outlet of an established business. This includes, first and foremost, a commercially viable product or service. Your franchisor should offer you discounts on bulk supplies of products and be able to help you find start-up capital (most established franchisors have special arrangements with the banks to help new franchisees) and suitable premises. To enable you to become fully operational—even if you're a novice at the business—you should be offered adequate initial training, after which you should have a programme of courses and seminars to continue your development and keep you abreast of changes affecting your sector. As well as giving you help and advice, your franchisor should encourage you to meet other franchisees in the network who'll be able to pass on useful insights and tips about the best way to manage your business.

Choose a franchise that best suits your needs

While you may have the dedication and commitment required to run a franchise, you should nevertheless choose one that most closely matches your aspirations and capabilities. There are events and services available that will help you to make the right decision. You could start by attending a franchise exhibition where you'll be able to compare and contrast different types of opportunities. The British Franchise Association (BFA), banks, and local business organisations often run seminars for potential franchisees, and the BFA can provide a franchisee information pack. Consultants attached to reputable franchise organisations can also help you to make the right choice.

Carry out some basic checks

Before you make your final decision about the franchise to go with, you should check out certain information. This will include examining:

- financial projections for your proposed outlet
- proof that the franchised product or service is viable and can be traded profitably
- a list of existing franchisees in the network and their trading performance
- what training will be available to help you establish your outlet
- evidence that the proposed franchise agreement will protect your rights

Particular care should be taken about joining a network that has no proven track record. However, organisations that are members of the BFA must follow certain rules, which include disclosing the information listed above.

Think about the franchise agreement

This is a legally binding contract between you and the franchisor. While you may be able to negotiate various aspects of the agreement, there are no hard and fast rules about what it should contain. The European Franchise Federation (EFF) has, however, put together a checklist for what it believes should constitute a good agreement. It must, for example, comply with national and EU laws and abide by the EFF's Code of Ethics; be clear and unambiguous in stating the rights, duties, and responsibilities of you and the franchisor; and reflect the interests of all members of the franchise network.

When evaluating the agreement, the EEF suggests you consider the following key issues:

- the rights granted to you and the franchisor
- your obligations and those of the franchisor
- the goods and services provided to you by the franchisor
- the terms and amounts of your payment for licences, management fees, and other costs imposed by the franchisor
- the duration of your agreement
- the basis for any renewal of your agreement
- the terms by which you may sell or otherwise transfer your interest in your franchise
- the terms by which you may use the franchisor's trade names, brand names, logos, store signs, and service marks
- the franchisor's right to adapt their franchise system to meet new or changed methods and market conditions
- your rights to terminate a franchise agreement before it expires
- the ownership of property, both tangible and intangible, provided to you by the franchisor and provisions for its surrender when an agreement is terminated

WHAT TO AVOID
Being unrealistic

Running a franchise involves a huge amount of time, effort, and money. Make sure before you take the plunge that you're prepared to commit what it will take to make the business a success. Talk to other franchisees to get a realistic idea of just how great the commitment must be.

Falling for the 'hard sell'

Don't be taken in by promises and the sales pitch from some organisations that may attend franchise exhibitions. If you find what appears to be a promising opportunity at an exhibition, before you sign anything take your time to think through carefully the proposals put to you. A reputable franchisor will encourage you to reflect before you commit yourself.

Signing up to a bad agreement

Be wary of generalisations in any franchise agreement. Make sure the terms apply specifically to you and your franchise, and that the details cover your particular requirements. Another thing to avoid is signing up to an agreement that does not last long enough to enable you to make a decent return on your investment. You should get a solicitor experienced in this area of commercial law to check the agreement before you sign; this added expense could save you a great deal in the longer term.

Setting up too close to an existing franchise

While your franchisor should make sure that you don't locate your business too close to other franchises in the same network, check that there are no similar outlets operated by other organisations. This can happen in some areas of retailing and food catering, for example, and if you're not careful you could end up with unnecessary competition.

RECOMMENDED LINKS

The British Franchise Association:
www.british-franchise.org.uk
The European Franchise Federation:
www.eff-franchise.com
Franchise Development Services:
www.franchise-group.com
Franchise World:
www.franchiseworld.co.uk

Understanding the Pros and Cons of a Mail Order Business

GETTING STARTED

The home shopping market in the United Kingdom has grown steadily over the last few years and is expected to be worth more than £35 billion in 2006. Mail order plays a major role in this and is thought to account for around 33% of the entire home shopping network. In the past few years the sector has started to embrace the Internet, partly because of the threat posed by e-commerce fuelled by the growth of online retail.

Mail order trading is a good way of creating relationships with customers without the overheads of retail premises, and small firms can usually afford to sell in this way. Niche businesses in sectors as varied as arts and crafts and organic foods can also employ this method to good effect, particularly when they're distributing goods across a wide geographical area.

Having said that, new and innovative ways of shopping—coupled with greater buying options from the large high street stores—have hit traditional mail order sales. Mail order trading is also littered with legal restrictions including provisions in the Consumer Protection (Distance Selling) Regulations, the Data Protection Act, and the Sale of Goods Act.

FAQS

How does a mail order business work?

Mail order firms generally sell goods through a catalogue but the growth of the Internet and direct mail have opened up new ways of reaching the market. Other ways of selling to the mail order customer include leaflets, brochures, and small advertisements in newspapers or magazines. Adverts for your catalogue or a specific product can be placed with the specialist media to help target the right customers—this may even include a printed order form for ease of use. Many mail order specialists now operate a website either to promote the business or sell to customers online.

How do I promote my mail order business?

Unlike a shop, which will attract passing trade, mail order consumers need to be told what you're offering and how or why they should buy it. If you're selling several different lines, or your product is particularly complicated, you can use leaflets or catalogues to show your products effectively. These provide photographs and descriptions of the goods, as well as an order form with your trading terms and conditions. The main disadvantage of using this method is that production costs can be high. One way round this issue is to charge for catalogues so that only serious potential customers request them. If they place an order, the catalogue cost can be refunded.

You can use direct mail to target very specific sections of the population, which is useful if you manufacture a specialist product. Additionally, some national papers and magazines have specific sections for mail order businesses.

What is the best way to ensure payment for goods?

Most small mail order firms ask for payment with the order, and it may be advisable to wait for a cheque to be cleared before the goods are sent. Make sure that customers don't send cash through the post, as this is a very insecure method. Credit card payments can be a convenient and safe means of remittance, and many customers prefer this payment method.

What legal issues should I be aware of?

The Consumer Protection (Distance Selling) Regulations 2000 apply when goods and services are sold by distance communication. The Data Protection Act 1998 sets rules for anyone keeping and processing personal information on individuals and, because of the nature of the business, mail order firms are bound to hold information of this type. If credit (subject to certain exemptions) is offered, the business may need a Category A Consumer Credit Business licence under the Consumer Credit Act 1974. Finally, if you're selling goods online, you must make sure customers see the terms and conditions of sale before they commit to a purchase.

MAKING IT HAPPEN
Find some customers!

Promoting your business is crucial if it is to survive in a very competitive marketplace, especially because mail order companies, by their very nature, aren't in the public eye in the same way as shops. Promotional campaigns are crucial so you must target them very carefully and thoroughly. Business is increasingly turning to the Web and customers will expect you to have some online presence. It may also be worth seeing if you can take payment via the site, and the information on your website should be updated regularly to encourage customers to return. You could also stay in touch with customers by e-mail, giving details of special offers, for instance. One of the main advantages of advertising in this way is that if the prices of any of your products need to be changed, the website can be altered immediately, which saves on the cost of printing a new price list or placing an advert.

Measure the effectiveness of your promotions

Assessing the success of any promotional activity you do is essential and one way to do this is to code your adverts in the press by placing an identifying letter or symbol on the reply slip to show its origin. If there isn't room for this, you could get customers to reply to a slightly different name or address depending on the media source in which you've placed the advert.

This way you'll get a better idea of which medium is the most effective for promoting your product.

Another way is to keep a record of:

- Where customer enquiries come from, such as media, personal recommendation, direct mailing, or other sources.
- Whether the enquiry becomes a sale. This will enable you to determine which adverts lead to sales (as opposed to just enquiries) and to target advertising even more effectively.

Respond to Enquiries and Orders

Respond to enquiries and orders promptly and efficiently, providing a good level of customer service. If you're unable to fulfil an order, or you know it will be delivered later than the usual delivery time, take the initiative and contact customers to let them know what's happening.

It may be a good idea to introduce a customer relationship management system into your business. These systems operate by integrating all of the information held on each customer and sharing this among your various business functions, such as accounts and sales. This allows you to deal effectively with all aspects of your relationship with a customer.

Take orders

Whether your order forms appear in print or online, do make sure that they're clearly laid out and request all the relevant information you need from the customer. This should include:

- name and address
- delivery address (if different from home or business address)
- code of item being ordered (if there is one)
- quantity of items being ordered
- total price of order
- credit card details (if that's the chosen method of payment)

Think about packaging and delivery

Managing the delivery process efficiently is the core element of customer service for mail order businesses: delivery delays can drive customers mad. The way you package your product for transportation is very important, as you'll want your goods to reach the customer safely and in good condition.

The kind of packaging you use will depend on the nature of the goods, the type and length of journey, the method of transport used, and how the goods will be handled at both ends. Although recycling is important in the packaging industry, it's vital that goods aren't compromised by using materials that may collapse or make them more susceptible to theft.

Labels on external packaging should show the package number, the destination, and something that enables the customer to identify it when taking delivery. This information should also be written on any documentation provided with the goods. Labelling must conform to the packaging legislation in the destination country with any marks or symbols on at least three visible faces.

The type of transport you choose will depend on the type of product you're selling and where it's being sent. The most common options available include road freight (such as couriers for door-to-door collection and delivery), Parcelforce, rail (bulk freight), and air (urgent long distance and overseas deliveries). As part of your customer service, you may decide to offer:

- free delivery
- free delivery for orders over a specified amount
- guaranteed next day delivery
- a surcharge for guaranteed delivery within 48 hours

You'll need to make sure that such guarantees can be met, and decide whether the expense is worth any corresponding increase in customers or loyalty.

WHAT TO AVOID
Using a Post Office Box number
When you're advertising, don't give a PO box as the reply address. They tend to give an impression of a business being evasive, and often contribute to a low response rate.

Confusing the customer
Take time to read through all the wording in your catalogue, website, or any other medium you use to advertise. Even better, get someone with a bit of 'distance' to read it through for you, so that you can be sure none of your material is confusing to your customer. Keep price, postage, and VAT costs separate so people can see exactly what they're paying for, and always give an estimated delivery date.

Upsetting customers
If you're selling a product via an advert, give a guarantee. Don't forget that you're expecting customers to buy after having seen only a few words and a drawing or photograph, so they must be able to send it back (perhaps even at your expense) if they're not happy with their purchase. Put yourself in their shoes and be aware of what *you* would expect if you were the customer.

Vague advertising campaigns
Time your advertising to run when it is most appropriate. If the item is a gift purchase, advertise during the run up to Christmas; if it's swimwear, do it in the months before the summer holidays. Always include a reply slip or telephone number in the advertisement so customers contact you to request a catalogue or order a product.

RECOMMENDED LINKS
Committee of Advertising Practice:
www.cap.org.uk
Direct Marketing Association:
www.dma.org.uk
Distance Selling Regulations–A Guide for Business, Department of Trade and Industry:
www.dti.gov.uk/ccp/topics1/pdf1/ bus_guide.pdf
Information Commissioner's Office:
www.informationcommissioner.gov.uk
National Newspapers' Mail Order Protection Scheme:
www.mops.org.uk
Office of Fair Trading:
www.oft.gov.uk

Evaluating an Existing Business

GETTING STARTED

It's often thought that buying a business is simpler than starting your own, but remember that many businesses are sold because they have inherent problems that prevent them from generating sufficient income. If you're buying a business, it's vital that you carry out comprehensive research and analysis in the same way as if you were setting the business up from scratch.

FAQS

What's my first step towards buying a business?

Your first step is to decide on the type of business you're looking for. Think about what size of business you want. Are you, for example, looking for a small local business, or are you aiming for a large national one? Also think about what business sector you're most drawn to—is it manufacturing, retailing, or perhaps services? Consider location too. Are you prepared to change your location and travel, or would you prefer to stay where you are and travel relatively short distances?

What should I be looking for in a business?

Look first and foremost for skills and experience. The most common reason for business failure is people taking on businesses outside their area of expertise, so think long and hard about the skills and knowledge that already exist in the potential business, and whether you can add to those skills. You also need to consider the products and/or services that the business provides. Again, ideally, you should be looking for a business which deals in a product or service that you have some experience of, especially if the operation is particularly complex or technical.

Remember to investigate the level of competition facing the business, especially locally. Make sure you know your competitors' strengths and weaknesses relative to the business you're considering buying, and what their share is of the market. Look at the size of the business, and find out how fast it has grown in the past, and whether

this rate is likely to continue, increase, or decline.

Another important factor to consider is location. Check that the business is located appropriately, for example, close to its target market (if location is relevant), and within reach of employees with the right skills. You'll also need to judge whether the business needs any major changes requiring a large investment of management time—you may be able to acquire a business at a lower price if this is the case. If the business is already successful, it can probably continue to operate in the same manner, regardless of a change of ownership.

Money is another key issue and you need to calculate how much needs to be invested in the venture. This is a crucial factor in determining whether to buy a particular business. Consider whether you'll be able to secure finance for future investment if it's required. Evaluate too the level of profitability of the business. Does it make the amount of profit you're looking for; does it have the potential to expand and grow?

How do I value the business?

Many people find it useful to employ a business transfer agent or financial adviser when they are having a business valued. The three methods often used are asset value, earnings multiple, and return on capital.

Asset value. To obtain the business's net asset value (that is, what it is worth, in basic terms), the value of the liabilities (that is, a business's financial obligations, such as outstanding debts, loan repayments, outstanding invoices etc) is subtracted from the value of the assets. The value for the entire business will be the net asset value, plus a value for goodwill representing the business's reputation and existing customer base.

Earnings multiple. The earnings multiple method requires you to apply a multiple to the earnings from the business. Earnings should take account of interest charges to be paid after purchasing the business, and any loans needed to make improvements. To come up with an earnings multiple, divide the company's market price by its after-tax earnings over a one-year period.

Return on capital. To find the return on capital, you'll need to define a desired rate of return. (Rate of return can be defined as a ratio of the profit made in a financial year as a percentage of the capital employed.) Then the income of the business before interest and tax should be calculated, and this figure should also be given as a percentage of the capital invested. If the figure is less than the desired rate of return, then any purchase should not go ahead.

MAKING IT HAPPEN
Evaluate the business

You'll need to carry out some research properly to evaluate any business you're considering for potential purchase. You should be able to obtain much of the information you require from the present owner; ask for details including the business plan, accounts, details of established customers, and so on.

It's a good idea to carry out a SWOT analysis (Strengths, Weaknesses, Opportunities, and Threats) on any potential business purchase. Consider the present position of the business in the market, its past performance, and its potential for growth. Look at its available resources, for example money, assets, manpower, and so on. Investigate the training, experience, and skills available within the business. Check its sources of supply, costs, reliability of material, stock supply, and relations with suppliers.

Find out who the competition is, where it is, and what its strengths and weaknesses are. Research your customers, making sure you know who and where they are, and how loyal they are. You'll need to examine external factors like industry trends, regulations, and political and economic developments. Consider much money you'll need for advertising and marketing. The way the business is promoted may have to change. Look at the business's distribution channels, asking yourself how reliable they are, and whether they can be maintained once the business changes hands. Calculate the profitability of the business after any initial capital outflow for improvements that need to be done before you start trading.

Work out a price

Obviously, if you become interested in purchasing a business, you'll need to value it and determine a reasonable price in conjunction with the seller. The price of a business may be derived from some of the factors mentioned in the previous section. It will also depend upon an appraisal of the land and buildings. The fair market value of the property is affected by a number of factors. These include the business's location in relation to its customers and suppliers, employees, and competition. The condition of the premises, for example whether improvements are necessary to bring them up to legally acceptable standards, is also an important consideration.

Financial considerations, such as the costs of property maintenance, transfer of title, licences, leases, property taxes, and so on, need to be taken in to account. There may also be problems over the transfer of a lease on premises. Some leases prohibit assignment.

External factors, such as current interest rates and the state of the property market, influence a property's value. So too will the future outlook, for example whether the property will continue to meet the requirements of the business as it grows. There will also need to be a valuation of fixtures and fittings. There may be equipment leases that need to be transferred (for example, the photocopier). Check for any contingent liabilities.

Consider other factors

You'll need to negotiate the transfer value of the stock. This should be cost or 'net realisable value' (NRV), whichever is lower. For redundant stock the NRV is zero. A recorded valuation and stock count should be carried out by a third party. You'll also need to engage an accountant to evaluate the business's books, bank statements, and tax records to get an accurate picture of the current financial situation and future profitability.

Valuing the goodwill of the business is especially important. Goodwill reflects the cumulative effect of the reputation of the business; its relationship with customers, suppliers, and competition; its market position, and the skills of the staff. You'll need to consider whether the existing staff are suitable for the business, and how they are likely to react to a new owner/manager. Think about how you'll replace those not keen to stay on. The effects of the Transfer of Undertakings (Protection of Employment) Regulations 1981 (TUPE) must be considered. If long-serving staff are transferred it will be expensive to make them redundant. Decide what benefits will be offered, for example, maternity benefits, holidays, and so on. National Insurance (NI) requirements, pension schemes, and personal liability insurance must also be considered.

Make sure that you evaluate the outstanding loans to the business, its relationship with its creditors, and its repayment history. Be realistic about whether you'll be able to obtain financing for the venture, and to repay the loan. Look at pro-forma income statements, balance sheets, and cash budgets. When you estimate how much income the business is likely to generate, it's important to be conservative, especially in the early stages.

WHAT TO AVOID
Rushing through the research stage

If you don't carry out thorough research, you may find you have made the wrong decision. Without enough information, facts and figures, and forecasts, a view of any business's prospects can be easily distorted and misleading.

Not exercising due diligence

You should always exercise due diligence when purchasing a business. You must make sure that what the vendor is saying is correct. Examine all accounts carefully. Ask yourself whether customers are likely to remain loyal once you have taken over the business, and whether suppliers will maintain the same relationship with you. If you don't exercise due diligence, you'll only have yourself to blame for any problems you could have discovered before the purchase.

Not setting a price before bidding

You should have a price band in mind before bidding, otherwise you'll be at a disadvantage. The seller may state an asking price outright, at which time the buyer must be prepared to negotiate. This way you shouldn't spend more than you can afford.

RECOMMENDED LINKS
Business Eye (Wales):
www.businesseye.org.uk
Business Link (England):
www.businesslink.gov.uk
Invest Northern Ireland:
www.investni.com
Business Gateway (Scotland):
www.bgateway.com

SEE ALSO
Small and Growing Businesses (p. 486)

A Guide to Business Regulations When Starting Up

GETTING STARTED

When you start up in business, there are many regulations with which you need to comply. This actionlist will help you to be aware of these regulations. It will also help you to work your way methodically through each of them before you start trading, to avoid penalties.

FAQS
What issues should I be thinking about?

There are several main areas to consider, all of which are explained in more detail below. You'll first need to tell the relevant authorities of your intention to set up in business, and register your business if necessary. You will also need to consider financial issues, such as income tax, National Insurance, Value Added Tax (VAT), corporation tax, and capital gains tax.

If you want to have new premises built, you may need to obtain planning permission. This can be a lengthy process, so do factor this into your overall start-up timetable. You may also need to apply for a patent, trade mark, or licence, and again, applying for these can take a long time. Remember that if copyright issues are likely to affect your business, you need to find out about these too.

If you are employing staff, you will need to comply with health and safety and fire safety regulations, and you will need to consider taking out insurance. Your business will also need to comply with other regulations to do with employing staff, such as the National Minimum Wage Act and Maternity and Parental Leave Regulations.

MAKING IT HAPPEN
Register your company

The status of your business venture will determine which specific regulations are applicable to it and who should be contacted. Further advice on all of the information given in this section should be sought from a solicitor, an accountant, or a relevant support organisation, for example, Business Link.

If you are a sole trader, or in a partnership, you must inform HM Revenue & Customs (HMRC), which governs income tax and National Insurance (NI) contributions, within three months of starting to trade. As a sole trader or a partner you are classed as self-employed, and therefore need to make arrangements for self-assessment of income tax and for paying your own National Insurance.

If you are an incorporated company, you are required by the Companies Act to register the name and address of your company with the Registrar of Companies at Companies House. Various other documents must also be lodged at Companies House, including the memoranda and articles of association of the company.

If a business operates as a sole trader or partnership under a name other than that of the owner/s of the business, there is a legal requirement for the name and address of the owner, or owners, of the business to be displayed at its premises and on its stationery. For limited companies, the registered name of the company must be displayed outside its office and on all relevant company publications, including e-mail. It is also important to verify the acceptability of the name itself with Companies House.

Understand financial issues

National Insurance and income tax must be paid. Self-employed persons should register for Class 2 National Insurance contributions on form CWF1 from HMRC. This form is then sent on to the appropriate Tax Office. If net profit is above a certain level, Class 4 contributions may have to be paid. All businesses that employ staff must register with

HMRC as employers, and they must deduct National Insurance contributions from employees' salaries.

Sole traders pay normal rates of income tax on the business's trading profits. In a partnership, each partner will be liable to pay income tax on their individual share of the business's trading profits. The HMRC's Self Assessment system, which is applicable to all unincorporated businesses, means that self-employed people must assess their own tax liabilities. Any business employing staff must make pay-as-you-earn (PAYE) tax deductions from employees' earnings, and pay these over to HM Revenue & Customs.

Your business needs to register for Value Added Tax (VAT) if its annual sales turnover exceeds a certain level. Current turnover threshold levels should be checked with HMRC. A business may also register voluntarily if its sales are below the threshold. Limited companies must pay corporation tax on any profit made from total sales and income gained from investment excluding certain allowable expenses. Capital gains tax (CGT) is applied to profits over a certain level gained from the sale of items such as land or investments. It may affect businesses run from home if the business owner decides to sell the house.

Be aware of health and safety issues

Employers are required to make sure that staff operate in a safe working environment and must regularly carry out a health and safety risk assessment. Various regulations are in force that cover, for example, working with computers, first aid, and basic conditions of work for employees including heating and lighting. If you are operating a factory or workshop, the Health and Safety Executive (HSE) should usually be contacted to register the business.

Implement fire safety procedures

If there are more than 20 people working in your building, then a fire certificate may be needed. If there are more than 10 people other than on a ground floor (including a basement), you will need to obtain a fire certificate. The Fire Precautions (Work-place) (Amendment) Regulations 1999 require all employers to assess their fire safety arrangements even if they already have their own certificate. The local fire brigade should be contacted to see whether a fire certificate is required.

Obtain planning permission if necessary

If the business is moving into a new building or changing the use of the building, the local authority's planning department may have to be consulted. If existing premises need to be altered structurally, or the business requires the installation of plant or machinery, the local authority planning department or building regulations department should definitely be consulted.

Understand the concept of intellectual property

Legislation exists to protect infringement of other people's intellectual property rights on designs, trade marks and copyright, or inventions that may already be patented. In addition, the business may generate certain intellectual property rights itself that may be of value and require adequate protection or exploitation. It is important to investigate these thoroughly and speak to appropriate sources such as the Patent Office or a solicitor before setting up in business.

Understand licences

If your business holds information about people on a database, the Information Commissioner's Office must be contacted to find out whether the business needs officially to notify the Commissioner of that fact. If it does, there are strict requirements to be met under data protection legislation. If the business is involved in lending/collecting credit, or in the hire of goods, it may need a credit licence, obtainable from the Office of Fair Trading.

Certain types of business require licences before they can operate. Speak to your local authority or business support organisation for advice on which licences would be relevant to your business.

Have insurance cover

Compulsory—Subject to some exemptions, a limited company employing staff (other than the owner/manager's immediate family) is legally required to maintain a minimum of £5 million employers' liability insurance. A copy of the certificate of insurance should be displayed at all business premises. Other compulsory insurance includes third party motor insurance on vehicles used for business. Periodic inspections of certain types of plant and machinery will require an annual inspection policy or contract.

Recommended—Public liability insurance, which covers bodily and property injury to the public, might be important if you have a walk-in retail business that receives many customers every day. Professional indemnity insurance covers legal liability for professional errors or omissions. It might be a good idea to seek advice from an accountant or tax specialist.

Employ staff

If your business intends to employ people, it needs to comply with certain regulations. These include the Maternity and Parental Leave Regulations 1999 (as amended), the National Minimum Wage Act 1998, the Working Time Regulations 1998 (as amended), and the Part-time Workers (Prevention of Less Favourable Treatment) Regulations 2000 (as amended). You are not allowed to discriminate against a person on the grounds of race, gender, disability, or sexual orientation. Employees must be provided with a written statement of their main employment terms.

There are payroll regulations which stipulate that all employees must be given itemised pay slips stating any deductions. You must inform HMRC when taking on an employee. They will set up a PAYE scheme and send you a new employers starter pack.

Contact them or the New Employers' Helpline (0845 6070143) for advice.

WHAT TO AVOID
Not doing your homework

It really pays to research every area thoroughly before you go ahead and start trading. This will not only save you time, but also money, as you can be heavily fined for not following regulations. Ignorance is not an excuse!

RECOMMENDED LINKS
Advisory, Conciliation and Arbitration Service (ACAS):
www.acas.org.uk
Business Eye (Wales):
www.businesseye.org.uk
Business Link (England):
www.businesslink.gov.uk
Companies House Enquiry Service:
www.companieshouse.gov.uk
Department for Environment, Food and Rural Affairs (DEFRA):
www.defra.gov.uk
Health and Safety Executive (HSE):
www.hse.gov.uk
Industrial Common Ownership Movement (ICOM):
www.icof.co.uk
Information Commissioner's Office:
www.informationcommissioner.gov.uk
HM Revenue & Customs:
www.hmrc.gov.uk
Invest Northern Ireland:
www.investni.com
Office of Fair Trading:
www.oft.gov.uk
Patent Office:
www.patent.gov.uk
Business Gateway (Scotland):
www.bgateway.com

SEE ALSO
Small and Growing Businesses (p. 486)

Setting Up a Business as a Private Limited Company

GETTING STARTED

Private limited companies balance the advantages of limited liability and better access to finance against greater administrative burdens and disclosure of the business's financial position. This actionlist looks at the advantages and disadvantages of companies, and describes how to set up a business as a company. It also discusses other relevant issues including administrative and accounting responsibilities, tax, National Insurance, and limited liability.

FAQS

What is a private limited company?

A private limited company has a legal identity separate to that of its owners; this is unlike a sole trader or a partnership, where there is no distinction. Companies have to comply with a wide range of legislation, particularly the Companies Act 1985 (as amended). There are two main types of limited company: public and private. Most small businesses that wish to trade as a company will take the route of a private (rather than public) limited company.

Public limited companies can offer their shares to the public and trade them on the Stock Exchange. The letters 'plc' (or the Welsh equivalent, 'ccc') must appear at the end of the business name. To trade as a public limited company, the business must have issued share capital of £50,000 or more. The owners of a company are its shareholders or 'members'. Public companies must have at least two shareholders.

A private company may be formed with one shareholder (a single member company). It must also have at least one director and a company secretary. Private limited companies cannot publicly trade their shares (these are usually held by employees, other businesses, family members, and acquaintances). There can be no more than 50 shareholders. If there is just one shareholder, he or she can be the sole director but not also the company secretary. In most small companies, the shareholders and directors will be the same people. Directors are often referred to as the 'board'.

What are the advantages of operating as a company?

The owners of a limited company have limited liability for the debts of the business, up to the value of their shareholding. If the business fails, the shareholders will simply lose the amount they have invested in the company. (A company may also be limited by guarantee. This means that members' liability is limited to an amount they have agreed to contribute if the company is wound up.)

Issuing shares in return for capital allows you to raise capital for expansion or other purposes. A limited company has a separate legal identity to that of its owners, so you can continue trading despite the death or resignation of a shareholder. Employees may be more motivated if they are able to own a share in the business. Suppliers and customers may perceive that limited companies have more credibility, which could be a competitive advantage.

What are the disadvantages of operating as a company?

You will have to comply with a wide range of complex and detailed legislation that is not applicable to sole traders and partnerships. There are also additional costs, including costs of incorporation and the recurring costs for statutory requirements such as auditing (compulsory when turnover exceeds £1 million). Public disclosure of the company's accounts can be seen as another disadvantage, and also, directors of new companies often still have to give personal guarantees to banks when seeking loans.

MAKING IT HAPPEN
Set up a private limited company
You must send the documents listed below to the Registrar of Companies (at Companies House, website given below) before a certificate of incorporation can be issued. The fee for registering a private company is currently £20.

Memorandum of Association. This describes the purpose of the company and its powers.

Articles of Association. This details the rights of the shareholders and the powers of the company's directors. A complete draft of the articles can be found in Table A set out in the Companies Act 1985. Most companies use this table as a basis for their articles and amend it to suit their particular requirements. You can also alter the Articles of Association later, using certain procedures laid down in the legislation.

Form 10. This is the 'Statement of the First Directors, Secretary and Registered Office'. It can be downloaded from the Companies House website.

Form 12. This is the 'Declaration of Compliance with the Requirements of the Companies Act'. It can also be downloaded from the Companies House website.

These documents are subject to certain checks, including confirmation of whether any of the prospective directors are on the disqualified directors' register. When the documentation is satisfactory, the Registrar of Companies will issue a Certificate of Incorporation. The company can then start trading.

Buy an 'off-the-shelf' company
Company registration agents and solicitors can provide ready-made companies. If you choose this option, all the documentation will be prepared for you and the company will be registered, naming the agency's own staff as directors and secretaries, but no business will be transacted. When you buy the company, the agency simply changes the company's details to match your business and notifies the registrar. An 'off-the-shelf' company can cost anything from £150 to £350. Although this method can be a lot quicker than doing it yourself, initial costs can increase considerably if changes to the documentation are needed to suit your needs.

Choose a company name
You cannot register the same name as another company, certain words are restricted, and names that may cause offence are not permitted. Check the index of company names kept by the Registrar of Companies at Companies House to make sure that another company is not already using your chosen name (you can search on the Companies House website for existing company names).

You must display the company name outside all your premises so that it can be easily seen and read. It must also appear on all company publications, including business letters, cheques, invoices, and notices. The company's directors and secretary may be fined if the business name is displayed incorrectly. The company's place of registration and registered number must also be displayed on business letters and order forms.

You must also display the letters 'ltd' or the word 'limited' after the company name. Private companies, limited by guarantee, can become exempt from including 'limited' in their name. However, they must still state on business letters and order forms that they are a limited company.

The tax implications of setting up as a company
Income tax and National Insurance. The directors of a company are treated as employees and must pay income tax on their earnings as well as Class 1 National Insurance contributions (NICs). The company must also pay NICs on behalf of its employees.

Corporation tax. Limited companies are eligible to pay corporation tax on the profits they make. The current standard rate of corporation tax is 30%, but rates vary depending upon the amount of profit you make. Companies are required to carry out self-assessment for corporation tax. The company's completed corporation tax return is due 12 months after the company's financial year-end. Corporation tax must be paid within nine months and one day from the end of the financial year. HM Revenue & Customs (HMRC) will send you reminders about this.

VAT. If the company's annual turnover reaches a certain level (£60,000 for 2005–6), it will also be required to register for VAT with HMRC. You may, however, register the business voluntarily if its turnover is lower than this threshold. This can have advantages, such as allowing your company to claim back VAT on purchases.

Legal responsibilities following incorporation

Administration. After incorporation (registering your company with Companies House) you must inform Companies House about the appointment of any new officers, the resignation of any officers, and changes to officers' names and addresses or other details originally registered on Form 10. There are strict time limits for the filing of such information, often as little as 14 days.

Once a year, every company must supply basic information to Companies House known as the 'annual return'. An annual return is a snapshot of general information about a company's directors and secretary, registered office address, shareholders, and share capital.

Accounts. Directors of limited companies must prepare, maintain, and submit accounts to Companies House on an annual basis, including a profit and loss account and a balance sheet. The accounts must start on the day of incorporation, and its first financial year (known as the 'accounting reference period') will end on the last day of the month of the anniversary of formation. For example, if your company is formed on 2 November 2006, your first financial year will end on 30 November 2007, and the sec-

ond financial year will start on 1 December 2007.

Your first set of accounts must be submitted to Companies House within 10 months of the end of the first financial year. There are automatic fines for accounts that are filed late. These accounts will be available to anyone who wishes to inspect them.

Northern Ireland

Company registration in Northern Ireland is dealt with by the Companies Registry, which is responsible to the Department of Enterprise, Trade, and Investment. Registering a company in Northern Ireland follows very similar procedures to the rest of the United Kingdom. It involves the submission of a Memorandum and Articles of Association, Form 21 (Statement of the First Directors, Secretary and Registered Office), and Form 23 (Declaration of Compliance with all the legal requirements relating to incorporation of a company). The standard registration fee is £35. Submission of accounts and annual returns must also be made to Companies Registry and they have similar procedures to the rest of the United Kingdom.

WHAT TO AVOID
Not using a solicitor or accountant
If you decide to set up your business as a company, it is important that you get advice from a solicitor or accountant, as the procedures involved can be quite complex. Company law changes constantly. Your solicitor or accountant should keep you informed of any new developments so that you can ensure that your business complies.

RECOMMENDED LINKS
Companies House:
www.companieshouse.gov.uk
Companies Registry (Northern Ireland):
www.detini.gov.uk
Association of Company Registration Agents:
www.chettleburghs.co.uk
HM Revenue & Customs:
www.hmrc.gov.uk

Setting Up a Business as a Non-profit Organisation

GETTING STARTED

A not-for-profit business, or non-profit organisation, is one that does not distribute its profit to its owners. All surpluses are put back into the business, or used for other charitable purposes in the community. Sectors including charities, the arts, education, and health care often operate in this way. This actionlist looks at various types of not-for-profit businesses, how they are set up and how they can obtain finance to fund the business.

FAQS

What kinds of not-for-profit businesses are there?

Social entrepreneurs use their business skills to address social problems rather than make a profit. It is common for them to set up a not-for-profit business to achieve this. Their aim is to improve the quality of life of a section of the community, often in some of the most deprived areas of society. Social entrepreneurs can set up all kinds of businesses, from youth clubs to mobile libraries. The School for Social Entrepreneurs works with local organisations around the UK to establish networks of local social entrepreneur programmes. Its website address is given below.

Charities generally aim to improve the welfare of others (people or animals) and often have to raise money to do so. Examples of large charities include Oxfam, Greenpeace, and Save the Children. These secure the majority of their funding through donations. There are many smaller charities, however, that generate their income through a combination of trading and donations, and these can be clearly identified as businesses (for example, performance arts organisations).

A **credit union** is a co-operative that gives members facilities for saving, borrowing, and other financial services, and is set up, owned, and run by its members. Members save together to create a pool of money from which low-cost loans are made. There must be at least 21 members for a credit union to be recognised.

MAKING IT HAPPEN

Setting up a not-for-profit business

Usually a not-for-profit business will either be an unincorporated association, or incorporated as a company, limited by guarantee, without share capital. There are also special registration requirements for charities and credit unions. The Registrar of Companies, for companies incorporated in England and Wales, is based at Companies House in Cardiff. For companies incorporated in Scotland, contact Companies House in Edinburgh, and for Northern Ireland, the Companies Registry in Belfast. Website addresses are given below.

Unincorporated associations

An unincorporated association does not have a separate legal identity to its owners. The association normally has a constitution that sets out its aims and objectives. It will also have a committee, normally elected during an Annual General Meeting, where members are nominated to serve as officers and members. Committee members are all personally liable for debts incurred by the business.

An unincorporated association cannot start legal action, borrow money, or enter into contracts in its own name. This is because it has no legal identity of its own, and in legal terms is only a collection of individuals. It also can't hold property without appointing trustees (usually committee members) to do so on its behalf. There are no formal registration requirements for setting up an unincorporated association.

Company limited by guarantee
The more usual route for a not-for-profit business is to incorporate as a company limited by guarantee. This type of company does not have shares or shareholders, instead it has members. Members agree, in the event of liquidation, to guarantee a sum of money that may be required to meet the demands of any creditors. The amount is defined in the Memorandum of Association. Companies, whether limited by guarantee or by shares, have to abide by the requirements of the Companies Acts.

Charities
The majority of charities in England and Wales need to register with the Charity Commission. Charities based in Scotland and Northern Ireland must register with HM Revenue & Customs (**www.hmrc. gov.uk**). If setting up a charity as a company limited by guarantee, you must submit the Memorandum and Articles of Association to the Charity Commission. The Memorandum and Articles should be agreed with the Charity Commission before incorporation, as this will save any difficulties later.

Credit unions
Credit unions must be authorised by the Financial Services Authority (FSA). In order to register, a credit union must identify that a 'common bond' exists between all members; this is to ensure that all members will abide by credit union principles. All credit unions must operate within the Credit Union Act 1979, which covers registration, members' eligibility, limits on loans and savings, the amount of interest that can be charged on loans, and distribution of profits. All credit unions must have a written set of rules that outline the duties of its officers and committees. The FSA is currently developing proposals for the future regulation of credit unions. The FSA's website address is given below.

Tax issues for the not-for-profit business
Any new business must register with HMRC. Charities have the absolute right not to pay tax on any income. Not-for-profit businesses can usually negotiate a tax exemption, but this is not automatic, and will largely depend on their sources of income. Businesses that are largely trading, for example, will have to pay tax like any other business. All businesses (including charities) need to register for VAT if their turnover is going to (or is expected to) exceed the annual threshold. However, some charity fundraising events, and sales of donated goods in charity shops, are exempt from VAT.

Annual accounts and audit
Limited companies may be required to have their end of year accounts audited. Under the Companies Act 1985 Accounts of Small and Medium-sized Enterprises and Audit Exemption (Amendment) Regulation 2004, small businesses with a turnover of up to £5.6 million are exempt from the audit requirement. However, they will still have to satisfy their boards of management and supporters that the money is well managed. Companies which are charities are exempt if their gross income is less than £90,000. Charities must submit their accounts to both the Charity Commission and Companies House.

Sources of help and finance for not-for-profit businesses
Many non-profit organisations look for **grant aid** to cover all their costs. Grant aid might come from large companies, grant-giving charitable foundations, or the government through a range of initiatives, the largest of which is the Single Regeneration Budget (visit the Office of the Deputy Prime Minister's website at **www.odpm.gov.uk** for further information). Grant aid may also be secured from the European Union Structural Funds (visit the Department of Trade and Industry website for further information). You should remember that there is far more demand for grant aid than can ever be met. (Website addresses are given below.)

Comic Relief, Scarman Trust, Community Action Network, and several other organisations have set up the partnership unLtd (**www.unltd.org.uk**), which has been awarded £100 million of Millennium Heritage Lottery finding. This money is used to make awards to individuals who wish to become social entrepreneurs. Levels of grant range between £500 and £2,500 for start-ups, and between £10,000 and £20,000 for those developing and expanding a project.

The **Local Investment Fund (LIF)** can lend between £25,000 and £250,000 to community, not-for-profit organisations in England which have been denied funding from banks, or which need top-up funding. The LIF is setting up Regional Community Loan Funds, of between £15,000 and £100,000 in eight English regions, too. LIF clients can also access ProHelp free of charge. This is a national network of professionals, for example architects, accountants, solicitors, marketing specialists, and IT consultants, who can provide strategic support, free of charge, to voluntary and community groups in their local area.

The Directory of Social Change provides information on grants as well as details on courses and conferences aimed at the voluntary sector and community organisations. The Charities Aid Foundation also aims to help not-for-profit businesses to make the most of their resources by providing advice and consultancy services. It can also provide small grants.

Further information and advice about sources of finance for not-for-profit businesses can be obtained from Business Links, Business Eyes, Business Gateways, and Invest Northern Ireland. The Charities Aid Foundation provides specialist financial services to charities and their supporters. FunderFinder is a website that helps individuals and not-for-profit organisations in the UK to identify charitable trusts that might give them money.

WHAT TO AVOID
Not getting the right advice
If the business wishes to register as a charity, it is advisable in all cases to contact the Charity Commission for advice, as charity law is extremely complex. The Charity Commission is the statutory organisation that regulates charities in England and Wales. The Commission seeks to ensure that charities operate within a framework that enables them to work effectively for the purposes for which they were set up. Community Action Network (CAN) was launched in 1998 as a learning and support network for social entrepreneurs, with the aim of strengthening communities in the United Kingdom. Using this network, CAN members share information about events, research and grants, as well as any useful contacts or advice to strengthen the network.

RECOMMENDED LINKS
Charities Aid Foundation:
www.cafonline.org
The Charity Commission:
www.charity-commission.gov.uk
Community Action Network:
www.can-online.org.uk
Companies House:
www.companieshouse.gov.uk
Companies Registry (Northern Ireland):
www.detini.gov.uk
Directory of Social Change:
www.dsc.org.uk
EU Structural Funds, Department of Trade and Industry:
www.dti.gov.uk/europe/structural.html
Financial Services Authority:
www.fsa.gov.uk
FunderFinder:
www.funderfinder.org.uk
Local Investment Fund:
www.lif.org.uk
School for Social Entrepreneurs:
www.sse.org.uk
Single Regeneration Budget:
www.urban.odpm.gov.uk/programmes/srb/index.html

SEE ALSO
Small and Growing Businesses (p. 486)
Understanding Business Models (p. 42)

Starting a Business While Under 18

GETTING STARTED

The rewards for anyone starting a business can be great, but it's a major decision for anyone, whatever their age. It's particularly difficult for those under 18, though, because of various legal requirements and other constraints. It's hard to know just how successful the businesses run by young people are, as they tend to operate invisibly, either within a 'training for business' scheme or in a form of partnership with a relative. There are, however, many successful young entrepreneurs and good sources of help for them. This actionlist looks at some of the issues faced by young people with great business ideas.

FAQS

Why might I want to set up a business at this age?

There are many reasons why you might want to do down this route. You may have a strong interest or skill in a certain business area; you may want more independence, and greater job satisfaction; the idea that any profits made will belong to you may also be a great incentive; you may look forward to feeling a sense of achievement and pride in the venture. If you're really serious about starting a business, you'll probably be a positive person, enthusiastic, and motivated to work hard and succeed. Also, you'll probably have fewer domestic commitments, like family or a mortgage, than many older people.

What problems will I face?

There are drawbacks to starting a business before the age of 18. Greater independence brings greater responsibility. Any business decisions will be down to you, and you'll also have to cope with any failures or problems faced by the business.

Lack of experience can cause serious problems in establishing credibility with both finance providers, for example, bank managers, and potential customers. They may feel that someone under the age of 18 could not know enough about managing a business. Some under-18s have work experience, but this is unlikely to be enough to convince potential backers or customers that they know what they're doing. You'll need to work much harder to prove yourself. Such lack of confidence in the manager's ability to run the business effectively can have an adverse effect on sales and profitability. Lack of qualifications, technical skills, and business training can also hinder anyone starting a business. This could cause problems of credibility, particularly with banks.

There are also legal issues to think about. Those under the age of 18 are legally described as 'young persons' and legislative requirements state that they may not work in certain business areas—for example, to sell alcohol a person must be 18 or over. Street trading and driving on public roads are both illegal for under-17s. If the planned business involves the use of certain industrial machinery, there may be age restrictions on its use; at the very least, full training will be required.

A young person may be unable to hire or lease equipment. However, it may be possible to set up a hire/purchase agreement through a trusted friend or relative, who would act as a guarantor for payments to a given company. Alternatively a 'contract' could be established by which to pay them. This brings up another problem, as 'young persons' cannot legally sign contracts. Again, it may be possible to have an arrangement with a relative by which they legally own the business, even though the under-18 is actually the owner. While this could seem an uncomfortable situation, it may be the only way around the legal constraints.

Another potential problem is the lack of business start-up finance for those under 18. A few specialised loan funds exist to help people that most lenders won't assist because of their age. However, many of these, such as the 'Northern Youth Venture Fund', are aimed at 18 to 30 year olds. It is also very difficult to open a business bank account in your own name at this age. This can affect the ability to sign cheques, make payments, and so on.

MAKING IT HAPPEN
Schemes for under-18s starting a business

The schemes mentioned below are available to those wanting to start a business while under 18. Some do not run all of the time in all areas of the country. A few of the schemes offer financial support. However, many treat the 16 to 17 age range as a time to plan for starting up after 18, so many students are encouraged to attend college instead of entering the world of business.

Shell LiveWIRE

Sponsored by Shell UK Ltd, Shell LiveWIRE is the only national organisation providing free, extensive support and advice to 16 to 30 year olds from before start up through to early growth. Every person making an inquiry receives an essential business kit which is tailored to their specific business idea. They are also put in touch with a local LiveWIRE co-ordinator. The annual Young Entrepreneur Awards give firms trading for less than 18 months the chance to compete for county, regional, and national prizes, gaining publicity along the way.

Young Enterprise

Young Enterprise is a national charity and a company which aims to educate young people about issues relating to starting and managing a business. The company achieves this through a series of Young Enterprise programmes, including.

1. Project Business UK (aimed at 14 and 15 year olds) gives students a practical insight into business life through business/works visits and activity-based sessions.

2. Company Programme (15 to 19 years) involves students setting up and managing their own business for one year, allowing them to learn about the practicalities of running a business in the real world. The scheme can also contribute to achieving business-related qualifications.

3. Team Programme is similar to the Company Programme but aimed at students with disabilities (15 to 19+ years).

4. Entrepreneurship Masterclasses are one-day seminars for those students who have already participated in the Company Programme.

Youth and Business

Youth and Business schemes are run by Teesside Learning and Skills Council (LSC). The schemes are not nationwide and vary according to location. The schemes are aimed at individuals between the ages of 16 and 18 considering starting up their own business. The individual works as a partner with the training company or LSC involved. Students are provided with advice, training, and guidance, and also a period of work experience. They also receive a weekly training allowance based on unemployment benefits, and some schemes train towards recognised qualifications such as the National Vocational Qualification (NVQ) in Owner Management—Business Planning (level 3). Much of the Youth in Business scheme centres on planning for business. This involves around six months of test marketing and research into the business idea.

The Prince's Trust

The Prince's Trust was established by the Prince of Wales in 1976 to help young people realise their full potential. Aimed at those aged 14 to 30 (or 14 to 25 in Scotland), the Trust offers support and financial assistance across a range of core programmes including business start-ups. Since 1983, the Trust has helped over 60,000 businesses, and its business programme currently offers: a low-interest loan of up to £5,000; a marketing grant of up to £250; advice lines and seminars; access to a volunteer business mentor.

Preparing for business

Most schemes, finance, and advice are available to people over 18. This makes it preferable to use the time between 16 and 17 to prepare for starting a business. Advice can be obtained from various organisations such as Job Centres, Learning and Skills Councils (LSCs) in England, Local Enterprise Councils (LECs) in Scotland, and the National Council for Education and Training in Wales, Business Links in England, Small Business Gateways in Scotland, Business Eyes in Wales, the Prince's Trust, the Prince's Scottish Youth Business Trust, and Chambers of Commerce. Trade associations may offer advice specific to a chosen business area. Making good use of the advice available will ensure that your planning is effective.

Gaining further qualifications may be essential to the success of some businesses. Professional qualification can gain credibility for a business. Any courses taken in further or higher education should be geared towards following a business career. Aim to combine specific subject knowledge with business skills, for example combining a photography with business NVQs or marketing training. If there isn't a specific course available for the business idea, continue developing your skills as a hobby, while undertaking more conventional business training.

You could negotiate with Job Centres to ensure that any training for work scheme offered to you is geared towards starting a business. Where possible, your work placements should be with small businesses, with any courses geared towards business start-up. Spend the time before you are 18 in gaining relevant skills, experience, or finance. This could be through part-time paid employment or a placement. While getting practical work experience, draw up a comprehensive business plan, seek advice, and research the market for your idea. Consider the costs of setting up, and think about premises, equipment, and labour requirements. Develop as complete a picture as possible of the way your business should be running in the future.

The moral support and advice of parents, relatives, and friends can be crucial in the early stages of business. You may need to rely on their financial assistance too, not only directly for the business, but also in terms of living expenses. Parental support can also be useful when establishing contacts, signing cheques, and so on. They could take responsibility for this side of the business until you reach 18.

WHAT TO AVOID
Not being fully committed

Only people who are entirely committed to the idea should attempt to set up in business. It's a long hard slog for anyone, whatever their age, so don't think that exuberance and enthusiasm will get you through. They'll certainly help a lot, but there are other things to bear in mind and you'll probably have to sacrifice some other areas of your life for a short time along the way.

Not being fully prepared

Plan your business approach as comprehensively as possible before you start up. A clear plan will be considered more positively by banks/sponsors/relatives and it will also be very useful to refer to when you start to manage your business once you're up and running. Make sure you're aware of legal and financial constraints that may affect you. You may need to think creatively to make your ideas become a reality.

Not getting the right advice and support

The nearest Business Link/Small Business Gateway/Business Eye or enterprise agency may be able to provide details of training schemes, loans, and grants available in a particular area. The Prince's Trust may be able to help with grants towards training or equipment for 14 to 18 year olds.

Not thinking through the alternatives

Do think long and hard about whether to want to start a business *now*. There are many advantages in completing your education and getting some work experience too. That's not to say for a moment that you should abandon your plans completely, just that you think about the timing thoroughly.

RECOMMENDED LINKS

Business Eye (Wales):
www.businesseye.org.uk
Business Link (England):
www.businesslink.gov.uk
Invest Northern Ireland:
www.investni.com
Prince's Scottish Youth Business Trust:
www.psybt.org.uk

Prince's Trust:
www.princes-trust.org.uk
Shell LiveWIRE:
www.shell-livewire.org
Business Gateway (Scotland):
www.bgateway.com
Young Enterprise UK:
www.young-enterprise.org.uk

SEE ALSO
Small and Growing Businesses (p. 486)

FINDING PREMISES

Renting a Business Property

GETTING STARTED

Many businesses occupy premises on a rental basis, covered by a lease or tenancy agreement. This actionlist explains what a lease is, and goes over some of the main issues you need to consider before signing a lease.

FAQS

What is a lease?

A lease is a legal document issued by the landlord of the premises covering the terms of the tenancy. It confers the exclusive right to occupy premises for a fixed term in exchange for the payment of rent.

Check with your solicitor that the conditions in the lease serve the purposes of your business and are reasonable.

MAKING IT HAPPEN

The description of premises

The description of the premises must be accurate, in order to avoid disputes. Be particularly wary of undefined boundaries, and ask for an accurate plan to be attached to the lease. Your legal rights should be stated in the lease and should include right of access from the nearest public highway. If you are renting part of a building, the right to use common areas leading to your section of the premises should also be included, as should the provision of essential services, for example, gas, electricity, and drainage. The landlord or tenant of adjoining premises is also expected to keep his or her property in good condition. Landlords have rights and obligations under the lease but must allow tenants to occupy the property without interference.

The term of a tenancy agreement

The term means the length of time the agreement is for. Make sure that the occupancy start date corresponds with the date on the lease. It may be difficult to withdraw if the premises are no longer required before the end of the term. Even if premises cease to be in use, you will be liable for payment until the lease lapses. For a small business, a shorter lease or periodic tenancy (from month to month, or quarter to quarter) may be more appropriate.

Some landlords may be prepared to offer a contract called a 'tenancy at will', or 'licence', which can be ended at short notice by either side. Such contracts don't offer any security of tenure and are excluded from the protection of the Landlord and Tenant Act 1954. If extensive alterations or improvements are intended, a short-term tenancy, tenancy at will, or licence is inadequate.

Your obligations as a tenant

On signing a lease, the tenant agrees to take responsibility for a number of things. These are explained in more detail below.

Rent

Make sure that the rent and its payment dates are clearly stated. Compare the rents of similar property in the area and, if possible, negotiate a rent-free period, for example, towards the costs of initial repairs or refurbishment. Consider instructing a General Practice Chartered Surveyor, experienced in commercial property, to negotiate on your behalf.

Repairs

These may be split into three stages. The first stage is before you occupy the property. It should be in a suitable state of repair, but if it is in poor condition, it will be necessary to prepare a schedule of condition with photographs. The second stage is during the lease. Be aware of your business's responsibility regarding repairs before occupying the premises. The third stage is the end of the lease. The property must be left in an acceptable state of repair. Businesses may be served with a schedule of dilapidation, itemising repairs that must be carried out.

Allowances should be made for fair wear and tear.

If the entire premises are leased, the landlord may expect the tenant to take full responsibility for all repairs (including structural). In this case, it is advisable to have a survey done and to have any defects remedied before signing the lease. It may be possible to negotiate an upper limit to the contributions made to the cost of repairs or an inclusive rent. Small businesses should go for an internal repairing lease with no liability for structural repairs.

Insurance
The tenant pays for insurance, although the landlord may initially make the payment, reclaiming pro rata from the tenant. Always make sure that insurance is adequate and that policy terms are reasonable.

Service charge
This applies to a multi-occupied building. The landlord will usually pay for common costs, for example, structural repairs, common areas, heating, and caretaker. This cost is re-charged to the tenants on a proportional basis (normally a ratio of floor areas). It is advisable to ensure that the basis of calculation is stated, that you have the right to see and check the landlord's expenditure, and that you are not paying for any empty areas.

Use
Leases usually contain restrictions on the use of the property. These may relate to a specific type of business, or to a nuisance, for example, noxious fumes and noise. The restrictions normally reflect those imposed by the planning authority. If the use may change in the future, discuss the possibility with both your landlord and the local authority. The lease should contain a clause which permits a change of use, subject to the landlord's approval and stating that he or she must act reasonably.

Assigning and sub-letting
Check that the lease allows you to sub-let to another business, or better still, to assign the lease. Sub-letting means that the business is still liable for the rent, whereas assignment transfers all responsibility to the new tenant. With leases made before 1 January 1996, the business can still be liable if the assignee defaults under the original contract with the landlord. For leases dated 1 January 1996 or later, complex new provisions exist. These mean that although the business might be obliged to guarantee the performance by the assignee of the lease (including the payment of rent and other monies), it cannot be liable for any default by subsequent assignees.

Alterations
Most standard leases prohibit the tenant from making alterations to the property unless the landlord finds it reasonable to do so. Before signing, consider any potential alterations that may be required, and remember that tenants are normally required to reinstate the property at the end of their lease.

Rent reviews
Leases normally contain a section stating that regular rent reviews will take place at specified intervals subject to contractual agreement. The section also indicates how new rents are agreed and disputes are resolved. Most standard leases only make a provision for rent to increase, but it is a good idea to try to make the landlord agree that rent can also be decreased. Rent is normally reviewed in relation to open market value at the date of review. If the landlord and tenant cannot agree on a rent, an independent arbitrator can be brought in, providing that this is a term of the lease.

Option to terminate the lease
Leases may contain an option to terminate before the end of the lease term on a specific date or dates. This is known as a break clause. One advantage is that if increased or decreased space is required, it is not necessary to wait until the lease ends. If a property is no longer suitable, but the lease term has not expired, it is possible to approach the landlord to see if he or she will accept a

surrender of the lease. This absolves the tenant from all future liability, but the landlord may not agree, or may require extra payment.

Guarantor

If the landlord insists that the business act as a personal guarantor, the business will be liable for paying the rent and other costs should it fail. A landlord may request that a third party, for example, an associate company, is obtained to act as guarantor. You may find it difficult to find someone to act on behalf of the business in this capacity. A returnable deposit may be an alternative to doing this. It is important to avoid giving guarantees.

Improvements

Tenants who carry out improvements beyond repairs at their own expense will not obtain any compensation from the landlord, even if the term is cut short, unless they follow a procedure of giving advance notice. A legal representative should be contacted for more information.

The end of a lease

At the end of the lease, businesses are protected against eviction by the Landlord and Tenant Act 1954. This protection cannot be enforced if the business is, or has been, in breach of its contract, or if the landlord wants to regain the premises for his own use. The Act entitles the tenant to request a renewal of the lease at an up-to-date rent. If it is not granted, compensation may be awarded for disturbance (but not for improvement).

Six to twelve months' notice by the landlord must be given, if the lease is to be terminated on the expiry date. If this is not given, the tenant can remain on the premises indefinitely, or can personally request a

new tenancy. Tenancy laws are complicated, and a solicitor should therefore be consulted.

If the lease is registered as being outside the Landlord and Tenant Act 1954, the rights of the tenant will be reduced. If the landlord and tenant have agreed to contract out of part II of the Act, the tenant is not entitled to compensation upon expiry. A tenancy of less than six months, a tenancy at will, and a licence are all excluded from the protection of the Act.

WHAT TO AVOID
Not doing your homework

Past or nearby tenants could be contacted for information about the landlord and how he or she performs their duties. You will need to check that the correct planning permission has been obtained to use the premises for your type of business.

Not getting the right advice

Be wary of one-sided lease agreements and seek professional advice if you are unsure. Avoid committing to a Full Repairing lease, particularly if the property is relatively old or is in a state of disrepair, except in circumstances where the tenant commits to such a lease in return for discounted rent or a rent-free period of occupancy.

RECOMMENDED LINK
Royal Institution of Chartered Surveyors: **www.rics.org**

SEE ALSO
Buying a Business Property (p. 75)
Complying with Fire Safety Regulations (p. 91)
Ergonomics at Work (p. 97)
Insuring a Business (p. 87)
Setting Up and Maintaining Your Home Office (p. 100)

Buying a Business Property

GETTING STARTED

Buying a property involves greater risks and financial commitment than renting, but sometimes it's the only way to get the right property for your business. Before making the choice, it's a good idea to list all of the factors affecting your decision, ranking them in order of importance. The main factors will be price, location, available finance, and whether the property meets the operational needs of the business. Everyone's needs are different and as few buildings are perfect, you'll probably have to compromise at some point. Once you've found your 'ideal' property, you'll need to make an offer, raise the finance, and go through the relevant legal procedures.

FAQS

Where can I find out about available property?

There are plenty of places where you can look for the kind of information you need. Try contacting local authorities, which keep a register of industrial property, estate agents, or the real estate departments of commercial companies. Check the ads in local and national newspapers, and specialist and trade magazines, and keep an eye out for notices or billboards posted on interesting looking premises. Don't forget also to spread the word among your personal contacts.

How do I evaluate my requirements when buying a property?

When choosing a building, you need to focus on which attributes are essential for your business to operate effectively. You may also need to decide whether it's preferable to convert an existing building or to buy purpose-built premises. The budget available for the actual purchase, and potential renovation/conversion will also need to be taken into account.

MAKING IT HAPPEN

Features to rank when evaluating potential buildings

You'll probably end up with a large number of buildings to choose from. The easiest way through the selection process is to list all the important features you require, and then score each property you see against each feature. A major constraint will be the price of the building. Costs can vary significantly. Try evaluating buildings on a 'cost per square metre' basis. Check whether the location qualifies for any financial incentives, for example, if it's located in a low-income area, as extra funding help can really make a big difference.

Location is key. Think about whether the location will be appropriate for your customers, and whether the facilities are appropriate. For example, does your business need to cater to passing trade? Would it be preferable to be nearer to a key customer or supplier? The location needs to be right for your staff, too. Make sure that the right staff can be recruited locally, and that there is access to reliable public transport. Staff should feel secure in the area, and have access to facilities such as nearby shops and banks.

Looking at surrounding businesses can also help you whittle down your list of potential properties. Are they growing or declining? Are any of them likely to be a nuisance, for example through noise or dust caused by the processes? Also, think about where your competitors are sited. Should the business be located near to competitors so that customers see at a glance how you differ?

The size of the building will be an issue. There should be a balance between sufficient space, not more than is needed or can be afforded, and enough space to allow for reasonable expansion. Floor space is allocated in square feet or metres so it's a good idea to keep in mind how large, for example, 500 or 1,000 square metres are, as a frame of reference. If it's too large, will it be possible to sub-let the extra space? An allowance of 11 cubic metres per person is recommended in the Workplace (Health, Safety and Welfare) Regulations 1992 Approved Code of Practice. New Royal Institute of Chartered Surveyors measuring practice states that building space should be quoted in metres squared primarily, with square feet listed as secondary information only.

Think about the physical nature of the building. The layout of the site itself should meet all of your business's operational requirements. Issues to consider are building density, the number of stories, and the condition of the building, in relation to the amount of money available for repairs. You also need to consider visitor flow, the availability of services, car parking (especially in residential areas), and accessibility (including stairs, lifts, and so on). Other issues to think about are security, storage, and lighting (natural and artificial).

Make an offer on a property

Once you've identified a suitable property, make an offer to the agent, making clear that the offer is conditional upon planning permission, a thorough building survey, and the Fire Officer's report. Your offer should also be conditional upon your ability to raise the required finances, the valuation, and whether or not the building is vacant possession, as well as upon certain contract conditions. For example, some new developments have maintenance charges with unregulated annual rises, so do check carefully that you won't get stung in this fashion.

After your conditional offer is accepted, employ a surveyor to undertake a full detailed structural survey. It's advisable to shop around for quotes from surveyors and to check which details the surveyor will evaluate. Ask friends, family, and other contacts if they can recommend a reliable surveyor if you're not sure where to start other than looking in the phone book. The survey will usually include a valuation for mortgage purposes.

Obtain advice on buying a property

You'll need to consult a number of officials and jump through some unavoidable hoops to make sure that the building can be used for the intended purposes.

Planning permission

This is the most important approval required (and the one which the business is most likely to need assistance with). It's required when building development or change of use occurs. Development is defined in Town and Country Planning legislation, and some situations do not require permission—contact your local authority planning department for more information. It will also be necessary to carry out a business search to find out more about the property and to research the planning authority's zoning area proposals, to make sure that the building will not be affected. You'll also need to find out about any restrictions due to preservation orders which could hinder development, and additional restrictions on the property because of local by-laws. Finally, make sure you identify the exact use of the building.

Building regulations

These regulations are administered by the Building Control Department of the local authority. Building regulations apply to the erection, re-erection, or extension of a building, the material alteration of a building, the material change of use of a building, and the provision, extension, or material change of use of a controlled service or fitting, in or in connection with a building.

Environmental health officers

Fire Officers grant fire certificates and are responsible for confirming that fire precautions are up to standard.

The HSE makes sure employees have a safe environment in which to work. Local authorities are responsible for ensuring health and safety guidelines are enforced in shops, offices, and some other service industries, while the HSE concentrates on larger-scale concerns, such as factories. Visit its useful website (**www.hse.gov.uk**) or contact its information line on 0845 345 0055 if you are unsure about any health and safety matters in relation to your business.

Legal aspects when buying a property

Before you buy, it's advisable to consult a solicitor or licensed conveyancer experienced in commercial property transactions. They can advise on contracts, planning regulations, financial research, history of building searches, and completion. They should also make sure that statutory regulations are met and that there are no outstanding notices on the property.

Stamp duty is payable by the purchaser on a property costing more than a certain amount. This is subject to alteration in the government's budgets. Since the Finance Act 1989, the freehold sale of a commercial building under three years old has attracted VAT at the standard rate (currently 17.5%). When VAT is paid on a building, stamp duty is due on the total price paid, not the price before VAT.

Financing the purchase of a property

Once you have decided on a building, the purchase will need financing. Property is usually financed over 20 or 25 years with the amount advanced as a loan being 60–70% of the property valuation. Lenders will expect a legal charge on the property for security. Once you have decided on a building, the purchase will need financing.

There are several sources of funding. If using high street banks, call around for the best rates of interest. Merchant banks may provide a large portion of money, but prefer proven businesses. Many will lend on an equity basis, meaning they take stock in the company in return for the capital loaned. You could also look at building societies, which may give mortgages for industrial and commercial purchases, and at local authority schemes, which are designed to help promote economic development (availability varies between different authorities).

WHAT TO AVOID
Not considering all the financial implications of buying freehold

Purchasing a building is a major undertaking, as it ties up a lot of capital in the building rather than in the business. Do make absolutely sure, then, that it's the right move for you and that buying a building won't damage your business overall. Most small businesses do grow, so you should consider carefully before buying a freehold. Remember that even when house prices are rising, commercial property values tend to rise at a slower rate. There is often no real financial advantage in buying instead of renting. Businesses should make sure that any advantages that do accrue are worth the cost. Also bear in mind that owning a property commits the business to additional expenditure, through obligations to undertake regular checks on electrical supplies and wiring for safety reasons. It's very important to be aware of the rateable value and rates payable on a property, as these can make a huge difference to the overall cost.

Not seeking the right advice

Seek advice from estate agents, local businesses, small business advisers, local authority development officers, and enterprise agencies when you need to make decisions about properties. It's also a good idea to talk to firms in the surrounding area about the property. It may be worthwhile asking why the previous tenant left. It's important to consult your solicitor once a property has been found, and to avoid signing anything straight away. Never be pressurised into agreeing to something you're not completely sure about: if in doubt, walk away and save your money—other properties will come up in time.

RECOMMENDED LINK
Royal Institution of Chartered Surveyors: **www.rics.org**

Choosing and Using an Architect

GETTING STARTED

If you are considering doing work of any sort to a building—whether new or existing—you should consult an architect. He or she will not only listen to your ideas, but will also be able to suggest alternative options. It is also part of the architect's service to help with planning permission and building regulations, and to make sure that the plan that is decided upon is strictly followed by the builders. You'll also need an architect if planning works to a listed building or a building in a conservation area, or when you are considering a change of use of a building or site. An architect will also be required when you have site or building development proposals, or planning or enforcement notice appeals (these often become necessary in cases where an architect was not appointed in the first instance).

FAQS

How do I choose an architect?

An obvious but potentially risky way of finding an architect is to select one from the Yellow Pages or online. Another is to base the choice upon a personal recommendation, or find out who designed projects that are similar to yours that you like. A recommended alternative to these methods is to contact client services at the Royal Institute of British Architects (RIBA), who act as a broker between clients and architects; they will provide a list of practices suitable for the potential project. The local public library should hold a RIBA Directory of Members in which the particular architect's expertise is mentioned. RIBA also has an on-line bookshop, and you may find the 'Engaging an Architect' series useful. (The RIBA website address is given below.)

It's not advisable to rely on 'fee-bidding' to locate appropriate services: it's important to choose an architect based on the quality of service and product, not solely on the fee. Ask to see a portfolio of the architect's work and visit completed buildings. It's also a good idea to check that your architect has worked on similar projects and has the appropriate design skills.

What is the architect's role?

The architect will discuss your requirements and help you to prepare a brief and an agreed action plan. He or she will then identify appropriate sites, carry out an evaluation and visit the proposed site before undertaking a feasibility study and investigating any statutory regulations applicable, as well as giving advice regarding other services the project requires. The architect will then prepare a timetable and details for planning permission/building regulation applications, as well as developing designs, working drawings, and models; determining the cost of the exercise and the deadline; and preparing production details.

He or she will also advise on appropriate procurement methods and prepare tender documentation, obtaining tenders and advising on them. They will negotiate with potential builders and draw up a building contract. Once the work has begun they will inspect the site and the progress made. The architect's role includes administering the building contract, submitting financial reports, giving advice on maintenance regimes, and finally providing drawings of the building as built. The full range of services is set out in the RIBA Standard Appointment documents.

MAKING IT HAPPEN

Find out about the conditions of appointment of an architect

When appointing an architect, a Conditions of Appointment document should be completed, checked and agreed upon. The points covered should include: the architect's authority and duty of care, use of consultants, site inspection, client's instructions, copyright assignment, suspension and termination, settlement of deposits, and governing law. There are standard forms for this purpose.

Investigate architects' fees and expenses

The Royal Institute of British Architects (RIBA) has a scale of indicative percentage fees based upon construction costs, building type, and nature of the work. Fees are usually charged by negotiation on an hourly basis for small jobs, or as a percentage of the building works for larger contracts. Any agreement should also include stage payments, suspension, resumption and termination, expenses and disbursements, variations, and VAT. Detailed guidance on these matters can be obtained by contacting RIBA.

Prepare for discussions

Once you've appointed your architect, the first stage of the work involves a discussion of the requirements, budget, timetables, and fees. After this discussion and the preparation of a full brief, the architect will draw up a plan of action which should be agreed In preparation for this discussion, it is a good idea for you to become familiar with ownership rights of the property, for example, rights of way or boundary fences. It is important for you to keep focused on what is to be achieved.

Plan the construction project

The second stage is for the architect to visit the site in order to evaluate what might be done. If a site has not been identified, the architect may be able to advise on appropriate locations and accommodation. A sketch proposal may be prepared at this stage as an initial point of discussion and agreement with you.

A feasibility study can then be undertaken by the architect, giving possible alternative options of spatial arrangements and elevational treatment. Restrictions may be imposed on the design by statutory items such as Town and Country Planning, building regulations, and fire and means of escape regulations. Health and safety legislation will have to be taken into account, as well as the Disability Discrimination Act 1995.

During this design process the architect will advise whether other consultant disciplines will need to be appointed, such as a quantity surveyor, structural engineer, landscape architect, mechanical and electrical engineering consultant, and a planning supervisor to deal with health and safety. The Construction (Design and Management) Regulations 1994 (as amended in 2000) affect work on all types of commercial and public buildings.

On smaller projects the architect may carry out their own survey of the land or building in question. The cost of this is usually based on an hourly rate, and is not included in the percentage fee quoted by the architect.

Preparation of the architect's designs

Once the plan of action has been agreed, the architect will organise meetings and surveys with all the other bodies involved in the project, which will enable cost estimates and outline proposals to be prepared. It's important to be aware that changes to the plans may be necessary as part of this planning process. Decisions on quality of workmanship, materials, and so on are made at this stage, to enable the quantity surveyor to monitor the costs. A planning application may be submitted, for which a statutory fee will be paid by you to the local authority. As planning approval cannot be guaranteed, it may be prudent to await consent before instructing the architect to prepare building regulations documentation. Again, you—as the client—will be responsible for statutory fees, one at the time of formal application, and further fees for site inspections.

Once planning and building regulation approvals have been obtained, the architect will be in a position to prepare detailed design drawings. The number of drawings will be dependent on the size and complexity of the project and may be used initially by the quantity surveyor to prepare a Bill of Quantities, and by the contractors at tender stage, and then on site during construction.

Architects and building contractors

The architect can now prepare production information and tender documents. These are then sent to contractors tendering for the work. The architect will provide advice regarding the suitability of tenders submitted. Once a contractor is selected, you can ask the architect to draw up a building contract between the business and the contractor.

Once the project is underway, the architect can visit the site at regular intervals to inspect the work being carried out. He or she will convene site meetings, to which you may be invited (or will otherwise be given the minutes), and will generally administer the terms of the building contract, give advice on maintenance, and arrange for drawings of the building pinpointing drainage lines, services, and so on, to be provided.

At various stages during construction, the architect will issue interim certificates for payment to the contractor. During the defects liability period (or retention period)—usually six or twelve months after practical completion of the project—an amount will be retained by the business until any defective work is satisfactorily completed.

Architects' services

In addition to construction projects, many practising architects can provide a range of additional services. These may include: surveying and inspection, furniture and interior design, cost estimating and financial advice, and undertaking negotiations.

WHAT TO AVOID
Choosing your architect on a 'fee basis'

The Royal Institute of British Architects (RIBA) fee scale is a guide to architects and clients based on historic data. Fees should be negotiated, and for larger contracts, it is important to meet the architect who will be dealing with the project, as dealings with them could last for a couple of years. This can help in avoiding personality clashes or misunderstandings over requirements. This can be a more important issue than the fee. Decisions should not be made on the basis of fee alone but on the overall value of service.

Not choosing the right architect for the job

For obvious reasons, you should select an architect who can demonstrate an ability to do jobs on time and on budget. Ask to see evidence of professional indemnity insurance and check that the sum covered for each and every claim is adequate. If required, architects will be happy to discuss undertaking some or all of the services with a commensurate variation in fees. The most useful advice is usually provided when still considering a project. It is a good idea to discuss ideas with an architect before being constrained by leases, loans, and so on. He or she may be able to identify suitable sites/premises for your business to consider. Remember that the architect is the expert and you may have to compromise on some aspects of your 'dream' premises: they may just not be possible in reality.

RECOMMENDED LINKS

Architects Registration Board:
www.arb.org.uk
Association of Consultant Architects
  (ACA):
www.acarchitects.co.uk
Client Services, Royal Institute of British
  Architects (RIBA):
www.architecture.com
RIBA Bookshop:
www.ribabookshop.com
RIBA Directory of Members:
www.ribafind.org
Royal Incorporation of Architects in
  Scotland (RIAS):
www.rias.org.uk
Royal Society for Ulster Architects:
www.rsua.org.uk

SEE ALSO
A Guide to Building Regulations (p. 81)

A Guide to Building Regulations

GETTING STARTED

The Building Regulations 2000 form the main United Kingdom legislation for the construction of, and changes to, all types of buildings. The regulations exist to protect anyone in or near a building. They also deal with energy conservation and issues concerning access and facilities for disabled people. For anyone involved in running a small business, it's therefore important to have a working knowledge of what the regulations involve. This actionlist provides a basic guide, but much more detailed information can be found on the websites listed at the end.

FAQS

In what instances are businesses affected by building regulations?

There are four main situations where building regulations apply:

1. the construction or extension of a building
2. a change of use of a building (even if the building itself is not changing, a change of use may require new ventilation or access arrangements that will need approval)
3. addition of extra fittings such as air conditioning and kitchen equipment
4. building changes such as underpinning or major structural modifications

Where can I find out exactly what is involved in and required by building regulations?

The building regulations and all associated approved documents, along with relevant other guidance, can be downloaded from the website of the Office of the Deputy Prime Minister. An up-to-date list of approved inspectors is available from the Association of Corporate Approved Inspectors' website. Both website addresses are given below.

MAKING IT HAPPEN

Comply with building regulations

Before you go ahead with making any changes to a building, you need first to have your plans checked and approved. You can do this in two ways—either through the local authority's Building Control department, or through an approved inspector. If you decide to use the local authority, there are two ways of obtaining approval:

1. Deposit of full plans

Your application should contain all relevant structural details and be submitted well in advance of starting on site. The local authority has to pass or reject plans within five weeks, but it can request an extension of up to eight weeks from the date of application. It will consult with all the necessary bodies such as fire, water, and highways before issuing a notice of approval. It can also request modifications to the plans or lay down conditions. If the plans are rejected, full reasons will be given in the notice.

2. A building notice

This is suitable for minor works, as the application needs only outline details. The notice allows for building works to start without the need for drawing up full plans, which can be costly.

Once a set of full plans or a building notice have been lodged with the local authority, two clear days' notice (so not weekends or bank holidays) must be given to the local authority before work starts. If work is started before approval is given on a full-plans submission, it may prejudice any future appeal against the local authority's decisions about the work.

If an approved inspector is used, he or she will discuss, check, and issue a plans certificate. An initial notice will be sent to the local authority and, once this has been accepted, the inspector will monitor the work as it progresses. You may start the work as soon as the notice is accepted by the local authority, as long as there are no further requests from the local authority within five days of lodging the notice. Work must not start if the notice is rejected. The inspector will issue a final certificate on completion.

If plans are rejected by the local authority, they may be altered and resubmitted, or an appeal may be lodged. For details of how to lodge an appeal, refer to the guidelines issued by the local authority.

Before you go ahead with making any changes to a building, you need first to have your plans checked and approved. You can do this by filing an application for a building permit with your local building inspector's office or building commission. In addition to the application, you may need to submit a proposal for the work that is to be done as well as evidence of liability insurance and a copy of your building contractor's licence.

Costs and fees

A fee is payable to the local authority for administering applications. However, each local authority sets its own charges depending on the type of work. Details of charges should be obtained direct from the local authority, who publish their fees and costs which are based on the Building (Local Authority Charges) Regulations 1998. If the work is solely for disabled people, Regulation 9 provides for an exemption from certain charges.

A full-plans application may involve a two-stage payment: the first stage is when the plans are submitted (plan charge), and the second follows a site inspection (inspection charge) if the local authority feels it is necessary to visit the site. The cost for submitting a building notice (building notice charge) will cost the same as the total of a plan charge and an inspection charge together, and is payable when the building notice is submitted to the local authority.

If the services of an approved inspector are employed, then the fee is negotiable but is usually based on a percentage of construction costs.

Enforcement of the building regulations

Before starting and during any work, the local authority may request additional information such as structural calculations. A building control surveyor monitoring the work will issue notification of any work contravening building regulations.

The approved inspector may make recommendations as work progresses. If the recommended amendments are not made within three months, a final certificate will not be issued and the inspector is obliged to notify the local authority, which in turn may use its powers of enforcement. The local authority can issue a notice insisting on alterations to the work or its complete removal within 28 days.

If the local authority is not informed of any relevant building works, it is entitled to prosecute. Currently the fine is a maximum of £5,000 plus £50 a day until the work is rectified. The local authority also has the power to undertake the work itself, even including demolition, and is entitled to start legal proceedings to recover its costs.

Other regulations relating to building

The list of related legislation is extensive and depends on the type of building work. Some of the most important are:

- the Construction (Design and Management) Regulations 1994, and 2000 amendment—these concern all owners of commercial property. Under these regulations, owners must appoint an individual as planning supervisor to co-ordinate the health and safety plan for the project. The regulations apply to all construction, maintenance, and demolition work
- the Construction (Health, Safety, and Welfare) Regulations 1996 (as amended)
- the Building Regulations (Approved Inspectors etc) Regulations 2000
- the Building (Disabled People) Regulations 1987 and the Building Standards (Scotland) Regulations 1990, as revised by the Building Standards and Procedure Amendment (Scotland) Regulations 1999
- The Fire Precautions Act 1971, as modified by the Fire Precautions (Workplace) Regulations 1997 and 1999 amendments
- The Party Wall Act 1996

Definitions relating to the building regulations

There are various terms which come up regularly in connection with building regulations, and it's useful to know exactly what is meant by each of them. Here is a list of the most common:

- *Local authority*: administrative office of local government
- *Building regulations*: legislation concerning building works
- *Planning permission*: official permission by the local authority to carry out building works
- *Approved inspector*: a qualified and registered surveyor who can oversee building works
- *Site inspection*: visit to building works by the building control surveyor
- *Full plans*: complete details of building works, including structural details
- *Plan charge*: fee payable on submission of full plans
- *Inspection charge*: fee payable if a site inspection is required
- *Building notice*: outline details of minor building works
- *Notice of approval*: confirmation that plans or details of building works conform to the regulations

WHAT TO AVOID
Not obtaining planning permission first

Before getting building regulations approval, it may be necessary to obtain planning permission. Normally, planning permission is applied for first; once approval has been granted, building regulations are then set in motion. If permission is neither sought nor granted beforehand, the penalties can be severe.

Not seeking professional advice

Building regulations can be complicated, so get professional advice if you feel out of your depth. The local authority's Building Control department can be contacted for guidance, free information booklets, and advice even before an application is made. You may also find the following books useful, both published by Blackwell in 2003: *The Building Regulations: Explained and Illustrated*, by Michael Billington; *The Scottish Building Regulations: Explained and Illustrated*.

RECOMMENDED LINKS
Association of Corporate Approved Inspectors:
www.acai.org.uk
Construction Industry Council:
www.cic.org.uk
National House-Building Council:
www.nhbc.co.uk
Northern Ireland Office, Department of Finance and Personnel, Building Regulations Section:
www2.dfpni.gov.uk/index.asp
Office of the Deputy Prime Minister:
www.odpm.gov.uk
Royal Institution of Charted Surveyors (RICS):
www.rics.org
Scottish Executive, Building Standards:
www.scotland.gov.uk
The Stationery Office:
www.legislation.hmso.gov.uk
Welsh Assembly Government, Housing Division:
www.wales.gov.uk

SEE ALSO
A Guide to Health and Safety at Work (p. 94)
Choosing and Using an Architect (p. 78)
Complying with Fire Safety Regulations (p. 91)
Insuring a Business (p. 87)
Obtaining Planning Permission (p. 84)

Obtaining Planning Permission

GETTING STARTED
The aim of the planning system is to balance the need for development with the need to protect the environment. To obtain planning permission, your business will need to apply to its local city, borough, or district council, or the development corporation if there is one in the area. Councils should grant permission unless there is a sound and clear-cut planning reason not to do so.

The Planning Inspectorate publishes two guides which you may find useful: *Making Your Planning Appeal* and *A Guide to Taking Part in Planning Appeals.*

The Stationery Office publishes four guides on the subject, *PPG1 General Policy and Principles, PPG4 Industrial and Commercial Development and Small Firms, PPG6 Town Centres and Retail Development,* and *PPG18 Enforcing Planning Control.*

FAQS
Is planning permission necessary?
You will need to check with your local council to find out if proposed developments will need planning permission. A fee will be payable for a formal decision, known as a lawful development certificate. In areas such as Conservation Areas, National Parks, and areas of outstanding natural beauty, tighter controls do apply.

Certain work is considered to be 'permitted development'. This includes internal alterations, unless the project will affect the exterior. However, internal alterations to a listed building may need listed building consent. Planning permission is not required for repairs to outside building works. Neither is it required for factory expansions, although this depends upon the size and volume of the extension. The expansion must also be related to the current use of the building, or the provision of staff facilities.

No planning permission is needed for demolition, although if it is a listed building or a building in a conservation area, other controls may apply. No planning permission is required for the exhibition of a sign if the sign displays the name of the firm or business, and the goods or services supplied. However, the sign must not exceed the sizes and heights specified by the local authority. The exception to this is when it is on a listed building, or a building in a conservation area. In general, no planning

permission will be required for using a domestic residence for business, unless the home will no longer be used mainly as a private residence. You will need to consider other factors too. For example, will the change in use result in a rise in traffic in the immediate area; and will it disturb the neighbours, or cause a nuisance, for example, in terms of noise or smells?

You will need to consult the local planning officer if you are planning to erect a fence with a height of over one metre. Building new premises nearly always requires planning permission, and the development plan of the area should be checked with the council to see if proposals are acceptable. Office and shop extensions require planning permission, and so will change of use, unless both the present and the proposed business fall within the same 'use class'. However, it is also possible to change use between certain classes. Use classes are set out by the Town and Country Planning (Use Classes) Order 1987, and changes of use are set by the Town and Country Planning (General Permitted Development) Order 1995. The classes include shops, financial and professional services, food and drink, business, assembly, and leisure. If a property does not fall within any category listed, it is termed 'sui generis', a use on its own.

What does the council look out for?
In considering a planning application, the council will take into account the character

of the area, road safety and traffic congestion, the need to reserve land for other purposes, and the adequacy of water disposal and sewerage. It will also consider the suitability of the site, any development plan policies relevant to the application, archaeological implications, and environmental impacts. The council will also be concerned with building regulations, listed building and conservation area consents, fire regulations, and even crime prevention and security.

MAKING IT HAPPEN
Apply for planning permission
Anyone can apply for planning permission. You may, however, prefer to appoint an agent to make the application on your behalf. The agent could be a solicitor or an architect, for example. If you, as the applicant, are not the true owner, or only have part ownership, of the property mentioned in the proposal, then you must inform those who do own or part own it. Planning permission decisions can take up to eight weeks, although large and complex applications can take longer.

Your first step is to inform the council of your plans. If necessary, your next step will be to ask to see the Development Plan, in order to assess any possible problems. You should then obtain the application form and find out how many copies to submit. You must then decide on the type of permission you want to apply for, and consult neighbours and people who may be affected by the proposal. Finally, you should submit your application, together with a certificate of ownership or notification, and the fee. (A list of fees can be obtained from the planning department of your local authority.)

Understand the different types of planning permission
There are several different types of planning permission.

Outline planning permission simply looks to see whether the development is acceptable in principle. It can only be applied for where the development involves the erection of a building. Detailed drawings

are not normally needed for outline planning permission. Permission, if granted, will be subject to certain conditions. It will be necessary to obtain approval for details, for example of appearance, landscaping, and design.

Full planning permission is required if the business intends to change the use of the property, or to legalise existing works which were built without the necessary permission. To obtain full planning permission, all of the details of the proposal should be submitted. Application for Renewal of Temporary Permission or Relief from Conditional Permission applies if the business intends to extend the time by which work must be started, continue a time-limited use, or retain planning permission without conditions.

After the application for planning permission
After you have applied, the application will be acknowledged. At this point, a discrete reference number will be issued. Your application will also be made available to anyone who wishes to see it. A report will be prepared for the planning committee. Applicants should hear within eight weeks unless there is a problem. Delays may occur if a site visit or further information is required. If the application is granted, the planned changes must be commenced within five years. After this time it will probably be necessary to reapply. When an application is rejected, the applicant must be told why.

Appeal against planning permission rejection
It is possible to appeal within six months of a planning permission proposal being rejected. Before appealing, applicants should make every effort to address the council's objections, either by negotiation or amendment. It is usual to opt for written representation. This is a relatively inexpensive option. However, it will require a lot of effort and time, and you should expect to wait for anything up to 18 weeks for a written appeal, and up to 24 weeks for an informal hearing.

WHAT TO AVOID
Not getting the right advice
This can be a complex area, and it is essential that you get the right advice. It is a good idea, if you are at all unsure, to use an architect or surveyor to assist with the proposal. If in doubt, applicants should consult an expert, or the local planning officer. If a business proceeds without planning permission, the consequences can be serious.

Not being prepared
The more prepared you are, the less likely it will be that delays will occur. It will be important to find out when the Planning Committee dates are, and to ensure that the information submitted meets the Committee timetable. It is advisable not only to consult the neighbours about a planning proposal, but also to contact other affected parties, such as the water and sewerage company, highway authority, and the Health and Safety Executive. It is also important to make sure that the information submitted with the application is complete and easily understood. It will be helpful to ask what additional information, such as photographs, may be required.

Worrying that it is taking too long
Planning permission is a fraught business and it's easy to lose your sense of proportion when the process seems to be dragging on for weeks. Remember that planning officers have a difficult job to do, and that it pays to be patient and respectful in any dealings with them. It is worth noting that planning applications are determined by elected members, not planning officers, who simply make recommendations. However, new council structures have led to the greater use of delegated powers for non-contentious applications.

Not abiding by the rules
Once the planning permission is obtained, it is essential that you make sure that any work carried out is as described in the approved plans.

Giving false information
It is a serious offence to give false information, or to withhold information, in order successfully to obtain a lawful development certificate. Penalties include a fine of up to £5,000 and two years' imprisonment.

RECOMMENDED LINKS
Office of the Deputy Prime Minister:
www.odpm.gov.uk
Planning Division, Welsh Assembly
  Government:
www.wales.gov.uk/subiplanning
Planning Inspectorate:
www.planning-inspectorate.gov.uk
Royal Town Planning Institute:
www.rtpi.org.uk

SEE ALSO
A Guide to Building Regulations (p. 81)

Insuring a Business

GETTING STARTED

Your business needs insurance against risks that might threaten its profitability, such as the theft of equipment, or a work-related injury to staff. Small businesses are more vulnerable to the impact of these incidents, as they often do not have the resources to cover unexpected expenditure.

This actionlist tells you what insurance your business is legally required to have and describes some optional types of insurance that you could use to protect your business.

FAQS

What insurance is compulsory for businesses?

As soon as your business employs someone (outside of your direct family), you are obliged to take out employers' liability insurance to cover all your employees' injuries or illness, whether they are caused on or off site. Employees include trainees and contract staff. By law you must have cover of £5 million, although most policies now automatically provide £10 million cover. You must exhibit a certificate of employers' liability insurance at each place of business and keep it for 40 years (see the 40-year rule below). You can be fined if you do not hold a current employers' liability insurance policy.

Any injuries or illness relating to motor accidents that occur while your employees are working for you may be covered separately by your motor insurance. All vehicles, whether cars, commercial vehicles, or motorcycles that are used on the road must be insured for minimum third party liability. Insurers normally need to know who will be using the vehicle for business purposes (especially any drivers whose age is under 25), what the business use entails, who owns the vehicle, and how it will be used. Make sure you check the licences of all your drivers. Remember that any serious motor convictions must be advised to your insurer.

What is the 40-year rule?

Employers must keep employer's liability insurance certificates, the ones you are required to display at each workplace, for not less than 40 years, starting with certificates issued in 1999. This is because claims for diseases can be made many years after the disease is contracted.

Health and safety inspectors have the right to see any certificates issued since 1999. These certificates can be kept electronically. You can be fined up to £2,500 for any day that you are without suitable insurance. If you do not display the certificate of insurance, or refuse to make it available to Health and Safety Executive inspectors when they ask, you can be fined up to £1,000.

Where can I go for more information?

The Employers Liability (Compulsory Insurance) Act 1969 and the Employers' Liability (Compulsory Insurance) Regulations 1998 are all published by The Stationery Office. *Employer's Liability (Compulsory Insurance) Act 1969: A guide for employers* is published by the HSE.

The Association of British Insurers (ABI) produces advice files specifically for smaller businesses. The National Enterprise Insurance Scheme is run by Local Enterprise Agencies and offers a range of independent professional advice to new and established businesses. The scheme helps businesses to identify basic insurance needs and can also help you get advice from an insurance broker.

All available website addresses for the above organisations are given below.

MAKING IT HAPPEN
Choosing an insurer

Any insurance company you use should be

authorised by the Insurance and Friendly Societies Division of the Financial Services Authority (FSA). Most are members of the Association of British Insurers. Check an insurer is authorised by calling the FSA's inquiry line (0845 606 1234) or visiting the website (**www.fsa.gov.uk**). It is always a good idea to shop around for advice and quotes.

Using the services of a reputable insurance broker will help you find the best product to suit your requirements, at the best value. A broker's services are usually free and they will search the market to obtain the best deal for you. Ideally, talk to insurance brokers or consultants who have experience of small businesses.

Different types of business insurance

There are a number of areas of risk for which insurance cover is prudent. Some of the main ones are given under the headings below.

Building and contents

Building and contents insurance can be important if you manufacture, repair, install, or even retail goods. Property cover can be provided for specific risks (such as fire or flood), or for a wide range of risks in one package. You should cover all your property, including buildings (if you own them), contents, stock, and fixtures. Note that since January 2004, most policies no longer automatically insure you for up to £100,000 against terrorist attack. You will need to arrange extra insurance if your property and possessions are at risk. If you rent, ask to see the landlord's insurance policy and check the range of protection that is in place.

Computer insurance

Computer insurance policies cover you for breakdowns and for loss of information. Check that your insurance covers the computer environment, including the e-mail and Internet access system. Different types of engineering insurance policies are available for machinery. These can include breakdown and statutory inspection cover.

Business interruption

Business interruption insurance (also known as consequential loss insurance) protects your company's income and overheads. This insurance compensates you for extra costs incurred and trading profits lost if your business suffers serious disruption, for example, after a fire. You are usually covered for an interruption period of up to 12 months from the date of any loss or damage. If damage to your office would increase the cost of working, you can claim added expense such as the cost of fitting temporary offices, removal costs and expenses, and increased rent and rates.

Legal insurance

The increasing volume of legislation affecting small businesses, and the financial and other penalties that may result in the event of non-compliance, has created an upsurge in demand for both helplines and commercial legal expenses if things go wrong. You can now get insurance for commercial legal expenses. A wide range of cover is available, ranging from employment matters, contractual disputes with customers, or accountants' fees following tax or VAT investigations.

Personal and public liability insurance

A director or officer of a company can be sued personally over an increasingly wide range of matters relating to the business. The personal liability of a director is unlimited. Legally, the directors of a company and the company itself are separate entities, and so both may be defendants, separately or jointly, in any legal action or prosecution. To protect the personal assets of individuals and, crucially, to cover the costs of their defence, directors and officers insurance is widely used. Modern insurance policies insure directors and senior managers, and extend to protect all other employees too. Directors and officers insurance extends to protect the company, rather than leaving it to fund its own defence, acting as a mechanism that also protects the value of a director's personal holding in the company.

Public liability covers you against accidents to members of the public, or damage to property that occurs as a result of your business activities. It also covers any related legal costs. This type of insurance is compulsory for certain types of business, for example health and fitness instructors.

Professional indemnity and product liability

Professional indemnity insurance covers you against being sued for giving poor advice or having been in some way negligent. This insurance is obligatory in certain professions such as medicine, law, accountancy, and financial services. It is now common in areas such as management and computer consultancy, engineering, and design. Cover usually includes breach of professional duty, breach of copyright, breach of confidentiality, libel and slander, and loss of documents.

Product liability insurance is the same principle as the professional indemnity, protecting you against claims arising from faulty products that you have sold, manufactured, or installed.

Key man

Key man cover pays a benefit to the business if a key employee, for example, a business partner, is lost through death or incapacity that would otherwise result in financial hardship for the business.

Income protection

Income protection insurance schemes cover employees in the event of long-term sickness, paying their salaries during the period of incapacity. This relieves your business of the burden of paying for a sick employee. The benefit is paid tax-free after a deferred period that is selected by the policyholder and is paid until retirement, recovery, or death.

Critical illness

Critical illness insurance provides a benefit in the event of diagnosis of any one of a list of serious illnesses, incapacities, or conditions. Benefits can be lump sum or income

based, and for any term. Premiums can vary dramatically, so independent advice and quotations are important.

Credit insurance

Credit insurance covers you against debtors who are unable to pay money owed to you because they have gone bankrupt.

Employee litigation

Employee litigation insurance covers you against claims brought by your employees on the basis of disability, race, and gender status.

Home workers

A growing number of start-up businesses begin in a person's home. Home workers' insurance may be needed as ordinary household insurance policies will not usually cover business risks such as employers', public, or product liability. If you work from home or use your car for business, your household and motor insurance may be invalidated.

WHT TO AVOID
Not taking time to think clearly

Take time to think clearly about the amount of insurance cover you need. Insure stock for its replacement cost price, without any addition for profit. Plant and machinery should normally be insured on a 'replacement as new' basis.

Not taking out sufficient cover

If you have too little cover, an insurance company can reduce any claim by the percentage to which you are under-insured.

Inappropriate excess on your insurance policy

Most insurance policies require you to pay an excess or deductible, covering the first part of any loss. Make sure the excess on your policy is appropriate. You can often negotiate a reduction in premiums by agreeing to a higher excess. If most of your claims fall beneath the excess threshold, you should consider switching to a policy with lower excess, but remember, it will cost you more. On the other hand, you may want to avoid making claims just above the excess, if they would mean increased premiums in subsequent years.

RECOMMENDED LINKS
Association of British Insurers (ABI):
www.abi.org.uk
Health and Safety Executive (HSE):
www.hse.gov.uk
National Federation of Enterprise Agencies (NFEA—through which you can find out about the Enterprise Insurance Scheme):
www.nfea.com
The Stationery Office:
www.legislation.hmso.gov.uk

SEE ALSO
A Guide to Building Regulations (p. 81)
A Guide to Health and Safety at Work (p. 94)
Buying a Business Property (p. 75)
Renting a Business Property (p. 72)

Complying with Fire Safety Regulations

GETTING STARTED
As well as endangering life, a fire can be a serious blow to any business. This actionlist will give suggestions on how you can prevent fires breaking out and measures you can take to minimise damage and danger should one occur. Businesses also have legal obligations to protect people in the workplace, and this is also explained.

FAQS
What are my legal obligations?
Three pieces of legislation lay down the general responsibilities of employers. The Fire Precautions Act 1971 applies to hotels (most of which require a fire certificate), and also to factories, offices, shops, and railway premises where people are employed to work. A fire certificate must be applied for where more than 20 people are employed at any one time (or more than 10 employed at any one time elsewhere than on the ground floor), and in the case of factories where explosives or highly flammable materials are stored or used. A Fire Officer will inspect the premises and either grant an exemption, issue a certificate if the premises are satisfactory, or notify the business of the action required to bring things up to standard.

The Fire Precautions (Workplace) Regulations 1997 provide the main legislation on duties and responsibilities for fire safety in the workplace. They are more far reaching than the Act, and emphasise the employer's responsibilities. They also require you to carry out a fire risk assessment and make a note of your findings if you employ five or more people. The Regulations apply to most workplaces (with very few exceptions), including those that also require a fire certificate under the Fire Precautions Act 1971.

The Fire Precautions (Workplace) (Amendments) Regulations 1999 amend the 1997 legislation. The main change to the 1997 legislation is to increase the number of workplaces to which the regulations apply by removing many of the excepted workplaces. As an employer, you have to prove that you have taken all reasonable steps to comply with the regulations: to identify the

hazards in the workplace and those people at risk; to provide appropriate fire fighting equipment and fire alarms as necessary, and to have clear routes to emergency exits. The risk can be significantly reduced by removing the hazards and therefore preventing an incident. The fire authorities and the courts also have more power in the implementation and enforcement of legislation.

Changes are afoot in England and Wales, however, led by the Office of the Deputy Prime Minister. New legislation, which is expected to come into force in 2006, will mean that fire certificates are not needed and instead emphasise the fire risk assessment requirements.

Other legislation operates in different parts of the United Kingdom. In Scotland, businesses should refer to the Fire (Scotland) Act 2005; in Northern Ireland, the Fire Precautions (Workplace) Regulations (Northern Ireland) 2001.

How do I carry out a risk assessment?
You can do this within a general health and safety risk assessment, or as a separate exercise. The risk assessment must consider features of the workplace, such as dimensions and layout, substances used or stored on site, the maximum number of occupants, the activities carried out there, and any other relevant circumstances.

Look for hazards such as combustibles, flammables, and sources of ignition, and consider who will be at risk because of them. Look for places where fire will spread rapidly, or where people might be trapped or injured trying to escape. If your business has five or more employees, you must write down your findings. Use your findings to try to reduce the chances of a fire occurring and to take steps to reduce death, injury, or damage to property should a fire occur. Draw up an emergency plan, detailing what to do in the event of a fire.

Inform employees of the assessment findings. If the workplace is shared with other employers, tell everyone of the risks that are found and the action taken (or required) to address them. Co-operation is the key, especially where shared escape routes, fire alarm systems, and so on, are involved.

✔ MAKING IT HAPPEN
Reduce risks

It is often possible to reduce risks quite cheaply, for example, by removing or reducing the amount of combustible/flammable materials, moving stored materials to a safer location, and removing or reducing the sources of ignition. Materials should not be stored in corridors, stairways or gangways, or obstruct an exit. Waste and rubbish are major fire hazards. Waste should not be allowed to build up and should be stored away from the premises until disposed of. If structural features of the workplace add to the risk, the cost of remedial work may be too high to justify. In such cases, the funds may be better spent on equipment for early detection and/or automatic fire fighting.

Detect and warn of fire

Detection of a fire may be rapid and straightforward in an open-plan office or rooms that are always occupied. Fires in storage areas and places that are often unoccupied could become serious before they are detected, and you may need to fit fire detection equipment in such areas.

You must have a way of giving warning in case of fire. This need not be a fire alarm system; a shouted warning, handbell, or whistle may be sufficient, as long as it is appropriate to the premises. Any warning method should provide audible warning throughout the workplace. The warning method should be tested, and a record kept that this has been done.

Identify escape routes

Make sure there are safe means of escape from the premises. The normal ways in and out will often be sufficient. A building with relatively recent Building Regulation approval (and which has not since been modified), or which has been inspected recently by the fire service and found satisfactory, will normally have acceptable means of escape. The distance people have to travel to an escape route should be limited so they reach safety quickly. A reasonable evacuation time is two and a half minutes. When timing this, consideration should be given to what people must do before leaving, for example, shutting down machines, taking security measures, and checking that areas are clear. If employees know exactly what to do, they will be able to clear the workplace more quickly. If times are too long, rearranging the workplace may cost less than providing extra escape routes.

Doors should ideally open in the direction of escape. They must open in the direction of escape when at the foot of a staircase, or if used by more than 50 people. Fire exits and escape routes must be useable at all times. Doors should be quick and easy to open without the use of a key. Lighting should be adequate: readily available torches may be sufficient in a small workplace, but emergency lighting units may be necessary in larger premises.

Exit signs may be required to mark the route. These should have graphic symbols and directional arrows on a green background. Text may also be used. Locate signs where necessary to indicate the route.

Have means of fighting fire

Fire-fighting equipment, such as fire extinguishers, should be available as appropriate and staff should be aware of its location and how to use it. There are several different types of extinguisher—water, foam, dry powder, and carbon dioxide—for different types of fire. They are usually colour coded by type for easy identification. A modern extinguisher will be predominantly red with a small area coloured to denote the contents, with pictograms to indicate the type of fire it is suited for. Sprinkler systems are becoming increasingly popular within the United Kingdom, despite their high cost. They are triggered in the event of a fire, and tackle the blaze early on. For certain new buildings under construction, fitting of sprinkler systems is compulsory. Fire blankets can be effective in putting out a fire but require the right technique in use. The equipment should be visually checked at least monthly, and the check should be recorded. It should be tested annually, usually by outside contractors, and the test recorded.

Give staff fire safety training

An employer may nominate someone to help with fire safety measures but still has overall responsibility. Staff must know who the nominee is. That person may need training, including using fire extinguishers. It is increasingly common within the workplace to appoint a Fire Safety Officer. All employees should be familiar with escape routes, how to give the alarm, where the fire extinguishers are, and how to use them. Written instructions should be displayed in the workplace and should also be given to every employee. New employees and anyone else spending some time on site should be taken through the procedure verbally by the person responsible for fire safety. Staff should also be made aware of any particular hazards and how they can ensure their own and other people's safety.

Act in the event of fire

A person discovering a fire must raise the alarm at once. Call the fire brigade; a person may be designated to do this upon hearing the alarm. Attempt to extinguish the fire if practicable, but it must be stressed to everyone that they must not put themselves at risk. Make sure that certain parts of the building have been cleared (a previously designated person may be responsible for this). Implement a system of checking that everyone has left the building, possibly by a designated person taking a roll call at the established fire assembly point. Don't take risks, use lifts, or return to the building after it has been evacuated.

WHAT TO AVOID
Not reviewing risk assessments
Risk assessments should be reviewed regularly, especially after changes in the workplace, activity, or staffing have occurred.

Not getting the right advice
The Health and Safety Executive can give advice related to specific manufacturing processes.

Not spreading the word
Draw up a fire precautions document, including responsibilities and fire instructions, and ensure that all employees receive a copy.

RECOMMENDED LINKS
British Safety Council:
www.britishsafetycouncil.org
FireNet:
www.fire.org.uk
Fire Protection Association (FPA):
www.thefpa.co.uk
Health and Safety Executive (HSE):
www.hse.gov.uk
Institute of Fire Prevention Officers:
www.fire.org.uk/IFPO

SEE ALSO
A Guide to Building Regulations (p. 81)
Buying a Business Property (p. 75)
Renting a Business Property (p. 72)

A Guide to Health and Safety at Work

GETTING STARTED

Businesses have a legal responsibility to protect the health and safety of their staff and others on their premises, and there is a range of laws to ensure that they do this. This actionlist explains the main steps you must take to ensure your business complies with health and safety regulations. It contains guidance on policy, obtaining a fire certificate, carrying out a risk assessment, reporting accidents, providing personal protective equipment, establishing a first aid procedure, and setting up a safety committee.

FAQS

What are my legal obligations with regard to health and safety?

The Health and Safety at Work Act 1974 requires every employer with five or more employees to produce a written policy on health and safety. The policy should contain a general statement acknowledging your legal responsibilities, an outline of the staff appointed to specific roles and their duties, and an outline of your procedures for ensuring appropriate standards are maintained. This might cover personal protective equipment, manual handling of loads, the use of display screens, safe handling of substances, maintenance records for plant and equipment, evacuation procedures in the event of fire, arrangements for first aid, the reporting of accidents, and staff training.

An appendix can also be helpful to record the legislation relevant to your business, your policies on specific issues such as smoking, drugs, alcohol, and HIV/AIDS, and how your staff will be informed about the policy and subsequent changes.

Under the Health and Safety at Work Act 1974, you must appoint a person to be responsible for putting the policy into practice. Make a formal list of duties, and ensure that everyone knows who the responsible person is. Their role will be to ensure that the safety standards and procedures outlined in the policy are adhered to on a day-to-day basis.

Where can I go for more information?

There are several organisations that provide advice about health and safety, including the British Safety Council, The Royal Society for the Prevention of Accidents (RoSPA), and the Health and Safety Executive (HSE). The website addresses for these three are given below.

The British Safety Council publishes a couple of useful guides, *Occupational Health* and *Update on Health and Safety Law*. RoSPA publishes a guide called *Essentials of Health and Safety at Work*, and the HSE also offers their own *Essentials of Health and Safety at Work*. Two other useful publications are *An A-Z of Health and Safety Law* by Peter Chandler, and *Manager's Guide to Health and Safety at Work* by Jeremy Stranks, both published by Kogan Page.

MAKING IT HAPPEN

Understand fire regulations

The Fire Precautions (Workplace) Regulations 1997 (amended 1999) apply to all workplaces. You must obtain a fire certificate from the fire officer if the premises are used for sleeping, treatment or care, leisure or entertainment, teaching, training, worship, or access to the general public. You will also need one if the premises are classed as a factory, shop, office, or railway, and at least one of the following conditions apply: 20 or more people are on the premises at any one time; 10 or more people work on floors above ground level; or explosives or highly flammable materials are used or stored on the premises.

Assess risk

Under the Management of Health and Safety at Work Regulations 1999, all employers (regardless of how many employees they have) and the self-employed are required to carry out a risk assessment. Businesses with five employees or more must record any significant risks discovered. The purpose of the risk assessment is to help you identify the measures that your business needs to take to comply with health and safety law.

You should examine whether employees are exposed to risk either because of the work they are doing, or by the condition of the premises, plant, equipment, or vehicles. You are also responsible for any risk posed to others, such as contractors and members of the public, which might arise out of the nature of your work, or the state of your premises.

Report accidents

Your responsibilities here are two-fold, involving an internal and an external procedure. To comply with the Health and Safety at Work Act 1974, you must establish an internal system for reporting and recording accidents. You also have to report work-related deaths, major injuries, diseases, and dangerous incidents to the Health and Safety Executive (HSE) and/or your local authority. This is stipulated in the Reporting of Injuries, Diseases and Dangerous Occurrences Regulations 1995 (known as RIDDOR).

Deaths, major injuries, and dangerous occurrences must be reported immediately, and followed up with a report submitted to the enforcing authority within 10 days. An accident which leaves a worker unable to do the full range of their normal duties for more than three days must be reported within 10 days. Records must be kept for three years from the date of the incident. The enforcing authority may request to see them.

Details of what must be reported, together with an accident report form, are set out in the free leaflet 'RIDDOR explained—Reporting of Injuries, Diseases and Dangerous Occurrences Regulations' (HSE31, rev 1). It is available from the HSE (website address given below).

Provide protective equipment

Under the Personal Protective Equipment at Work Regulations 1992, employers must provide suitable safety equipment (such as hard hats, reinforced footwear, and reflective jackets) for use at work wherever there are risks that cannot be adequately controlled in other ways. You will have to assess what type of equipment is suitable to offer protection against the hazards of the job, and to ensure compatibility where more than one item of equipment is needed.

You must ensure that the personal protective equipment is kept clean and in good repair, stored correctly, and replaced when necessary. Your employees must be given adequate information about the equipment, and be properly trained to use it.

First aid

Employers must have facilities to offer first aid to employees if they are injured or become ill at work. The Health and Safety (First Aid) Regulations 1981 and Code of Practice and Guidance outline the requirements.

Your first task is to assess the level of first aid likely to be needed. To do this, consider the nature and degree of risk, the number of employees involved, and the location of the business. Extra consideration should be given to employees working in isolated locations, travelling through remote areas, or using potentially dangerous tools and machinery. The HSE has guidelines on the number of first aid personnel a business should have, depending on the number of employees and the assessment of risk.

The procedures for first aid should be detailed in your health and safety policy, and all staff should be made aware of them. You should also set up a first aid post. At least one notice should be posted in each premises indicating the location of the first aid kit, and the names and locations of the trained first aiders and appointed persons. A first aider is someone who has passed a training course in administering first aid at work, and holds a current first aid at work certificate. The training has to be approved by HSE. The certificates are currently valid for three years, and employers need to arrange refresher training before they expire.

An appointed person is an employee who is selected to take charge in the event of illness or an accident. Their responsibilities will include calling an ambulance if needed, and restocking the first aid box. An appointed person is not a certified first aider, so they should not attempt to administer first aid.

Think about a safety committee

Under the Safety Representatives and Safety Committees Regulations 1977 (SRSCR), recognised trade unions have the right to consult with employers about workplace safety. If requested, the employer must set up a safety committee to supervise the implementation of health and safety policy. If it is not a recognised trade union, then the Health and Safety (Consultation with Employees) Regulations 1996 apply. These require employers to consult their employees either directly or via elected safety representatives. However, unlike the SRSCR, the regulations do not make any formal provision for safety committees.

Train employees

Employers have an obligation to provide training for new employees as part of the induction process. This needs to cover safety systems used in the workplace, fire safety and evacuation procedures, the health and safety policy, and the identity of employees responsible for first aid, fire safety, and the reporting of accidents.

Secure premises

Contractors and visitors to your premises are entitled to the same considerations of health and safety as your employees, and they should follow the same safety procedures. The premises should also be secured against unauthorised entry.

WHAT TO AVOID
Not getting the right advice

For more detailed information, as well as practical advice, the Health and Safety Executive website is very useful (address given below).

Not keeping employees informed

A health and safety law poster must be displayed in your premises. Entitled 'What You Should Know', it is available from HSE Books (see website below).

Not keeping the HSE informed

If you plan to use premises as a factory, make sure that you inform the HSE (in writing) at least a month before you start (this is required to comply with the Factories Act 1961).

RECOMMENDED LINKS

British Safety Council:
www.britishsafetycouncil.co.uk
HSE Books:
www.hsebooks.co.uk
Health and Safety Executive (HSE):
www.hse.gov.uk
Institution of Occupational Safety and Health (IOSH):
www.iosh.co.uk
International Institute of Risk and Safety Management:
www.iirsm.org
Royal Society for the Prevention of Accidents (RoSPA):
www.rospa.co.uk

SEE ALSO
A Guide to Building Regulations (p. 81)
Buying a Business Property (p. 75)
Ergonomics at Work (p. 97)
Insuring a Business (p. 87)

Ergonomics at Work

GETTING STARTED

Ergonomics concerns the adaptation of equipment, procedures, and surroundings to the people who use them. Its aims involve creating a safe, comfortable, and stress-reduced environment by selecting the right products and systems to customise a workspace for an individual. Ergonomics is normally associated with computer seating and work stations, though it can apply equally to assembly-line work and production, construction, and maintenance.

This actionlist looks at the concept of ergonomics, particularly within the office environment. It then suggests how you might apply the concept to your working surroundings, creating and maintaining a workplace that increases comfort and reduces stress for everyone working in that space.

FAQS

What are the benefits of ergonomics?

Managers have only recently recognised the benefits ergonomics can bring to their companies. It can improve production and efficiency levels, quality of service, and reduce staff turnover and insurance premiums. Benefits for employees include increased motivation and job satisfaction, less pain and fewer injuries, reduced absenteeism, and a greater sense of general well-being in the workplace.

What can happen if ergonomics are ignored?

If ergonomic practices are not followed in the workplace, there may be a number of consequences, ranging from the relatively minor to serious injury. These include general symptoms, such as stress and fatigue, which can build up slowly over a period of time. In some cases, in particular those involving prolonged and repetitive activity, the worker may suffer physical injuries caused by poor posture, applying excessive force, making repetitive movements, and taking too few recovery breaks. Computer-based injuries are commonly known as Repetitive Strain Injury (RSI), Work Related Upper Limb Disorder (WRULD), and Cumulative Trauma Disorder (CTD). RSI includes work-related injuries to the muscles, tendons, and nerves of the limbs; back and wrist injuries are the most common ailments. Workers in construction and main-

tenance, who regularly use vibrating hand tools, may suffer hand-arm vibration syndrome (HAVS), the most common of which is 'white finger'. Employees working with VDUs and computers, or workers doing precise assembly tasks, are prone to blurred vision or unusual eye irritability.

MAKING IT HAPPEN
Raise ergonomic awareness

Carry out a diagnostic test of working areas to identify any potential risk factors that may cause discomfort or stress. It is essential to involve all employees in this process, as far as possible, to make them feel they have some control over their working environment. You could start by asking which tasks involve prolonged activity that may lead to physical discomfort, and whether any aspects of the job cause stress. Find out whether particular tasks cause stress or discomfort and which equipment or furniture could improve the working environment.

On the basis of the diagnostic test of the workspace and an awareness of potential problem areas, make the changes necessary. They will help reduce the risk of strain or injury and will enhance the working environment. To optimise any ergonomic practices put in place, it is advisable to train employees on the best ways of using the equipment or furniture, as well as on the principles behind it.

Be aware of ergonomic problems in the workplace

Workplace seating is a common problem and the position and height of chairs and desks are not always suitable. The chair should fit the user, be comfortable, and support the back. No chair is suitable for every worker for every task, therefore adjusting a chair may be essential. Chair backrests and armrests can both help to reduce strain on the back.

Computers and VDUs are another problem area. The glare and/or reflections on monitor screens may make it difficult to read information clearly on the screen. Desks should be positioned perpendicular, rather than parallel, to windows in order to help minimise reflections. Using anti-glare filters or screens can also be a useful remedy. Some office lighting, such as unshielded fluorescent strip lighting, is not suitable for use with VDUs. Indirect lighting should be used, such as uplighters or lights with suitable diffusers, which provide glare-free lighting for personal computers. Individual task lighting could be provided for hard-copy work.

The temperature in the office needs to be regulated, as the indoor climate can sometimes be too warm, too cool, or draughty. Furthermore, electrical equipment dries the air, and static build up around a computer screen attracts dust. A comfortable temperature for office work is between 20 and 24 degrees Celsius.

Selecting ergonomic equipment

Once risks have been identified, consideration can be given to the design of the workspace. People vary in height and weight, in physical strength, sensory abilities (vision, hearing, and so on), their ability to handle information and make decisions, and general health. It is therefore essential to take account of these attributes when providing a comfortable and safe workspace and equipment.

Choosing ergonomic office furniture is essential if the working environment is to be improved for employees. The manager should be aware of the performance criteria and standards of various office products, know what they are looking for, and buy from a reputable, knowledgeable manufacturer. Going for the cheapest option may not always result in obtaining the right piece of equipment.

Devising a product check list, like the one below, is a good idea before selecting office furniture. For example:

- Is the item convenient and easy to use?
- Is the item easy to adjust, and does it come with clear instructions?
- Are the materials of the product durable and of good quality?
- Does the item offer good fit and comfort?
- Does the item cause any discomfort if used for a prolonged period of time?
- Is the item made by a reputable manufacturer?
- Does the item conform to International/European/British Standards?

A number of manufacturers sell ergonomic office equipment in the United Kingdom. Using ergonomic office equipment may prevent injury in the first place, avoid an injury recurring, or be useful for workers with disabilities. Examples are an ergonomic mouse to reduce strain on the wrist and lower arm muscles; a keyboard to reduce RSI by using palm rests; and anti-glare computer screens to reduce eyestrain.

Follow best practice

No amount of ergonomic furniture and equipment in the workplace can compensate for bad practice. It should be ensured that every employee takes a number of preventative measures to reduce the risks of fatigue, stress, and work-related injuries in the workplace. This can be achieved by distributing best practice leaflets throughout the organisation, and holding ergonomic awareness training sessions.

Highlight the important areas for improvement and point out the benefits, for example, improving posture can result in reduced risk of back and wrist injuries. Suggest other simple measures, such as taking frequent short breaks throughout the working day (which is far better than taking one or two long breaks). This can be combined with doing frequent stretching exercises and breathing exercises to loosen up the muscles and reduce tension.

There are a few ergonomic tips which, if followed by you and your employees, should help reduce the risks of injury and stress. When you lift heavy loads, keep your knees bent and your back straight. Avoid extremes in reaching, twisting, or lifting, and keep any items you use frequently within arm's reach.

Adjust the backrest and armrests of the chair you use to allow you to sit in an upright position without slouching. The backrest should follow the natural 's' curve of your spine. The height of the chair should be adjusted so that your wrists, hands, and forearms are horizontal with the desk. Your feet should be placed flat on the floor; use a footrest if you need to. Keep your head up and your shoulders relaxed. Your legs and feet should fit comfortably under the desk, so remove any obstacles that prevent this.

Your computer monitor should be at a comfortable distance from the eyes. Make sure there is space on the desk to rest hands and wrists, so that you can keep movement of the wrists to a minimum. Adjust the brightness and colour contrast of your computer screen and make sure that all screens are reflection-free and clean. Avoid long periods of repetitive activity; for example, alternate computer-based work with other tasks, such as filing, telephoning, or photocopying.

Know the relevant legislation
Although applying ergonomic practices to the workplace is a matter of common sense, it is the business's responsibility to be aware of health and safety legislation in order to create and maintain a safe working environment. A large number of Acts and Regulations outline how this can be done, and some are listed here:

- Health and Safety at Work Act 1974
- Management of Health and Safety at Work Regulations 1999
- Workplace (Health, Safety, and Welfare) Regulations 1992

- Health and Safety (Display Screen Equipment) Regulations 1992
- Provision and Use of Work Equipment Regulations 1998

WHAT TO AVOID

Doing too little too late
Ergonomics should be used in the workplace to help prevent problems. Ergonomic awareness should not just be introduced after a problem becomes apparent, although this is often a common reason for introducing ergonomic practices.

Insufficient training
Running staff training programmes is crucial to raising awareness and gaining commitment to ergonomic practices. Employees should be trained on the best ways to use ergonomic furniture and equipment in their workspace. The reasons for adjusting the equipment to suit their needs should be highlighted.

Not selecting the right equipment
Make sure that the ergonomic equipment you select is suitable for your business and your staff. Carry out a diagnostic test of the workplace before making any decision. An ergonomic consultant could be employed if it is not clear what the best ergonomic practices for the workplace are, or if complicated changes need to be made.

RECOMMENDED LINKS
HSE Books:
www.hsebooks.co.uk
Health and Safety Executive (HSE) Information Centre:
www.hse.gov.uk
Ergonomics Society:
www.ergonomics.org.uk

SEE ALSO
A Guide to Health and Safety at Work (p. 94)
Buying a Business Property (p. 75)
Renting a Business Property (p. 72)

Setting Up and Maintaining Your Home Office

GETTING STARTED

Many people choose to work from home these days, and most new businesses start off in the home of their owner-managers. If you're thinking about basing your company where you live to begin with, you may need to get used to a new way of working, especially if you've previously been working in a more formal, structured setting. To start, ask yourself the following questions:

- Can I handle the social isolation of a home office on a full-time basis?
- Am I a self-starter?
- How do I rate as a decision-maker, organiser, book-keeper, and secretary?
- Could I separate business and personal life if both were under the same roof?
- Am I a workaholic and would an office at home worsen that problem?

FAQS

Is working from home as wonderful as it sounds?

Yes and no. For convenience, cost, and comfort, there's nothing quite like a home office. Low overheads, no commuting hassles, no office politics, and setting your own hours are a few of the pluses. On the minus side, there's only you—and if you're not disciplined, you'll be spending more time with the children, the pets, or in front of the fridge than working where you belong. It can be a simple formula for failure.

How can I make a home-based business seem professional to customers?

It depends on the type of business, but start with a professional attitude and then get some good-looking business cards and stationery. Think about adding an attractive logo and using a two-colour design on business cards, letterheads, and envelopes. Having a well-produced flyer or brochure that describes your business is also a plus: good quality customer service will do the rest.

E-commerce is relatively easy to conduct from a home office, especially with a website that attracts customers. Clients don't really need to know whether you work at home or in a sophisticated office building, so long as you get the job done for them. As with your other materials, the website should reflect the personality and professionalism of your business.

What sort of investment is necessary to equip a home office?

This, too, depends on the type of activity you'll be doing—whether it be business or teleworking, or a personal or family office. But generally, spending between £1,000 and £3,000 should make you well equipped and comfortable. Make a list and plan a sensible budget beforehand; you don't want to blow your entire savings on setting up the office, then have nothing to spend on attracting business.

MAKING IT HAPPEN

Plan the layout of your office

Planning a home office involves deciding where to locate the office, how to decorate it, and how to furnish it. You should give lots of thought to this, as it will be the hub of a small business and you'll be spending a lot of time there. Some people even make a scale drawing of the room they intend to use, then place to-scale furniture in there to decide on the best layout. Some office furniture suppliers also provide this service.

Take account of tax considerations

As you're planning to use the office for a small business, HM Revenue & Customs will allow you to deduct certain expenses connected to the business. For that reason, the office must be completely dedicated to the business and not merely a spare bedroom with a fold-up desk and your cordless phone. Good record-keeping is very important if you plan to deduct expenses and part of the mortgage interest, utilities, and phone bills for business activity.

Make sure you're comfortable and have the right equipment

Office décor is important. Besides getting the right atmosphere (lighting, paint/wallpaper, floor covering), think about practical items too: do you have enough phone points and sockets in the room to support the office equipment? Beyond that, having comfortable, functional furniture will allow you to work productively.

Your package of office equipment will depend on the type of business you're in, but will probably include computer(s) and peripherals, software, phones and phone service for voice, fax and computer, and perhaps even a separate copier and/or scanner. Add a digital camera if you plan to put photos of yourself or your products on your website. If you don't have a broadband connection to the Internet already, do consider upgrading: it will make life a lot easier as you'll be able to work online and still be able to use the phone (handy if you're discussing a document or website with someone else). You'll also be able to open attachments much more quickly. Broadband isn't available everywhere, and the service is especially limited in some rural areas. If you visit www.broadbandchecker.co.uk, you can type in your postcode and phone number and you'll be told whether broadband is available in your area, along with a list of service providers. Finally, don't forget that you'll need storage space for files, records, and other general office supplies.

Impose proper discipline on yourself

One of the most difficult aspects of the home office is the home itself—it's all too easy to be distracted by jobs round the house, watch TV, weed the garden, get involved with family things, have a snack in the kitchen, and otherwise avoid the work that awaits you in your office. Two factors will help avoid the home trap: being excited about your office space and the work—and discipline. Set regular office hours, have a separate business phone, organise your time, and stick to your deadlines.

Don't let yourself get isolated

Being isolated in your home office, you may develop a tendency to cocoon yourself in there or to avoid keeping in touch with the outside world, both of which can be unhealthy.

Having a business gives you plenty of opportunity to break away from the office to meet other people socially and professionally. Even if much of your business is conducted over the phone and by computer, it's still important to network. Invite customers and prospective customers to lunch, if they happen to do business nearby. Join a local community group or professional organisation to stay connected and also to generate local interest in your business. Get physical exercise away from the home. Join an evening class. All these things will help keep you connected, bring in new ideas, and generate lots of personal energy—things you'll value when working alone.

WHAT TO AVOID
You go halfway with the office arrangement

Starting a home office on the dining-room table is not a good idea, nor is committing only half-heartedly to making a guestroom into a real office. If you don't treat the office seriously, there's a better than even chance you won't take your work seriously either.

Carve out a separate space and dedicate it as the office. You'll feel better and your work will benefit from that decision.

You succumb to workaholic syndrome

If, while working in an office setting, you've had a tendency to stay there until the work is done, operating from home is a workaholic's dream come true. With the office only a few rooms away, there's a temptation to 'get one last thing done' after dinner or at weekends.

It's important to be professional about your business, but it's also important that you don't let the office become your new home. Set hours, try to manage your work-flow into those hours, then shut the door and leave it all behind.

You get swamped by family issues

Lots of women see working at home as the answer to two issues—making a living and raising a family. If it were easy to mix children and work, parents would have been doing it at their offices long ago.

That said, it isn't entirely impossible either. The trick is balance. You can't afford to be at the beck and call of your children, but you certainly don't want them to feel totally ignored. Racing from the office to untangle toys and do the washing every hour will soon turn your work world upside-down. Closing the door and ignoring the family will have an equally unfortunate effect.

Obviously, day care is an option. Consider it for the days that you might need to concentrate on your most important work. On days you set aside for more mundane tasks, such as paying bills, book-keeping, research on the Internet, and so forth, you might find it easier to have the family there.

You lack certain office job skills

When working for other companies, you probably relied on others with jobs that complemented your own. When you are your own boss, working from your home office, you have a lot more duties besides the specific ones that 'bring home the bacon'. You'll be responsible for executive and marketing decisions, financial and administrative details and deadlines, as well

as clerical and reception work. Until your business becomes profitable enough to employ other people, it's all down to you.

This is where a business plan makes sense. You need to work out the details of how you'll charge for your products or services. Be careful to account for the 'cost of doing business', which includes the clerical and administrative things, too. Add in a 'fudge factor' and some profit. Assuming that you'll work a 40-hour week, set your sights on making a living in 30 hours, then use the other 10 hours to take care of the other parts of the business—marketing, promotion, invoicing, book-keeping, and business errands.

If you feel you lack the skills to juggle all of these things, or don't have the interest in becoming your own secretary, perhaps you're not cut out for a home business. But if you want to give it a try, you can certainly learn what you need to know about the care and feeding of a small business from books, the Internet, or your local small-business advisory service.

RECOMMENDED LINKS
Entrepreneur:
www.entrepreneur.com
HM Revenue & Customs:
**www.hmrc.gov.uk/menus/
   b_taxpayers.htm**
Money *Guardian*:
www.money.guardian.co.uk

SEE ALSO
Buying a Business Property (p. 75)
**Computers, Information Technology, and
   E-commerce (p. 503)**
**Drawing Boundaries: How to Manage
   Working at Home (p. 103)**
Renting a Business Property (p. 72)

Drawing Boundaries: How to Manage Working at Home

GETTING STARTED

Many small businesses are run from the home of the owner-manager. Working from home has become much easier over recent years, especially as technology has become more sophisticated, but for some people (especially those who have been used to working in larger companies) it can take a while to get used to working in a less-structured setting. This actionlist offers some advice on how to work productively from home.

FAQS

Will I be able to concentrate on my work when at home? There are so many distractions.

If you decide to work from home, you absolutely must carve out a separate work environment within your house or flat and create some boundaries around your working day too. It is hopeless trying to balance your laptop on your knee in the kitchen whilst you attempt to avoid intrusions from family or friends; you need to set rules for yourself and others so that everyone can support your efforts rather than sabotage them.

I'm really looking forward to being my own boss, but also enjoy very much the buzz of being in the office. How can I find this level of stimulation?

If you're an extrovert and enjoy the energy of having other people around, build this into your working life. If your business has an office elsewhere, split up your week into days there and days working at home. If you work from home full-time, schedule visits and meetings regularly so that you feel involved with and energised by others.

MAKING IT HAPPEN

Plan, plan, plan

Once people get used to working from home, they often find they prefer it to working in an office. However, to be successful, you need to plan ahead. You will need all the elements of a 'real' office: furniture, computer, software, telephone, fax, an e-mail account, and so on. Spend some time setting up your office as you will probably spend much more time in it than you envisage. Make sure you have a dedicated telephone line so that calls related to work and home don't get confused. Experiment with different office layouts until you feel comfortable with your arrangements.

Create boundaries

If you have other people at home, make sure you create boundaries around the time you set aside for working. Non-work interruptions can be frustrating when you're trying to complete a task. Set up boundaries by establishing in advance how you are going to manage your time at home, including things like the beginning and end of your working day. It also helps to have a separate room to call your office, with a door you can close so you won't be disturbed. If you live with others, stick to your guns and people will soon get the message.

If your work requires you to receive visitors, try to find an area where they won't be distracted by your domestic arrangements. Having to ignore the pile of washing on the kitchen floor can be very off-putting when the point of the meeting is anything but domestic. If you are unable to avoid these situations, find a local hotel or restaurant where you can meet for an hour or two. Again, this is about creating boundaries that will enable you to maintain focus and create an impression of professionalism.

Establish a routine

It is important to differentiate your day between being 'at work' and 'at home'. If your working and resting time becomes confused, it can feel as if you are always on duty, and when you do take a break you can feel guilty that you are not finishing a project. This differentiation comes naturally when you have to travel to and from work, but when you're no longer commuting you'll need to make this shift in your head yourself. It could be signalled by a new routine; making a cup of coffee, taking it to your desk, closing your door, and switching on the computer. Once you've done this a few times, this routine creates the boundary within which you can work effectively.

Plan your day so that you don't find yourself wasting time. The advantage of working from home is that you have greater control over interruptions. People will no longer be able to wander past your desk at will and ask you for some information or, worse, to do something for them. A great deal of time is wasted in these 'Oh, by the way...' moments that happen mostly because you are accessible or visible.

Take a break

Make sure you take breaks throughout the day. It's commonly understood that powers of concentration diminish after about twenty minutes, and continuing to work after this time can lead to a point where thinking becomes a struggle. Taking a break, perhaps a short walk, can re-energise your thinking capability. Of course, breaks need to be balanced by the need to be productive. Try not to get distracted by picking up something else that needs doing. You will only end up wasting time and lowering your efficiency by spreading your energies too thinly.

Maintain your work/life balance

Make sure you plan for the end of the day also. It is far too easy to remain sitting in your workspace well into the evening and ignore the private side of your life. Keeping a work/life balance is just as important for those who work from home as it is for office workers. As you won't have to factor commuting time into your day any more, make sure you use the extra time well by doing whatever it is you enjoy, whether it be meeting friends, spending time with your family, pursuing a hobby, or taking some exercise.

Find out about your tax status

If you are self-employed, you will find that having an office in the home may qualify you for tax concessions. Tax relief is available on your mortgage interest, heating and telephone bills, and the cost of capital equipment and services needed to support your business. HM Revenue & Customs (HMRC) or your accountant will guide you on what tax benefits you may receive. Anyone starting a new business must register with HMRC within a strict time period. Visit their website (details below) for full information. As of April 2005, if your income is going to reach £60,000 in a 12 month period you must register for VAT beforehand. This threshold figure tends to change annually during the Budget, so do contact your local VAT registration office or find more information at **www.hmrc.gov.uk** if you're at all unsure about your situation.

WHAT TO AVOID
Losing your focus

For those who enjoy dynamic environments and the cut and thrust of being in a busy office, working from home may not be enjoyable. It is tempting for this type of person to create dynamism for themselves by finding activities that distract them from their own company. Flitting around from task to task can create a feeling of being in the flow but may not be very productive. Time spent at the beginning of the day creating a 'to do' list can focus your energy and ensure that there is a valuable output to the day's activities.

Not switching off

It is very easy for people to work beyond the call of duty when the office is located in the home, especially during the hectic first stages of a new business. 'I'll just go and answer a few e-mails...' can become a lengthy session in front of the computer that eats into private time. Try to discipline yourself to keep to the 'rules' that you have set, with only occasional exceptions.

Losing track of the time

If you get a buzz from working with others, you might be tempted to get on the phone as a substitute for their presence around you. It's all too easy to spend a lot of your day in this way and find that you have to work long into the evening to actually achieve anything worthwhile. Again, this is a question of discipline. Give yourself time when you can talk to others, but keep control of it. A large

clock on the wall in front of you is the most basic but best reminder of how long you are spending on each activity.

RECOMMENDED LINKS

Home-Workers.com:
www.home-workers.com
HM Revenue & Customs:
www.hmrc.gov.uk

SEE ALSO
Setting Up and Maintaining Your Home Office (p. 100)

FIGURING IT OUT

Financing a New Business

GETTING STARTED
New businesses need finance to cover the cost of equipment and expenses before sales generate enough cash to make the operation self-supporting. This actionlist describes the main ways of financing your business (equity finance, loan finance, and grants). It explains how to work out the amount of finance you need, and what proportion of debt to equity is advisable.

FAQS
What is a business angel?
A business angel is someone who is willing to invest money in a business. The amount available from angels is usually much less than from venture capitalists, but they are often willing to take bigger risks.

What is equity finance?
Equity, or shareholder capital, is the money introduced into a business by the owners. If it is a company, then the equity is introduced in exchange for shares. Investors expect a share of the business's profit. In the case of limited companies, this takes the form of dividends. The person starting a business will normally introduce equity capital, but it can also be raised from external investors, including business angels and venture capitalists. Investors will be looking for an annual dividend, which often can be quite small, and a good return when they sell their shares. Equity is best suited, therefore, to businesses that expect to grow quickly.

What is loan finance?
Loan finance is money that is borrowed from a finance company, such as a bank. Loans are repaid over a period of time, at either fixed or variable rates of interest. The lender will usually require security against a business or personal asset. Terms can vary in length from one year to 25 years, and will usually be determined by the asset that is being financed. The interest rate will reflect the lender's perception of the risk in providing the loan. Loan finance can be provided in different ways.

An overdraft is money that a business can borrow from a bank up to an agreed limit. It provides a business with short-term finance, effectively by running a negative balance on the bank account. This is a particularly good way of funding short-term requirements, such as providing working capital during the course of each month.

Term loans are funds borrowed for a fixed term. Usually, such loans are repayable in equal instalments over the term of the loan, although sometimes they can be repaid in a lump sum at the end of the term. Term loans are more attractive than overdrafts for long-term borrowing because repayments are fixed and the cost is usually less. However, lenders are increasingly writing into the small print that term loans are repayable on demand. If the loan has been used to finance capital assets, this could cause problems.

Creditor finance is an excellent way of 'borrowing' money, effectively at no cost. Typically, suppliers may give 30 to 60 days' credit for their goods or services before payment is due. If you can sell your product or service and get paid before paying your creditors, then it will generate cash into the business. Your business may have to establish a trading record before credit is given, and it can be withdrawn at any time.

Debtor finance is particularly useful if your business is growing rapidly and is providing credit accounts to its customers. Instead of waiting for your own customers to pay your invoices within a 30- or 60-day period, you can use the services of a third party invoice discounting or factoring firm. Factoring can be an expensive way of speeding up cash flow, but it may reduce administration costs since the factor normally takes on the role of invoice clerk.

Grants are usually 'one off' payments providing a percentage of the costs towards a specific purpose, usually for capital expenditure, but sometimes for a specific activity such as taking part in an exhibition or trade fair. Amounts vary depending on the scheme. A grant may be available from the government, the European Union, the local authority, or a related organisation. Grants are usually treated as income to the business and, as such, are shown on the profit and loss account. There are several sources of grant aid worth investigating when starting in business, and whenever you are buying equipment.

Capital asset finance can often be done through 'off-balance-sheet' finance. There are different ways of doing this. Financial leasing allows you to finance the use of an asset rather than owning it. The equipment remains the property of the leasing company; the business has the legal right to use the equipment for the period of the lease, provided that the lease payments are up to date. In a lease purchase arrangement, you have an option to purchase the equipment at the end of the lease period. Through hire purchase, you pay regular instalments to a third party, normally a finance house, to purchase ownership of plant and machinery from a supplier. The finance house will own the equipment throughout the period of the agreement, until the last instalment has been paid.

◢ MAKING IT HAPPEN
Work out how much capital you need
The working capital of a business is its current assets (typically stock, cash at the bank, and debtors) minus its current liabilities (typically trade creditors, other creditors such as PAYE and VAT, and your bank overdraft). This information is summarised on the balance sheet, although this only gives a snapshot of the working capital requirements at a specific moment in time. Generally, this is the finance required for the short-term running of the business.

The amount of working capital needed will vary during the course of the year and even during the course of a month. You need to allow for the maximum likely working capital requirement. Consideration needs to be given to the variation that can occur within each month. As a rule of thumb, it makes sense to aim for minimum working capital of a month's average sales multiplied by the number of months it takes to collect payment. If you want to be more accurate, then use the following procedure:

1. Determine the average number of weeks that the raw material is in stock.
2. Deduct from this figure the credit period from suppliers, in weeks.
3. Then add the average number of weeks to produce goods or service, the average number of weeks finished goods are in stock, and the average time customers take to pay.
4. Take the total, and divide it by 52 (the number of weeks in the year). Multiply the result by your estimated sales for the year. The answer will give you a figure for the maximum working capital required.

It would be more accurate to use the cost of sales (direct and fixed), rather than the full selling price, but the above calculation is close enough. If your business is growing, then you need to use the budgeted sales figures, and it is advisable to calculate your working capital needs on a regular basis.

Understand gearing and interest cover
Gearing is the proportion of debt to total capital in the business. The more debt there is relative to equity, the higher the gearing. Introducing more equity, or retaining more of the profits, can reduce the gearing ratio. Most banks look for a gearing of no more than 50%; in other words, your debt should be no more than half of the total capital.

Once you have built up a track record with your bank, you should be able to attract medium-term loans (three- to seven-year loans) to cover the cost of plant and equipment. Established companies may be able to raise long-term debt as a debenture or convertible loan stock, which normally receives a fixed rate of interest and is repayable in full at the end of the term. Long-term debt is usually included with the capital on the balance sheet. The banks will also be more comfortable with a higher gearing, though they still do not like to see it too high. Lease and hire purchase companies will not have as great a concern about gearing as the banks. They will, however, be interested in your cash flow and whether you can afford the repayments.

If you expect to grow quickly and do not have enough of your own money to provide the necessary finance, then you may need to look for equity early on. Banks will be reluctant to keep on providing additional working capital, as that simply increases the gearing and increases their risk. Growing too quickly is often known as 'over-trading' and is a major cause of business failure. The banks will also want to reassure themselves that you can afford the interest on the loan. So they will look for profits that are at least three or four times the expected interest charge.

WHAT TO AVOID
Not thinking ahead
Regularly calculate the total level of funding required for the next year, and split the funding into fixed asset requirements and working capital requirements. Think carefully about the term, the cost, the suitability, the timescale, and any security required. Remember that cost should not be the sole criterion. Keep your lenders informed of your financial position, giving ample warning if you are likely to need to increase your overdraft, for example.

Not changing with the times
In times of recession, keep as much of your debt as possible as fixed medium-term loans, and keep your overdraft requirement to the minimum. In times of expansion, when finance is more readily available, it may be more cost-effective to use an overdraft.

RECOMMENDED LINKS
British Venture Capital Association:
www.bvca.co.uk
Factors and Discounters Association:
www.factors.org.uk
The Prince's Trust:
www.princes-trust.org.uk

SEE ALSO
Addressing Cash-flow Problems (p. 148)
Applying for Grants and Funding (p. 117)
Budgeting (p. 499)
Controlling Costs (p. 123)
Drawing Up a Budget (p. 126)
Preparing a Successful Business Plan (p. 114)
Understanding the Role of the Bank (p. 111)
Venture Capital (p. 553)

Understanding the Role of the Bank

GETTING STARTED

Every entrepreneur understands you need a bank account to facilitate payments and receipts, but banks can help your business in other ways too. They provide a range of banking services such as overdrafts, term loans, and equity, as well as financial services like insurance and pensions. This actionlist explains how to choose the best bank for you, and looks at some of the services banks can offer.

FAQS

What is the best way to choose a bank?

Banking is intensely competitive nowadays, so it pays to gather as much information as possible on the services offered. All the major banks have customer charters, or codes of practice, with full details of their charges and tariffs, so you should be able to estimate the likely cost to your business. All the banks offer incentives for new customers, for example free banking for the first 12 months; you should only consider these incentives when there's little to choose between other more important factors. However, most businesses require a loan or overdraft at some point in their development, so ask different banks about this before deciding where to open your business account.

Relationships are critical. You should seek advice and recommendations from professionals and small businesses in the same area, for example your local enterprise counsellors or your solicitor, to help find a bank with a good track record. This is probably the most important factor. The relationship between a business and the local enterprise agency is a crucial factor for most banks when they consider financing a business. The chosen bank should, in turn, also have good relations with the local enterprise networks. Finally, talk to the bank manager to help you decide whether this is someone with whom you can work.

How do I open a business bank account?

Opening a business bank account is, like opening any other bank account, pretty straightforward, although it does involve some red tape caused by the Government's drive to crack down on money laundering—so be prepared to provide appropriate identification. If you are seeking a loan, banks can often give very fast answers, especially if you need less than £10,000, but expect them to make inquiries about your credit history.

MAKING IT HAPPEN
Borrowing from the bank

Banks offer a number of different arrangements, each tailored to suit various business needs. The most flexible and simple form of borrowing is the **overdraft**. This provides a business with short-term finance, so do not use it for anything that will take a long time to repay (such as fixed assets). The interest rate charged is usually linked to Bank Base Rate, and should be agreed at the outset. In addition, an arrangement fee (a percentage of the amount borrowed, normally around 1.5%) may be payable. Overdrafts also often attract annual renewal fees.

It is important to be aware of the charges connected with exceeding the agreed overdraft level. Charges may be levied at a set amount every time you exceed the agreed level, or per day when the agreed overdraft limit is exceeded. Additional interest will be charged, and banks usually charge for informing the account holder (by telephone, letter, or additional statement). There are also charges for returned cheques. Monies provided by an overdraft are repayable on demand.

A **loan** is the ideal form of finance to purchase fixed assets. (A fixed asset is a long-term asset of a business, such as a piece of machinery or a building.) The loan term will be geared to the expected working life of the asset being bought. The interest rate may be fixed, which helps accurate budgeting and protects the business's cash flow in times of rising interest rates. Loans with variable rates are also available. Depending on your circumstances, you may be able to negotiate a capital repayment holiday. The banks can offer insurance to cover disruption to repayments, and loans can be linked to an endowment or pension policy with life and disability cover also available.

Ask the bank to confirm the loan terms and conditions in writing, and analyse them carefully before proceeding. When considering loans, banks normally require a business plan and references from a small business adviser. An arrangement fee is usually charged, often in the region of 2%.

Few banks will provide an unsecured loan to a business. The bank will normally expect the business to have something to act as security against the loan (property, for example). Alternatively, the bank may ask the directors of your business to provide personal guarantees on the loan. If the only impediment to you being given a loan is lack of suitable collateral, then you may qualify for the Small Firms Loan Guarantee Scheme; in this case, the government will guarantee 75% of the loan (for an additional premium on the interest rate), which should enable the loan to proceed.

Banks provide other services, which may be charged for separately on an 'as used' basis, and will be in addition to normal bank charges. Such services can make your banking much more flexible. For example:

- open credit arrangements enable the business to withdraw cash regularly from a branch of the bank other than the branch holding the account
- your credit cards or payment cards can have facilities for multiple use, and statements can be broken down to show clearly areas of expenditure
- electronic funds transfer enables funds to be transferred from a business account to another account at another branch or bank on the same day

Banks can also help with payment issues. For example:

- banker's references are inquiries carried out on behalf of a business into the creditworthiness of its suppliers and customers
- night safes enable cash or cheques to be deposited outside normal banking hours. There is usually a set quarterly charge plus a charge per usage
- stopped cheques are where the bank is instructed not to pay a cheque that has been issued
- special presentations allow you to request express payment of a cheque that has been paid into your business account
- sterling drafts are similar to cheques but are drawn on the head office of the business's bank, thus ensuring payment

Additional bank services

Many banks offer a range of international trade services for businesses trading in overseas markets whose suppliers or customers are based abroad. All the banks have systems and services in place to offer current, deposit, and loan accounts in euros and other major currencies. You may be able to ask for cross-border payment services, and your bank may be able to offer its clients a factoring service for customers in the United Kingdom or overseas.

Online banking services are increasingly available, allowing users to deal with the bank via the Internet. This allows instant access to information about their account, saving time and paperwork. It also means users can integrate their internal computerised account system more efficiently with that of the bank. Telephone banking is offered by many banks. As with online banking, this can be used to check accounts, transfer money, pay bills, and so on.

To meet legal requirements and to ensure that the business is covered for unforeseen events, businesses require insurance cover. The banks all have arrangements or partnerships to provide appropriate cover. They can also help with life cover, pensions, and personal savings if required. Linked savings accounts with competitive interest rates can help your business make the most of surplus funds. Reserve accounts allow money to be put aside for tax, VAT, and working capital.

Many banks offer free business counselling to new businesses to identify potential difficulties, and suggest new facilities and services that may be helpful. Most major banks publish literature on business start-up and offer comprehensive information services.

WHAT TO AVOID
Not giving the bank enough appropriate information

You expect an efficient and helpful service from your bank; the bank also has expectations of you. Banks do not like surprises, so keep them informed about your business, particularly if you have a loan. If you think that your requirements may change, give the bank good warning. As far as possible, run your accounts and loans in accordance with your agreement with the bank. The bank will then be far more likely to respond positively if you need, for example, to borrow more money. Once your business is up and running, send the bank a copy of your annual accounts each year. If you have a loan, this may be a condition; but even if you haven't, it may help if you think you may need a loan at some point.

Exceeding an overdraft limit without permission

If you overdraw your account without prior arrangement, or exceed your overdraft, you will be charged interest on the unauthorised borrowing, as well as being charged for the letter the bank sends you informing you of the interest charge.

Using an overdraft instead of a loan

Beware of 'easy' overdrafts. A bank may offer an overdraft facility rather than a loan. Overdrafts are usually more expensive than a loan and are repayable on demand, so only use an overdraft for working capital requirements.

Being unaware of the bank's charges

Watch out for hidden charges. People new to business are often surprised by the range of charges imposed on them by the bank in contrast to the free banking personal customers receive, though recently the banks have begun to reduce some of the charges imposed on business customers.

RECOMMENDED LINKS
Banking Code Standards Board:
www.bankingcode.org.uk
British Bankers Association:
www.bba.org.uk
Financial Ombudsman Service:
www.financial-ombudsman.org.uk

SEE ALSO
Budgeting (p. 499)
Financing a New Business (p. 108)

Preparing a Successful Business Plan

GETTING STARTED

Many new owner-managers write business plans with the sole purpose of convincing a financier to lend them money for starting up. However, a good business plan do much more than that and also help you build a stronger foundation for your business. It can help you to clarify your business purpose to yourself and communicate it to your partners and staff; predict future scenarios and address them before they threaten the success of the business; and set targets and objectives so that you can monitor your business performance.

Your plan must be a coherent description of how your business will move from where it is now to where you want it to be in the future. Obviously each business will be different, but the headings below are useful stepping stones to include in your business plan and will make sure that you cover the most important aspects.

FAQS

What should I say about my business?

Be as specific as possible about the kind of business that you are starting. Describe your business in terms of a mission statement or 'executive summary' that clearly summarises its purpose and is easily understood by you, your staff, customers, and potential investors. If you cannot describe your business in these terms, rethink your business idea; focus on the core activities and direction.

What should I use as my starting point?

Try to envisage where you might want your business to be in five years' time, so that you can start to move towards that point. For instance, you might work towards becoming a market leader, an innovator, a specialist, a good employer, a large concern, or a supplier of superior quality.

MAKING IT HAPPEN

Make sure you cover all the important issues in your business plan

As well as being very specific about the type of business you are starting, and thinking ahead to where you want to be in five years, there are a number of important elements that you will need to include in your business plan.

Current market situation

To earn enough revenue, your business must be able to achieve a share of the markets available. To do this, you'll need to have a thorough understanding of your market environment, including its size and the share that you can realistically achieve. The size of your share will depend on:

- market trends—find out what influences your target market now, and how your product can take advantage of this
- target customers—describe who your target customers are and how many there are; also justify your estimate of the market share you aim to get
- competition—list your competitors and describe their products; also describe how your product will be different

Current target customers

Define the characteristics of the target groups of customers that could buy from your business. Make a list of the features that your products have, and the associated benefits that these features can provide to your customers, then build up a picture of your target customers. For individuals, describe them in terms of characteristics like age, income, location, lifestyle, and marital status. For businesses, consider location, numbers of employees, public or private sector, industry type, and turnover. Carry out some research into how many customers there are in your target group, and how much they spend, and also try to identify trends that tell you whether this group is growing or shrinking.

Competitor analysis

Competitors may be in the same (direct competition) or similar (indirect competition) business to you. The level and strength of competition in a market indicates how difficult it will be to gain a share of the market. However, it is not simply the number of competitors that you should be concerned about; analyse the following aspects of each competitor's business:

- their products: are their products and services the same as yours? Do your competitors provide something that you don't?
- their customers: are your competitors targeting the same customer segments as your business?
- their share of the market: how large is it, and could you take some of it?
- their strategies: in how they grow, market themselves, and price their products. Can you learn from how they conduct business, or do it better?
- their operations and facilities: what levels of service are customers demanding?

Marketing strategy

With a clear understanding of your market, you can define your overall strategy. Break this down into objectives and targets relating to the volume and share of the market (or market segments) you hope to achieve, and when you intend to achieve them by. Ask yourself, for example:

- who are your initial marketing targets?
- what products, services or particular deals will you be offering?
- is there a specific volume, value, or share of these markets that you hope to achieve?
- when do you hope to achieve these targets by?
- why are you choosing these markets first?
- who will you target next, in the next 6 or 12 months?

Marketing plan

Now that you have a coherent marketing strategy, you need to be clear about how you are going to make it happen. A detailed marketing plan must explain how you will go about achieving each of your marketing targets and objectives, either by particular target segment, by type of marketing activity, or both. Such a plan will include some, or all of the following:

- the marketing methods you will use for each segment of the target market
- the specific action you are going to undertake
- a timescale or timetable for each marketing activity
- the people or organisations that are going to carry it out
- the estimated costs to undertake particular marketing activities
- how you will monitor and review progress
- how you will handle the response to your marketing

It will also be important to identify how you will manage the overall marketing plan, in other words ensuring that the entire budget is not spent in the first couple of months, monitoring results, adjusting the plan, and introducing new tactics as you go along.

Sales targets and objectives

Your marketing plan, when implemented, needs to be converted into perhaps the most important business goal of all: sales revenues. Set out your forecasts in terms of sales of different product types by volume and value; sales from different customer groups; and sales from different distribution channels.

Operational requirements

Information about your operational requirements will be required for your financial forecasts, while other information will be needed for your basic operational planning. Outline your plans for premises, equipment, staff, suppliers, and compliance and licensing, and estimate the respective costs involved.

Current financial requirements and financial forecasts

Your business plan should include a breakdown of your financial requirements, the sources of finance you have available to you, and any additional amount that you may need. This breakdown should include: the cost of starting your business; your personal budget; details of your own personal finance that you intend to invest, as well as of additional finance; a detailed cash flow forecast that will help estimate how much available cash you will have in any particular month; a profit and loss forecast to help estimate when your business will start to make a profit (which will be essential to your medium-term success); and a balance sheet forecast to provide you with a snapshot of the trading position of your business, to identify what your business will owe, what it will own, and how financially strong it will be at a particular point in the future.

Management processes

Even if you are the only person involved in your business, it is still important to consider your key skills, responsibilities, and management processes. Consider:

- management team—outline skills and experience
- key staff and responsibilities—summarise roles and contribution to the business. Be sure to cover these tasks: marketing and sales, finance, recruitment, product development, general management, and administration
- monitoring and co-ordination—set out how you plan to monitor performance and to co-ordinate the key roles in the business

Business risks

Your plan should include an honest awareness of the risks involved, as well as how you plan to minimise them. Consider which of the following risks are relevant to your businesses: lack of management experience; no trading history; economic uncertainties; reliance on key staff; reliance on a few suppliers; reliance on a small customer base; bad customer debts; partnership difficulties; increased competition; security and insurance against burglary and loss; and failure to meet your sales targets. Show that you have thought about all of these issues and that you have contingency plans for coping with them should they occur.

Present your plan professionally

Once you have researched and drafted all the necessary information, you can compile the plan. Produce a simple but stylish cover for it, not forgetting to include the business name, your address, your phone numbers, e-mail address, and the date. Put an edited, proofed, and double-checked final draft together. Use a transparent plastic cover with a binder, and letter-quality printer and paper. The order should be cover, title page, executive summary, contents page, contents, and appendices.

WHAT TO AVOID
Producing unrealistic sales forecasts

It is a good idea to produce more than one sales forecast, including one for the worst-case scenario so that you can show how you would deal with that. If you are over-optimistic you may not be able to make the necessary repayments. Make sure that any market research is comprehensive enough to give you realistic sales targets.

Not proof-reading the plan

To give your plan the best chance of impressing all the right people, it's essential that it's accurate and mistake-free. Ask two other people to read it through thoroughly to check that nothing has gone awry: if you can, ask a friend or family member who isn't directly involved in your business to check it, as he or she will have a bit more 'distance' than you do and will be able to give you a more objective view.

RECOMMENDED LINKS

Business Eye (Wales):
www.businesseye.org.uk
Business Link (England):
www.businesslink.gov.uk
Invest Northern Ireland:
www.investni.com
Business Gateway (Scotland):
www.bgateway.com

SEE ALSO
Financing a New Business (p. 108)

Applying for Grants and Funding

GETTING STARTED

A grant is financial assistance, usually for a specific project, given to a business by an awarding body. The grant might help you to develop a new product, buy equipment, or run a training scheme. A grant is usually a one-off payment and will provide funding that covers a percentage of the costs of the project. Unlike loans and venture capital, a grant does not have to be repaid, unless you fail to comply with the specific terms and conditions of the scheme. This actionlist gives information about what grants are available, where to apply for them, and how to make the application.

FAQS

What can I get a grant for?

Grants are available for a variety of projects, but each individual scheme will offer funding for a specific purpose. Whether or not you qualify for a grant can also depend on other factors such as the kind of business you run, the size of the business, whether the project will create jobs, and where your business is located. The sorts of areas which a grant might cover include consultancy, design, advertising, marketing, and promotion. Grants are also obtainable for business expansion and relocation, improving business premises, and security, and also for businesses going into exporting. They can be awarded for starting up a business, market testing, and capital equipment. Grants are also available for co-operatives and community enterprises, and for environmental improvements. There are grants for information technology (IT) and e-commerce, new technology and innovation, and research and development (R&D), as well as recruitment and training.

Where can I get a grant?

At local or regional levels, you may be able to get a grant from organisations such as Business Link (England), Business Gateway (Scotland), Business Eye (Wales), and Invest Northern Ireland. Grants are also provided by local authorities, enterprise agencies, the Government Office for the Region (GOR), and Regional Development Agencies (RDA). The Chambers of Commerce and the Learning and Skills Councils (LSC) also provide grants.

Nationally, grants are available from various government departments and agencies, such as The Department of Trade and Industry (DTI), The Countryside Agency, UK Trade & Investment, and The Department for Environment, Food and Rural Affairs (DEFRA). Grants are also available from organisations such as The Prince's Trust, the Crafts Council, and the English Arts Board.

At a European level, grants are usually not available directly to businesses. Instead, the European Commission provides finance to local or regional grant administering bodies via its four Structural Funds. These are the European Regional Development Fund (ERDF), the European Social Fund (ESF), the European Agricultural Guidance and Guarantee Fund (EAGGF), and the Financial Instrument for Fisheries Guidance (FIFG). These grants can usually be accessed through local and regional organisations such as those listed above.

How long does a grant application take?

The application process for some grants can take several months (see below), so if your project needs funding immediately it'd be a good idea for you to investigate alternative sources of finance, such as loans. Also bear in mind that businesses are usually required to meet some of the costs of the project (usually at least 50% of overall expenditure), so you'll have to be prepared to raise some finance as well.

It's always worth finding out whether your business could attract grant funding, but it may be risky to base any business idea *solely* on the presumption that you'll get it. Most grant funding is conditional and your business will need to meet the specific criteria of the grant programme.

MAKING IT HAPPEN
Before applying
Your first step is to contact your local Business Link, Business Gateway, Business Eye, or Invest Northern Ireland office. Most will have a directory of assistance available locally, nationally, and at a European level. Their advisers will be able to put you in touch with the relevant grant-awarding bodies, and will also be able to help you through the application process.

You will then need to contact the awarding body and check that your project meets the specified criteria of the scheme. It's important at this stage to find out whether it is actually worth applying, as grant application forms can take a lot of time and effort to complete. If you do decide to proceed, ask them to send you an application form and more detailed information about the grant.

Many schemes will require you to supply a project plan or proposal. Within this you will need to include a project description. This should detail the aim of the project, and also how the project will benefit your business. You will also need to give information about the people who will run the project, and what experience, knowledge, and skills they have. Don't forget to include the cost of the project, as well as its length and key deadlines, and make sure you explain where the project is located. You will also need to make a convincing case as to why your project needs the support of the grant. Outline what would happen if the support wasn't provided, and state clearly how much money is required. Give details of how you intend to fund your share of the project's costs. You will need to work out how the project complies with the criteria set by the grant provider. Give details about your business, when it was set up, its activities, and so on, as well as financial information about the business. This might require the submission of accounts and forecasts.

Make the application
Read any guidance notes that are supplied with the application. These will give you information on how to complete the form. Application forms will differ widely. The proposal should follow the format required, be clear and concise, and should be tailored to the grant you are applying for.

For national and European grants, you may have to submit two forms. These will be a short initial form to assess your eligibility for the grant, and then a second form providing detailed information about your business and the project you intend to undertake. It is a good idea to speak to someone involved with administering the grant. They will be able to help you with completing the form. Alternatively, seek the assistance of a Business Link adviser or accountant to help you with your application.

Your business plan will provide a lot of the detail for your grant application. You should make sure that your business plan is up to date and includes information about your experience, future plans, and financial requirements.

After the application
When you have completed the application, make sure that you check it over thoroughly and that you've supplied all the information required. After you've sent in your application, the awarding body may contact you to get more information to help with the assessment. They may also ask you to come to an interview or visit your business themselves.

If your application is successful, you'll probably receive a formal letter offering the grant. This will probably include the agreed programme of work, eligible costs, start date, and the time scale. You'll probably have to accept the conditions that apply to the offer within a given period of time. Read the letter carefully, as you will be signing up to a legally binding agreement.

It's likely that you'll have to wait some time before getting a decision on your grant application. This could range from a few weeks (for local grants) to a year (for national and European grants). Again, bear this in mind and make sure you have some alternative sources to pursue, especially if you need finance quickly.

WHAT TO AVOID
Not completing the application form properly

If your application is incomplete, it will take longer to process and is more likely to be rejected. Also, if you provide incorrect information the grant may be reclaimed: in other words, you'll have to pay it all back. You must be honest and do check with the funding body if there are any parts of the application form or process that you're not sure about.

RECOMMENDED LINKS
Business Eye (Wales):
www.businesseye.org.uk
Business Link (England):
www.businesslink.gov.uk
Invest Northern Ireland:
www.investni.com
Business Gateway (Scotland):
www.bgateway.com

SEE ALSO
Budgeting (p. 499)
Financing a New Business (p. 108)
Preparing a Successful Business Plan (p. 114)

Controlling a Budget

GETTING STARTED

Controlling budgets is a headache for businesses of all sizes. Many smaller businesses start off on the right foot by putting in place a good book-keeping system, but then fail to exercise proper financial control and end up in trouble. The only way to make sure that you make a profit is to control the budget efficiently. To do this, you need to estimate your sales income reasonably accurately, estimate your costs precisely, and keep both under control. You also need to charge the right price for your end product in your chosen market(s). It is important to collect all financial documents in a methodical way, and to keep all your figures up to date on a daily basis. This actionlist will look at some of the most common problems in controlling a budget, and suggest ways to tackle them.

A book which you might find useful on this subject is *Cash Flows and Budgeting Made Easy*, written by Peter Taylor and published in 2002 by How To Books.

FAQS

What is budgeting?

Each year you should prepare a business plan for the business, including your best forecast of sales. A budget is simply that forecast turned into figures. In other words, it is an estimate of sales income together with the costs required to produce those sales.

What is financial control?

Financial control is different from book-keeping. Book-keeping is about recording the figures—in other words income and expenditure, receipts and payments, and assets and liabilities. Accurate book-keeping, of course, is a prerequisite for effective financial control, and computerised accounting packages make accurate book-keeping far easier.

You then, however, need to use the figures as a basis for effective financial control. It can be difficult to keep the complete picture in your head all the time, so calculating a few simple ratios or using a graph are both good techniques to help you keep up to date.

MAKING IT HAPPEN

Set targets

Each year, set objectives and prepare a business plan. Define your objectives in financial terms, as well as in terms of marketing, quality, and people. If a venture capitalist or business angel has invested in your business, his or her primary concern will often be the rate of return on investment (often referred to in financial documents as 'ROI'). If you've invested your own money into the business, you may be expecting smaller returns initially, planning for your business to provide higher returns over a longer period.

Keep the books

A reliable, easy-to-use accounting system is essential for straightforward effective financial control. Make sure that you keep proper records. The information to record includes: any sales orders received; invoices issued by the business for sales; purchase orders placed by the business; invoices received by the business for purchases; cash receipts, and cash expenditure. Turning this information into graphs, tables, and charts can help to reveal trends, which in turn will help you to revise your forecasts and future planning. A range of accessible computer software, such as Microsoft Excel, will help you to do this.

Carry out a monthly check

Bring the cash book up to date and carry out a bank reconciliation every month. The cash book balance represents the business's liquidity; it is the cash immediately available to the business.

Prepare an operating statement by combining the revenue, direct costs, and overhead costs. This records income and expenditure (as does the profit and loss account), not receipts and payments. It ignores some items such as depreciation or bad debts. Each month, you should compare your actual performance with your forecast both for the month and, ideally, for the year to date. You can then look at some simple ratios and the variances.

Analyse the available information

Carry out a ratio analysis. Do this by defining your costs as a percentage of the sales income. This gives you a very quick method of determining whether or not you are on target. If your costs are rising as a percentage of your sales income, then you know that you have a problem to address. Consider your gross profit margin. If the margin is falling, it could be a sign of trouble. Ask yourself the following questions. Has wastage increased? Have costs increased? Monitoring changes closely will help you to react to any problems, preventing them from escalating any further.

Then carry out a variance analysis. A variance is the difference between your target and your actual performance. Variance analysis looks at the differences themselves, rather than comparing different figures, as happens in ratio analysis. Review figures for: sales, inquiry and order position; material and labour usage; overheads; cash position/cash forecast; stock; and capital expenditure. As you work through the analysis, remember that analysing variances means thinking about more than just differences in cash; there may be major variances even though the overall cash position remains more or less as forecast. Make sure you understand why the figures are changing. There are various possible reasons; for example, it is possible for a reduction in raw material cost to be cancelled by increased wastage?

Manage cash

The operating statement shows the net trading profit but does not show the liquidity (that is, the cash position of your business, and the ability to meet payments). It is important, therefore, that you also prepare a monthly cash-flow statement. This reflects when money is received or paid out and includes items such as drawings, VAT, or tax, which are not regarded as trading expenses. All the figures should be readily available from the cash book.

Remember the importance of actively controlling the budget. Generating the figures is only the first part of the process; you must then take some action. Keep a tight grip on anyone who owes the business money (your debtors). If the level of debtors rises, this could be because your sales are increasing or because your debtors are taking longer to pay. Make sure you define in your terms of trade how quickly you expect debtors to pay, and then ensure that they stick to these guidelines. Put processes in place to deal with late payments or debtors who continually delay their payments.

Similarly, try not to get on the wrong side of your suppliers by taking too long to pay *them*, as they may withdraw your credit facilities. To gain the most benefit, you need to take the maximum amount of credit possible without abusing your agreed terms. Take care to ensure your PAYE and VAT payments are made on time, otherwise you could incur substantial penalties.

Controlling your debtors and creditors carefully will ensure that you're controlling your working capital carefully. If you're building up large sums of cash, do something worthwhile with them, even if only to move it to an account that pays you a better rate of interest. If you expect to need additional working capital, for example because debtors are rising as your sales increase, then talking to the bank—or your investors—early will reassure them that you really are in control of your business, and they will be more likely to help.

Watch your stock levels carefully. Consider how much stock you have tied up in raw materials, work in progress, and finished goods. If you have too much stock, you may be using excessive storage space and tying up money that could be used in other ways.

WHAT TO AVOID
Setting too many targets
Choose a small number of appropriate targets and focus on a handful of key issues, such as revenue growth, profit, and cash flow. Compiling and analysing huge amounts of information can be time-consuming and not always of great use if the major points are buried underneath too much detail.

Letting your books get out of date
You need up-to-date financial records before you can control your budget properly, so record transactions accurately and promptly.

Losing track of cash
The key to making a profit is through the careful control of cash, so that you can pay your debts as they fall due.

RECOMMENDED LINKS
Institute of Credit Management:
www.icm.org.uk
bizhelp24:
www.bizhelp24.com

SEE ALSO
Budgeting (p. 499)

Controlling Costs

GETTING STARTED

The basis of any successful business is that income should exceed expenses. One way to improve profitability is to increase the sales of your business, but you can also enhance profitability by cutting down on your costs. A business that can do this will be able to release more resources for growth in the good times, and will be in a better position to survive in a recession. This actionlist gives some suggestions on ways to control (and in some cases reduce) the costs of your business.

FAQS

Which costs do I need to control?

To be able to *control* costs, you first have to know exactly what they are. Start by identifying each cost clearly, and make sure that you keep records of all bills, receipts, and so on. Review your costs regularly, basing the timing on when your accounts are normally completed. It is not enough to calculate whether the business is in profit or loss, important though that is; you also need to be aware of what normal costs are, so that you can spot anomalies and take action to address them. Some costs will be more important to control than others, so you need to work out what the *business's* critical costs are, and concentrate on reducing them.

Who is responsible for controlling costs?

Cost control is the responsibility of everyone working in the business. If you have a team of people working for you, all your employees have countless opportunities to affect costs throughout each day. You need to be aware that if employees are unhappy at work, they are in a position to do a lot of damage, if only through what they *don't* do. For example, if they're bored, frustrated, or feel undervalued, they're less likely to feel that the business's welfare is their focus. If they're motivated and feel part of the business, on the other hand, they'll work economically without supervision. Rising to the challenge of providing this kind of environment for your employees is a test of good management; one approach is to involve employees by asking them to come up with ideas to reduce costs. As your staff

are on the 'front line' they're bound to have some practical suggestions that may really have a significant impact. If you do decide to ask your staff for their input, though, be careful with the way you phrase your request. Unless the company is in dire straits and you are genuinely thinking of making redundancies, don't give them the impression that their jobs are on the line as part of this cost-cutting measure!

Many people assume that because the volume of expenditure is so much larger than they are used to in home life, any savings they might make are insignificant. Every little does help, though, so let your team know that cutting back on what look like insignificant costs will help the business overall.

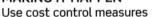

MAKING IT HAPPEN
Use cost control measures

One effective cost control measure is to carry out a cost—benefit analysis. Try to build in cost awareness as part of your general planning processes across all areas of the business. Whether you're planning ways to develop yourself, your staff, or the company's direction in general, think of how the overall impact of any decision should be understood in terms of business profitability. In other words, the benefits of a particular course of action should be set against the cost. For example, a person may be assigned to carry out a piece of research that could, in fact, be done quicker by a consultant, or bought off the shelf. It can be hard to keep a professional distance when you have to make hard decisions about a project or issue that you have invested a lot in personally, but this is exactly what you have to do if money is tight: you must be pragmatic.

Another method of cost control is value analysis (VA), which involves a detailed examination of each part of a product, service, or system to work out if there is any way in which its costs could be reduced without affecting quality. Value analysis is usually done as a group exercise and it is therefore a good way to involve employees and increase general awareness of cost control. Each aspect of the product should be brought under the spotlight. The group has to decide, for example, whether the product is really necessary; whether it can be made with cheaper materials; whether it is actually cheaper to buy than to make; whether it can be made more quickly; or whether it can be simplified to reduce potential faults. Other aspects to look at might be reducing the material that is used to make it, or reducing wastage. Economising on the use of raw materials can be a very effective cost-saving measure.

Also look at your company's purchasing methods and, as a first step, see if you could get a discount by buying in bulk from your suppliers if you don't do this already. Be prepared to haggle and regularly review the cost of supplies and suppliers. In fact, no bill or invoice that your business receives should be taken for granted. For example, if you rent your business premises and you feel the rent is too high, don't just accept the status quo, but talk to your landlord about the possibility of reducing it. Alternatively, if you feel that rates are too high, you can appeal to have the rateable value reduced; contact your local HM Revenue & Customs (HMRC) valuation office for the relevant forms. Stock control is another potential area for savings, as accurate control will reduce storage and working capital costs. Providing effective security should reduce the cost of stock lost through theft. For example, if your business manufactures products that have a high market price (or if you're a wholesaler), do check that you're protecting your stock well. For example, electronic equipment, pharmaceuticals,

alcohol, and cigarettes are the type of thing that people might try to steal. Your insurance should cover theft, of course, but it's much better to keep your stock secure so that you don't lose money as a result of someone else's actions.

Look at potential areas for cost savings

Staff costs often offer the greatest potential scope for savings, although it would be wise not to launch wholescale into redundancies until you've thought through your actions to their logical conclusion. You may be able to manage with fewer people on your team, but then again there's a risk you could pare back your staff numbers so much that the business just can't function. It's perfectly valid to investigate whether your staff are delivering value for money, though. Are they being motivated and managed well? Also check that their pay is appropriate for the work they do. You are trying to cut costs, of course, and too much is clearly expensive, but if salaries are too low, you'll end up with a high staff turnover rate that may ultimately damage performance.

One environmentally-friendly way of making your business run more leanly is to cut down on energy costs. Encourage your employees to use energy as responsibly at work as they do at home (where *they* are paying the bills). Many people today are concerned about the environment, and this can motivate them to save energy. It's easy to forget that some of the biggest savings available to businesses lie within some of their most basic costs, such as gas and electricity. Have your meters double-checked, especially if the business uses a lot of energy, and set thermostats correctly. Something as basic as insulation can really help you shrink your bills and produce long-term savings, and you may even be eligible for a grant to help pay for it. The BusinessLink website has a very helpful section on energy efficiency at work under the 'Health, safety and environment' option—see below for the address.

Telephone calls are another basic company cost offering potential savings. Some private phone calls made from the office are necessary, but don't allow staff to take advantage. Make sure that you outline a policy for the use of phones for personal calls and agree and circulate it. Staff should also be made aware of any possible disciplinary action that could be taken against them for breach of the policy. It is possible to get itemised bills for each extension, which should discourage misuse of phones. Staff should also be trained in the efficient use of the telephone, to reduce the length of calls.

Photocopiers are easy to use and the expense can soon get out of control if usage is not monitored. Make sure that all copies are logged, allocated to a cost centre, and that the initials of the person taking the copy are recorded. Staff should be charged for personal copies, and discouraged from making unnecessary copies. Someone should be made responsible for monitoring copying, and usage should be reviewed regularly. Make sure that all staff know exactly how to use all the facilities on the copier. This in itself can reduce costs; for example, printing double-sided copies can save time and money.

Some staff may be tempted to take office stationery home for their own use, so it might be worth keeping the stationery cupboard locked and making someone responsible for issuing materials. Recycling can again play a useful role here: scrap paper can be recycled as stapled writing pads, for example, and used laser printer cartridges can be sent off to be refilled at a discount price. In fact, all waste should be considered for potential recycling or resale to recycling companies. For example, there are companies who will buy industrial plastic waste for recycling.

Finally, make sure you have a clear expenses policy. It is possible to reduce misuse of expenses by drawing up guidelines so that everyone understands what is, and is not, acceptable. Expense claims should be cleared by a manager before being paid. Make sure that expenses for individuals are reviewed periodically, and anomalies investigated.

WHAT TO AVOID

Making false economies
Don't cut back on the wrong things. If you reduce the level of service your customers are used to, you'll probably end up losing the business money. Similarly, if you make working conditions too harsh (for example, by cutting back on pay, benefits, and training) your staff will become demoralised and won't perform as well as they could—indeed, you run the risk of them leaving.

Ignoring rising costs
Confront cost problems immediately rather than put them off and hope they'll go away. They won't go anywhere. It's much better to act sooner and to stop the problem from escalating.

RECOMMENDED LINKS
Business Link:
www.businesslink.gov.uk
BRE Research and Consultancy:
www.bre.co.uk
Energy Saving Trust:
www.est.org.uk

SEE ALSO
Budgeting (p. 499)
Drawing Up a Budget (p. 126)
Financing a New Business (p. 108)

Drawing Up a Budget

GETTING STARTED

Every business needs to plan its spending on the basis of what it expects from sales income; without this tool, you can't be sure that your business will survive. Budgeting is simply the name given to the process of working out what you expect your business to earn and spend in a given period. It also gives you the ability to check how the business is doing from week to week, or month to month; without this check, you can easily overspend. This actionlist explains how you can make use of your budget, and how to draw one up.

FAQS

What can I use a budget for?

It's important that you use your budget as a control mechanism. At the end of each month, you should enter the actual figures for sales and expenses next to the figures that were forecast. If there are substantial differences between the budgeted figures and the actual figures, then you need to do something about it. For instance, if your sales are too low, you may need to reconsider your marketing strategies. If sales, on the other hand, are higher than planned, then you may need to reconsider your staffing levels or raw material supplies, in order to cope with the rising demand. Also, if your expenditure is too high, you'll need to find ways to bring costs down.

How do I estimate sales and expenditure?

The starting point for drawing up a budget is for you to estimate future sales and expenditure. The sales budget can be split into the number of different products your business plans to sell; the number of units of each product that you plan to sell; the price that you plan to sell each unit for; and the place or area where you plan to sell them.

You'll need to split your expenditure budget into production costs or variable costs (such as materials, power, and subcontractors); overhead costs or fixed costs (such as rent and salaries); and capital costs (equipment).

 MAKING IT HAPPEN

Budgeting for sales

If your business is a new one, forecasting sales will be particularly tricky for you, because you don't have actual sales from the past on which you can base your expectations. Instead, you'll have to make sure that your budget is based on good research. It must also be closely tied to a realistic marketing plan that will generate the sales you expect. It's important not to just guess your sales figures. Also, don't start by looking at your planned expenditure and then just deriving a sales forecast to cover the cost.

Make the sales budget as detailed as you can. You need to make it very clear what you plan to sell, and at what price. Set out your expected sales on a monthly or quarterly basis. If your business sells a range of products, make sure that you prepare sales budgets for each of them. If your products are sold in more than one area, then you may find it helpful to have a sales budget for each area.

Budgeting for expenditure

Now that you have prepared the sales budget, you have the basic foundations for working out what your expenditure will be. For your purposes, the expenditure budget can be split into a production budget and an overheads budget. If you know how many products you'll sell, you can work out the direct costs of producing them. These direct costs will then make up the production budget, and will vary with the level of production. The overhead costs will stay more or less constant.

The production budget

The production budget is made up of items like the materials and components that go into the product.

If you have a sales team, you also need to include commission paid to them. (If sales people earn a regular retainer as well, this retainer would normally be regarded as a fixed cost.) Make sure that you include the cost of subcontractors, where people are being paid as independent contractors to perform a certain, defined job.

Discounts are usually shown in the budget as a direct cost.

There are some expenses, such as depreciation, that are usually treated as fixed overheads. However, if you want to be particularly accurate with your production budget, you could include these, especially if you can clearly associate them with specific products.

The overheads budget

Once you have prepared the production budget, you'll need to consider the other costs that the business will incur. These will include the salaries for you and your staff, National Insurance contributions, and pension contributions. You'll also need to include rent and company insurance, and telephone, Internet, and e-mail account costs. Any interest on money that you have borrowed will also need to be included in your overheads.

If your business is in manufacturing, it's likely that the above will represent a relatively small proportion of the total costs. On the other hand, if you have a service sector business, it's likely that overheads will represent a very high proportion of the cost. Include all overhead costs, including interest payments and drawings (how much money you plan to take out of the business). Remember that you are taxed on the total profit (if you are self-employed), so allow for this too. If your business is registered as a company, and you expect to take high dividends, make sure that you budget for this as well.

Your business may aim to allocate the overheads to each product, or may prefer to retain overheads as a single budget. Whichever path you choose, it's important that you ensure that the price for each product makes a reasonable contribution to the overheads.

Budgeting for the full cost of production

You're now in a position to pull together the production budget and the overheads budget into a single production cost budget. If there is more than one product or service, then there will be a production budget for each. There will also be variable overheads for you to add for each product. There is no need for you to split fixed overheads across products at this point, since the object of this exercise is for you to be able to determine the total costs.

Capital expenditure budget

If you expect to buy capital equipment, you'll need to decide how you'll pay for it (whether in cash or through a loan), and make sure that you budget for these payments in the relevant months. This is essential information if an accurate forecast is to be prepared, particularly where the business may have to take out a loan to finance the purchase and will have to meet a repayment schedule that includes interest.

If the business decides to lease equipment, it's important to make sure that you read all the small print. While the selling is carried out by a supplier, the leasing is done by a finance company. Usually the conditions are more favourable for them than for your business. On the other hand, the organisation leasing the equipment to you usually has a responsibility to ensure the equipment keeps working, even if the supplier can no longer support it.

Cash flow

If you operate your business on a cash basis, in other words taking in cash for your sales and paying cash for your purchases, then it's fairly easy to see if you are living within your means because you'll have cash left over at the end of the month if you're making a profit. Very few businesses, however, operate like this. It's far more likely that you'll be selling goods or services in one month, and not receiving payment until the following month, or the month after that.

Similarly, you may be buying raw materials one month, but not paying for them for at least another four weeks. A budget will help you keep track of your cash flow in and out of the business, and keep control.

Once the budgets have been prepared, you can use the data that has been accumulated in order to prepare financial forecasts. This will include a cash flow forecast, but you should also include a forecast of the profit and loss statement, and the balance sheet. The cash flow forecast should set out, on a month-by-month basis, all cash inflows and outflows from the business for the following 12 months, to help you to determine your working capital needs. The profit and loss forecast will help you to check that your business remains profitable.

WHAT TO AVOID
Not setting realistic targets
If you set realistic targets, you'll be able to tell whether sales and expenditure have gone to plan, and you'll also be able to foresee problems and opportunities in time to take action.

Not bothering to prepare a cash-flow forecast
It's important to remember that a cash-flow forecast is as important as the budget itself. While the budget can tell you if your business is generally profitable, it might not alert you to cash-flow problems.

RECOMMENDED LINKS
Institute of Credit Management:
www.icm.org.uk
bizhelp24:
www.bizhelp24.com

SEE ALSO
Budgeting (p. 499)
Controlling Costs (p. 123)
Financing a New Business (p. 108)

Getting to Grips with Income Tax

GETTING STARTED

Income tax is payable on an individual's income in any particular tax year if it exceeds an annual threshold. The government writes and re-writes tax law and the courts have the job of interpreting exactly what it means, in any particular circumstance. HM Revenue & Customs (HMRC) inspectors are responsible for the collection of tax and National Insurance in the United Kingdom.

Income tax can be collected from a whole range of sources. These include: employment salary and benefits; the net profit from a sole business; the partnership profit share in the case of partnerships; dividends paid on shareholdings; investments; pensions; foreign income; income from property; and trust income.

It is particularly important, if you are self-employed or run a small business, that you maintain a good grip on your tax liability and plan ahead so that you can meet your tax bills. This actionlist aims to act as a guide and a reminder to help you run your tax affairs smoothly.

FAQS

What is income?

Tax is charged on income arising from an enterprise. It can be described as the fruits of an endeavour, rather than just the receipt of money. This means that in most circumstances, gifts or transfers of capital are not counted towards your income in a tax year—although they might have to be taken into account for capital gains tax purposes instead. Any occupation or profession that produces an annual sum in terms of money can be a source of 'income'. Even a one-off job producing income is included.

Who has to pay income tax?

As has often been said, nothing is certain in life except death and taxes. So if you are resident in the United Kingdom, or working for a UK employer, the income tax rules apply. The Pay As You Earn (PAYE) system means that most employees have the correct tax deducted at source by their employers. If you are self-employed, you need to fill in a self-assessment form each year and, depending on when you submit this to HMRC, either calculate the tax you need to pay yourself, or have it calculated for you by them.

How much is it?

Tax is only payable if your total income for a tax year exceeds certain limits. In the United Kingdom, for the tax year 2005–06, personal allowances for individuals start at £4,895 per annum as a tax-free allowance. Tax on any income above that level is then paid at the following rates:

- a starting rate of 10% on the first £2,090 of income above the personal allowance
- the standard rate of 22% on the next £32,400
- the higher rate of 40% on the remainder of your income (there is no upper limit)

Personal allowances apply to everyone aged 0 to 64 years, and the basic allowance is due whatever your total income. This basic allowance can be augmented with an additional amount for those over 65, and again at 75, if the individual has a moderate income.

MAKING IT HAPPEN
Recognise that tax is a cost of running a successful business

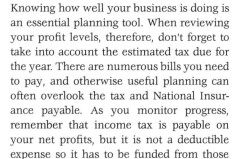

Knowing how well your business is doing is an essential planning tool. When reviewing your profit levels, therefore, don't forget to take into account the estimated tax due for the year. There are numerous bills you need to pay, and otherwise useful planning can often overlook the tax and National Insurance payable. As you monitor progress, remember that income tax is payable on your net profits, but it is not a deductible expense so it has to be funded from those profits.

Plan for your tax bills

It is important to know when your tax is payable and how much it is likely to be—and then to set aside sufficient funds to pay it. The date of payment for the self-employed, whether sole traders or in partnership, is dependent on your accounting year end. Businesses can make up annual accounts to any date to suit their particular trade, and that date falls within a particular tax year. The tax on those profits and a payment on account of the next year is payable on the 31 January and 31 July following the 5 April of that tax year.

Take advantage of all the allowances available

Under self-assessment, it is up to you to make sure that you claim any and all allowances that you are eligible for. HMRC adopts a file-now/check-later process which means that it is unable to consider whether you have filled the form in to your best advantage. Take time to ensure everything you can claim is included in your accounts and tax return. It is a good idea to get proper advice from an accountant, as there are usually ways of organising things to ensure that you make optimum use of your allowances.

Check as you go

Deductions when calculating profits have to be made in accordance with recognised accountancy principles. Items like wages come off your gross income, but capital expenses are not deductible in the same way; there is a delay in receiving tax relief for most of these items. This may mean you have to plan carefully to fund your tax bills if capital investment has been high in particular years.

Get good advice

Tax law is continuously being modified. If in doubt, seek help—and always check with a professional adviser before relying on being able to deduct expenses or claim allowances.

WHAT TO AVOID
Spending your tax fund

When starting in business there is a delay before you have to pay your first tax bill. It can come as a nasty surprise if, when payment time does eventually come, you find that you did in fact make a healthy profit but have spent all the money. Even if every penny went back into the business, the Revenue will have little sympathy with if you get behind with tax payments. Interest, penalties, and court action will swiftly follow if you are unable to pay.

Comparing one year with another

The annual nature of tax means that every tax year will involve a different set of figures. Annual changes to allowances and rates are proposed by the chancellor in the Pre-Budget Report each November, and finalised by the Queen's speech. In some years, an incoming government makes amendments. From your own point of view profits may fluctuate; after a bad year it may take a while to increase your profits, but when you do, the tax will have to be paid.

Not preparing accounts soon enough

Individuals are now responsible for providing the Revenue with enough information to be able to calculate the tax bill themselves. Since the self-assessment system came into effect, tax has to be paid in January and July following the 5 April. This can mean that if your accounting date is 5 April you have less than ten months to work out and fund the tax bill. If the return is filed later than 30 September after the tax year ends, you also have to work out the tax due yourself rather than having it done by the tax office.

RECOMMENDED LINK
HM Revenue & Customs:
www.hmrc.gov.uk

SEE ALSO
Budgeting (p. 499)
Taxation (p. 551)

Getting to Grips with National Insurance

GETTING STARTED
National Insurance (NI) is a contribution towards state benefits such as pensions and unemployment and incapacity benefits. Contributions are paid by everyone who works, whether as an employee or on a self-employed basis, and by all employers. Businesses that employ staff are required to collect and pay the employers' and employees' contributions each month. The self-employed have a separate arrangement. This actionlist explains how National Insurance works.

FAQS
How are contributions assessed?
Contributions are assessed according to the National Insurance (NI) class into which a person fits. Some people may fall into more than one class. **Class 1** is for individuals in employment. There is no liability for employee or employer National Insurance Contributions (NICs) on wages at, or below, the current earnings threshold (£82 per week for 2005/06). Both employee and employer have to pay contributions on all earnings above the threshold. There is an Upper Earnings Limit for employees' contributions, but not for employers' contributions.

Employers providing benefits in kind such as company cars for employees have a further National Insurance liability under **Class 1A**. Contributions are payable on the amount charged to income tax as a taxable benefit. Childcare benefits provided by an employer are exempt from these contributions.

Everyone who is self-employed pays **Class 2** contributions. There is a Small Earnings Exception, below which National Insurance Contributions are not payable. **Class 3** contributions are voluntary. This allows people to protect their right to contributory benefits, even if they're not liable to National Insurance Contributions under Class 1 or 2.

The self-employed are liable to pay **Class 4** contributions as well as Class 2. Class 4 is set as a percentage rate of profit between lower and upper thresholds (between £4,895 and £32,760 in 2005/06).

Is anyone exempt from paying National Insurance Contributions?
Some employees will not be liable for any National Insurance Contributions. These include those who are under 16 years old, and also those who have reached pensionable age (currently 60 years old for women, and 65 for men). If an employee has more than one job and will pay the maximum amount from one of the jobs, he or she doesn't need to pay contributions on his or her employment with the second employer. However, the employer must still pay employer's contributions for them. The self-employed who reach pensionable age are exempt from Class 2 and Class 4 contributions.

What forms do I need?
When you first tell HM Revenue & Customs that you are employing people, they will send you their employers' pack, which includes a number of forms to be used if you intend to maintain a manual payroll system.

The **Deductions Working Sheet P11** is for keeping weekly or monthly records. Each of your employees will have a P11, on which are recorded their personal details, National Insurance number, and details of National Insurance and tax contributions each time they are paid.

The **End of Year Summary P14/P60** form must be returned at the end of the year to the Inspector of Taxes. There should be one for each employee, containing the employee's details, and total National Insurance Contributions and tax paid. The P60 must be given to employees by 31 May each year.

The **Payslip Booklet P30BC** contains bank credit slips that are completed monthly. Every month, or every quarter if the business is a PAYE small employer, your business must fill in and send a P30BC payslip to the HM Revenue & Customs Accounts Office, together with any payment of National Insurance Contributions and tax deducted in the previous month or quarter.

The **Employer's Payment Record P32** is used to record tax details, and National Insurance payment details, as well as Statutory Sick Pay (SSP) and Statutory Maternity Pay (SMP) recovered in the year. There are also columns covering tax credits and student loan deductions.

The **Employer's Annual Return P35** must be returned at the end of the tax year to the Inspector of Taxes. You must submit this form by 19 May.

MAKING IT HAPPEN
Assessing how much National Insurance is payable

National Insurance contributions are assessed on gross pay. There are many payments that might be made to employees. Some are included in National Insurance liability, while others are exempt. These payments include income tax deduction, arrears of pay (such as a back-dated pay rise), and commission. They also include Christmas, productivity, and completion bonuses, as well as holiday pay (subject to certain exemptions), Statutory Sick Pay, and Statutory Maternity Pay. Payments made to company directors in anticipation of future earnings are also included. You will find that although this list is not exhaustive, it does include most elements of gross pay for National Insurance liability purposes.

Not included in gross pay are board and lodging provided free, uniforms purchased for staff, personal, unexpected gifts made to an employee, redundancy, termination or pay in lieu of notice payments (though this may be chargeable if it is in the contract or if it is the norm to pay it) and compensation awarded by an employment tribunal.

Collection of National Insurance contributions (NICs)

National Insurance Contributions on wages are deducted at source under the PAYE scheme. If you use a manual payroll system, HM Revenue & Customs will provide you with tables to calculate the amounts due, and forms on which to record your calculations. If you run a computerised payroll system, the software will do all the calculations for you, and will also provide the summaries that you need to complete the HM Revenue & Customs return.

Class 1A contributions are generally calculated at the end of the tax year and then paid direct to HM Revenue & Customs. The self-employed can pay Class 2 contributions by monthly direct debit. Class 4 contributions are collected with income tax each year in January and July. Voluntary contributions can be paid by quarterly bill or direct debit.

Claiming back National Insurance contributions

In certain circumstances, some or even all National Insurance contributions can be claimed back. There are also provisions for over-payment or under-payment on the business's part, or by deductions made from employees' pay.

Statutory Maternity Pay (SMP)

Your business may be entitled to Small Employers' Relief if Class 1 contributions of £45,000 or less have been paid in the qualifying tax year. (The qualifying tax year is the last complete tax year before the employee's qualifying week. The qualifying week is the 15th week before expected childbirth.) All the employer's NICs paid on SMP can be recovered, plus 4.5% compensation. If the business is not entitled to relief, it can recover 92% of the NI paid on SMP. This is reclaimed by deduction from the monthly NI and tax payments. The amount due to be recovered should be recorded on the employee's form P11.

Statutory Sick Pay (SSP)

The business may qualify for the Percentage Threshold Scheme, designed to reimburse employers who have a high percentage of workers off sick at any one time. It is not restricted to small businesses. You can perform the following calculation to assess whether the business qualifies. Add together the employer and employee NI Class 1 contributions for the tax month, then multiply by 13%. If the total SSP payments for the month come to more than this calculation, the business can recover the difference through its NICs.

WHAT TO AVOID
Deducting too much from employees' pay

If you accidentally deduct too much from employees' pay, you can refund them and amend your pay records if the error is from the current tax year.

Underpaying Class 1 Contributions

If you underpay an employee's Class 1 contributions you have no right to recover the underpayment from the employee after the tax year the mistake was made in. You as an employer have to pay the underpayment to HM Revenue & Customs. If you discover the mistake within the relevant tax year you can make further deductions from the employee's pay during that year to recover the underpayment.

RECOMMENDED LINKS

HM Revenue & Customs Business Support Team for your area:
www.hmrc.gov.uk/bst/index.htm

SEE ALSO
Budgeting (p. 499)
Taxation (p. 551)

Getting to Grips with Corporation Tax

GETTING STARTED
If your business is set up as a company, then the company will have to pay corporation tax on its profits. If you are a partner in either a traditional partnership or limited liability partnership, or a sole trader, you will not pay corporation tax, but you will pay income tax instead. This actionlist aims to give you some advice on the most common problems. For extra advice, HM Revenue & Customs offer a Helpline for the Newly Self-Employed on 0845 915 4515.

FAQS
Which profits get taxed?
Trading profits are liable to tax. These profits are the money from your business trading activities, minus expenses. That means, if you make products to sell, you will pay tax on the profits of selling your products, once you have deducted the cost of making the product. The same applies if you sell a service; once you have calculated how much it costs to provide the service, and deducted the cost from the price of selling the service, the amount of profit left will be subject to corporation tax.

Capital gains are also taxed. This is the money earned by selling company assets. If you sell, for example, property belonging to the company, the difference between the original price paid and the price it is sold for (that is to say, the profit from the sale) is subject to corporation tax. The only way to avoid this is by reinvesting the profit back into the company, for example, by buying another property.

What are the different rates of corporation tax?
The main rate of corporation tax is 30% for the financial year ending 31 March 2006. However, there are lower rates for companies with taxable profits of less than £1.5 million. You should note that all your profit is taxed at the same rate once you reach a specified threshold, though there is some marginal relief for profit levels below £1.5 million.

There is also the small companies' rate. For the purposes of corporation tax, 'small' is defined by the company's profits. For companies with profits below £300,000, the small companies' rate of 19% applies. For companies with profits below £10,000 the rate is zero. In addition, there is marginal relief between £10,000 and £50,000, and between £300,000 and £1.5 million. This means that you are not hit with the full charge if you exceed the threshold.

The rates are summarised in the table below:

Profit	Percentage tax rate
Up to £10,000	0.00
£10,001 – £50,000 (effective rate)	23.75
£50,001 – £300,000 (small companies' rate)	19.00
£300,001 – £1.5m (effective rate)	32.75
Greater than £1.5m	30.00

What relief and allowances apply to corporation tax?
Relief and allowances must be claimed on the company's tax return, or an amended return. Depreciation cannot be deducted. Instead, allowances are given for acquisitions of industrial buildings, fixtures, plant, equipment, and motor vehicles. Expenditure for the purposes of the trade can be set off against profit—for example, wages, salaries, energy, rent, rates, stationery, telephone, cleaning, and advertising expenditure.

You can claim relief on charges on income, such as patent royalties or covenants to charities. You can also claim relief for trading losses. These can be set against income or gains of the current or previous accounting period. If the loss is not claimed for some other relief, it will automatically be carried over and set against future profits. If the company ceases to trade, the previous 12 months' losses can be set against trading profits of the previous three years.

MAKING IT HAPPEN
Understand the collection of corporation tax

Companies are expected to work out their own tax liability and to pay their tax without prior assessment by HM Revenue & Customs (HMRC). You are liable to penalties if you do not make a tax return by the statutory filing date.

File a corporation tax return

The company's completed corporation tax return will be due 12 months from the company's accounting date or three months from the HMRC notice, whichever is later. It must be on an official form or an accepted substitute. Incorrect or fraudulent returns incur interest and penalties.

Three months after the end of the accounting period, HMRC will send the company a notice to send in a return form, plus the form itself. If your company is liable for corporation tax but does not receive this notice, contact HM Revenue & Customs before the due date to avoid penalties.

HMRC may carry out an inquiry into the tax return; they will let you know when this is to take place. At the end of the inquiry, HMRC will tell you of any necessary adjustments and the company will have 30 days to amend the self assessment.

Understand the payment of corporation tax

Corporation tax must be paid within nine months and one day from the end of the accounting period (the due date). Large firms (those with taxable profits of £1,500,000 or more) must pay their tax quarterly. HMRC will send a payslip and pre-paid envelope three months after the end of the accounting period, and then a further two reminders just before and just after the due date. The company's payment should go to the HMRC Accounts Office. Interest (linked to commercial rates) is payable on under/over payments from the due date.

WHAT TO AVOID
Underpaying corporation tax

If your company has underpaid corporation tax, the additional tax should be paid as soon as it is discovered. If the company has paid too much, it will not be reimbursed until after the company corporation tax return has been filed.

Not filing on time

The Inspector should be informed as soon as figures are finalised, to avoid incurring penalties. If circumstances out of the company's control prevent filing on time, make sure you tell the Inspector in advance; HMRC may extend the deadline. Late returns incur fixed penalties that increase substantially if this happens repeatedly.

If your figures are not finalised by the time corporation tax is due, and an exact assessment cannot be made, then corporation tax should be estimated and that amount paid by the due date. If it is not paid, HM Revenue & Customs will collect any outstanding tax (together with any interest which has accrued), once it has received the company's corporation tax return.

RECOMMENDED LINKS
HM Revenue & Customs Business Support Team for your area:
www.hmrc.gov.uk/bst/index.htm
HM Revenue & Customs' Corporation Tax Self Assessment Orderline:
www.hmrc.gov.uk/ctsa

SEE ALSO
Budgeting (p. 499)
Taxation (p. 551)

Getting to Grips with VAT (Value Added Tax)

GETTING STARTED

If your business's turnover is more than £60,000 a year, you will have to register with HM Revenue & Customs (HMRC) as a Value Added Tax (VAT) vendor and charge VAT on all goods and services that you provide. The disadvantage to this is that it involves some administrative effort on your part, but a balancing advantage is that it lets you claim back the VAT that you pay to suppliers.

At the end of each VAT accounting period (usually each month or quarter), you complete a one-page form for HMRC known as a VAT return. This must be returned, and the money paid, within a month of the end of the VAT accounting period. This actionlist explains who is liable for VAT, and how to register. The telephone number of the VAT National Advice Service is 0845 010 9000, and the HMRC website address is given below.

FAQS

What are the different rates of VAT?

There are currently three rates of VAT. The standard rate of 17.5% covers all those goods and services that are not exempt, zero, or reduced rated. The reduced rate (5%) is charged on domestic fuel and power, as well as other domestic energy-saving products. The renovation and conversion of certain buildings is also subject to the reduced rate. The zero rate (0%) applies to specified categories of goods including children's clothes, exports (outside the European Union), food (excluding fast food, restaurant meals, and catering supplies), books, and newspapers. Exempt goods include insurance, finance, some education and training, lotteries, and transactions involving land or existing buildings.

If your product consists of both zero-rated and standard-rated goods (for example, food in a decorative container), there may be occasions when VAT will be charged at a proportional rate. Customs and Excise have special retail schemes to assist retailers selling a mix of standard and zero-rated products.

Do I need to register for VAT?

You need to register for VAT as soon as your annual turnover exceeds £60,000 a year. (This is the rate for the financial year 2005–06. The rate normally changes each year, so do check after every Budget. The Business Link website has a helpful summary of up-to-date tax thresholds.) You can work this out simply by totalling the past 12 months' sales (taxable supplies). You can also register for VAT if it looks likely that you will exceed the limit of £60,000 in the next month's trading. If your business acquires goods with an annual value in excess of £60,000 from other European Union countries, or supplies goods with an annual value of £70,000 under the United Kingdom's distance selling arrangements, then it must register for VAT.

Registration is straightforward. All you need to do is complete and submit form VAT1 to Revenue & Customs within 30 days from the end of the month when taxable supplies reached £60,000, or within 30 days from the date when it became clear that taxable supplies would exceed the annual limit.

A business cannot register for VAT if it only makes exempt supplies. If the business's taxable supplies are zero-rated, you can apply for exemption from registration. If a business makes taxable and exempt supplies, you may be 'partly exempt'.

MAKING IT HAPPEN

Charging VAT

VAT must be charged from the date your business became liable for registration, not from the actual date of registration. Before you are issued with a VAT number, VAT should not be shown separately on invoices; rather, a tax invoice should be issued as soon as the number is received. Any customers who are VAT registered should be informed that they will be sent a tax invoice within 30 days. Retailers do not have to provide a VAT invoice for every transaction. However, if a taxable person requires it, the retailer must issue a tax invoice.

Keeping account of VAT

Once your business is VAT registered, you must ensure that you keep a VAT account. This record will usually be made up of tax invoices. It must be kept up to date, show all supplies made and received, and show a VAT summary for every tax period the tax return covers. Records must be kept for six years.

Businesses collecting more VAT from their sales of goods and services than they pay out in business purchases, make up the bulk of VAT-registered businesses.

VAT accounting schemes

HMRC have different schemes for businesses to choose from, depending on their trading circumstances. The standard accounting scheme is an arrangement whereby your output VAT is levied as soon as you issue a sales invoice, and your input VAT is reclaimable as soon as a purchase invoice is received. The cash accounting scheme applies to businesses with a taxable turnover of less than £660,000. Instead of accounting for VAT using issued and received tax invoices, you account for receipts and payments as they are made.

After a year's registration for VAT, businesses with a turnover of less than £660,000 can join the annual accounting scheme, in which you only make one annual VAT return. Businesses with a taxable turnover of less than £150,000 can join this scheme as soon as they register for VAT. If your business has a taxable turnover of less than £150,000 you may be able to join the flat-rate

scheme. Under this scheme, businesses calculate their VAT payment by using a fixed percentage of their VAT-inclusive turnover. Different percentages have been assigned to different trade sectors. You still have to issue tax invoices, but you will not need to keep full records of invoices issued and received.

WHAT TO AVOID
Not sending back your return on time

If a business has not made its return or sent the full payment due on time, it is regarded as being in default. HMRC will inform the business that if it defaults again within a 12-month 'surcharge period', a penalty will be applied.

Not sending back your return at all

If HMRC do not receive a return from you, they will send a computer-generated assessment that demands payment of tax. Over recent years they have taken a harder line in relation to businesses that do not submit returns or pay on assessment. In some circumstances Revenue & Customs will treat underpayments as either civil or criminal fraud, with much heavier penalties including, for the latter, a possible term of imprisonment.

It may be that you have a genuine problem completing your VAT return, for example because of an IT systems failure. If this is the case, HMRC can be approached to approve an estimate of the tax. This must be done as soon as the problem is discovered and before the due date for the return. If your business takes this action, it may be able to avoid incurring a default that might otherwise apply if the return or payment were delayed.

RECOMMENDED LINK
HM Revenue & Customs:
www.hmrc.gov.uk

SEE ALSO
Budgeting (p. 499)
Taxation (p. 551)

Getting to Grips with Benefits in Kind

GETTING STARTED

The taxation of benefits can affect anyone paid under Pay As You Earn (PAYE). Employers can also be subject to taxation on the 'perks' they provide. You can be affected whether you are a sole trader, paid by a limited company, or in a partnership. It is important to be aware that providing employees or directors with the use of anything free of charge could be affected by tax legislation. This actionlist aims to raise your awareness of what constitutes a benefit in kind, and suggests alternative ways of rewarding your employees.

FAQS

What is a benefit in kind?

Anything paid for, or given to, an employee to use can be classed as a benefit. If the cost to you is not included in the salary figures subject to PAYE it could be a benefit in kind for tax purposes. You may think that this is confined to the more glamorous items, such as chauffeur-driven luxury cars. It may surprise you to learn that even things that an employee might consider an inconvenience, such as a brightly liveried company van parked at home overnight, are considered by HM Revenue & Customs (HMRC) to be benefits in kind.

Who has to pay the tax?

Employees have to pay tax and National Insurance on benefits as if they were earnings. As an employer, you are obliged to notify HMRC of any benefits you provide so that they can be included in the code number. The company also has to pay Employers' National Insurance on the value of the benefits. Make sure you find out how often you need to pass on this information to HMRC; in the case of some benefits, you need to report on them every quarter or run the risk of being fined.

Why can't we just sort it out at the end of the financial year?

Some benefits need to be notified to HM Revenue & Customs quarterly, and financial penalties will be imposed if you fail to inform HM Revenue & Customs of any benefits' details. For this reason alone, management and payroll staff need to be right up to date.

MAKING IT HAPPEN

Identify the benefits you provide

The best way to avoid problems later on is to be absolutely aware of the tax implications of offering remuneration packages that include 'perks' to your employees. It is important that you take early responsibility, by researching the most cost-effective way to reward your employees. Benefits in kind can be powerful recruitment and retention tools, but they also bring compliance responsibilities.

Cost the whole benefits package

If you can source the items (for example, vehicles) that your employees need to use more effectively and cheaply than they can, it makes sense to pass that saving on. However, you need to consider carefully if the end use is wholly for business. If it is not, you must decide whether to provide this benefit free of charge, at cost, or at retail price. Providing key staff with company cars has traditionally proved popular, but the related tax cost has increased significantly in recent years. It is worth reviewing the current cost of all benefits, as in some cases the tax cost may exceed the true value to the employee. Make sure that you cost the alternatives as well. For example, you might consider paying a tax-free mileage allowance to the employee to use their own vehicle on business trips.

Know your benefits

To be a benefit in kind, an item must have been provided by the employer for the employee to have, or to use. You, as the employer, will not have recouped the cost of the item from the employee. Also, the item will not be used for wholly business purposes, and the employee does not refund the cost of private use. If all these criteria do apply, then you have given your employee a benefit in kind which would otherwise be taxed as pay if you gave them the money rather than the goods.

The main classes of benefit in kind often provided include vehicles, for example cars, motorcycles, and vans. They also include fuel for private journeys, including travel between home and work, and parking costs. Expenses for travel, subsistence, and telephone calls are also considered to be a benefit in kind, as are health care and insurance, and incentive schemes. Any discounts, or goods provided for the employee's own use are considered benefits in kind, and so is any entertainment provided by the company, such as office parties.

Be aware of tax-free 'benefits'

There are situations where you provide facilities or refund business expenses incurred out of the employee's own pocket. HMRC will allow you to claim a dispensation in limited cases, and letting them know what you intend to pay for, and in what circumstances, should allow you to take advantage of this valuable relaxation of the rules. If it is clear that no benefit accrues to the employee, it is accepted that a dispensation saves everyone considerable paperwork. Some things that can be covered by this include certain travel and overnight subsistence, canteen meals, and workplace parking. Childcare, relocation costs, and re-employment counselling are also included, as are sports and training, pooled vehicles, and mobile phones.

Know the consequences

When you give someone a benefit, you must remember that it is not only a business expense; it is costing the employee tax on the benefit. Careful planning is also essential to prevent exposure to hidden costs in Employers' National Insurance. Getting the compliance paperwork wrong can result in

an adverse tax inquiry, or financial penalties.

WHAT TO AVOID
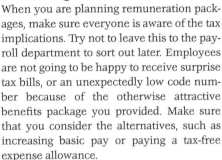
Not realising tax is a factor

When you are planning remuneration packages, make sure everyone is aware of the tax implications. Try not to leave this to the payroll department to sort out later. Employees are not going to be happy to receive surprise tax bills, or an unexpectedly low code number because of the otherwise attractive benefits package you provided. Make sure that you consider the alternatives, such as increasing basic pay or paying a tax-free expense allowance.

Not keeping good records

It is vitally important to be able to support your remuneration strategy with complete paperwork. It is no good trying to convince HMRC that no private use was made of an asset, if you didn't actually record what happened during the year. The tax year runs to 5 April each year so it may well not tie in with your accounting year end. You need to notify HMRC and your employees of any benefits by 6 July each year, so records need to be accurate and up to date. It is not only the financial information that is important here. Especially with cars, it is essential to have detailed records of business and private mileage. You also need to know who the vehicles have been made available to and (in the case of pool vehicles) where they were kept overnight. The quality and accuracy of your records will help to avoid fines for poor record keeping. If you find it difficult to calculate the value of benefits provided, you can negotiate a PAYE Settlement Agreement with HMRC to pay over the agreed tax due.

Thinking HMRC won't bother to check

HM Revenue & Customs has dedicated staff who spend their time looking for errors on the part of employers. Their job is to collect the correct amount of tax, and if you get it wrong you will have to pay back the tax and National Insurance, plus interest and penalties. Make sure you carry out a comprehensive review now, in order to save time and money later.

Not keeping up to date

The Chancellor of the Exchequer's annual Pre-Budget report usually changes various rates and allowances, as well as revising benefits in kind legislation. This is a good place to start looking out for upcoming changes in the rules so that you can plan ahead to deal with any costs and paperwork.

RECOMMENDED LINK
HM Revenue & Customs:
www.hmrc.gov.uk

SEE ALSO
Budgeting (p. 499)

Getting to Grips with the Tax Credit System

GETTING STARTED
The tax credit system is designed to ease the tax burden for people on lower incomes. Under this system (which has touched over one million small businesses), employees and the self-employed can claim, as can people caring for children—and there is also an element of help for employees with disabilities, and employees over 50 years old.

There are two main elements to tax credits: working tax credit (WTC) and child tax credit (CTC). This actionlist explains what is involved in the credits, who is eligible to claim them, and who is responsible for ensuring that anyone eligible receives the benefits.

FAQS
What exactly is involved in tax credits?
Working tax credit (WTC) can apply to working people on relatively low incomes, where they work an average of at least 16 hours per week. The effect of the WTC is to reduce the amount of tax deducted, or to pay a credit where necessary. If the claimant is employed, the responsibility for paying WTC falls on the employer. Employers need to be aware that they have to pay it, in addition to wages, on behalf of the government. The amounts are funded from the money you would normally send to HM Revenue & Customs for PAYE and National Insurance deductions.

Child tax credit (CTC) is for children, and is paid directly into the main carer's bank account. This replaces the tax allowance which previously reduced the amount of tax paid by the main earner of a family.

Who can claim?
Individuals or couples can claim. In the case of a couple, a joint claim has to be made. For both types of credit, you must be UK resident or a European Economic Area (EEA) citizen working in the United Kingdom.

WTC—this is paid to the person working more than 16 hours per week. If both people in a couple both work, one person must be nominated to receive the whole amount, and it cannot be divided between them both. It can, however, be requested that the amount due is paid into a joint account. The main classes of claim are:

- individuals over 16 years of age in low-income households with children
- the working disabled
- workers paid for at least 16 hours
- workers paid for over 25 and 30 hours
- people over 50 and returning to work after receiving certain benefits

Approved childcare costs can be an added element of WTC, which is always paid directly to the person with main responsibility for childcare.

CTC—this is paid directly to the person who is mainly responsible for caring for the child or children. Employers are not involved with any payment processes, as the payment goes straight into the claimant's bank account. It is paid to qualifying people on the following basis:

- to the carer responsible for at least one child
- in respect of children until the September following their 16th birthday, or to 19 if continuing in full time education
- you do not need to be in paid employment to receive CTC

How are the credits made up?
The amount paid to an individual is initially based on income or hours worked. Claimants will be notified of the range by which family income can rise or fall before needing to notify a change in financial circumstances.

WTC is made up of the following elements: basic; lone parent; couples; over 25 and 30 hours work; disability; severe disability; 50 plus (if you have returned to work at age 50 after 6 April 2003); and childcare.

CTC is made up of the following elements: family basic; a child element for each child; disability; severe disability; and extra payment for babies under one year old. If family earnings rise above a relatively high amount, the CTC will be reduced in line with the rise in income.

When do claims need to be made?
The new system came into effect on 6 April 2003. Claim forms were sent out to all known claimants who were already in receipt of the children's tax credit. Claims must be lodged within three months of becoming eligible for the credit, otherwise entitlement will lapse.

Can credits be backdated?
Tax credits can only be backdated for three-month periods, making it essential to put forward claims in good time. Changes in eligibility criteria should be notified to HM Revenue & Customs as quickly as possible, because the credits can be recovered from the date of a past change in circumstances.

MAKING IT HAPPEN
Remember practical considerations
Employers are required by law to make WTC payments to their eligible employees after receiving an official notice to pay from HM Revenue & Customs. The WTC payments are funded by diverting the PAYE and National Insurance contributions, together with any student loan deductions that would normally be sent off to HM Revenue & Customs on behalf of staff.

Careful planning is required to budget for the payments as in practice, it's an additional payment on top of wages, made initially by you (the employer) on behalf of the government. Payroll staff need to be able to show it separately on the payslip. There may be very little warning that an amount is due to be added to staff wages each week or month, and if there is little cash leeway, you may find it difficult to fund the extra

payments—even though ultimately you will be able to recover them from HM Revenue & Customs. One issue to note, however, is that this system of payment via the employer is likely to be phased out by Spring 2006: visit the HMRC website to keep up to date.

Apply promptly to the tax office if you need funding
Small businesses have the opportunity to request funding from HM Revenue & Customs to cover the payments due, so review your projected cash flow as soon as you receive notification that you'll have to pay the credits to any of your staff. You should apply as soon as possible so that the money goes into your bank before you need to pass it on to the employee.

Keep employees informed
If you receive a notification for payment, let the employee know that you will be making the payments on time. Reassure him or her that it will be dealt with confidentially. The general advice about claiming can be shared with staff, so that everyone is aware of the changes they need to tell HM Revenue & Customs about, and how to claim.

WHAT TO AVOID
Getting your timing wrong
Employees are told when to expect payments, and that their employer has been authorised to make payment with their wages. A small business, with low deductions to make each week or month, may have chosen to pay the PAYE amounts over quarterly. A previous cash-flow advantage from this can disappear because employees have to receive their WTC with weekly or monthly pay. Remember to keep all your bank details up to date so that you receive the amounts into the right accounts.

RECOMMENDED LINK
HM Revenue & Customs:
www.hmrc.gov.uk

SEE ALSO
Budgeting (p. 499)

Repaying Employees' Student Loans

GETTING STARTED

The Student Loan Scheme (SLS) was set up by the UK government to allow students to borrow money to help them meet their costs and expenses while studying in higher education. The SLS is administered by the Student Loans Company (SLC), but repayments are the responsibility of HM Revenue & Customs (HMRC) and collected through the Pay As You Earn (PAYE) or self-assessment tax systems. All companies employing new or recent graduates will have to manage the repayment of their employees' student loans by making deductions from their salary and paying the deductions to HMRC through the PAYE system. This actionlist is a guide to your duties and responsibilities as an employer.

FAQS

As an employer, when do I start making student loan repayments?

An employer should only start to make deductions from an employee's salary when formally advised to do so by HMRC or through the employee's P45. Student Loan Repayments (SLRs) usually start in the April following completion of studies. HMRC will send you a Start Notice, form SL1, which will identify the employee and instruct you to start making deductions. The notice will give a start date, which is usually at least six weeks from the date of issue. You should only start to make deductions on the first payday after that start date.

If an employee starts work with you having had a previous job, then he or she should have a P45 from their previous employer. The P45 has a box that is marked 'Y' if student loan deductions (SLDs) should continue to be made. If this box is completed then you should set up your payroll system for deductions to be made for the employee from the next payday. If the employee does not have a P45 then you should complete a P46, which is a form you use to tell HMRC about the employee in this situation. You then need to do nothing more until HMRC issues a Start Notice to you.

How do I calculate how much to deduct?

How much employees repay on loans is directly related to their income. If the employee began his or her higher education course on or after 1 September 1998, repayments are set to start once the student is earning £1,250 per month (£288 per week), which equates to £15,000 per annum. Once the employee is earning above this level he or she pays 9% on any earnings above the threshold. HMRC provides student loan deduction tables for employers using manual payroll systems, to help calculate the amounts to deduct at different income levels. Most computerised payroll systems will automatically run the repayment calculations.

Who do I contact if I have a query?

If your employee has any queries over the process for repaying their student loan or the deductions that you are making, then they should contact the SLC directly.

If you, as the employer, have any queries about the process of student loan deductions, then you should contact the HMRC helpline. You should not contact the SLC, as they will not give information to a third party.

When do I stop making deductions?

If an employee's salary falls below the threshold level then payments will automatically be temporarily suspended. The only other time that you will stop making deductions is when HMRC advises you to do so, usually through the issuing of a Stop Notice, form SL2. This notice will tell you when to stop making the deductions and normally gives you at least six weeks to do so.

You cannot stop making deductions because your employee requests you to do so.

MAKING IT HAPPEN
Set up your payroll system
The repayment of student loans through the PAYE system means that the process can be tied in with the regular payroll system. Most businesses now use computerised payroll systems that greatly simplify the process, and make the administration of these additional requirements fairly straightforward. If you do not run a computerised system, it may be worth looking at using the services of a payroll bureau.

Check that you are meeting your responsibilities
Employers have the following responsibilities regarding student loan repayments:
- making student loan deductions when asked to do so by HM Revenue & Customs
- providing employees with a wage slip which records the amount of deductions
- keeping records of the deductions made for each employee
- paying the deductions to HM Revenue & Customs
- providing HM Revenue & Customs with details of the SLRs that have been deducted
- when an employee leaves, identifying on his or her P45 that the individual is liable to make SLRs

Payments of the deductions should be sent to HM Revenue & Customs accounts centre with your income tax and National Insurance contributions. This payment should be made by the 19th of the month following the month of pay, and the SLR should be included with your income tax figures.

Ensure you complete the right tax forms
SLRs must be recorded on several key HM Revenue & Customs end of year tax forms:
- P35 summary of tax
- P14 end of year summary
- P60 certificate of pay

The HM Revenue & Customs processes the end of year tax forms and passes details of the specific deductions made from each employee to the SLC, so that the correct repayment amounts can be applied to outstanding loans.

WHAT TO AVOID
Miscalculating earnings
SLRs are non-cumulative, and so you should not take into account earnings from an earlier pay period when calculating the deduction in the current pay period. If you find that you have deducted too much then you should repay to your employee the amount wrongly deducted and make a similar adjustment to your next PAYE payment.

Thinking employers alone are responsible for repayments
It is not the employer's responsibility to identify which of their employees are liable to make SLRs, and when to stop making these payments. It is up to HM Revenue & Customs to keep you informed.

RECOMMENDED LINKS
HM Revenue & Customs:
www.hmrc.gov.uk
Student Loans Company:
www.slc.co.uk

SEE ALSO
Budgeting (p. 499)

Managing Creditors and Debtors

GETTING STARTED

All businesses have trading relationships with both suppliers and customers. At any point in time, those suppliers who are extending credit to your business by letting you pay for goods or services after you have received them, are known as your creditors. Customers who owe you money for goods or services that you have supplied are known as your debtors.

The balance between when you need to pay your creditors and when you receive payment from your debtors has a major effect on the cash flow of your business. Getting the balance right is important in determining what cash will be available to your business in the short term, and for identifying the cash needs (often referred to as 'working capital') of your business as it grows.

FAQS

Why do I need to manage creditors and debtors?

Knowing how much you owe, how much you are owed, and when payments are due to be made or received, allows you to forecast your cash flow over several months and ensures that you will have enough money in the bank for other regular business payments, such as salaries and rent. This can be particularly important for businesses that are seasonal, or that have a high spend with their suppliers several months before their customers pay them.

How does this effect the working capital required by a business?

When the value of your creditors equals the value of your debtors, there is no effect on the working capital needs of your business, assuming payment terms are the same. However if the value of your debtors increases relative to the value of your creditors, then the working capital used by your business rises. This is a typical situation faced by businesses as they grow. If you are able to increase the value of your creditors while maintaining the value of your debtors then you can reduce the working capital needed by your business.

What are standard payment terms?

There are no firm rules for credit terms, but there are accepted practices that are widely adopted. Normally the credit period is either based on the date of the invoice, or on the month of the invoice. The most standard credit term based on the date of invoice is 30 days—that is, the invoice is due for payment 30 days after the date on the invoice. If you are providing several invoices to a customer in any one month, it is normal to use 'net monthly terms'. This means that all invoices for a particular month are grouped and paid together at the end of the following month. Using net monthly terms greatly simplifies the process for both supplier and customer, reducing the payment process to only once a month, irrespective of the number of invoices issued.

What is debtor finance?

For many businesses the amount owed by their debtors is the largest single element of their balance sheet. If your business is trading in a business-to-business environment, there is the potential to use the services of a third-party finance company who will make money available to you, based on the security of your debtor balances. This service is called 'factoring' and can range from the provision of just finance against your debtor list to a full sales ledger and credit-control service. The initial advance payment is usually up to 80% of the value of the invoice, with the remaining balance being due either at an agreed maturity date, or when your customer pays the factor. This type of service is especially useful for fast-growing businesses who can suffer from a shortage of working capital.

What is creditor finance?

This is the term used for 'borrowing' money from your creditors to fund your working capital. It is typically used by retail businesses, where you sell your products or services for cash, and yet obtain credit from your suppliers.

Are trade suppliers my only short-term creditors?

Although trade suppliers are usually viewed as being the creditors of your business, you should actually include all of the organisations that you owe money to in the short term. This means that the term 'creditors' is more formally split between trade creditors—which will include your trade suppliers to your business—and other creditors, which will include organisations such as HM Revenue & Customs (HMRC) if you are an employer, or if you are VAT registered.

✓ MAKING IT HAPPEN

Managing your creditors and debtors is vitally important to the smooth and effective operation of your business. Doing this effectively will save you money, and may even make the difference between your business surviving or failing.

Manage the relationship with your creditors

Suppliers are vital to the operation of your business and the role that they play is often undervalued. For many suppliers, how you manage the payment of their account is a key to a successful long-term relationship. The main issues for a good working relationship with your suppliers are for you to be:

■ professional in your handling of their account, by conforming to the agreed credit terms, and not wasting their time through poor administration

■ honest with them if you have cash-flow problems and are unable to meet their normal payment terms

■ straightforward in your commercial negotiations—look to negotiate better terms from your suppliers, but base this on the volume of business and how this has grown over a period of time, and the fact that you manage your account well

Use a credit card to obtain credit

In situations where it is difficult to obtain credit from your suppliers, then you should consider using a credit card to make payment for goods. This has the effect of giving the supplier immediate payment, but also giving you 30–50 days credit. However, there can be an additional charge added to the invoice of 1–3%, and it is essential that you pay it off promptly or you will incur further cost.

Manage the relationship with your debtors

If providing credit to your customers is important to your business, then it is vital to set up effective credit-control procedures.

Get your customers to complete an account application form, giving details about their business and its legal structure, and details of references. Supply them with a copy of your standard terms and conditions of sale, and make sure they are aware of (and acknowledge) your payment terms, and what their credit limit is. Keep records of quotations and delivery notes to ensure that disputes can be quickly resolved (by you providing the missing information, if needed), and ensure that you have efficient accounts administration systems that allow you to send invoices promptly, and follow up with regular statements and reminders.

Monitor your customers' payments. If you are unhappy with them then speak to the person who places the order as well as the finance department. If they still do not pay, be prepared to halt supplies and to take further action to collect the debt if necessary. You may even decide to withdraw credit facilities if a customer is a persistently poor payer.

You should produce a regular debtors list, preferably in balance order, so that you can easily review how much each business owes to you, and how old their debt is. You need to concentrate your efforts on those customers that have the oldest and largest debts to ensure that your time is used most cost-effectively.

WHAT TO AVOID
Taking a narrow focus
Do not focus all of your efforts on getting better payment terms from your creditors at the expense of managing your debtors more effectively. If your business regularly struggles to pay its creditors because of slow payment from your debtors, this will be an indication that your business does not have sufficient working capital. You will then need to decide if you can manage your debtors better, and reduce the average credit period given, or whether you will need to get additional finance into the business to increase your available working capital.

RECOMMENDED LINKS
Better Payment Practice Campaign:
www.payontime.co.uk
Factors and Discounters Association:
www.factors.org.uk

SEE ALSO
Addressing Cash-flow Problems (p. 148)
Budgeting (p. 499)
**Issuing Invoices and Collecting Debts
  (p. 154)**

Addressing Cash-flow Problems

GETTING STARTED

Running out of cash is probably the biggest cause of small businesses failing. There are many reasons behind a cash crisis, so it's crucial that you understand them and know how to prevent a short-term problem leading to business failure. No matter how good your balance sheet may look in terms of physical assets and outstanding debtors, your ability to convert these to actual cash at critical times can make the difference between survival and failure. This actionlist looks at some of the main causes of cash-flow problems, and suggests some ways of overcoming such problems.

For more information on cash-flow issues, you might like visit the 'Small Business—Information and Cash Flow' website, which offers resources and links for small businesses on credit management, cash flow, debt collection, and related topics. The website address is given below.

FAQS

How does the behaviour of my customers affect my cash flow?

Slow payment by your customers is a main cause of cash-flow problems. Remember that a sale is only completed when your invoice has been paid in full. Many businesses concentrate on generating new sales, but fail to set up credit-control procedures until they actually experience cash-flow problems. These procedures should be in place from the start.

If a key customer becomes insolvent this can also cause cash-flow problems. If your business is very dependent on a few major customers, you are always exposed to the risk of one of them having their own financial problems, which could result in you not getting paid. This could be disastrous if the income from that client makes up a big chunk of your overall revenue and you are relying on that money to pay your creditors or employees.

How does poor planning affect cash flow?

Poor financial planning can cause huge problems. Your business must plan for certain payments, such as Value Added Tax, Pay As You Earn tax, and personal or business tax bills. You need to build these payments into your cash-flow forecasts and then make sure that sufficient funds will be available at those key times. Also make sure

that any purchase of equipment is scheduled for payment when your cash position is stronger, or is structured over a longer period to reduce its impact on your cash flow.

If your business plan focuses on turnover, and neglects profit, you can also end up with a cash-flow crisis on your hands. A business is only able to generate a positive cash flow by generating profits from its trading activities. If you prioritise the turnover of your business, then you may improve sales but this might lead to spending more than you earn (a problem known as negative cash flow). This can be a particular problem if the business has to invest in new equipment and staff as it grows, as these costs are often incurred well in advance of you receiving your additional sales revenue.

Another common reason for cash-flow problems is inappropriate planning for stock purchases. It's very tempting to overcommit, especially as many suppliers will offer you discount incentives to purchase larger quantities of their goods; on the face of it, this could look very attractive because it holds the promise of making you a larger profit. However, you need to think carefully before committing to large orders of stock, particularly while you are establishing your business. If you order bulk purchases and then the items quickly go out of fashion or have a short shelf life, you can be left with stock that you cannot sell but that you still have to pay for.

How does the rate of growth of my business affect cash flow?

Another common reason for problems with cash flow is insufficient working capital. This means that there is not enough money initially invested in the business to allow it to operate effectively on a day-to-day basis. It can also be a problem when a business grows rapidly and needs to produce more than normal without having the income to fund that growth; this is called over-trading.

► MAKING IT HAPPEN
Plan effectively

Preparing a cash-flow forecast and then putting it to good use is the basis for avoiding many cash-flow problems. The forecast allows you to anticipate most cash-flow problems that could occur during the normal course of running your business. It also allows you to do a sensitivity analysis, in which you can test the effect of lower sales or slower payment on your cash flow, all of which will help you know what strains your business could stand if things do get tight.

Build good relationships with suppliers and customers

Tight credit-control procedures are an absolute must, so make them your priority. Start with only giving credit to approved customers (whose references you've checked out), keep an eye on when their accounts are due for payment, and make sure that they pay according to your agreed terms. It's a good idea to confirm in writing any deals you arrange so that customers can't claim that they didn't really understand what the payment system was. Also make sure that you have efficient administration procedures for raising your invoices promptly and sending statements to your customers. Basically, the sooner you invoice, the sooner you'll get paid!

Offering incentives for early payment is another good way to encourage your customers to pay more quickly. You could do this by offering a discount if they either pay on delivery, or within a certain number of days (typically between 7 and 14 days) from the invoice date. Typical levels of discount are between 2% and 5%, but the exact level will depend on your profit margins and on how important early payment is to you. It's probably wise to only adopt this measure for a limited period, otherwise customers will begin to expect a discount from you, which may be bad news for your business in the long term.

As your business grows, aim to negotiate better credit terms with your suppliers. Initially, this may be achieved by progressing from paying at the time of purchase, to having a 30-day credit account. If the majority of your customers expect to have 60-day credit accounts, then you should try to agree 60-day payment terms with your suppliers.

Get help

Debtor finance is an option for businesses that are growing rapidly and you could investigate using the services of an invoice discounter or factoring company. These companies enter into an arrangement where they will provide your business with an advance (usually 80%) on the value of your invoices, as soon as these invoices are raised. Interest is then charged on the balance drawn, and there is a service charge. Factoring companies can also take control of collecting payments from your customer directly, which can save you the costs of using your own staff to manage this process.

An agreed overdraft facility with your bank allows you to borrow money as and when required, up to an agreed limit. It is a relatively cheap way to finance working capital if you have large variations in cash flow during the course of a month (or if your business is very seasonal), because you only pay interest on the amount actually borrowed. However, relying continually on your overdraft can be expensive; more importantly, it may also highlight that your business needs additional working capital, or a longer-term form of finance. With an overdraft, you are also exposed to 'repayment on demand', which means that your lender can ask for full repayment at any time; a 'term loan' with fixed monthly instalments is safer from your point of view, as the lender can usually only demand full repayment if you default on your instalments.

If your business needs to invest in new equipment, but does not have the cash, then you can look to fund this with asset financing, in the form of a term loan, a hire purchase loan, or a leasing deal. This avoids the large cash outflow on the full price of the equipment, and gives you a fixed level of repayment over a set period (usually between two and five years). In situations where the asset is being used as security for the finance, it is likely that you will still need to provide at least a 10% deposit.

WHAT TO AVOID
Not thinking ahead
Don't be taken by surprise. Keep a close eye on your bank balance and your debtors' book and look ahead a few weeks at what expenditure you will have to make. Cash-flow problems are best caught early, and the more time you can give yourself to respond, the better.

Procrastinating
Don't be fooled into thinking that cash-flow problems will resolve themselves; they won't go away! Talk to your bank and your suppliers as soon as you think there might be a problem. This way, you assure them that you are at least doing your homework, even if there are difficult times ahead. If you don't act, you run the risk of affecting your relationship with your bank, suppliers, and customers. Your bank will be far more receptive to dealing with your cash-flow problems if you approach it before the problem occurs.

RECOMMENDED LINKS
Institute of Credit Management:
www.icm.org.uk
Small Business—Information and Cash Flow:
www.credit-to-cash.com

SEE ALSO
Budgeting (p. 499)
Financing a New Business (p. 108)
Managing Creditors and Debtors (p. 145)

Coping in a Cash-flow Crisis

GETTING STARTED

Many businesses face a cash-flow crisis at some point in their existence. Good financial management should generally prevent this but there are some circumstances that are difficult to avoid, especially in a company's early days. Events such as a major customer refusing or becoming unable to pay their debts can often saddle small businesses with cash-flow problems.

Running out of cash is probably the biggest cause of small businesses failing. There can be many reasons behind a cash crisis, so it's essential that you understand them and know how to prevent or mitigate short-term problems which might otherwise lead to business failure. No matter how good your balance sheet may look in terms of physical assets and outstanding debtors, your ability to convert these to cash at critical times can make the difference between survival and failure.

FAQS

What are the main causes of cash-flow problems?

Typical causes of cash-flow problems include:

- slow payment by your customers
- a key customer becomes insolvent owing you a large sum of money
- insufficient working capital
- focusing on turnover instead of profit
- poor financial planning
- buying too much stock

How can you spot when you're heading for a crisis?

Sometimes a cash-flow crisis will suddenly jump up and hit you, such as when a major debtor announces out of the blue that they cannot pay what they owe. Clearly, you can't always predict that things like this are going to happen, but you can take some steps to soften the blow. Spotting the problem in advance and doing something about it early is still the best step you can take, though, so try to bear this in mind, especially if you have one or two very large customers that you rely on.

You can spot the warning signs by keeping a close eye on your balance sheet. Is the number of debtors rising when everything else is constant? Are your stock levels, especially of finished goods, rising? If the answer to either of these is yes, then you may need to take remedial action.

You also need to keep a close eye on your profit and loss account, although it may take longer to spot problems. Is your profit falling? Worse, are you losing money? If the answer to either of these is yes, then your available working capital will be reducing, and this spells trouble.

MAKING IT HAPPEN

Make sure that you have procedures in place to safeguard, as far as possible, against cash-flow disasters. Even if these can't be prevented, the procedures you've worked out should at least enable you to spot the warning signs and take emergency action.

Control your finances effectively

The best form of preparation is an effective and robust system of financial control. Preparing a cash-flow forecast and—crucially!—putting it to good use is the basis for avoiding many cash-flow problems. The forecast allows you to anticipate most cash-flow–related issues that could occur during the normal course of running your business. It allows you to do a 'sensitivity analysis' in which you can test the effect of lower sales or slower payment on your cash flow.

Make sure that you're costing your products or services accurately and that what you charge for them will let you make a profit. Adopt tight credit-control systems and establish procedures for managing the whole process of giving your customers credit. Start by giving credit only to approved customers; check when their accounts are due for payment and that they pay according to your agreed terms. If you have efficient procedures for raising invoices promptly and sending statements to your customers, you won't be adding to payment delays yourself.

Consider encouraging your clients to pay more quickly by offering a discount if they pay either on delivery or within a certain number of days (typically 7–14 days) from the invoice date. Generally the discount is between 2% and 5% of your sale price, but the exact level will depend on your profit margins and on how important early payment is to you.

To speed up payments, you could use the services of an invoice discounter or factoring company. These companies enter into an arrangement where they will provide your business with an advance (usually 80%) on the value of your invoices as soon as they're raised. Interest is then charged on the balance drawn and there is a service charge. Factoring companies can also take control of collecting payments from your customer directly, which saves you the costs of using your own staff to manage the process. This type of service is particularly suitable for businesses that are growing rapidly because they reduce the likelihood that you'll run out of working capital. However, you may still suffer if a major customer goes down because the factor will usually recover the outstanding debt from you.

As your business grows, you may be able to negotiate better credit terms with your suppliers. Initially, this could be achieved by progressing from paying at the time of purchase, to having a 30-day credit account. If the majority of your customers expect to have 60-day credit accounts, you should aim to agree 60-day payment terms with your suppliers.

An agreed overdraft facility allows you to borrow money as and when required, up to an agreed limit. It's a relatively cheap way to finance working capital if you have large variations in cash flow during the course of a month (or if your business is very seasonal), because you only pay interest on the amount actually borrowed. However, if you're continually relying on your overdraft it can be expensive; more importantly it may also highlight that your business needs a longer-term form of finance. With an overdraft, you're exposed to 'repayment on demand', which means that your lender can ask for full repayment at any time.

If your business needs to invest in new equipment but doesn't have the cash, you may be able to fund this with a term loan, a hire purchase loan, or a leasing deal. This avoids the large cash outflow on the full price of the equipment, and gives you a fixed level of repayment over a set period (usually two to five years). In situations where the asset is being used as security for the finance, it's likely that you will still need to provide a deposit.

It's also sensible to manage your business so that you aren't reliant on just one or two major customers, as you'll be dangerously exposed if one of them has a problem. Spread your customer base as widely as you can, aiming for at least five or six customers.

Build up your working capital availability by retaining some of the profit in your business. This will provide a reserve when you need to buy equipment or have unexpected expenditure to deal with, but will also provide a cushion against possible cash-flow problems.

Take emergency action if all else fails

If you're hit with a cash-flow crisis you have to act very quickly if the business is to survive. The first thing to do is to make an accurate assessment of the scale of the problem. Prepare an updated cash-flow forecast and decide if you'll be able to trade out of your difficulty. If this seems unlikely, look carefully at how much support you need and whether you can provide this from your own personal resources.

If the answer is no, you'll have to go to the bank and explore the possibility of increasing your overdraft. Even if you think you can trade out of the problem, it may be sensible to inform your bank at an early stage in case you discover later that you do need additional working capital after all.

If the bank is unwilling to help, or can only provide partial support, the next step is to inform your creditors. It's sensible to talk to larger creditors directly, explain your position and ask them for longer to pay. It's especially important to talk to HM Revenue & Customs if you have employees and therefore hand over PAYE monthly. They can be very understanding if they think that you're being straight with them and that a little leniency now will result in full payment later. If necessary, offer them reduced payments now with the outstanding balance in instalments as your business recovers. If they are crucial suppliers, you need to keep them on your side or else you won't be able to continue trading.

You should also consider developing a business disaster plan, which will help the business cope with any unexpected events that could damage cash flow. This enables you to prepare for the aftermath of incidents such as computer viruses, major power cuts, loss of key personnel, natural disasters, and terrorist attacks.

If all these options fail, you may have no alternative but to consider the future of your company. If your business runs into severe financial difficulties and becomes insolvent, you must cease trading. The options then are either to seek the appointment of a receiver or liquidate the business. In commercial law this process can involve terms such as insolvency, receivership, administration, liquidation (winding up), and bankruptcy.

WHAT TO AVOID
Being taken by surprise

Keep a close eye on your balance sheet, your debtors, and your bank balance. Look ahead at your cash-flow requirements for the next few weeks and consider what receipts you expect and what payments you'll have to make. Cash-flow problems are best caught early and the more time you can give yourself to respond the better.

Procrastinating

Cash-flow problems rarely resolve themselves—they require positive action. Talk to your bank and your creditors as soon as you suspect there may be a problem. This way, you assure them you're at least doing your homework, even if there are difficult times ahead. If you don't act you run the risk of affecting relationships with all your key stakeholders including the bank, suppliers, and customers. Your bank will be far more receptive to dealing with your cash-flow problems if you approach them before the problem occurs. It is bound to be a worrying time for you, but burying your head in the sand won't help and you'll feel better for doing something about the problem.

RECOMMENDED LINK
bizhelp24:
www.bizhelp24.com

Issuing Invoices and Collecting Debts

GETTING STARTED

When your business supplies goods or services to its customers, you need to record these transactions formally with a document called an invoice. This document becomes particularly important when you let your customers defer payment for the transaction, by offering them credit. From the date that the invoice is issued, until it is paid, the value of the invoice is regarded as a debt to the business. This actionlist explains the invoicing procedure and offers advice on how to deal with customers who won't pay up on time.

FAQS

Why do you need to issue invoices?

An invoice is a formal record of trading between two parties. It confirms details of the goods or services supplied, and the prices charged. It is used as the basis for all financial management and accounting processes in a business, and is a key document in business tax records. An invoice that is issued by your business to confirm a sale is then a crucial document for the customer, as it acts as proof of purchase.

Are there different types of invoices?

Yes. Three types of invoice documents can be used.

1. Pro-forma invoice—this is issued by a business when it does not have credit facilities set up with its customer, and acts as a request for payment for goods prior to despatch. This ensures that payment is received, and is often used when two businesses have not traded before.

2. Standard invoice—a standard document issued to confirm a trading transaction. It is normally classed as a sales invoice by the business that has sold the goods, and as a purchase invoice by the buyer. When an invoice is issued by a VAT-registered business, it is known as a VAT invoice. This must provide specific information about the rate and amount of VAT charged.

3. Credit note—this is issued to cancel an original invoice or part of an invoice when goods are returned or a pricing error has been made. If the original invoice has been settled prior to the credit note being issued, then the buyer will be entitled to alternative goods up to the value of the credit note.

What details should be included on an invoice?

All invoices need to convey certain key pieces of information as supporting evidence for tax and VAT purposes, and to avoid queries from customers which may lead to delays in payment. These are:

- a unique identifying number
- your business name, address, its legal status, and VAT number (if relevant)
- a date of issue, which becomes the tax point
- your customer's name (or trading name) and address
- a description of the quantity and type of goods or services supplied, along with the price charged, and, where appropriate, the VAT charged
- the payment terms for the invoice

Must an invoice always be issued?

You do not always need to issue an invoice to your customer, but you will need to keep a record of the transaction. For example, many retail businesses issue till receipts to their customers rather than fully-detailed invoices. This is fine for small one-off transactions that are paid for at the time of purchase but most business-to-business transactions require an invoice to be issued, and this is especially important if you and your customer are VAT-registered.

Is there anything that can be done if the customer will not pay the invoice?

First of all, you need to find out as soon as possible why your customer won't pay the invoice. If it is a simple issue, such as a genuine pricing or quantity error, then it should be simple to resolve. However, if the reason given is not acceptable and a compromise cannot be reached, you will need to take action to recover the money owed. This can be done in several ways:

- using the County Courts and the small-claims procedure for debts of less than £5,000
- instructing a solicitor to pursue the debt for you. This may just involve him or her sending a letter on your behalf, or managing the whole process of pursuing your claim through the court process
- engaging the services of a debt collection agency, who will either manage the process for a fixed fee, or work on a commission of the debt that is collected

You need to balance the time that it will take for you to pursue your customer for payment, against the costs involved with using the services of a solicitor or debt collection agency.

✒ MAKING IT HAPPEN

If your business only issues a small number of invoices then you can use a computer and word-processing package, or even manually write out the invoices. You will need to produce two copies, one for your customer and one for your own records. This simple approach can work well, but once you start to offer credit or have the complication of being VAT registered, it makes more sense to use an integrated accounts system that manages both invoicing and credit control.

Set up procedures for credit control

If you offer credit to your customers, then issuing a sales invoice is just *part* of the sales process—the transaction is not completed until the invoice has been fully settled. Many businesses are very successful at selling their goods or services and yet still fail because they are unable to collect the money owed to them, so it's vital to set up processes that minimise the risk of your customers failing to pay you.

Make sure that credit is only offered to creditworthy customers, and that you agree payment terms with them in advance. Check the accuracy of invoices before you send them out, and provide customers with monthly statements showing their account balance. When credit terms are exceeded, send reminder letters and follow up with telephone calls, and be prepared to put a customer's account on hold if there is no good reason for non-payment. Finally, don't be afraid to charge interest under the Late Payment of Commercial Debts (Interest) Act 1998.

Investigate reasons for non-payment

Even when you adopt these procedures there are going to be situations that lead to an invoice not being paid on time. You will then have to decide on the best approach to recover your debt, and a lot will depend on the approach of your customer, their size and importance to your business, and the size of the debt. There are several reasons for non-payment.

Habitual slow payer. Sometimes new customers are won suddenly, and it is only after you've supplied them for a while that you find out why: their previous supplier had closed their account because of continuing problems with late payment. This type of customer will go through long delaying tactics as a matter of course, and can waste a huge amount of your (or your finance department's) time in chasing them. Undertaking credit checks can help to minimise this risk, but often it is only by adopting very tight credit control and setting low credit limits initially that you can limit the problem. If the problems continue you may then have to decide between charging higher prices to reflect your extra costs, or refusing to give your customer credit.

Disputed invoices. Misunderstandings about the terms of a transaction are quite common, and the easiest way to avoid them is to make sure that each stage of the sales process has been documented. If this information is not complete, you may have to face negotiating a compromise with your customer, which should mean that you get paid for at least part of the invoice. If there is no room for compromise and you believe that your case is strong, then you should look at formal recovery of your debt as the best way forward—although the process can be time consuming and expensive. If the dispute does end up in court, you will need to be able to demonstrate that you have explored all avenues to resolve it, so you should document the process carefully.

Financial difficulty. This is probably the most common reason for non-payment of an invoice, and is often masked by your customer behind lots of other reasons. You need to identify whether this is a short-term cash-flow glitch or a major financial problem that is likely to result in your customer becoming insolvent. In situations where a customer faces a short-term difficulty, it may be possible to agree to payments by instalment over a specific period. If you do agree to this approach, make sure you confirm it in writing and then monitor the situation carefully to ensure that your customer maintains these special payments.

If a customer's business faces long-term or extreme cash-flow problems it is likely to be unable to pay your debt. Knowing the legal status of your customer's business is important under these circumstances, because this will determine how you can pursue the recovery of your debt. Often the best that you can hope for is that you can claim title to the goods that you have supplied, which may still have some value to you. For this reason, you should ensure that a retention-of-title clause is used in all of your terms of sale and all invoices which involve the sale of goods.

WHAT TO AVOID
Delaying sending out invoices
Issue invoices promptly after a sale. Taking too much time will lead to delays in you getting paid because payment terms will be based on the invoice date and not the date that you supplied the goods or services.

Being over-sympathetic to customers' financial problems
If there's no valid reason for non-payment, don't delay the process of debt collection because you're worried about upsetting your customer. This may just lead to your business being owed more, and possibly not getting paid at all if the customer's business ceases trading.

RECOMMENDED LINKS
Her Majesty's Courts Service:
www.hmcourts-service.gov.uk
Credit Services Association (information about Debt Recovery Agencies):
www.csa-uk.com
Better Payment Practice Campaign:
www.payontime.co.uk

SEE ALSO
Budgeting (p. 499)
Managing Creditors and Debtors (p. 145)

Understanding the Role of Price

GETTING STARTED

The price that you charge for your product or service needs to reflect your costs on the one hand and the strength of the market on the other. Setting a price too high can result in lost sales, while undercharging can eat into your profits and possibly lead to you being unable to deliver on your contracts. This actionlist contains advice on how to go about calculating prices, in a way that will suit both your business and the market. One book on the subject that you might also find useful is *Power Pricing: How Managing Price Transforms the Bottom Line* by Robert J. Dolan and Hermann Simon, published in 1996 by Simon & Schuster.

FAQS

What is the difference between price and cost?

The *cost* of producing your product or service is the total costs for the business, both direct and fixed, divided by the number of products that you sell. The *price* that you charge depends on what the market will stand, that is, on what the customer will pay. The difference between price and cost is profit—or loss!

How do I work out how much I can charge?

You need to research the market carefully in order to determine the price that you can charge. This is most difficult when you are starting up, since you have little information on which to base your pricing decisions, other than reviewing the prices charged by your competitors and your own market research with potential customers. Once you are in business it becomes easier, since you can adjust your prices and review the effects they have on demand.

Will charging less than my competitors win customers?

Many people have difficulty calculating the cost of their products or services and, as a result, let their competitors effectively set the price, thinking that as long as they undercut that price, then they will succeed. However, cost leadership is a strategy that often fails for small businesses since they lack the economies of scale necessary to make the price really competitive, and end up losing money as a result.

What is gross profit?

The gross profit is the selling price less the direct costs involved in making the product or delivering the service. Direct costs (sometimes known as variable costs, because they vary with the output) include such items as raw materials, bought-in components, and sub-contracting. Fixed costs (sometimes known as overheads—items such as rent, utilities, depreciation, and insurance) are then deducted from the gross profit, resulting in the net profit. So you need to sell enough at your chosen price to cover all the direct and fixed costs, and make a profit as well.

What is the breakeven point?

The breakeven point is the point where the income from sales exactly equals all the costs incurred by the business. More sales will result in a profit; fewer sales will result in a loss.

Can I change the price once it is set?

The price can always be changed, but there is often customer resistance to the raising of a price if the rise is too great, or if you change it too frequently.

MAKING IT HAPPEN ✔
Remember the two-step process

There are two steps in setting price: the first step is to determine the costs of delivering a product or service; the second step is to set a price that is high enough to cover the costs, but low enough to be competitive.

Research the market

You need to start with an idea of what you may be able to sell and the price at which you might be able to sell it. This information comes from your market research. It is necessary to have sensible estimate of likely sales volumes, otherwise you will not be able to calculate the direct costs. This is less important if you are selling a service where there are very low, if any, direct costs. But it is very important if you are in manufacturing, particularly if the direct costs (like raw materials) are of a high value. Prepare an income and expenditure forecast using different prices. Estimate what effect a price increase will have on your sales. Consider the prices offered by your competitors. If your prices are much higher, are you offering sufficient extra benefit to entice customers to buy from you?

Calculate the costs

There are a number of different ways of allocating costs to products and services, but the key requirement is to know all the costs—direct and fixed—for an expected level of sales. Don't forget to include depreciation and your deductions if you are self-employed. Once you have the cost, then you have the bare minimum price for a given level of sales.

Provided the costs are less than the price that you set when you did your market research, you will make a profit—assuming, of course, that you also sell the volumes that you predicted.

Carry out a breakeven analysis

Once you know your costs and estimated selling price, you are in a position to calculate how many products, or hours of your time, you need to sell to break even (that is, to cover all your costs).

One way to calculate the breakeven point is to draw a graph that shows sales volume on the horizontal axis and money on the vertical axis. First show the overhead costs. This will be a horizontal line since these costs are, generally, fixed for all volumes of production.

The direct costs can then be added to the overhead costs to give total costs for a given volume of output. A line representing total costs can be plotted. The sales income can then be plotted to show how much income will be generated for a given volume of sales. Remember that sales income starts at zero for zero sales.

The point where the sales income equals the total cost shows the breakeven point. A higher price will achieve breakeven with fewer sales. A lower price may attract more customers, but will require higher sales to break even. The further above breakeven that a business can operate, the greater its margin of safety.

Set targets

Once you have determined your price and defined the breakeven volume that you need to sell, set an annual target, broken down into monthly targets, designed to generate a reasonable profit.

It can often be helpful to plot the targets for sales and actual sales on a graph to monitor progress regularly. If the business does not achieve its targets you will need to take remedial action.

Review

Review your sales volumes and income regularly. Ensure that you are making a profit; if you are not, you will need to take corrective action, perhaps involving changing the price.

WHAT TO AVOID
Setting the price too low

The greatest danger when setting a price for the first time is to pitch it too low. Raising a price is always more difficult than lowering one, yet there are great temptations to undercut the competition. It is clearly important to compare your prices to your competitors', but it is essential that your price covers all your costs and contributes towards your profit.

Failing to cost accurately

Many businesses run into difficulties, and some fail, because they do not cost their work accurately. They fail to check the actual costs of a job against the estimated costs. While they cannot turn back history and re-price, they can at least amend their prices for future sales. Not doing this is likely to result in failing to achieve targets for profit and profitability.

Under-utilising assets
Many businesses buy expensive equipment and fail to include all the depreciation when they are costing. If you are buying expensive equipment, you need to think carefully about how you will recover the cost.

RECOMMENDED LINK
Bizpeponline (offers business software and tools that help with pricing, budgeting, forecasting, and other business issues):
www.bizpeponline.com

SEE ALSO
Budgeting (p. 499)
Pricing (p. 536)
Setting Prices (p. 160)

Setting Prices

GETTING STARTED

Setting the price of a product or service is often regarded as a financial issue, but in reality it's also a marketing issue. Clearly the price has to cover all the costs and generate a profit—the business won't survive otherwise—but equally, you won't necessarily want to charge the most that you could get away with because you want customers to think that you offer good value for money, and you want repeat business. This actionlist looks at some of the main issues for you to consider when setting your prices.

FAQS

How do I set the price?

Setting a price is a two-part exercise. First, you need to calculate all of your costs, and then divide this figure by the number of products, or days of service, that you expect to sell. This gives a minimum price, at which your business can break even but not make a profit. Second, you need to research the market to determine the maximum price that could be achievable for your product or service. You can then set your actual price somewhere between the two.

If my price is lower than my competitors', will I sell more?

Many businesses believe that if they set their price lower than their competitors, then they will win greater market share. This is known as 'cost leadership'. Small businesses, however, are usually too small to achieve the economies of scale necessary to enable them to fix a really competitive price. If you are in this position, you need to 'differentiate' your product or service in order to secure a competitive edge. This could be done on the basis of better quality, better service, or quicker delivery, for example. You may find that quicker delivery is an extra benefit for which your customers might be willing to pay.

What happens if I increase my prices?

Fixing a price is a juggling act between strategy, pricing, and cash flow. If your price is too low, the income may not cover all your costs. If the price is too high, even with a well-differentiated product, you may have difficulty attracting enough customers.

However, maximising profit does not necessarily mean selling high volumes at low profit. It may be possible to sell low volumes at high profit. The challenge that you face is to find the right balance.

In general, changing the price will cause a change in demand. Small businesses often find that they can put up the price without losing too many customers, thus increasing profitability. But you also need to understand the potential effect that a price change will have on your customers. It's a good idea to warn them that prices are going to rise, and to explain why. A good relationship with your customers can improve their perception of the value you are offering.

How much flexibility do I have?

The amount of flexibility that you have largely depends on the way that your product or service is perceived in the marketplace. A cost leadership strategy gives you almost no flexibility, because you have to respond to the price set by your competitors. A differentiated strategy is based on demonstrating how your product or service is quite different from your competitors'; the particular benefits of what you offer give you more flexibility in setting your price.

I know how important pricing is, but should I think about *free* giveaways as well?

It's certainly something to consider. Used carefully, offering existing or prospective customers free access to your product or service can have a real and very positive effect on sales. For example, existing customers will be thrilled that you think so highly of them and this will engender a lot of goodwill in turn. They'll feel they have more of a bond with you, which will make them less likely to buy from a competitor and much more likely to tell colleagues and friends about your company.

Prospective customers like free giveaways as they can try out new products without risk. The key thing in this situation, though, is to make them want to *stay* with you after the free trial is over. The only way to do this is to be sure that what you're offering is the best option around—if you're not, what are you going to do to change that situation? In both cases, though, you should only do free giveways in such a way that you don't get left hopelessly out of pocket with nothing to show for it. Offer customers something that doesn't cost you very much but which has a high perceived value for others.

MAKING IT HAPPEN
The marketing mix

The marketing mix, often referred to as the four Ps (product, position, price, and promotion), covers the different aspects of marketing. It's the marketing mix that conveys your message to your customers.

Your price needs to reflect the position that you want to adopt in the market place. If you adopt a position of quality, you will want (and will probably need) to charge a premium price. If your product or service is regarded as mass-produced, and therefore of lower quality, then the price should be at the bottom end of the spectrum.

Pricing strategies

There are a number of possible pricing strategies that you could adopt:

- **Cost-based pricing** is when total costs are calculated and a mark-up is added to give the required profit. The mark-up is usually expressed as a percentage of the cost. Different types of businesses will apply varying mark-ups, for example, the mark-up on jewellery is enormous compared to the mark-up on food products.
- **'Skimming'** is where you initially charge a relatively high price to recover investment costs quickly if the product is new. As your

competitors follow your lead and launch their own products to compete and enter the market, you lower the price.

- **Negotiating prices individually** with customers, based on the quantities they are prepared to buy. If you wish to sell to a particular market, then you might sell one product or service more cheaply (as a **loss leader**) to gain market entry. You balance this by selling other products or services at a higher price. This can be risky, as the danger is that everything becomes a loss leader.
- **Expected price** involves finding out what the customer expects to pay. If you are selling a high-quality product, do not underprice. Often the customer expects to pay more (for instance, if the product or service has a certain 'snob' value), and you could diminish the premium value of your product or service if you under-price, making it less attractive to the customer.
- **Differential pricing** is where you charge different segments of your market different prices for the same service; for example, you may decide to offer discounts to certain people, such as pensioners or the unemployed, or charge lower rates for quiet periods.
- **Lifetime pricing** is a technique you can adopt if your product price is higher than your competitors' and you want to encourage customers to look at the cost of ownership over the *lifetime* of the product. This might work well if, for example, your product is likely to last longer, thus reducing depreciation. Also, the cost of maintenance may be lower, reducing the annual cost.

WHAT TO AVOID
Relying on cost leadership

Do not simply aim to undercut your competitors; cost leadership is a difficult strategy for small businesses to pursue. Instead, aim to differentiate your product or service.

Not selling enough

Ensure that you are selling enough products at your chosen price to cover all of your costs and to generate a profit. Keep a careful eye on your sales and if you are not selling enough at your chosen price, then you need to take remedial action.

Treating price as a simple calculation

It's best to regard price as part of the marketing mix, rather than a straight financial calculation. You need to consider all the parts of the equation carefully. Research the market thoroughly to make sure that you are familiar with your competitors' pricing strategies and your customers' needs.

RECOMMENDED LINK
Professional Pricing Society:
www.pricingsociety.com

SEE ALSO
Budgeting (p. 499)
Pricing (p. 536)
Understanding the Role of Price (p. 157)

Creating a Balance Sheet

WHAT IT MEASURES
The financial standing, or even the net worth or owners' equity, of a company at a given point in time, typically at the end of a calendar or fiscal year.

WHY IT IS IMPORTANT
The balance sheet shows what is owned (assets), what is owed (liabilities), and what is left (owners' equity). It provides a concise snapshot of a company's financial position.

HOW IT WORKS IN PRACTICE
The format of a company's balance sheet is strictly defined by the 1985 Companies Act. Essentially, assets must be in balance with liabilities and shareholders' equity. In other words, assets must equal liabilities and owners' equity.

Assets include cash in hand and cash anticipated (receivables), inventories of supplies and materials, properties, facilities, equipment, and whatever else the company uses to conduct business. Assets also need to reflect depreciation in the value of equipment such as machinery that has a limited expected useful life.

Liabilities include pending payments to suppliers and creditors, outstanding current and long-term debts, taxes, interest payments, and other unpaid expenses that the company has incurred.

Subtracting the value of aggregate liabilities from the value of aggregate assets reveals the value of owners' equity. Ideally, it should be positive. Owners' equity consists of capital invested by owners over the years, and profits (net income) or internally generated capital, which is referred to as 'retained earnings'; these are funds to be used in future operations.

As an example:

ASSETS	
Current:	**£**
Cash	8,200
Securities	5,000
Receivables	4,500
Inventory & supplies	6,300
Fixed:	
Land	10,000
Structures	90,000
Equipment (less depreciation)	5,000
Intangibles/other	
TOTAL ASSETS	129,000

LIABILITIES	
	£
Payables	7,000
Taxes	4,000
Misc.	3,000
Bonds & notes	25,000
TOTAL LIABILITIES	39,000
SHAREHOLDERS' EQUITY (stock, par value shares outstanding)	80,000
RETAINED EARNINGS	10,000
TOTAL LIABILITIES AND SHAREHOLDERS' EQUITY	129,000

TRICKS OF THE TRADE

- The balance sheet does not show a company's market worth, nor important intangibles such as the knowledge and talents of individual people, nor other vital business factors such as customers or market share.
- The balance sheet does not express the true value of some fixed assets. A six-year-old manufacturing plant, for example, is listed at its original cost, even though the price of replacing it could be much higher or substantially lower (because of new technology that might be less expensive or vastly more efficient).
- The balance sheet is not an indicator of past or future performance or trends that affect performance. It needs to be studied along with two other key reports: the income statement and the cash-flow statement. A published balance sheet needs to include prior period comparatives.

RECOMMENDED LINK

Conetic.com:
www.conetic.com

SEE ALSO

Accounting (p. 494)

Reading a Balance Sheet

GETTING STARTED
A balance sheet will tell us something about the financial strength of a business on the day that the balance sheet is drawn up. That situation changes constantly, so you could say it is more like a snapshot than a film. Although the method of producing a balance sheet is standardised, there can be a certain element of subjectivity in interpreting it. Different elements of the balance sheet can tell you different things about the how the business is doing.

This actionlist gives an overview of a balance sheet and looks at a brief selection of the more interesting figures that help with interpretation. It's important to remember that a lot of these figures do not tell you that much in isolation; it is in trend analysis or comparisons between businesses that they talk more lucidly.

FAQS
What is a balance sheet?
A balance sheet is an accountant's view, the book value of the assets and liabilities of a business at a specific date and on that date alone. The term 'balance' means exactly what it says—that those assets and liabilities will be equal. In showing how the balance lies, the balance sheet gives us an idea of the financial health of the business.

What does a balance sheet not do?
A balance sheet is not designed to represent market value of the business. For example, property in the balance sheet may be worth a lot more than its book value. Plant and machinery is shown at cost less depreciation, but that may well be different from market value. Stock may turn out to be worth less than its balance sheet value, and so on.

Also there may be hidden assets, such as goodwill or valuable brands, that do not appear on the balance sheet at all. These would all enhance the value of the business in a sale situation, yet are invisible on a normal balance sheet.

MAKING IT HAPPEN
Here is a very simple company balance sheet:

		£
Fixed assets		1,000
Current assets	700	
Less current liabilities	400	
Net current assets		300
		1,300
Less long-term loans	200	
Net assets		1,100
Profit and loss account		500
Share capital		600
Shareholders' funds		1,100

Define the individual elements
- *Fixed assets*—items that are not traded as part of a company's normal activities but enable it to function, such as property, machinery or vehicles. These are tangible assets (meaning you can kick them). This heading can also include intangible assets (you cannot kick them). A common example is 'goodwill', which can arise upon the acquisition of one business by another.
- *Current assets*—items that form the trading cycle of the business. The most common examples are stock, debtors, and positive bank balances.
- *Current liabilities*—also items that form the trading cycle of the business but represent short-term amounts owed to others. Examples will be trade creditors, taxes, and bank overdrafts—broadly, any amount due for payment within the next 12 months from the date of the balance sheet.

- *Net current assets*—not a new figure, but simply the difference between current assets and current liabilities, often shown because it may be a useful piece of information.
- *Long-term loans*—debt that is repayable more than one year from the date of the balance sheet.
- *Net assets*—also not a new figure, but the sum of fixed assets plus net current assets less long-term loans. In other words, all of the company assets shown in its books, minus all of its liabilities.
- *Profit and loss account*—the total of all the accumulated profits and losses from all the accounting periods since the business started. It increases or decreases each year by the net profit or loss in that period, calculated after providing for all costs including tax and dividends to shareholders.
- *Share capital*—the number of shares issued, multiplied by their nominal value. The latter is the theoretical figure at which the shares were originally issued and has nothing to do with their market value.
- *Shareholders' funds*—not a new figure, but the sum of the profit and loss account plus the share capital. It represents the total interest of the shareholders in the company.

Learn to interpret them

Note that balance sheets differ between one industry and another in the sense of the range and type of assets and liabilities that exist. For example, a retailer will have little in the way of trade debtors because it sells for cash, or a manufacturer is likely to have a far larger investment in plant than a service business like an advertising agency. So the interpretation must be seen in the light of the actual trade of the business.

Reading a balance sheet can be quite subjective—accountancy is an art, not a science and, although the method of producing a balance sheet is standardised, there may be some items in it that are subjective rather than factual. The way people interpret some of the figures will also vary, depending what they wish to achieve and whether they see certain things as being good or bad.

Look first at the net assets/shareholders' funds

Positive or negative? Our example, being a healthy business, has net assets of a positive £1,100. Positive is good. If there were 600 shares in issue, it would mean that the net assets per share were £1.83.

If it had negative assets (same thing as net liabilities), this might mean that the business is heading for difficulty unless it is being supported by some party such as a parent company, bank, or other investor. When reading a balance sheet with negative assets, consider where the support will be coming from.

Then examine net current assets

Positive or negative? Again, our example has net current assets of a positive £300. This means that, theoretically, it should not have any trouble settling short-term liabilities because it has more than enough current assets to do so. Negative net current assets suggest that there possibly could be a problem in settling short-term liabilities.

You can also look at NCA as a ratio of current assets/current liabilities. Here, a figure over one is equivalent to the NCA having a positive absolute figure. The ratio version is more useful in analysing trends of balance sheets over successive periods or comparing two businesses.

A cut-down version of looking at NCA considers only (debtors + cash)/(creditors), thus excluding stock. The reasoning here is that this looks at the most liquid of the net current asset constituents, and again a figure over one is the most desirable. This is also a ratio that is more meaningful in trends or comparisons.

Understand the significance of trade debtor payments . . .

Within current assets, we have trade debtors. It can be useful to consider how many days' worth of sales are tied up in debtors—given by (debtors × 365)/annual sales. This provides an idea of how long the company is waiting to get paid. Too long, and it might be something requiring investigation. However, this figure can be misleading, where sales do not take place evenly throughout the year. A construction company might be an example of such a business: one big debtor incurred near the year end would skew the ratio.

...and trade creditor payments

Similar to the above, this looks at (trade creditors × 365)/annual purchases, indicating how long the company is taking in general to pay its suppliers. This is not so easy to calculate because the purchases for this purpose include not only goods for resale but all the overheads as well.

Recognise what debt means

Important to most businesses, this figure is the total of long and short-term loans. Too much debt might indicate that the company would have trouble, in a downturn, in paying the interest. It's difficult to give an optimum level of debt because there are so many different situations, depending on a huge range of circumstances.

Often, instead of an absolute figure, debt is expressed as a percentage of shareholders' funds and known as 'gearing' or 'leverage'. In a public company, gearing of 100% might be considered pretty high, whereas debt of under 30% may be seen as on the low side.

WHAT TO AVOID
Believing that balance sheet figures represent market value

Don't assume that a balance sheet is a valuation of the business. Its primary purpose is that it forms part of the range of accounting reports used for measuring business performance—along with the other common financial reports like profit and loss accounts and cash-flow statements. Management, shareholders, and others such as banks will use the entire range to assess the health of the business.

Forgetting that the balance sheet is valid only for the date at which it is produced

A short while after a balance sheet is produced, things could be quite different. In practice there frequently may not be any radical changes between the date of the balance sheet and the date when it is being read, but it is entirely possible that something could have happened to the business that would not show. For example, a major debtor could have defaulted unexpectedly. So remember that balance sheet figures are valid only as at the date shown, and are not a permanent picture of the business.

Confusion over whether in fact all assets and liabilities are shown in the balance sheet

Some businesses may have hidden assets, as suggested above. This could be the value of certain brands or trademarks, for example, for which money may never have been paid. Yet these could be worth a great deal. Conversely, there may be some substantial legal action pending which could cost the company a lot, yet is not shown fully in the balance sheet.

SEE ALSO
Accounting (p. 494)
Reading a Cash-flow Statement (p. 173)

Creating a Profit and Loss Account

WHAT IT MEASURES

A company's sales revenues and expenses over a period, providing a calculation of profits or losses during that time.

WHY IT IS IMPORTANT

Reading a P&L is the easiest way to tell if a business has made a profit or a loss during a given month or year. The most important figure it contains is net profit: what is left over after revenues are used to pay expenses and taxes.

Companies typically issue P&L reports monthly. It is customary for the reports to include year-to-date figures, as well as corresponding year-earlier figures to allow for comparisons and analysis.

HOW IT WORKS IN PRACTICE

A P&L adheres to a simple rule of thumb: 'revenue minus cost equals profit'.

There are two P&L formats, multiple-step and single-step. Both follow a standard set of rules known as Generally Accepted Accounting Principles (GAAP). These rules generally adhere to requirements established by governments to track receipts, expenses, and profits for tax purposes. They also allow the financial reports of two different companies to be compared.

The multiple-step format is much more common, because it includes a larger number of details and is thus more useful. It deducts costs from revenues in a series of steps, allowing for closer analysis. Revenues appear first, then expenses, each in as much detail as management desires. Sales may be broken down by product line or location, while expenses such as salaries may be broken down into base salaries and commissions.

Expenses are then subtracted from revenues to show profit (or loss). See the next page for a basic multiple-step P&L layout.

P&Ls of public companies may also report income on the basis of earnings per share. For example, if the company issuing this statement had 12,000 shares outstanding, earnings per share would be £5.12; that is, £61,440 divided by 12,000 shares.

TRICKS OF THE TRADE

- A P&L does not show how a business earned or spent its money.
- One month's P&L can be misleading, especially if a business generates a majority of its receipts in particular months. A retail establishment, for example, usually generates a large percentage of its sales in the final three months of the year, while a consulting service might generate the lion's share of its revenues in as few as two months, and no revenues at all in some other months.
- Invariably, figures for both revenues and expenses reflect the judgements of the companies reporting them. Accounting methods can be quite arbitrary when it comes to such factors as depreciation expenses.

RECOMMENDED LINK

Biz/ed:
www.bized.ac.uk

SEE ALSO

Accounting (p. 494)

MULTIPLE-STEP PROFIT & LOSS ACCOUNT (£)

NET SALES			750,000
Less: cost of goods sold			450,000
Gross profit			300,000
LESS: OPERATING EXPENSES			
Selling expenses			
Salaries & commissions	54,000		
Advertising	37,500		
Delivery/transportation	12,000		
Depreciation/store equipment	7,500		
Other selling expenses	5,000		
Total selling expenses		116,000	
General & administrative expenses			
Administrative/office salaries	74,000		
Utilities	2,500		
Depreciation/structure	2,400		
Misc. other expenses	3,100		
Total general & admin expenses		82,000	
Total operating expenses			198,000
OPERATING INCOME			102,000
LESS (ADD): NON-OPERATING ITEMS			
Interest expenses	11,000		
Interest income earned	(2,800)		8,200
Income before taxes			93,800
Income taxes			32,360
Net Income			**61,440**

Reading a Profit and Loss Account

GETTING STARTED
A profit and loss account is a statement of the income and expenditure of a business over the period stated, drawn up in order to ascertain how much profit the business made. Put simply, the difference between the income from sales and the associated expenditure is the profit or loss for the period. 'Income' and 'expenditure' here mean only those amounts directly attributable to earning the profit and thus would exclude capital expenditure, for example.

Importantly, the figures are adjusted to match the income and expenses to the time period in which they were incurred—not necessarily the same as that in which the cash changed hands.

FAQS
What is a profit and loss account?
A profit and loss account is an accountant's view of the figures that show how much profit or loss a business has made over a period. To do this, it is necessary to allocate the various elements of income and expenditure to the time period concerned, not on the basis of when cash was received or spent, but on when the income was earned or the liability to pay a supplier and employees was incurred. While capital expenditures are excluded, depreciation of property and equipment is included as a non-cash expense.

Thus if you sell goods on credit, you will be paid later but the sale takes place upon the contract to sell them. Equally if you buy goods and services on credit, the purchase takes place when you contract to buy them, not when you when you actually settle the invoice.

What does a profit and loss account not show?
Most importantly, a P&L account is not an explanation of the cash coming into and going out of a business.

MAKING IT HAPPEN

Here is a simple example of a profit and loss account for a particular year:

Sales		1,000
Opening stock	100	
Purchases	520	
	620	
Closing stock	80	
Cost of sales		540
Gross profit		460
Wages	120	
Other overheads	230	
		350
Net profit before tax		110
Tax		22
Net profit after tax		88
Dividends		40
Retained profit		48
Retained profit brought forward		150
Retained profit carried forward		198

Note that the presence of stock and purchases indicates that the business is trading or manufacturing goods of some kind, rather than selling services.

Defining the individual elements

- *Sales*—the invoiced value of the sales in the period.
- *Stock*—the value of the actual physical stock held by the business at the opening and closing of the period. It is always valued at cost, or realisable value if that is lower, never at selling price.
- *Purchases and other direct costs*—the goods or raw materials purchased by the business for resale—not capital items used in the business, only items used as part of the direct cost of its sales. In other words, those costs which vary directly with sales, as distinct from overheads (like rent) which do not.

Where a business holds stock, the purchases figure has to be adjusted for the opening and closing values in order to reach the right income and expenditure amounts for that period only. Goods for resale bought in the period may not have been used purely for that period but may be lying in stock at the end of it, ready for sale in the next. Similarly, goods used for resale in this period will consist partly of items already held in stock at the beginning of it. So take the amounts purchased, add the opening stock and deduct the closing stock. The resulting adjusted purchase figure is known as 'cost of sales'.

In some businesses there may be other direct costs apart from purchases included in cost of sales. For example, a manufacturer may include some wages if they are of a direct nature (wages of employees directly involved in the manufacturing process, as distinct from office staff, say). Or a building contractor would include plant hire in direct costs, as well as purchases of materials.

- *Gross profit*—the difference between sales and cost of sales. This is an important figure as it measures how much was actually made directly from whatever the business is selling, before it starts to pay for overheads.

The figure is often expressed as a percentage

ratio, when it is known as the 'gross profit margin'. In our example the GPM is 460:1,000—or 46%. Ratios are really only useful as comparison tools, either with different periods of the same business or with other businesses.

- *Overheads*—the expenses of the business which do not vary directly with sales. They include a wide range of items such as rent, most wages, advertising, phones, interest paid on loans, audit fees, and so on.
- *Net profit before tax*—the result of deducting total overheads from gross profit. This is what the business has made before tax is paid on that profit.
- *Tax (or corporation tax)*—this will not actually have been paid in the year concerned, but is shown because it is due on the profit for that period. Even then the figure shown may not be the actual amount due, for various reasons such as possible overpayments from previous years. Tax can be a very complex matter, being based upon a set of changeable rules.
- *Net profit after tax*—the result after deducting the tax liability—the so-called bottom line. This is the amount that the company can do with as it wishes, possibly paying a dividend out of part of it and retaining the rest. It is the company's reward for actually being in business in the first place.
- *Dividends*—a payment to the shareholders as a reward for their investment in the company. Most publicly listed companies of any size pay dividends to shareholders. Private companies may also do so, but this may be more for tax reasons. The dividend in the example shown is paid out of the net profit after tax, but legally it is not permitted to exceed the total available profit. That total available profit is comprised of both the current year's net profit after tax and the retained profit brought forward from previous years.
- *Retained profit*—the amount kept by the company after paying dividends to shareholders. If there is no dividend, then it is equal to the net profit after tax.
- *Retained profit brought forward*—the total accumulated retained profits for all earlier years of the company's existence.

- *Retained profit carried forward*—the above figure brought forward, plus the current year's retained profit. This new total will form the profit brought forward in the next accounting period.

How to interpret the figures

A lot of accounting analysis is valid only when comparing the figures, usually with similar figures for earlier periods, projected future figures, or other companies in the same business.

On its own a P&L account tells you only a limited story, though there are some standalone facts that can be derived from it. What our example does show, even in isolation, is that this business was successful in the period concerned. It made a profit, not a loss, and was able to pay dividends to shareholders out of that profit. Clearly a pretty crucial piece of information.

However, it is in comparisons that such figures start to have real meaning.

The example figures reveal that the gross profit margin was 46%, an important statistic in measuring business performance. The net profit margin before tax was 110:1,000, or 11%. You could take the margin idea further and calculate the net profit after tax ratio to sales as 88:1,000, being 8.8%. Or you could calculate the ratio of any expense to sales. In our example, the wages:sales ratio is 120:1,000, or 12%.

If you then looked at similar margin figures for the preceding accounting period, you would learn something about this business. Say the gross margin was 45% last year compared with 46% this year—there has been some improvement in the profit made before deducting overheads. But then suppose that the net profit margin of 8.8% this year was 9.8% last year. This would tell you that, despite improvement in profit at the gross level, the overheads have increased disproportionately. You could then check on the ratio of each of the overheads to sales to see where this arose and find out why.

Advertising spending could have shot up, for example, or perhaps the company moved to new premises incurring a higher rent. Maybe something could be tightened up.

Another commonly used ratio

Another ratio often used in business analysis is return on capital employed. Here we combine the profit and loss account with the balance sheet by dividing the net profit (either before or after tax as required) by shareholders' funds. This tells you how much the company is making proportionate to money invested in it by the shareholders—a similar idea to how much you might get in interest on a bank deposit account. It's a useful way of comparing different companies in a particular industry, where the more efficient ones are likely to derive a higher return on capital employed.

WHAT TO AVOID
Assuming that the bottom line represents cash profit from trading

It does not! There are a few examples where this is the case: a simple cash trader might buy something for one price, then sell it for more; his profit then equals the increase in cash. But a business that buys and sells on credit, spends money on items that are held for the longer term such as property or machinery, has tax to pay at a later date, and so on, will make a profit that is not represented by a mere increase in cash balances held. Indeed, the cash balance could quite easily decrease during a period when a profit was made.

RECOMMENDED LINK
The Motley Fool UK:
www.fool.co.uk

SEE ALSO
Accounting (p. 494)
Reading a Cash-flow Statement (p. 173)

Reading a Cash-flow Statement

GETTING STARTED
In their annual report, most public companies must publish a cash-flow statement—together with the profit and loss account and a balance sheet. As the name suggests, the purpose of a cash-flow statement is to explain the movement in cash balances or bank overdrafts held by the business from one accounting period to the next.

The balance sheet shows the assets and liabilities at the end of the period, with comparative figures for the start of it. The profit and loss account shows how much profit was generated by the business in the period. The cash-flow statement is the third part of the financial picture of the business over the period.

FAQS
What is a cash-flow statement?
Over an accounting period, the money held by a business at the bank (or its overdrafts) will have changed. The purpose of the cash-flow statement is to show the reasons for this change. If you look at the actionlist on profit and loss (**Reading a Profit and Loss Account (p. 170)**), one of the common mistakes illustrated was the erroneous belief that the profit was equal to the cash generated by a business. It is not, but the cash-flow statement is the link between profit and cash balance movements. It takes you down the path from profit to cash. The figures are derived from those published in the annual accounts, and notes will explain how this derivation is arrived at.

What does a cash-flow statement not show?
In the same way that a profit and loss account does not show the cash made by the business, a cash-flow statement does not show the profit. It is entirely possible for a loss-making business to show an increase in cash, and the other way round too.

MAKING IT HAPPEN
Here is a simple example of a cash-flow statement for a particular year:

		£
Net cash inflow from operating activities		7,020
Returns on investments and finance costs		
Interest paid	820	
Less interest received	90	
Net cash outflow from finance costs		(730)
Taxation		(1,060)
Capital expenditure		
Sale of fixed assets	760	
Less purchase of fixed assets	4,420	
Net cash outflow from capital expenditure		(3,660)
Dividends paid		(1,530)
Net cash inflow before financing		40
Financing		
New loans	1,000	
Loan repayments	(300)	
Finance lease repayments	(100)	
Net cash inflow from financing		600
Increase in cash		640

Define the individual elements

- *Net cash inflow from operating activities*—broadly this is the profit of the business, before depreciation plus the change in debtor and creditor balances. There may also be other items included here. In the statutory annual accounts of companies, there will be an explanation to show how this net cash inflow figure is derived from the profit and loss account and balance sheet. Depreciation is excluded because it does not represent a cash cost.

Debtor and creditor balance changes are included here because they represent an inflow or outflow of cash to the business. Thus if customers owe you less or more at the end of a period than at the beginning of it, it follows that there must have been cash flowing in or out of the business as a result. A reduction in debtors means that cash has come in to the business, and the reverse for an increase in debtors. The same applies to the creditor balances of suppliers. An increase here means a cash inflow, with a decrease denoting an outflow.

- *Returns on investments and finance costs*—these figures comprise interest received on cash balances, less interest paid on debt. There could be other forms of investment income here, such as dividends on shares owned.
- *Net cash outflow from finance costs*—this is not a new figure but the net result of the above items, identified as returns on investments. In our example the result is an outflow of cash. That is, the interest paid on debt exceeded the interest received on cash. It could in some circumstances be the other way round, where for example a business has substantial cash balances earning interest.
- *Taxation*—self explanatory, this is the outflow of cash arising from corporation tax paid by the business. It can on occasion be an inflow, where the company has obtained a repayment of corporation tax for some reason.
- *Capital expenditure*—this is cash expended on fixed assets bought for the business, less cash received from the sale of assets no longer required by the business.

- *Net cash outflow from capital expenditure*—this is not a new figure but the net result of the above items, identified as expenditure on new fixed assets less receipts from the sale of disposals of such items. In our example there is a large outflow, which generally would be the norm. It can happen sometimes though that a business realises more from the sale of fixed assets in a particular period than it expends on items acquired.
- *Dividends paid*—self-explanatory; this is the outflow of cash arising from paying dividends to shareholders.
- *Net cash inflow before financing*—this is not a new figure but a subtotal of the items above. In our example, the figure of £40 shown happens to be an inflow but it could just as easily have been an outflow. There is no typical figure here; it is just as common to see net inflows as outflows.

It is important to understand what this figure represents. It is the net cash result of running the business in the period concerned, after paying tax to the government and dividends to the shareholders. However, as its label indicates, it doesn't include any financing.

- *Financing*—this term includes the raising of new loans, the repayment of old ones and other methods of financing such as issuing new shares. In the example, the company borrowed £1,000 in new loans, which creates a cash inflow of that sum, and repaid £300 on old debt plus a further £100 on equipment leases (which are another form of finance), making a net inflow on finance of £400.
- *Increase in cash* (the bottom line)—adding the net inflow of £600 from finance to the £40 generated by business operations gives us an overall net cash inflow of £640. This is the bottom line. It means that we have £640 more in the bank at the end of the accounting period than at the beginning of it.

Learn to interpret the figures

As suggested above, the cash-flow statement is the third section of the primary set of accounting documents used to explain and analyse businesses. It is a 'derived schedule', meaning that the figures are pulled from the profit and loss account and balance sheet statements, linking the two.

Its purpose is to analyse the reasons why the company's cash position changed over an accounting period. For example, a sharp increase in borrowings could have several explanations—such as a high level of capital expenditure, poor trading, an increase in the time taken by debtors to pay, and so on. The cash-flow statement will alert management to the reasons for this, in a way that may not be obvious merely from the profit and loss account and balance sheet alone.

The generally desirable situation is for the net position before financing to be positive. Even the best-run businesses will sometimes have an outflow in a period (for example in a year of high capital expenditure), but positive is usually good. This becomes more apparent when comparing the figures over a period of time. A repeated outflow of funds over several years is usually an indication of trouble. To cover this, the company must raise new finance and/or sell off assets which will tend to compound the problem, in the worst cases leading to failure.

Cash is critical to every business, so the management must understand where its cash is coming from and going to. The cash-flow statement gives us this information in an abbreviated form. You could argue

that the whole purpose of a business is to start with one sum of money and, by applying some sort of process to it, arrive at another and higher sum, continually repeating this cycle.

WHAT TO AVOID
Confusing 'cash' and 'profit'

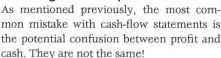

As mentioned previously, the most common mistake with cash-flow statements is the potential confusion between profit and cash. They are not the same!

Not understanding the terminology

It is clearly fundamental to an understanding of cash-flow statements that the reader is familiar with terms like 'debtors', 'creditors', 'dividends', and so on. But more than appreciating the meaning of the word 'debtors', it is quite easy to misunderstand the concept that, for example, an increase in debtors is a cash outflow, and equally that an increase in creditors represents an inflow of cash to the business.

RECOMMENDED LINK
The Motley Fool UK:
www.fool.co.uk

SEE ALSO
Accounting (p. 494)
Reading a Balance Sheet (p. 165)
**Reading a Profit and Loss Account
  (p. 170)**

Creating a Cash-flow Statement

WHAT IT MEASURES
Cash inflows and cash outflows over a specific period of time, typically a year.

WHY IT IS IMPORTANT
Cash flow is a key indicator of financial health, and it demonstrates to investors, creditors, and other core constituencies a company's ability to meet obligations, finance opportunities, and generally 'come up with the cash' as needs arise. Cash flow that is wildly inconsistent with, say, net income, often indicates operating or managerial problems.

HOW IT WORKS IN PRACTICE
In its basic form, a cash-flow statement will probably be familiar to anyone who has been a member of a club that collected and spent money. It reports funds on hand at the beginning of a given period, funds received, funds spent, and funds remaining at the end of the period.

That formula still applies to a business today, even if creating a cash-flow document is significantly more complex. Cash flows are divided into three categories: cash from operations; cash-investment activities; and cash-financing activities. Companies with holdings in foreign currencies use a fourth classification: effects of changes in currency rates on cash.

CRD Ltd
Statement of Cash flows
For year ended 31 December 20__

CASH FLOWS FROM OPERATIONS	£
Operating Profit	82,000
Adjustments to net earnings	
Depreciation	17,000
Accounts receivable	(20,000)
Accounts payable	12,000
Inventory	(8,000)
Other adjustments to earnings	4,000
Net cash flow from operations	**87,000**

CASH FLOWS FROM INVESTMENT ACTIVITIES	
Purchases of marketable securities	(58,000)
Receipts from sales of marketable securities	45,000
Loans made to borrowers	(16,000)
Collections on loans	11,000
Purchases of plant and land and property assets	(150,000)
Receipts from sales of plant and land and property assets	47,000
Net-cash flow from investment activities:	**(−121,000)**

CASH FLOWS FROM FINANCING ACTIVITIES	
Proceeds from short-term borrowings	51,000
Payments to settle short-term debts	(61,000)
Proceeds from issuing bonds payable	100,000
Proceeds from issuing capital stock	80,000
Dividends paid	(64,000)
Net cash flow from financing activities	**106,000**
Net change in cash during period	72,000
Cash and cash equivalents, beginning of year	27,000
Cash and cash equivalents, end of year	**99,000**

TRICKS OF THE TRADE
- A cash-flow statement does *not* measure net income, nor does it measure working capital.
- A cash-flow statement does not include outstanding accounts receivable, but it does include the preceding year's accounts receivable (assuming these were collected during the year for which the statement is prepared).

- Add to a cash inflow any amounts charged off for depreciation, depletion, and amortisation, since cash was actually spent.
- Cash equivalents are short-term, highly liquid investments, although precise definitions may vary slightly by country. These should be included when recalculating the movement of cash in the period.
- There are alternative ways to present cash flow from operations. Some texts, for example, omit earnings and adjustments, and list instead cash and interest received, cash and interest paid, and taxes received.

RECOMMENDED LINK

International Accounting Standards Consultancy:
www.iasc.co.uk

SEE ALSO

Accounting (p. 494)

Calculating Accounts Receivable Turnover

WHAT IT MEASURES
The number of times in each accounting period, typically a year, that a firm converts credit sales into cash.

WHY IT IS IMPORTANT
A high turnover figure is desirable, because it indicates that a company collects revenues effectively, and that its customers pay bills promptly. A high figure also suggests that a firm's credit and collection policies are sound.

In addition, the measurement is a reasonably good indicator of cash flow, and of overall operating efficiency.

HOW IT WORKS IN PRACTICE
The formula for accounts receivable turnover is straightforward. Simply divide the average amount of receivables into annual credit sales:

sales / receivables = receivables turnover

If, for example, a company's sales are £4.5 million and its average receivables are £375,000, its receivables turnover is:

4,500,000 / 375,000 = 12

TRICKS OF THE TRADE
- It is important to use the average amount of receivables over the period considered. Otherwise, receivables could be misleading for a company whose products are seasonal or are sold at irregular intervals.
- The measurement is also helpful to a company that is designing or revising credit terms.
- Accounts receivable turnover is among the measures that comprise asset utilisation ratios, also called activity ratios.

RECOMMENDED LINK
The Motley Fool UK:
www.fool.co.uk

SEE ALSO
Accounting (p. 494)
Calculating Asset Utilisation (p. 185)

Calculating Acid-test Ratio

WHAT IT MEASURES
How quickly a company's assets can be turned into cash, which is why assessment of a company's liquidity is also known as the quick ratio, or simply the acid ratio.

WHY IT IS IMPORTANT
Regardless of how this ratio is labelled, it is considered a highly reliable indicator of a company's financial strength and its ability to meet its short-term obligations. Because inventory can sometimes be difficult to liquidate, the acid-test ratio deducts inventory from current assets before they are compared with current liabilities—which is what distinguishes it from the current ratio.

Potential creditors like to use the acid-test ratio because it reveals how a company would fare if it had to pay off its bills under the worst possible conditions. Indeed, the assumption behind the acid-test ratio is that creditors are howling at the door demanding immediate payment, and that an enterprise has no time to sell off its inventory, or any of its stock.

HOW IT WORKS IN PRACTICE
The acid-test ratio's formula can be expressed in two ways, but both essentially reach the same conclusion. The most common expression is:

(current assets – inventory) / current liabilities = acid-test ratio

If, for example, current assets total £7,700, inventory amounts to £1,200, and current liabilities total £4,500, then:

(7,700 – 1,200) / 4,500 = 1.44

A variation of this formula ignores inventories altogether; distinguishes assets as cash, receivables, and short-term investments; then divides the sum of the three by the total current liabilities, or:

cash + accounts receivable + short-term investments / current liabilities = acid-test ratio

If, for example, cash totals £2,000, receivables total £3,000, short-term invest-

ments total £1,000, and liabilities total £4,800, then:

(2,000 + 3,000 + 1,000) / 4,800 = 1.25

There are two other ways to appraise liquidity, although neither is as commonly used: the cash ratio is the sum of cash and marketable securities divided by current liabilities; and net quick assets is determined by adding cash, accounts receivable, and marketable securities, then subtracting current liabilities from that sum.

TRICKS OF THE TRADE
- In general, the quick ratio should be 1:1 or better. It means a company has a unit's worth of easily convertible assets for each unit of its current liabilities. A high quick ratio usually reflects a sound, well-managed organisation in no danger of imminent collapse, even in the extreme and unlikely event that its sales ceased immediately. On the other hand, companies with ratios of less than 1 could not pay their current liabilities, and should be looked at with extreme care.
- While a ratio of 1:1 is generally acceptable to most creditors, acceptable quick ratios vary by industry, as do almost all financial ratios. No ratio, in fact, is especially meaningful without knowledge of the business from which it originates. For example, a declining quick ratio with a stable current ratio may indicate that a company has built up too much inventory; but it could also suggest that the company has greatly improved its collection system.
- Some experts regard the acid-test ratio as an extreme version of the working capital ratio because it uses only cash and equivalents, and excludes inventories. An acid-test ratio that is notably lower than the working capital ratio often means that inventories make up a large proportion of current assets. An example would be retail stores.
- Comparing quick ratios over an extended period of time can signal developing trends

in a company. While modest declines in the quick ratio do not automatically spell trouble, uncovering the reasons for changes can help find ways to nip potential problems in the bud.

- Like the current ratio, the quick ratio is a snapshot, and a company can manipulate its figures to make it look robust at a given point in time.
- Investors who suddenly become keenly interested in a firm's quick ratio may signal their anticipation of a downturn in the firm's business or in the general economy.

RECOMMENDED LINK
Business Owner's Toolkit:
www.toolkit.cch.com

SEE ALSO
Accounting (p. 494)

Calculating Amortisation

WHAT IT MEASURES

Amortisation is a method of recovering (deducting or writing off) the capital costs of intangible assets over a fixed period of time. Its calculation is virtually identical to the straight-line method of depreciation.

Amortisation also refers to the establishment of a schedule for repaying the principal and interest on a loan in equal amounts over a period of time. Because computers have made this a simple calculation, business references to amortisation tend to focus more on the term's first definition.

WHY IT IS IMPORTANT

Amortisation enables a company to identify its true costs, and thus its net income, more precisely. In the course of their business, most enterprises acquire intangible assets such as a patent for an invention, or a well-known brand or trademark. Since these assets can contribute to the revenue growth of the business, they can be—and are allowed to be—deducted against those future revenues over a period of years, provided the procedure conforms to accepted accounting practices.

For tax purposes, the distinction is not always made between amortisation and depreciation, yet amortisation remains a viable financial accounting concept in its own right.

HOW IT WORKS IN PRACTICE

Amortisation is computed using the straight-line method of depreciation: divide the initial cost of the intangible asset by the estimated useful life of that asset. For example, if it costs £10,000 to acquire a patent and it has an estimated useful life of 10 years, the amortised amount per year is £1,000.

$$£10,000 / 10 = £1,000 \text{ per year}$$

The amount of amortisation accumulated since the asset was acquired appears on the organisation's balance sheet as a deduction under the amortised asset.

While that formula is straightforward, amortisation can also incorporate a variety of non-cash charges to net earnings and/or asset values, such as depletion, write-offs, prepaid expenses, and deferred charges. Accordingly, there are many rules to regulate how these charges appear on financial statements. The rules are different in each country, and are occasionally changed, so it is necessary to stay abreast of them and rely on expert advice.

For financial reporting purposes, an intangible asset is amortised over a period of years. The amortisable life—'useful life'—of an intangible asset is the period over which it gives economic benefit. Several factors are considered when determining this useful life; for example, demand and competition, effects of obsolescence, legal or contractual limitations, renewal provisions, and service life expectations.

Intangibles that can be amortised can include:

Copyrights, based on the amount paid either to purchase them or to develop them internally, plus the costs incurred in producing the work (wages or materials, for example). At present, a copyright is granted to a corporation for 75 years, and to an individual for the life of the author plus 50 years. However, the estimated useful life of a copyright is usually far less than its legal life, and it is generally amortised over a fairly short period.

Cost of a franchise, including any fees paid to the franchiser, as well legal costs or expenses incurred in the acquisition. A franchise granted for a limited period should be amortised over its life. If the franchise has an indefinite life, it should be amortised over a reasonable period not to exceed 40 years.

Covenants not to compete: an agreement by the seller of a business not to engage in a competing business in a certain area for a specific period of time. The cost of the not-to-compete covenant should be amortised over the period covered by the covenant unless its estimated economic life is expected to be less.

Easement costs that grant a right of way may be amortised if there is a limited and specified life.

Organisation costs incurred when forming a corporation or a partnership, including legal fees, accounting services, incorporation fees, and other related services. Organisation costs are usually amortised over 60 months.

Patents, both those developed internally and those purchased. If developed internally, a patent's 'amortisable basis' includes legal fees incurred during the application process. Normally, a patent is amortised over its legal life, or over its remaining life if purchased. However, it should be amortised over its legal life or its economic life, whichever is the shorter.

Trade marks, brands, and trade names, which should be written off over a period not to exceed 40 years. However, since the value of these assets depends on the changing tastes of consumers, they are frequently amortised over a shorter period.

Other types of property that may be amortised include certain intangible drilling costs, circulation costs, mine development costs, pollution control facilities, and reforestation expenditures. They can even include intangibles such as the value of a market share or a market's composition: an example is the portion of an acquired business that is attributable to the existence of a given customer base.

TRICKS OF THE TRADE
- Certain intangibles cannot be amortised, but may be depreciated using a straight-line approach if they have a 'determinable' useful life. Because the rules are different in each country and are subject to change, it is essential to rely on specialist advice.
- Computer software may be amortised under certain conditions, depending on its purpose. Software that is amortised is generally given a 60-month life, but it may be amortised over a shorter period if it can clearly be established that it will be obsolete or no longer used within a shorter time.
- Under certain conditions, customer lists that were purchased may be amortised if it can be demonstrated that the list has a finite useful life, in that customers on the list are likely to be lost over a period of time.
- While leasehold improvements are depreciated for income tax purposes, they are amortised when it comes to financial reporting—either over the remaining term of the lease or their expected useful life, whichever is shorter.
- Annual payments incurred under a franchise agreement should be expensed when incurred.
- The Internet has many amortisation loan calculators that can automatically determine monthly payments figures and the total cost of a loan.

RECOMMENDED LINK
Best Software:
www.bestsoftware.com

SEE ALSO
Accounting (p. 494)
Calculating Depreciation (p. 193)

Calculating Annual Percentage Rate

WHAT IT MEASURES

Either the rate of interest that invested money earns in one year, or the cost of credit expressed as a yearly rate.

WHY IT IS IMPORTANT

It enables an investor or borrower to compare like with like. When evaluating investment alternatives, naturally it's important to know which one will pay the greatest return. By the same token, borrowers want to know which loan alternative offers the best terms. Determining the annual percentage rate provides a direct comparison.

HOW IT WORKS IN PRACTICE

To calculate the annual percentage rate (APR), apply this formula:

$$APR = [1 + i/m]m - 1.0$$

In the formula, **i** is the interest rate quoted, expressed as decimal, and **m** is the number of compounding periods per year. For example:

If a bank offers a 6% interest rate, paid quarterly, the APR would be calculated this way:

$$
\begin{aligned}
APR &= [1 + i/m]m - 1.0 \\
&= [1 + 0.06/4]4 - 1.0 \\
&= [1 + 0.015]\,4 - 1.0
\end{aligned}
$$

$$
\begin{aligned}
&= (1.015)\,4 - 1.0 \\
&= 1.0614 - 1.0 \\
&= 0.0614 \\
&= 6.14\% \ APR
\end{aligned}
$$

TRICKS OF THE TRADE

- As a rule of thumb, the annual percentage rate is slightly higher than the quoted rate.
- When using the formula, be sure to express the rate as a decimal, that is, 6% becomes 0.06.
- When expressed as the cost of credit, remember to include other costs of obtaining the credit in addition to interest, such as loan closing costs and financial fees.
- APR provides an excellent basis for comparing mortgage or other loan rates; in the United Kingdom, lenders are required to disclose it.
- When used in the context of investment, APR also can be called the 'annual percentage yield', or APY.

RECOMMENDED LINK

Investorguide.com:
www.investorguide.com

SEE ALSO
Accounting (p. 494)

Calculating Asset Turnover

WHAT IT MEASURES
The amount of sales generated for every pound's worth of assets over a given period.

WHY IT IS IMPORTANT
Asset turnover measures how well a company is leveraging its assets to produce revenue. A well-managed manufacturer, for example, will make its plant and equipment work hard for the business by minimising idle time for machines.

The higher the number the better—within reason. As a rule of thumb, companies with low profit margins tend to have high asset turnover; those with high profit margins have low asset turnover.

This ratio can also show how capital-intensive a business is. Some businesses (software developers, for example), can generate tremendous sales per pound of assets because their assets are modest. At the other end of the scale, electric utilities, heavy industry manufacturers, and even cable TV firms, need a huge asset base to generate sales.

Finally, asset turnover serves as a tool to keep managers conscious of the company's balance sheet along with its profit and loss account.

HOW IT WORKS IN PRACTICE
Asset turnover's basic formula is simply sales divided by assets:

sales revenue / total assets

Most experts recommend using average total assets in the formula. To determine this figure, add total assets at the beginning of the year to total assets at the end of the year and divide by two.

If, for instance, annual sales totalled £4.5 million, and total assets were £1.84 million at the beginning of the year and £1.78 million at the year end, the average total assets would be £1.81 million, and the asset turnover ratio would be:

4,500,000 / 1,810,000 = 2.49

A variation of the formula is:

sales revenue / fixed assets

If average fixed assets were £900,000, then asset turnover would be:

4,500,000 / 900,000 = 5

TRICKS OF THE TRADE
- This ratio is especially useful for growth companies to gauge whether or not they are growing revenue—for example, turnover—in healthy proportion to assets.
- Asset turnover numbers are useful for comparing competitors within industries. Like most ratios, they vary from industry to industry. As with most numbers, the most meaningful comparisons are made over extended periods of time.
- Too high a ratio may suggest overtrading: too much sales revenue with too little investment. Conversely, too low a ratio may suggest undertrading and an inefficient management of resources.
- A declining ratio may be indicative of a company that overinvested in plant, equipment, or other fixed assets, or is not using existing assets effectively.

RECOMMENDED LINK
Biz/ed:
www.bized.ac.uk

SEE ALSO
Accounting (p. 494)
Calculating Asset Utilisation (p. 185)

Calculating Asset Utilisation

WHAT IT MEASURES
How efficiently an organisation uses its resources and, in turn, the effectiveness of the organisation's managers.

WHY IT IS IMPORTANT
The success of any enterprise is tied to its ability to manage and leverage its assets. Hefty sales and profits can hide any number of inefficiencies. By examining several relationships between sales and assets, asset utilisation delivers a reasonably detailed picture of how well a company is being managed and led—certainly enough to call attention both to sources of trouble and to role-model operations.

Moreover, since all the figures used in this analysis are taken from a company's balance sheet or profit and loss statement, the ratios that result can be used to compare a company's performance with individual competitors and with industries as a whole.

Many companies also use this measure not only to evaluate their aggregate success but also to determine compensation for managers.

HOW IT WORKS IN PRACTICE
Asset utilisation relies on a family of asset utilisation ratios, also called activity ratios. The individual ratios in the family can vary, depending on the practitioner. They include measures that also stand alone, such as accounts receivable turnover and asset turnover. The most commonly used sets of asset utilisation ratios include these and the following measures.

Average collection period is also known as days sales outstanding. It links accounts receivable with daily sales and is expressed in number of days; the lower the number, the better the performance. Its formula is:

**accounts receivable / average daily sales
= average collection period**

For example, if accounts receivable are £280,000, and average daily sales are 7,000, then:

280,000 / 7,000 = 40

Inventory turnover compares the cost of goods sold (COGS) with inventory; for this measure, expressed in 'turns', the higher the number the better. Its formula is:

cost of goods sold / inventory

For example, if COGS is £2 million, and inventory at the end of the period is £500,000, then:

2,000,000 / 500,000 = 4

Some asset utilisation repertoires include ratios like debtor days, while others study the relationships listed below.

Depreciation / Assets measures the percentage of assets being depreciated to gauge how quickly product plants are ageing and assets are being consumed.

Depreciation / Sales measures the percentage of sales that is tied up covering the wear and tear of the physical plant.

In either instance, a high percentage could be cause for concern.

Income / Assets measures how well management uses its assets to generate net income. It is the same formula as return on assets.

Income / Plant measures how effectively a company uses its investment in fixed assets to generate net income.

In these two instances, high numbers are desirable.

Plant / Assets expresses the percentage of total assets that is tied up in land, buildings, and equipment.

By themselves, of course, the individual numbers are meaningless. Their value lies in how they compare with the corresponding numbers of competitors and industry averages. A company with an inventory turnover of 4 in an industry whose average is 7, for example, surely has room for improvement, because the comparison indicates it is generating fewer sales per unit of inventory, and is therefore less efficient than its rivals.

TRICKS OF THE TRADE

- Asset utilisation is particularly useful to companies considering expansion or capital investment: if production can be increased by improving the efficiency of existing resources, there is no need to spend the sums expansion would cost.
- Like all families of ratios, no single number or comparison is necessarily cause for alarm or rejoicing. Asset utilisation proves most beneficial over an extended period of time.
- Studying all measures at once can take up a lot of time, although computers have trimmed hours into seconds. Management teams in smaller organisations may conduct asset utilisation on a continuing basis, tracking particular measures on a monthly basis to stay abreast of operating trends.

RECOMMENDED LINK
Powerinvestor.com:
www.powerinvestor.com

SEE ALSO
Accounting (p. 494)
Calculating Accounts Receivable Turnover (p. 178)
Calculating Asset Turnover (p. 184)

Calculating Contribution Margin

WHAT IT MEASURES

The amounts that individual products or services ultimately contribute to net profit.

WHY IT IS IMPORTANT

Contribution margin helps a business decide how it should direct or redirect its resources.

When managers know the contribution margin—or margins, as is more often the case—they can make better decisions about adding or subtracting product lines, investing in existing products, pricing products or services (particularly in response to competitors' actions), structuring sales commissions and bonuses, where to direct marketing and advertising expenditures, and where to apply individual talents and expertise.

In short, contribution margin is a valuable decision-support tool.

HOW IT WORKS IN PRACTICE

Its calculation is straightforward:

sales price – variable cost = contribution margin

Or, for providers of services:

total revenue – total variable cost = contribution margin

For example, if the sales price of an item is £500 and variable cost is £350, the contribution margin is £150, or 30% of sales.

This means that 30 pence of every sales pound remain to contribute to fixed costs and to profit, after the costs directly related to the sales are subtracted.

Contribution margin is especially useful to a company comparing different products or services.

Obviously, Product C in the table below has the highest contribution percentage, even though Product A generates more total profit. The analysis suggests that the company might do well to aim to achieve a sales mix with a higher proportion of Product C. It further suggests that prices for

	Product A £	Product B £	Product C £
Sales	260	220	140
Variable costs	178	148	65
Contribution margin	82	72	75
Contribution margin (%)	31.5	32.7	53.6

Products A and B may be too low, or that their cost structures need attention. Notably, none of this information appears on a standard income statement.

Contribution margin also can be tracked over a long period of time, using data from several years of income statements. It can also be invaluable in calculating volume discounts for preferred customers, and break-even sales or volume levels.

TRICKS OF THE TRADE

- Contribution margin depends on accurately accounting for all variable costs, including shipping and delivery, or the indirect costs of services. Activity-based cost accounting systems aid this kind of analysis.
- Variable costs include all direct costs (usually labour and materials).
- Contribution margin analysis is only one tool to use. It will not show so-called loss leaders, for example. And it doesn't consider marketing factors such as existing penetration levels, opportunities, or mature markets being eroded by emerging markets.

RECOMMENDED LINK

Business Owner's Toolkit:
www.toolkit.cch.com

SEE ALSO

Accounting (p. 494)

Calculating Cost of Goods Sold (COGS)

WHAT IT MEASURES

For a retailer, COGS is the cost of buying and acquiring the goods that it sells to its customers. For a service firm, COGS is the cost of the employee services it supplies. For a manufacturer, COGS is the cost of buying the raw materials and manufacturing its finished products.

WHY IT IS IMPORTANT

Cost of goods sold may help a company determine the prices to charge for its products and services, and the volume of business that it needs to maintain in order to operate profitably.

For retailers especially, the cost of the merchandise sold is typically the largest expense, and thus an absolutely critical business factor. However, understanding COGS is an important success factor for any business because it can reveal opportunities to reduce costs and improve operations.

COGS is also a key figure on an income statement (also called the profit and loss account), and an important consideration in computing income taxes because of its close relationship to inventories, which taxation authorities treat as future income.

HOW IT WORKS IN PRACTICE

Essentially, COGS is equal to a company's opening stock of goods and services, plus the cost of goods bought and direct costs incurred during a particular period, minus the closing stock of goods and services.

A critical consideration is the accounting policy that a company adopts to calculate inventory values, especially if raw materials prices change during the year. This may happen often, particularly when inflation is high. Visit the website of the Institute of Chartered Accountants in England and Wales (www.icaew.co.uk) for information on stocks and work in progress.

COGS for a manufacturer will include a variety of items, such as raw materials and energy used in production, labour, benefits for production workers, the cost of raw materials in inventory, shipping fees, the cost of storing finished products, depreciation on production machinery used, and factory overhead expenses.

For a retail company such as Marks and Spencer, COGS is generally less complex: it is the total amount paid to suppliers for the products being sold on its shelves.

COGS is calculated as follows:

Stocks at beginning of period	£20,000
Purchases during period	+ £60,000
Cost of goods available for sale	= £80,000
Less inventory at period end	– £15,000
Cost of goods sold (COGS)	= £65,000

Because the counting of inventory is an exhaustive undertaking for retailers, doing it quarterly or monthly would be open to error. Accordingly, taxation authorities allow them to estimate cost of goods sold during the year.

Determining these estimates requires details of the gross profit margin (retailers typically use the preceding year's figure). This figure is then used to calculate the cost ratio.

Begin by assuming that net sales are 100%, then subtract the gross profit margin, say 40%, to produce a cost ratio of 60%: 100% – 40% = 60%. A monthly COGS calculation then looks like this:

Inventory at beginning of month	£10,000
Purchases during month	+ £25,000
Cost of goods available for sale	= £35,000
Less net sales during month	– £28,000
Cost ratio 100% – 40%	= 60%
Estimated cost of goods sold	= £16,800
	(£28,000
	× 60%)

There is one sample to review, because calculating COGS for manufacturers requires additional factors:

Inventory at beginning of year	£20,000
Purchases during year	+ £50,000
Cost of direct labour	+ £15,000
Materials and supplies	+ £12,000
Misc. costs	+ £3,000
Total product expenses	= £100,000
Less inventory at year end	– £15,000
Cost of goods sold (COGS)	= £85,000

TRICKS OF THE TRADE

- Anyone who wants to determine COGS must maintain inventories and know their value!
- Because goods returned affect inventory values and, in turn, cost of goods sold, returns of goods must be reflected in COGS calculations.
- Merchandising firms may use different inventory accounting systems, but the choice has no bearing on the actual costs incurred; it only affects allocation of costs.
- COGS should not include indirect costs like administration and marketing costs, or other activities that cannot be directly attributed to producing or acquiring the product.

RECOMMENDED LINK
Biz/ed:
www.bized.ac.uk

SEE ALSO
Accounting (p. 494)

Calculating Creditor and Debtor Days

WHAT THEY MEASURE

Creditor days is a measure of the number of days on average that a company requires to pay its creditors, while debtor days is a measure of the number of days on average that it takes a company to receive payment for what it sells. It is also called accounts receivable days.

WHY THEY ARE IMPORTANT

Creditor days is an indication of a company's creditworthiness in the eyes of its suppliers and creditors, since it shows how long they are willing to wait for payment. Within reason, the higher the number the better, because all companies want to conserve cash. At the same time, a company that is especially slow to pay its bills (100 or more days, for example) may be a company having trouble generating cash, or one trying to finance its operations with its suppliers' funds. Ultimately, companies whose creditor days soar have trouble obtaining supplies.

Debtor days is an indication of a company's efficiency in collecting monies owed. In this case, obviously, the lower the number the better. An especially high number is a telltale sign of inefficiency or worse. It may indicate bad debts, dubious sales figures, or a company being bullied by large customers out to improve their own cash position at another firm's expense. Customers whose credit terms are abused also risk higher borrowing costs and related charges.

Changes in both measures are easy to spot, and easy to understand.

HOW THEY WORK IN PRACTICE

To determine creditor days, divide the cumulative amount of unpaid suppliers' bills (also called trade creditors) by sales, then multiply by 365. So the formula is:

(trade creditors / sales) × 365 = creditor days

For example, if suppliers' bills total £800,000 and sales are £9,000,000, the calculation is:

(800,000 / 9,000,000) × 365 = 32.44 days

The company takes 32.44 days on average to pay its bills.

To determine debtor days, divide the cumulative amount of accounts receivable by sales, then multiply by 365. For example, if accounts receivable total £600,000 and sales are £9,000,000, the calculation is:

(600,000 / 9,000,000) × 365 = 24.33 days

The company takes 24.33 days on average to collect its debts.

TRICKS OF THE TRADE

- Cash businesses, including most retailers, should have a much lower debtor days figure than non-cash businesses, since they receive payment when they sell the goods. A typical target for non-cash businesses is 40–50 days.
- An abnormally high creditor days figure may not only suggest a cash crisis, but also the management's difficulty in maintaining revolving credit agreements.
- An increasing number of debtor days also suggests overly generous credit terms (to bolster sales) or problems with product quality.

RECOMMENDED LINK

Global Investor:
www.finance-glossary.com

SEE ALSO

Accounting (p. 494)

Calculating Current Ratio

WHAT IT MEASURES

A company's liquidity and its ability to meet its short-term debt obligations.

WHY IT IS IMPORTANT

By comparing a company's current assets with its current liabilities, the current ratio reflects its ability to pay its upcoming bills in the unlikely event of all creditors demanding payment at once. It has long been the measurement of choice among financial institutions and lenders.

HOW IT WORKS IN PRACTICE

The current ratio formula is simply:

current assets / current liabilities = current ratio

Current assets are the ones that a company can turn into cash within 12 months during the ordinary course of business. Current liabilities are bills due to be paid within the coming 12 months.

For example, if a company's current assets are £300,000 and its current liabilities are £200,000, its current ratio would be:

300,000 / 200,000 = 1.5

As a rule of thumb, the 1.5 figure means that a company should be able to get hold of £1.50 for every £1.00 it owes.

TRICKS OF THE TRADE

- The higher the ratio, the more liquid the company. Prospective lenders expect a positive current ratio, often of at least 1.5. However, too high a ratio is also cause for alarm, because it indicates declining receivables and/or inventory—signs that portend declining liquidity.
- A current ratio of less than 1 suggests

pressing liquidity problems, specifically an inability to generate sufficient cash to meet upcoming demands.

- Managements use current ratio as well as lenders; a low ratio, for example, may indicate the need to refinance a portion of short-term debt with long-term debt to improve a company's liquidity.
- Ratios vary by industry, however, and should be used accordingly. Some sectors, such as supermarket chains and restaurants, perform nicely with low ratios that would keep others awake at night.
- One shortcoming of the current ratio is that it does not differentiate assets, some of which may not be converted easily to cash. As a result, lenders also refer to the quick ratio.
- Another shortcoming of the current ratio is that it reflects conditions at a single point in time, such as when the balance sheet is prepared. It is possible to make this figure look good just for this occasion: lenders should not, therefore, appraise these conditions by the ratio alone.
- A constant current ratio and falling quick ratio signal trouble ahead, because this suggests that a company is amassing assets at the expense of receivables and cash.

RECOMMENDED LINK

Business Owner's Toolkit:
www.toolkit.cch.com

SEE ALSO

Accounting (p. 494)

Calculating Days Sales Outstanding

WHAT IT MEASURES

A company's average collection period, or the average number of days it takes a firm to convert its accounts receivable into cash. It is also called the collection ratio.

WHY IT IS IMPORTANT

Knowing how long it takes a company to turn accounts receivable into cash is an important financial indicator. It indicates the efficiency of the company's internal collection, suggests how well a company's customers are accepting its credit terms (net 30 days, for example), and is a figure that is routinely compared with industry averages.

Ideally, DSOs should be decreasing or constant. A low figure means the company collects its outstanding receivables quickly. Typically, DSO is reviewed quarterly or yearly (91 or 365 days).

DSO also helps to expose companies that try to disguise weak sales. Large increases in DSO suggest that a company is trying to force sales, either by accepting poor receivable terms, or selling products at discount to book more sales for a particular period. An improving DSO suggests that a company is striving to make its operations more efficient.

Any company with a significant change in its DSO merits examination in greater detail.

HOW IT WORKS IN PRACTICE

Regular DSO requires three figures: total accounts receivable, total credit sales for the period analysed, and the number of days in the period (annual, 365; six months, 182; quarter, 91). The formula is:

accounts receivable / total credit sales for the period × number of days in the period = days sales outstanding

For example: if total receivables are £4,500,000, total credit sales in a quarter are £9,000,000, and number of days is 91, then:

4,500,000 / 9,000,000 × 91 = 45.5

Thus, it takes an average 45.5 days to collect receivables.

TRICKS OF THE TRADE

- Companies use DSO information with an accounts receivable ageing report. This lists four categories of receivables: 0–30 days, 30–60 days, 60–90 days, and over 90 days. The report also shows percentage of total accounts receivable that each group represents, allowing for an analysis of delinquencies and potential bad debts.
- A rarely-used related calculation, best possible DSO, shows how long it takes a company to collect current receivables:

current receivables / total credit sales for the period × the number of days in the period = best possible DSO

So, current receivables of £3,000,000 and total credit sales of £9,000,000 in a 91-day period would result in a best possible DSO of 30.3 days (3,000,000 / 9,000,000 × 91).

- Only credit sales of merchandise should be used in calculating DSO; cash sales are excluded, as are sales of such items as fixtures and equipment, or land and property.
- Properly evaluating an acceptable DSO requires a standard for comparison. A traditional rule of thumb is that DSO should not exceed a third to a half of selling terms. For instance, if terms are 30 days, acceptable DSO would be 40 to 45 days.
- A single DSO is only a snapshot. A fuller picture would require at least quarterly calculations. Some companies review DSO monthly.
- DSO can vary widely by industry as well as company. For example, clothing wholesalers have to have the goods on retailers' shelves months before they will be sold and the retailer is able to cover invoices. However, a computer wholesaler with a lengthy DSO suggests trouble, since computers become obsolete quickly.

RECOMMENDED LINK

Dun & Bradstreet:
www.dnbcollections.com/kdso.htm

SEE ALSO

Accounting (p. 494)

Calculating Depreciation

GETTING STARTED

Depreciation is a basic expense of doing business, reducing a company's earnings while increasing its cash flow. It affects three key financial statements: balance sheet; cash flow; and income (or profit and loss). It is based on two key facts: the purchase price of the items or property in question, and their 'useful life'.

Depreciation values and practices are governed by national tax laws, which must be monitored continuously for any changes that are made. Accounting bodies, too, have developed standard practices and procedures for conducting depreciation.

Depreciating a single asset is not difficult: the challenge lies in depreciating the many assets possessed by even small companies, and is intensified by the impact that depreciation has on income and cash-flow statements, and on income tax returns. It is essential to depreciate with care and to rely on experts, ensuring that they fully understand the current government rules and regulations.

FAQS

What is depreciation?

It is an allocation of the cost of an asset over a period of time for accounting and tax purposes. Depreciation is charged against earnings, on the basis that the use of capital assets is a legitimate cost of doing business. Depreciation is also a non-cash expense that is added into net income to determine cash flow in a given accounting period.

What is straight-line depreciation?

One of the two principal depreciation methods, it is based on the assumption that an asset loses an equal amount of its value each year of its useful life. Straight-line depreciation deducts an equal amount from a company's earnings throughout the life of the asset.

What is accelerated depreciation?

The other principal method of depreciation is based on the assumption that an asset loses a larger amount of its value in the early years of its useful life. Also known as the 'declining-balance' method, it is used by accountants to reduce a company's tax bills as soon as possible, and is calculated on the basis of the same percentage rate each year of an asset's useful life. Accelerated depreciation also better reflects the economic value of the asset being depreciated, which tends to become increasingly less

efficient and more costly to maintain as it grows older.

What can be depreciated?

To qualify for depreciation, assets must:
- be used in the business
- be items that wear out, become obsolete, or lose value over time from natural causes or circumstances
- have a useful life beyond a single tax year

Examples include vehicles, machines and equipment, computers, office furnishings, and buildings; plus major additions or improvements to such assets. Some intangible assets also can be included under certain conditions.

What cannot be depreciated?

Land, personal assets, stock, leased or rented property, and a company's employees.

MAKING IT HAPPEN

In order to determine the annual depreciation cost of assets, it is necessary first to know the initial cost of those assets, how many years they will retain some value for the business, and what value, if any, they will have at the end of their useful life.

For example, a company buys a lorry to carry materials and finished goods. The vehicle loses value as soon as it is purchased, and then loses more with each year it is in service, until the cost of repairs exceeds its overall value. Measuring the loss in the value of the lorry is depreciation.

Straight-line depreciation is the most straightforward method, and is still quite common. It assumes that the net cost of an asset should be written off in equal amounts over its life. The formula used is:

**(original cost – scrap value) /
useful life (years)**

For example, if the lorry cost £30,000 and can be expected to serve the business for seven years, its original cost would be divided by its useful life:

(30,000 – 2,000) / 7 = 4,000 per year

The £4,000 becomes a depreciation expense that is reported on the company's year-end income statement under 'operation expenses'.

In theory, an asset should be depreciated over the actual number of years that it will be used, according to its actual drop in value each year. At the end of each year, all the depreciation claimed to date is subtracted from its cost in order to arrive at its 'book value', which would equal its market value. At the end of its useful business life, any un-depreciated portion would represent the salvage value for which it could be sold or scrapped.

For tax purposes, some accountants prefer to use accelerating depreciation to record larger amounts of depreciation in the asset's early years in order to reduce tax bills as soon as possible. In contrast to the straight-line method, the declining-balance method assumes that the asset depreciates more in its earlier years of use. The table below compares the depreciation amounts that would be available, under these two methods, for a £1,000 asset that is expected to be used for five years and then sold for £100 in scrap.

While the straight-line method results in the same deduction each year, the declining-balance method produces larger deductions in the first years and far smaller deductions in the later years. One result of this system is that, if the equipment is expected to be sold for a higher value at some point in the middle of its life, the declining-balance method can produce a greater taxable gain in that year because the book value of the asset will be relatively lower.

The depreciation method to be used for a particular asset is fixed at the time that the asset is first placed in service. Whatever rules or tables are in effect for that year must be followed as long as the asset is owned.

Depreciation laws and regulations change frequently over the years as a result of government policy changes, so a company owning property over a long period may have to use several different depreciation methods.

Straight-line Method

Year	Annual Depreciation	Year-end Book Value
1	£900 20% = £180	£1,000 – £180 = £820
2	£900 20% = £180	£820 – £180 = £640
3	£900 20% = £180	£640 – £180 = £460
4	£900 20% = £180	£460 – £180 = £280
5	£900 20% = £180	£280 – £180 = £100

Declining-balance Method

Year	Annual Depreciation	Year-end Book Value
1	£1,000 40% = £400	£1,000 – £400 = £600
2	£600 40% = £240	£600 – £240 = £360
3	£360 40% = £144	£360 – £144 = £216
4	£216 40% = £86.40	£216 – £86.40 = £129.60
5	£129.60 40% = £51.84	£129.60 – £51.84 = £77.76

TRICKS OF THE TRADE

- With rare exceptions, it is not possible to deduct in one year the entire cost of an asset if that asset has a useful life substantially beyond the tax year.
- To qualify for depreciation, an asset must be put into service. Simply purchasing it is not enough. There are rules that govern how much depreciation can be claimed on items put into service after a year has begun.
- It is common knowledge that if a company claims more depreciation than it is entitled to, it is liable for stiff penalties in a tax audit, just as failure to allow for depreciation causes an overestimation of income. What is not commonly known is that if a company does not claim all the depreciation deductions it is entitled to, it will be considered as having claimed them when taxable gains or losses are eventually calculated on the sale or disposal of the asset in question.
- While leased property cannot be depreciated, the cost of making permanent improvements to leased property can be (refurbishing a leased office, for example). There are many rules governing leased assets; they should be depreciated with care.
- Another common mistake is to continue depreciating property beyond the end of its recovery period. Cars are common examples of this.
- Conservative companies depreciate many assets as quickly as possible, despite the fact that this practice reduces reported net income. Knowledgeable investors watch carefully for such practices.

RECOMMENDED LINKS

Business Owner's Toolkit:
www.toolkit.cch.com
Encyclopedia.com:
www.encyclopedia.com

SEE ALSO

Accounting (p. 494)
Calculating Amortisation (p. 181)

Calculating EBITDA

WHAT IT MEASURES
A company's earnings from ongoing operations, before net income is calculated.

WHY IT IS IMPORTANT
EBITDA's champions contend it gives investors a sense of how much money a young or fast-growing company is generating before it pays interest on debt, tax collectors, and accounts for non-cash changes. If EBITDA grows over time, champions argue, investors gain at least a sense of long-term profitability and, in turn, the wisdom of their investment.

Business appraisers and investors may also study EBITDA to help gauge a company's fair market value, often as a prelude to its acquisition by another company. It is also frequently applied to companies that have been subject to leveraged buyouts—the strategy being that EBITDA will help cover loan payments needed to finance the transaction.

EBITDA, and EBIT, too, are claimed to be good indicators of cash flow from business operations, since they report earnings before debt payments, taxes, depreciation, and amortisation charges are considered. However, that claim is challenged by many—often rather intently.

HOW IT WORKS IN PRACTICE
EBITDA first appeared as leveraged buyouts soared in popularity during the 1980s. It has since become well-established as a financial-analysis measure of telecommunications, cable, and major media companies.

Its formula is quite simple. Revenues less the cost of goods sold, general and administrative expenses, and the deductions of items expressed by the acronym, or:

revenue – expenses (excluding tax and interest, depreciation, etc.) = EBITDA

or:

revenue – expenses (excluding tax and interest) = EBIT

This formula does not measure true cash flow. A communications company, for example, once reported £698 million in EBIT but just £324 million in cash from operations.

TRICKS OF THE TRADE
- A definition of EBITDA isn't as yet enforced by standards-making bodies, so companies can all but create their own. As a result, EBITDA can easily be manipulated by aggressive accounting policies, which may erode its reliability.
- Ignoring capital expenditures could be unrealistic and horribly misleading, because companies in capital-intensive sectors such as manufacturing and transportation must continually make major capital investments to remain competitive. High-technology is another sector that may be capital-intensive, at least initially.
- Critics warn that using EBITDA as a cash-flow indicator is a huge mistake, because EBITDA ignores too many factors that have an impact on true cash flow, such as working capital, debt payments, and other fixed expenses. Interest and taxes can and do cost a company cash, they point out, while debt holders have higher claims on a company's liquid assets than investors do.
- Critics further assail EBITDA as the barometer of choice of unprofitable firms, because it can present a more optimistic view of a company's future than it has a right to claim. *Forbes* magazine, for instance, once referred to EBIDTA as 'the device of choice to pep up earnings announcements'.
- Even so, EBITDA may be useful in terms of evaluating firms in the same industry with widely different capital structures, tax rates, and depreciation policies.

RECOMMENDED LINK
The Motley Fool UK:
www.fool.co.uk

SEE ALSO
Accounting (p. 494)

Calculating Economic Value Added

WHAT IT MEASURES
A company's financial performance, specifically whether it is earning more or less than the total cost of the capital supporting it.

WHY IT IS IMPORTANT
Economic Value Added measures true economic profit, or the amount by which the earnings of a project, an operation, or a company exceed (or fall short of) the total amount of capital that was originally invested by the company's owners.

If a company is earning more, it is adding value, and that is good. If it is earning less, the company is in fact devouring value, and that is bad, because the company's owners (shareholders, for example) would be better off investing their capital elsewhere.

The concept's champions declare that EVA forces managers to focus on true wealth creation and maximising shareholder investment. By definition, then, increasing EVA will increase a company's market value.

HOW IT WORKS IN PRACTICE
EVA is conceptually simple and easy to explain: from net operating profit, subtract an appropriate charge for the opportunity cost of all capital invested in an enterprise—the amount that could have been invested elsewhere. It is calculated using this formula:

net operating profit less applicable taxes – cost of capital = EVA

If a company is considering building a new plant, and its total weighted cost over ten years is £80 million, while the expected annual incremental return on the new operation is £10 million, or £100 million over ten years, then the plant's EVA would be positive, in this case £20 million:

£100 million – £80 million = £20 million

An alternative but more complex formula for EVA is:

(% return on invested capital – % cost of capital) original capital invested = EVA

TRICKS OF THE TRADE
- EVA is a measure of pound surplus value, not the percentage difference in returns.
- Purists define EVA as 'profit the way shareholders define it'. They further contend that if shareholders expect a 10% return on their investment, they 'make money' only when their share of after-tax operating profits exceeds 10% of equity capital.
- An objective of EVA is to determine which business units best utilise their assets to generate returns and maximise shareholder value; it can be used to assess a company, a business unit, a single plant, office, or even an assembly line. This same technique is equally helpful in evaluating new business opportunities.

RECOMMENDED LINK
Stern Stewart & Co:
www.sternstewart.com

SEE ALSO
Accounting (p. 494)

Calculating Elasticity

WHAT IT MEASURES
The percentage change of one variable caused by a percentage change in another variable.

WHY IT IS IMPORTANT
Elasticity is defined as 'the measure of the sensitivity of one variable to another'. In practical terms, elasticity indicates the degree to which consumers respond to changes in price. It is obviously important for companies to consider such relationships when contemplating changes in price, demand, and supply.

Demand elasticity measures how much the quantity demanded changes when the price of a product or service is increased or lowered. Will demand remain constant? If not, how much will demand change?

Supply elasticity measures the impact on supply when a price is changed. It is assumed that lowering prices will reduce supply, because demand will increase—but by how much?

HOW IT WORKS IN PRACTICE
The general formula for elasticity is:

**elasticity = % change in x /
% change in y**

In theory, x and y can be any variable. However, the most common application measures price and demand. If the price of a product is increased from £20 to £25, or 25%, and demand in turn falls from 6,000 to 3,000, elasticity would be calculated as:

−50% / 25% = −2

A value greater than 1 means that demand is strongly sensitive to price, while a value of less than 1 means that demand is not price-sensitive.

TRICKS OF THE TRADE
There are five cases of elasticity:
- E = 1, or *unit elasticity*. The proportional change in one variable is equal to the proportional change in another variable: if price rises by 5%, demand falls by 5%.
- E is greater than 1, or just *elastic*. The proportional change in x is greater than the proportional change in y: if price rises by 5%, demand falls by 3%.
- E = infinity, or *perfectly elastic*. This is a special case of elasticity: any change in y will effect no change in x. An example would be prices charged by a hospital's emergency room, where increases in price are unlikely to curb demand.
- E is less than 1, or just *inelastic*. The proportional change in x is less than the proportional change in y: if prices are increased by 3%, demand will fall by 30%.
- E = 0, or *perfectly inelastic*. This is another special case of elasticity: any change in y will have an infinite effect on x.

There are more complex formulae for determining a range of variables, or 'arc elasticity'.

Elasticity can be used to affirm two rules of thumb:
- demand becomes elastic if consumers have an alternative or adequate substitute for the product or service
- demand is more elastic if consumers have an incentive to save money

RECOMMENDED LINK
Investopedia.com:
www.investopedia.com

SEE ALSO
Accounting (p. 494)

Calculating Interest Cover

WHAT IT MEASURES
The amount of earnings available to make interest payments after all operating and non-operating income and expenses—except interest and income taxes—have been accounted for.

WHY IT IS IMPORTANT
Interest cover is regarded as a measure of a company's creditworthiness because it shows how much income there is to cover interest payments on outstanding debt. Banks and financial analysts also rely on this ratio as a rule of thumb to gauge the fundamental strength of a business.

HOW IT WORKS IN PRACTICE
Interest cover is expressed as a ratio, and reflects a company's ability to pay the interest obligations on its debt. It compares the funds available to pay interest—earnings before interest and taxes, or EBIT—with the interest expense. The basic formula is:

$$EBIT \ / \ interest \ expense \ = \\ interest \ coverage \ ratio$$

If interest expense for a year is £9 million, and the company's EBIT is £45 million, the interest coverage would be:

$$45 \ million \ / \ 9 \ million \ = \ 5{:}1$$

The higher the number, the stronger a company is likely to be. Conversely, a low number suggests that a company's fortunes are looking ominous. Variations of this basic formula also exist. For example, there is:

$$operating \ cash \ flow \ + \ interest \ + \\ taxes \ / \ interest \ = \\ cash\text{-}flow \ interest \ coverage \ ratio$$

This ratio indicates the firm's ability to use its cash flow to satisfy its fixed financing obligations. Finally, there is the fixed-charge coverage ratio, which compares EBIT with fixed charges:

$$EBIT \ + \ lease \ expenses \ / \ interest \ + \\ lease \ expense \ = \\ fixed \ charge \ coverage \ ratio$$

'Fixed charges' can be interpreted in many ways, however. It could mean, for example, the funds that a company is obliged to set aside to retire debt, or dividends on preferred stock.

TRICKS OF THE TRADE
- A ratio of less than 1 indicates that a company is having problems generating enough cash flow to pay its interest expenses, and that either a modest decline in operating profits or a sudden rise in borrowing costs could eliminate profitability entirely.
- Ideally, interest coverage should at least exceed 1.5; in some sectors, 2.0 or higher is desirable.
- Interest coverage is widely considered to be more meaningful than looking at total debt, because what really matters is what an enterprise must pay in a given period, not how much debt it has.
- As is often the case, it may be more meaningful to watch interest cover over several periods in order to detect long-term trends.
- Cash flow will sometimes be substituted for EBIT in the ratio, because EBIT includes not only cash but also accrued sales and other unrealised income.
- Interest cover also is called 'times interest earned'.

RECOMMENDED LINK
The Motley Fool UK:
www.fool.co.uk

SEE ALSO
Accounting (p. 494)

Calculating Marginal Cost

WHAT IT MEASURES
The additional cost of producing one more unit of product, or providing service to one more customer.

WHY IT IS IMPORTANT
Sometimes called incremental cost, marginal cost shows how much costs increase from making or serving one more, an essential factor when contemplating a production increase, or seeking to serve more customers.

If the price charged is greater than the marginal cost, then the revenue gain will be greater than the added cost. That, in turn, will increase profit, so the expansion in production or service makes economic sense and should proceed. Of course, the reverse is also true: if the price charged is less than the marginal cost, expansion should not go ahead.

HOW IT WORKS IN PRACTICE
The formula for marginal cost is:

   change in cost / change in quantity

If it costs a company £260,000 to produce 3,000 items, and £325,000 to produce 3,800 items, the change in cost would be:

   £325,000 – £260,000 = £65,000

The change in quantity would be:

   3,800 – 3,000 = 800

When the formula to calculate marginal cost is applied, the result is:

   £65,000 / 800 = £81.25

If the price of the item in question were £99.95, expansion should proceed.

TRICKS OF THE TRADE
- A marginal cost that is lower than the price shows that it is not always necessary to cut prices to sell more goods and boost profits.
- Using idle capacity to produce lower-margin items can still be beneficial, because these generate revenues that help cover fixed costs.
- Marginal cost studies can become quite complicated, because the basic formula does not always take into account variables that can affect cost and quantity. There are software programs available, many of which are industry-specific.
- At some point, marginal cost invariably begins to rise; typically, labour becomes less productive as a production run increases, while the time required also increases.
- Marginal cost alone may not justify expansion. It is best to determine also average costs, then chart the respective series of figures to find where marginal cost meets average cost, and thus determine optimum cost.
- Relying on marginal cost is not fail-safe; putting more product on a market can drive down prices and thus cut margins. Moreover, committing idle capacity to long-term production may tie up resources that could be directed to a new and more profitable opportunity.
- An important related principle is contribution: the cash gained (or lost) from selling an additional unit.

RECOMMENDED LINK
The Motley Fool UK:
www.fool.co.uk

SEE ALSO
Accounting (p. 494)

Calculating Payback Period

WHAT IT MEASURES
How long it will take to earn back the money invested in a project.

WHY IT IS IMPORTANT
The straight payback period method is the simplest way of determining the investment potential of a major project. Expressed in time, it tells how many months or years it will take to recover the original cash cost of the project—always a vital consideration, and especially so if you are evaluating several projects at once.

This evaluation becomes even more important if it includes an examination of what the present value of future revenues will be.

HOW IT WORKS IN PRACTICE
The straight payback period formula is:

cost of project / annual cash revenues = payback period

Thus, if a project cost £100,000 and was expected to generate £28,000 annually, the payback period would be:

100,000 / 28,000 = 3.57 years

If the revenues generated by the project are expected to vary from year to year, add the revenues expected for each succeeding year until you arrive at the total cost of the project.

For example, say the revenues expected to be generated by the £100,000 project are:

	Revenue	Total
Year 1	£19,000	£19,000
Year 2	£25,000	£44,000
Year 3	£30,000	£74,000
Year 4	£30,000	£104,000
Year 5	£30,000	£134,000

Thus, the project would be fully paid for in Year 4, since it is in that year the total revenue reaches the initial cost of £100,000.

The picture becomes complex when the time-value-of-money principle is introduced into the calculations. Some experts insist this is essential to determine the most accurate payback period. Accordingly, present-value tables or computers (now the norm) must be used, and the annual revenues have to be discounted by the applicable interest rate; 10% in this example. This produces very different results:

	Revenue	Present value	Total
Year 1	£19,000	£17,271	£17,271
Year 2	£25,000	£20,650	£37,921
Year 3	£30,000	£22,530	£60,451
Year 4	£30,000	£20,490	£80,941
Year 5	£30,000	£18,630	£99,571

This method shows that payback would not occur even after five years.

TRICKS OF THE TRADE
- Clearly, a main defect of the straight payback period method is that it ignores the time-value-of-money principle, which, in turn, can produce unrealistic expectations.
- It also ignores any benefits generated after the payback period, and thus a project that would return £1 million after, say, six years, might be ranked lower than a project with a three-year payback that returns only £100,000 thereafter.
- Under most analyses, projects with shorter payback periods rank higher than those with longer paybacks, even if the latter project higher returns. Longer paybacks can be affected by such factors as market changes, changes in interest rates, and economic shifts. Shorter cash paybacks also enable companies to recoup an investment sooner and put it to work elsewhere.
- Generally, a payback period of three years or less is desirable; if a project's payback period is less than a year, some contend it should be judged essential.

RECOMMENDED LINK
Business Owner's Toolkit:
www.toolkit.cch.com

Calculating Return on Assets

WHAT IT MEASURES

A company's profitability, expressed as a percentage of its total assets.

WHY IT IS IMPORTANT

Return on assets measures how effectively a company has used the total assets at its disposal to generate earnings. Because the ROA formula reflects total revenue, total cost, and assets deployed, the ratio itself reflects a management's ability to generate income during the course of a given period, usually a year.

Naturally, the higher the return the better the profit performance. ROA is a convenient way of comparing a company's performance with that of its competitors, although the items on which the comparison is based may not always be identical.

HOW IT WORKS IN PRACTICE

To calculate ROA, divide a company's net income by its total assets, then multiply by 100 to express the figure as a percentage:

net income / total assets × 100 = ROA

If net income is £30, and total assets are £420, the ROA is:

30 / 420 = 0.0714 × 100 = 7.14%

A variation of this formula can be used to calculate return on net assets (RONA):

net income / fixed assets + working capital = RONA

And, on occasion, the formula will separate after-tax interest expense from net income:

net income + interest expense / total assets = ROA

It is therefore important to understand what each component of the formula actually represents.

TRICKS OF THE TRADE

- Some experts recommend using the net income value at the end of the given period, and the assets value from beginning of the period or an average value taken over the complete period, rather than an end-of-the-period value; otherwise, the calculation will include assets that have accumulated during the year, which can be misleading.
- While a high ratio indicates a greater return, it must still be balanced against such factors as risk, sustainability, and reinvestment in the business through development costs. Some managements will sacrifice the long-term interests of investors in order to achieve an impressive ROA in the short term.
- A climbing return on assets usually indicates a climbing stock price, because it tells investors that a management is skilled at generating profits from the resources that a business owns.
- Acceptable ROAs vary by sector. In banking, for example, a ROA of 1% or better is a considered to be the standard benchmark of superior performance.
- ROA is an effective way of measuring the efficiency of manufacturers, but can be suspect when measuring service firms, or companies whose primary assets are people.
- Other variations of the ROA formula do exist.

RECOMMENDED LINK

MSN Money:
www.moneycentral.msn.com/investor

SEE ALSO

Accounting (p. 494)

Calculating Return on Investment

WHAT IT MEASURES
The overall profit or loss on an investment expressed as a percentage of the total amount invested or total funds appearing on a company's balance sheet.

WHY IT IS IMPORTANT
Like return on assets or return on equity, return on investment measures a company's profitability and its management's ability to generate profits from the funds investors have placed at its disposal.

One opinion holds that if a company's operations cannot generate net earnings at a rate that exceeds the cost of borrowing funds from financial markets, the future of that company is grim.

HOW IT WORKS IN PRACTICE
The most basic expression of ROI can be found by dividing a company's net profit (also called net earnings) by the total investment (total debt plus total equity), then multiplying by 100 to arrive at a percentage:

$$\text{net profit / total investment} \times 100 = \text{ROI}$$

If, say, net profit is £30 and total investment is £250, the ROI is:

$$30 / 250 = 0.12 \times 100 = 12\%$$

A more complex variation of ROI is an equation known as the Du Pont formula:

$$(\text{net profit after taxes / total assets}) = (\text{net profit after taxes / sales}) \times \text{sales / total assets}$$

If, for example, net profit after taxes is £30, total assets are £250, and sales are £500, then:

$$30 / 250 = 30 / 500 \times 500 / 250 = 12\% = 6\% 2 = 12\%$$

Champions of this formula, which was developed by the Du Pont Company in the 1920s, say that it helps reveal how a company has both deployed its assets and controlled its costs, and how it can achieve the same percentage return in different ways.

For shareholders, the variation of the basic ROI formula used by investors is:

$$\text{net income + (current value − original value) / original value} \times 100 = \text{ROI}$$

If, for example, somebody invests £5,000 in a company and a year later has earned £100 in dividends, while the value of the shares is £5,200, the return on investment would be:

$$100 + (5,200 − 5,000) / 5,000 \times 100$$
$$= (100 + 200) / 5,000 \times 100 =$$
$$300 / 5,000 = .06 \times 100 = 6\% \text{ ROI}$$

TRICKS OF THE TRADE
- Securities investors can use yet another ROI formula: net income divided by shares and preference share equity plus long-term debt.
- It is vital to understand exactly what a return on investment measures; for example, assets, equity, or sales. Without this understanding, comparisons may be misleading or suspect. A search for 'return on investment' on the web, for example, harvests everything from staff training to e-commerce to advertising and promotions!
- Be sure to establish whether the net profit figure used is before or after provision for taxes. This is important for making ROI comparisons accurate.

RECOMMENDED LINK
Investopedia.com:
www.investopedia.com

SEE ALSO
Accounting (p. 494)

Calculating Return on Sales

WHAT IT MEASURES

A company's operating profit or loss as a percentage of total sales for a given period, typically a year.

WHY IT IS IMPORTANT

ROS shows how efficiently management uses the sales pound, thus reflecting its ability to manage costs and overheads and operate efficiently. It also indicates a firm's ability to withstand adverse conditions such as falling prices, rising costs, or declining sales. The higher the figure, the better a company is able to endure price wars and falling prices.

Return on sales can be useful in assessing the annual performances of cyclical companies that may have no earnings during particular months, and of firms whose business requires a huge capital investment and thus incurs substantial amounts of depreciation.

HOW IT WORKS IN PRACTICE

The calculation is very basic:

operating profit / total sales × 100 = percentage return on sales

So, if a company earns £30 on sales of £400, its return on sales is:

30 / 400 = 0.075 × 100 = 7.5%

TRICKS OF THE TRADE

- While easy to grasp, return on sales has its limits, since it sheds no light on the overall cost of sales or the four factors that contribute to it: materials, labour, production overheads, and administrative and selling overheads.
- Some calculations use operating profit before subtracting interest and taxes; others use after-tax income. Either figure is acceptable as long as ROS comparisons are consistent. Obviously, using income before interest and taxes will produce a higher ratio.
- The ratio's operating profit figure may also include special allowances and extraordinary non-recurring items, which, in turn, can inflate the percentage and be misleading.
- The ratio varies widely by industry. The supermarket business, for example, is heavily dependent on volume and usually has a low return on sales.
- Return on sales remains of special importance to retail sales organisations, which can compare their respective ratios with those of competitors and industry norms.

RECOMMENDED LINK

Investopedia.com:
www.investopedia.com

SEE ALSO

Accounting (p. 494)

Calculating Working Capital Productivity

WHAT IT MEASURES
How effectively a company's management is using its working capital.

WHY IT IS IMPORTANT
It is obvious that capital not being put to work properly is being wasted, which is certainly not in investors' best interests.

As an expression of how effectively a company spends its available funds compared with sales or turnover, the working capital productivity figure helps establish a clear relationship between its financial performance and process improvement. The relationship is said to have been first observed by the US management consultant George Stalk while working in Japan.

A seldom-used reciprocal calculation, the working capital turnover or working capital to sales ratio, expresses the same relationship in a different way.

HOW IT WORKS IN PRACTICE
To calculate working capital productivity, first subtract current liabilities from current assets, which is the formula for working capital, then divide this figure into sales for the period.

sales / (current assets – current liabilities) = working capital productivity

If sales are £3,250, current assets are £900 and current liabilities are £650, then:

3250 / (900 – 650) = 3250 / 250 = 13

In this case, the higher the number the better. Sales growing faster than the resources required to generate them is a clear sign of efficiency and, by definition, productivity.

The working capital to sales ratio uses the same figures, but in reverse:

working capital / sales × 100% = working capital to sales ratio

Using the same figures in the example above, this ratio would be calculated:

250 / 3250 = 0.077 × 100% = 7.7%

For this ratio, obviously, the lower the number the better.

TRICKS OF THE TRADE
- By itself, a single ratio means little; a series of them, several quarters' worth, for example, indicates a trend, and means a great deal.
- Some experts recommend doing quarterly calculations and averaging them for a given year to arrive at the most reliable number.
- Either ratio also helps a management compare its performance with that of competitors.
- These ratios should also help motivate companies to improve processes, such as eliminating steps in the handling of materials and bill collection, and shortening product design times. Such improvements reduce costs and make working capital available for other tasks.

RECOMMENDED LINK
The Motley Fool UK:
www.fool.co.uk

SEE ALSO
Accounting (p. 494)

Defining Assets

WHAT THEY MEASURE

Collectively, the value of all the resources a company uses to conduct business and generate profits.

Examples of assets are cash, marketable securities, accounts and notes receivable, inventories of merchandise, buildings and property, machinery and office equipment, natural resources, and intangibles such as patents, legal claims and agreements, and negotiated rights.

WHY THEY ARE IMPORTANT

No business can continue for very long without knowing what assets it has at its disposal, and using them efficiently. Assets are a reflection of organisational strength, and are invariably evaluated by potential investors, banks and creditors, and other stakeholders.

Moreover, the value of assets is also a key figure used to calculate several financial ratios.

HOW THEY WORK IN PRACTICE

Assets are typically broken down into five different categories:

- *Current assets.* These include cash, cash equivalents, marketable securities, inventories, and prepaid expenses that are expected to be used within one year or a normal operating cycle. All cash items and inventories are reported at historical value. Securities are reported at market value.
- *Non-current assets, or long-term investments.* These are resources that are expected to be held for more than one year. They are reported at the lower of cost and current market value, which means that their values will vary.
- *Fixed assets.* These include property, plants and facilities, and equipment used to conduct business. These items are reported at their original value, even though current values might well be much higher.

- *Intangible assets.* These include legal claims, patents, franchise rights, and accounts receivable. These values can be more difficult to determine. FR10, published by the Accounting Standards Board of the Institute of Chartered Accountants for England and Wales, is essential reading for dealing with this issue.
- *Deferred charges.* These include prepaid costs and other expenditures that will produce future revenue or benefits.

TRICKS OF THE TRADE

- Assets do not necessarily include everything of value, such as the talents of individuals, an organisation's collective expertise, or the value of a customer base.
- Classic definitions of assets also often exclude or undervalue trademarks, even though there is universal agreement that these, for example, the three-point star of Mercedes-Benz or Coca-Cola's red logo, can have enormous value.
- Fixed assets are valued at their original cost, because of the prevailing opinion that they are used for business and are not for sale. Moreover, current market value is essentially a matter of opinion.
- Determining the value of patents can be challenging, because a patent has a finite lifespan, its value declines each year, and its useful life may be even shorter.
- Some experts contend that the principal assets of 'knowledge-based' businesses such as consulting firms or property development companies are, in fact, its people. In turn, their aggregate value should be calculated by subtracting the net value of assets from market value.

RECOMMENDED LINK

Investorwords.com:
www.investorwords.com

SEE ALSO

Accounting (p. 494)

MARKETING YOUR IDEA

Choosing Your Marketing Strategy

GETTING STARTED

Defining and implementing a rock solid marketing strategy is probably the single most important factor that will contribute towards the long-term sustainable success of any business venture, yet most businesses don't have one. Even if businesses do have a strategy, it is often then not followed and implemented 100% from top to bottom. For that reason, small businesses that do have the vision to create a dynamic, customer-focused marketing strategy, and also the determination to put it into practice, usually have the competitive edge. It is these businesses that will have a real opportunity to do something special. They will create the 'buzz' that will set them apart from their competitors.

This actionlist gives more information about how to choose, implement, and maintain a dynamic marketing strategy. A book that you may find useful to read on the subject is *101 Ways to Market Your Business*, written by Andrew Griffiths, and published by Allen & Unwin.

FAQS

What is a marketing strategy?

A marketing strategy isn't the same as a marketing plan. A marketing strategy involves choosing a realistic, measurable, and ambitious goal that you think your business can achieve on a sustainable basis. With a marketing strategy, each marketing tactic you use is focused completely on reaching and beating that overall goal.

What is a marketing plan?

A marketing plan will include all of the tactics and actions that are designed to achieve the overall strategic goal. It will also include a timetable for their implementation. In other words, the plan will detail what you will do to make the strategy happen.

Why don't most businesses have a strategy?

The vast majority of businesses in all sectors market themselves in the same way as their competitors. They use supply-driven marketing messages based on product features; they design unfathomable websites; they create bland straplines and statements about what their business does. They do this because it is easy. Businesses also do this because their owners/managers know their products and services better than anyone else; as a result, they promote themselves in terms that they understand, but that their customers don't. They also do it because they look at what their competitors are doing and fall into the trap of doing the same things. Instead, what they should be doing is differentiating themselves by creating a unique, accessible proposition that gives them a real competitive edge.

MAKING IT HAPPEN
Set your sights

The first thing to do is to decide on your ultimate goal. Every business will have different strategic objectives for its own specific situation. No matter how high you set your sights, your marketing strategy should drive everything that your business does to achieve that objective.

You might aim to double turnover in twelve months; to maximise the value of your business in three years in order to sell it; or to increase your market share three fold in six months. You will only make the most of your chances of achieving or surpassing your goal by following a well thought out, meticulously implemented marketing strategy. With your business's marketing efforts accurately aimed and 100% focused on the needs of the target market, you are far more likely to succeed. If the aim is wrong, and your understanding of the market is wrong, your marketing will be mediocre at best, and useless at worst.

Choose the right marketing strategy

Your business can achieve competitive advantage if you choose a marketing strategy that sets it apart from everyone else. There is (sadly) no magic formula for doing this. You can't just import or implant an off-the-shelf strategy into a business and hope that it works; it's down to you to choose and define your marketing strategy in your own business situation.

There are, though, a number of key factors that will help you choose the right strategy. You need to know exactly who your customers or target prospects are, and where they are located; what these people want and need, why they need it, how they need it, and when they need it. You'll have to be confident enough to develop or create a unique selling proposition (USP) that you can offer to completely fulfil your customers' needs. You must then test your proposition in your chosen market first. Once that's done, you'll need to analyse the results and use them refine the proposition as appropriate until you're sure it's right.

Implement your strategy

You should only attempt to implement your strategy fully when you are absolutely sure that your unique selling proposition is right. Your task then is to get your message across to your market, making sure that your USP is articulated in all of your marketing messages, campaigns, and sales channels. It is important that you recognise when your proposition is working so that you can then market it fast, first, and aggressively in your sector—only in this way will you achieve an unassailable lead over your competitors.

Keep ahead of the game

In the 1990s everyone spoke about being 'market-led'. Today, market conditions change at bewildering speed. Any number of factors can play a part in this, including technology, customers' tastes, fashions, trends, media influences, and so on. If you want your business to survive in the 21st century, you must make the right choice of target market. You then need to focus everything the business does on providing unique value and benefits to meet the needs of that chosen market, and you need to do this better than your competitors.

Your business and your marketing strategy cannot stand still. What is unique today is widespread tomorrow, and unwanted the day after that. The vital ingredient in a truly dynamic marketing strategy is to strive continually to discover new and better ways to add value for your customers, and keep your proposition unique in your chosen market.

Every single time you put your strategy into action, you will also learn something new about your customers' needs, and whether your proposition is right for them. The implementation of your marketing strategy should be a continuous process of creating a proposition to satisfy your customers; testing it; and learning from it. You can learn from it by recognising what is right and doing more of it, or changing what is wrong as soon as you realise it isn't working.

WHAT TO AVOID
Missing the target

The most important aspect of any marketing strategy is making sure that you have chosen the right market at which to aim your products and services. You may have utterly convincing sales messages and advertising copy, and you may be brilliant at selling and articulating the benefits of your service. If you haven't selected the right target audience in the first place, however, or if you haven't understood what that audience needs, you will almost certainly fail. Make sure you select the right market, with the right profile of consumers who have a propensity to buy your products or service. Then you will be able to aim your proposition, and the benefits it brings, directly at them.

Standing still

To succeed in your market you need to keep up to date with changes in customer preference and buying patterns. You also need to keep up with the seemingly relentless changes in technology and other external forces. If you don't make the effort to move forward constantly, your competitors will steal your market share, your biggest customers, or your intended new market, before you have a chance to do anything about it.

Lack of focus

The biggest mistake is to stop focusing on your market. You have to make sure that you are continuing to provide the unique value and benefit your customers need and expect from your service. Take your eye off the marketing ball for a second, and your strategy will fall flat on its face.

RECOMMENDED LINKS

Business Link:
www.businesslink.gov.uk
Chartered Institute of Marketing:
www.cim.co.uk
Internet marketing:
www.it-advice.org

SEE ALSO

Market Research and Competitor Intelligence (p. 526)
Planning Marketing (p. 214)
Profiling Your Competitors (p. 220)
Researching the Size of Your Market (p. 211)

Researching the Size of Your Market

GETTING STARTED

It's important to find out what potential your business has to generate revenues and profits in your chosen market sector, and the only way to do this is to carry out thorough market research. The better the data you have about your market, the better equipped you will be to make informed decisions about your business. Good market research will help you establish the most important objective of all—in other words, your sales targets. Your financial backers, business partners, key staff, and other key stake holders will also have a keen, if not vested, interest in your sales potential and the market share you believe you can realistically achieve.

Before you can estimate the share of the market you want to attain, you'll need to have researched the *overall* size of the market. Its size could be calculated in terms of its volume (that is to say, the number of buyers), and its value (in terms of annual total spend), or both. This actionlist will help you to do this. A book which you may find useful on the subject is *Marketing Research Toolbox: A Concise Guide for Beginners*, by Edward McQuarrie, published by Sage Publications.

FAQS

What do I need to know about my customer group?

Assuming you have already accurately profiled the customer group that you consider to be your ideal market audience, you need to know how many potential buyers the group consists of, and how much they currently spend.

What else do I need to know before I set my sales targets?

Once you have found out how many potential buyers you have, and how much they spend at the moment, you need to find out whether your market is growing or declining. You then need to decide what sales levels you are going to aim for.

MAKING IT HAPPEN

Find out the number of potential buyers

Your target audience will be made up of groups of businesses, groups of individuals, or both. Calculating the size of this overall market, that is to say the number of people who could potentially buy from you, will only be possible once you have considered who they are, their unique characteristics, and where they are located. It may be the case in your business situation that your potential customers live close to you as you offer a service that people generally will

travel only a short distance to purchase—you could run a sandwich bar or café, for example. For other services, people are prepared to travel a reasonable distance, for example, up to an hour, to buy something. In other instances, distance is not an issue, as consumers will buy by mail order or via the Internet.

You need to ask yourself whether location or proximity to your service is an issue for your target audience. This will help you to scope the potential size of your market when you add this factor into the profile of your customers' buying characteristics. You'll then be able to target the number of buyers you think you can reach with your marketing.

Research how much buyers spend in the market

Establishing how many buyers there are for your service is only part of the equation. You will also need to understand how much these buyers are prepared to spend on a product or service such as yours, in terms of each time they buy, and in terms of how frequently they buy.

Knowing your market size is meaningless unless you can attach a value to the volume of potential buyers you have. That value is also meaningless unless you understand the repeat purchase rate, in other words how many times they buy or use your service in weeks, months, or over a year. This information is vital when forecasting sales revenues for your business plan or forthcoming budget.

Establish if the market is expanding or declining

Once you know how many buyers you have, how much they spend, and how often they buy, you need to look at the market *potential*. Will your market be the same size in six or twelve months' time, for example? Look at the trends, to see if they suggest that your customers will be spending more, the same, or less. Try to predict whether there will be any more buyers seeking your type of product or service.

There may also be other target audiences with similar buying characteristics and needs that you will be able to access through your marketing. Don't get fixated on the size of your market now; you'll end up missing opportunities to reach a wider audience in a year's time without even realising it. Similarly, watch out for—and act on!—signs that customer numbers are falling or that they're buying less frequently: don't leave it too late.

Think about your target market share

Once you've come up with a target market share to aim for, you can work out the precise marketing effort, methods, channels, and budget you'll need to achieve it. Also remember that you'll need to bear in mind what your competitors are up to: what could you learn from or improve on, based on their approach? If your market is a growing one, it's likely that you'll have more competition as time goes on, so keep on top of trends and try to predict whether your competitors will have new, better value, more innovative services than yours. You will need to keep a very close eye on their marketing activities; for example, special promotions, free gifts, guarantees, after-sales service, and so on. This might give them the edge over your business, and a chance to steal a greater share of the market you have targeted or established for yourself.

Find information about market size and trends

Business and market information is available from a variety of sources. Some is free, but you will probably have to pay for more in-depth statistics, trends, and forecasts. The reference section of your local library will have a business section carrying published market reports on hundreds of sectors. They will also have government statistics, trade magazines, and national and local business directories. If they do not have the publications themselves, they should have a directory of them, together with details of their costs and where you can source them. Contact your local council if you want local population or business information.

The Internet is also a good place to start, but wading through the sheer volume of information available can be time-consuming, especially for the less experienced Web user. Having said that, using one of the main search engines and carrying out a search using terms containing the name of the market sector you are in, the type of information you need, a product name, geographic area, and suppliers' or competitors' names, should bring up a good range of relevant websites for your business.

For information on market trends in the United Kingdom, try Mintel, KeyNote, or Euromonitor—or National Statistics Online, which gives information about statistics and trends (website addresses are given below). For details of potential business buyers, there are a number of good directories including Thomson Directories, Yellow Pages, and the British Chambers of Commerce. If you are just starting up, or are a newly established business, try Enterprise Quest. The website addresses for all of these are given below.

WHAT TO AVOID
Not being up to date

Do be 100% sure that your estimates of the size of your market are based on current data and trends. If you make decisions based on out-of-date information, or fail to spot the trends in your sector, you'll either miss the opportunities to obtain a greater share of the overall market, or your competitors will steal your market share.

Taking your eye off the target
Research regularly: it shouldn't be a one-off exercise! If you don't keep tabs on what's happening to the size and structure of your market, you'll lose touch with your existing audiences and potential new customers.

Failing to spot the trends
Do try to always look at the 'bigger picture' in your sector, rather than just one particular aspect of the market, or the statistics relating to it. Look for trends in terms of potential buyers you could reach, the average value of purchases they make, and how often they are buying. Keep an eye out for new entrants in your sector, and the share of the overall market they are taking.

RECOMMENDED LINKS
Chambers of Commerce:
www.chamberonline.co.uk

Chartered Institute of Marketing:
www.cim.co.uk
Enterprise Quest:
www.enterquest.net
Euromonitor:
www.euromonitor.com
KeyNote:
www.keynote.co.uk
Mintel:
www.mintel.co.uk
National Statistics Online:
www.statistics.gov.uk
Thomson Directories:
www.thomweb.co.uk
Yellow Pages:
www.yell.com

SEE ALSO
Choosing Your Marketing Strategy (p. 208)
Market Research and Competitor Intelligence (p. 526)
Profiling Your Competitors (p. 220)

Focus On: Planning Marketing
Malcolm McDonald

GETTING STARTED

Most managers accept that some kind of procedure for planning a company's marketing helps to sharpen their focus, making the complexity of business operations manageable and adding a dimension of realism to the business's future plans. This procedure is known as marketing planning. It is a managerial process with a logical sequence of activities leading to the setting of marketing objectives and the formulation of plans for achieving them.

As with any plan, it needs to be as clear and simple as possible. This also needs to be reflected in the sales approach, which has to be as straightforward for customers as possible and remove any obstacles to actually making the sale. This actionlist explains how to cope with market uncertainty by:

- developing a *strategic* marketing plan
- developing a *tactical* marketing plan
- reviewing current thinking about markets and marketing

FAQS

Why is it important to plan marketing?

The contribution of marketing planning to the success of a business, whatever its size or area of activity, lies in its commitment to detailed analysis of future opportunities to meet customer needs. It offers a wholly professional approach to selling to well-defined market segments those products or services that deliver the desired benefits. Such commitment and activities shouldn't be mistaken for budgets and forecasts, which have always been a commercial necessity. Marketing planning is a more sophisticated approach concerned with identifying what sales are going to be made in the longer term and to whom, in order to give revenue budgets and sales forecasts a real chance of being achieved.

What are the main features of marketing planning?

Successful marketing planning is the cornerstone of developing strong, durable, and robust businesses. Overcoming an organisational culture that acts as a barrier to effective marketing planning is essential if performance is to be optimised and long-term goals are to be achieved. Given the complexity of the rapidly changing business environment and the high number of variables that influence business performance, it is necessary for managers or owner-managers to have an effective means of making the situation manageable. Thorough and detailed analysis of how to meet future customer needs provides a sophisticated and reliable method for building long-term success. Marketing planning enables your business's vision to become a reality.

MAKING IT HAPPEN
Review current thinking

From an extensive review of the current research into strategic marketing planning, five principal conclusions emerge.

- There is a clear consensus about the benefits of the strategic marketing planning process.
- Strategic marketing planning and the marketing orientation that accompanies it are clearly associated with improved performance across most market situations.
- In unsuccessful companies, the process of strategic marketing planning is poorly adhered to in practice, and is frequently used as a pretext for inadequate budgeting and tactical programmes.
- Although the degree of formality of the process can range from a highly creative, entrepreneurial approach to the more structured, rational process described

here, there is universal consensus among strategic thinkers and planners that some kind of managerial planning process has to be used to manage the link between a business and its environment.

In large, multi-national, multi-product, multi-cultural businesses, then, it is usual to find a structured process for marketing planning; in smaller businesses with fewer complex products or markets, the management of the process outlined here tends to be much less formal and structured. The process and the steps, however, are the same in all consistently successful companies.

Understand the level of marketing plan

There are two principal kinds of marketing plan.

The strategic marketing plan. A strategic marketing plan is a plan for three or more years. It is a written document outlining how owner-managers or managers perceive their own position in the market relative to their competitors (with the advantage they have over their competitors accurately defined), what objectives they want to achieve, how they intend to achieve them (strategies), what resources are required (budget), and what results are expected. Three years is the most common strategic planning period. Five years is the longest, but is becoming less common because of the speed of technological and environmental change. Strategic marketing-driven plans are not to be confused with scenario planning or the kind of very long-range plans formulated by a number of Japanese companies (which often have planning horizons of between 50 and 200 years!).

The tactical marketing plan. A tactical marketing plan is the detailed scheduling and costing of the actions necessary for achieving the first year of the strategic marketing plan. The tactical plan is thus usually for one year.

Develop the contents of a strategic marketing plan

The contents of a strategic marketing plan are as follows:

- mission statement, setting out the raison d'être of the business and covering its role, business definition, distinctive competence, and future indications.
- financial summary, summarising the financial implications over the full planning period.
- market overview, providing a brief picture of the market, including market structure, market trends, key market segments, and (sometimes) gap analysis.
- SWOT analysis, analysing the strengths and weaknesses of the business compared with competitors against key customer success factors, and considering opportunities and threats, usually for each key product or segment.
- issues to be addressed, derived from a SWOT analysis (of strengths, weaknesses, opportunities, and threats) and usually specific to each product or segment.
- portfolio summary, offering a pictorial summary of the SWOT analysis that makes it easy to see at a glance the relative importance of each of the four elements; it is often a two-dimensional matrix in which the horizontal axis measures the organisation's comparative strengths and the vertical axis measures its relative attractiveness.
- assumptions, listing the underlying assumptions critical to the planned marketing objectives and strategies.
- marketing objectives, usually consisting of quantitative statements (in terms of profit, volume, value, and market share) of what the business wishes to achieve; they are usually given by product, by segment, and overall.
- marketing strategies, stating how the objectives are to be achieved. They often involve the four Ps of marketing: product, price, place, and promotion.
- resource requirements and budget, showing the full planning-period budget, giving in detail the revenues and associated costs for each year.

Develop the contents of a tactical marketing plan

The contents of a tactical marketing plan

are very similar, except that they often omit the mission statement, the market overview, and SWOT analysis, and the plan goes into much more detailed quantification by product and segment of marketing objectives and associated strategies. An additional feature is more detailed scheduling and costing of the tactics necessary to achieve the first year's planned goals.

Complete the process of marketing planning

This involves:

- identifying what sales will be made in the longer term and to whom, in order to turn revenue budgets and sales forecasts into reality.
- analysing your strengths and weaknesses compared with competitors' against key customer success factors, and similarly review the business's opportunities and threats.
- completing the strategic marketing plan before the tactical plan. Write your strategic marketing plan to cover three or more years, defining competitive advantage, objectives, strategies, and budgets.
- building marketing strategies round the four Ps of marketing: product, price, place, promotion.
- writing a tactical marketing plan, detailing schedules and costing for the specific

actions necessary to achieve the first year of the strategic plan.

WHAT TO AVOID
Failing to implement the marketing plan successfully

A business's culture is the biggest barrier to implementing effective marketing planning. People may simply want to do what they have always done, or they may misunderstand (or not be told) why a new approach is needed. The solution is to keep everyone informed about the marketing plan: what it is, how it will work and why it will succeed.

Disorganised planning

The output of the process (the plan) needs to spell out how a business expects to achieve its objectives. However, people may view the planning process as an academic exercise, or they may not have the skills or experience to plan effectively. Also, strategic marketing planning needs to precede tactical marketing planning. The planning process is universal, although how formal its implementation is will vary from business to business.

RECOMMENDED LINKS
Marketing Research Association:
www.mra-net.org

Focus On: Marketing—The Importance of Being First
Al and Laura Ries

GETTING STARTED

Most managers believe the basic issue in marketing is convincing a prospective customer that you have a better product or service. Not true.

The basic issue in marketing is creating a new category you can be first in.

Marketing is not a battle of products, it is a battle of *perceptions*. To win the battle of perceptions you have to become the leader in a category. Prospects assume the leader must be better because 'everybody knows the better product or service will win in the marketplace'. How do you become the leader? You launch a new category you can be first in. It doesn't have to be a big technological advance. Sometimes the simple ideas are the easiest to get into the mind. And where do you win the battle? You win the battle inside the mind of the prospect.

This actionlist explains how to dominate your market sector.

FAQS

For a small company, how do the principles of marketing differ from those that apply to a large company?

The principles are exactly the same, only a small company usually manages to stay small by ignoring these principles. The truth is, every large company was once a small company that became big by doing the right things. The biggest mistake a small company can make is thinking of themselves as a small company instead of thinking of themselves as a big company in its gestation period.

How does a market leader achieve its leadership?

Not by introducing a better product or service. Invariably the leader in the category got to be the leader by being the first brand in a new category. Some examples:

- Coca-Cola, the first cola.
- Dell, the first personal computer sold direct.
- Domino's, the first home delivery pizza chain.
- Red Bull, the first energy drink.

What big companies introduced these brands? None. They were all started by small entrepreneurs like Tom Monaghan (Domino's Pizza) and Dietrich Mateschitz (Red Bull). Most of these companies started small, then grew up over an extended period of time.

Some consultants have called this leadership phenomenon 'the first mover advantage', but that is not so. It's an advantage, but it's not the reason that most leader brands were first in their categories. It's the 'first minder' advantage. That is, the brand that gets into the mind first is the winner, not the brand that was first in the category. Du Mont made the first television set; Hurley, the first washing machine; Red Rock, the first cola, the MITS Altair 8800 was the first personal computer; but these and many other brands failed to get into the minds of their prospects. You don't win in the marketplace. You win in the mind.

If you weren't first in your category and you can't win by being better, what can you do?

The answer is obvious: start a new category you can be first in. Marketing is more a battle of categories than it is a battle of products. Winning companies think category first and product second. They try to categorise what they do, not in terms of being better, but in terms of being different.

When Procter & Gamble introduced Tide many years ago, they could have called the product a 'new, improved soap'. Tide was a soap then, and Tide is a soap today, in the sense that soap is a 'cleansing agent'. But Tide was made from synthetic materials rather than the fats and lye found in traditional cleaning products like Ivory, Oxydol, and Rinso. Tide could have been called a synthetic soap, but that would have nailed the brand to the soap category. So Procter & Gamble called Tide the 'first detergent', a totally new category, and even today Tide is the leading brand of detergent in the United States.

MAKING IT HAPPEN
Create a new category you can be first in

When Michael Dell set up the Dell Computer Corporation, he could have sold his 'better' products through conventional computer retailers, but he didn't. Instead he launched the first brand of personal computer sold direct by phone. Today Dell is the world's largest selling brand of personal computer and still doesn't sell any computers through conventional computer retailers.

Get the launch right

Before you launch (or relaunch) a new product or service, ask yourself:

- What is the name of the category? Not a name that you might like, but a name the industry gives the category.
- What is the brand name of the leader in the category? Not necessarily the sales leader, but the brand that customers perceive to be the leader.

If there is no dominant brand, or at least not a dominant brand in the mind of most prospects, jump right in with your product or service and try to quickly establish your leadership. Cut prices, cut deals, hire sales people, launch massive publicity campaigns, do everything you can to seize the leadership position before someone else does.

Promote your brand as the leading brand. 'It's so easy to use', says AOL, 'no wonder it's number one'. Leave no piece of marketing material or website or TV advertisement or radio commercial without mentioning your leadership. Leadership is the most important aspect of any marketing campaign. Why? Prospects assume the better product or service will win in the marketplace. Therefore, if you are the leader, you must have the better product.

If there is a dominant brand, then move on and set up a new category you can be first in. But make sure you have a new name to match the new category. You can get in serious trouble if you try to use an existing name.

You can't dictate the category name. Only the industry and the media can do that. Therefore, you have to launch your new brand with publicity and get the media to establish the category name for you.

Avoid falling into the 'better product' trap

Odd as it might seem, a small company is more likely to make the 'better product' mistake mentioned above than a large company. Cynical marketing people who don't really care about 'building a better product' often populate large companies. Their focus is on marketing, distribution, packaging, display and other sophisticated ways to hype sales. It's the small company entrepreneur who believes deeply in the superiority of his or her product that is most likely to bet the ranch on this strategy.

However, unless you are already the leader in some aspects of what you do, these programs are bound to fail. People just naturally assume that the leader must have the better product or service.

WHAT TO AVOID
Failing to establish a new category or product sector

There's almost always a way to set up a new category. Unfortunately, most companies refuse to even consider the possibility of a new category because 'there's no market'. Of course, there's no market. If there were, it wouldn't be a new category. That's the most difficult thing to overcome. You have to have faith that you can succeed in getting acceptance for a new category. Furthermore, a new category doesn't necessarily represent a big, technological advance. Soapsoft, the first liquid soap, was a big commercial success. How difficult is it to take a tub of soap and liquefy it?

Using an existing name for the new product sector

How difficult is it to take regular beer and add water? Miller Lite, the first light beer, was a big success, but ultimately paid a big penalty for it. Instead of creating a new brand to match the new category, the company used a line extension name which just about killed their regular beer brand (Miller High Life) and caused them to lose their light beer leadership to the competition. A new category needs a new name.

RECOMMENDED LINK
Marketing Research Association: **www.mra-net.org**

Profiling Your Competitors

GETTING STARTED

Competitor information helps you protect and grow your business. To keep one step ahead—or at least in roughly the same place!—as your direct competitors, you need to need to build a detailed profile of them, their strengths, weaknesses, and relationships with customers, as well as thinking more widely about competition for your customers and their spending. To help you do this, compare the performance of your business with that of your main competitors by measuring factors that are important to quality of service, and use the comparison as the basis for a programme of performance improvement.

Whether you sell yourself or you have a sales team, competitor information can be obtained from many different sources. Publications, the press, and the Internet have information readily available that can help you compile intelligence on competitors, and corporate brochures and annual reports are also excellent sources of published information. Maintain a file of press cuttings on your competitors' activities, using their trade publications as a source.

Published industry surveys can provide a useful insight into purchasing patterns, and competitors' websites can provide valuable information on their resources, plans, and capabilities.

FAQS

Why is competitor intelligence so important?

Competitive activity can have a significant impact on your own plans. If you are about to run a marketing campaign or new product launch, competitive activity could limit its effectiveness—so you need to know about it. You may also identify growing threats to important accounts. Unless you monitor activity and take appropriate action, your business faces an unknown risk.

Who are my competitors?

Many small companies already know their main, direct competitors. Often they have worked with them or encountered them at trade events or heard of them through customers. It is dangerous, however, to assume you know all the competitors.

It is often useful to think laterally about who might be in competition for your customers. Many products and services could be classed as non-essential, and so customers may be choosing to spend their discretionary budget between two very different market sectors. In addition, as a specialist, you could find yourself in competition with a larger company who give away a competing service as a promotional device.

Should competitor research be carried out internally or by an independent research company?

You can carry out the research internally, provided you have the resources. Much of the source material is in the public domain, so you should be able to obtain it yourself—and you must never ignore the wealth of information you already have in your company, or can gain through your own contacts. However, if you wish to research customer attitudes (to compare your company with the competition), you may need to use an independent research organisation. Customers may not be completely honest with your own representatives.

How reliable is published competitor information?

You have to make assumptions about the accuracy and quality of any published information that is used for research. Much of the material will be published to provide information for customers, so it is unlikely to be misleading. However, realistically, you can only use the latest and best information that is reasonably available.

MAKING IT HAPPEN
Identify the competitive threat

Competitor information helps you to identify how you can protect your most important business and, more positively, how you can strengthen your position with customers in situations in which your competitors are currently holding a larger share of the business than you. These are the main questions:

- How many competitors do you have? Are they direct or indirect?
- Who are your major competitors—those who threaten your most important customers?
- How much of your business do they threaten? Quantifying the threat helps you prioritise.
- Where are your main competitors located? How do they compare in size? Are they growing? Map them and track them.
- How do your products compare with competitive offerings? What about price? Distribution? Image and reputation? Service quality?
- What are customers' attitudes towards your competitors and towards your own company?
- Which customers might switch to competitors and why?
- How strong are competitors' relationships with key customers or key decision-makers? How long have competitors been dealing with them?
- Have you got the skills and resources to overcome the competitive threat?
- Are any competitors making inroads into businesses in which you are currently the dominant supplier?
- Who are your competitors' main customers?
- Have your competitors invested in links with customers that would make it difficult for other suppliers to make inroads?
- Can you (or your customers) identify weaknesses in your competitors?
- Which of your competitors' customers do you want to win?

Compare key competitive factors

Listed below are a number of factors that are important to meeting customer needs. You can score these factors (0–10, where 10 is the best in the market) to see how your business and your main competitors compare. The results should be used as the basis for a programme of performance improvement. As far as possible you should give priority to the things that matter *to your customers* rather than your own opinion:

- evidence of an excellent service culture—for example, problems quickly resolved by frontline staff rather than reference to higher managers
- high levels of after-sales service and support offered
- product adapted readily to meet customer specifications
- evidence of commitment to quality measurements such as ISO9002, Investors in People or similar industry schemes
- promises made to customers, for example in sales literature offering money-back guarantees or precise delivery schedules
- evidence of feedback encouraged, for example comment forms or Freephone telephone number made widely available
- flexible approach to pricing, such as the use of price incentives or finance schemes to appeal to different types of customer. Willingness to negotiate prices for important customers
- staff knowledgeable about the product and willing to share this knowledge and give advice to customers
- good reputation with agents, distributors, or other intermediaries
- overall reputation. For example, how do your staff or customers rate the company?

Use the salesforce

If you have one, the salesforce can obtain competitor information from many different sources. By talking to customers, salespeople can find out about competitors' direct sales calls, marketing campaigns, special offers, and new developments. They can also obtain similar information from retailers or distributors. Crucially, they can get a feel for customers' awareness and attitudes towards your competitors.

Analyse published information

Information is readily available from publications, the press, and the Internet that can help you compile intelligence on different aspects of competitors' business, including:

- main markets
- customers
- resources and financial performance
- product range
- new products
- plans for growth

Obtain competitor literature

Corporate brochures and annual reports are available for some companies. You can sometimes obtain copies from exhibitions or customers, or as downloads from competitors' websites. Often, by just visiting your competitors' offices you can pick up brochures and leaflets.

Monitor the press

Maintain a file of press cuttings on your competitors' activities, using their trade publications as a source, or (depending on your budget), you might consider using a press cuttings agency to gather material for you. Smaller companies can give a member of staff (for example, a sales person) responsibility for gathering and keeping data on a particular competitor.

Analyse industry reports

Published industry surveys can provide a useful insight into purchasing patterns in different market sectors. You can sometimes obtain information on competitors, market share, and industry trends.

Check the Internet

Competitors' websites can provide valuable information on their resources, plans, and capabilities. As well as checking the company information and product pages, you should read any customer case studies on the site and monitor the news section to find out about new developments. Trade publications are increasingly available in electronic editions, making it easier for you to monitor the press.

Visit exhibitions

Competitors' exhibition stands can be valuable sources of information. Most organisations only participate in exhibitions that are important to their current or future business plans.

Monitor competitors' promotional activities

Analysing competitors' promotional activities will help you to respond to their activities. By monitoring their advertising, promotions, exhibition presence, press activities, and Internet information, you can assess possible strategies. These are some of the possible scenarios:

- heavy advertising expenditure could indicate a competitor trying to win greater share or attempting to remedy losses in that market
- price promotions may indicate that your competitors want to be perceived as value-for-money suppliers, or it may be an emergency response to declining sales
- press announcements about new production facilities could indicate that your competitors are trying to increase their business significantly. They may become more cost-effective and able to offer lower prices, or may be taking on additional overheads that they must finance
- announcements about new branch or dealership openings could mean that competitors are expanding into new territories
- recruitment drives may signal a change in direction, a growth strategy or a sudden loss of staff

All of these can mean that your competitor is spending more money, and you might compare this with published accounts (available at Companies House or through credit reference agencies) to gain an indication of their financial health.

Marketing and trade publications can be useful sources of information on competitor marketing activity.

Appoint a research company

If you do not have the internal resources to monitor competitive activity, you can use an independent research company to carry out all the tasks outlined above. You can also ask them to explore customer attitudes to competitors. Customers may be more willing to provide this information to an independent organisation.

Consider benchmarking

Benchmarking compares your performance with that of other, similar companies. Competently done, it will give you a baseline assessment of your company's efficiency and some insight into where competitors may be gaining competitive advantage over you.

WHAT TO AVOID
Overlooking the obvious sources

Some competitor intelligence is freely available from the Internet, the press, and other published sources and, most of all, from your staff, your customers, and your competitors themselves. Information from these sources can provide a valuable starting point for developing detailed competitor profiles.

Ignoring competitor information

Competitor information is only valuable if you use it to refine your own strategies or take defensive action to protect your business. Simply gathering information without analysis or action is wasteful.

Acting on incomplete information

Be cautious about acting on competitor intelligence. Published sources can only provide a partial picture, and more strategic information is likely to be confidential. This means that you may make incorrect assumptions in planning your response to competitor action.

Using out-of-date information

Records should be carefully checked and maintained. Using poor quality data can ruin the best campaigns.

RECOMMENDED LINK
Market Research Society:
www.marketresearch.org.uk

SEE ALSO
Choosing Your Marketing Strategy (p. 208)
Researching the Size of Your Market (p. 211)

WORKING WITH CUSTOMERS

Carrying Out Market Research

GETTING STARTED

Businesses of all sizes need to keep on top of changes or developments in their chosen markets so that they can make sure that the product or service they offer fits the bill. This actionlist gives you some ideas on how to carry out different types of market research.

Telephone interviews are a quick and cost-effective way to obtain opinions from a sample of customers. This type of research can be used to assess your customers' reaction to a change in the product or service, or to measure awareness of a company or product. One of the downsides of this approach, however, is that it can be difficult to reassure people that you are carrying out legitimate research—most people will think you're trying to sell them something!

Postal surveys are ideal for customer satisfaction surveys or detailed surveys that take time to complete. However, it can be difficult to obtain a worthwhile rate of response, and you, as the researcher, have little control over the process. Incentives may be needed to improve response and there is a risk of incomplete responses.

Group discussions or focus groups are ideal for identifying issues of concern to customers and assessing customer reactions to potential changes. This type of research is open-ended and can highlight important customer issues that the researcher may not be aware of. However, group discussions are not representative and can be influenced by a dominant member of the group.

The personal interview is ideal for obtaining detailed information on attitudes to products and services or getting feedback from specific individuals. Personal interviews allow in-depth discussion of complex topics and give you greater control over the response.

An omnibus survey is a cost-effective method of researching several topics at the same time. The same survey is used to carry out regular research on a number of different products by telephone or personal interview. You should check that the other topics in the survey are compatible with your own products.

FAQS

Can we carry out market research ourselves, or should we use a consultancy?

Market research is a professional discipline and depending on your industry and what you need to find out, you may get more meaningful results by using a consultancy. They are trained to detect possible errors in research results, and their independence is reassuring to people who are being interviewed. The main problem for small businesses is, naturally, the expense. Review your budget and see if you can afford outside help.

You can carry out a limited amount of research yourself, developing and mailing questionnaires or carrying out limited telephone interviews. Again, there is a risk that people may feel that your research is a thinly disguised sales pitch.

How do I carry out quick and effective research?

Without incurring great costs, you often have the opportunity to research your own customers. Every time you or a member of your staff meet a customer you can discover important information during the course of a normal conversation. Record this information and create opportunities to share it.

More formal research may include a space on delivery notes or invoices, enclosures with products, or follow-up phone calls to ask customers' opinions. Be cautious about asking for too much (or too personal) information, though, as this puts people on their guard and makes them much less likely to help you.

How reliable are the results from focus groups?

The results are as reliable as the quality of the participants and the people who run the sessions. For example, very bossy or loud participants can dominate a group and influence the course of discussions. Also, if the person running the discussion asks the wrong questions, the resulting discussion may prove worthless. Make sure those in charge are well briefed and know what your goals are.

We have limited resources for research. Should we participate in an omnibus survey so that we can make the best use of our budget?

An omnibus survey is an ideal way to share expensive research resources and reach a large audience. However, you must be sure that the audience is relevant to your company's business. Ask for a profile of the research audience and check the names of other organisations which have used the survey. If there is a reasonable match to your own business, it could be a cost-effective solution.

▶ MAKING IT HAPPEN
Interview customers by telephone

Telephone interviews are a quick and cost-effective way to obtain opinions from a sample of customers. They can be used to assess customer reaction to a change in the product or service, or to gauge satisfaction ratings compared to competitors. The make-up of the sample is crucial; it is more important to know the views of valuable customers than those who haven't bought from you for a while, or who tend not to spend a lot of money on your products and services. Do remember, though, that some people don't like being 'cold-called' and may not want to participate. It might be worth sounding out some key customers in advance by e-mail, on your website, or via a newsletter if you have one, as you'll get

much more useful information from someone who actually wants to take part in your research.

Speed up research

The main benefit of telephone research is speed: a large number of interviews can be conducted in a short space of time, and data can be gathered and processed quickly. Telephone interviews also cost considerably less than personal interviews. As long as they are brief and to the point they are non-intrusive and easy to arrange. A customer may be too busy for a personal interview, but willing to spend a short time on the phone. Again, it may be worth sounding people out in advance.

Be careful about a senior decision-maker at another business being contacted by a junior member of your staff or an independent researcher, though—they may prefer to hear from you directly if you have a good relationship with them—and always bear in mind the effect on the customer's relationship with you.

Don't confuse telephone research with selling

Telephone interviews have limited scope because people may not be prepared to spend a long period of time on the telephone. It can also be difficult to get across complex concepts by telephone.

Follow industry guidelines:
- define the target audience
- draft a questionnaire and test it with colleagues
- make the calls at times likely to be convenient for the target audience, but check when you call that it is convenient; if not, offer to call back
- identify the purpose of the call and give an indication of the likely duration
- use faxes, if necessary, to send more detailed information for discussion

Use postal surveys or questionnaires

Questionnaires are very difficult to compile well and those who do it well have honed their skills over many years. If you feel a questionnaire is crucial to your research, it may be worth contacting a questionnaire specialist to help you out. Other types of postal surveys are delivered directly to customers, and they can be a quick and relatively inexpensive method of obtaining information. They are ideal for customer satisfaction surveys, or detailed surveys, that take time to complete; but it can be difficult to obtain a reasonable rate of response, and you cannot assume that the responses will be representative of all customers.

Assess the value of postal surveys

Postal surveys are relatively inexpensive. The costs include outward and return postage and stationery. They are precise and can be targeted at specific customers or prospects. They are also voluntary, because there is no pressure on the customer. The main problem, however, is the low response rates; incentives may be needed to improve them. There is also a risk of questionnaires and survey forms being returned incomplete, or incorrectly completed. You may face a slow response because there is no time pressure on the customer (unless you introduce one, by offering a discount or incentive if customers respond within a certain time limit), so you must take this into account in your planning.

Improve the response from postal surveys

Response rates can be influenced by many different factors. For many consumer goods markets, less than 5% would be normal and 15% or more would be extremely high. For highly involved customers in some sectors, you might anticipate much more. If you need to improve response think about:

- offering an incentive, such as entry into a prize draw, for returned questionnaires
- simplifying the questionnaire
- reassuring the customer that information will be kept confidential
- enclosing a stamped addressed or business reply envelope

Hold a group discussion

In group discussions—sometimes called 'focus groups'—existing and prospective customers are invited to discuss a particular topic, usually under the guidance of a researcher. They are ideal for exploring and, possibly, identifying issues or problems which concern customers, and assessing customer reactions to potential changes.

There is no limit placed on what the group can discuss, and this format can highlight important customer issues that the researcher may not be aware of. Many customers welcome the opportunity to discuss products and services with their colleagues and have an opportunity to contribute to change. The disadvantages are that group discussions are not representative, and they can be biased or influenced by a dominant member of the group. It is also difficult to quantify results.

You need to be cautious in planning group discussions. By and large they should not be used to identify only what is wrong with a product or service and it may cause problems to have several, important, customers in the same room. Groups composed entirely of customers with grievances will also have limited value: it's unlikely that you'll be able to get past their individual complaints.

To set up a group discussion:

- invite eight to ten customers; this number is controllable, but with fewer people it may be difficult to maintain discussion
- thank customers for participating and put them at their ease
- record the discussion if possible, using a tape recorder
- advise people that their comments are being recorded and that all material will be treated in confidence
- if conducting a group amongst consumers (not your customers) you might consider providing participants with a gift for taking part
- consider using more than one group to gather a range of views

You could also consider using an independent researcher to run the discussion.

Conduct personal interviews

In a personal interview, a customer and an interviewer work through a series of pre-determined questions. The personal interview is ideal for key customers and for obtaining detailed information on attitudes to products and services, or initiating the process of getting feedback. The interview can take place in a customer's home or office, or in a public place. It can be prearranged by telephone, post, or personal contact.

Personal interviews allow for a more in-depth discussion of complex topics and give you more control over the response. They also offer greater accuracy, and results are easy to analyse. Meeting people in a working environment can give an indication of their real purchasing intentions. The main disadvantages are the time and cost of recruiting interviewers and conducting interviews, and the risk of interviewer bias.

Before you carry out personal interviews, you should identify the groups or individuals you wish to contact. You should advise the customer about the length of time the interview is likely to take, and respect the confidence of the customer.

Carry out an omnibus survey

An omnibus survey is a cost-effective method of researching several topics at the same time. The same survey is used to carry out regular research on different products, by telephone or personal interview. They are suitable for measuring attitudes and behaviour towards different types of products and services, or monitoring changes in attitude among groups of consumers.

Before participating in the survey, you should check that the other topics in the survey are compatible with your own products, and that the overall length of the survey is not excessive. It may reduce costs, but the audience may not give enough attention to all topics.

WHAT TO AVOID

Asking obvious questions

Remember that you already know a good deal about your customers and their attitudes and behaviour. In a business-to-business market, you may know more than your customer.

Assuming formal market research is necessary

For many smaller companies (and some quite large ones) expensive research does not meet their needs. Companies with just a handful of very important customers would do better to concentrate on their relationships with these key accounts. For example, local retailers will often know their own area well, and the best 'research' they could do is to talk to their regular customers.

Choosing the wrong research technique

Each research technique has different applications, benefits, and disadvantages. You have to decide whether you need depth of information, speedy results, or cost-effective research. A market research consultancy may be able to provide advice on a suitable approach, but you need to have a very clear picture of your needs.

Relying on limited results

If time or resources are scarce, some research programmes may provide limited results. It's important to put the research findings in context, and take account of the limited findings when you are making important decisions. Market research consultancies use proven techniques to evaluate results, and should advise you to use their findings with caution.

RECOMMENDED LINK

Market Research Society:
www.marketresearch.org.uk

SEE ALSO

Getting More Feedback from Customers (p. 230)

Getting More Feedback from Customers

GETTING STARTED

Customer feedback is essential for improving products and services, and for identifying and correcting any problems at an early stage. Offer customers a choice of feedback methods to encourage them to respond, but make sure that all methods are as easy to use as possible. For high-value goods, a structured follow-up mechanism encourages customer comments on purchases.

FAQS

What is the best feedback mechanism?

For customers, the choice of feedback mechanism is probably a matter of personal preference. Some may prefer the anonymity of a postal questionnaire or response through a website. Others may wish to discuss their concerns and get an immediate response over the telephone. To boost your chances of getting as much feedback as possible, give customers a choice.

Do we need to use incentives to encourage feedback?

Customers may provide feedback if they feel strongly enough about an issue. Someone who has a serious complaint is likely to let you know. However, customers who have less pressing comments may not bother, feeling that their feedback is unimportant. Incentives may encourage them, but only if the incentives are appropriate.

Should we use an independent research organisation to obtain feedback?

Using an independent research organisation demonstrates to customers that you take their feedback seriously, and provides an objective, independent channel for comments. You may also find that customers are willing to talk to a research organisation about issues that they might be reluctant to discuss with your company directly. You must, however, be sure that the costs of employing a market research company are justified in the light of what you may discover. You and your own staff (if you have any)—especially field staff and sales

people—may already know a great deal about customer opinion.

MAKING IT HAPPEN

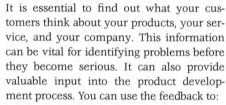

Find out what customers think

It is essential to find out what your customers think about your products, your service, and your company. This information can be vital for identifying problems before they become serious. It can also provide valuable input into the product development process. You can use the feedback to:

- improve products
- tailor products and services to the needs of individual customers
- identify new product opportunities
- highlight potential problems
- develop focused marketing and customer service plans
- strengthen customer relationships
- reduce customer losses

You can also use the feedback as part of your promotional message.

Talk to customers before you develop a new product

By explaining your plans and involving customers in product development, you can strengthen relationships and provide a service that is mutually beneficial. Questions could include:

- How can we improve the current product?
- What problems need to be overcome?
- What new features would customers welcome?
- Do the plans represent an improvement?
- Would customers make more use of a product that included the features they have highlighted?

Ask about purchasing experience

When a customer buys a product, include a brief questionnaire with it, asking about the customer's buying experience. Questions could include:

- Where did you buy the product? How often do you buy it?
- Why did you choose the product?
- What other (competing or complementary) products do you buy, and how often?
- Why did you choose the retail outlet?
- Where did you hear about the product and retail outlet?
- How did you find the service offered by the retailer?
- Would you visit the retailer again?
- Do you have any specific comments about the product or retailer?

The questionnaire could take the form of a reply-paid card, and should be brief.

Follow up a product sale

If the product has a reasonably high value, you could set up a follow-up mechanism to find out about the customer's experience in using the product. Typical intervals would be a week after purchase, a month after purchase, and six months after purchase. The first follow-up would check that the customer had no initial problems, while the subsequent follow-ups would ask about the customer's experience in using the product. Having a scale such as 1–5 (where 1 is 'very poor' and 5 is 'very good') enables comparisons over time.

Follow up servicing and maintenance

The standard of after-sales service can be critical in determining overall customer satisfaction with your company. After every service or maintenance visit, contact customers to ensure that they were satisfied with the standard of service they received. Questions could cover:

- convenience of booking a service
- punctuality and response times
- standard of service
- attitude of staff
- availability of spare parts

It is a good idea to use scales as described above to enable comparisons over time.

This kind of follow-up can be handled by a reply-paid questionnaire or telephone call.

Set up a customer satisfaction programme

Customer satisfaction has become one of the most important issues facing businesses in every market. Customer satisfaction programmes are known by many different names, such as customer service, customer satisfaction, and customer focus. Their common theme is meeting the customers' requirements and ensuring that all aspects of the business contribute to customer satisfaction. The intention is to build repeat business. If customers are satisfied with the product and the standards of service they receive, they will return to the business or the retail outlet again and again, for both major and minor purchases.

Measure satisfaction regularly

A customer satisfaction index takes the results from a number of satisfaction surveys, and allocates a numerical value to key customer satisfaction indicators. A local outlet is then given an overall index of performance, which can be compared with other outlets and measured on a year-on-year basis. The survey questionnaire asks customers to respond to questions with a scale of satisfaction: fully satisfied, very satisfied, satisfied, not satisfied, very dissatisfied. Alternatively, customers can be asked to respond on a numerical scale, where, for example, 1 is very dissatisfied, and 10 is very satisfied. They can also provide written comments on aspects of the service and, in some cases, ask for specific actions, such as an explanation from a departmental manager.

Set up a customer hotline

As well as formal mechanisms, you should also set up facilities to encourage customers to provide feedback at any time. A telephone hotline allows customers to call with queries or complaints about any aspect of your products or service. Calls to the hotline should be free, and the telephone number should be included in all your customer communications. The hotline should be staffed by people trained in customer handling techniques, and it should be continuously monitored to ensure that customers receive a suitable response. All calls should be recorded so that the call patterns can be analysed to identify any recurring problems.

Include a feedback mechanism on your website

You should include a simple feedback mechanism on your website. This provides a similar function to the telephone hotline, and provides customers with an alternative, easy-to-use channel for complaints, queries, and other issues. Users should have to complete only minimal personal details, such as name and e-mail address, before submitting their comments. Alternatively, you can allow users to submit their comments anonymously.

Use incentives to encourage feedback

You will increase response if you offer an incentive such as a free gift. You could also set up a regular prize draw for visitors who submit comments.

Establish a user group

You can encourage feedback and build a sense of community by setting up a user group. The user group would operate as a forum for discussing all issues of concern to customers, such as quality, performance, standards, and future developments. The group would include representatives from your own company and from a cross-section of your customers. The comments from the user group provide valuable feedback on current performance, and help to identify needs that can be met through new product development.

Respond to feedback

Let visitors know that you have received their comments, and thank them for their feedback. When you have taken corrective action, tell them what you have done, so they see that their effort is not wasted. This can encourage further feedback. If a visitor highlights a serious problem, keep them informed about progress.

WHAT TO AVOID
Failing to act on feedback

The most important way to encourage feedback is to demonstrate that you can respond. The point of gathering feedback is to identify concerns and problems before they become serious; however, unless you act on that feedback, the exercise will be wasted. Industry experience indicates that customers who have a problem resolved are far more likely to remain customers than those who receive no response. If you act on customer input during the product development process, it indicates a high level of partnership and helps to strengthen customer relationships.

Making it difficult to provide feedback

If you want to encourage feedback, make it easy for your visitors. Calls to telephone hotlines should be free. Postal surveys and questionnaires should have the return postage paid. Any questionnaires should be brief, and should not ask for much personal information. You should also provide facilities on your website for customers to provide feedback or submit a response to a survey using an electronic form.

Poor complaints management

If you do not record and analyse complaints and other feedback, you may not spot emerging trends. A series of complaints on the same issue indicates a recurring problem that could be dangerous to your company if it is not resolved quickly. Set up a formal mechanism for recording all feedback.

RECOMMENDED LINK
Chartered Institute of Marketing:
www.cim.co.uk

SEE ALSO
Carrying Out Market Research (p. 226)
**Involving Customers in Product or
  Service Development (p. 233)**

Involving Customers in Product or Service Development

GETTING STARTED

For some people, 'new product development' means inventing something wonderfully new. In reality, though, the vast majority of new products are modifications of existing ideas. In some cases, 'new product development' can also mean adding an element of service onto a (physical) product.

The power of new product development is that your business may be able meet a customer's need more closely than the competition. Involving customers creates the possibility of your product or service being tailor-made for them, thereby encouraging loyalty.

FAQS

Is there a risk in letting customers evaluate new products before launch?

There are two risks. Firstly, the customer may be extremely disappointed with the product if quality is poor. Secondly, there is a risk that competitors could find out about your plans indirectly. The quality issue is one that you should deal with: if a product is not right, it should not be given to customers in any form—it is not enough simply to promise future improvements. The security risk of a leak to competitors can be minimised through disclosure and confidentiality agreements, although these provide no real guarantee. Having said that, the advantages of involving customers outweigh the risks, so evaluation is worthwhile.

How practical is it for customers and suppliers to collaborate on product development?

There are different levels of collaboration. Some may involve regular meetings to provide input and review progress. These meetings can be held on site or remotely, using video-conference links. In some cases, customer staff may work alongside the supplier team for all or part of the project. Secondment like this can provide other benefits for the customer by improving the technical knowledge of their staff.

Does pre-announcement put new product launches at risk?

Some companies, particularly in the IT sec-

tor, have put themselves under unnecessary pressure by trying to meet a series of pre-announced release dates. The schedule may not allow proper time for development, resulting in failure to meet the date, or the release of a product that is not ready. Both are potentially damaging.

MAKING IT HAPPEN

Ask customers before you launch your product

If you are planning a new product or redeveloping an existing one, ask your customers for their views on the existing product and what they would like to see in a new one. By explaining your plans and involving customers in product development, you can strengthen relationships and provide a service that is mutually beneficial. Questions could include:

- How is the product used?
- How can we improve the current product?
- What problems have been encountered?
- What new features would customers welcome?
- Do the plans represent an improvement?
- Would customers make greater use of a product that included the features they have highlighted?

Set up a user group

You can encourage feedback and build a sense of community by setting up a user group, which can be online and may allow customers to share experiences or solve one another's problems. The user group can operate as a forum for discussing issues of mutual concern to customers such as quality, performance, standards, future developments, and customer concerns. The group would include representatives from your own company and from a cross-section of your customers. Comments from the user group provide valuable feedback on current performance and help to identify needs that can be met through new product development.

Ask customers to evaluate new products

Customer evaluation, or beta testing, is well established in the software industry. Customers test new products or upgraded versions before they are released to the market. They identify any problems in using the software, thus providing valuable feedback on product performance.

Issue new product announcements

Another valuable practice from the IT industry is to pre-announce new products. For example, a company will set a number of release dates during the coming year when it will release new versions of products. The company outlines the new products and gives customers the opportunity to provide input to the development process. The major benefit for customers is that they can align their own business development plans to the release dates.

Work in partnership with customers

Product development can be a joint initiative where you work closely with specific customers to develop products that meet their specific needs. This approach is a valuable one where:
- your customers have developed partnership sourcing to take advantage of your technology
- your customers have technology and technical skills that complement your own, and a joint project can produce more effective results
- you want to strengthen relationships with key customers by working in partnership on joint development projects

Understand your customers' markets

The new products you develop could enable your customers to improve their competitive performance, so it is important to understand their markets. Tell customers about your product plans and ask them for input to your development process. By building a detailed picture of their markets, you can align your own plans with them, and develop products that are tailored to their needs.
- What are their main markets?
- What is their position in the marketplace?
- Who are their main competitors?
- How are their products regarded in the marketplace?
- What are the key success factors in the market?
- What are the long-term product trends?
- What new technical developments will be needed to succeed?
- Could innovation by you help your customers to succeed?
- Are your customers considering entry into new markets?
- Do you have product development plans that are relevant to the new market?

Understand customer strategies

It is equally important to understand your customers' business strategies: their corporate direction and key objectives, and how they aim to succeed. By aligning your product development objectives with theirs, and showing how your products or services can help them to achieve their strategic business objectives, you can improve the chances of your new products being successful.

There are two possible approaches to customer-focused product development. Where your customers want to become market leaders through innovation, your new product programmes can help them develop the right level of innovation without investment in their own skills. Where they want to succeed through competitive pricing, you can help them reduce overall costs by developing cost-effective products.

Assess the value of your products and services

Products that help your customers to meet their strategic business objectives can increase the chances of new product success. The more your customers depend on your new product, the more demanding they will be. If you can keep up with their demands, try to anticipate and meet them —and you'll not only help yourself but also create barriers for your competitors.

For example, if your customer must develop new products quickly in order to retain and protect market share, your own new products can be critical to their product development programme.

Analyse your customers' technical requirements

When you're assessing new product development opportunities, think about how your products can help your customers. They can use your skills in a number of ways:

- improving the performance of their own products and services by using your design and development skills. They may gain privileged access to your technical skills to improve their own competitive performance.
- using your technical expertise to enhance the skills of their own technical staff, enabling them to make a more effective contribution to their own product development process
- using your technical resources to handle product development on a subcontract basis. This provides your partners with access to specialist resources or to additional research and development capacity, to improve the performance of their product development programmes
- using your technical expertise to develop new products that they could not achieve themselves. This provides your customers with new technology, and allows them to diversify in line with your specialist skills
- using your design skills to improve through-life costs (the total cost of owning and using a product, including purchase price, maintenance, and any other related costs). By carrying out value engineering studies on your customers' products, you may be able to reduce overall costs and improve reliability by designing components that are easier to assemble and maintain.

WHAT TO AVOID
Not involving your customers sufficiently

Product development should be focused on customer needs. Although most companies carry out research before development, the research may not provide the detailed input that is essential. Product development may also be driven by technology, with no clear market focus. The more your customer depends on your product, the more likely it is to succeed, so involving customers can pay real dividends.

Ignoring user groups

There are many examples of companies who have set up user groups in response to a crisis and then failed to use them. This can be frustrating for customers and wasteful for the companies. User groups provide a valuable perspective on products and services, and their feedback can provide real benefits for the product development process.

Failing to understand customer strategies

Where the supplier/customer relationship is that of a partnership, products are developed and customised to help customers meet their business objectives. It is essential, therefore, to understand customers' markets and business strategies so that your product plans can be integrated with theirs.

RECOMMENDED LINK
Chartered Institute of Marketing:
www.cim.co.uk

SEE ALSO
Getting More Feedback from Customers (p. 230)

Converting Leads into Sales

GETTING STARTED
If you are trying to grow your business, finding leads (that is, potential new customers) is just the beginning. Before they can benefit you in any way, you need to turn those leads into sales. This actionlist offers a systematic approach to doing this, and to making sure that the leads are of the right kind in the first place—which will cut down on wasted time and resources.

FAQS
How far can services such as telemarketing take over from the salesforce?
These services can be used to handle many of the sales team's routine functions: carrying out initial research, qualifying prospective customers, making appointments, and maintaining regular contact. Despite these benefits, they're no substitute for face-to-face selling if that's important to your customer relationships, so make sure they're appropriate for your business.

What is the best way to measure lead conversion?
Measuring sales as a percentage of initial leads is too simplistic an approach: it is more effective to measure at each stage of the process. For example, only 50% of initial leads may turn out to be suitable prospective customers. If the leads have been well qualified, the sales team may be able to convert 20% of the final prospect list. Measuring results at each stage helps you focus the right level of resources and plan future lead-generation programmes.

Should we try to get as many leads as possible?
The quality of the leads is as important as the number. Following up a large number of unsuitable leads is a waste of resources, but getting as many good leads as possible is important to any company that wants to expand its business.

MAKING IT HAPPEN
Qualify your leads
Your lead-generation programme may have given you large numbers of leads, but not all of them will convert to sales. Some may be poor prospects, while others may simply be gathering information rather than planning a purchase. Good prospects have the following characteristics:

- the financial resources to purchase your product
- the authority to make a purchase decision
- a genuine need for your product or service
- the desire to learn more about your product
- plans to make a purchase in the near future

Telemarketing can be used to qualify the leads. Call the contact and ask for more details of their inquiry so that you can send information tailored to their needs. Just sending a brochure, with no accompanying letter and no understanding of the prospective customer's needs, is a waste of money.

Qualifying questions can include:

- Are you the person who makes the purchasing decision? If not, who does?
- Is your company currently buying this product?
- What quantities do you buy, or how much do you spend on the service?
- When are you likely to make your next purchase?
- What information do you need on our product and company?

Choose a one-step or two-step process
In the case of some products and services, the lead-generation and sales conversion processes can be combined. These are known as one-step programmes, and are equivalent to direct selling operations. They are suitable for:

- inexpensive products
- information services such as newsletter or magazine subscriptions
- office supplies

- software
- low-value financial offers

In a two-step programme, the prospective customer (prospect) requests initial information. You send the information and then continue following up until the prospect is ready to buy. Two-step programmes are suitable for:

- expensive offers
- complex technical products
- professional services
- high-value financial services

Plan the conversion process

Lead conversion can be a long-term continuous process, the duration of which depends on the complexity of the product and of the decision-making process. For example, how many people are involved or how important is the product to the customer (or the customer's business)?

For a complex product, the process could be:

- identifying key decision-makers
- sending information to key decision-makers
- arranging meetings with decision-makers
- providing sample products for evaluation by the customer
- bidding for a contract against competition
- final negotiations
- purchase
- after-sales service and support

You must decide how you will handle each stage of the process, who will be involved in the sales team, and how you will manage communications with the prospect.

Another example could be where the product and the purchasing process are simpler, but the prospect is reluctant to change suppliers. The conversion process could take a long time, so you must plan a programme to maintain contact and move the prospect away from the existing supplier. Actions could include:

- personalised direct mail with product information
- regular updates on new developments in the company
- targeted special offers to encourage the customer to try the product

Allocate responsibility

Normally, the marketing department generates leads and the sales department follows up. It is important for the two departments to work together to integrate their activities and ensure that the company focuses on the kind of high-quality prospects it really needs. Sales departments frequently complain about the quantity and quality of leads. They want as many leads as possible so that the final number of new sales is high; however, they may also complain if too many of the leads are of poor quality and do not meet the right criteria. Collecting a large number of high-quality leads can be a difficult balancing act. Some sales teams prefer to do their own qualifying, while others prefer to leave that to others so that they can concentrate on face-to-face meetings with prospects.

Back the sales team with telemarketing

Telemarketing can be used to enhance the performance and productivity of the salesforce. The telemarketing team can be responsible for following up sales leads, qualifying prospects, setting up appointments, and maintaining contact with longer-term prospects. This frees the salesforce to increase the number of face-to-face meetings and to concentrate on the most likely prospects. The integration of telemarketing with the salesforce can play an important part in reducing overall sales costs. The cost of keeping a sales team on the road continues to soar, and it may not always represent the most cost-effective way of reaching the right people.

Maintain a contact diary

A contact diary can help you plan the conversion process and make sure that the sales team does not miss any important contact opportunities. It also ensures that the sales backup team integrates its follow-up activities with the field salesforce. Computer software is available which allows sales teams to operate a sales diary and record details of meetings and other follow-up activities. The same software can be used by the management team to monitor progress and ensure that no important contacts are overlooked. Contact diaries can include details on the customer, the customer's likes and dislikes, availability for meetings or telephone calls, their buying limits/authorisation, and even personal information that helps maintain a relationship with them.

Track progress

It is essential to track progress at each stage of the conversion process. If the prospect is important, you may wish to allocate additional resources to win the business. If a prospect is of only minor importance but is taking time and resources, you may want to refocus the efforts of the salesforce. The progress from initial lead to customer goes through a number of stages:

- raw lead: an initial enquiry from any source
- suspect: an enquiry that has been qualified and has the potential to become a paying customer
- prospect: a lead that has been qualified in more detail
- inactive lead: a prospect who will not buy now but has future potential
- dead lead: a prospect who has little potential to become a customer
- customer

You might also include lapsed customers in this process as a source of qualified leads.

Choose the right contact frequency

A single mailshot, telephone call, or direct response advertisement may produce results, but a series of quality contacts will have greater impact and ensure you meet your response targets. Multiple direct marketing activities raise levels of awareness with each contact; follow up contacts who have not responded; and move individual respondents further along the decision-making process.

Use personalised contact

Personalised one-to-one mailings are an ideal form of communication for companies with detailed information on their prospects. The letter reflects the individual prospect's main interests and concerns, and the offer can be tailored to the prospect's needs. Subsequent mailings can build an individual relationship with the prospect.

WHAT TO AVOID
Focusing on the wrong prospects

Sales teams have a natural tendency to deal with friendly prospects and avoid the difficult ones. From a business perspective, however, they may be dealing with the wrong people. The qualifying process should be used to identify the most important prospects in order to improve the targeting of the salesforce.

Poor management

Lead conversion can be a long, complicated process, so it is essential to monitor progress and manage the programme carefully. Lead conversion can use a lot of salesforce and telemarketing resources, and careful planning can make sure that it is carried out effectively.

Putting all the burden on the salesforce

In some organisations, the salesforce is given total responsibility for generating leads, qualifying them, and converting them into sales. This may not represent the best use of salesforce resources. Telemarketing or other tools can be used to supplement the salesforce and take over routine tasks.

RECOMMENDED LINK
Chartered Institute of Marketing:
www.cim.co.uk

SEE ALSO
Handling Customer Inquiries (p. 247)

Retaining Existing Customers

GETTING STARTED

Just about every business will depend to a certain extent on repeat sales from customers who have already bought from them. In fact in some cases, repeat sales from existing customers will be the biggest revenue-generating source. However, many business owners just don't understand this and fail to realise that establishing a long-term relationship with a loyal customer base is as important, if not more important, than getting sales from new customers in the first place.

If your business is one of those where customers are likely to come back and buy the same product or more products from you over and over again, then it will be vital that you do everything you can to keep them satisfied and loyal to your business for as long as possible. This actionlist contains some ideas on how to ensure that this is the case. One book on the subject you may also find useful is *The Loyalty Effect: The Hidden Force Behind Growth, Profits and Lasting Value* by Frederick Reichheld, published by Harvard Business School Press in 1996.

FAQS

Why do I need to bother with customers when they've already bought from me?

Now that you've worked out your ideal market audience and made those all-important first sales, your business will only really outstrip your competitors in the long term when you truly understand why those customers have bought from you. Was it your price? Your products? Because of a special offer? Once you know why you've attracted these customers, you'll have a unique opportunity to persuade them to buy from you again and again.

How can I gain the edge over my competitors?

Even if you are lucky enough to be the first into a new market, it won't be long before someone else follows suit. Think carefully about what can you do to make sure customers stay loyal to you as long as they are in the market for your service. Can you create a unique selling proposition (USP) that will lock them into *your* business rather than the competition? The vast majority of businesses concentrate on achieving a profit from first time or single sales and don't appreciate that meeting the needs of their customers over the longer term will reap far greater benefits.

MAKING IT HAPPEN

Identify what unique benefits you can offer

People do not buy products for their features. They buy to satisfy their needs and will aim to acquire something that will provide them with a valuable solution from which they will benefit them personally. To succeed in your marketing and create a long-term loyal customer base, you will need to identify the unique value that you can provide over and above your basic product or service offering. It is this value, the unique combination of benefits to your customers, that must be at the core of your marketing strategy, and which your competitors will not be able to match.

Offer value that will make customers loyal to you

The key to this is not to think about individual features of your service, but to concentrate on how the benefit within that product or service impacts on your customers' long-term personal needs. These needs often fall into the following categories.

- **A feeling of belonging.** People like people, and they like to do what other people like themselves are doing—for example, being in associations, or in membership schemes. They like being part of a cause and surrounding themselves with people they consider to be their peers. Can you offer something to your customers to satisfy their sense of belonging? Is there something that they can join as part of their purchase of your service? Could you set up a user group? Can you publish a top sellers' list for your products?

- **Self-improvement and self-esteem.** Just as with belonging, people will often choose to purchase something that makes them feel better, fitter, healthier, or just more important. Do you recognise something in your customer's requirements where your product or service can help them satisfy this need? Can you include this in your USP and marketing message?
- **Being reminded that they have made a good choice.** For customers in many situations, the purchase decision is fraught with fear of making the wrong choice. Look for ways you can remind or reward your customers for making the right purchase by buying from you. Can you think of ways to make it a risk free, 100% secure experience for the buyer—for example through extended warranties, money back guarantees, or free after-sales support for long periods? Can you make this better than what your competitors are offering?
- **A sense of achievement.** Is there a way that you can make your customers feel that, by buying from you now and in the future, they are going to put themselves in a much better situation or position than they were in before? Can you create something unique in your after sales service? Is it possible to offer some form of loyalty points scheme, future discounts, or reward scheme that delivers more benefits the longer they remain as your customer?
- **Being educated about your service.** Do you go out of your way to tell customers regularly and in detail about the wise decision they have made in buying from you? Do you let them know how they can get even more benefits by buying again, or can access special offers in the future only available to loyal customers of your business? Publishing a customer newsletter with informative, interesting, and relevant information

about how they can make best use of and get more value from your service, is a very popular method of achieving this.

- **Getting a personal and relevant service, exactly when they need it.** More than anything else your purchasers will place the greatest long-term value on your business and your product if they feel they will continue to receive personal attention and care from you whenever they need it. They must be made to feel that they are your most important customer every time they deal with you. Are there ways you can make the sales experience with your firm more fun, more exciting, more rewarding, more personal, and more relevant than it is at the moment? More importantly, can you make this a better experience than is being offered by your competition?

Make sure that your USP aims to keep them loyal

Gaining the loyalty and trust of your customers can only be achieved if they feel you are fulfilling their exact needs, and that they will continue to receive value from you that meets their needs in the future. Your USP needs to communicate the loyalty-building value that your service will provide—that your competitors cannot match. Every time your customer wants to re-purchase your type of product or service, your marketing proposition must make it as difficult as possible for them to say no to you. Does your USP express this value strongly enough? Think of the services that you repeatedly buy from other suppliers yourself. Why do you remain loyal to them? What is it that makes you want to keep on purchasing from them? If you can recognise what this is, you should aim to replicate the same value in the service you provide to your own customers.

WHAT TO AVOID
Letting customers forget
You have done all the hard work and built up a solid customer base, so don't let them forget why they bought from you, or the extra value they can receive by continuing to buy from you in the future. Your loyalty-building

strategy should look for continual ways to communicate with and educate your customers about the benefits of your service: competitions, special offers, new product lines, open days, and so on. A newsletter, especially by e-mail, is a very popular and cost-effective way of doing this. If you let them forget you are there, or what you can offer them, they will eventually buy from someone else instead.

Failing to make them feel appreciated

Each customer must feel as if he or she is the most important one you have. If they feel neglected, they're much more likely to try a different service and give one of your competitors a try instead. If you have the names and addresses of your customers, aim to write to them and thank them for their custom on a regular basis. When they first buy from you, ask them if they would like to receive advance details of special offers or new products in the future. If they agree, ask for their telephone number,

e-mail, or other contact details and make sure you communicate with them regularly.

Whenever possible, reward them with loyalty-building discounts and offers for repeat purchases, or ask them individually—as one of your most valued customers—for their views and opinions about how they use your service, and how you can improve it for them. If they feel appreciated, their loyalty and their trust in you and your service will almost certainly follow.

RECOMMENDED LINK
CRM Daily:
http://crm-daily.newsfactor.com/perl/ section/lylt/

SEE ALSO
Communicating Customer Service (p. 245)
Corporate Hospitality (p. 256)
Involving Customers in Product or Service Development (p. 233)
Public Relations (p. 541)
Selling and Salesmanship (p. 546)

Extending a Product with Service

GETTING STARTED

'Service' is a business concept that's often overlooked or relegated to somewhere inbetween maintenance and problem-solving. Done properly, though, service can be a key differentiator between your business and the competition. Meeting customer requirements in the most appropriate and efficient way adds enormously to the perceived value of your product, and can sometimes increase the profitability of your relationship.

FAQS

My product is a market leader. Why would services be important?

Services can add further value to a product, providing incremental income and increasing customer loyalty. Services provide you with an opportunity to working with a customer long after the initial sale and to develop your relationship with them.

I already offer free installation and maintenance with my products. Does that add value?

Yes. But whilst some customers may expect this, others may not, or may not value this service. Many companies have recognised the importance of service to certain customers, and have changed their service strategy accordingly. Instead of offering free service to everyone, they have upgraded the services, increased the range of services offered, and therefore, in some cases, started charging customers. Although customers may initially object to being charged for something that seemed to be free, they may see the value of a service that now more closely meets their needs.

I don't have the skills or resources to deliver services. How can I offer my customers a service?

You can either build your own service team through recruitment and training, or work in partnership with a specialist organisation which will deliver service on your behalf.

My customers have their own internal service people. Why should they want to use my services?

Many companies have internal service departments. They can be expensive to maintain, however, and are sometimes lacking in essential skills—for example, they may not be trained in the latest software. By demonstrating the potential savings and benefits of outsourcing a service, you can persuade them to switch to you.

MAKING IT HAPPEN
Differentiate your product with service

Service is proving to be a key differentiator in many market sectors. In many companies, however, the role of the service department should be more than simply maintenance and problem-solving. For example, a company supplying industrial dishwashers to the restaurant trade has to respond quickly to breakdowns—replacing the machine if necessary rather than simply scheduling a repair visit. So, to take full advantage of the service opportunity, it is important to explain the benefits of effective service to customers, and present your service operations as convenient, cost-effective, and strategically important.

Meet key service attributes

These are some of the key features that customers may be looking for in a service offer:

- one contact point, simplifying contact and service administration
- direct contact with a technical specialist, providing an immediate response to problems or queries wherever the customer is located
- quality support to a standard such as ISO 9000, giving independent reassurance that service standards are high

- support round the clock which means that it is available when the customer needs it, and minimises interruption of their business
- a choice of service levels, which can be aligned to customers' needs
- investment in support means long-term commitment to the customer

Provide one contact point for service resources

Whether your customers have a technical query, a service request, or a product enquiry, or need advice, guidance, or information, they should be able to call one number for direct access to all your support resources. Ideally, you'll have specialists on the spot to deal with their requests. If they can't answer the query straight away, make sure that the right person calls the customer back.

Offer direct contact with technical specialists

Your customers may have a technical query, and want to talk to an experienced specialist straight away. When they call the technical help desk, they should be talking to a highly skilled person with extensive technical support and field experience. It may mean locating support staff in accessible locations to be able to make visits quickly and efficiently.

Provide good support

When your customers have a service request, they should be able to contact a central service point where a service co-ordinator ensures that the right specialist help is available. Service co-ordinators should ensure that customers get the fastest and most effective response to their requests. In some cases, service points can deal with requests directly but if not, they can assign an engineer to visit the customer site within agreed times. All service processes should be assessed to ISO 9000. If customers have any queries, there should be an 'escalation procedure' to move a customer complaint up to a more senior team member if the person dealing with the complaint initially cannot resolve it. This

should ensure a prompt resolution of any problems.

Offer flexible service options

You can provide your customers with a choice of flexible service options to suit their operational needs and to increase their loyalty. If your customers have in-house support, you can support their team with an efficient spares delivery service, or manage their spares for them. You can also offer to enhance the skills of your customer's in-house team with training, advice and guidance, technical support, and access to specialists. You may go as far as offering consultancy on a fee basis, utilising your specialist knowledge to help your customer.

Invest in support

High-quality service for your market may require a significant investment in the service infrastructure; the right premises, efficient service communications, and a sophisticated service management system to enable you to enhance your response and performance even further. It may require you to appoint one person with specific responsibility for customer service or, perhaps, develop a dedicated support website.

Add value to a product

Improving your customer service may add value and help to differentiate your products and services from the competition. By analysing the products and services in your range (and those of your competitors), you can add relevant value and improve a customer's perception of your business. Some examples are:

- business services that free up customer staff to do more important tasks, or help managers perform their jobs better. Training, for example, can ensure that staff make more effective use of the products the company buys
- complementary services to make a consumer product more attractive, such as film processing offered with a camera
- convenience services added to a basic service to enhance it. Insurance companies,

for example, might add a helpline or list of approved repairers to help their customers recover more quickly from an accident

Develop product/service packages
To add value to products and to increase customer loyalty, put together 'bundles' of products and services that reflect customer needs. The list below shows examples of this.

'Adding-in' services
- specialist package holidays, including flights, hotel, and guides
- a building company includes plans and planning application services

'Leaving-out' services
- 'fastfit' car repair centres, without non-essential services
- specialised conveyancing services without using solicitors

Added value services
- home delivery of fast food or videos
- support and advice through helplines

Changing distribution channels
- direct sales, bypassing retailers, such as organic vegetable 'box schemes'
- electronic delivery, such as delivery of technical drawings and specifications

WHAT TO AVOID
Offering only basic services
Basic services such as installation, maintenance, and upgrades are available from many different service organisations. They do not differentiate you and they do not add value. Higher-value services, requiring skill, knowledge, or experience, are the keys to success.

Failing to invest in a service infrastructure
Customers expect a quality service. That means you have to invest in people and infrastructure. Ideally, your services should conform to recognised industry standards. If you fail to deliver the right standard of service, you could damage customer relationships.

Missing service opportunities
Customers require many different services during the time they own a product. Their requirements could include advice, consultancy, and design before the sale; installation, and training; followed by maintenance, upgrading, and other after-sales services. Each of these represents an opportunity to earn incremental income and maintain contact with the customer.

RECOMMENDED LINK
Chartered Institute of Marketing: **www.cim.co.uk**

Communicating Customer Service

GETTING STARTED

Your business won't survive without customers, and you need to get across how much you value them. To communicate well externally, you need to have in place a clear, consistent, internal communications strategy too. If you have a team of people working with you, let them know how they each contribute to your business's success, and that the way they interact with your customers is a key part of this.

FAQS

Who is responsible for customer service?

Everyone in a business contributes to overall customer satisfaction, even if their jobs do not involve direct customer contact. Broken delivery promises, inaccurate invoices, or poor telephone handling can cancel out the benefits of a good product or service.

Why are award programmes important to the success of customer service?

Customer service staff are in the front line, facing difficult customers and frequent problems. Award programmes can help to maintain motivation and demonstrate that their contribution is important.

Isn't customer service the same as marketing?

Certain aspects of customer service—understanding customer needs, delivering a service, tailoring the offer to meet customer requirements—are the same, but the scope of marketing is much broader.

Is customer service just a set of personal skills?

Personal skills are important, but a company can put in place processes and programmes that improve the customer's experience and make it easier and more convenient for the customer to do business.

MAKING IT HAPPEN
Communicate clearly

When a company changes its focus towards customer service, it is essential that everyone is involved. Change creates an atmosphere of uncertainty, so it is vital that everyone understands, the important issues, and feels that they can contribute to the success of the change. In an atmosphere of uncertainty, customer service levels can be adversely affected.

Build understanding

Organisational changes can have a significant impact on employees, suppliers, and distributors—so it is vital that they are thoroughly briefed. Change can be a powerful positive factor rather than a cause for concern, and change can demonstrate that a business is committed to improvement and progress.

Encourage commitment

Implementing a customer service policy requires commitment and involvement from all employees. Before implementing a programme, it is sensible to find what the level of commitment is, and to include staff in discussion. The most important part of the process is the follow-up. Too many employees believe views will be ignored.

Encourage improvement

As far as possible, training should be offered to all staff to help them understand the importance of customer care. A customer satisfaction guide could be issued, describing the most important elements of customer service and the standards which apply.

Maintain motivation

Motivation and award programmes can help to maintain high levels of interest in the customer service programme and build a high level of commitment to the programme's success. Award programmes that reward continued improvement in levels of customer satisfaction maintain momentum, and give customer service programmes a high profile. They are therefore valuable in building team spirit and a commitment to excellence.

Provide a vision

Clear visions and strong, motivating language focus attention on the importance of customer service programmes. It is also essential that the programme is led from the top. A key figure should be involved personally in every aspect of the programme—talking to groups of employees and using every public relations opportunity to raise its profile.

Develop champions

The leader cannot achieve all the objectives alone, so it is essential that other people with influence can take on the role of supporting the message throughout the business. Management commentators often call these people 'champions'. Their task is build commitment and enthusiasm for change. They may be the very people who could undermine change if left out of the process, though.

WHAT TO AVOID
Treating customer service as a departmental function

Customer service is often left only to those staff who are directly involved with customers. This is too limited a view, because customer service is relegated to a sales or complaints handling process.

Managing customer service at departmental level

If customer service is treated as a line management function, staff will not appreciate its critical importance to the success of the business. Customer service must be led from the top, with the direct involvement of a senior manager.

Failure to develop customer service skills

It's a common misconception that customer service quality depends solely on personal skills. Customer service standards can be improved through training and through the introduction of customer service programmes.

Low recognition

Customer service has long suffered from low perceived status. Motivation and reward programmes, together with leadership from the top, can help to redress the balance.

RECOMMENDED LINK
Chartered Management Institute:
www.managers.org.uk

SEE ALSO
Corporate Hospitality (p. 256)
Handling Customer Inquiries (p. 247)
Handling Customer Problems (p. 250)
Retaining Existing Customers (p. 239)

Handling Customer Inquiries

GETTING STARTED

Businesses need mechanisms to cope with inquiries or requests for help from both existing and potential customers. This actionlist offers some information on the different options open to you.

Helplines are essential for delivering support, service, advice, and information to customers, and add value to a business. To provide the best service, use staff with extensive, up-to-date product knowledge and strong interpersonal skills, and train them in customer service techniques to ensure they can deal effectively with different types of query or problem. To maximise the benefit to users of the service, deal with queries immediately where possible, or arrange to call the customer back on more complex queries, and ensure that the customer is satisfied with the response at the end of the conversation.

FAQS

Should helpline services be offered free to customers?

Helpline services fall into a number of categories: support, help with problems, advice, and useful information. The support categories should be free because they are essential for customer satisfaction. The information services can also be seen as a customer service, something that adds value to the original purchase. You may feel it strengthens customer relationships to continue offering them free. Information services offered to the general public are valuable services that can be charged, usually through a premium rate number.

Which staff should work on the helplines?

Trained customer service staff can help customers report a problem effectively and may be able to offer advice or help up to a certain level. When the query goes beyond their level of knowledge, you should have a two-stage process in which the customer service representative takes the initial call, and arranges for a specialist to call the customer back within an agreed time.

Can a helpline service be handled by an external organisation?

Provided the external organisation's team undergoes thorough training, there is no reason why the helpline cannot be outsourced. The practice is common in the computer industry.

MAKING IT HAPPEN
Set up a helpline

The most important thing about a helpline is that it really needs to *help*, so there are a number of rules to remember when setting one up.

- Make it convenient: offer customers a Freephone facility to encourage contact, and set opening times to suit customer calling patterns.
- Get the right staff: use staff with extensive, up-to-date product knowledge, and make sure that they are trained in customer service techniques so that they can deal effectively with different types of query or problem.
- Provide the right back-up: helpline staff need to have access to any existing product, technical, or service databases, as well as guidelines on the actions they can take to deal with different types of complaint. Make sure they also have lists of contacts for authorisation of different types of action and information.
- Make the service fast and reliable: deal with queries immediately or arrange to call the customer back on more complex queries, and operate an 'escalation procedure' (see below for more information) to deal with complaints that cannot be resolved within agreed time scales.

- Check and double check: follow up to make sure that if a customer was promised a return call within an agreed time scale, it did happen and that he or she is satisfied with the response.

Plan helpline staffing levels

There's nothing worse that getting to a helpline but then being kept on hold for a long time. It really is crucial to get your staffing levels right, so ask your telephone supplier to provide a report on the number of calls to the helpline number, as well as the average waiting time, and then analyse the pattern of calls during the day/week/month/year, identifying the peaks and troughs. This will help you to determine the current and planned level of calls per day; the ratio of staff to calls, and therefore how many helpline staff you need.

If you have very marked peak and off-peak periods, decide whether you can meet demand using current staff resources, or whether it might be beneficial to use technologies such as voicemail to handle some of the incoming calls. If you can afford it, you could also consider using an external call handling service to manage overload or peak traffic.

Identify helpline skills

Make sure that your staff meet a checklist of appropriate helpline skills. These might include product knowledge, telephone technique, and technical, product service, administrative, and customer service skills.

Develop helpline skills

Regardless of how good your staff are, there are always ways in which you can help them improve and develop their skills. Assess the skills required for different types of helpline service, compare these with the current skills of your helpline staff, and identify the areas that need to be improved. Implement training and monitor performance improvements, ensure that staff know how to use any new technology, and obtain customer feedback to evaluate performance.

Provide customer information for helpline staff

Your staff will be able to provide a prompt response and personal service if they've been given enough customer information. Make available the information you already have, such as existing customer records, data generated by responses to advertisements or promotional activities, and so on, and make sure it is checked and updated. Take the opportunity to capture customer information each time a customer calls, and add further information that is appropriate to the helpline service, such as service records. Use a simple code to access information quickly, for example, name, account number, and postcode, and include prompts to contact customers with details of new products and services.

Set up helpline escalation procedures

There are always some calls that cannot be dealt with immediately, so you need to have an escalation procedure in place to make sure they don't slip through the net. Identify critical types of helpline requests, including technical support, complaints, and breakdowns, and set target response times for such queries. Appoint a supervisor to monitor conformance to target response times; escalate any queries that exceed target times to a designated manager, and monitor the responses to escalated queries.

Record helpline usage

In order to make sure you are meeting demand properly, you need to record helpline usage. How many calls does your helpline receive: per day; per week; per month; per year? What types of call does it receive and what is the volume of each type of call? Which customers are the most regular helpline users? Which media generate most inquiries to the helpline? What is the impact of promotional campaigns on helpline activity? Which products receive most/least: complaints, queries, or requests for support? What are the most frequent complaints, queries, and requests for support? Which type of request uses most resources?

What is the average call time for different types of request?

Promote the helpline service

Above all, make sure customers know what help is available to them. Include the help-line number in advertisements, publications, website pages, and other promotional material, as well as on invoices, delivery notes, instructions, user guides, and other product documentation.

WHAT TO AVOID

Putting the wrong people on the helpline

The people who run the helpline should have good customer handling skills, and a level of product and technical knowledge that enables them to provide the right answer or put the customer in contact with the right specialist.

Inadequate resources on the helpline

When customers call a helpline, they are looking for a quick response. Phones that go unanswered for long periods of time show poor customer service. Putting a customer in a queue of other callers is satisfactory only for a short period of time.

Failing to call the customer back

If you cannot deal with queries immediately, let the customer know when someone will get back to him or her, and then check that the return call has been made.

RECOMMENDED LINK

Call Centre Association:
www.cca.org.uk

SEE ALSO

Communicating Customer Service (p. 245)
Converting Leads into Sales (p. 236)
Handling Customer Problems (p. 250)

Handling Customer Problems

GETTING STARTED

Even the most professional service companies will inevitably face a problem with a customer that, if left unresolved, may lead to a loss of business. Customers who know that their problems are taken care of are more likely to be fully satisfied with the services that are available. A key factor in resolving customers' problems is the ability to reassure them that help is on the way. Having in place a process to respond quickly and effectively to a problem enables a company to deliver the highest standards of customer care at a time when the customer most needs it.

This process, sometimes called incident management, is particularly suitable for larger companies or if the customer is likely to suffer a great deal of inconvenience because of the incident. However, the principles can be applied to any business, however small.

- In developing a response and support strategy, you should set a wide range of business objectives.
- The incident management approach is to appoint one person, trained in customer service skills, to deal with a customer throughout an incident.
- The role of the personal incident manager is to take responsibility for the provision of appropriate services.
- An incident management programme has two main elements—the infrastructure to deliver the service, and the personal skills to provide the right level of customer care.
- Skilled staff are essential to the effective delivery of the service, and training may be necessary.
- Many equipment manufacturers use incident management techniques to support their customers after a disaster.

FAQS

Should incident management form part of all service offerings?

It depends on the type of service that is offered. If the service is critical to the customer's business process—telecommunications or computing, for example—incident management would be important. Disruption to those services could damage the customer's business.

Why is a personal incident manager necessary?

During an incident, effective co-ordination of support services and regular communication with the customer are essential. By appointing a single person to take responsibility for co-ordination and communication, you can guarantee continuity and reassure the customer by giving them a single point of contact.

Is it possible to plan for future incidents?

It isn't just possible; it is essential. Industry research indicates that a high proportion of companies who did not have a documented plan failed to recover lost business. Planning is just as important as quality support services.

MAKING IT HAPPEN
Deal with customer incidents

Customers who know that their problems are taken care of are more likely to be fully satisfied with the services that are available, and will be happier to deal with the same company in the future. Quality experts found that a key factor in delivering time-guaranteed services was the ability to reassure customers that help was on the way. Customers would then be prepared to wait until help or support arrived, even if there was a long gap between reporting the incident and having it resolved. Other research has shown that customers whose complaints are satisfactorily dealt with are likely to be more loyal than those who had no complaint in the first place.

Identify opportunities for incident management

A number of scenarios can be used to identify situations where support like this could be valuable.

- The customer could suffer a great deal of inconvenience and stress as a result of the incident. Reducing the stress and inconvenience would help to demonstrate high levels of care and increase customer satisfaction.
- The incident could threaten the efficiency of the company business, and measures must be taken to limit the damage.
- The customer does not have the skills and resources to resolve the problems on the spot, and is dependent on external forms of support.
- The customer has paid for a support package and has agreed to a certain level of response. The company must respond within the agreed levels.
- The speed of response is seen as a competitive differentiation and is positioned as an integral part of the service package.
- Failure to deal with the incident quickly could have a critical effect on the customer's business or personal activities.
- The incident could have legal implications, and the customer needs high levels of advice and guidance.

Set objectives for incident management

In developing a response and support strategy, you should set a wide range of business objectives:

- to provide the highest levels of quality response and customer support throughout an incident
- to minimise inconvenience for the customer
- to ensure that incidents are resolved promptly within agreed time scales
- to ensure that support resources are deployed effectively to maximise customer satisfaction

Introduce incident management

The incident management approach is to appoint one person, trained in customer service skills, to deal with a customer throughout an incident.

Incident management can be applied to any service-led organisation where the customer needs to be kept informed, for example, maintenance and support services for vital equipment or disaster recovery services, where the customer faces difficult and unfamiliar decisions and needs support.

Appoint a personal incident manager

The role of the personal incident manager is to take responsibility for the provision of appropriate services and to reassure the customer that help and support are on the way. In the smaller company, this may be a senior manager, even the managing director, but whoever takes the role must have the authority to take appropriate action. The personal incident manager:

- takes the incoming calls from the customer, establishes the location, and identifies the form of support needed
- provides individual guidance to the customer on action to be taken, with an indication of the support that will be provided
- deals with the customer's immediate queries
- makes detailed arrangements to put support services into operation
- monitors the progress of support services and keeps the customer up to date if possible

Offer disaster recovery services

Many equipment manufacturers use incident management techniques to support their customers after a disaster such as fire, accident, or system breakdown. If the customer loses essential equipment such as computers or telephones for an extended period, this could seriously threaten the future of their business. Industry research shows that only a minority of companies dependent on the computer have a formal disaster recovery strategy, and points out that loss of a system for more than a few days could put them out of business.

Plan and implement disaster recovery

A disaster recovery programme has a number of stages:

- helping the customer identify critical activities that should be covered in the event of a disaster
- training staff and managers to prepare for a disaster by simulating the conditions of an emergency
- preparing a contingency plan
- providing replacement equipment and services in the event of an incident
- providing support and project management resources during an incident
- providing full support to restore normal service

Throughout a disaster, the customer would have access to an incident manager who would co-ordinate the rescue and recovery activities, and provide advice, guidance, and support. The principle is similar to that of the personal incident manager, where customers are given reassurance that incidents will be resolved, and that they can be sure of the highest standards of support throughout the incident.

Create the infrastructure for incident management

The programme has two main elements: the infrastructure to deliver the service, and the personal skills to provide the right level of customer care. The infrastructure requires a significant investment to ensure that the service can be delivered rapidly and efficiently throughout the country. Depending on the complexity of the project, it might include:

- communications to provide a rapid response to customer queries, and put the service into operation
- a trained support team to deliver the service
- quality-controlled suppliers to support the direct response team
- a control centre to manage the operations and co-ordinate the response
- a network of contacts and suppliers to provide the specialist services that form part of the response

Develop the right skills

Skilled staff are essential to the effective delivery of the service. The skills requirements would include:

- incident management skills, to deal with customers who may be in stressful situations
- project management skills, to co-ordinate and implement a response
- technical skills, to deliver the service
- communications skills, to co-ordinate the elements of the programme

WHAT TO AVOID
Failing to communicate with the customer during an incident

Research shows that customers who receive regular progress updates feel reassured that they are getting the right level of support. Anxiety levels are high during an incident, but regular communication helps customers deal with the incident and contributes to overall customer satisfaction.

No escalation procedure

A company should have a formal escalation procedure for dealing with customer incidents. If support staff cannot resolve an incident within an agreed time scale, the incident should be reported to a more senior manager, who would then commit more resources. If there is no escalation procedure, the incident can get out of hand and damage customer relationships.

Failure to train staff in customer care

An incident creates high levels of stress in an organisation, and support staff must be trained to deal with this.

RECOMMENDED LINK
Chartered Institute of Marketing: **www.cim.co.uk**

SEE ALSO
Communicating Customer Service (p. 245)
Handling Customer Inquiries (p. 247)

Increasing Customer Lifetime Value

GETTING STARTED

'Customer lifetime value' (CLV or LTV) is a way of measuring how much your customers are worth over the time they buy your products and services. Increases in customer retention can increase sales and profits significantly. It is important to retain customers, but not at the cost of other essential marketing activities.

Putting customers into key categories helps clarify analysis, and acts as the basis for marketing activities designed to improve customer lifetime value.

FAQS

What's the difference between customer lifetime value and customer loyalty programmes?

Customer loyalty programmes are designed to retain as many customers as possible, regardless of their real value. The customer lifetime value calculation indicates the contribution individual customers make to profitability.

Why are lapsed customers important?

If they can be 'revived', they tend to behave like new customers and become regular buyers once again, with good potential lifetime value.

Is customer retention more important than acquisition?

Acquisition should never be neglected, because existing business may decline for reasons outside your control. Industry experience indicates, however, that existing customers make a comparatively greater contribution when marketing costs are taken into consideration.

Do we want to retain all our customers?

Not necessarily. Some customers may not be profitable. Using customer lifetime value, you can calculate the cost and contribution of each customer.

MAKING IT HAPPEN

Apply the customer lifetime value concept

Customer lifetime value is a way of measuring how much your customers are worth to

you, over the length of time that they remain your customers.

The lifetime for customers will vary from industry to industry, and from brand to brand. The lifetime of customers should come to an end when their contribution ceases to be profitable unless steps are taken to revitalise them.

Benefits from customer lifetime value

Industry experience indicates that a number of benefits apply:

- A 5% increase in customer retention can create a 125% increase in profits.
- A 10% increase in retailer retention can translate into a 20% increase in sales.
- Extending customer life cycles by three years can treble profits per customer.

Identify categories of customer

Before calculating customer lifetime value, it is possible to analyse your customers according to four key attributes. This can help to clarify analysis and act as the basis for marketing activities to improve customer lifetime value:

- Frequency—how often they purchase (regular customers are more likely to purchase in the future)
- Recency—how much time has elapsed since the last purchase (recent customers are more likely to purchase again)
- Amount—how much they spend (higher-spending customers are likely to be more committed)
- Category—what sort of product they buy (some products will be more profitable than others, and some may be one-off purchases)

Calculate lifetime value
In a consumer business, customer lifetime value is calculated, in practice, by analysing the behaviour of a group of customers who:
- have the same recruitment date
- are recruited from the same source
- bought the same types of product

In a business-to-business environment, a similar approach can be used:
- Isolate particular customers, and examine them individually.
- Analyse the behaviour of different groups, segmenting your customer database by factors such as industry, annual turnover, or staff numbers.

The basic calculation has three stages:
- Identify a discrete group of customers for tracking.
- Record (or estimate) each revenue and cost for this group of customers, by campaign or season.
- Calculate the contribution, by campaign or season.

Refine the calculation
Other factors can be introduced to make the calculation more relevant. In a business-to-business environment, for example, it may be the sales representatives who generate sales. In this case, the calculation should include the representative's 'running costs' and the cost of any centrally produced sales support material.

Evaluate a campaign
The table shows the calculations for a group of customers who were recruited through a direct response advertising campaign that ran in the spring of year 1. The table tracks their expenditure over a five-year period.

Divide the total contribution by the number of customers in the group. Say there are one thousand customers: the average lifetime value per customer is £7. But this compares favourably with a short term analysis which, in the first year, would show a loss of £3 per customer recruited.

Analyse the results
A company may offer different products or brands, which are marketed under different cost centres. If a customer is a customer of more than one cost/profit centre, there is a choice of approaches:
- examine customers of each brand and ignore multi-purchases
- build a more detailed model that combines and allocates the cumulative costs as well as the cumulative profit in the appropriate proportions

Use customer lifetime values to improve marketing performance
There are four important applications:
- setting target customer acquisition costs
- allocating acquisition funds
- selecting acquisition offers
- supporting customer retention activities

In the example above the decision was taken in Year 4 to reduce marketing costs on this group of customers. Equally valid may be an increase in expenditure aimed at reactivating customers—this is a classic retention activity.

Set target customer acquisition costs
If a customer is expected to generate more than one sale, the allowable cost can be greater than the cost allowed for the first sale—the classic loss-leader approach to customer acquisition, illustrated in the example

Year	Annual Customer Expenditure	Annual Marketing Costs	Annual Net Contribution
0	£12,000	£15,000	£–3,000
1	£10,000	£6,000	£4,000
2	£8,000	£6,000	£2,000
3	£7,000	£6,000	£1,000
4	£6,000	£4,000	£2,000
5	£5,000	£4,000	£1,000
Totals	**£48,000**	**£41,000**	**£7,000**

table above. However, overspending on customer acquisition can also be ruinous. A reasonable calculation is to recruit only from those sources that yield new customers at less than half the estimated lifetime value. On that basis, the worst sources will have a cost per customer close to a lifetime value, while the average cost per customer should be far lower.

Allocate acquisition funds
Different recruitment sources will provide customers with different lifetime values. After identifying those values, spend more on the best sources.

Select acquisition offers
The lifetime value of a customer may depend on the type and value of their initial purchase. In turn, this can lead to decisions about which products and offers to use when advertising externally, or when considering how to upgrade existing customers.

Support customer retention activities
Once the typical lifetime value of a group of customers is known, companies can decide how hard to work at retaining them. It is not a foregone conclusion that all customers are worth having. Activities should be tailored to the customers who are most valuable.

Increase value with new offers
A financial services company can increase customer lifetime value by cross-selling a range of different products and services.

WHAT TO AVOID
Trying to retain the wrong customers
Customer retention costs money in terms of sales and marketing funds, so do bear in mind that not all customers are worth keeping. You should carefully select the customers who are likely to yield the highest returns over a period of time, and prioritise the allocation of marketing resources to these.

Offering customers a limited range of products
When you have identified the most valuable customers, you need to have a wide range of products or services to offer them. Cross-selling and up-selling are the best ways to increase customer lifetime value, but this can be difficult with a limited product range. Customers are your company's most valuable asset; think about 'share of customer wallet' rather than just share of market.

Spending too much on acquiring new customers
Customer lifetime value analysis reinforces a traditional marketing rule of thumb, that it costs less to retain existing customers than to acquire new ones. Overemphasis on new business development could be a bad move, since existing customers are easier to sell to.

RECOMMENDED LINK
Peppers + Rogers:
www.www.1to1.com

Corporate Hospitality

GETTING STARTED

Corporate hospitality within a business can really help improve staff morale, perhaps by motivating a sales team, raising customer awareness, building team working skills, or celebrating a special occasion. There are many advantages to this approach, including improved communications and understanding, a stronger organisational spirit, and a reduction in staff turnover through boosted loyalty and greater motivation.

FAQS

What are the advantages and disadvantages of internal corporate hospitality?

Corporate hospitality may be used to improve staff morale, perhaps by motivating a sales team, raising customer awareness, building team working skills, celebrating a special occasion, or increasing business profits. Advantages can include improved communications and understanding, an improved organisational spirit, and a reduction in staff turnover through improved loyalty and greater motivation.

You do, however, need to be aware of some of the disadvantages to this approach. If you're holding a social event, make sure that all employees have an equal opportunity to attend. Give as much notice as you can so that people can make arrangements, such as finding a babysitter if they have children. Rather than concentrating on evening events, you may want to hold some at lunchtime too, so that those who have to travel a long way home can also come along. Also think very carefully about whom you wish to reward. For example, a gift given to one individual may be regarded as favouritism. It's important to exercise discretion and to be aware of the potential risks of damaging staff morale.

Do think long and hard about running a corporate event for employees purely because you think staff morale is low. There may be more practical reasons for staff discontent, for example salary or promotion problems, or lack of equipment, and team building activities are unlikely to rectify such problems—they could even compound them if your staff think you're spending what could be their bonus on a big party. Get to the root of the problem first and then decide whether a corporate event is the best way of solving it.

What are the advantages and disadvantages of external corporate hospitality?

External corporate hospitality promotes your business to existing or potential clients, providing an environment to meet clients socially, and using the informality of a social event to find out more about the client's needs in an unpressurised way. The expectation is that it will help you to develop business contacts, and the business to sell more products and services.

Corporate hospitality can help to increase customer loyalty, differentiate your business from the competition, target the best prospects (your existing customers), increase word-of-mouth recommendations, raise and maintain the profile of your business, and build positive relationships. The main disadvantages are that external clients may not be able to accept this hospitality, and that there may also be considerable costs involved.

MAKING IT HAPPEN
Types of corporate hospitality event

There are many events and activities on offer to choose from. Make sure the activity is appropriate for your purpose, and put the emphasis on having fun!

Spectator events

A small business is unlikely to have the budget required to entertain clients and/or staff at lavish major spectator events such as the Henley Regatta or Wimbledon. However, you could think about inviting clients and/or staff to popular events such as rugby, golf, football, horse racing, opera, music, or the theatre.

Social events

You may want to invite existing clients to a lunch, dinner, or a party. Social events for staff are more likely to be linked to a special occasion, such as Christmas or New Year, or for hitting a specific sales target.

Participation events

Common examples of this type of event include multi-activity days, rock climbing, and sailing. Don't force employees into taking part in physical activities if they don't want to, however—that really will damage morale. It's essential that you obtain adequate insurance cover so that your business is covered in the event of accidents. Unless the client is a personal friend, it's unlikely that a participation event would involve clients—it might be embarrassing if a client lost spectacularly! Try to think of innovative events that would appeal to men and women equally.

Family occasions

Think about showing your appreciation for an employee on a special occasion, for example a wedding or the birth of a child, by offering a gift. Alternatively, you may decide to run an informal family fun day in the form of a small local gathering with side-shows and attractions for the children, such as a bouncy castle or an arts-and-crafts section. Celebrating a family occasion with a client is unlikely, as it's usually considered a private affair, outside of the business relationship.

Team-building events

These are a common form of corporate incentive for staff, but the quality of them can vary—as anyone who saw David Brent disrupting the team seminar in the first series of *The Office* will know. The traditional outward-bound day may not be suitable, as it places physical rather than mental demands on the participants, and therefore may not be universally popular. Work-related simulation activities, for example running a fictional business, may be more appropriate. The key to the success of such an activity is that the purpose is clearly communicated to all those involved—so explain to everyone why they are doing the activity, and that they are not just having a fun day out. The greatest benefits can be derived from such events when they are followed through, and when the lessons learned from the activity are applied to the workplace. While team-building is thought of as an employee activity, some companies/suppliers may have a long history of trading with the business, so that their employees could also be invited to join in team-building events.

Using event organisers

If you enjoy organising small-scale events personally, such as the staff Christmas party or a business lunch, you might want to take charge yourself, or ask a colleague to take responsibility for it. Alternatively, you may decide to engage the services of an event organiser to carry out the planning and staging of larger events. There is stiff competition in this field, with a wide range of event organisers, suppliers, and venues to choose from. The Corporate Hospitality and Event Association (CEA) has a directory of members including caterers, suppliers, event organisers, and venues. Members of the CEA operate to a code of conduct and ensure that customers are dealing with a reputable and responsible business. Event organisers work in close collaboration with outside suppliers, including hotels, tent and marquee hire companies, audio and visual equipment hire companies, and so on. They use a wide variety of venues, ranging from large stately homes to small hotels.

Event organisers usually offer a package tailored to your needs and objectives, time-table, budget, and guest profile. The price depends on the number of people being entertained, the type/number of activities chosen, the duration of the event, and whether catering and accommodation are included. Choose an organiser who offers an inclusive event price, and be aware of hidden costs, such as staff accommodation and meals. Ask to see the organiser's terms and conditions so that you know what is in the small print; for example, what happens if an event is cancelled due to bad weather (you can take out insurance to cover this). In addition, check that the event organisers have adequate public liability insurance.

Costs of corporate hospitality
Budget carefully for the cost of providing corporate hospitality, and set aside money in your marketing budget at the beginning of the financial year, rather than using surplus money that may be left over at the end. You may need to cut out corporate hospitality altogether if there is a downturn in business. All instances where a client/ member of staff has been entertained are a legitimate business expense, and should be included in the corporate hospitality budget. These include all business lunches with existing and potential clients, and the staff Christmas party.

Corporate gifts
Corporate gifts can be used as part of your marketing strategy, targeted either at an individual or a group of people. They can also be used to offer a goodwill gesture or to serve as a reminder to customers. Gifts may be given as a staff incentive too, or as a special award. Corporate gifts should be appropriate to the event and reflect something about your business. For example, you could have a Christmas card bearing your company logo, or a fun item such as a pen or small notebook. It's also often a good idea to leave a reminder of your business name with a client. The gift need not be expensive but should be of appropriate quality. More expensive items may give the impression that the client is valued more highly. However, be aware that local authorities and some private companies do not allow their employees to accept gifts at all, as an extravagant gift may be seen as an attempt to bribe an official, or influence a contract.

Offering a corporate gift to an employee may be seen by the tax authorities as payment in lieu of wages, or as a bonus.

WHAT TO AVOID
Poor planning
Arrange events well in advance, and choose a suitable time, activity, and location. Don't leave it to the last minute, as this will prove stressful for you or the organiser, and also mean that not everyone you'd like to attend can come along.

Not arranging insurance
The importance of the employer's duty of care towards their employees cannot be overstated. Make sure you take out public liability insurance.

Not evaluating events
Evaluate each event properly once it's over. For example, you could measure events for your customers for quantifiable results, such as increased sales.

Not taking allowable expenses into account
Contact HM Revenue & Customs to find out what are considered to be allowable business expenses.

RECOMMENDED LINKS
Association for Conferences and Events (ACE):
www.martex.co.uk/ace
Corporate Event Association:
www.cha-online.co.uk
EventServiceNet:
www.eventservicenet.co.uk
HM Revenue & Customs:
www.hmrc.gov.uk
Society of Event Organisers:
www.seoevent.co.uk

SEE ALSO
Communicating Customer Service (p. 245)
Managing Key Accounts (p. 259)
Retaining Existing Customers (p. 239)
Selling and Salesmanship (p. 546)

Managing Key Accounts

GETTING STARTED

It's said that 80% of the average business's income will come from just 20% of its customers, so it makes sense to dedicate time and resources to keeping those key accounts satisfied. More than this, you also need to ask yourself how you could better serve the needs of these key accounts, to build loyalty and more business with them.

Your business needs both a commitment and a strategy to manage its key accounts. The first step is to understand and appreciate the need to allocate resources. Research in the United States suggests that larger businesses have been consciously reducing their number of suppliers. The positive side of this is that, if you as a supplier successfully meet your key customers' needs, you're likely to progressively capture more of their business. One of the results is that customers come to rely on your special insight into their needs, and the cost (to them) of changing suppliers then grows.

Your strategy then needs to outline what you want to achieve with your key accounts, and how you plan to achieve this. Make sure that there is a particular person (preferably a senior manager or director) in your business who has the final responsibility of ensuring that each key customer is happy with your service. If you have a formal customer relationship management (CRM) system, this should support your key account strategy by recording the date and nature of all contact with the clients. One book you may find useful for more ideas is *Key Account Management and Planning: The Comprehensive Handbook for Managing Your Company's Most Important Strategic Asset* by Noel Capon, published in 2001 by Free Press.

FAQS

Why is key account management necessary?

The loyalty of your big customers is too important to leave unmanaged. What would happen, for example, if the salesperson dealing with a big customer were to resign suddenly and leave certain important duties undone? Years of trust and co-operation could be undermined. On a more day-to-day level, your important customers need to know that they can turn to someone senior in your business if there are problems in the business relationship.

How do you identify a key account?

This will obviously depend on how many customers you have, and whether they are evenly spread in terms of the amount that each of them spends with you. As a rule of thumb, you could view any customer who brings in substantially more business than average as a key account. Your challenge will be to see how many of these customers you can treat in a preferential way, given the limits of your time and resources.

Do you need key account managers?

Many small businesses will not have the capacity to appoint a large number of people to work exclusively as key account managers. In reality, you'll probably want to build the job of account manager into jobs that already exist in your business. For instance, as the owner of your business, you'll most likely have an important role to play in managing key accounts; but you'll do this in addition to the various other responsibilities that you have. In the same way, you could get certain senior staff to take on responsibility for other customers, in addition to their core responsibilities.

MAKING IT HAPPEN
Implement a system

To manage your key accounts successfully, you need to build your contact with them into an on-going process, so that:

- someone senior is allocated responsibility for looking after each key account
- regular contact is maintained with—and feedback requested from—each key customer

- targets are set for the revenue expected from each key account
- the health of the relationship with each key customer is monitored regularly

Develop and empower senior staff

Your big customers want to feel that they have the ear of a decision maker in your business. They need to know that if they are dealing with your business through your key account manager, that person must be experienced and authorised to take decisions so that problems are quickly resolved. From your point of view, this requires an on-going effort to develop the management and people skills of your employees. Especially as your business grows, you'll need to delegate these important responsibilities and rely on others to retain your customers' loyalty.

Consider a customer relationship management (CRM) system

As communications technology allows businesses and the individuals within them to become more efficient, you might find it difficult to keep track of each contact with a customer. If you're prioritising the management of key accounts, you may want to build this into a formal CRM system. This is generally provided as a computer program, and can hold contact details of all your customers, as well as details of their orders and communications with your business. The value of these systems is that they allow important information to be shared among different people in your organisation, so there is no duplication of contact with the client and everyone within your business is fully up to date. It's particularly useful when a problem arises and the history of an order needs to be tracked, or when the relevant person is out of the office and someone else needs the latest information on a transaction.

Keep it personal

One of the main advantages of making individuals responsible for managing key accounts is that trust and co-operation can be built up on a personal basis. Even in our high-tech world, it's still true that people prefer to do business with people they like and trust. Being systematic about this relationship need not detract from the person-to-person value.

WHAT TO AVOID
Waiting for complaints

Be proactive in finding out what your key customers feel about your service. Contact them regularly for feedback; do not wait for them to come to you with a complaint. This also creates an opportunity to talk to them about their own activities, and to get early warning of any future work that your business might be able to gain from them.

Becoming complacent

The danger of having a regular customer for a long time is that you can easily take their business for granted, and get complacent about your attitude to them. Make sure that everyone in your business from the receptionist to the book-keeper is aware of who the key accounts are, so that they are particularly well received whenever they interact with the business.

Putting all your eggs in one basket

By concentrating your efforts on your key accounts, you run the risk of paying insufficient attention to your other customers; indeed, it may even detract from your efforts to find and nurture new customers. This makes you over-reliant on just a few customers, where the effect of losing their business could be disastrous. In addition to posing an unacceptable strategic risk for your business as a whole, this situation could also put your key customers in a position of too much strength, where they are able to negotiate terms and prices that you would not otherwise accept.

RECOMMENDED LINKS

Business Link:
www.businesslink.gov.uk
The Graduate School of Business at Colombia University:
www.keyaccountmanagement.com

COMMUNICATING WITH
YOUR CUSTOMERS

Perfecting Your Pitch: Preparing Presentations

GETTING STARTED

Presentations are useful in many situations, such as pitching for business, putting a case for funding, and addressing staff meetings. Few people like speaking formally to an audience, but there are many real benefits—and as you gain experience in giving presentations, you'll probably find that it becomes less of a worry, and even enjoyable. This actionlist will give you some suggestions for preparing the content of your presentation, looking at the objectives that you hope to achieve, pitching it right for your particular audience, and getting your points across in the best way.

FAQS

What objectives should I set?

The starting point for any presentation is to set clear objectives. Ask yourself why you're giving the talk, and what you want your audience to get out of it. Also consider whether using speech alone is the best way of communicating your message, and whether your presentation would benefit from using visual aids and slides to further illustrate its main points. When you're planning and giving the presentation, keep your objectives in mind at all times—they'll focus your thoughts. Having clear reasons for giving the presentation will make sure that you're not wasting anyone's time, either your audience's or your own.

What do I need to know about the audience?

Before you plan your presentation, try as best you can to find out who is going to be in your audience, and their expectations. For example, the tone and content of a presentation to the managing director of another firm will be very different to one addressed to potential users of a product. It's important that you know the extent of the audience's knowledge about the topic you'll be discussing. Their familiarity with the subject will determine the level at which you pitch the talk. Try to appeal to what will motivate and interest these people.

MAKING IT HAPPEN

Write your speech

When it comes to presentations, there is no substitute for detailed preparation and planning. While everyone prepares in different ways, all of which develop with experience, here are a few key points to bear in mind while you're preparing.

Start by breaking up the task of preparing your speech into manageable units. Once you know the length of the presentation—say 15 minutes, for example—break the time up into smaller units and allocate sections of your speech to each unit. Then note down all the points you want to make, and order them logically. This will help you develop the framework and emphasis of the presentation.

Keep your presentation short and simple, if you can, as it'll be easier for you to manage and remember. If you need to provide more detail, you can supply a written handout to be given out at the end. A shorter presentation is usually more effective from the audience's point of view, too, as most people dislike long speeches, and will not necessarily remember any more from them.

Avoid packing your talk with facts and figures—your audience may become confused and you could lose the thread as well. If you do need to back up what you're saying, you could use graphs or charts to get across the message in a clear, pictorial form. Aim to identify two or three key points, and concentrate on getting these over in a creative fashion.

Use visual aids and equipment

With any presentation, you'll need to consider whether to use visual aids, which can range from the simple—such as acetates for an overhead projector (OHP)—to the more sophisticated —such as a computer package like PowerPoint. Remember that visual aids should only be used as signposts during the presentation, to help the audience focus on the main point. It's important not to cram too much information on to one visual aid, as you'll probably lose the attention of your audience while they try to read everything on it. Make sure the audience can see the information by using big, bold lettering, and bear in mind that images are often far more effective than words.

At its most basic, a personal computer can be used to develop and produce a series of slides which can be printed onto acetates for use on an overhead projector. A more common usage is to link up the PC with a projector in order to show the information on a large screen.

If you're going to use slides, you should try to standardise them to make them look more professional. Use templates where possible to make sure that they don't blend together, and again, try not to put too much information onto a single slide, or it will become difficult to read. A sensible guideline is to include no more than six points per slide, and to keep the number of words you use for each point to the absolute minimum. Think of what you're writing as the prompts for what you want to say.

The most common presentation packages are Microsoft PowerPoint and Corel Presentations. Both of these will allow you to develop a presentation using slide templates and give you the option of using charts, graphics, or even photographs to bring your information alive. Packages such as Photo-Shop or Paint Shop Pro will also allow you to scan in or manipulate photographs, or you could also use some of the available animations for transitions between slides.

You should pay particular attention to the layout and text on the slides and remain consistent throughout. Select a background that contrasts well with the text, and colours that are strong and stand out. It may also be a good idea to include the business's logo on all of the slides. It's important, always, to proofread your slides and acetates. There is nothing more noticeable, or more unprofessional, than a typo or grammatical error projected to ten times its size on a screen!

Practise as many times as you can to make sure that you're very familiar with your speech—allow plenty of time for rehearsal before the event. Once you're confident that your presentation is right, resist the temptation to change it. Remember, *you* may have heard the speech many times, but the audience will be hearing it for the first time. It's also a good idea to practise your speech using the equipment you intend to use; slide projectors and video machines should be tested in advance to make sure you know how to operate them. Make sure you have a contingency plan to cope with any unforeseen mishaps. For example, you could take printouts of your slides along with you so that if your computer breaks down and there's an OHP to hand, you can show them that way. Finally, during your rehearsals, time your speech so that you can check that it's neither too long nor too short. Remember that you'll probably need to allow time at the end for a question-and-answer session. Resist the temptation to bring your script into the presentation and instead write the main points on numbered cards, known as cue cards, to provide reminders.

Prepare the venue

Make sure that an appropriately-sized room has been organised for your presentation; take into account the number of people you're expecting, and check that there is enough seating, lighting, ventilation, and heating. If you're presenting at your office or on other 'home turf', provide some refreshments for participants such as tea, coffee, and water.

You also need to make sure there will be no interruptions, for example by phone calls, fire drills, or people accidentally entering the room. Whether you're presenting at your own office or elsewhere, you must make sure that any equipment or props you need are available and set up properly before the presentation starts. If you're presenting away from your office, at a conference or a client's premises for example, it's a good idea to visit the site beforehand to make sure it provides the necessary facilities.

WHAT TO AVOID
Not researching your audience
A good knowledge of the audience is absolutely crucial in finding the correct pitch. It's no good blinding your audience with technical jargon if they only have a basic grasp of the subject. Similarly, a very knowledgeable audience will soon switch off if you spend the first few minutes going over the basics.

Going on for too long
If your presentation absolutely has to be longer than 20 minutes, it may be a good idea to insert some breaks so that your audience remains fresh and interested.

Forgetting to check the room and equipment
This can be disastrous! Imagine, for example, arriving and finding that there is no facility for delivering PowerPoint presentations, and you have no other method of showing slides. Make sure you're familiar with the environment in which you'll be presenting.

RECOMMENDED LINKS
Mind Tools:
**http://www.mindtools.com/CommSkll/
  PresentationPlanningChecklist.htm**
SpeechTips.com:
www.speechtips.com/preparation.html

SEE ALSO
Deliver Presentations (p. 265)
Presentation/Speaking (p. 534)

Perfecting Your Pitch: Deliver Presentations

GETTING STARTED

A presentation is an ideal environment for you to promote your ideas, your products, or your services. You have a captive audience, are able to provide them with relevant information, and can answer any questions they may have on the spot. For a presentation to be a success you need to speak clearly and fluently, to hold the attention of the audience, and to leave them wanting to know more.

Some people are natural presenters while others find it more difficult, but practice and feedback from previous audiences will help you develop your presentation skills. This actionlist will give you some ideas for structuring, preparing, and delivering your presentation.

FAQS

How should I structure my presentation?

Structure is essential for any presentation: there should be an introduction, a main body, and a conclusion. You can be witty, controversial, or even outrageous if the mood of the presentation allows, but whatever approach you try, your chief aims are to arouse the audience's curiosity and to get your message across.

What's the best way to introduce my presentation?

The introduction to your presentation needs to attract your audience's interest and attention. A good opening is also important for your own confidence, because if you start well, the rest should follow easily. Plan your opening words carefully for maximum impact: they should be short, sharp, and to the point. Let your audience know how long your presentation will take, as this will prepare people to focus for the period of time you expect to speak. Summarise what you'll be discussing, so that they can work out how much information they'll need to absorb. Explaining the key points in the first few sentences will also help your mind to focus on the task in hand, and refresh your memory on the major points of your presentation. It sometimes helps to get started if you can learn your first few sentences by heart. Let your audience know if you're happy to interact with them throughout the presentation. Alternatively, inform them that you'll be holding a question and answer session at the end.

What should I do in the main body of the presentation?

The main body of the presentation will be dictated by the points that you want to make. Use short, sharp, and simple language to keep your audience's attention, and to ensure that your message is being understood. Include only one idea per sentence and pause after each one so as to make a mental full stop. Use precise language to convey your message, but make sure that your presentation sounds spontaneous—it shouldn't sound like a chapter from a textbook. You need to convey your message clearly, without masking the salient points with waffle. Stick to your original plan for your presentation and don't go off at a tangent on a particular point, missing the thread of your presentation. Why not try using metaphors and images to illustrate points? This will give impact to what you say, and help your audience to remember what you've said.

How should I conclude my presentation?

You should close by summing up the key points of what you've covered. The closing seconds of your presentation are as crucial as the opening sentence as they give you a chance to really hammer home your point. To make the most of this, think about what action you'd like your audience to take after the presentation is over and then inspire them to do it.

MAKING IT HAPPEN
Make sure you've practised

Nothing will make you more confident about your presentation than practising. Run through it by yourself a few times or, even better, ask a friend, colleague, or family member to listen to you.

Think about posture and delivery

Once you've practised the core part of your presentation, you can move on to think about some techniques to do with your posture, and the way that you deliver your presentation, that can be used to improve its impact. Firstly, keep up good eye contact and address your audience directly throughout your presentation. Try to be aware of your stance, posture, and gestures without being too self-conscious. Don't slouch, as you'll look unprofessional, but stand up straight: this will make you look more confident and also help you project your voice better. Even if you're nervous, don't fiddle with pens, pencils, your hair, or clothes: all these things are distracting for an audience, and will mean that they're missing important points in your presentation.

Remember that your audience has come to learn something, so be authoritative, sincere, and enthusiastic; if *you* don't sound as if you believe in yourself, your audience won't be interested. Also think about the way in which you're speaking. Most people need to articulate their words more clearly when addressing an audience. There's usually no opportunity for the audience to ask you to repeat a word you've missed, so aim to sound the vowels and consonants of words clearly. Also be aware of your vocal expression and try to vary volume, pitch, and speed of delivery to underline your meaning, and so that you maintain your audience's interest. Try not to use too many acronyms that are specific to your business or industry, as you can't be completely sure that everyone in the audience will know what they mean. If you do need to use them, introduce them and explain them early in your presentation so that everyone can keep up.

Close your presentation

It's tempting (and, if you're a nervous presenter, comforting) to have the full version of your speech in front of you, but it's best to avoid this and use cue cards instead. These will have a few headings referring to the main subject areas of your speech, and a few key points. In this way you can remember the key points you want to convey, but you have the freedom to talk naturally about them, rather than speaking from an over-rehearsed script, and this will make you seem more spontaneous. You may, though, want to write out the introduction in full on your first card to get you off to a good start.

Be careful when using visual aids and equipment in the presentation as these can also be distracting for an audience. Use a pen to point out details on the overhead projector itself, rather than the screen, as this is much clearer. Flipcharts should be written on quickly in long hand, but try not to turn your back on the audience as you write. Commonly available presentation packages often have a facility to enable you to link to specific slides. If a specific topic needs further explanation, you could also have a built-in series of links so that you can move to some extra slides to explain a particular point. If you intend to use sophisticated technology, then have a technician on hand to help out. Make sure you have a contingency plan in case your technology crashes: a back-up disk or extra copies of a hand-out are good plans.

Finish on a high note

As you draw your presentation to a close, remember to summarise briefly your key points and whatever you want your audience to 'take away' from the time you've spent talking to them. You might also want to take a few questions from the audience: in fact, taking all the questions at the end is a good idea for nervous presenters, as it means that they won't have their train of thought interrupted while they're speaking.

We all deal with questions in a different way, but some good general pointers are as follows:

- give your audience an idea of how much time you have to spend on the questions. This may be an issue if you're just one of several people speaking, because if you run over, everyone else will start running late.
- if someone asks you a question and you don't know the answer, be honest and tell them that you'll find out what they need to know and get back to them separately. This will save time, and also prevent you from giving an incorrect answer. Try to get back to them within two working days.
- if the question is a general discussion point, you could always try throwing the question open to the floor; you may be able to get an interesting discussion going between the members of your audience.

WHAT TO AVOID
A lack of enthusiasm
If *you* don't have any interest or excitement in your own speech, then don't expect your audience to be interested or excited. Listening to a single voice for 20 minutes or more can be difficult for an audience, so you must try to inject enthusiasm into what you're saying. You could consider planning some kind of interaction with your audience, too, in the form of activities or discussion.

Speaking too quickly
Don't rush your presentation; it's important to take your time. It's hard not to rush, especially if you're nervous and want the whole thing to be over as soon as possible, but the audience will find it hard to understand or keep up with you if you talk too fast. Make sure you summarise your main points every five minutes or so, or as you reach the end of a section. This will help to clarify the most important issues for your audience, and it's then more likely that they'll

remember the central issues long after you've finished your presentation.

Not checking equipment
There is nothing more irritating for an audience who have all made an effort to turn up on time, than to have to sit around and wait while you struggle to get your laptop to work, or sort your slides out. Make sure everything is exactly in place well before your audience begins to arrive. If you're planning to use sophisticated technology, it might be a good idea to have an expert colleague on hand just in case.

Not interacting with the audience
Be careful not to look at the floor during your presentation, or to direct your speech at one person. Try to draw your whole audience into the presentation by glancing at everyone's faces, in a relaxed and unhurried way, as you make your points. Keeping in tune with your audience in this way will also help you judge if people are becoming bored. If you do detect this, you could try to change the tempo of your presentation to refocus their attention.

RECOMMENDED LINKS
BusinessTown.com:
www.businesstown.com/presentations/ index.asp
iVillage.co.uk:
www.ivillage.co.uk/workcareer/survive/ prodskills/articles/ 0,,156471_156690,00.html
SpeechTips.com:
www.speechtips.com/delivering.html

SEE ALSO
Managing Key Accounts (p. 259)
Perfecting Your Pitch: Preparing Presentations (p. 262)
Presentation/Speaking (p. 534)

Writing a Sales Letter

GETTING STARTED

Most small businesses need to sell by mail in some shape or form. A sales letter is a low-cost selling tool that can be adapted and modified according to circumstances. A good letter by itself can be enough to get the message across, but in most cases sales letters are used in conjunction with other promotional materials such as brochures, samples, and reply envelopes. Some mailings allow for an instant response, often in the form of an order, while others may set the scene for follow-up telephone calls and personal visits in the hope of establishing a longer-term relationship. As the first contact with a client, it's essential that the sales letter sets the right tone, and this actionlist explains how to do just that.

FAQS

How can I use sales letters?

A sales letter can be used in a variety of ways. It could be the first step in preparing the customer for a phone call or visit, perhaps raising questions that will be answered later.

It may aim just to raise general awareness about the product or service as part of an overall promotional effort, in which case it doesn't need to contain all of the information the client requires, as that can be supplied through other media. However, it's difficult to measure the results of letters with vague objectives, and if your business sells to a select group, this type of letter will be a complete waste of time. Letters to a select group are different from letters to a wider audience. If contacts represent good sales potential, each letter should be written with their particular needs in mind. Letters can also be adapted for a variety of different groups that you might approach at different times.

If you are targeting customers repeatedly —for example, to inform them about new products, new offers, tax-related offers, and seasonal offers—the sales letter should take each offer into account, reinforcing the basic promotional message while providing enough variety so as not to bore the reader or make them feel pestered. Sometimes, a sales letter is used to accompany responses to inquiries requesting information, and this presents an ideal opportunity to sell.

MAKING IT HAPPEN

Plan the letter

You need to set down on paper exactly what you want the letter to do. List your points under three headings: Inform, Sell, and Encourage Action.

It's easy to miss out basic information in a letter in an effort to sell the benefits of something, so remember to include the product name, the price, the business name and address, and order details. If necessary, include more detailed information about the product as well as brochures, other inserts, an envelope, and some sort of reply device.

To sell your product, you have to be persuasive and get customers to view it favourably. Remember, there are limits to what a letter can achieve, and the recipient may need a number of opportunities to decide, so think about making your letter part of a sales drive, including offers, telesales, etc.

Encourage the customer to take further action progressing towards a sale, for example, by reading enclosures, sending or phoning for more information, or placing an order. Follow up inquiries for further information promptly with further mailings or telesales, and make sure arrangements are in place before the next letter is sent.

Think about the contents

Position key information at the beginning of your letter, and expand on it later. If you have a special offer running, mention it in the first paragraph to attract the reader's attention and to make them read on. Make sure you describe how the product works and what it is meant to do in a way that enables the potential customer to visualise it. If you want to draw attention to certain features, why not highlight them with bullet points? You can always expand and give more detailed product information in brochures.

Describe your product's benefits clearly and simply, and try to think of the product from the customer's viewpoint. For example, if the photocopier you offer allows your customer to print documents direct from his or her personal computer so that there's no need to invest in a printer as well, tell them how much money they could save. Don't be afraid to spell out the benefits.

Avoid making exaggerated claims and remember that using this method, customers don't have a chance to ask questions as they would if you were selling to them. If you do make claims, back them up with examples, such as endorsements from current users and case histories. If your business has large or well-known customers, enclose a testimonial from them, but make sure that they are sincere, specific to the product, and signed by the user.

Encourage immediate action wherever possible. Ask for a response, and keep asking for it throughout the letter. Make it easy for the reader to take the next step, by enclosing part filled-out forms, reply-paid envelopes, and Freephone numbers. Give incentives if you can and reward prompt action; for example, with a time-limited discount. Give the reader the option to send for more information, perhaps with samples or a demonstration, and record the details of customers who go to the trouble of doing this, for future sales efforts.

At the end of the letter, reinforce your message by repeating the offer, the guarantee, the cost, and the value of the product or service.

Think about the presentation

Direct mail is a popular method of promotion, and prospective customers are often inundated with it. You must distinguish your business from the others so that its mailings stand a chance of being read and not put straight in the bin—materials of an unusual size or colour should stand out, for example. Keep samples of the opposition's mailing materials on file so that you can see and learn from what others are doing.

When you address your letter, avoid 'Dear Sir/Madam' if possible and try to find out the recipient's name, taking care to spell it correctly. Getting someone's name wrong will almost certainly guarantee that your letter is thrown away, unread. Alternatively, you could use more informal non-specific titles that work well with your product or service. For example, if you're selling ski equipment, you could begin your letter with 'Dear Skier'. Don't ever use 'Dear Friend', though, and avoid sexist titles at all costs.

The top of the letter is, clearly, key for attracting attention but a good sign-off is just as important, so you could use a postscript to announce or reinforce a special gift or offer. A headline will grab initial attention and can be used to state a major benefit of the product or service, and also helps the reader to decide at a glance if the letter is of interest. Break the letter up into short paragraphs with subheadings which gives the reader an overview of the contents at a glance. The reader can then read the sections that most interest him or her.

Keep the tone of the letter natural, conversational, warm, and easy to read. Use short words and sentences, and avoid jargon and complicated grammar or vocabulary. Use 'you' rather than 'I' or 'we'. Remember that you are addressing an individual person, not a crowd.

Choosing an appropriate typeface and colour scheme will have a big impact on how easy the letter is to read. Black on white is easier to read than the reverse, for example. Avoid using uppercase too much— it will lose any impact you might have wanted—and it goes without saying that it's a nightmare to read very small type. Important words can be emphasised by underlining, italics, and bold, but take care not to vary the typeface too much or the reader will be distracted by the look rather than the content of the page.

An example sales letter

Mr. F Giles
Windy Hill Farm Shop
Nr Cottington
Countyshire
OB29 3YZ

ASHBURY COUNTRY PRESERVES—A TASTE OF SUMMER

Send for our discount sample pack now!

Dear Mr Giles

For a limited period only, Ashbury Country Preserves are providing farm shops in Countyshire with an opportunity to test our exclusive range of pure fruit preserves at discount prices.

An Exclusive Product
Made with fresh fruit harvested from our own farm set in the rolling Anyshire countryside, Ashbury Country Preserves are made to Lady Blagington's original recipe. Our preserves provide the traditional real fruit taste that discerning country shoppers are looking for. A growing number of outlets now stock Ashbury Country Preserves. Exclusive food shops in both town and country find this high-quality food product is a reliable seller and an attractive addition to their stock range.

An Attractive Offer
Packed in distinctive octagonal 1lb jars, with attractive floral labels and lid covers, our preserves contain only fresh fruit and sugar. Each jar (strawberry, raspberry, and blackcurrant) retails at £2.00. We supply at £1.00 per jar, but discounts are available for long-term purchasing commitments. Our introductory pack represents a price of 50p per jar. Supplies are delivered in packs of 36. We will also supply a distinctively-painted wooden display stand to regular customers by agreement. Our brochure and order form are enclosed.

An Elite Market
Ashbury Country Preserves are ideal for the high-quality food retailer. We supply a select group of retail outlets in the Home Counties and London with our exclusive range. Established customers include Plockington Hall Visitors Shop, the Garlic Sausage Deli chain, and the famous Carrobs department store.

I do hope you will be able to take advantage of our offer, which lasts until March. I will be telephoning you shortly to discuss our products, but if you have any queries in the meantime, please do not hesitate to call.

Yours sincerely

Jenny Jumper
Sales Executive

VIEWPOINTS

CONTENTS

Viewpoint: Avril Owton—The Cloud Hotel

Avril Owton's extraordinary experiences in life and business are the embodiment of the show business saying that the show must go on. A member of the world-famous dancing troupe the Tiller Girls in the 1960s, Avril was left to take charge of a struggling hotel business when her husband died suddenly in 1991. Since then, Avril has transformed the 18-bedroom Cloud Hotel near Brockenhurst in the New Forest, and regularly passes on her experiences to other female entrepreneurs around the world.

Here she describes how she adapted to such a radical change in her life, turned her business around, and set up an organisation to help other entrepreneurial women.

A CHANGE OF CIRCUMSTANCE

'I didn't actually start my business, but I married into it 32 years ago. My husband owned the Cloud Hotel and was the chef here, but I only took the reins in 1991 when he died very suddenly at a very young age. I had to take over the running of the hotel the day after his death, even though I had a young family to look after as well—everything just landed on me.

'When my husband died, the hotel wasn't in that good a state. It had no en suite facilities, for example, and had barely been ticking along. Selling up and moving on seemed to be the best option initially, so I put the hotel on the market for £325,000. There were no takers, though, so I had no choice but to stay on and to try to get the hotel back on track. This meant a very steep learning curve as at that time, I had no business experience at all. My husband had been a chef and had also taken care of the financial side of things, while I'd worked in the hotel as a waitress and chambermaid. Before we married, I'd been a dancer and I always say that when I started running the hotel, I didn't know a bottom line from a chorus line! Now, though, I have 26 staff—including 4 chefs—and turnover has improved by 700%.'

THE BENEFITS OF BEING THE BOSS

'You have much more freedom of choice when you're your own boss, and more control too. Even though turning the hotel round has involved a huge amount of hard work, I love to see the place growing—it gives me a real buzz. It'll be time to give up only when I don't feel like that any more.

'I think the most difficult part of being your own boss, whatever the industry you work in, is recruiting and retaining staff. I always employ people based on their personality rather than their skills; you can teach people the skills they need, but if someone's not suited temperamentally to a job in this industry, there's not much you can do. A warm personality is so important, as is being able to work well as part of a team. I like staff to stay with us for as long as possible, as I find it keeps standards high and retains lots of knowledge within the business.'

LEARNING FROM GOOD ADVICE. . .

'The best pieces of business advice I've heard came from a conference I attended. Bob Paton, an American restaurateur, was speaking and he said that to be success-ful, you had to do three things: be unique; be good at what you do and enjoy it; and tell the world.

'I found the last piece of advice the hardest to put into practice, especially as people (and women in particular) in the UK aren't very good at that sort of thing. It really does put you on the map, though, so it's important to put yourself forward for opportunities that come your way, and to keep on top of it all. I engaged a PR consultant to start the ball rolling and we worked together for quite some time until his retirement. I was a little worried about being over-exposed at one point, so while I do still have some external PR help now, it's on a much more ad hoc basis.

'Don't assume that newspapers or magazines wouldn't be interested in you— they're always on the look out for stories, so both sides can benefit. It does take a while, but you do learn to cope with this element of the job and not be shy about it. Having faith in yourself is the main thing. As Mary Kay Ash—a hugely successful American entrepreneur—said, "if you think you can do it, you can. If you think you can't, you're right". I believe I could do almost anything now and not let it faze me.'

. . .AND PASSING IT ON TO OTHERS

'Over recent years I've spoken at many international conferences and I enjoy them very much. I like to pass on the advice above to other women in business and encourage them to never give up. There's an old saying in show business that if you're standing up and breathing, you're on, and that translates to business too: you just have to keep going.

'Everyone makes mistakes, but you will learn from them and they'll make you sit up and raise your standards. When I refurbished the hotel to add in en suite facilities, I was up to my eyes in debt, and I was also taken for a ride by some builders who took advantage of my inexperience. It was a lot to deal with, but you do learn and move on. For example, keeping an eye on figures is extremely important for any small businesses. In the hospitality industry—whether it be a hotel, pub, or restaurant—your cash flow is very good, as people pay as they leave. You don't have to invoice them and wait for them to pay in 90 days, for example. I always do regular reports on costs, though, as you do need to keep a very tight rein on them and to scrutinise your overheads closely.'

Wessex Women

'I also work closer to home to help other women entrepreneurs and in 2002 founded Wessex Women. I'd been asked to set up an organisation for business-women in my area, so sent a mailshot to 30 women who lived locally and it took off from there. We now have a database of over 120 women. It's a great way for female entrepreneurs and women with business ideas to meet, exchange ideas, and have some fun along the way: we invite speakers to visit us and organise social functions too. It's a good way for women to help each other out, both in terms of getting more business and of creating good networking opportunities.

'I'm delighted to work with women's networks—I'm the vice-president of the British Association of Women Entrepreneurs, the UK branch of a worldwide organisation, and have also been nominated for an award by Everywoman.co.uk (I was a judge on those awards in 2005 too). Women have so much hidden talent and part of the problem for them, I think, is that they don't have enough confidence in their own abilities; men tend not to hold themselves back in this way. The more you learn, though, the more you can do: so many exciting opportunities can open up for you, and I really enjoy encouraging others to reach their full potential. In this country, I feel that too many of us are embarrassed to say, "I'm successful". It's good to be proud of what you've achieved and to say "I've done this—you could do it too".'

Visit the Cloud Hotel at: **www.cloudhotel.co.uk**

Viewpoint: Daniel Nabarro—Figleaves.com

Daniel Nabarro is founder and Chairman of Figleaves, an online retailer of lingerie, men's underwear, hosiery, swimwear and activewear. It has grown rapidly since its first incarnation in 1998, as Easyshop—a company selling 'stuff for women'. In 2000, they dropped the perfume and other extras to focus on lingerie, and rebranded as Figleaves. It is now the UK's leading online retailer of 'intimate apparel', and ships orders to 66 countries.

The company is dedicated to making the shopping experience as easy and enjoyable as possible, and combine the latest innovations in online shopping with great customer service, competitive pricing and a range of products to suit customers of any size, sense of style or budget. As a result, they have won an impressive array of awards, including:

- Online Retailer of the Year 2004
- Drapers Awards: Lingerie Retailer of the Year 2003
- UK Fashion Exports Awards: e-tailer award 2003
- Growing Business Awards: International Initiative of the Year 2003

STARTING OUT

'I am a serial entrepreneur—this is my third business. After selling my first company, I set up a networking company for estate agents. Unfortunately, the time wasn't right for this and I had to move on, after losing money.

'In 1998 I started investing in retailing on the internet—a company called Easyshop. We initially sold "stuff for women"—lingerie and perfume. In October 2000 we dropped the perfume and rebranded as Figleaves. Buying this domain name was a stroke of luck—a US business which had run into financial difficulties sold it to us for £80,000, at a time when people wanted six- or seven- figure sums for anything decent. As the Chief Executive, Michael Ross, said: "It was the best £80,000 we ever spent, because I could not imagine a more perfect name. The name is everything. It's exactly what you want from a dotcom name because it's suggestive without being descriptive."

'We started with a staff of four, and now employ 160 people. We have an office in New York, with 12 staff, 80 people in our warehouse in Suffolk and the rest in our office in London. A major challenge we face is getting great staff—as shopping online is still in the embryonic stage, there are few people with the experience and expertise in the business. We generally find the person, then teach them what they need to know. The company has been built up by myself and the Chief Executive Michael Ross, who joined in 1999.

'Initially, we did no market research. The idea sprang from the realisation, during journeys round London, that (almost!) everyone was wearing underwear, and that there was a huge market to be tapped.

'At first we were experimenting—as we started selling online, we used the

Internet to help us understand the nature of the market. We do more research now, using online questionnaires and focus groups.

'We have no plans to diversify from our current range of "intimate apparel"— underwear, swimwear, nightwear. . . Anything that touches your skin, really. Buying from our website is a better consumer experience than going into a shop. We have a vast range, more sizes—and the embarrassment factor is removed.'

THE GRAND DESIGN

'Our ambition was to become a global leader in selling lingerie online. This was slightly tongue-in-cheek at first—but we have got there! After six years, we are now the second most visited online retailer of intimate apparel in the world, after Victoria's Secret.

'Over the next 3 to 5 years, we plan to dramatically increase sales. We are doing very well in the UK, but the US market is 5 times bigger so we see a huge opportunity there. Our brand is much less known in the US than the UK, and we want to address this. We also see opportunities in Europe and Asia.'

THE ART OF E-TAIL

'We have been investing in some impressive developments on the website. With 220 brands, it can be very confusing for the consumer. We want to make the website even more easy to use, and the shopping experience even more enjoyable.

'While planning for developments on our website, we carry out a process that we call "AB Testing". We may build two pages, which perform the same function but are designed in different ways. We then test these two sites against each other, observing how customers perform on the different pages, and see which works best. At first the testers may be split 50/50, but we will tweak and develop until it is maybe 20/80—then go with the favoured site design. This testing comes at a relatively low cost, but can have amazing results.

'The website isn't the only major investment. We have also invested heavily in merchandising systems, financial control systems, logistics. . . At the moment I have 400,000 pieces available for next day delivery.

'We are now able to scale up at Christmas with no problems. Some days there may be three times as much activity as normal, but we can deal with this. At first the staff used to leave the office to help in the warehouse, but now that isn't necessary. Now we've got it right over here, we plan to use the same systems in the US and elsewhere.'

WERE I TO START OVER AGAIN. . .

'. . . I don't think I would do anything differently. We have been very prudent in the way we have run things—but mistakes are inevitable, and all part of the learning process. In fact, I think I learned more from my failed second venture than from anything else. The timing of our setup was good, not too early—and I wouldn't want to be any later. Anyone coming in now would be at a serious disadvantage.

'We don't tend to advertise offline—instead we rely on gaining a word-of-mouth reputation, and on doing deals with online partners. We have relationships with search engines and portals such as MSN. When advertising online what you pay depends on the performance of the ad, whereas with billboards you pay the money then hope for the results. We prefer the performance-based option.

'I would say that ideas are worthless—it's all about execution. Forget about how wonderful the idea is. How are you going to get the income and control expenses?

'I wouldn't call what I do working for myself—more for my company. And I love what I do. Every day there are new challenges, and the buck stops with me!'

Visit Figleaves at: **www.figleaves.com**

Viewpoint: Rebecca Jordan—Gapwork.com

The Small Business Service forecasts that in 2006, companies owned by women will account for 20% of all businesses in the United Kingdom. Gapwork.com was founded in 2000 by Rebecca Jordan and Kirsty Weir and is at the forefront of that movement.

The Leeds-based business already has a diverse and successful range of services: the principal business is a travel information service for young people who are planning to work or travel abroad before university, but Rebecca and Kirsty have also branched out into services for 'golden gappers'—the over 50s who didn't have time for a gap year when they were younger. In addition, they have set up Clear Content, an editorial service which works with advertising agencies, financial institutions, and government departments (amongst others) to produce top-quality print and online communications.

Gapwork.com has gone from strength to strength in just five years and Kirsty and Rebecca have been garlanded with awards, including Sunday Express Young Entrepreneurs of the Year 2003. Here Rebecca explains how the company started.

THE BIG IDEA

'I had had grand plans of doing a law conversion degree and becoming a solicitor in a desperate bid to get a proper job after leaving university. These plans were scuppered by the arrival of my first baby three months after I finished my Finals, and I was contemplating a life of domesticity when I had a conversation with a friend that gave me an idea for a website. He was a bar manager in London, and was looking for a temporary summer job in France. He complained that there was nowhere to go to find information about working abroad, which I found odd, but after some research, discovered was true. Then another friend of mine, Kirsty Weir, came back from her career break in Australia. I chatted to her about it and with her marketing background she saw that there was an opportunity to set up a website to help young travellers find work abroad. That's how gapwork.com started. It was a combination of having a good idea and being at a crossroads in life that prompted us to start a business.'

RESEARCHING THE MARKET

'We knew that there was a massive demand for gap year information that simply wasn't being supplied. We were familiar with the market as everyone we knew was taking career breaks and gap years—we'd done it ourselves. To get a better handle on the market's size, we found out from UCAS and the Australian Tourist Commission about the growth in students deferring entry to university and going to Australia on working holiday visas. When we moved into the schools market and started selling to careers services in schools it was relatively easy to find out how many schools with sixth forms there were in the UK through the Department for Education and Skills. We built our own database and started selling gap year books and CD ROMs directly into schools.'

PROS AND CONS

'The hardest part of running your own business is, I think, dealing with staff; recruiting good people and learning how to manage them can be a big challenge. Human beings are all very different and individual—something you learn very quickly in business! Kirsty and I enjoy working with each other still: coming up with new ideas, getting them into the market, and seeing them flourish is all a buzz. We are about to launch a range of home-learning books for pre-school children, which is something we would never have dreamt of trying to do 4 years ago. The learning curve is incredibly steep when you are a start-up, but you would never learn as much if you were working for someone else.'

LEARNING POINTS

'You learn from everything you do: mistakes and failures are as valuable as successes. We have always asked lots of people for advice. When we were starting up and had to write a business plan we would pester top people at Deloitte or Ernst & Young who we read about and get their advice! Family and friends who are running their own business are always good for some tips as well, but be aware that they might be biased. In fact, when listening to advice, you always have to bear in mind that everyone has their own agenda, however helpful they want to be. At the end of the day, you should have the courage of your own convictions and decide what is best for you and your business.'

Visit gapwork.com at: **www.gapwork.com**

Viewpoint: Paul Ward—J P Filpak

A good location can be a huge advantage when you set up a small business and Paul Ward, who founded J P Filpak Ltd in 2004, is certainly in the right place for his line of work. Based at the heart of the chemical industry in Widnes, Cheshire, J P Filpak is a contract packing and blending company which offers a wide range of services to industries such as printing inks, cleaning, food, and oil manufacturing.

Paul started his company armed with over 15 years' industry experience and a determination to make a go of working for himself. Here he describes his route into the chemical industry, what prompted him to set up his own company, and how he's hoping to put something back into his local community too.

FROM THE ARMY TO INDUSTRY

'I actually came to the chemical industry via the Army. I joined as medic when I was 18 and was stationed in Germany, Northern Ireland, Canada, and Norway. My main claim to fame from that time was delivering two babies! I left the Army after three and a half years and became a paramedic on ambulances but that didn't pay too well, so I left to work at a temping agency.

'I then got a job at Joseph Crosfield, a large chemical manufacturer in Warrington. I worked at the pilot plant on new projects and developed an interest in chemistry. I was made redundant, unfortunately, but then joined Croda Resins in Liverpool. Over the course of three years, I went from working as a process operator to supervisor to lab technician and had a large amount of in-house training on chemical blends. At the same time, I was studying at night school at Halton College. I'd found out I was dyslexic while I was in the Army, so I re-took some exams and went on to gain GCSEs, O levels and A levels, including chemistry. I also taught myself how to use a computer and got lots of extra IT training on top. I was at night school for 8 years in total, which was a really big commitment, but it's all been very worthwhile.'

MAKING THE BREAK

'I was at Croda for ten years in all and was promoted to shift manager and then production manager, but left to become site manager at Prism Chemicals, which is also in Liverpool. My job at Prism meant managing the whole depot, looking after new projects, and developing new business. At that time, Prism was a subsidiary of a larger group, and it seemed like most of the investment in the company was going to the London office. I felt a bit like a fall guy: I'd agree to take on work on behalf of the company and then find out that the owners wouldn't invest in the equipment we needed to make the deals happen. I became incredibly frustrated, knew I could handle things better myself, and started planning how to do just that.

'I spent about two years planning how I could go it alone. I did a great deal of market research and also made as many contacts as I could in the chemical industry: every time I spoke to a supplier or contact, I'd make a note of their name, what they did, and their contact details, and built it up into a database. It's been really useful and I'm now contacted by people who I've built good working relationships with along the way. I finally resigned from Prism in May 2004 and J P Filpak opened on 23 June 2004.'

NO REGRETS

'It's great to be your own boss and I think that being free to make your own decisions is definitely the best part of it. I'm not it for the money, to be honest with you. I set up the business because I didn't want to have any regrets in life—I didn't want to look back and think "I wish I'd had a go at. . .". The urge to start my own business was so strong that at times I felt like it was eating away at me—I was thinking about it so much that I couldn't sleep at night and even kept a notepad by the side of the bed so that I could write down any ideas that came to me.

'In terms of staffing, there was just me at first but my dad also helped out for 6 months; I could not have got through the first few months without his help. He then went back into retirement and I now have a small team in the manufacturing unit. I had some experience of using recruiting agencies via my old job so could have gone down that route, but actually I prefer to have friends and family working for me. My sister-in-law and her friend work for me full-time, and my parents-in-law work part-time. I'm hoping that one of my brothers will be joining me soon too, to help out on the sales side as well as with the chemical blends.

'What I do find hard is having the responsibility of other people working for me. If there's just you, it's easy to look after number one and you can take a few rash decisions here and there and know that they'll only affect you. When you've got people working for you, though, you have to make more qualified decisions and weigh up the pros and cons more. I'm also not that keen on the accountancy side of things. It's not one of my strengths, but because we're a limited company we have to have an accountant, so I can rely on some help there. On a financial note —and with some hindsight—I think some more capital when I set up would have been an advantage. My wife and I re-mortgaged the house and took out a loan to finance the setting up of the company, but I didn't want to take on more debt beyond that and have tried to stick to a tight budget.'

SOME SOUND ADVICE

'The best piece of advice I've been given? That you should never rely on anyone but yourself. I'm also a big believer in learning from your mistakes and in spreading the risk in a business venture by not putting all your eggs in one basket.

'Never burn your bridges either. For example, Prism was sold three months after I left and the new owners asked me to come back. I explained that I'd started my own business, but we've still been able to work together. I do sales and marketing for them via my own company and earn commission and we also have joint ventures: I do large projects for them, and they send smaller work my way. I left the company on good terms and it's all worked out well.'

HELPING THE LOCAL COMMUNITY

'My philosophy is that if I can help someone else, I'll do it. It's good to help others benefit from what you have. One way I'm hoping to do this is to generate some funds for an amateur rugby league team in Widnes I used to play for, West Bank. I remembered what it was like when I was playing and we used to be looking about for kit before a game, so I'm going to donate ten pence from every sale of our wet wipes—we produce all types, industrial and personal—to the club. It might also increase sales too, so everyone will benefit if the idea takes off. I mentioned the idea to one of the local papers in Widnes and they featured it in article, so fingers crossed!'

Visit J P Filpak at: **www.jpfilpak.co.uk**

Viewpoint: Pam Shipperbottom—Let's Do Lunch Ltd

Pam Shipperbottom is a mother of three and co-founder of Let's Do Lunch Ltd. Set up in May 2004 by Pam and Laura Illsley, the company provides healthy, organic school dinners for the pupils of Lethbridge Primary School in Wiltshire.

RESPONDING TO A NEED

'Our company came about in response to the proposed closure of the kitchen at Lethbridge Primary school. We both felt very strongly that a freshly prepared and nutritionally balanced hot meal at lunchtime is a vitally important part of the children's day. We realised that it was essential to improve the quality of school meals that had previously been offered to the children. I am completely passionate about locally-sourced organic food and have fed my family organic food for the last 7 years. We had previously lived in India for 2 years and had shopped at local markets and eaten fresh, locally-produced food. Although our choice of food wasn't as vast as in this country, what we ate was full of flavour.

'When we returned to this country and I started shopping in supermarkets again (which, strangely, I had been really looking forward to) I found myself continually disappointed at the poor quality and lack of flavour in the food I was buying—in particular the meat and vegetables. This led me to look for alternative sources of food. I came across a wonderful place called Abbey Home Farm which is, in my opinion, the best farm shop around selling organic vegetables, fruit, meat, dairy, bread and an amazing range of other food products. It also has the best vegetarian café I have ever come across. This find opened up a whole new way of purchasing and eating food for my family and myself, and I can honestly say I have never looked back! So for me what had happened at Lethbridge was an ideal opportunity to get locally-sourced organic food on the menu.

'We put an initial proposal to the head teacher in February 2004 which he accepted in principle. We then conducted a feasibility study, which among other things enabled us to gauge interest from parents. In May 2004 we presented our plans to the governing body, and it was at that meeting we got the go-ahead to provide Lethbridge with cooked lunches from 1st September 2005. We responded to a need, really—and before we knew it had set up a limited company!'

THE START-UP

'Laura [Illsley] and I are joint partners—we developed the idea and provided the initial funding for equipping the kitchen etc. Some people set up complicated business plans, but we had none of that. Obviously we made sure that it would work financially, but in general we tackled issues on a daily basis—when we needed advice or help we found out who to contact and contacted them.

'At first it was very difficult to keep track of what we were spending each month. We have more of an idea now, and are much better at keeping tabs on spending.

'I work on the business full-time, but Laura is a direct marketing manager so does that job for four days a week. At the moment we employ one cook and three assistants, but we are working on expanding the business, setting up in four more schools for September 2005. Once that is up and running, we will have a dozen more members of staff.

'We were incredibly lucky to do what we did at a time when there were pockets of people around the country with the same concerns as us—in particular the Soil Association. As a result, we have had loads of free publicity which we just couldn't have got otherwise, and it is through that that other schools have contacted us. We have been inundated with calls! I don't think we would do anything differently were we to start over—we wouldn't be where we are now if we had done it badly. However, Laura would probably say that if we had been more organised and had more business savvy there would have been less stress. Neither of us had started or run a company before, so there was a very steep learning curve. I have to say upon reflection that we both enjoy it enormously, and continue to gain a great deal of satisfaction from feeding adults and children the best quality locally-sourced organic food available at costs which are affordable.

'The local authority caterers announced in June 2005 that they were to terminate all contracts from that July, so would no longer be providing primary schools with hot meals. They explained that this was due to dwindling numbers of pupils staying for hot lunches. Our company has experienced a very different picture, however, with the numbers of pupils staying for hot lunches increasing steadily, along with the number of interested schools.'

BUILDING RELATIONSHIPS

'When we were planning the start-up, we contacted Jeanette Orrey, the school meals policy advisor for the Soil Association. With her help and our persistence and dedication, we have managed to steadily increase the amount of locally-sourced organic ingredients that we use in our recipes.

'Both Jeanette and the Soil Association have been extremely helpful. In return, we have been a good story for them, a vehicle to help them highlight an issue they are fighting for. Our long term aim is to go for the soil association organic certification stamp, which will take a lot of work—but will be worth it. I think that it is very wise to create such mutually beneficial relationships.'

A BALANCING ACT

'There is very little that I haven't enjoyed about this start up. I suppose the worst aspect would be the stress involved in the initial stages. You can never escape! When you're working the adrenaline keeps you going—it's only when you go on holiday that you realise how tired you are.

'It has been very tricky balancing my home life with work demands—it is always later than I think! My husband runs his own company, Applied Acumen, a business improvement company, so we are both constantly juggling our commitments. It is tricky for me, having to be at particular places at particular times and working in the evenings. I think I'm beginning to get the balance right, though. I now have an office at home, an office at the school and a laptop, which allows me much more flexibility. I have no more sleepless nights, which must be a good sign!

'Our hard work is more than repaid by the amazing sense of achievement felt by our staff—they really feel that they are doing something worthwhile. One of the ladies who works in our kitchen says, on an almost daily basis, how happy she is doing what she is doing. She has spent years working in school kitchens, but only now does she feel that she has learnt how to cook!'

A LOCAL BUSINESS

'We have set up various spin-off ventures: there are children's cookery classes; parents can join their children for lunch; senior citizens can come for lunch; and this year we have also started a vegetable box scheme and a meat box scheme.

'It has been really nice working with like-minded people within the community, and being able to employ local people. The food that we serve has travelled from 10 miles away, not 1,000 miles—and it's fresh.

'Organic food may be slightly more expensive, but it tastes so much better. You may not notice when you switch from non-organic to organic, but if you've been eating organic food for a while and then try non-organic food, that is when you will really notice the difference.'

LOOKING FORWARD

'We have been overwhelmed by the success, really. We have been approached by an agent to write a book with our recipes and ideas, and the BBC has shown interest in filming a documentary, looking at our supply chains and locally-sourced organic food.

'As for expansion, we are looking at primary and secondary schools locally, we are primarily interested in creating a niche in our local area. The secret is to expand slowly and not get too big for our boots. We are making sure that we have got it right at Lethbridge first. We have been able to make our working model a kind of flagship for our area and an example to which other schools can aspire, with our help. We have recently been contacted by private companies who are looking to improve the quality of food on offer to their staff, so this may become an exciting new growth area.

'I think the key is that our model doesn't cost the school a penny. It runs itself and pays for itself, unlike other catering companies which charge for management fees, utilities etc. Some even charge for ingredients on top of the cost of the meal paid for by parents! They are making so much profit out of schools that just don't have the money. What really gets to me is the way they compromise the quality of the food in order to maximise profit margins—it's just not right. We have shown that it can be done another way.'

Contact *Let's Do Lunch*: **letsdolunch@appliedacumen.co.uk**

Viewpoint: Rachel Duffield—The Lighthouse Bakery

As we saw on p. 13 of this section, a good location will definitely boost your chances of making your small business work. If it's close to the type of customers you want to reach, so much the better. The Lighthouse Bakery is an excellent example of this great combination.

Rachel Duffield and Elizabeth Weisberg set up the Lighthouse Bakery in Clapham, South London, in 2000. The bakery uses artisan—traditional—methods to produce its wide range of British, European, and American breads, pastries, and cakes. None of the bakery's products uses chemical improvers or artificial enhancers.

The bakery has a strong attachment to its local community and has many committed customers. Here Rachel explains how the business has grown and how it spreads the message about the importance of good bread in a carb-phobic world.

STARTING UP

'Neither Liz nor I had worked in the food industry before, so opening the bakery was a new departure for both of us.

'Liz attended the National Bakery School in London before we opened, where she gained a good grounding in the basics of bread making. The school is mainly aimed at those hoping to work in in-store bakeries in large supermarkets, whereas we are an artisan bakery—we bake every day and use no chemicals or additives in our recipes. All of our bread is fermented over a long period of time and hand-moulded: no two loaves look the same.

'The School's aims weren't the same as ours, then, but the course gave Liz a useful background view. In terms of the actual nuts and bolts of setting up a business, I had some useful experience as I'd previously been the chief executive of an intellectual property business. The bakery is very different from my previous business, mainly in that you're actually making something. It's like baking at home but clearly on a much bigger scale. It's great to see something fabulous coming out of the oven; it's a wonderful feeling you never get tired of.'

SMALL IS BEAUTIFUL

'The business is still relatively small in terms of staffing; there were three of us at the very beginning but we now have a team of fifteen. One other big difference between my previous business and the bakery is swapping mental stress for physical stress; we're up at 2 a.m. and working until 6.30pm which can take a big toll. We make the most of our free time, though, and take two weeks off in the summer and over Christmas. Any spare cash we have is invested in people; we try to grow our team as a bigger one will, obviously, help spread the work load and make our lives easier.

'We started off with quite a small range of products but became more adventur-ous as we got to know our customers better and found our feet. We're all involved with testing out new ideas—some are ours, some come from our customers. It takes time to develop new ideas and find out if they're practical, but we try to fit the ones that *will* work into our schedule.

'It is a challenge working with the public, and I firmly believe everyone should do it for six months! 95% of our customers are wonderful but you'll always get some who are rude—it's amazing how many people never say thank you or who point at something rather than ask you for it. Thankfully, though, people like this are very much in the minority and the feedback we get more than makes up for it; it's extremely rewarding.'

NEXT TIME. . .

'I think if I were to do this all over again, I'd try to make sure there was definitely a lot more time before the shop opened in which to plan how it should look. As neither Liz nor I had run a shop before, we didn't know how long that aspect would take and it's important to make sure that a shop's layout is practical as well as enticing.

'Because of time pressures, we ended up slotting into the previous owners' shop layout rather than coming up with one that definitely suited us. We had to make the best of a difficult situation, really, as there were some issues related to the lease and sorting these out took so long that we were only able to take possession of the shop at the last minute. We had just a week before our planned opening date and obviously we dedicated this time to making sure our range was how we wanted it to be, and as a result the shop itself got neglected a bit. We've made it look beautiful, don't get me wrong, but it could be more practical in its layout.'

TO GROW OR NOT TO GROW?

'We've no plans to expand with another shop at the moment. It could make us a lot of money but we feel it would take us away from what we do best; running a small, community-based business. We are based in a reasonably affluent area of South London and I think that has helped us make a positive start. Our customers appreciate good food and don't mind paying a little extra for it. I know nearly all of them by name, and I'd hate to lose that personal aspect of what we do. We also feel that we might lose control of the business if it grew too quickly. We are, however, planning to start another business—its working title is Atelier Light-house—which will be a purely wholesale venture.

'Offering an online service isn't something we're investigating at the moment either, and nor are we enticed into the mail order market The cost of sending a loaf through the post is prohibitive, so it just wouldn't make sense, to be honest— it could cost roughly £4 to post a loaf that you could buy for £1.20.

'We've had a lot of very positive publicity for the bakery, which I find good and sad at the same time. Obviously it's very good news for us, but sad that fantastic bread is such a rarity. We're actually a big fish in a small pond: there are only ten artisan bakeries in London, for example, and some of them are wholesale and so don't sell to the public.

'Thankfully we've not suffered as a result of the nation's current obsession with a low-carb diet! We often have people coming into the shop who think they suffer from "intolerances", but I tend to think that they're more fads than real problems: people tend to bandy about these catch-all phrases without understanding them properly. There are lots of home bakers in this area too, but they haven't affected business either because we stock baking ingredients (like flour) as well as our own products. Customers come in to pick them up and then buy a loaf for the freezer or something while they're here. It's heartening to see a real movement towards appreciating good bread.'

Visit the Lighthouse Bakery at: **www.lighthousebakery.co.uk**

Viewpoint: Kim Buckland—Liz Earle Naturally Active Skincare

Having a clear vision for your business—and finding just the right person to work with—are essential for any small company, as Kim Buckland can attest.

Kim set up Liz Earle Naturally Active Skincare in 1995 with the former beauty journalist, Liz Earle, to produce a range of skincare products made from high-quality botanical ingredients. Eleven years on, the business has gone from strength to strength and sells its products by mail, online, in selected retail outlets, and on the television shopping channel QVC.

Excellent customer service is a particularly high priority for the business and its philosophy of quality and service feature prominently on its content-rich website.

Here Kim explains what prompted her to make the break from her previous full-time job to the challenges of a start-up.

THE 'EUREKA!' MOMENT

I'd always wanted to do something for myself, but for a long time I didn't know what. I was looking for a good opportunity, though, and the right one came to me in a 'Eureka!' moment.

'I was driving in central London with my husband when suddenly I knew *exactly* what I wanted to do and shouted at him to stop the car. I called Liz right away, as she was a key part of my plans. The idea was to create a range of premium quality skincare products that were affordable, pampering, full of genuinely high levels of botanical ingredients, and developed by a trusted beauty expert. I've known Liz for over 20 years and she was absolutely the right person to work with: she has years of expertise in this area, has published over 30 books on health and skincare and also has a passion for working with the best botanical ingredients.

'I left a message asking Liz to call me back as soon as she could and we met up, started planning with a blank piece of paper, and never looked back.'

MAKING THE MOVE

'I was very excited about starting up the business with Liz, but was also sad to be leaving John Frieda Professional Haircare, which I'd enjoyed tremendously. I was there for eight years in all and it was a great experience. The company has a very clever business strategy which took three haircare brands to no. 1 status in the UK and US—I learned a lot while I was there and this has been invaluable in starting up and growing our business.

'When we started out, there was just me and Liz, but now there are 170 of us. It's been great to see our people develop while they've been working with us, and there's a great atmosphere. Being based on the Isle of Wight has been a real advantage; we have a beachfront office with beautiful views just 1½ hours from London and a dynamic, loyal, and friendly local workforce. Many of our friends and family work with us, and our team share our passion. I love going to work—it's not a chore at all.

'In terms of downsides to starting your own business, I don't think I realised how long the hours would be, and that you'd be on the go 24/7—your brain just doesn't switch off and your home and work lives become very integrated. You really do end up doing everything yourself when you're starting out—my particular pet hate was buying all the office equipment and keeping the stationery cupboard stocked!'

BACKING UP IDEAS WITH RESEARCH

'We researched our market carefully when we set up the company, but not by asking people to fill in questionnaires while standing on street corners! As part of my job at John Frieda, I'd spent a lot of time in stores watching people looking at products on the shelves and buying, or deciding not to buy. Even though my own role focussed on hair care products, I was always checking out the skin care, so I had a good grasp of the market and products available at that time.

'As far as I could see, there was nothing that combined the look and performance of a premium product with genuinely high levels of botanical ingredients, affordability and a "trusted expert" as the creator, and that's the niche that we've found.'

KEEPING FOCUSSED

'Everything we do is for us, in that when we come up with new products, we concentrate on what everyone in our team feels they need in their beauty lives, rather than on what the competition is doing. This means we stay focussed on the five things that are very important to us:

1. developing products that really work—our customers can see a real difference in their skin when they use them
2. using genuinely high levels of carefully sourced botanical ingredients in our formulations
3. creating pampering products that are a treat to use
4. being affordable—our prices are inbetween the high street and premium brands
5. offering a brand that people can trust via Liz's name and experience'

BENEFITING FROM ADVICE

'Right from the very beginning, Liz and I had some trusted advisors whose experience we could really rely on and I highly recommend it to others. It's great to be able to talk through ideas or problems with other people and to get their perspective on things.

'I also had some wonderful advice from former colleagues. Gail Federici, the former president of John Frieda Professional Haircare, was extremely supportive from day one. She said "make this for yourselves and you won't go far wrong". John Frieda himself said that "if you want a decision now, the answer's no".' Being bounced into taking a quick decision is never a good idea. There are lots of business books that encourage quick decision-making, but I have learned it's always better to take the time to think things through carefully first. Take a step back and try to look at things objectively.

'Some people find it surprising that we do take our time when it comes to decision making, but our motto is "quality and service always". We try to abide by that in every single area of what we do.'

Visit Liz Earle Naturally Active Skincare at: **www.lizearle.com**

Viewpoint: Carl Lyons—ReCreate

When it comes to setting up their own company, many people are tempted by one of the traditional options open to them; coffee bars, beauty salons, hairdressing salons, and restaurants are perennial favourites, for example. Changes are afoot, however, and life skills coaching is now an area of growing interest. ReCreate, which was established by Carl Lyons in 2002, is in the vanguard of that movement.

Carl is a qualified Ayurvedic consultant, clinical hypnotherapist, and life coach and ReCreate's mission is to '[help] groups or individuals achieve excellence in their physical, mental and spiritual health in every area of life'. Carl and his colleagues feel that 'good health is good business' and they offer a variety of services and products to individuals and organisations, integrating a holistic approach to life within a corporate setting.

ReCreate has grown strongly over the past four years as a result of word-of-mouth recommendations from satisfied customers. Here Carl describes what prompted him to change his own life and to do what he loves.

MAKING THE CHANGE

'After graduating with a degree in mechanical engineering from Liverpool University, I joined ICI as a project consultant. After about 10 years of senior roles, I began to feel as if I'd "fallen out of love" with my job and that it was time to review my life and find out what I was truly passionate about. It struck me that in working for someone other than ourselves, most of spend all our lives giving our best resources to someone else! After a lot of thought, I realised it was time to leave and to take a new direction.

'Part of my job at ICI was training people in negotiation skills, and I got a huge amount of enjoyment from helping people learn about themselves as part of the training. I'd also always been interested in health—physical, emotional, and spiritual—and as a result of that, I began to learn about Ayurvedic medicine and its principles. Ayurveda is a holistic and very practical approach to life in that it acknowledges that we all have responsibilities, but holds that good health is key to meeting them. I lived and studied in India, which was a life-transforming time for me. When I returned to the UK, I took a degree in Ayurvedic medicine in London, although my interest was from the perspective of helping people reach their full potential, rather than giving therapy.

'Once I completed my degree, I started to think about what I wanted to do next. I had a corporate background coupled with a keen interest in a holistic way of life —a reasonably rare combination. Jobs fusing the two just didn't seem to be out there, so starting my own company seemed the best thing to do.'

GOOD HEALTH MEANS GOOD BUSINESS

'This is where ReCreate comes in. The business was started four years ago and it aims to take that holistic approach to life into a business environment so that both companies and individuals feel the benefit. I have two associates and we feel that what we do can change the way business is done. Many people in business these days find themselves slaves to the bottom line and their shareholders, but we help them to get off that treadmill and to find themselves again.

'I very much enjoy being able to contribute directly and positively to other people's lives. It's very rewarding to see clients find a better sense of self and of purpose. I hope that that in turn filters back out to a company's customers: when we understand ourselves more, we become better people overall and better employees.

'I still deliver most of ReCreate's training work myself, but we do also use associates if necessary. We take a lot of time to find the right people to work with us and they need to have the right combination of life skills and experience—it's hard to tell someone how to change the way they live for the better if you've not been through the process themselves. Charisma, experience, and good presentation skills are all very important.

GETTING THE TIMING RIGHT

'For a business to be a success, the entrepreneur has to be passionate about what she or he is doing, but good timing is invaluable too. I think we've benefited from being in the right time at the right place; there has been a revolution in the workplace over the past 10 years or so and people are much more aware of the importance of finding personal fulfillment at work, and also of balancing their career with their personal life so that they can be successful in both arenas. People are raising their expectations in life, and our aim is to give them a framework that enables them to reach their goals.

'When we first started up, it was a big challenge to get clients to understand what we do. They had no reference point, in a way, and it was hard at times to get them to see that we didn't just offer stress management advice. We help develop "soft" skills (that is, people-related knowledge), and businesses can find these difficult to measure. We found, though, that once we'd got our foot in the door and begun our work, our clients could see that the results were spectacular.'

Growing the right way

'The business has grown organically, really, and we now secure most of our work via recommendations from existing clients, which is great. Our reputation and results find new business for us. We're now at a crucial stage in our growth, though, and need to manage it carefully. Like most businesses we'll need to find the right balance between expanding at a sensible rate and staying true to our core purpose.

'We'll need to do plenty of market research to help us decide on the right growth strategy, I think. In all honesty, we didn't do a great deal of research early on because our service and products were so unique. When we first started up, I relied on my own intuition and drive to make the business a success as we were offering a service that people don't necessarily know that they need; we're creating a need not responding to it, so by extension we're *creating* a market rather than slotting into someone else's.

'Media coverage has also helped our business grow. My first book, *Skilful Living*, was published in December 2004 by Middlesex University Press, and I also appeared regularly as a consultant on BBC1's Heaven and Earth Show, where I used the principles of Ayurveda to help a viewer make a positive, lasting change to his hectic lifestyle. The ReCreate website had a huge increase in traffic as a result, which has been great.'

KEEPING THE FAITH

'If you are thinking of setting up a business, I think you have to have a strong connection to what you want to deliver as well as an eye for the practicalities that will help make your ideas become a reality.

'I started the business at home to keep the overheads down and I still work from my home office. The line between life and work can become blurred, and you need to be motivated and self-disciplined to keep them separate. It can be difficult to start your business from home if you enjoy the company of others and I did find it lonely at times.

'You need to be ready to do whatever it takes to make your idea work. For me, the long hours and effort needed to make things happen didn't feel like a sacrifice as I felt completely in control of my own destiny; in a way, the business was like a form of self-expression. I felt completely that I was on a mission. What I do for a living is a real and very rewarding part of me. The key things to remember are that you need to listen to yourself, not others and that you need a strong sense of belief in what you're trying to do—you won't get anywhere without that.'

Visit ReCreate at: **www.recreatelife.co.uk**

Viewpoint: Chris Tomaszewski— Stella Books

Stella Books in Tintern, Monmouthshire, and Rose Books in Hay-on-Wye, Herefordshire, are two parts of a family business run by Chris and Cliff Tomaszewski, and daughters Maria & Sonia. The bookshops' aim is to be 'the premier source for rare and out of print books' and they do this by combining their physical presence with an information-packed website that helps them sell to customers around the world. The staff's relationship with customers is one of the business's strengths, and this was rewarded in 2003 when the shops topped the category for Outstanding Customer Service in the Viking Direct UK Business Awards.

Early converts to the benefits of working electronically, the Tomaszewskis were able to trade globally relatively quickly in their business life as they'd invested time in cataloguing their books on computer. As soon as the Internet boom began in the late 1990s, they were able to upload their listings onto their website right away. They now have a worldwide mailing list of more than 55,000 customers and are among the top 2-3% of UK Internet booksellers in terms of volume of books online.

Here Chris describes how her family's business reflected, and grew out of, their love for children's and illustrated books.

THE BOOKS BEHIND THE BOOKSHOP IDEA

'We had no bookselling experience when we set up Stella Books, but we did have a business background: my husband and I had worked in the computer industry for over 20 years. Cliff's interest in books was the catalyst, really, and I too became interested via some Beatrix Potter books I saw when visiting the Potter family farm in the Lake District. When I said I wished I could find a complete set of the books, Cliff suggested trying to get first editions of them all. I didn't think they'd exist, but they did and that was my first foray into collecting. My interest in children's books grew from there and expanded to take in all the classics, including Winnie the Pooh and Rupert Bear.

'Between the two of us, Cliff and I started to build a huge library. Like any other addiction, we had to sell some items to be able to afford new things, so we placed an advert in a collectors' magazine and were thrilled when we sold our first book! At around this time, our younger daughter, Maria, was studying business and looking for her next step after she'd completed her course. As Maria is hard of hearing, we thought that working from home with her computer was a good option, and this actually became the embryo of the business idea. We decided to make our hobby of buying and selling books work commercially and Maria took it from there: she worked from a room in our house, dealing with customers, answering their queries, and sending out the catalogues that helped grow the business.

'As time went on, we could see that the business had potential, so the next challenge was to decide on how to move forward. In 1992, that opportunity came along when a commercial property in Tintern became available. We decided to go for it. We bought one room in the shop and Maria began to work from there. The business thrived under her management and we invested a lot of money in stock, which we saw as our pension. Then in 1995, Rose's Books in Hay-on-Wye came up for sale. It was another great opportunity: a beautiful shop, and one that specialised in children's books to boot. We decided to strike while the iron was hot and Maria moved to Hay, to a flat above the shop.

'The staff in the Tintern shop pulled together and managed on their own for about a year, but we realised that they would need another manager. It was time for another big decision and in 1996, after two years of planning, I decided to leave my job. It was a nerve-wracking time—I was giving up a lot, including a company car and international travel—but it was time for a change and I've never looked back.'

THE INTERNET BOOM

'One thing we did buy into early on was using computers to make our lives easier and enable us to provide a better service for our customers. We compiled a full listing of all the titles we had using a Windows package, Microsoft Works. At the time, there were hardly any computer packages specifically designed to help booksellers and the only packages that could have helped cost £10,000, so we decided to write our own. We paid £150 for a software licence and took it from there. It was great to work with a tailor-made package, and it meant—and still means—that whatever direction we took the business in, the software could follow.

'When we started up in Tintern, lots of the local booksellers came round to sniff us out. Nearly all of them were surprised that we were using computers to help the business—they didn't understand how useful they could be, and thought we should be out instead buying and selling books. Clearly we needed to do that too, but we really reaped the benefits of being organised so early on. By 1998, when the use of the Internet really took off, everyone wanted to do it! This time was really a turning point for the business: we were one of the first online booksellers in the UK and we still have one of the biggest volumes of sale. Our catalogue now includes over 50,000 books and the hard work in the early days has paid off.'

THE IMPORTANCE OF PLANNING

'All in all, planning is essential for businesses of all sizes. If you don't know where you're going, how will you ever get there? I don't think we would do anything different, even with hindsight; we would still use the same approach. Obviously you can't plan for every eventuality, but learning from mistakes is the best way to learn in any situation. Having said that, researching your market is one thing not to leave too late. We did plenty of market research before we opened the Tintern shop and really benefited from it.

'Thousands of visitors every year come to Tintern to visit the Abbey, so we worked out how many of those people would come to Tintern village while they were nearby, what proportion of those would visit our shop and then what proportion of that final number would buy a book from us. We were then able to put these figures into a business plan, confident that we had a reasonable idea of what our customer base was. When we were actually up and running, we could measure our estimates in terms of footfall (that is, how many people come into the shop). Researching your market is crucial, I think: what's the point of offering a product or service, however brilliant an idea it is, if no-one wants it?'

IN A NUTSHELL

'There are some downsides to running your own business—lack of money in the early days (everything we earned we ploughed back into the business) and holidays being two of them (we're open seven days a week)—but if you enjoy what you do, it's all worth it. I love being my own boss and being able to shape the future direction of the business.'

Visit Stella Books and Rose Books at: www.stellabooks.com

Viewpoint: Bruce Walker—Bruce Walker Engravers

Bruce Walker is a sculptor and glass engraver working in Kirriemuir, near Dundee.

His work mainly consists of commissions for glass engraving, although his real passion is stone sculpture—mainly in granite. He sells his pieces locally, from his studio and gallery in a craft unit in the centre of Kirriemuir. He has run his own business for 30 years.

MAKING THE MOST OF AN OPPORTUNITY

'I trained in Aberdeen in the early 1960s, in the granite industry. The place where I did my apprenticeship had some links with Aberdeen's Grays School of Art, so I was able to go to art school for part of my apprenticeship. I made the most of that opportunity! I developed a technique of engraving on granite, but one lunchbreak I found a piece of broken window and decided to see if the technique worked on glass. It worked very well—which is how my two specialities came about!

'To start off with I was working in the granite industry during the day and doing glass engraving commissions at night, for extra cash. When I realised that I was earning almost as much from my part-time glass engraving as from my full-time job, I decided to take the plunge. That was 30 years ago now, so I must be doing something right!'

A LOCAL BUSINESS, WITH A SIMPLE GOAL

'I hardly advertise at all, and have no Internet presence—although I would like to set up a website to be able to advertise my sculptures, to reach a wider market. My customer base has grown by word of mouth, really, so I sell mainly within the neighbourhood. I like the fact that the bulk of my work is local. I get customers from all walks of life—even royalty—but I treat them all the same.

'I mainly do presentation work in glass for weddings, christenings etc. Basically whatever people want—which can make for some strange commissions! An example of this is when I was asked to engrave a plate for someone who was leaving the police fingerprint department. They got hold of his fingerprint, and I copied it onto a plate for them to present to him. He was over the moon! They tested my recreation out on the computer, and it matched this person's records perfectly!

'My initial aim was very simple—to be an artist but also to make a living. I have stuck to this through many years and hardships (health problems etc), but I have succeeded. Through all this, my wife has been a very strong influence, never letting me give up. I would pass on her main lesson—never give up. You may come across huge difficulties, but you just have to pull yourself back together and get on with it.

'The best part of what I do is that I do what I love as a full-time job. I am so fortunate. So many people can't wait for Friday night, can't wait to retire. I'm just not like that at all—the word 'retirement' just doesn't feature in my vocabulary. As an artist, the older you get the more you see, and the more you see the more you want to communicate. This means that my art becomes more important to me the older I get. I'm doing bigger things now than ever before. I am a firm believer that humanity is here for a reason—we are all part of something bigger. So to waste our time is just not good. I have a real passion for living.'

THE ESSENTIALS
'On a more mundane note, I have found that banks have changed drastically since I first set up in business. They used to be our friend, and interested in our business—now they seem to be dominated by greed, and to have no interest in what we're doing. I used to know my bank manager, but now I have to phone someone in another town, who I've never met, who doesn't know me, and who doesn't care.

'It is essential to find a good accountant and a good lawyer—preferably people who care about what you're doing, who can become your friend. And a good banker —although as I have said, that may be harder to find!

'I would say that in order to have the drive to overcome all the inevitable hurdles, you need a passion. You need the belief that what you have chosen to do *is* your life. You should be genuinely interested in your product. If not, it won't be a good product. So you need drive and passion—and, of course, enjoyment.'

Visit Bruce Walker at: **Bruce Walker Engravers, 3 Cumberland Close, Kirriemuir DD8 4EF (Tel: 01575 575 252)**

Check before you post!

Even if you're in a tearing hurry to get your letter out there and work its sales magic, do take time to read it over before you send it. Your computer can help with checking your spelling, but it's much better to ask someone else to read it over for you as they will have a bit more 'distance' than you do—it's easy to agree with yourself! Also, spellcheckers often can't catch grammatical errors or instances where you've used the wrong word; if that word is spelt correctly in itself (if you've used 'their' when you meant 'there', for example) the spellchecker won't pick it up, so a second opinion is doubly helpful.

WHAT TO AVOID
Not treating the mailing package as a whole

Refer frequently to the other parts of your mailing package to encourage the reader to read the letter several times. It might be a good idea to test a draft letter out on some established customers, and ask for their feedback.

Not making the most of previous mailings

If your business does a lot of direct mail selling, invest in a personal computer and a laser printer if you haven't got one already. This makes it easier to customise the basic letter for a variety of purposes. You can also keep a mailing database and carry out mail merges so that letters can be personally addressed. Microsoft Word gives helpful advice on creating mail merge documents, and once you get the hang of it, you'll find they don't take long at all.

RECOMMENDED LINK
Just Sell:
www.justsell.com

SEE ALSO
Creating Impressive Direct Mail Material (p. 288)
Direct Marketing (p. 505)
Improving the Response to Direct Mail (p. 292)

Selling by Mail Order

GETTING STARTED

Mail-order trading has developed as businesses have recognised it as a good way of selling to customers without incurring the overheads of retail premises. Small, specialist catalogues have performed well by using this strategy, particularly in selling niche items like hand-made shirts, kitchen equipment, and luxury and organic foods. Lakeland Limited, the kitchen and homeware stockist, is a good example of how this route can lead to a successful business with longevity. Lakeland now has stores around the country, but their catalogue is still a popular option for many of their customers. This actionlist looks at the advantages and disadvantages of mail-order selling, and also explains some of the legal implications.

FAQS

What are the advantages of selling by mail order?

Selling by mail order is good for cash flow because payment is in advance for goods that the business may not even need to stock, and round payment terms are of 30 or 60 days for purchases. Costs can be kept down because there is no need to rent high street premises, and little or no need for holding stock. Flexible working hours can be introduced, bringing in staff at busy times. If the business is a specialist retail or manufacturing outfit, setting up mail order is a good way of extending your catchment area. Also, mail order can be used with all customer income levels.

What are the disadvantages of selling by mail order?

People may be reluctant to send money to an unknown firm at a distant address. You will need to send frequent mailshots with offers to attract more sales. Mail order also imposes limitations on what product(s) can be sold.

MAKING IT HAPPEN

Choose the product

You need to consider whether there is a market for the item you have chosen; customers should see the advertised product and need it enough to send for it. Try to choose a product that is not generally available and that doesn't require demonstration. You will also need enough of the product to fulfil orders. It should be reasonably cheap, even with postage, and must be straightforward to pack and send. If possible, choose a group or set of products. This encourages people to keep coming back, especially if there is money off future items.

Promote it

Unlike a shop, which will attract passers-by, people need to be told what your mail-order business offers, and how and why they should buy it. There are various ways to get your message across. Direct mail is one. You can rent lists of names and addresses from a list brokerage service until you have built up your own. Data can be broken down specifically, so that tiny sections of the population who are very likely to buy can be targeted.

If you are offering several items, or your product is complicated, then using leaflets or catalogues will be the best means of promotion. Production costs for such materials can be high, so consider charging for catalogues. That way only serious potential customers will request a copy; you can offer to refund the cost if the customer then orders.

Small advertisements are another way to sell. Place adverts in special-interest media to narrow down the target market. Some national papers and magazines have specific sections for small mail-order businesses. To increase the response rate, make sure your timing is right, and don't squeeze too much information into a tiny space. Use a good headline and a few words, with a drawing rather than a photo. Coupons have a good response rate; respondents fill them in and you send them a more comprehensive leaflet or catalogue.

Giving a guarantee is a must; you are expecting customers to buy having seen only a few words and a drawing, so they should be able to send the product back at the business's expense. Don't use box numbers: they have a low response rate and can give the impression that your firm is being evasive. Keep price and postage separate and give a delivery time (though if you are selling goods zero-rated for VAT, the business could offer 'free postage' and, provided it is VAT-registered, recover VAT from HM Revenue & Customs).

Websites can be used to promote your business and generate orders. It may also be worth investigating taking payment via the site.

Track inquiries

It is important to be able to assess the success of targeting. Make sure that all your coupons are coded with an identifying letter or symbol, to show their origin. If there is not room for this, then a slightly different name or address could be used for each media source.

Keep a record of where each inquiry comes from (media, personal recommendation, direct mailing, and so on), and whether the inquiry becomes a sale. This allows you to determine which adverts lead to sales, as opposed to just inquiries, and to target advertising even more effectively in the future.

Aim to break even on the cost of mailing with your first set of orders. Then convert the requests into regular, loyal customers. This conversion rate should be significantly higher than the initial response rate. If brochures and leaflets are sent out and there is little or no response, some inquirers could be telephoned and asked why.

Get paid

The traditional system of offering cheap credit through agents is declining in popularity; most people want to buy only for themselves. Most small mail-order firms ask for payment with order. It's a good idea to wait for a cheque to be cleared before the goods are sent.

If possible, credit cards should be accepted. Customers prefer this as it is convenient and offers protection: if an individual item bought by credit card costs over £100 but less than £25,000, under the Consumer Credit Act 1974 the customer will be reimbursed by the card company should the business go into liquidation.

Package and deliver

Managing the delivery process efficiently is the core element of customer service for mail-order businesses. Test different packaging in Royal Mail conditions by sending items to and from the business. A separate packaging area should be set up with materials to hand. The importance of secure, efficient packaging should be emphasised to staff.

Think about how your business will deliver. Possible offers include free delivery, or free delivery for orders over a specified amount; and guaranteed next day delivery, or a surcharge for guaranteed delivery within 48 hours. Your business needs to decide whether such guarantees can be met, and whether the expense is worth the corresponding increase in customers and customer loyalty.

The British code of advertising, sales promotion, and direct marketing

These codes have been agreed by the advertising industry. They apply to catalogues, circulars, newspaper and magazine adverts, direct mail, brochures, and circulars. A catalogue should state that goods can be returned if applicable. It should also give any limitations to the offer. It should state the VAT due, unless the advert is exclusively trade. It should also give an estimated delivery time. Subject to certain exclusions, all orders should be fulfilled within 30 days. If delivery will take over 30 days, customers should be offered a refund. If they choose to wait, either fortnightly reports or a firm date should be given. Written statements of terms and conditions should be provided for customers.

Lists and databases should be run against the Mailing Preference Service (MPS) Consumer File, which lists the addresses of people who have chosen not to receive direct mail, to ensure their accuracy. Lists that are over six months old should not be used unless they have been corrected. If information will be disclosed to other businesses, consumers should be given the chance to object. Also, personal information should be relevant and not excessive.

Be aware of legal issues

The European Directive on Distance Selling was adopted in May 1997 and covers the supply of goods and services at a distance. Your business should be aware of any changes that this directive makes to existing UK legislation.

The Data Protection Act 1998 covers personal data, that is to say information on a living, identifiable individual. Data controllers must register with the Data Protection Commissioner. There are eight principles of good practice, including that data be fairly and lawfully obtained, that it is held only for the purpose specified in the register entry, and that adequate security measures are taken to prevent unauthorised or accidental access to, alteration, disclosure, or loss and destruction of information.

If credit (subject to certain exemptions) is offered, your business may need a Category A Consumer Credit Business credit licence under the Consumer Credit Act (CCA) 1974.

Consider voluntary protection schemes

Many mail order businesses adopt one of the voluntary codes of practice designed to protect customers' details and money. The Mail Order Protection Scheme (MOPS) covers most adverts in national newspapers that ask for payment with order (excluding most classified advertisements). If the business is cleared, it pays a fee to the common fund based on advertising costs (this is used to pay customers for goods up to £100 should the advertiser go into liquidation). To join the scheme you must provide the latest accounts, a bank reference, details of your stock levels, details of advertising agencies used, and your advert and product details.

The Mailing Preference Service allows people to have their details removed from the lists of companies that subscribe. The Mail Order Traders' Association (MOTA) has a code of practice for catalogue mail order. Although its members are leading general catalogue companies, its Office of Fair Trading-agreed code has useful guidelines for practice.

WHAT TO AVOID
Not being prepared

Make sure that you have the resources to set up this type of business. It may look like an easy way of selling, but you need to be certain that you have the right product and that you have pinpointed the right market for it.

Worrying about lack of response

Your business may only get a few replies initially, but if these lead to high-price, high-margin sales, then it can be worth it.

RECOMMENDED LINKS

Advertising Standards Authority (ASA) and Committee of Advertising Practice (CAP):
www.asa.org.uk
Committee of Advertising Practice:
www.cap.org.uk
Direct Marketing Association (DMA):
www.dma.org.uk
Mailing Preference Service:
www.mpsonline.org.uk

SEE ALSO
Direct Marketing (p. 505)

Telemarketing

GETTING STARTED

Telemarketing is a marketing strategy that uses telecommunications and computers, or a manual contact system, to make sales calls and build leads for the sale of your product or service. This actionlist looks at the best ways to structure your own telemarketing operation and considers the use of an independent telemarketing agency.

FAQS

How do I set up an in-house telemarketing operation?

Office design can significantly affect performance, so if your budget allows, use a consultant experienced in call centre design. The office should be arranged so that individuals can make or answer calls in private yet still feel part of a team. Good sound insulation is essential. Workstations should be comfortable, and equipment should include lightweight headsets and antiglare computer screens. Workstations and equipment should meet the Health and Safety (Display Screen Equipment) Regulations 1992.

Think carefully about recognition and remuneration. In the case of outgoing calls, you could consider a results-based scheme. For staff handling incoming calls, you could offer bonus payments for hitting cross-selling (selling customers different products within your range) or up-selling (selling customers a higher-priced version of a product they have bought previously) targets. You could run a pilot scheme to evaluate variable factors such as lists, people, markets, equipment, and management, before embarking on a full programme.

How do I introduce a telemarketing programme?

A telemarketing operation won't reach its full potential in isolation, and needs to work with other parts of the business—co-operation is the key to success. Everyone involved in marketing, sales, and production needs to understand the reasons for its introduction, what benefits it will bring, and the impact it will have. Sales people may feel threatened by telemarketing, so you

must explain how telemarketing will *complement* their activities rather than replace them.

The first step is to do an overview of the business operations and then to identify the telemarketing objectives. Then carry out a cost-benefit analysis and draw up a detailed step-by-step plan for implementing and running the operation. Best practice guidelines can be obtained from the Direct Marketing Association. In particular, you will need to be aware of the guidelines in respect of politeness and times of calling, and the use of the Telephone Preference Service if the business is planning to make calls to consumers who are not current customers. Check the provisions of the Telecommunications (Data Protection and Privacy) Regulations 1999.

MAKING IT HAPPEN
Implement a telemarketing programme

First you need to target your telemarketing programme. Identify the targets for outgoing calls by analysing existing customer life-cycles, looking at how recently a customer bought something, how frequently he or she buys, and the value of their purchases. Prospects can also be identified by geographical location, from lapsed customers, and from bought-in lists of names. Incoming calls are usually generated through advertising, which must itself be targeted. Ideally, rank target groups by potential return on investment.

Second, you must test your telemarketing programme. There are specific methods for calculating how big a sample to try, but for a campaign of any real size it is advisable to work on 500 to 1,000. After determining the sample size, you can work out the level of human and telephone resources needed for the trial period. The trial gives your business a chance to monitor results and modify the details of the programme.

Third, you need to implement your programme, depending, of course, on the test results. Budgets must be set for the programme, and you will need to consider the investment required, operating costs, the cost-saving benefits of the programme, and the extra revenue likely to be produced through additional orders.

Fourth, you should evaluate the programme. You will need to work out costs, and productivity levels in terms of rates of response and conversion (contacts into sales). Telemarketing should produce quantifiable results. With accurate figures, it is possible to establish future activity budgets and be able to compare the cost-effectiveness of telemarketing against alternative sales and marketing methods, or as a support to the existing methods.

Use databases for telemarketing

You'll need to buy or develop a database to store information on customers and prospects. Databases range from simple systems (like a computerised card index system) to relational databases that allow data to be analysed in various ways. Think about what categories of information the database should hold, potential data entry methods (for example, directly during the customer's telephone call, or later by transfer from paper records), how the information will be accessed, how reports will be generated, and quality standards and procedures (to keep data accurate and up-to-date).

Your business's own database is the ideal source of telephone contacts, but you might want to to think about buying in appropriately-sourced contact lists from a specialist agency. Do shop around: list-provision is a competitive business and similar lists may be available through several brokers at different prices. Be aware that lists go out of date very quickly. The quickest way to check the accuracy of a list is by phone.

Telemarketing businesses need to comply with the Data Protection Act 1998. If the business uses a bought-in database, it is important to make sure that it has been screened against the list provided by the Telephone Preference Service (TPS), which helps people make sure their telephone number is not made available to organisations who may wish to offer them services they do not want; the TPS's website address is given at the end of this actionlist.

Call management

Call management affects the service provided to callers and the cost-effectiveness of your telemarketing operation. There are two main methods of managing incoming calls.

1. A Special Automatic Caller Distributor (ACD) transfers incoming calls to the first available person, or plays a message indicating that the caller is in a queue. ACDs also produce useful call-management information.

2. Call Sequencers answer calls with a message saying that the call will be taken as soon as possible, or giving the caller an option to leave voicemail for a return call.

ACDs and Call Sequencers can be located on the premises and are available from a number of companies. Additionally, caller-controlled systems let callers select the person or department with whom they wish to speak by pressing buttons on their telephone, or through voice recognition.

Recruit and train for the telemarketing operation

The performance of a telemarketing operation depends on the people manning the phones. They must be skilled in creating rapport, overcoming objections, responding to criticisms, and directing conversations. When you're looking for staff to work in this role, it makes sense to do your initial evaluation of them over the phone so you can hear them in action. Ask yourself whether they come across as genuine, interested individuals who enjoy contact with people; whether they are clear communicators; and whether they listen well, taking in all the information they are given. Would they perform well in a demanding atmosphere without becoming discouraged? This is particularly important, as rejection is an inevitable part of the job. Training is vital; appropriate courses for telemarketing managers and staff are widely available.

Lead and motivate staff in a telemarketing operation

All telemarketing teams need a leader; someone with excellent interpersonal skills and the ability to motivate staff. Team leaders should start and finish each day with upbeat team briefings. Before making calls, it is important that everyone knows his or her target for the day. At the end of the day, results can be discussed and the day should be closed on a positive note. The team leader should be located near the team, and team members should be encouraged to swap information and raise problems.

Think about using scripts

Telemarketing staff need to direct every conversation in a planned and controlled, yet natural, way. You will need to develop a script or structured call plan covering all stages of the conversation, from greeting callers and answering questions to taking orders and signing off. Many telemarketing departments provide their agents with computer-based scripts. These often have built-in intelligence; for example, when an answer is filled in by an operator, the computer provides the most appropriate question to ask next. Information from callers can be typed directly onto a form on-screen.

Writing a multi-option telemarketing script is a specialised skill; it's worth hiring a professional to do it. Allow your team to spend time role-playing first; you could, for example, tape trial conversations and check that they sound natural. Well-prepared scripts should control the message being delivered and ensure that customers receive correct information. They also ensure that the right information is collected and make it easier to analyse results. However, there

can also be drawbacks; in the hands of the inexperienced, scripts can sound false and contrived and they can diminish initiative in more experienced staff.

Consider using an outside telemarketing agency

Some telemarketing agencies specialise in inbound telemarketing, others in outbound, but many operate in both fields. Make sure you know exactly what services *your* business requires and try to visit each agency in person, seeing how it works and talking to the staff. Check the agency's client list; ask permission to contact several clients for references; and find out about the agency's database system and what management information it can provide. Ask for a written response to your brief, with detailed costing. Don't forget to confirm that the agency has the capacity to handle full implementation to your timescale if the trial goes well.

Monitoring performance is essential, so arrange for regular reports on all key activities, including lost calls, response rates, and data quality. If people are declining an offer, try to find out why—changing the script might help. Finally, reward outstanding results, and thank staff personally, to keep their motivation high.

WHAT TO AVOID
Not researching thoroughly

Whatever type of business you're in, keep up to date with what your competitors are doing. It will set you a benchmark if you're starting to use telemarketing, or may help you raise your game if you're doing it already.

Not getting an 0800 number

It is worth considering getting an 0800 telephone number; calls made to these numbers are charged to the business. They are available from several telecommunications companies and are popular in telemarketing.

Complying with Data Protection Legislation

GETTING STARTED

The 1998 Data Protection Act has significantly changed the rules concerning the use of customer data, and applies to small companies as much as it does to larger ones. From now on, both paper and computerised records must comply with the Act, which also refers to the use of data for telemarketing.

Companies must also be open about how they use data and must follow sound information-handling practice. Furthermore, data must be available to the individual (usually your customer) who 'owns' it.

All data users must register with the office of the Information Commissioner and comply with the principles of the Act. You (and your company) will then be listed on the register as a 'data controller'.

The key principles of the Act are that data must be:

- fairly and lawfully processed
- processed for limited purposes
- adequate, relevant, and not excessive
- processed in accordance with the data subject's rights
- accurate
- secure
- not transferred to other countries without adequate protection

Companies should use customer data to benefit customers. Many simply hold data without using it. You should reassure customers that you treat their data with the highest levels of confidentiality and use data, within the spirit of the Act, to contact customers with information that you believe may be of interest to them.

Above all, make it clear to consumers how they benefit from giving you information and make it easy for them to respond, change their details, or decline to be contacted.

FAQS

How do I know if my data has to comply with the Act?

Even if you only hold a small number of customer names and addresses, they constitute data under the terms of the Act. By and large, however, the Act is concerned with data relating to private individuals and not companies. You may find that even if your customers are companies, you also keep data on individuals within those companies. If in doubt, check.

My company is part of a larger group. Can I pass customer data to other companies in the group?

You should ask the customer's permission before passing data to any other parties, even internal ones.

Do I need permission to collect data?

Yes, you should tell the owner of the data and give him or her the opportunity to opt out of giving you information. Any holding or use of data must be done 'fairly' and usually this means one or more of the following:

- the individual has given his or her consent
- it is necessary for the performance of the contract with the individual
- it is a legal obligation
- it is necessary to protect the vital interests of the individual; or to carry out public functions
- it is necessary in order to pursue the legitimate interests of the data controller or third parties (unless it could prejudice the interests of the individual)

How long can I hold data on a customer?

The Act does not specify a time limit, but recommends that it should not be held longer than necessary. It is in the spirit of the Act that you should not just hold data, but should use it to benefit the customer; for example, by providing him or her with information that you believe is useful.

What happens if data is inaccurate?

According to the Act, data must be accurate and up to date. That puts the onus on you to maintain it properly and check with customers that it is accurate.

Can I use data for telemarketing?

Yes, but again you must ask permission from individuals or companies before sending faxes, and individuals have a right to opt out of telephone calls. Companies cannot insist on no telephone calls, but you would be well-advised to consider such a request seriously! Both individuals and companies must give permission before you can use automated call systems—a point not well known.

MAKING IT HAPPEN
Check all your records

The use of customer data changed significantly when the 1998 Data Protection Act came into force. The 1994 Act only covered data held electronically which could be processed on a computer. However, the 1998 version includes paper records.

Remember that paper records must comply as well

In theory, this means that if you have a box of file cards with names and addresses, you should register that information with the Data Protection Registrar (Information Commissioner). Many sales and customer service teams still use this type of filing, even in relatively large companies.

Use data properly

The basic premise behind the Data Protection Act is: if you have data, use it properly. The Act works in two ways.

- Firstly, it places obligations on data users. They must be open about how they use data and must follow sound information-handling practice which is specified in the Act.
- Secondly, the Act gives every individual access to information held about him or herself. It also allows them to have the information corrected or deleted where appropriate if it is wrong, and gives the right to seek compensation for damage and associated distress through the courts.

Register your data

Under the Data Protection Act, all data users must register with the Information Commissioner. Once registered, users must comply with the principles contained in the Act. They must:

- obtain and process personal data fairly and lawfully
- hold the data only for the purposes specified in the register entry
- only hold accurate data which is relevant and not excessive for the purpose for which it is held
- make sure personal data is accurate and, where necessary, kept up to date
- not hold data for longer than necessary

The Information Commissioner has a helpline to find out more: 01625 545 745.

Use customer data to benefit customers

Not all companies comply with the spirit of the Act. According to research, some of the organisations holding most data, particularly in financial services, don't seem to use it at all, resulting in poor communications with customers. Many companies have simply been collecting data and not really putting it to good effect. The data is itself very valuable, but customers may feel that they have handed over a great deal of information on their lives without seeing any benefit. The issue of data collection becomes even more complicated with the growth of the Internet. Not only will data collection be faster; consumers will expect higher levels of service than ever.

Be aware of Internet data
The issue of regulation for the Internet is a difficult one. The World Wide Web is based on principles of freely available information on a worldwide scale. However, consumers need to be protected so that they can use the Internet with confidence.

Check data accuracy
Recent changes to the Data Protection Act mean that companies must ensure the data they hold is accurate and up to date. As part of your commitment to customer service, you should aim to offer customers useful and timely information that meets their individual requirements. To do this you might hold contact details, together with information on customers' personal interests which they have provided in the past. Because circumstances change, make sure that you have your customers' correct details and check that they are happy for the company to continue to contact them.

Customers have a right under the Data Protection Act to ask for a copy of the information you hold on them and to have any inaccuracies corrected.

Get the customer's permission
Ask customers to let you know if they do not wish you to give this information to other parties. Tell them that you would like to continue contacting them. However, if the customer prefers you not to, ask them to let you know. If they do not reply within a specified time frame, tell them that you will assume that it is okay to continue contacting them.

Reassure customers about data
Customers should be assured that you treat their data with the highest levels of confidentiality. You should not disclose their information, without their consent, to third parties, any party within your own business, dealers or other businesses acting on your behalf.

Use the information to maintain contact
If you have data, you can use it—within the spirit of the Act—to contact customers with information about products and services that you believe may be of interest to them.

You can also use the information for marketing, research or sales tracking purposes. Customer names and addresses may also be used to process orders and maintain accounts with the company or its dealers.

Make it easy for customers to respond
Allow customers to respond to requests for permission to contact them by post, fax or e-mail. Let them know that they should reply if they would like you to stop communications, or if they want to change contact details. Provide a helpline that customers can call if they need any further information on your data policy or on the data you hold.

WHAT TO AVOID
Storing data and not using it
The Act says that you should not hold data for longer than necessary. Consumer attitudes say that they should see some recognisable benefit for providing the information.

Using inaccurate data
The onus is on the company to check that data is accurate. This means contacting customers to ensure that information is up to date and correct.

Failing to register data
The 1998 version of the Act widened the scope of data protection to include paper records, so even small organisations with apparently simple customer records must comply.

Making it difficult for customers to respond
The Act says that you must give customers access to any data you hold on them. That means you must make it easy for customers to contact you.

RECOMMENDED LINK
Data Protection Agency:
www.dpa.gov.uk

SEE ALSO
Carrying Out Market Research (p. 226)

Raising Awareness of Your Brand

GETTING STARTED
Brand awareness is an important factor in customer purchasing decisions. Brand values relate to many areas, from product attributes to less tangible aspects of a company's reputation. By identifying the key values of your brand you can establish how your products, your services, and your company are perceived by different types of customer.

FAQS
Can a small company use branding?
Absolutely. You have to understand your own brand, since you will have a brand or corporate image in your market whether you like it or not! Smaller companies increasingly compete with large, well-known, brands—sometimes globally—so the aim of branding is to differentiate your company or product and to convey its unique attributes.

How important are brand values?
Branding is frequently perceived as a consumer marketing discipline. However, industry experience indicates that business-to-business purchasing is a complex process influenced by intangible perceptions as much as by hard facts on product performance.

MAKING IT HAPPEN
Identify the most important elements of a brand
The key attributes of a business brand may include:
- fitness for purpose—is it the best at what it does?
- value for money—if not offered at always the lowest price, does it represent a good deal compared to the competition, even if it isn't better?
- quality—is it simply better-built or better-managed?
- extendability—does the brand work in many related markets?
- company reliability—does the brand come from a good 'stable'?
- proven products—is the brand associated with established successes?

- investment in product development—is innovation significant?

Find out what is important to your customers
Although these brand values can be applied to business products in general terms, it's vital to understand how individual customers rank the values. This can be determined in several ways, described below.

Talk to customers
This is the simplest way to find out what they value, but take care not to talk exclusively about the physical benefits of a product. There will almost certainly be aspects of service that are as important. You should also ask 'open' questions about the competition for example:
- Who else have you looked at?
- What do you think of them?
- What is their biggest strength or weakness?
- What do other people think of them?

Carry out customer surveys
To find out what your customers consider important, carry out a survey; if your budget runs to it, this should be done through a market research company so that respondents feel the survey is independent. It should ask respondents how they rank the different brand values, and how they believe your company and a number of competitors compare across these values.

Run a focus group
A focus group can be used to cover the same ground as the customer survey, but it enables you to cover the subject in greater depth, and to raise issues that you may not

anticipate or that would normally be outside the scope of a survey. Focus groups are ideal for identifying branding issues that concern customers, assessing customer reactions to potential changes, or identifying any problems customers are experiencing.

Review industry trends

Industry associations and publishers produce regular surveys into buying behaviour in their industry sector. These surveys can highlight issues that concern the whole market.

Find out about customer purchasing requirements

An increasing number of business customers use formal criteria to evaluate potential suppliers and monitor their performance. These purchasing criteria indicate the factors that your customers believe are important, and can help to identify the key messages you should include in your own brand communications.

Communicate through all channels

Advertising and marketing communications are the most important media for raising awareness. However, there are several other direct and indirect channels, including:

- products—the design and brand symbolism can convey significant brand values
- services—the way you deal with customers can demonstrate your commitment to their needs
- packaging—this can carry messages regarding your brand
- distribution facilities—these can give an impression of your approach and values
- websites—they must be consistent with your key brand values
- customer service facilities—they must deliver the promise of the brand

Assess your product branding

Do your products communicate your key brand values? The most important values are listed above, but you should include every aspect of your company that your customer may experience.

If customer research shows that you are perceived as poor in any of these areas, or if customers are not aware of your strengths, you must look closely at your product development programme. Also review your customer communications to see how customers build their image of your brand.

Brand your services

Service capability can also help to differentiate a company from its competitors. Many companies have underestimated the importance of service to their customers, and as a result haven't adequately communicated their service capabilities. The right services can help customers improve their own business performance and can supplement their own resources, so raising awareness of service capability is an important aspect of brand communication. You can increase awareness through product advertising, product literature, direct marketing, and product public relations, as well as through service communications.

Communicate brand values through packaging

Packaging raises awareness of brand values by the way in which it reflects the corporate identity. The right packaging can visually support your brand through the use of your logo, slogans, promises and company values.

Don't forget to include your branding distribution facilities

Your distribution facilities can affect awareness of your brand. Again (if your budget allows) vehicles, uniforms, and premises should carry the same logo and key messages as other mediums of communication.

Distribution is an area that is frequently overlooked in branding programmes, but it can make an important contribution to customer perceptions of your company. For example, the cleanliness of a delivery van shows a level of professionalism.

Build brand values through your website

An effective e-commerce website is one in which the various technical and design components all work together to generate customer interest, build trust, communicate product value, and support convenient profitable transactions. Even if you don't sell directly from your website, the key is that your customer must feel they have gained something from the visit that exceeds the 'cost' (even if only in time) of visiting.

Brand through customer service facilities

Your customer service facilities have a major impact on the way your customers perceive your company. Customer contact takes place both before and after a sale, and these contacts can prove critical in shaping customer attitudes. When your customer service team handles enquiries, orders, or complaints effectively, it creates awareness of positive brand values.

Monitor levels of brand awareness

Customer perceptions change over a period of time. Continuous research should be carried out to monitor customer attitudes. This type of research is known as tracking research, and it helps to measure the effectiveness of brand communications programmes.

WHAT TO AVOID

Failing to monitor customer perceptions

Regular research is critical. You must know how you are perceived by your customers so that you can plan the way your brand is represented in the future.

Overlooking individual customer preferences

Industry research may give you a broad view of the brand values that are important to customers. However, it's more important to understand how individual customers—particularly your most important customers—rank individual values. This can be achieved only by continuous detailed research into individual customer needs.

Ignoring important communication channels

Brand values are communicated through many different channels, not just advertising and marketing media. Customers' attitudes and perceptions are shaped by packaging, customer service, distribution, and products as well as by other factors. Make sure every aspect of your business reflects the brand values that are important to your customers.

RECOMMENDED LINKS

British Brands Group:
www.britishbrandsgroup.org.uk
Institute of Practitioners in Advertising:
www.ipa.co.uk

SEE ALSO

Planning a Cost-effective Direct Marketing Campaign (p. 284)
Planning an Advertising Campaign (p. 303)
Producing Press Material (p. 296)

Planning a Cost-effective Direct Marketing Campaign

GETTING STARTED

Direct marketing works most effectively when it is aimed at a precise audience that cannot be easily reached by any other medium. A campaign should be carefully planned in accordance with the target market and the product or service concerned. Short-term results can be measured accurately and directly by the level of response, so the effectiveness of a campaign can be assessed quickly. There are, however, many different factors that can affect the outcome, such as product price or the quality of the campaign material. As with any direct approach, it is essential to make it as easy as possible for customers to respond.

FAQS

Is direct marketing the same as direct mail?

No. Direct marketing (DM) is any marketing activity that depends on a direct and measurable response. Conventional advertising can be 'direct', as can telephone, fax, e-mail and, of course, the Internet. Direct mail is direct marketing communication sent by post, and therefore often has a poor reputation because of the amount of unsolicited mail that people regularly receive.

Can direct marketing be used to sell products?

There are many situations in which you can use direct marketing to build direct sales. You may not have a salesforce or a retail network, so customers can only buy direct from you. If you want to sell to niche markets, or if your customers are widely spread or even global, direct marketing may be the only cost-effective way of reaching them. If you decide to sell direct, you must ensure that the products themselves are suitable for selling through direct marketing—that is, that they do not have to be demonstrated, or inspected by the customer.

How does direct marketing build relationships with customers?

The stronger your relationship with your customers, the more opportunities you have to influence the future direction and success of your business. If your company depends on a few key customers for most of its business, you can use direct marketing to improve customer loyalty by building long-term relationships with them. You may also need to use it if your customers want to rationalise the number of suppliers, and you want to remain on the approved list.

Is direct marketing only effective for reaching a small audience?

There are numerous examples of successful large-scale mailings. However, the key to direct marketing success is reaching the right people in a cost-effective way. Large-scale mailings based on poorly researched mailing lists may yield results, but there will also be a high level of wastage. The more precise your mailing, the more likely you are to succeed.

MAKING IT HAPPEN
Set campaign objectives

Direct marketing objectives can be initially expressed in general terms:

- encouraging prospects to buy directly in response to a direct marketing campaign
- generating leads for the salesforce or retail network
- supporting salesforce activity
- improving the effectiveness of other forms of communication
- raising awareness of a company, product, or service among clearly identified customers and prospects
- maintaining effective contact with customers and prospects

- building relationships with customers and prospects

However, these general objectives should be translated into precise, measurable objectives, for example:

- raising awareness of your product range among 35% of technical directors in the mechanical engineering sector
- ensuring that purchasing managers of your ten top corporate customers are contacted at least once a fortnight
- increasing direct sales of supplies by 15%

Define the target market

Do you want to reach all customers and prospects, or are you targeting specific groups? Direct marketing is a precise medium, so your campaign could be aimed at just a few key decision-makers or thousands of potential users. To plan your direct marketing campaign, you should ask questions such as:

- Who buys your type of product?
- Who influences the purchasing decision?
- How many prospective customers (prospects) do you want to reach with the direct marketing campaign?
- How many prospects can you normally convert to customers, and how long does it take?
- How do they currently get information about your products?
- Is direct marketing the best (or only) way of reaching the target audience?

The more information you have about your target audience, the more precise you can make your campaign. In an ideal world, direct marketing would allow you to communicate one to one with every prospect, but, in practical terms, you are more likely to be communicating with groups that share certain characteristics. For example, you could reasonably expect that 'all fleet managers in the North East of England managing more than thirty vehicles' would have similar needs in respect to their day-to-day job.

Plan campaign timing

A direct marketing campaign can run at any time, so you do not have to consider advertisement publication dates. However, timing may be dictated by other factors—lead times

for producing mailing material, seasonal purchasing patterns, product availability, or tender dates. These are some of the factors to consider in planning the timing of your campaign:

- When is your customer likely to be making the buying decision?
- How long is the selling or buying process? How many stages are involved? Who is involved?
- Does your direct marketing campaign have to tie in with the timing of any other marketing activity, such as an exhibition, advertising campaign, or salesforce visit?
- If you are launching a new product, when will the product be available?
- How long will it take to produce the material that is to be mailed?
- When will you be able to follow up the campaign?
- What will you do if you get fewer responses than you need *or* more than you can handle?

Decide on your contact strategy

A single mailshot, telephone call, or direct response advertisement may produce results, but a series of appropriate contacts will have greater impact and ensure you meet your objectives. There are several benefits from repeated contacts:

- raising levels of awareness with each contact
- educating potential clients about your product/service
- following up those who have not responded
- moving individual respondents further along the decision-making process
- maintaining contact during extended decision-making processes

There is no hard-and-fast rule about the frequency of individual campaigns; a company trying to get a prospect to make a decision may make contact several times a week, while a company aiming to maintain long-term customer loyalty may only need to contact customers monthly or quarterly.

Develop a response mechanism

Action is a vital ingredient of any direct marketing campaign, and it is essential that you make it easy for your prospects to respond. First, decide if your prospects are to place an order, request a sales visit, or ask for further information. Then decide which of the five basic types of response mechanism is the most appropriate: post, telephone, faxback, e-mail, or website address.

Keep track of the campaign

You must be prepared to keep records of every aspect of your campaign. You will have to set up the systems to capture data before your campaign (or test campaign) starts. Aim to know at the very least:

- what was sent (the offer, the pack/letter, and so on) and to whom (the lists used and reason for selection)
- the anticipated response (for example, percentage initial response and percentage purchase)
- the actual response
- the costs and the return—in other words, did your campaign make a profit?

Test the campaign

Part of the flexibility of direct marketing is that you can test your approach before committing resources to the full campaign. There are several variables that can be tested:

- the target audience—the most important element
- the offer—what exactly you are offering for sale (including any incentive)
- the creative approach—the look and feel of the communications
- the response mechanism—how easy it is to respond, for example, using a Freephone number or Freepost
- frequency and timing—including the way you follow up inquiries

The test campaign can be carried out in a number of ways:

- on a sample of the target market
- in a defined sales or geographic territory
- in a particular sector of the target market

The most effective test campaign is the one that achieves the highest response levels; committed DM organisations test continuously to drive down their costs and drive up response rates. Indeed, every campaign should be considered a 'test' to improve on previous campaigns. Each best-performing campaign then becomes the 'control' against which others can be evaluated.

Plan split campaigns

Testing your campaign may reveal that different approaches work more effectively in different market sectors. If budget allows, you can develop a series of campaigns that vary the offer, the creative approach, frequency, timing, or other factors—but ensure you keep track of these variables so that you can use the best-performing campaign format next time.

Set target response levels

In the long term, a campaign may increase awareness, improve customer relations, or cut the cost of sales. However, the simplest and most immediate measure of a direct marketing campaign is the response level it generates. In setting your target response levels, you should aim for a realistic figure that is within budget. Note that:

- response levels as low as 1 or 2% are regarded as the industry norm for large companies sending mail to 'cold' lists
- response rates in the region of 5% are therefore regarded as high
- response rates in the region of 10–20% have been reported by companies who have integrated other forms of marketing communications
- far higher response rates can be experienced by specialist companies communicating vital information to a very committed list of supporters

Many different factors can affect the level of response, including price, quality of the mailing list, the promotional offer, and quality of copy and design. A test is very often the only way to set an initial target response rate for future campaigns.

WHAT TO AVOID
Using DM unnecessarily

While the principles of direct marketing can help any company in its communications and selling, sometimes direct *mail* is used when the existing channels are preferable. Customers who are used to a personal visit and face-to-face negotiations may feel aggrieved if you try and deal with them at a distance.

Failing to set measurable targets
The results of a direct marketing campaign can be measured precisely by the number of responses. This makes it a particularly accountable medium. It is therefore important to set realistic, measurable objectives. If your target is to generate leads from 2% of the target audience, this will determine how many people you mail, the type of offer you make, and the response mechanism you provide. It will also tell you very quickly if your budget balances—how many of those leads need to convert into customers to cover your costs?

Poor audience selection
With direct marketing you can communicate with a single prospect or with 50,000. However, there may be more cost-effective ways of communicating with 50,000 prospects. Direct marketing works most effectively when it is aimed at a precise audience that cannot be easily reached by any other medium and, crucially, when you want a response. For example, you may find there

is a specialist magazine or newsletter that precisely covers your target market.

No integration with other communications
If your marketing budget is split between different communications activities such as advertising, sales promotion, and press and public relations, it is essential that each activity works as effectively as possible. You can use direct marketing in conjunction with other methods of communication. If you place advertisements in publications that only reach a general audience, you can reinforce the advertisements with personalised communications to selected prospects. If your advertisements include a response mechanism, keeping to direct marketing principles will ensure effective follow-up. You can also tailor your product and corporate literature to the information needs of different market sectors by including direct marketing material.

RECOMMENDED LINKS
The Direct Selling Association:
www.dsa.org.uk
The Institute of Direct Marketing:
www.theidm.co.uk

SEE ALSO
Raising Awareness of Your Brand (p. 281)

Creating Impressive Direct Mail Material

GETTING STARTED

When you are marketing your product or service, you may find you need an effective and precise marketing tool that you can personalise in order to more accurately reflect the needs of customers and prospective customers. If so, direct mail may be what you need. It can be eye-catching and creative, and allows you to include different types of enclosure to provide additional details on the product or service being offered.

Another benefit of direct mail is that it's easy to measure its results precisely, so that you can assess how you've done with a particular campaign or approach. As part of this process, you need to include an easy response mechanism for the customer, such as a reply-paid envelope, or contact details such as an e-mail address, so that your customers can give you feedback.

FAQS

Don't customers just throw direct mail in the bin?

No, but attitudes vary enormously. According to research (Direct Mail Information Service, 2004), 60% of people open direct mail, but only 40% open *and read it*. Business managers opened 70% of their direct mail but, on average, filed only 20%. Executives are now also starting to employ growing numbers of direct mail 'filterers', who open their mail for them and decide whether it's worth passing on.

Is it possible to create effective direct mail?

Yes, but like any other marketing activity, you'll get the best results from working towards a specific objective. The more information you have, the more focused the work. Direct mail is a very precise medium, so it is possible to create highly customised and attractive mailings that meet the information needs of your chosen prospective customers (prospects).

How far can personalisation go in direct mail?

Of course, mailings to a small number of customers can easily be personalised, and should be. Provided you have the budget, larger mailings can be personalised down to individual level (one-to-one marketing). As an example, you could write individual letters to each of your prospects, or include an incentive tailored to their individual preferences. Practical financial constraints usually prevent this degree of personalisation, so most companies concentrate on limited customisation, addressing specific sector concerns or tailoring special offers to different types of business.

Can the quality of direct mail creative work be measured?

Direct mail is an extremely accountable medium, and the results can be measured precisely, making it possible to judge whether or not a particular creative approach has worked. However, creative work is only one of the factors that influence campaign success, so many companies test different creative approaches to try to identify how they affect results. Remember, though, that the offer's recipient is more important than the presentation of the offer itself, so targeting should be your priority.

MAKING IT HAPPEN
Create good-quality mailing material

Direct mail is the most precise marketing medium, but campaigns will only be effective if they combine precise targeting with good creative work.

In theory anything can be sent by post, but most mailings consist primarily of printed material—letters, leaflets, and brochures. Three-dimensional objects can be mailed and can stimulate interest, but they must be relevant and cost-effective. A striking envelope design can also add impact to a mailing. The Post Office has a dedicated team to provide all the information you need to ensure your mailings conform to their regulations, and to help set up freepost and business reply services.

Use direct mail letters effectively

Letters are a universal communications medium and an integral element of any direct mail campaign. They can be used on their own as a personalised form of communication, and can also be used to support and personalise other standard mailing items. Letters can be customised easily and cost-effectively to meet different sector marketing requirements.

Personalise letters

Personalised one-to-one mailings are an ideal form of communication for companies with detailed information on their prospects. The letter should reflect the individual's main interests and concerns, and the offer can be tailored to the individual prospect. Subsequent mailings can build an individual relationship with the prospect.

The key features of this type of letter are:

- it is personalised to the individual reader
- it offers direct and valuable benefits
- it builds future relationships with the customer by promising regular offers

Letters can also be customised by market sector, offering specific benefits to groups of customers.

Use letters to support other mailing material

Direct mail letters can also be used to accompany other material—a product brochure, management guide, or even an invoice, for example. The letter can customise the mailing by including information specific to the individual prospect or market sector, or by making a further offer to the prospect.

Include enclosures

Enclosures can include:

- catalogues
- sales leaflets or brochures
- price lists
- management reports or surveys
- information on special offers
- samples, free gifts, or incentives

There are a number of criteria for selecting enclosures:

- they should be relevant to the prospect's needs
- they should not make the mailing impractical or costly because of size or weight
- they should improve response, size of order, or frequency of order—if they do not they are an unnecessary cost

Treat envelopes creatively

Postal authorities specify a number of preferred envelope sizes which help them to handle mail more efficiently. Companies using specific postal response services such as Freepost or Business Reply use the preferred layouts indicated in the authority's design specification. However, using nonstandard envelope sizes can add greater impact to a mailing. Envelopes can be designed in a number of ways to achieve greater impact:

- they can include advertising messages
- addresses can be handwritten to add a personal touch
- they can incorporate corporate design elements such as logos or company colours

But be aware of occasions when a clearly, but wrongly identified envelope may depress response, such as an item that looks like a routine statement.

Create three-dimensional enclosures

Three-dimensional enclosures can add impact and novelty value to a mailing. They can be used to send product samples by mail, to send promotional items, or to improve response by creating interest. However, it is important that they are relevant to the prospect's needs, that they do not make the mailing too expensive, and that they do not contravene postal regulations.

Include a response mechanism

If your mailing is designed to stimulate action, it should include an easy-to-use response mechanism such as a reply-paid card or envelope, or contact details such as a Freephone telephone number, e-mail address, or website address.

Use professional creative and production services

Quality and impact are essential to the success of a direct mail campaign. Creating an effective direct mail item requires professional skills, and is best handled by suitably experienced people. Although many of the direct mail processes are straightforward, your company may not have the skills or resources to achieve the best possible results. External specialists provide a range of direct mail services, including copywriting and design, printing letters, and producing three-dimensional enclosures.

Specialists include:

- direct mail agencies
- advertising agencies
- marketing communication consultancies
- design consultancies
- creative consultancies
- printers

However, there may be occasions when you decide to create simple direct mail items yourself.

Write persuasive copy

Use a powerful headline to get the attention of the reader. Words such as 'free', 'new' and 'improved' attract attention, while price benefits such as 'sale' and 'reduced' are also useful. Keep your writing style simple, with short sentences and paragraphs; in longer mailing items, use headings and subheadings to make sure that the reader picks up key messages without having to read the complete text. Tell your prospects what they need to know in order to make a decision about your product or service. Your message should deal with your customers' most important concerns and requirements. Describe benefits to the prospect, not features of the product: for example, a power drill that features extremely high operating speeds may be technically interesting, but the benefits to a builder are greater productivity and the opportunity to finish a job quickly. Offer the prospect a clear, powerful proposition. Your copy should encourage the prospect to take action—contact the company for more information, ask for a demonstration, or order immediately to qualify for a promotional offer. Describe your biggest benefit first, then remember that everything that follows should be designed to make the potential customer move on to the next stage.

Create a well-designed layout

Design quality is also important in getting a message to prospects clearly and effectively:

- keep the layout simple to ensure immediate comprehension
- use photographs, diagrams, or illustrations if they help to clarify a point or create impact
- use the most legible type faces and sizes to make text easy to read
- use bold headings or a larger type size for the headline or to emphasise important statements

WHAT TO AVOID
Using mailing unnecessarily

When customers already know your company and do business with you, it can be off-putting for them to be treated as 'prospects'. Always check that your mailing is an effective means of communicating.

Producing standard mailing material

Direct mail is a precise medium. You can use that precision to talk to specific customer groups or individual prospects with tailored messages and offers. Too many mailings fail to address prospects' individual needs and concerns. Research will help you to identify the key messages for different prospects, and to build them into your mailing.

Failing to plan

All mailing activity must be planned with sufficient time and resources. Rushing a mailing can lead to embarrassing and costly mistakes. Not anticipating response can lead to disappointed customers.

Failing to measure

Direct mail campaigns are measured on their results: they should deliver enquiries or sales. If they do not deliver results, even the most creative campaigns should be considered failures. Make sure that you set realistic targets for your campaign. If you do not reach the targets, change the targeting, the offer, the format, or timing—until you find one that delivers the results you want.

Making mailings too complex

Some mailings contain so much material they can be daunting to deal with, so the prospect may lose interest.

RECOMMENDED LINKS

The Institute of Direct Marketing:
www.theidm.co.uk
Royal Mail:
www.royalmail.com

SEE ALSO

Improving the Response to Direct Mail (p. 292)
Writing a Sales Letter (p. 268)

Improving the Response to Direct Mail

GETTING STARTED

The simplest and most immediate measure of a direct marketing campaign is the response level it achieves. Many different factors can affect response rates; it is important to test the variables before committing all your resources to a particular approach, and you should aim for a realistic figure that is within your budget.

- Do try as far as you can to define your target market precisely. The more precisely you target, the better your response rates will be. Make it easy for your prospects to respond, and test your approach before committing resources to the full campaign.
- Performance can be improved by integrating the campaign with other marketing activities.
- If budget allows, you can develop a series of split campaigns. A series of mailings will make sure that you meet your response targets.
- Getting the mailing list right is vital. Check all internal sources of information and be sure that they are up to date. Customer records invariably generate the highest response rates when they are mailed with relevant information.
- If you are moving into new market sectors, internal lists may not provide the information you need. To achieve a high response rate, check how closely the list matches your customer profile.
- You could commission a special tailored list that matches your requirements exactly.
- Keep refining your lists. To improve response and reduce waste in your mailing campaigns, it is important that your lists are regularly checked for accuracy.
- Personalised one-to-one mailings are an ideal form of communication for companies with detailed information about their prospects.
- Direct mail response levels can increase significantly when telemarketing is used.

FAQS

Why are direct mail responses so low?

The figures quoted are industry averages. They can vary upwards or downwards depending on the industry and the type of mailing. Remember that a small percentage of a mass mailing can provide you with a reasonable level of new prospects. To put the response rates into perspective, compare the response and the cost of response with an equivalent spend on advertising.

Should direct mailing always be tested?

If it is practical, test direct mail on a small proportion of the market. Although direct mail is a precise medium, testing can refine the process even further. With so many variables in a mailing campaign, you can test different elements individually and plan your full campaign on the basis of the best response rate.

Should direct mail effectiveness be measured by response or by sales?

The ultimate test of any marketing campaign is an increase in profitable sales. However, direct mail on its own cannot deliver sales. Sales depend on pricing, the quality of your products, sales representatives, customer service, competitive activity, and many other factors. Direct mail should be given a specific role and measured by how it fulfils that role.

MAKING IT HAPPEN
Set target response levels

- Response levels as low as 1 or 2% are regarded as the industry norm.
- Response rates in the region of 5% are regarded as high.
- Response rates in the region of 10–20% have been reported by companies who have integrated other forms of marketing communications.

Define your target market precisely

Do you want to reach all customers and prospects, or are you targeting specific groups? Direct marketing is a precise medium, so your campaign could be aimed at one key decision-maker or thousands of potential users. The more precisely you target, the better your response rates will be.

Integrate the campaign with other marketing activities

Direct marketing campaigns can run at any time. However, performance can be improved by integrating the campaign with other marketing activities such as an exhibition, advertising campaigns, or salesforce calls. With integrated campaigns, overall awareness levels among customers and prospects will be much higher. Your direct marketing offer will have a much higher chance of success.

Choose the right campaign frequency

A single mailshot, telephone call, or direct response advertisement may produce results, but a series of quality contacts will have greater impact and make sure you meet your response targets. Multiple direct marketing activities provide a number of benefits:

- they raise levels of awareness with each contact
- they follow up contacts who have not responded
- they move individual respondents further along the decision-making process

Make it easy for prospects to respond

If you want to improve response rates, clearly you have to make it easy for your prospects to respond. Website or e-mail addresses, Freepost, and Freephone facilities provide easy-to-use response mechanisms that can boost response. You should monitor the response levels from different sources to see which are the most effective.

Test your campaign

To guarantee the success of your campaign, you should test your approach before committing resources to the full campaign.

There are a number of variables that can be tested:

- the offer
- the creative approach
- the target audience
- the response mechanism
- frequency and timing
- integration with other communications programmes

Use split campaigns

If budget allows, you can develop a series of campaigns that vary by offer, creative approach, response mechanism, frequency, and timing.

Improve your mailing lists

Getting the mailing list right is vital. Basic mailing lists simply include names, addresses, job titles, and telephone numbers of customers and prospects. The basic list can be refined by adding information about buying patterns, lifestyle, and many other factors, all of which provide a comprehensive picture of customers and prospects.

Check all internal sources of information

Your customer records are probably your most valuable asset as they invariably generate the highest response rates when they are mailed with relevant information. The most important sources are:

- customer records
- customer correspondence, including records of complaints
- warranty records
- service records
- sales prospect files
- salesforce reports
- records of lapsed customers
  Simple segmentation of your internal lists might give you categories such as:
- customers who have bought in the last six months
- lapsed customers
- customers who spend over £X a year

Add external sources of information

Your internal lists are likely to yield high response rates, but if you're moving into new market sectors, they may not provide the information you need. External lists are available from a number of different sources, including list brokers, magazine publishers, directory publishers, trade associations or professional institutes, commercial organisations, and retailers. To achieve a high response rate, check how closely the list matches your customer profile.

Commission a special list

Standard lists may not give you the degree of match you need. The successful preparation of a tailored list is directly related to the quality of the brief, and you should provide the supplier with a detailed description of your target audience.

Keep refining your lists

- Make sure that the list is kept up to date with new customer and prospect data.
- Include coupons and other reply mechanisms with every form of communication, and add the responses to your lists.
- Encourage the salesforce to provide up-to-date customer and prospect information.
- Maintain an active search programme in appropriate websites, magazines, and newspapers to identify new prospects for your list.

Check the accuracy of lists

To improve response and reduce waste in your mailing campaigns, it is important that your lists are regularly checked for accuracy. The two main problems are:
- duplication, where the same individual appears several times on the same list, possibly in different guises, for example as Ron Smith, R.T. Smith, and Mr Smith
- out-of-date information, where the original recipient has moved, or, for business mailings, changed jobs

Use personalised letters

Personalised one-to-one mailings are an ideal form of communication for companies with detailed information about their prospects.

If the database or mailing list holds complete names and other information, direct mail letters can be personalised in a number of ways:
- including the name in the address and greeting only: 'Dear Mr Jones'
- including the name throughout the text: '. . . and Mr Jones, you'll be glad to know that you've won a special prize. . .'

Use telemarketing

Direct mail response levels can increase significantly if used in conjunction with telemarketing. Telemarketing offers a range of benefits because it is:
- selective: contact can be initiated and maintained with all or selected groups of customers and prospects
- precise: the calls can be targeted
- flexible: the offer and the message can be varied
- fast: calls can be made immediately
- responsive: because telemarketing is interactive, it encourages response
- measurable: the effectiveness of a telemarketing campaign can be measured precisely

WHAT TO AVOID
Setting unrealistic response rates

Direct mail is a precise medium, but it's all too easy to set unrealistic targets for response: figures such as 5% or 6% would be seen as extremely high in many industries, for example. If you want a much higher response rate, you may need to use other marketing media or invest more in the campaign.

Failing to integrate direct mail with other activities

Direct mail works most effectively when it is part of an integrated marketing campaign. Advertising can be used to raise the company profile. For example, direct mail would be used to reach specific prospects with a targeted offer, and telemarketing could be used to back up the mailing with follow-up calls. Response rates from integrated campaigns are generally higher because direct mail is given a specific task within that campaign.

Poor mailing lists

Good response rates depend on the quality of your mailing lists. If your lists contain duplicate addresses, out-of-date information, or incorrect data, response is bound to be poor. Refine your lists continuously to make sure they're working hard for you.

RECOMMENDED LINK

The Institute of Direct Marketing:
www.theidm.co.uk

SEE ALSO

Creating Impressive Direct Mail Material (p. 288)
Writing a Sales Letter (p. 268)

Producing Press Material

GETTING STARTED
Newspaper, television, trade press, and radio journalists are always looking for stories. Supply information in the form of press releases, feature articles, or advertorials—in the right format and to the right person—and you can gain great publicity for your organisation.

FAQS
Will the press be interested in us?
Journalists are always looking for stories and they work under great pressure, so a well-written, informative, and current press release is always welcome. They won't, however, be interested in you unless you have a story to tell. Like customers, editors will want to know what makes your company different from others. Local media will be interested in how you fit in with the community; and the trade press will be more interested in new products and ideas.

It is worth developing a relationship with editors in order to understand how you can help them. By concentrating on the kind of news and story they want, you can save yourself time and increase the chances of your story being published.

Should we produce our own press material or use the services of an external agency?
An external agency can take a more object-ive view of your press material and may have experience of writing for the publica-tions on your distribution list. That means they can tailor material for individual publi-cations and ensure that it is printed. They may, however, lack product knowledge and require considerable training to achieve the right results. If your company produces complex technical products, you may split the task—keeping technical press releases in-house, and using an external agency to produce company or business material. Do check out their rates and fees carefully before you place work with them, though, as their costs may be well outside your budget.

Can we use the same press release for all the publications on our distribution list?
You can issue a single release, but you will increase the chances of getting into print if you tailor information to the needs of indi-vidual publications; for example, your local newspaper will have a different take on your news than a trade publication. By talking to journalist, reading previous issues, and studying publishers' readership data, you can identify the type of material that is likely to be printed or broadcast.

What should we do if an editor does not publish the information in a press release?
There's no cast-iron guarantee that your piece will get published, so don't see it as a 'given'. There could be a number of reasons for non-publication that are outside your control, such as lack of space, the release missing the copy date, or another story coinciding with your release. Your story may appear in the next issue if space allows. On the other hand, the editor may have decided simply that your information was wrong for the publication or not news-worthy. A quick call to the editor may help you find out the reason. If your material was unsuitable, you may be able to provide something more relevant for future issues.

MAKING IT HAPPEN ✔
Plan your press release
A press release is a piece of information dis-tributed to newspaper, television, or radio journalists which is published or broadcast as a piece of news. It can cover a variety of topics, including:

- information on new products or services
- information on developments in a company
- news of new appointments or promotions

An effective press release should contain news rather than thinly disguised advertising, and it should reflect readers' interests.

The release may be used without modification if it is newsworthy, timely, and if space permits. The press release may be cut to fit available space without any further reference to you. In some cases, a journalist or editor may contact you for further information and rewrite the item in the style of the publication. It is often a good idea to provide additional background information to help journalists in this task. Information such as product specifications, contact details, or alternative photographs are useful. Some companies offer such information specifically for journalists on a section of their website. Sometimes the information may not be used, because it is not newsworthy or not relevant to the readership. Alternatively, although the main press release may not be used, an accompanying photograph may be used with a caption.

Produce your press release

The following guidelines will help you produce an effective press release:

- Press releases should be typed double-spaced.
- The source of the release should be clearly identified.
- A contact name for further information should be provided.
- Any limitations on use or timing of publication should be clearly highlighted, for example, 'not for publication before. . .'.
- The most important information should be included in the early paragraphs. If an editor is short of space, the press release will be cut as simply and quickly as possible, probably from the bottom upwards.
- Quotes are useful and are frequently used by editors.
- Photographs or diagrams add value to the release and may help to ensure publication.
- The style of writing, even the length of sentences and paragraphs, should match the targeted publication as far as possible.

Distribute your press release

Press releases can be delivered by hand or by post, depending on quantity. They can also be sent by e-mail or placed on a website so that they can be picked up by visiting journalists. Wherever possible, they should be sent to a named individual. Information on editorial contacts, with details of their special interests, is available in the *PR Planner*, which is updated regularly. If you do not want the information published before a certain date for reasons of commercial security, include an embargo—'not for publication before. . .'.

Time your press release

Check the publication dates of magazines or newspapers on your distribution list. This information is available in publications such as *British Rate and Data*, *Willings Press Guide*, or the *PR Planner*. An editorial copy date will be indicated. Ensure that your release reaches the editor by that date at the latest.

Plan feature articles

A feature article, which could be 500–2,000 words in length, is published in a magazine and credited to an organisation. The article may be on technical or business developments in an industry, or on other subjects that provide practical or topical information for readers. The article may form part of an industry survey. This type of feature provides an opportunity for organisations to demonstrate their expertise and professionalism.

Feature articles can cover a variety of topics, including surveys of new industry or technical developments, practical 'how to' articles, or reviews of research projects.

If it is reasonably well written, the article may be used without modification; it will be published when space permits, or may be used as part of a special survey. In some cases, a journalist or editor may contact you for further information and rewrite the item in the style of the publication.

Produce feature articles

An effective feature article should reflect readers' interests and contain information that is useful to them. It should also bring them up to date with recent developments.

The following guidelines should help you prepare a feature article:

- feature articles should be typed double-spaced
- length should be discussed with the editor, but is likely to be between 500 and 2,000 words, with 1,000 words as the average
- a contact name for further information should be provided
- photographs or diagrams, with a caption for every item, add value to the article

Distribute feature articles

Feature articles should only be sent to one publication at a time, although they can be modified for use in other markets. Wherever possible, they should be sent to a named individual. Information on editorial contacts, with details of their special interests, is available in the *PR Planner*, which is updated regularly. In some cases, the initiative may come from the publication and the editor will provide you with details of requirements.

Time feature articles

Check the publication dates of magazines or newspapers on your distribution list. This information is available in *British Rate and Data*, *Willings Press Guide*, or the *PR Planner*. An editorial copy date will be indicated. Ensure that your release reaches the editor by that date at the latest. You should also ask the editor for a list of special editorial features. The article may be suitable for inclusion in a survey.

Produce advertorials

An advertorial is a special category of feature article, combining advertising and editorial, which is used to promote products and services. These are the key characteristics of an advertorial. It:

- may include a reader offer, such as a chance to participate in a competition
- should be identified as an 'advertisement feature'
- is produced in the form of an editorial rather than in a conventional advertise-

ment format, even though the space is paid for

The writing guidelines are similar to those for press releases and feature articles, but you are paying for the space and you have considerably more control over what is published. Newspapers and journals will often help with the layout.

WHAT TO AVOID
Writing information that is not suitable for a publication

It is important to study the publications that are on your distribution list. Editors know very quickly what is relevant or interesting to their readers. If your material is not suitable, it will not be used. Study the editorial content and check the readership figures, which are usually available from the publication.

Providing news stories that are out of date

'Old news is no news' and that means a story could be wasted. It's easy to get the timing right with a daily or weekly publication, but it can be tricky to decide on the right date to send a news story to a monthly publication. The publication can provide you with the dates when your copy will be required, but you have to make sure that those dates tie in with your own schedules. If you have to release a sensitive news story early to catch a publication date, you can protect your interests by putting an embargo clause on the release, saying 'not for publication before. . .'.

Confusing editorial with advertorial

A press release or feature article should provide factual, newsworthy information. It should not be a blatant advertisement for the company. Editors are not keen on items that are thinly disguised advertisements.

RECOMMENDED LINK
Institute of Public Relations:
www.ipr.org.uk

SEE ALSO
Raising Awareness of Your Brand (p. 281)

Setting Advertising Objectives

GETTING STARTED

Clear objectives for a communication campaign are essential, whether it is intended to generate leads or encourage brand switching. These objectives should be in place well before a campaign begins, so that each campaign has a specific task. In addition, the desired results should be measurable so that you can be sure the campaign is worth the investment.

FAQS

What can communications achieve?

Communications are about influencing the customer or potential customer in the way they make decisions. No matter how good your communications, they cannot overcome the problems caused by poor products, inefficient service or distribution, or uncompetitive pricing.

Should advertising be judged on sales results?

Advertising should certainly be measured, but there may not be a direct correlation between advertising and sales. Advertising may generate a large number of leads, but the salesforce may not be able to convert those leads to sales.

Should advertising agencies be judged solely on the results they deliver?

There has been a trend towards judging agencies on measurable results. This has been driven partly by the increasing importance of direct marketing agencies who claim to be driven by results, and partly by the desire of marketing executives to increase accountability. Some agencies have gone so far as to base their fees on results, rather than traditional agency payment. The problem is that results are dependent on so many other aspects of marketing. An agency could claim that it has no control over the performance of the salesforce or the quality of the product. It is essential therefore that you agree on a definition of success.

Is it possible to set a number of different objectives for the same advertising campaign, particularly when budgets are limited?

It *is* possible, but it may not be a good idea. An effective campaign has a single focus with a specific measurable result. By mixing objectives, you may achieve only part of the outcome you want.

MAKING IT HAPPEN
Set the right objective

You must have clear objectives for your campaign. There are many different advertising objectives, so identify a specific task for a specific campaign. This might be:

- raising awareness of a company, product, or service within a clearly identified target market
- communicating the benefits of a product or service
- generating leads for the salesforce or retail network
- encouraging prospects to buy directly through a direct response campaign
- persuading prospects to switch brands
- supporting a special marketing event such as a sale or an exhibition
- ensuring that customers know where to obtain the product
- building confidence in an organisation

Whatever your general objectives, you should be clear how much of that is dependent on the communications and how much dependent on other aspects of your marketing effort, such as the sales force (if you have one).

Make the objectives measurable

To ensure you design a cost-effective campaign that delivers results, advertising objectives should be translated into precise, measurable targets, as in the following examples.

Consumer product

- target market: 500,000 ABC1 prospects in the South of England
- marketing objective: achieve high level of product understanding
- advertising objective: persuade 15% of targeted prospects to request a free sample

Business product

- target market: 5,000 specialist machinery designers in (specified) industrial processes
- marketing objective: increase market share to 20% (that is, recruit 1,000 new clients)
- advertising objective: persuade 40% of prospects to request product fact file

Raise awareness

This objective is usually the starting point for advertisers, and is especially important if your company is entering new markets where you do not have an established reputation, or you are trying to influence important decision-makers who may not be aware of your company. Awareness advertising can also be used if you are launching new products which appeal to specific sectors of your market, or if research shows that customers and prospects are not aware of the full extent of your products and services.

This type of objective would be important for a company launching a new range of products. For example, to raise awareness of its new range, one company planned to advertise in a group of special interest consumer magazines aimed at its target audience. The advertisements included the telephone number of an information line that generated a large number of inquiries. Editorial articles in the same group of publications backed up the advertising by providing more detailed information for consumers. You should, however, be wary of specifying awareness targets. Awareness on its own will not sell products and, if this is

your aim, you will have to integrate your campaign carefully with other elements of your marketing to meet your targets. Likewise awareness amongst the general public is very different from awareness in a very small, specialised market, so you should be clear about who you are trying to reach.

Communicate benefits

Product advertising should lead on benefits. This type of advertising is important when research shows low awareness of product benefits. It should also be used if your products have recently been improved, or if you need to counter competitors who have introduced products with similar or better benefits.

For example, if research shows that your company's products are perceived as old-fashioned or poor value for money, you need to take action to correct this impression and communicate the real benefits of your products.

Generate sales leads

Advertising's role is to provide leads that can be followed up by a field salesforce or telemarketing team. Lead generation is important if marketing success depends on the performance of the salesforce. Sometimes, customers or prospects have a complex decision-making structure, and you cannot identify some of the decision-makers. Advertising that generates inquiries can identify the right people and open the door for the sales team. It can also be used to identify prospects when you are entering new market sectors where you do not have an established customer base. The final use for this type of campaign is to generate leads for agents, distributors, or retailers who handle your local marketing.

Sell through direct response

Direct response advertising is the most measurable form of advertising. The advertising budget provides a direct return in terms of incremental sales. This objective can be important if customers can only buy direct from you. In an increasing number of markets, customers prefer the convenience of buying direct and you have to decide whether to bypass your existing distribution channels. If you are targeting niche markets which are not covered by retail outlets, direct response can be used to complement your distribution channels. Selling direct is not always a practical proposition. Where product inspection or demonstration is important, direct response may not be appropriate.

In the personal computer market, for example, manufacturers found that businesses and individuals were willing to buy personal computers 'off the page' or via the Internet. The products were regarded as commodities and the resulting price competition put pressure on margins. The result was a considerable growth in the level of direct sales, with manufacturers using large format advertisements or inserts in computer and business publications. Direct selling meant that the manufacturers could reduce prices by avoiding the cost of selling through retail outlets.

Encourage brand switching

Brand-switching advertising plays an important role in winning new customers as the first stage in a customer relationship programme. It helps you to increase market share or maintain share against competitive actions, and is also important if you are introducing new products that offer greater benefits than competitive products.

Support a marketing event

This objective can be important in a number of situations; for example, taking part in an exhibition where an important new product will be launched, or holding a sale, or promoting a seminar or other customer event at which you wish to ensure customer participation. Advertising helps to build traffic for your event and ensures that the event attracts the right prospects. A company that sponsors senior executive seminars as a way of building its credibility could run advertisements in the business press to promote a seminar.

Help customers obtain the product

Advertising can help to drive business to retail outlets or distributors, or improve the performance of your distribution network by showing the range of services available from the outlets. It can also counter competitive action, if, for example customers are using other distributors to obtain spare parts and service. To win back this important business, advertising could show locations of retail outlets and explain why the authorised distributor should be the first choice for customers.

Build customer confidence

Capability advertising or corporate advertising is sometimes dismissed because it is difficult to measure, but it is important when a company has been undergoing significant change, or is entering new markets where it's not established. It also provides support when a company is trying to win key account business, or if competitors are threatening important business.

WHAT TO AVOID
Setting objectives that cannot be measured

Advertising objectives should be measurable for two important reasons. First, to ensure that advertising represents an adequate return on investment. Second, to measure the effectiveness of the campaign itself, so that future advertising can be improved or modified to deliver better results.

Setting objectives that are too general

A general objective, such as raising awareness, is important, but is often seen as the only objective. Advertising objectives should be closely linked to marketing objectives, so that advertising is used to carry out specific tasks within an overall marketing framework. You should be sure that what you want to achieve is possible with communications, and acknowledge the importance of other elements of your marketing— crucially the product itself or your pricing strategy.

Failing to integrate communications objectives with other marketing objectives

It is important that some advertising objectives, such as generating more leads, should be integrated with the other activities that will increase sales. It may be necessary to increase salesforce training to improve the team's ability to convert leads into sales. Advertising alone cannot be expected to deliver sales.

RECOMMENDED LINK

Institute of Practitioners in Advertising: **www.ipa.co.uk**

SEE ALSO

Planning an Advertising Campaign (p. 303)
Preparing an Advertising Brief (p. 310)
Selecting and Working with an Advertising Agency (p. 306)

Planning an Advertising Campaign

GETTING STARTED

Any communications campaign needs to have clear, measurable objectives, whether it is designed to communicate product benefits or to support an event. In order to achieve these objectives, it must also be planned carefully. There are eight main stages to consider, from defining the target market to setting a budget.

FAQS

Do I need an advertising campaign?

Often the term advertising campaign is used when the more holistic term 'communications campaign' would be more appropriate. Strictly, advertising only refers to paid-for space or time in media such as newspapers or radio. On the other hand, direct mail, sales promotions, exhibitions, or any of a range of communication tools can be used in a campaign to support your marketing. To decide if you need a communications campaign, you should be fairly sure that the problem you want to address can be solved best by communications. For example, finding new customers or prospective customers is often best accomplished by advertising or direct mail, but converting inquirers into customers may be better dealt with by you or your sales team (if you have one) directly.

Who is responsible for campaign planning—the client or the advertising agency?

Both parties contribute. The client sets the overall marketing objectives and the specific communications campaign objectives. The agency develops an advertising strategy based on those, but may seek to modify the campaign objectives. Timings will be determined by the client's product and marketing plans, together with practical considerations such as publication dates and lead times.

Why is it necessary to plan a campaign in so much detail?

To be effective, advertising and communications must meet specific measurable objectives. The objectives affect choice of media, creative strategy, overall budget, and lead times. Overlooking any of those details could weaken the effectiveness of the campaign.

Should planning be applied to the creative process?

There is an assumption that creative work takes place in a vacuum. Like any other marketing activity, it must be directed towards an objective. The more information a creative team has, the more focused its work.

MAKING IT HAPPEN
Set campaign objectives

It is important to set clear objectives for an advertising campaign. It is essential to identify a specific task for a specific campaign. This might be:

- raising awareness of a company, product, or service within a clearly identified target market
- communicating the benefits of a product or service
- generating leads for the salesforce or retail network

To ensure you design a cost-effective campaign that delivers results, advertising objectives should be translated into precise, measurable targets.

Identify key planning activities

There are eight main stages in planning an advertising campaign:

1. Define the target market

Who is your campaign aimed at?

An understanding of your audience will influence the media you select and the creative treatment of your advertisement. To define your target market, you should ask questions like these:

- Who buys your type of product?
- Who influences the purchasing decision?
- In business buying, who are the important decision-makers?
- Do you need to communicate with the actual buyers or those who influence the purchasing decision?
- How many potential buyers are there?
- How many users are currently buying your product and what is your share of the market?
- Which prospects do you want to reach with the campaign and where are they located?
- What are the characteristics of these people (for example, age, sex, income, job title), and what are their most important considerations in choosing a brand or a supplier?
- What does research tell you about their attitudes towards your company and your products?
- How do they currently receive information about your products?
- What is the role of advertising in reaching the target audience?

2. Select media

There are four important factors to consider in selecting campaign media:

- how closely the audience profile of the medium matches your target audience
- the comparative costs of reaching the target audience through different media
- whether the frequency of the medium matches the timing of your campaign
- the creative opportunities of the medium for the communication of your message

3. Plan campaign timing

When should your campaign run? You have to consider a number of factors first in relation to the purchasing pattern of your products:

- When are your customers making their buying decisions?
- Do you know when your customers hold product/purchasing review meetings?
- If you are launching a new product, when will the product be available?

- Does your advertising campaign have to tie in with the timing of any other marketing activity, for example, an exhibition, direct marketing campaign, or salesforce call?
- How quickly will you be able to follow up the campaign?

You also have to take into account production and media lead times:

- What is the next available publication or broadcasting date?
- When does the media owner require your advertisement?
- How long will it take to produce the advertisement?

4. Decide campaign frequency

Campaigns raise levels of awareness with each appearance and increase the number of opportunities to see the advertisement. They also move individual respondents further along the decision-making process and maintain contact during an extended process. Campaigns reinforce the impact of the message by repetition and provide an opportunity to communicate multiple or complex messages about the company or the product range.

Frequency is determined by a number of factors:

- frequency of publication, that is, how often the publication appears
- frequency of broadcast: radio or television commercials can be broadcast many times during the same day, if the budget allows
- your budget, although a number of appearances in the same medium will earn a discount that makes the entire budget go further
- the behaviour of consumers or buyers: if a buying decision is made only annually then timing may be more crucial than frequency

5. Plan creative treatment

To achieve good results, you must develop a comprehensive creative brief. These are the main elements:

- campaign objectives
- description of the target audience
- the main concerns of the target audience: why they buy; what they consider; how they view different products and suppliers

- the main benefits of the product or service: why the product is different from competitive offerings; what is new; why the benefits are important
- the core message or proposition—what the prospect is being offered: the opportunity to sample or buy; further information; a sales visit; an incentive; or a discount
- the planned response: should the prospect contact the company, send off an order, wait for a phone call, or simply absorb the information?
- the media—size and mechanical details
- the supporting activities—telemarketing, advertising, sales follow-up, tie-in promotions

6. Develop a response mechanism

Action is a vital ingredient of any advertising campaign and it is essential that you make it easy for your prospects to respond. First, decide which action your prospects are to take:

- place an order
- arrange a sales meeting
- request further information
- visit a retail outlet
- try the product

Review the cost, convenience, and practicality of response options, including telephone, post, fax, e-mail, and website.

7. Set a budget

A campaign budget will include direct, indirect, and variable costs. Direct costs include the production costs of advertisements, including design, writing and production, and media costs. Indirect costs include the cost of setting up response handling, either by internal resources or an external supplier, and the management costs of planning and controlling the campaign. Variable costs include the cost of handling the campaign response—for example: Freephone costs and telephone resources, or costs of Freepost services; the cost of meeting the response—supplying and distributing the material that is requested; and the cost of servicing the

response—sales or telemarketing costs in dealing with the potential volume of new business.

8. Set schedules

To set a campaign schedule, work back from the launch date and work out how long each individual activity will take.

WHAT TO AVOID
Poor targeting

Without a clear picture of your target market, advertising can be wasteful. You should always aim for the best match between the audience and your ideal customers—subject, of course, to your budget.

Failing to integrate advertising plans with other marketing activities

Advertising must be integrated with other related marketing tasks. Poor salesforce performance, for example, could waste the contribution of a highly successful advertising campaign that provided a large number of sales leads.

Trying to take shortcuts on lead times

Advertising lead times are influenced by a number of factors, including publication dates, production lead times, and product availability.

Trying to achieve advertising objectives with inadequate resources

If companies try to achieve targets without committing the right budget, it will mean either that advertisements do not appear frequently enough to have impact, or that production quality is sacrificed.

RECOMMENDED LINK
The Advertising Association:
www.adassoc.org.uk

SEE ALSO
Preparing an Advertising Brief (p. 310)
Selecting and Working with an Advertising Agency (p. 306)
Setting Advertising Objectives (p. 299)

Selecting and Working with an Advertising Agency

GETTING STARTED

If your budget will stretch and you are able to engage an advertising agency to help you spread the word about your product or service, you need to choose an agency that can provide the right selection of services. These can include consultancy, strategy, creative work, media, and integration with other communications activities. Important factors in selecting an agency include its approach, reputation, and financial stability. If you choose your agency carefully, you're much more likely to avoid the problems that cause breakdowns in the agency/client relationship.

FAQS

Do I need an advertising agency?

Many small to medium-sized companies don't. However, the skills offered by agencies are just as specialised as those offered by your accountant. Many agencies will be able to offer services other than advertising, including direct marketing, sales promotion, and public relations. Indeed they may not call themselves an 'advertising' agency at all. Agencies that offer a wide range of skills are often called 'full-service' agencies. If you know what you want to achieve, but are not sure if advertising is the best course, discuss the issues with a number of different agencies.

I want to work with a specific agency, but they already handle the account of a competitor. Should I work with that agency?

This problem occurs frequently, particularly when agency mergers occur, and the new group finds that its client lists include conflicting accounts. The decision to continue handling conflicting accounts is sometimes taken by the agency, and sometimes by the clients. It can be particularly difficult if the agency is seen as an industry specialist, with considerable expertise in a particular market. Sometimes the problem can be resolved by handling the conflicting accounts through separate agency teams.

How do I know that an agency can maintain its standards in day-to-day business, once they have won the initial pitch?

Sometimes agencies field a special senior team to win new business, and then hand the day-to-day account to a completely different team. Since a good relationship between agency and client is so important, you should insist on meeting the team who will actually work on the business.

Is it essential to appoint an agency to handle advertising campaigns?

A full-service agency may not be essential, particularly if you have the resources to handle part of the task internally. Creative consultancies, media specialists, or integrated agencies can take on specialist tasks.

MAKING IT HAPPEN

Choose the right type of agency

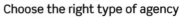

Depending on the type of agency, you can use a comprehensive service or specific services including:

- initial consultancy
- development of an advertising strategy
- creative proposals, copywriting, design, and production of advertisements
- media planning, negotiation, buying, and administration
- integration of advertising with other communications activities

Whatever you decide, ask to see examples of previous campaigns and for an honest appraisal of their effectiveness.

Work with a full-service advertising agency

Full-service agencies handle all aspects of an advertising programme. You should select a full-service agency if you do not have any internal skills or resources for handling advertising, or if extensive advertising is important to the achievement of your marketing objectives.

Use a media independent

A media independent only handles media planning and buying, and so is likely to be interested only if you are spending a considerable amount on buying space in newspapers and magazines or airtime on TV or radio. By concentrating on media, the independents can often negotiate better deals with them than full-service agencies. Many smaller advertising agencies use media independents to handle their media buying. If you can handle campaign planning and creative work in other ways, but do not have any internal skills or resources for media planning and buying, then you should use a media independent.

A media independent could prove useful if you spend a large amount of your budget on media, and you want to take advantage of specialist buying skills to get better positions or lower rates. You may find that certain media will not deal with you, because you are an advertiser. In that case, a media agency can provide valuable support.

Choose creative independents

Creative independents only handle creative work such as copywriting and design. By specialising in this way, the independents can often achieve more effective advertising than full-service agencies. You would have to handle campaign planning and media in other ways. There are three types of creative independent:

- freelance staff, either combined writer/art director teams, or individuals

- design consultancies offering advertising as part of a communications service
- specialist creative independents—small agencies that either have their own creative teams, or manage freelance teams

Again, you should consider using a creative independent if you can handle campaign planning and media in other ways, but do not have any internal skills or resources for creative work. If advertising is a small part of your marketing activity, you could develop effective campaigns by taking advantage of specialist creative services.

Work with an integrated agency

Integrated agencies handle all aspects of an advertising programme, and integrate advertising with other media. Agencies offer integrated services in two forms:

- as a single integrated agency, in which all campaigns are handled by the same team
- as an agency group, in which non-advertising campaigns are handled by specialist companies within the group

An integrated agency may be suitable if other tools, such as direct marketing, publications, and sales promotion are as important as advertising, and you want all of the activities integrated and handled professionally. Any extra cost incurred will be well worth it.

Use the media's own expertise

One alternative to using an agency is to ask the newspaper, magazine, or radio station to help. Often they will offer basic design or writing services free of charge. However, they are rarely as skilled as specialists, and you may find it difficult to make your advertising stand out or to maintain consistency over time.

Evaluate advertising agencies

There are a number of important factors in selecting an agency:

- approach: what is the agency's philosophy, and how does it work in practical terms?
- track record: what campaigns has the agency produced, and how effective have they been?

- reputation: does the agency have an established reputation in your market? Are you able to approach other clients to give their assessment of the agency?
- accountability: how does the agency measure the performance of its campaigns?
- client relationships: what is the current client list, and how many of these clients are enjoying long-term relationships? What is the average length of account tenure?
- disciplines: does the agency offer all disciplines from within its own resources, and can it offer the full range of services?
- staff: does the agency have the staff to handle complex, large-scale programmes? What is the consultancy's recruitment and personal development policy?
- financial stability: what is the agency's recent performance? Does it have the stability and resources to sustain an effective level of service over the long term?

Check agency performance

According to Henley Centre research, clients believe the ten most important questions regarding agency performance are:

- Does it take the trouble to understand your business?
- Can it use creativity effectively to sell your products?
- Does it have real creative flair?
- Does it get work done on time?
- Does it have a good understanding of your consumers?
- Does it believe in defining advertising objectives beforehand?
- Does it keep costs within budget?
- Does it use research to aid its creative work?
- Is it strong on media buying?
- Is it thorough and hard-working?

Obtain information about advertising agencies

There are a number of useful sources of information about agencies:

- The Institute of Practitioners in Advertising and the Marketing Communication Consultants Association publish information about agencies.

- Individual agencies provide videos of their agency credentials or will send, or present in person, their portfolio of work. Larger agencies have their details available through the Advertising Agency Register and most agencies have websites or, at the least, brochures available.
- *Campaign*, *Marketing*, and *Marketing Week* magazines publish regular news about agencies and their clients, and your own trade publications may mention agencies which specialise in your market.
- Talk to friends and colleagues, even if in different businesses, to find out which agencies are reliable.

Avoid problems in client/agency relationships

Reports in the trade press highlight a number of factors that create conditions for a breakdown:

- The client believes that the advertising has not delivered results, or has not had the planned effect on the marketplace.
- The agency feels that poor results are caused by marketing, product, or management problems on the client side.
- The client does not like the advertisements for subjective reasons.
- The agency fails to understand the client's business.
- A failure of communication means that the agency cannot respond to the client's real needs.
- Frequent changes in the agency team or client team make continuity difficult.
- Poor agency administration can let down good creative work.
- Relationships can become stale.

WHAT TO AVOID
Choosing the wrong size of agency

A large agency may have the resources and scale to support national or international campaigns, but if your account is small, you may get poor service from a junior team. It may be more appropriate to work with a smaller agency, where you will get personal service from the senior people.

Choosing the wrong type of agency

Agencies, like any other business, develop specialities. Their expertise may not coincide with your needs. The most important division is between a consumer and a business-to-business agency but, beyond that, agencies develop expertise in certain industries or markets. Look carefully at the agency's client list to find the right match.

Relying on a creative pitch

Agency selection is frequently made on the basis of a pitch—a presentation that shows how an agency would tackle a specific project. Although the presentation gives an insight into the agency's working methods, it is an artificial guide to potential performance.

Not sharing information with the agency

Clients often expect a lot from a new agency, but can be disappointed when the agency does not know something 'obvious' about the client's business. The agency can only know what you know *if you tell them.* If you are concerned about confidentiality, discuss this and get a signed agreement from the agency management.

Not discussing the budget in enough detail

Agencies work for a fee and, like you, will want to make a profit. You will only get good service when they feel your business is worthwhile for them. From the outset discuss how much you plan to spend and what you want to achieve—competent agencies will tell you from the outset what is possible.

RECOMMENDED LINKS

Institute of Practitioners in Advertising:
www.ipa.co.uk
Institute of Sales Promotion:
www.prca.org.uk

SEE ALSO

Planning an Advertising Campaign (p. 303)
Preparing an Advertising Brief (p. 310)
Setting Advertising Objectives (p. 299)

Preparing an Advertising Brief

GETTING STARTED

To get the most from working with an advertising agency, you need to make a start by putting together a comprehensive creative brief. This must cover all aspects of the project: background, objectives, research, competitors, product information, and the target audience. It's worth spending time on making the briefing information as complete as you can, or you run the risk of wasting time and money on a campaign that has little impact.

FAQS

Why is a detailed brief important?

It will start the campaign on exactly the right foot. An imprecise and undetailed brief may mean that the work is aimed at the wrong audience. Provide the agency or consultancy with as much information as possible so that they can produce a campaign that achieves results.

Who should be involved in setting a creative brief?

The people who evaluate a creative brief should also be involved in setting or approving the brief. It can be difficult to deal with objections and criticism from someone who does not understand the brief. On the client side, the briefing team is likely to include the marketing executive, sales executive, and any relevant marketing specialists such as promotions or direct mail executives. The person who has the final say—whether it is you yourself or your business partner—must be involved in defining the brief. The team should also include product or research specialists to provide detailed information on the product and prospective customers. The agency team should also be involved in preparing the brief, although this does not always happen in practice.

Should an agency brief always have measurable objectives?

The more specific the brief, the easier it is to assess the results of the creative work. It is not always possible to set a measurable objective, but this should be the goal. Agencies may argue that results depend on factors outside their control, but it should be possible to isolate the communications objectives and identify a way of measuring them. A direct response campaign, for example, can be measured by the number of responses, while a corporate campaign could be assessed through attitude surveys conducted before and after the campaign.

MAKING IT HAPPEN

Plan the campaign approach

How will you present your message? Most publications and commercial broadcast media carry high volumes of advertising. Your advertisement must achieve immediate impact to succeed. There are three essential checks that can be applied to creative work in any media:

- it must have immediate impact
- it must meet the needs of the reader or viewer
- it must stimulate a response

Provide background Information

Your briefing of the agency or consultancy should begin with the background to the project:

- What is the overall aim of the project?
- What threats and opportunities does the business face?
- Why is the project being produced?
- How does the project fit into the overall marketing programme?
- Why is it necessary to advertise and what is it intended to achieve?

The background material should include any research that you have carried out or used. You should ensure that the project works in the context of other marketing activities (your own and competitors').

Produce a comprehensive brief

To achieve good creative results, you must develop a comprehensive creative brief. These are the main elements:

- campaign objectives
- description of the target audience
- the main concerns of the target audience: why they buy; what factors they consider; how they view different products and suppliers
- the main benefits of the product or service: why the product is different from competitive offerings; what is new; why the benefits are important
- the core message or proposition: what the prospect is being offered—the opportunity to sample or buy, further information, a sales visit, an incentive or discount
- the planned response: should the prospect contact the company, send an order, wait for a phone call, or simply absorb the information offered?
- the media: scope and practical details
- the supporting activities: telemarketing, advertising, sales follow-up, tie-in promotions

Information of this kind would enable writers and designers to approach the creative process in a disciplined, logical way. Great creative ideas may occur in a vacuum, but they are more likely to be a response to a clearly defined problem.

The creative brief is important whether you are using external suppliers or carrying out the creative work internally.

Set out objectives

The brief should set out a number of objectives, including the overall corporate objective and the marketing objective. State the communications objectives and how they contribute to the wider marketing objectives. For example, you may want to make potential customers in a new region aware of your product in order that sales staff can work more effectively.

The campaign objectives should be detailed and specific. Examples could include:

- generate 3,000 prospects and convert 3% of them
- ensure that key decision-makers understand the product's business benefits
- raise awareness among 20% of the target audience

Provide access to any research information

The creative team should be aware of any relevant research information, including:

- customer surveys, interviews, or analysis
- industry surveys
- competitor analysis
- product reviews
- press comment on the product or company
- feedback from focus groups
- results of previous campaigns

Include information on competitors

The brief should include detailed information on:

- which competitors provide a similar product or service
- how the competitive offering compares
- the product's key benefits against the competition
- how competitors are perceived by customers

This information can help creative teams identify some of the key benefits that will differentiate the product from competitors' offerings. It will also show how other companies have tackled the problem of describing the product.

Provide comprehensive product information

The product or service should be described in detail:

- what it is
- what it is used for
- how it operates
- the main benefits for the customer
- the advantages over competitor products

If the team can use or experience for themselves your product or service in the same way as a customer, then this will greatly enhance their understanding.

Describe the target audience

Describing the target audience helps the creative team to focus on the key decision-makers:

- What types of company buy the product?
- Which business sectors are they in?
- How big are these companies?
- Who are the main decision-makers?
- What is their role in the decision-making process?
- What are their business concerns?
- What is their perception of your company and its products?

Establish target perceptions

The creative team should be aware of any key messages that are important to the target audience. The task of the creative team is not to invent these messages; it is to communicate them as effectively as possible. The brief should therefore set out the perceptions that the target audience have now, and those they should hold once the campaign is finished.

Get approval of the brief

The brief should be circulated to all members of the group involved in briefing and approving the project. No creative work should begin until the brief has been signed off by everyone involved. Once the brief has been approved, members should not be able to change it without good reason.

Be clear about payment terms

Some agencies will present their ideas without expecting payment, but most would rather not. If you cannot pay for initial ideas, make this clear before expecting anything of value from the team. If, however, you *can* pay, agree the amount and establish who will own the ideas once the initial presentation is finished.

Describe the review process

Let the creative team know how their work will be reviewed and evaluated. This can take place at a number of levels:

- review by the agency and client teams
- evaluation in focus groups
- pilot campaigns in test markets

WHAT TO AVOID
Making the brief too specific

It is possible to make a brief too specific, thereby ruling out creative approaches that may achieve outstanding results. For example, setting out the creative approach in the brief before the creative team has had an opportunity to consider it will produce very limited results. The creative team needs information to focus their attention on the problem, not suggestions on how the problem should be solved.

Not integrating creative work

Although the brief should allow the agency creative team complete freedom, it is equally important that creative work across different media should be integrated. If advertising is the dominant medium, and a team is working on direct marketing, they should relate their approach to the advertising theme. Repetition of the same creative theme across different media reinforces the key messages and can improve overall awareness.

Concentrating too hard on creativity, and not enough on results

Creative work should be accountable. The agency may have a brilliant, award-winning creative idea, but if it fails to produce the intended results it may be a waste of money. The creative team should therefore be aware of the specific objectives of the campaign; it is not enough just to get attention.

RECOMMENDED LINK
Institute of Practitioners in Advertising: **www.ipa.co.uk**

SEE ALSO
Selecting and Working with an Advertising Agency (p. 306)
Setting Advertising Objectives (p. 299)

Working with Your Local Community

GETTING STARTED

Corporate social responsibility (CSR) started as little more than corporate philanthropy and involvement in the community. However, CSR is about far more than that. It's about taking a responsible approach to every aspect of your business. It covers almost any activity of a business, so there is a good chance that you may be doing something already. Every business has an impact on society—through what it produces, how it employs and develops its staff, how it purchases supplies and sells its products or services, how it affects the environment, and how it acts in the community. Social responsibility can help any business to succeed. It can build sales, develop the workforce, encourage enthusiasm, and increase trust in the business as a whole. Businesses are stronger and work better when they have the support and respect of all their stakeholders; their customers, suppliers, staff, and communities.

This actionlist aims to introduce you to some of the ideas behind corporate social responsibility, and to suggest some ways in which you could take your business forward in this respect. For further information, you may be interested to contact the Small Business Service, which has a Benchmarking Index module that can help you assess your current approach to social responsibility. This can be found on the Small Business Service website (address given below).

FAQS

Is corporate social responsibility relevant to small businesses?

Corporate social responsibility is not just for large corporations—it's essential for all businesses to think about their role in the community and their responsibilities to all of their stakeholders. Corporate social responsibility is about business behaviours that not only deliver commercial objectives, but that also have a positive social impact. It is for their own long-term good, as well as for reasons of principle, that businesses should aim to be responsible in all their activities, and to embrace the principles of sustainable development in their widest sense.

What are the key principles of social responsibility?

Businesses can help to improve the lives of their customers, suppliers, staff, and shareholders by enabling them to share in the wealth the business creates. They should deal honestly with their suppliers and competitors, and act as good citizens in their local communities. Sincerity, truthfulness, and keeping promises not only contribute to credibility, but also to the effectiveness of

business transactions. Businesses clearly have to respect the rule of law, but in many cases it makes good economic sense to do rather more than the legal minimum.

Why is corporate social responsibility important?

Customers, suppliers, and employees are all becoming more interested in the way that businesses behave. A good reputation can open doors, win loyalty, and create staff enthusiasm. Social responsibility is about getting business benefits from being a good corporate citizen. It is not random philanthropy. Done well, it raises your profile in the most positive way. Responsible businesses do not just gain respect; they can gain real business benefits too.

Can small businesses afford a social responsibility programme?

Businesses can choose to support community initiatives with money, but in most cases being responsible is simply about guaranteeing the right behaviour. There may be a cost associated with this, in the sense that behaving irresponsibly is cheaper, but in the long run behaving responsibly will enhance your reputation and do more to help you retain customers and staff.

How do you get the best value for social responsibility?

As with every other aspect of your business, you need to review carefully your activities and make sure that you are getting a return, whether it is in terms of your team feeling more motivated, lower staff turnover, a better reputation locally, or higher sales.

MAKING IT HAPPEN
Reflecting stakeholder needs

Businesses need to provide customers with the highest quality products and services consistent with their specified needs. You need to treat customers fairly, ensure health and safety, and respect human dignity. You can also engage with customers in social projects. This is often called 'cause-related marketing' and can increase customer appreciation of a product while simultaneously delivering a social benefit.

Every business has an interest in being an employer of choice. In a competitive job market, this can be a real advantage. This means paying staff fairly, providing a good working environment, communicating openly and honestly, respecting staff suggestions, avoiding discrimination, and promoting personal development and continuous learning. Increasingly, this means making sure that staff can balance their work and the rest of their life, with appropriate flexibility in working patterns.

Businesses have a responsibility to manage assets effectively to provide investors with a fair and competitive return. Different businesses will take different views about what constitutes the most appropriate level of social engagement; but the importance of sustainable behaviour is now being reflected in legal requirements.

Businesses have a responsibility to deal fairly with suppliers. The relationship should be free from coercion and should aim to foster stability in return for value, quality, and reliability. Some businesses, for example, prefer suppliers whose values reflect their own. This can mean avoiding sub-contractors who have poor labour practices. Small businesses often think that this does not apply to them, but you may find yourself caught up by human rights requirements if you supply larger organisations. One obligation that applies to every business is to pay suppliers on agreed terms.

Businesses, of whatever size, see involvement in the local community as part of being a good corporate citizen. It is no longer enough to argue that businesses contribute to society simply by creating jobs and wealth. Enlightened self-interest plays a part; businesses understand they need an educated and healthy workforce to work for them, a healthy business sector to provide suppliers and customers, and a 'licence to operate'.

Community investment is more than just giving money to a good cause. While that is clearly important, a great deal of good can come from other approaches, such as giving away old equipment, or getting staff involved with community organisations. Think of ways in which you can use your business' core skills in your local community; if you've a great design team, for example, you could offer to produce a programme for a local social event. There may be good opportunities for mutually beneficial arrangements so that you get some return, perhaps in terms of publicity and reputation.

Some basic steps to take

The first thing to do is to look at your own practices systematically. If you don't yet have a statement of business principles, think about creating one. Ideally, it should insist on honesty, integrity, and fairness in all aspects of your business. You could consider committing the business to an external code or set of business principles, that provide a framework for you and your stakeholders to measure your progress on environmental, social, and community issues. You might also consider using some of your marketing budget to associate your business with a social cause.

Consider how your stakeholders feel about the business. Identify your most important stakeholders and their concerns, and relate them to your business interests. Think about ways in which you could be more socially responsible in your relationships with your stakeholders. You could set out to seek mutually beneficial relationships with contractors, suppliers, and customers, as well as with other stakeholders, such as communities and local government. Make sure that you pursue ethical supply-chain management. Remember to promote your business principles at all times: if you have a website, make a feature of your code of practice so that visitors can see how important it is to you and your team.

Now is a good time to review your business's current policies and processes. One useful area to think about is waste recycling, and the use of renewable sources of energy and materials. Are there any ways to avoid materials that are known to be toxic, or to damage the environment? Do some research (ask others in your local business community if they can help or suggest some useful ways forward), and then introduce a social and environmental strategy, and set targets for your business. You could, perhaps, establish an environmental management system (EMS) with objectives and procedures for evaluating progress. The Institute of Environmental Management and Assessment has some useful resources for businesses at:

www.iema.net/readingroom

It's important to measure how well you perform, and to make it clear to your staff that you care about this. They need to know how serious you are before they take any steps in the right direction themselves. Celebrate successes that you achieve along the way—remember that people feel good about getting social responsibility right. Also let others know how your initiative is going: include a passage on this area in your annual review, mention it in newsletters, or even produce a special report. Do tell people what you're doing and aiming for, as it will affect their view of your business.

In order to be socially responsible, you must respect your own rights and those of your staff. You can do this by providing good and safe working conditions, and introducing health and safety policies that your staff understand and adhere to. It's also important to develop and make the best use of the talents of your staff. Provide training opportunities and mentoring, so that you can promote from within your business where possible; this will help keep morale high if people can see that their hard work and commitment is being rewarded. Also encourage your staff to be involved in the planning and direction of your company. Your commercial success depends on their commitment and talents, so show that you appreciate that; by being open to job-sharing, flexitime, and other family-friendly policies.

Encourage staff volunteering in the community, as well as supporting the community with financial contributions and help in kind. Look for opportunities to make surplus products and redundant equipment available to local schools, charities, and community organisations. You can also help your local community by buying from local suppliers.

WHAT TO AVOID
Treating social responsibility as an isolated activity

The most common mistake is seeing social responsibility as an add-on, or 'nice-to-have', rather than as an integral part of your business strategy. Try to get out of this mindset and see social responsibility as one of the ways in which you can build the reputation of your business. In other words, you should treat it as seriously as you treat all the other aspects of running your business.

RECOMMENDED LINK
Business Link:
www.businesslink.gov.uk

SEE ALSO
Small and Growing Businesses (p. 486)

GROWING YOUR
BUSINESS

Analysing Your Business's Strengths, Weaknesses, Opportunities, and Threats

GETTING STARTED

SWOT (Strengths, Weaknesses, Opportunities, and Threats) analysis is a method of assessing a business, its resources, and its environment. Doing an analysis of this type is a good way to better understand a business and its markets, and can also show potential investors that all options open to, or affecting a business at a given time have been thought about thoroughly.

The essence of the SWOT analysis is to discover what you do well; how you could improve; whether you are making the most of the opportunities around you; and whether there are any changes in your market—such as technological developments, mergers of businesses, or unreliability of suppliers—that may require corresponding changes in your business. This actionlist will introduce you to the ideas behind the SWOT analysis, and give suggestions as to how you might carry out one of your own.

FAQS

What is the SWOT process?

The SWOT process focuses on the internal strengths and weaknesses of you, your staff, your products, and your business. At the same time, it looks at the external opportunities and threats that may have an impact on your business, such as market and consumer trends, changes in technology, legislation, and financial issues.

What is the best way to complete the analysis?

The traditional approach to completing SWOT is to produce a blank grid of four columns—one each for strengths, weaknesses, opportunities, and threats—and then list relevant factors beneath the appropriate heading. Don't worry if some factors appear in more than one box and remember that a factor that appears to be a threat could also represent a potential opportunity. A rush of competitors into your area could easily represent a major threat to your business. However, competitors could boost customer numbers in your area, some of whom may well visit your business.

What is the point of completing a SWOT analysis?

Completing a SWOT analysis will enable you to pinpoint your core activities and identify what you do well, and why. It will also point you towards where your greatest opportunities lie, and highlight areas where changes need to be made to make the most of your business.

MAKING IT HAPPEN

Know your strengths

Take some time to consider what you believe are the strengths of your business. These could be seen in terms of your staff, products, customer loyalty, processes, or location. Evaluate what your business does well; it could be your marketing expertise, your environmentally-friendly packaging, or your excellent customer service. It's important to try to evaluate your strengths in terms of how they compare to those of your competitors. For example, if you and your competitors provide the same prompt delivery time, then this cannot be listed as a strength. However, if your delivery staff is extremely polite and helpful, and your competitor's staff has very few customer-friendly attributes, then you should consider listing your delivery staff's attitude as a strength. It is very important to be totally honest and realistic. Try to include some personal strengths and characteristics of your staff as individuals, and the management team as individuals. Whatever you do, you must be totally honest and realistic: there's no point creating a useless work of fiction!

Recognise your weaknesses

Try to take an objective look at every aspect of your business. Ask yourself whether your products and services could be improved. Think about how reliable your customer service is, or whether your supplier always delivers exactly what you want, when you want it. Try to identify any area of expertise that is lacking in the business, as you can then take steps to improve that aspect. For example, you might realise that you need some more sales staff, or financial help and guidance. Don't forget to think about your business's location and whether it really does suit your purpose. Is there enough parking, or enough opportunities to attract passing trade?

Your main objective during this exercise is to be as honest as you can in listing weaknesses. Don't just make a list of mistakes that have been made, such as an occasion when a customer was not called back promptly. Try to see the broader picture instead and learn from what happened. It may be that your systems or processes could be improved so that customers are contacted at the right time, so work on boosting your systems and making that change happen rather than looking about for someone to blame.

It's a good idea to get an outside viewpoint on what your weaknesses are as your own perceptions may not always marry up to reality. *You* may strongly believe that your years of experience in a sector reflect your business's thorough grounding and knowledge of all of your customers' needs. Your customers, on the other hand, may perceive this wealth of experience as an old-fashioned approach that shows an unwillingness to change and work with new ideas. Be prepared to hear things you may not like, but which, ultimately, may be extremely helpful.

Spot the opportunities

The next step is to analyse your opportunities, and this can be tackled in several ways. External opportunities can include the misfortune of competitors who are not performing well, providing you with the opportunity to do better. There may be technological developments that you could benefit from, such as broadband arriving in your area, or a new process enhancing your products. There may be some legislative changes affecting your customers, offering you an opportunity to provide advice, support, or added services. Changes in market trends and consumer buying habits may provide the development of a niche market, of which you could take advantage before your competitors, if you are quick enough to take action.

Another good idea is to consider your weaknesses more carefully, and work out ways of addressing the problems, turning them around in order to create an opportunity. For example, the pressing issue of a supplier who continually lets you down could be turned into an opportunity by sourcing another supplier who is more reliable and who may even offer you a better deal. If a member of staff leaves, you have an opportunity to re-evaluate duties more efficiently or to recruit a new member of staff who brings additional experience and skills with them.

Watch out for threats

Analysing the threats to your business requires some guesswork, and this is where your analysis can be overly subjective. Some threats are tangible, such as a new competitor moving into your area, but others may be only intuitive guesses that result in nothing. Having said that, it's much better to be vigilant because if a potential threat does become a real one, you'll be able to react much quicker: you'll have considered your options already and hopefully also put some contingency planning into place.

Think about the worst things that could realistically happen, such as losing your customers to your major competitor, or the development of a new product far superior to your own. Listing your threats in your SWOT analysis will provide ways for you to plan to deal with the threats, if they ever actually start to affect your business.

Use your analysis

After completing your SWOT analysis, it's vital that you learn from the information you have gathered. You should now plan to build on your strengths, using them to their full potential, and also plan to reduce your weaknesses, either by minimising the risk they represent, or making changes to overcome them. Now that you understand where your opportunities lie, make the most of them and aim to capitalise on every opportunity in front of you. Try to turn threats into opportunities. Try to be proactive, and put plans into place to counter any threats as they arise.

To help you in planning ahead, you could combine some of the areas you have highlighted in the boxes; for example, if you see an external opportunity of a new market growing, you will be able to check whether your internal strengths will be able to make the most of the opportunity. Consider whether you have enough trained staff in place, and whether your phone system would be able to cope with extra customer orders. If you have a weakness that undermines an opportunity, it provides a good insight as to how you might develop your internal strengths and weaknesses to maximise your opportunities and minimise your threats.

The basic SWOT process is to fill in the four boxes, but the real benefit is to take an overview of everything in each box, in relation to all the other boxes. This comparative analysis will then provide an evaluation that links external and internal forces to help your business prosper.

WHAT TO AVOID
Focusing just on a few issues

Don't just focus on the large, obvious issues, such as a major competitor encroaching on your business. You need to consider all issues carefully, such as whether your Internet system provides everything you need or whether your staffing levels are as they should be.

Completing your SWOT analysis on your own

Do take advantage of other people's contribution when you're completing your SWOT analysis; don't try and do it alone. Other people's perspectives can be very useful, particularly as they may not be as close to the business as you are. This distance can often help them see answers to thorny questions more easily, or to be more innovative: we all get stuck in a rut at points.

Using your analysis for the next ten years

Don't do a SWOT analysis once and then never repeat the exercise. Your business environment will be constantly changing, so use SWOT as an ongoing business analysis practice.

Relying on SWOT to provide all the answers

Use SWOT as part of an *overall* strategy to analyse your business and its potential. It is a useful guide, not a major decision-making tool so don't base major decisions on this analysis and nothing else.

RECOMMENDED LINKS

Business Eye (Wales):
www.businesseye.org.uk
Business Link (England):
www.businesslink.gov.uk
Invest Northern Ireland:
www.investni.com
Business Gateway (Scotland):
www.bgateway.com

SEE ALSO

Identifying Opportunities for Your Business (p. 321)
Small and Growing Businesses (p. 486)

Identifying Opportunities for Your Business

GETTING STARTED

The business world today is a fast-moving one, and the pace of change can at times seem bewildering. The environment in which your business operates is changing all the time, and there are many different factors that influence it. There are continual changes in your market, your customers' needs and preferences, the technology you use, your sales channels, and the way you can deliver your products or services. These changes can bring threats to your business, but they will also, undoubtedly, bring opportunities.

It's important that you regularly take a step back and try to analyse the way in which your business currently operates. Think about the factors that may promote change. Try to identify threats, and make sure you are prepared for them. It is also important, however, that you spot the many opportunities that arise. This actionlist will give some advice on how to spot opportunities, and make the best of them.

A book that you might find helpful is *Marketing Plans That Work*, written by Malcolm McDonald and Warren Keegan and published by Butterworth-Heinemann. The website address for the Chartered Institute of Marketing is given below.

FAQS

What is my current success based on?

Too simple a question? Not really. If you can explain how you became successful in the first place, you have more chance of being able to repeat that success again. Carry out an analysis of your current strengths and weaknesses, and try to establish how these are contributing to your current success, or lack of it.

What opportunities can I identify?

Write down a list of the opportunities you think you can exploit. These opportunities might be a natural extension of what you are doing already, or an adaptation of what you currently do. Alternatively, they could involve branching out into something completely different.

Which opportunity can I exploit most quickly, and most profitably?

Most businesses will be able to say that there are many new opportunities for them. What's more difficult, though, is identifying those opportunities that have realistic potential. Before you plunge headlong into pursuing every opening that arises, try to identify the one prospect that provides the most immediate, long-term, profit-making potential for you. Try to be honest with yourself; decide if the opportunity you are selecting is really the one that will have the greatest impact on your business's future.

How can I prepare my business for change?

The needs of the market change continually. Trends can be influenced by technology, fashion, lifestyle, and the economy as a whole. No small business can avoid these effects. Try to identify the trends that are affecting your business now, and over the next 12 months. Try to spot the opportunities those trends will create, as well as the threats they may pose. You need to think about how to prepare your business to adapt its products, prices, marketing methods, sales channels, or overall customer experience in order to make the most of these opportunities.

MAKING IT HAPPEN

Attracting new customers

Look at the way you acquired your existing customers. Do you understand why they buy from you? It may be that you have used different methods to attract customers, so try to identify which is your most productive method of generating business. By doing this, it may be possible to repeat this success. Speak to your existing and former customers to find out what attracted them to you and what might have turned them off. Ideally, this will help you keep your existing customers happy for longer and may also tempt former customers back!

Retaining existing customers

Work out your current client retention rate and think about ways in which you could improve it. It may be that you already have an existing, loyal customer base, where there is a high degree of trust in the service you provide. However, there may still be potential to offer add-ons to your current service. Look out for opportunities to generate or improve repeat levels of sales. You might consider offering new products, or adaptations of products, or upgrades of your existing service to your customers.

Find out your average sales value per customer, and think about ways in which you can improve it. Try to encourage feedback from your customers and ask if there is anything they need that you currently do not supply. You may be able to build some of these things into your service. It may also be worth carrying out a formal piece of research with a sample of your customers, to help identify opportunities for new services or products.

Expanding your customer base

Think about whether there are customer groups that you do not sell to at present, but who you believe would benefit from your services. Write a list of specific businesses, or business types, to whom you don't currently sell, and then identify reasons why they might buy from you. If you sell to individual consumers, make a list of specific groups of individuals who could benefit from your service. Write down the characteristics that made this group distinctive, for example their age, gender, race, occupation, income, hobbies, membership of clubs and associations, and so on. Write down a list of the benefits that your existing products and services can provide to these groups of people.

Unique selling propositions

A key question to ask yourself when assessing whether you can exploit the opportunities you are facing is how you can make yourself different from your competitors. There must be something about your business, products, or the way that you market your service that sets you apart. You will not be able to exploit your opportunities if you provide the same products and services at the same prices and in the same way that your competitors do.

Identify your unique selling proposition (USP). Make a list of all your main competitors; it may be helpful to do this in the form of a grid. Write down areas where you can do something more, better, cheaper, faster, or just differently than them. Identify any specific locations where your competitors don't operate. Find out if they supply to any customer groups that you currently don't. From your list, try to identify two or three key areas where you can position your service or product as being different, or better, than that of your rivals.

The way you differentiate products, prices, customer service levels, marketing messages, money-back guarantees, upgrade offers, or overall company image will ultimately determine whether you will succeed in capitalising on new market opportunities.

Partnerships with other businesses

It is unlikely that any small business on its own will be able to meet all of the opportunities that it is facing, and exploit their full potential. It can often prove very worthwhile to work with other businesses that offer complementary services to your own, and which are aimed at the same, or similar, customer groups. By doing this you can open the doors to opportunities for your business that you would otherwise be unable to develop. There are several ways in which you could work in partnership with another business. For example, you could access their products to sell to your existing customers. You could develop a new product or service based on a combination of your own and another business's product. Both businesses could share costs in joint marketing campaigns, for example at trade fairs, in catalogues, or in brochures. Alternatively, another business might be able to sell your product to a customer group that you currently do not reach. These 'piggyback' marketing relationships are increasingly popular, and can help small businesses to develop opportunities very quickly and effectively.

WHAT TO AVOID
Spreading yourself too thinly
You must try to avoid a scattergun approach to pursuing the opportunities you are facing. Don't spread your ideas so thinly, that you end up being ineffective in everything you try to achieve.

Being unrealistic
If you are not selective enough, and have not sufficiently considered the full impact on your ability to develop or deliver a new product or service, or carry out a marketing campaign to a new target audience, you will not make the most of the opportunities that exist. If you do not honestly assess what you have done right and wrong in the past, there is a real danger of repeating previous mistakes, and failing to achieve your considerable potential.

RECOMMENDED LINK
Chartered Institute of Marketing:
www.cim.co.uk

SEE ALSO
Analysing Your Business's Strengths, Weaknesses, Opportunities, and Threats (p. 318)
Small and Growing Businesses (p. 486)
Understanding the Effects of Growth (p. 331)
Understanding the Role of Partnerships for Small Business (p. 334)

Taking the Decision to Diversify

GETTING STARTED

If you're considering options for diversifying your business, you must be very clear about the strengths or weaknesses of your current position. If market opportunities beckon and you decide to move into new areas, will you be working to your core strengths and will you have the skills and know-how necessary for success? Alternatively, if you're planning to diversify into new areas because you're struggling in your current line of activity, could you be making your existing weakness worse by moving into a market for which you lack the necessary knowledge and experience?

Diversification can be of great benefit to businesses working to their core disciplines and strengths, but it could be disastrous if the right competencies, motivation, and commitment are lacking. You could also find yourself diluting what expertise you have. Before you take the plunge, carry out a thorough appraisal of your strengths and weaknesses and think also about the threats you're likely to face.

FAQS

What should I regard as the strengths of my business?

One of the main strengths of any business should be its employees. Do your staff have a sufficiently wide range of skills and experience? Do you provide training and encourage your people to continually develop their skills? Are your employees adaptable? Any decision you take to diversify is likely to involve considerable changes to the way your business operates, and could put considerable new pressures on your employees.

A sound way of assessing your strengths is to evaluate whether your business does well in producing innovative and attractive products, unique services, or high levels of customer loyalty. You may, for example, provide good customer service, have particular marketing expertise, or perhaps environmentally-friendly packaging that attracts buyers.

Scrutinise your strengths to see how well they compare against those of your competitors. If you all provide roughly the same level of customer service and support, don't list this as a strength as it doesn't differentiate you from the others. It can be hard to be objective about your own business as you're so close to it, but you do need to be hard-headed and realistic when you're thinking

about strategic plans, as there is a lot at stake.

What weaknesses should I look out for?

Again, try to be as objective as possible on this front. You shouldn't simply be looking for mistakes that have been made, such as failures to respond promptly and effectively to a customer's complaints. These may be the sort of problems that can be remedied easily and shouldn't be classed among the more fundamental weaknesses. If a product's sales are disappointing, is it because its quality is poor compared with those of your competitors? Put that down as a weakness. If you're a retailer with premises in the wrong location, or you don't have enough parking space to attract passing trade, that's another weakness—and you should think about relocating sooner rather than later!

Look at every aspect of your business and examine whether the products or services need to be improved. Make sure your customer service is reliable and consistent. Do you have dependable suppliers? Are there areas of expertise that are lacking in your business? Do you need more financial help or guidance, or are you short of sales staff? Is your approach to marketing not up to scratch?

Being unaware of these issues or ignoring inherent weaknesses could leave you badly exposed if you do choose to diversify. It's always good to seek out the views of independent outsiders—perhaps an accountant or business adviser with knowledge about your existing enterprise and the new area of activity you're planning to move into. They will be able to help identify particular weaknesses that could undermine you.

What kind of threats should I be aware of?

There'll be some obvious threats, like the presence of a powerful competitor with a superior range of products moving into the market. Technological change may also pose a major threat—if your systems or processes haven't been brought fully up to date, you could face severe problems in making your products or services competitive.

Some threats may be less tangible or a matter of guesswork, so you must try to avoid your analysis becoming too subjective. On the other hand, if you're complacent about the threats you face, you may be unable to react quickly enough to change. If you take a realistic approach you should strive to put in place contingency plans to deal with most of the major problems likely to affect your type of business, especially in terms of the sector in which you're hoping to get involved. Again, do remember that the advice of expert outsiders will be invaluable, as they could point out threats which you have overlooked or been totally unaware of.

▶ MAKING IT HAPPEN
Draw up a plan

Once you've carried out a thorough appraisal of your operations you can draw up a business plan for your new venture. At the same time, start to address and remedy the weaknesses you've identified, while also building on your underlying strengths. Some of the most successful businesses are able to turn threats into opportunities by developing effective plans to counter the threats and gain a march over their competitors. You need to have well-trained staff in place to cope with the demands and challenges that diversification will bring. They should have a thorough grounding in, and

access to, any new areas of knowledge that will be needed. Check that your IT and phone systems are adequate to deal with larger volumes of customer enquiries and make sure the new processes and tools you'll need are put in place and tested well ahead of the launch of your new venture. It's important to develop a cohesive view of the capabilities of your business, to enable you to harness whatever new resources are necessary, and to help guarantee, as far as possible, a successful outcome to your diversification.

WHAT TO AVOID
Failing to focus on all the issues

It's not just the obvious threats, such as major new competitors encroaching on your chosen market, that you need to be aware of. Think broadly and carefully about a range of factors. For example, do you have an Internet-based purchasing system that allows customers to place orders online? Do you have a well-designed website that provides the right kind of information about your products or services, and contributes to your marketing efforts? Business is increasingly being conducted via the Internet, so make sure your staff have the necessary skills to facilitate this.

Trying to do it alone

Don't trust only your own judgement about the changes you're planning. It's essential to get the views and perspectives of outsiders to give you an honest appraisal of the prospects for your business when you diversify. They'll be able to distance themselves from your business to a much greater extent, providing a more objective view.

Diversifying before you're ready

If you don't act to remedy any weaknesses you may already have, they're likely to become magnified and could prove fatal when you diversify. Many businesses have come to grief by chasing tantalising opportunities and attempting to move away from core disciplines when they've been ill equipped and unready. If you do decide to diversify, try to ensure that the new area of activity complements wherever possible the inherent culture and competencies of your business. Focusing on core disciplines and remedying weaknesses has been the secret of many of the most successful companies around the world: they have built on their strengths.

RECOMMENDED LINKS

Abbey – expanding and diversifying:
www.anbusiness.com/business_advice/ expanding_diversifying.shtml
Winning Business Network:
www.consultfma.co.uk/diversification/ docs/Diversification_Intro.doc

Franchising Your Business

GETTING STARTED

If your business has suitable branded products or services and you're looking to grow it with relatively low risk, then franchising could provide a worthwhile route. The process can involve considerably less capital investment by you than other approaches to growth, because the franchisees you appoint will invest their money—and their time—in creating new outlets under your organisational umbrella. You will, though, need to undertake a considerable amount of planning and research to make sure that your business is suitable for franchising and to enable you to create a successful franchise network.

FAQS

What is a franchise?

In basic terms, a franchise is a legally binding agreement between you (the franchisor) and another business (the franchisee) that enables it to use your trade name and trade mark, and supply your branded services or products under licence. The franchisee will pay a fee in return for your granting them a franchise licence, and they'll have to comply with any terms and conditions set by you in the agreement. Another definition of franchising put forward by the European Franchise Federation describes it as 'a system of marketing goods, products, or services, based on a close and ongoing collaboration between legally and financially separate and independent undertakings'.

What is a franchise network?

This is an association of independently-owned businesses selling a range of products or services developed by an umbrella organisation. They are linked together by common brand identities and the support activities they share, such as marketing, advertising, and training.

How will I make money from franchising?

There are two sources of income from franchising: fees and the profit you could make from supplying materials to your franchisees. The fees come in the form of a one-off initial payment—the franchise fee—for granting a licence, and an annual management charge for the support services you provide, which should include training and

development. The latter fee is usually calculated as a percentage of your franchisees' turnover. In order to attract suitable franchisees, it's accepted practice to keep the franchise fee low and to provide good value for your management charge. Where the supply of materials is concerned, you can make money by buying in bulk and then reselling to your franchisees, but you must make sure that in doing so, you keep within the law regarding commercial practices. If you have any doubts or queries, take appropriate legal advice and contact the organisations listed below.

What are my obligations to franchisees?

Franchisees will expect you to provide them with a range of support services in addition to a protective framework that will involve monitoring the quality and standards of your network. Attracting good and reliable franchisees may rely a lot on how seriously you take, and fulfil, these obligations. The support services should include:

- product and service development
- marketing, advertising, and public relations
- protection of intellectual property (such as copyrights, brand names, patents, and trade marks)
- purchasing, financial, and administration services for the network
- communications between your franchised outlets
- quality control
- training

Most franchisees will expect you to help them raise capital for their outlets. One of the best ways to do this is by putting together some sort of support package with a bank. You should also consider putting together a franchise handbook that will set down specific rules and approaches to things like local marketing, use of brand names, and so on. That way, all concerned parties are completely clear about who is doing what, how, and when.

MAKING IT HAPPEN
Make sure your business is suitable for franchising

Not every type of business is suitable for franchising, but it usually works well where a wide variety of products or services are involved—for example, where there is a strong demand being created for new or innovative goods targeted towards niche or specialist markets. If your business offers products or services with a broad appeal, or which satisfy a common need, franchising may be a good way for you to grow. This would apply, for example, if you have an existing and profitable outlet supplying branded items that have a high profile and a strong reputation with customers. Many businesses that are now high-street names have managed their growth via franchising, including The Body Shop, Blockbuster Video, and Thornton's.

Franchising is not so good a choice if your business supplies products or services with a short market life (if it is catering to the latest fad, for example), or with low profit margins. Similarly, if you offer services that involve high skill levels and prolonged training, such as accountancy, or which rely on repeat business from customers with a strong sense of loyalty, franchising is unlikely to be the right option. This might also be the case if the business is dependent on a geographically-defined market, as would be the case with a tourist attraction. Enterprises with high levels of audit and control requirements—a financial institution such as a bank, for example—are unsuitable too as these outlets can't operate as separate legal entities, which is essential with franchises.

Before deciding whether franchising is right for your business, study the expert advice available on the British Franchise Association's website (address given below).

Prepare your business for franchising

As part of the careful research and planning you need to do to prepare your business for franchising, you should identify the elements of your operations that can be adopted in each franchised outlet. You can't franchise a concept or an idea, so you should have a business format that has been tried, tested, and shown to have a good track record in a particular marketplace. Your brand name has to be strong enough to attract suitable franchisees. Where appropriate, you should have proven manufacturing processes or distribution systems.

Among the things you'll need to develop are a new accountancy system and a business plan for your franchising activities. You'll find it a great help to do SWOT (strengths, weaknesses, opportunities, and threats) analyses for each geographical area in which you'd like to establish an outlet. You'll need to devise and set up support services for your franchisees, as well as initial and ongoing training programmes that will enable even relative novices to learn about the various facets of your business and how to then run their own franchises successfully. There will be technical issues in all of these aspects of franchising your business, so you should be prepared to call in professional advice at each stage of the process.

The British Franchise Association advises potential franchisors to run a pilot operation for at least 12 months, preferably at more than one location to test the business concept in different geographical areas. When this has been successfully carried out and fine tuning has been done, you can then prepare a prospectus to attract suitable franchisees.

Recruit franchisees

It will be important for you to be able to attract franchisees of the right calibre to be certain your network is successful, so do be wary of badly-run franchise recruiting agencies. Put in place a thorough vetting process for candidates that will allow you to attract highly motivated applicants. You could consider:

- attending franchise exhibitions
- advertising in newspapers and trade magazines
- setting up or adapting your business website to promote your franchising opportunities
- registering yourself with reputable franchise centres and brokers

Draw up franchise agreements

A franchise agreement is a contract between you and the franchisee. You'll be able to negotiate various aspects of the agreement and there are no hard and fast rules about what it should contain. The European Franchise Federation (EFF) has, however, put together a checklist for what it believes should constitute a good agreement. It must, for example, comply with national and EU laws and abide by the EFF's Code of Ethics. It must also be clear and unambiguous in stating the rights, duties, and responsibilities of you and the franchisee; and reflect the interests of all members of your network.

When evaluating the agreement the EFF suggests you consider the following key issues:

- the rights granted to you and the franchisee
- your obligations and those of the franchisee
- the goods and services provided by you to the franchisee
- the terms, and amounts, of the payments for licences, management fees, and other costs you impose on the franchisee
- the duration of your agreement
- the basis for any renewal of your agreement
- the terms by which the franchisee may sell or otherwise transfer their interest in a franchise
- the terms by which the franchisee may use your trade names, brand names, logos, store signs, and service marks
- your right to adapt the franchise system to meet new or changed methods and market conditions

- the franchisee's right to terminate the agreement before it expires
- the ownership of property, both tangible and intangible, provided by you to the franchisee and provisions for its surrender if an agreement is terminated

Think about whether or not you'll be granting exclusive geographical licences to franchisees, and how big the respective areas will be. Also think about whether you'll allow them to pursue other business interests, possibly competing ones, at the same time.

Bear in mind the advantages of franchising . . .

One of the chief advantages of franchising is that it provides you with an opportunity to expand your business for minimal investment. Other major advantages include: a predictable income stream from franchisees; a centralised system that spreads the costs over a wider network thus reducing the individual costs for each franchisee; and the fact that you'll be able to concentrate on developing and growing your business because there is no need for you to be involved in the management of individual outlets.

. . . but remember there are some disadvantages too

Because you'll have no direct control over the running of individual outlets, one bad franchisee could damage the reputation of your entire network. You should train or recruit specialist staff to conduct the training of franchisees and carry out the central management of your network. The process of starting your franchising operation will be complicated and you'll have to rely on expensive professional or specialist help and advice.

WHAT TO AVOID
Having unrealistic expectations

Don't overestimate the early growth rates of your franchise network and don't assume the franchise fee will generate profits, as it's usually the annual management fees that produce real returns. You'll need to have a realistic idea of what your initial costs will be, and these will need to include professional advice from lawyers and consultants.

Seeing franchising as a panacea for other problems

If your business is experiencing financial or other potentially fatal problems, franchising is highly unlikely to provide a solution. Franchising is a way of growing viable businesses and a variety of conditions need to be met to enable this to succeed (as explained above).

Appointing unsuitable franchisees

Don't be afraid to reject applicants who fail

to pass your vetting process. A ratio of ten enquiries to one successful applicant is normal, and ratios as high as 100:1 are not uncommon.

RECOMMENDED LINKS

The British Franchise Association: **www.british-franchise.org**
The European Franchise Federation: **www.eff-franchise.com**
Franchise Development Services: **www.franchise-group.com**
Franchise World: **www.franchiseworld.co.uk**

Understanding the Effects of Growth

GETTING STARTED
All businesses need to plan strategies for growth or run the risk of declining, often suddenly. The most successful approach to growth is an integrated one, in which the business's owner or management team look at how all aspects of the business can work together to reap the benefits of growth. For example, a successful new sales promotion strategy put together by the marketing department has brought in many new customers. In principle, this is fantastic news, but what will happen if the customer services department hasn't taken on enough new staff to deal with new accounts, or if the despatch department cannot cope with the increased demand in orders? All that effort will be wasted, so put plenty of time into planning and look at the whole picture so that you understand exactly what growth means for your business.

FAQS

How do I keep control of a growing business?
Many businesses that start small get by without a proper plan of exactly whom they will serve, how they will focus their resources, and what they aim to achieve. However, as a company grows, it becomes more difficult to operate effectively without a solid and detailed plan. It's a good idea to prepare a business plan (or adapt the one you have already written in the past) to plot the future direction of your company and to address the demands of growth. Consult a business adviser for help with this important task unless you are completely confident and focused.

How do I make sure that the growth is sustainable?
If your business has tended to grow without specific marketing efforts, you may need to find out more about your market before you can be confident the growth will continue. If you're not sure where the increased customer demand is coming from, you cannot be certain it will last.

As a start, find out where your most ready markets are and get a better picture of what they want. Look carefully at how your customer base is evolving as it grows; there may be segmentation occurring which requires you to push your product in the direction of new markets. Try to anticipate which areas you should be expanding into next.

What are the legal implications of growth?
If your business started life on a 'sole trader' basis (or even as a partnership) you may, after a period of growth, have to consider whether incorporation as a limited company would be more beneficial. This change would involve more paperwork and compliance requirements, but would limit your personal financial liability. This is important to consider as turnover grows and your business's financial requirements and risks begin to dwarf your personal resources.

Issues of contractual liability also become more pressing as the size and number of your transactions increase. In time there will be more at stake, and you need to protect yourself and your business with good contracts and terms—both with your suppliers and your customers.

It's very important that you do your research properly and get good professional advice, preferably from your accountant and a solicitor experienced in commercial law, before you make any major decisions. Discuss your options well in advance of any big change.

MAKING IT HAPPEN
Find finance for growth

Growing a business without the necessary working capital or investment is difficult at best, and at worst could endanger the whole enterprise. Supplying larger orders or providing a service to more customers invariably means investing in productive capacity long before you get a return on that investment. Sources of finance to help you do this will depend on how much you need and what exactly you need it for.

Bank loans are a common form of finance for growing businesses. These range from long-term loans (for property or fixed assets) to overdraft facilities (for short-term fluctuations in cash flow). Getting substantial amounts of investment finance may require you to relinquish part of your ownership—for instance, selling shares in your company or taking in another partner—and could involve venture capitalists or business angels.

Take on new employees

Moving from operating as a sole trader to a partnership or an employer can be a difficult step to take as it represents many changes for the owner-manager. However, if the business is to grow, it may be an essential progression.

Entrepreneurs have to learn to delegate tasks and relinquish control of some business operations in order to create the capacity for growth. The recruitment of appropriately skilled individuals, who are trustworthy, reliable, and dedicated to the job, is important. Success depends on the efforts of others, not just the entrepreneur's motivation.

Taking on employees involves substantial costs. When considering cash flow, you will need to take into account the costs of recruitment, training, pension contribution, employee liability, National Insurance, taxes, health and safety regulations, and personal records, as well as the cost of a salary.

Be selective about who you employ, as it is important to ensure that they will fit in with you or your other employees. Employee dissatisfaction results in low quality products, an unpleasant atmosphere, and general disruption to the flow of business.

An alternative to taking on more employees may be to bring in a partner. Before establishing a partnership, you will need to decide exactly how responsibilities will be split and how soon the partner will have full business control. It is particularly important that you completely trust and feel able to work with the new partner.

Consider subcontracting some work if you are reluctant to employ people directly, though do make sure you assess the firms to whom you intend to subcontract work carefully; an irresponsible company will damage your reputation. Subcontracting may also be a way to increase your customer base, especially if the subcontracted firm offers parallel goods or services to your own.

Consider relocation

Many small firms are initially run from small, low-cost premises—often the home of the owner-manager. As the business expands, so will the work area needed. For some idea of what to expect, consider how expensive it is to move house. For a firm to open additional branches, considerable strategic planning is needed to ensure success. You should be concerned not only with site selection, financing, and staffing, but also with the degree of independence each site will have and the adequacy of information and accounting systems.

Increase efficiency

To deal with the challenges of growth it is essential to run a well-designed operation. If you need to increase capacity, make sure you allow plenty of time to test out new systems and products and ensure that they work properly. It is all too easy for costs to get out of control. Ensure you invest in suitable cost-control systems as you increase capacity—you may need help to do this. Are you working to optimum efficiency? There is no point expanding inefficient systems into bigger ones.

Telework

Teleworking may be an appropriate way to deal with growth. Having employees working from home reduces the pressure on space, decreases overheads, and keeps the office size to a minimum.

WHAT TO AVOID
Not being fully committed to growth
Decide once and for all whether you really are committed to further business growth. There is little point in expanding the business if you decide that you prefer working in a small operation. Are you prepared to deal with the challenges of increased responsibility? Don't fall into 'the grass is greener' trap and think that growing the business won't take up that much of your time and energy. It will, and you need to be sure you have the right people and systems in place to help you do it (see below).

Not having the capabilities to run a larger team of employees
Expanding the business will mean that you'll have to learn how to develop and manage a larger working team or employ a manager to help you do that. Be brutally honest with yourself and conduct a 'time audit', that is, a detailed breakdown of how you spend your day. Be realistic about how much time you have to spare from the day-to-day running of the business to manage growth. If you think that you can't do it all yourself, think about what new systems and how many new staff you'll need to make sure you can all cope. If you think you can

incorporate the extra responsibilities into your day, you might want to undertake a professional management qualification yourself or attend some courses on managing staff.

Not having enough funds to generate growth
You must make sure that you fund all your plans to increase capacity. Again, be realistic and be prepared to limit your objectives or delay growth plans until you can commit safely to the levels of funding they require.

RECOMMENDED LINKS
Business Eye (Wales):
www.businesseye.org.uk
Business Link (England):
www.businesslink.gov.uk
Invest Northern Ireland:
www.investni.com
Business Gateway (Scotland):
www.bgateway.com

SEE ALSO
Identifying Opportunities for Your Business (p. 321)
Small and Growing Businesses (p. 486)

Understanding the Role of Partnerships for Small Business

GETTING STARTED
Small businesses can enter into partnerships with other businesses working towards a mutually-agreed goal. They can be long-term partnerships (for example, developing a new product), or short-term (for entering a new market). Partnerships are especially useful if you are seeking to exploit the new opportunities and challenges created by today's global marketplace. By teaming up with another business possessing complementary skills, you can achieve the strengths needed to exploit new opportunities and undertake new challenges. Inevitably there are risks involved; however, many of the potential problems can be anticipated and avoided by taking sensible steps in advance.

FAQS
What are the benefits of partnerships?
Clearly the overriding benefit of developing partnerships is obtaining access to the extra resources brought by the other partner, and achieving goals which would not be possible alone. When the partner business is operating in another country from your own, there can be additional benefits of access to international markets or new products to import. There are other important advantages too.

- Businesses that would otherwise only be able to reach a new market by over-committing themselves can do so without risking the rest of the business.
- By pooling resources, smaller businesses have more chance of winning a large contract, as they will be seen as being more secure and reliable.
- Partnerships allow small businesses access to technology, know-how, and customers that they could not have reached on their own.
- Partnerships can increase your databases of customers and contacts.

MAKING IT HAPPEN
There are several steps you will need to take before choosing a partner to work with.

Decide what you want from a partner
What are the general aims of the partnership? Are you aiming to gain access to a new market, develop a new product, or raise its profile in a certain area? Although details can be worked out at a later date, you need to decide whether your partner will be expected to input money, technological know-how, publicity, and so on.

For many reasons, joint ventures based on equal partnerships work best, and by teaming up with another small business, each party is able to contribute without either feeling they are working for the other. However, it is important to resist the urge to approach a business which is very similar to yours. It is better to team up with one that offers complementary skills and services so that you can both contribute without being in direct competition. There will also be less disagreement over which business has most to gain from the partnership.

Make inquiries
In England, some Business Links run schemes for finding partners, and the services of a network broker can also assist in establishing a partnership. Similar services are available from Scottish Development International, Invest Northern Ireland, and WalesTrade International.

A listing of European businesses seeking partners to co-operate in research and development activities is available through the European Commission's CORDIS database. Access to these services is through the CORDIS website.

Informal links with local entrepreneurs may develop into partnerships. It may be worthwhile studying the local business community for suppliers/customers who might be interested in a partnership. They may also know of other businesses that might consider the possibility of teaming up.

Some specialist consultancy firms provide support to businesses interested in entering new markets in a specific country or industry sector. Their services often include help in finding and approaching a partner in the new market, and further advice in establishing and developing the joint venture.

Businesses seeking partners sometimes place advertisements in the local press, trade magazines, or on the Internet. You should check these sources for suitable partners, but it is important to investigate any business thoroughly before agreements are signed. If you are a member of a trade association, advisers there may be able to offer you support and advice.

There are also a number of formal joint venture programmes offering support, assistance, and finance for businesses seeking partners. Contact your local Business Link, Business Eye, Business Gateway, or Invest Northern Ireland office for information.

Investigate possible partners

Once a likely candidate has been found and a positive response received, you need to make certain checks. Doing this before you finalise your commitment will make sure that a partner can be trusted. Check that there are no court judgments against them, whether they pay suppliers on time, and what their customer service record is like. If you are working with another business, some of its reputation may rub off onto your business so it is important that it is good.

Assess whether you can work together

Many partnerships, especially between small businesses, break up because of personality clashes. A good working relationship must be developed if the partnership is going to work. In many ways working with someone who has a different business style can be helpful, for example, one partner may be less cautious, and the other more so.

However, it is important that the business ethos of the two firms is similar; for example, if one partner regards employees as his or her greatest asset, whereas the other considers employees just to represent a huge wage bill every month, it may be very difficult to work well together.

Form the partnership

The aim of the partnership should be clear from the outset, and put into writing. You should seek legal advice when drafting the formal agreement. The written plan should not only cover goals, financial contributions (such as profit sharing, purchasing, and expenses), and any joint training, but also factors such as any time limit on the partnership and how to end it if necessary. You should make provision for any intellectual property issues which may occur; joint product development, especially technological development, could leave both parties in joint ownership of a patent or copyright. This could cause problems if the partnership dissolves on a negative footing.

Trust is essential; if partners are continually checking up on each other, there is not much hope for the strength of the venture. You are not obligated to reveal everything about the business to the other party if it is not relevant to the project in hand. However, you should decide on how much information the other business can have access to, for example, will it have access to your existing customer base? It is important not to give away unnecessary information, and to think carefully before revealing anything that is confidential. You should try to ensure that, as far as possible, both parties are making an equal contribution to the project, for example in terms of technology or sales leads.

Work together, not as rivals

It is important that you maintain an open working relationship with your partner and avoid treating them like a rival. As with any project, ample time should be given to strategy, planning, promotion, implementation, and back up such as after-sales care. You should also ensure that employees are given adequate time to get to know their counterparts they will be working with in the partner business, and if possible, joint training should be given to both sets of employees to inform them of the goals of the project. Good communication is also essential for all parties affected by this arrangement—so make sure you keep employees informed of progress so that they can feel a part of any success.

WHAT TO AVOID
Not doing enough research into your potential partner

You really need to find out as much as you can about any potential business partners. If you're not fully aware of the way the other business works and what their objectives are for the partnership, disputes can arise. For example:

- personality clashes develop with other managers—these can be especially invasive in smaller businesses, where the owner of the firm is likely to have imprinted his or her style on the business, working methods, and staff
- one party feels it is contributing more, and effectively carrying the other
- one side takes a disproportionate share of the profits
- there is a mismatch between the two parties in terms of goals
- disputes arise over legal issues such as ownership of copyright material or other intellectual property, which has been produced/developed by the partnership

Not putting the agreement into writing

It is easy for different businesses to enter a partnership with differing ideas and goals. Similarly, it is surprising how often two parties will come away from the same meeting with different ideas of what was agreed. Although each may have slightly different aims to achieve, the overall aim of the project should not be in doubt and the best way to achieve this is to have a written agreement signed by both parties.

RECOMMENDED LINKS
Business Eye (Wales):
www.businesseye.org.uk
Business Link (England):
www.businesslink.gov.uk
Community Research and Development Information Service (CORDIS):
www.cordis.lu
Invest Northern Ireland:
www.investni.com
Scottish Development International:
www.scottishdevelopmentinternational.co
Scottish Enterprise:
www.scottish-enterprise.com
Business Gateway (Scotland):
www.bgateway.com
UK Trade & Investment:
www.uktradeinvest.gov.uk
WalesTrade International:
www.walestrade.com

SEE ALSO
Identifying Opportunities for Your Business (p. 321)
Small and Growing Businesses (p. 486)

Timing the Decision to Export

GETTING STARTED

The lure of foreign markets can be tempting for a small business looking for new customers, especially when your national market is becoming saturated. Such an expansion, however, needs to be thoroughly researched and carefully considered to ensure that the timing is right, both for the business and the market being considered. For a start, your business needs to have proved the success of its products or services closer to home, where the risks and costs of entry are generally going to be lower. This should be reflected not just in customer satisfaction but also in the commercial success of your business over a number of years; it is essential to proceed from a strong financial position if you want to develop markets abroad.

You will need to establish the commitment of your management team, based on in-depth knowledge of exactly what will be involved in the export effort. This support will be important in getting over the many (and unexpected) hurdles of entering a market for the first time. Be prepared to hold back on pursuing your ideas until everyone is 'on board'. Once this commitment is solid, you can develop the plans, capacity, and systems for your business to launch an export programme confidently.

Thorough analysis and understanding of the market you want to enter is vital. Your research and PLEST (political, legal, economic, socio-cultural, and technological) analysis should provide you with a reliable insight into your new market to assess whether this is the right time to enter an export market.

FAQS

How long does the planning take?

It is possible to fast-track the export planning and development process so that you can be winning your first export orders within six months. On the other hand, the circumstances of your business might require a year or two before you feel comfortable to start exporting. As a practical guideline, you could aim at achieving some progress within a year, but be aware that unexpected problems might force you to take longer.

Is it important to pioneer new markets?

There is obvious merit to being among the first to exploit a new export market, but the risk of being a pioneer may outweigh the possible benefits. It is usually businesses with deep pockets who venture into uncharted territory, and other businesses following will learn by the earlier mistakes. When considering the timing of a new market entry, be aware of all the unknown factors that could cost you dearly. Start with small orders, for instance, and make sure all agreements are in writing and signed by both parties.

Where can I find out more about the impact of the euro on UK exporters?

Twelve countries in Europe (Austria, Belgium, Finland, France, Germany, Greece, Ireland, Italy, Luxembourg, The Netherlands, Portugal, and Spain) have adopted the euro as their single currency and become the 'eurozone'. While the United Kingdom is not part of this group, many of its businesses are affected by it, especially those who trade with partners in the 'eurozone' or those whose supply chain passes through there.

There is a good deal of information for you to tap into if you are unsure of how the euro affects you. UK Trade & Investment (**www.uktradeinvest.gov.uk**) is an excellent source of advice and it offers many links to other sources, including the Treasury's Euro Information site: **www.euro.gov.uk**, which aims to provide businesses of all types with relevant information on this topic. The 'Business Impact' section of this site offers an interactive assessment of how your business is, or may be, affected and also provides access to a series of factsheets for further reading. The Department of Trade and Industry (**www.dti.gov.uk**) and Business Link (**www.businesslink.gov.uk** or call on 0845 7567765) also offer advice.

MAKING IT HAPPEN
Conduct a PLEST analysis
A PLEST analysis—standing for political, legal, economic, socio-cultural, and techno-logical—of the market you plan to enter will ensure that you appreciate all the important factors that impact on your work there.

- **Political factors.** The political arena influ-ences the regulation of businesses and the spending power of consumers and other businesses. Consider issues like: How stable is the political environment? What is the government's overall economic policy? Is the government likely to change tax regu-lations soon? What is the government's position on marketing ethics? Does the government have a view on culture and religion? Is the government involved in regional trade agreements?

- **Legal factors.** Every country has its own legal structure and legislation. You need to make sure that your products or services will not be infringing any legislation, and that your exporting processes fully comply with customs regulations. Other issues to consider could include packaging and related environmental legislation; and your marketing strategy, as many countries over recent years have adopted new advertising constraints, covering issues such as adver-tising certain products like alcohol and tobacco, and advertising directly aimed at children.

- **Economic factors.** Consider the state of the economy you are planning to enter. This is especially important when planning for international marketing. You need to look at issues like interest rates, the level of inflation, the employment level per cap-ita, long-term prospects for the economy, and gross domestic product.

- **Socio-cultural factors.** The social and cul-tural influences on business vary from country to country, so you should consider questions like: What is the dominant religion? What are the attitudes to foreign products and services? Does language affect which products make it into the market? How much time do consumers have for leisure? What are the respective roles of men and women within society? What is the average life span? Are the older generations wealthy? Does the population have a strong opinion on green issues?

- **Technological factors.** Technology is vital for your competitive advantage, so con-sider these questions: Will technology help reduce the cost and quality of products and services? Do the technologies offer consumers and businesses more innovative products and services such as Internet banking and new generation mobile tele-phones? How is distribution changed by new technologies? Does technology offer businesses a new way to communicate with consumers?

Set time-bound objectives
Within the constraints of your particular business and sector, set some time frames that you can work towards. You need to take into account the level of funding available to implement your plans; the revenue that you expect from your capital outlay; the extent to which your export business will strengthen its position, and the extent to which exports further the overall mission of your business.

Test and modify your product first
In your export development plan, give yourself time to test your product in the market and to make any modifications that might be necessary. Do this before launch-ing a full-scale marketing campaign so that you can deliver, from the start of proper trading, a final product closer to local requirements.

Build up skills and capacity
From your market research, you will develop sales forecasts to use in developing production and supply plans. When timing your export launch, make sure you give

yourself enough time to employ and train the necessary people, and to install the systems you will need to meet the demand you expect. You will be working hard to get these new export customers, but you will not be able to keep them if you have not developed the capacity to deliver on new order levels.

Choose the moment

There may be factors peculiar to your new market that you need to consider when timing your entry. If certain trade barriers or customs duties are being changed or removed, this could present a good opportunity to start trading with a lead on competitors. There may also be certain times of year that see more trade in your sector, particularly if it is seasonal. You would need to consider the conditions on the supply side (for instance, if you are exporting fruit when it is in season at home) and the demand side (where you would want to enter the new market at a time when those fruits are in short supply).

WHAT TO AVOID
Rushing in

The size of a market is no guarantee of its willingness to let in new entrants. Indeed, large markets are often those most heavily contested by big and small players due to the high stakes. Take your time in doing

your research and in finding the best point of entry.

Unrealistic expectations of quick returns

Most small businesses will be constrained in their export efforts by their limited funds and resources, so your export plan will be tailored to take account of your individual situation. With this in mind, be careful not to expect miracles from a new market. If you are working through an agent or distributor, they might give an overly optimistic forecast of what they might sell; you need to know enough about the market to make a realistic assessment of these forecasts, so that you do not expect too much, too soon. This can be particularly dangerous if your export effort is drawing on cash or resources that are vital to your core, local market.

RECOMMENDED LINK
UK Trade & Investment (the Government export promotion agency): **www.uktradeinvest.gov.uk**

SEE ALSO
Exporting (p. 514)
Exporting for the First Time (p. 343)
Importing (p. 518)
Small and Growing Businesses (p. 486)

Exporting—Methods of Market Entry

GETTING STARTED

Many first-time exporters feel unsure about the best way to approach their export market and how to manage a complex marketing and distribution process from a distance. This actionlist explains the various ways to approach market entry and also suggests how to choose a sensible market entry method for your business.

FAQS

What do the terms 'direct' or 'indirect' exporting mean?

Direct exporting means actively developing your venture into overseas markets. This approach requires a great deal of preparation and considerable investment of time. You could employ someone to take charge of part of the process, or to act as a representative in the chosen market. Alternatively, you may choose to manage the whole process yourself. Examples of direct exporting include joint ventures, using agents, or selling via trade fairs.

Indirect exporting usually means exporting via customers in the United Kingdom, which may eliminate the need for travelling abroad and dealing with complex export processes. However, it still requires considerable commitment. It can be a useful route into selling abroad for small-to-medium enterprises (SMEs), and provides a means of testing product viability in new markets.

Where can I go for advice and information on exporting?

UK Trade & Investment (**www.uktradeinvest.gov.uk**) offers a range of market research, programme planning, and promotional support to exporters. Export Explorer is a scheme that aims to help new or inexperienced exporters take part in export missions into western Europe. Support and assistance is also delivered through local business advice organisations such as Business Links and Chambers of Commerce, in conjunction with commercial teams in British Embassies abroad.

The British Exporters Association (BExA) aims to link first-time exporters with profes-sional services. It can also give details of regional Export Clubs, groups of business people who meet informally to discuss exporting issues. Members may be able to recommend agents or give advice on methods they have used. The embassies and Chambers of Commerce often have local expertise and contacts in certain markets. They are a useful source of practical information on import and export legislation.

Trade associations often have links with international groups or lists of contacts in export markets. Some have well-developed export services and can arrange joint ventures and trade fair visits, as well as provide general advice. All the major banks have international divisions that should be able to provide useful contacts and give general advice on the financial implications of particular export options.

Many solicitors have specialist expertise on contract law abroad and should especially be consulted when signing up an agent or distributor. Freight forwarders are an important part of the distribution process and can also provide advice on terms and paperwork. It may also be helpful to consult the national and trade press of the proposed export market and any international export journals. Often export representatives seeking customers will advertise in these publications.

MAKING IT HAPPEN

Choose an exporting method

Look carefully at your proposed market and customers. Clarify the existing channels of distribution for your business's particular type of product. A trade visit will provide a good opportunity to study the local business structure. Are there any legislative issues which will affect sales, such as restrictions on choice of representatives? How do existing customers prefer to do business? For example, many large organisations are not keen on unsolicited approaches but channel all their buying through an agent.

In many cases, the nature of the product or service being exported will determine the selection of entry method. Make a list of any factors that may affect the way the product should be sold, using experience of the UK market where applicable. For example, what level of technical backup and promotional investment will be required? Think about your available resources, such as staff time, language skills, technical and marketing resources, as well as finance. How will domestic business be affected if technical staff are busy dealing with problems abroad?

Find out about methods of entry

Commission agents seek orders on behalf of a client in return for an agreed commission on each order. The agent is briefed on appropriate prices and terms and then approaches businesses within a designated area. Agents legally bind the business they represent to any contracts they sign for product orders. They generally seek sole agency rights for a country or region. Agents do not deal with shipping or payment, which must be arranged separately from the United Kingdom. An agent will accept no credit risk on stock unless they are a 'del credere' agent, charging a higher commission to compensate for the credit risk involved.

Distributors hold stocks of products from which they fulfil local orders. Unlike agents, they usually take legal title to the goods, buying from a business and selling on their own account at prices that they fix themselves. They usually also oversee the export process. It is normal to grant the distributor an agreed area of operation and to take orders from that area only through them.

Sell direct using the business's own resources

It is possible to sell direct to individual customers or outlets abroad. This may be appropriate where the customer base is narrow or limited, for example, luxury goods stocked by a small number of exclusive outlets, and when there is little need for servicing or after sales care. However, selling direct will involve considerable resources of time and money.

Attend trade fairs

Fairs and exhibitions are held throughout Europe and beyond, attracting customers and suppliers involved in various trades. If your business is considering exhibiting, contact the relevant trade association and UK Trade & Investment, the agency combining the export activities of the DTI and the Foreign Office. Its Trade Fair Support can provide financial advice and technical help. Even if your business doesn't exhibit, there will be opportunities to make contacts, research the market, find agents or wholesalers, and develop sales leads.

Consider franchising

Franchising involves selling a business as a ready-made package to local operators in return for fees and other income, for example a percentage of annual profits. Franchising is a means of expanding rapidly while limiting management responsibility. The operation must be unique in some way to be a viable franchise. The franchisee contributes towards capital and resources as well as paying a licence fee, whilst the business is expected to provide a range of support, including training and technical services.

Consider licence agreements

A business can grant another firm the right to use its product names, technical specifications, processes, or patents, by drawing up a licence agreement. A fee (which may or may not include royalties) is charged for the licensed rights. Licensing may depend on the business securing protection for intellectual property rights in the country concerned and may also require approval.

Consider joint ventures

There are many types of joint venture. It may be possible to identify a suitable UK firm that is willing to enter into a partnership to begin exporting. This provides an opportunity to pool resources and expertise, but it is important to find a firm with strengths that balance your existing weaknesses. Export clubs can be a good means of locating potential partners.

You could make an arrangement with a compatible business abroad. You might, for example, agree to manage each other's export trade, or combine in a joint operation to enter a specific market or markets. This often involves joint investment. Another option is to work with an international firm. Large international companies, whether UK-based or in the export market, often seek new products for their sales portfolio. If initial research indicates that a product could work well within a particular business's range, this 'piggy back' method is worth exploring.

Investigate export houses

Export houses are firms with a detailed knowledge of international sales, who specialise in financing and servicing exports. The price paid for the product on offer will reflect their costs, but in some cases the importer pays the export house fees.

Export consultancies are generally small consultancies specialising in particular markets and services. They usually accept responsibility for all aspects of export administration or will offer particular services and support.

Export merchants buy products outright from the manufacturer and sell them abroad. They usually take delivery and make payment in the United Kingdom, and often specialise in certain products. When dealing with a new product, they will require an agreement to protect their investment in building overseas sales, and they may also request that you agree to certain product or packaging changes to meet their market requirements.

Confirming houses place orders with manufacturers and suppliers on behalf of overseas organisations and attend to all transport arrangements. They can also act as agents for UK manufacturers and seek orders from their overseas contacts.

The Crown Agents

The Crown Agents make purchases on behalf of the public sector, for example foreign governments, armed forces, and transport authorities. They are responsible for paying suppliers within the UK.

Buying houses

Large overseas businesses, for example, grocery or retail chains, often have buying houses in the United Kingdom. These have huge purchasing budgets, and although businesses usually still have to deal with the physical process of exporting, they are guaranteed fairly large-scale sales.

WHAT TO AVOID
Not researching thoroughly

Different markets and countries operate in different ways. In many countries, particularly those in the Middle East and Africa, government regulations may dictate the choice of representation (usually an approved agent), and may stipulate the level of commission. It is important to remember that the best method in one market may not work in another. Many businesses which export to a number of markets deal directly in some areas, while using UK intermediaries to sell to other territories.

RECOMMENDED LINKS
British Exporters Association (BExA):
www.bexa.co.uk
Export Credit Guarantee Department (ECGD):
www.ecgd.gov.uk
The Institute of Export:
www.export.org.uk
Invest Northern Ireland:
www.investni.com
Scottish Development International:
www.sti.org.uk
SITPRO (Simpler Trade Procedures Board):
www.sitpro.org.uk
WalesTrade International:
www.walestrade.com

Exporting for the First Time

GETTING STARTED
Exporting can be a rewarding way for a small firm to develop and grow. At the same time, it presents challenges and risks that are different from those in the domestic market. This actionlist will help you identify potential problems and plan for them.

FAQS
Why should I export?
There are many reasons why small firms seek to export. These might relate to the personal aims of the owner or manager (new challenges, credibility, added wealth, and so on). They might also relate to the commercial needs of the business (increased turnover and profits, reduced reliance on the home market, and so on).

When is the right time to begin exporting?
Exporting should be seen in the wider context of the strategic business plan. The potential rewards are massive, but a substantial investment is required to achieve them. Beware of overstretching your resources. Often, additional finance and evidence to show that the investment will pay off may be required.

Before you commit your business to the additional costs of export activity, carry out a business 'fitness check', to assess whether it is in a condition to sustain the additional effort required (or, indeed, to maintain current levels of activity properly). Five areas that should be of particular concern are: your knowledge of the market; your production, distribution, and sales capacity; your flexibility to meet market needs; the financial resources available to you; and management, staffing, and skills resources.

MAKING IT HAPPEN
Know the key factors for success
Successful exporters demonstrate management commitment to exporting and will have carried out thorough research and planning. They will have conducted market visits and research validation and will have developed contacts and relationships. They will have a feel for foreign cultures and languages and an eye for detail in export documentation and procedures. They will also have put the emphasis on quality.

Avoid potential problem areas
A number of problems can arise that may not appear to be directly related to exporting. The added challenge of exporting, whether successful or not, can show up the flaws in a business. Growing firms can find it hard to recruit staff with the right knowledge and experience. Recognise your limitations and be prepared to use appropriate external advisers. They can provide strategic guidance, commission research, and act as a sounding board for problems.

The cost of breaking into foreign markets is frequently underestimated. The venture should be seen as an investment, covering the initial costs of research, developing contacts, and the losses incurred before sales begin to cover the extra cost. It may be necessary to explore separate financial arrangements in order to support any exporting ventures. Pricing is another potential problem area. Having established the market potential for the product or service, the price the market will bear is crucial in determining how profitable the returns will be.

Accepting substantial new business without thinking through all the implications can be risky and may cause operational problems. cash-flow problems destroy many promising firms, and payment can take longer for exports. Stock control is a particular issue in terms of capital and prompt delivery. The administration of orders, insufficient production capacity, and extensive transit times may produce delays unacceptable to the customer.

All investment of management and staff time, money, and costs must be taken into account. It will be necessary to consider: UK factory costs; export packing; inland transport and handling costs; export transport costs; insurance costs; overseas handling and transport costs. There are also taxes: any customs duties payable overseas, including VAT; freight forwarders' charges, inclusive of documentation; any direct office costs, including any salesperson's commission; overseas agents' charges; advertising; cost of money and credit, and the cost of cover against exchange rate risk when applicable.

Work with other organisations

A lot of advice, information, and support is available to exporters through business support organisations, much of it free or subsidised. UK Trade & Investment, the Foreign Office and Department of Trade and Industry (DTI) export agency, provides a number of useful market research, export counselling, and trade mission services. Points of contact include: the local Business Link in England; Scottish Development International; WalesTrade International, and Invest Northern Ireland.

There are also organisations that can provide the necessary expertise to help a business to develop an export market. Chambers of Commerce provide specific export training and services, for example, documentation, letters of credit, and certificates of origin. They also undertake trade missions, often sponsored by UK Trade & Investment, and act as host to local export clubs. Export Consultancies are, usually, small consultancies specialising in particular markets and services. They take on all aspects of export marketing and administration, or provide particular services, for example, training, to assist with exporting issues.

Commission Agents will seek orders on the behalf of the business and charge an agreed commission on all orders from their territory, even if they did not obtain the order. Agents also generally seek sole agency rights for a country or region. Distributors act as agents and hold stocks of the product, from which local orders are supplied. Often distributors buy from the business and sell for their own account, at local prices, which they fix themselves.

Buying houses are often specialised, buying products outright from the manufacturer and undertaking to sell them abroad. They usually require an agreement that protects their investment in building up the overseas sales of the product. Confirming houses place orders with manufacturers and suppliers on behalf of overseas organisations and attend to all the shipping arrangements. They may also act as agents for United Kingdom manufacturers, and often seek orders from their overseas contacts and principals.

Crown Agents make purchases on behalf of overseas governments, and a number of large organisations. HM Revenue & Customs will provide technical advice and information on export procedures, duties, restrictions, refunds, and product classification.

Think about transportation and distribution

There are many unfamiliar issues involved in the exporting of goods, including aspects of transport and distribution that may have not been a problem in the past. The following paragraphs cover some of these issues.

Freight forwarders offer comprehensive documentation and transportation services, not necessarily using their own transport. They undertake door-to-door services for shipments. An efficient freight forwarder will take advantage of the keen competition between transport operators to secure the best prices. The British International Freight Association can assist with finding a local forwarder. You might also consider using a freight forwarder to deal with documentation. Simple typing errors can lead to long and costly delays at overseas customs. The UK network of Chambers of Commerce offers a comprehensive export documentation and certificates of origin service.

Suitable packaging should be used to ensure that goods reach their destination undamaged at the most economical cost.

For export, packaging may have to be tougher and/or meet specific legal standards. Particular attention should be paid to any printed descriptions on the packaging. Another issue is the terms of delivery. The point at which the business's responsibility for the goods ends and that of the overseas buyer begins is determined by the contract terms. As there is a wide range of options available, it is essential that the business is fully aware of its responsibilities regarding insurance and contractual obligations.

Manage the risks

If you explore foreign markets directly, reduce the initial financial investment and risk by focusing on one, or fewer, markets. In exporting it is even more important that delivery promises are kept and products are acceptable and reliable. The administration and documentation and the physical distribution of products can be handled efficiently by external specialist companies. Marketing, including overseas visits, can be contracted out to self-employed export marketing specialists.

There are various types of risks to consider when exporting. Insurance will cover straightforward commercial risks such as those encountered during transportation. More critical is the risk that an overseas buyer may refuse to accept delivery of goods ordered, or may take delivery, refuse to pay, and disappear. It is therefore essential to put all of the terms (Incoterms) of the contract in writing, and select a secure method of getting paid (normally through a bank), which is appropriate to the risk involved.

Political risks can vary from political instability (military coups) to the sudden imposition of restrictions by a government on payments for importers. Currencies may fluctuate wildly or cease to be convertible into other currencies, making them effectively valueless. Current assessments of political and economic risks can be obtained through UK Trade & Investment Country Reports or through discussions with British Embassy commercial staff overseas.

Interest rate risks can be especially important in the case of high-value capital ventures, where there is a long period of time between the initial planning work and final payment for the product. In such cases, costings should take account of the charge for the money required. There is also a risk that the rate of exchange between sterling and the buyer's currency will change between the agreeing of terms and the completion of the deal. Hedging mechanisms are available that enable exporters to protect themselves from exchange rate changes, and banks can provide further details.

WHAT TO AVOID
Exporting when your business is unfit

Exporting can put pressure on a business. It is essential that your business is running efficiently before taking on the added complications of exporting.

Not getting the right advice

Take full advantage of the free advice and information available. Some of the subsidised services can assist with finding partners who can give the right type of support for your business's own products and markets.

RECOMMENDED LINKS

British Chambers of Commerce:
www.chamberonline.co.uk
British Exporters Association:
www.bexa.co.uk
British International Freight Association:
www.bifa.org
Department of Trade & Industry:
www.dti.gov.uk
Scottish Development International:
**www.scottishdevelopment
 international.com**
Simpler Trade Procedures Board (SITPRO):
www.sitpro.org.uk
UK Trade & Investment:
www.uktradeinvest.gov.uk
WalesTrade International:
www.walestrade.com
Invest Northern Ireland:
www.investni.com

SEE ALSO
Export Documentation (p. 346)
Exporting (p. 514)
Timing the Decision to Export (p. 337)

Export Documentation

GETTING STARTED

To the small business exporter, the documentation required can seem daunting, but it is worth getting documentation right; having the correct information, knowing where and when to send it, and to whom, speeds up the processing of individual transactions and inspires confidence in the business. Indeed, where letters of credit are involved, you won't get paid without the relevant documentation. Export documentation is subject to frequent change and amendment, and requirements vary from country to country so do your homework well or seek advice if you're unsure of any legal requirements.

FAQS

Why would I need to use export documentation?

Documentation is used for a variety of purposes in the export process. It can help to reduce delayed shipment and delivery, describe cargo, allow customs clearance; to indicate the ownership of goods for collection purposes or in the event of dispute; and to obtain payment. Documentary requirements often depend on the Incoterm used. (Incoterms are standard trade definitions most commonly used in international sales contracts, and help traders in different countries to understand one another. Information on the Incoterms is hosted on the International Chamber of Commerce website, the address of which is given below.)

What types of export documentation are there?

Most export documentation falls into one of five of the following broad categories: commercial, official, transport, insurance, and financial documents.

Many export documents are now a part of the United Kingdom Aligned System of Documents, managed by the Simpler Trade Procedures Board (SITPRO). This system implements the United Nations Layout Key for Trade Documents. It basically means that the same piece of information is in the same place on all documents. This makes the completion, checking, and comparison of related documents much easier.

Who can I ask for assistance with export documentation?

SITPRO (Simpler Trade Procedures Board) has developed a range of systems for preparing paperwork quickly, cheaply, and accurately without repetitive retyping, and offers advice to individual businesses on export needs. HM Revenue & Customs advises on export documentation requirements for United Kingdom or European Community purposes, VAT, controlled goods, and legislation. Customs officers oversee the key aspects of export transactions, such as documentation, legislative standards, and duty.

Local Chambers of the Chambers of Commerce can help with information and advice on all aspects of export/import documentation, and will usually have experienced staff to advise on specific problems. The Department of Trade and Industry's Export Control Organisation can tell you if your particular product is exportable only under licence, can give details of any restrictions, and tell you how to obtain the relevant licence.

Freight forwarders offer a range of services covering the physical transportation of goods for export, usually including packing and documentation. The British International Freight Association (BIFA) can help you contact such companies. Export management and documentation services are also an option; the British Exporters Association (BExA) can help in finding sources of assistance.

● MAKING IT HAPPEN

Commercial documents

There are three types of commercial document. The commercial invoice is a bill for the goods, a basis for the assessment of import duty, evidence of value in case of an insurance claim, and in some cases a contract of sale. It describes the product, including shipping marks, price, and so on. It must be completed according to the requirements of customs authorities in the export market.

The pro forma invoice may be needed in advance if the importer has to get an allocation of foreign exchange, or an import licence. It can also be used to send commercial samples and other 'free of charge' consignments. Blank or nil value pro formas are illegal in all countries.

Finally, there is the Export Cargo Shipping Instruction (ECSI). This is the instruction from the exporter to the forwarder or carrier. It sets out the terms and conditions for the movement of goods, and who is responsible.

Official documents

There are many different kinds of official documents. The Single Administrative Document (SAD) is known as the C88 in the United Kingdom. It is used for exports, imports, and goods transiting the European Union.

Export licences are required for certain goods to be exported legally, for example drugs, chemicals, antiques, military-related items, high-technology industrial goods, and scientific instruments, under the Export of Goods (Control) Orders. It is the exporter's responsibility to ensure that their goods are covered if necessary. The Department of Trade and Industry's Export Control Organisation can be contacted for further information. Contact the Department of Culture, Media and Sport for specific information related to antiques and works of art.

Certificates of Origin (C/O) are required by some countries when goods are imported. They are available from Chambers of Commerce for goods of EU origin. Documentary proof of origin (usually the manufacturer's invoice) must also be sub-

mitted to the Chamber. Movement Certificates are required where goods are being exported from the European Union to a country covered by EU trade agreements. These certificates ensure preferential tariff treatment. They must be stamped by UK Customs before dispatch. Certificates of Health are often required for food, livestock, agricultural, and horticultural products. These certificates are issued by a state-appointed veterinary inspector or health board, this being DEFRA (Department for Environment, Food and Rural Affairs) in the United Kingdom.

The Clean Report of Findings (Pre-Shipment Inspection Certificate) applies mainly in developing countries, where foreign currency is rationed, and where priority may be given to medical supplies, food, and so on. The report is issued by an independent inspection house, appointed to check that the goods being shipped are those on the pro forma invoice, and that they conform to quality, price, and quantity requirements. Checks are also made once shipment is complete. Contact the inspection agency as early as possible if you believe that inspection may be required.

Individual countries have their own very specific requirements relating to import licences and special requirements. Many require import licences for certain goods, and some for all imports. Others prohibit certain goods entirely. Although it is normally the customer's responsibility to comply with import documents, it makes sense for you to confirm that they are doing so.

Transport documents

The **maritime bill of lading** is issued and signed by the designated carrier once the goods to be exported have been placed in its care. It serves as evidence of a contract between the exporter or importer and a shipping company to transport the goods; it also acts as a receipt for goods. It may describe the condition of the goods when transferred to the shipper, and it also serves as a document of title indicating the person, or business, who has the right to possess the goods.

The bill should show relevant information, for example date and point of dispatch, and the shipper's name and destination port. The reverse side gives details of the terms on which the transporter is carrying the goods, and indicates limitations on its liability. Bills are usually completed in sets of two or three, one being forwarded immediately, another sent later in case of loss, while a number of copies are kept as records.

Goods can be consigned 'to order', which means the importer can give someone else authority to collect them on arrival. In this case, the bill of lading will be endorsed by the exporter. If the consignee (importer) is named, the goods will only be released to them.

Bills of lading can be issued in several forms, for example a 'shipped' or 'shipped on board' bill signifies that the goods have been received and placed on board ship, while a 'received for shipment' bill indicates that the goods have been received by the ship owner, but have not been placed on board. Other types of bills cover 'combined transport', for example over land as well as sea, and containerisation.

The **sea waybill** serves the same purpose as the bill of lading except that it is not a document of title.

An **air waybill** receipt issued by an airline when goods are received for transport, which travels with the cargo. It is similar to a bill of lading, but cannot serve as a document of title.

A **Parcel post receipt** is issued by the Royal Mail as proof of dispatch. It is not a document of title. A similar receipt would be issued by Parcelforce Worldwide.

The **CMR** (Convention relative au contrat de Transport International de Marchandises par Route) accompanies goods transported by road. The **CIM** (Convention International de Marchandises par Chemin de Fer) accompanies goods dispatched by rail. Neither is a document of title, but both function as receipts and evidence of the contract of carriage.

The **dangerous goods note** (DGN) is required when shipping hazardous, or potentially hazardous, goods. The exporter must provide the transporter—that is the shipping, haulage, or air company—with full details of the goods, including the official 'class' of danger to which they belong. You should also be aware of packing and marking requirements for hazardous cargoes. A new version of DGN came into force in July 1999, which implemented various changes including new declarations, updated completion guidelines, and so on. For air transport, the International Air Transport Association (IATA) Dangerous Goods Declaration should be used.

The **standard shipping note** (SSN) is usually completed by the exporter and is the receiving document for ports and container bases in the United Kingdom. It advises recipients of the necessary information to handle the goods. The SSN was also amended in July 1999. The note may now be used for goods classified as hazardous by a mode of transport other than that for which the SSN is being used, for example goods classified as hazardous under the IATA Dangerous Goods Regulations.

ATA (Admission Temporaire, or Temporary Admission) **Carnets** are particularly useful where the exporter is taking goods through a number of countries, for example to a trade fair, but will bring them back to the United Kingdom. Carnets are issued by selected Chambers of Commerce on payment of a fee and relevant security, and serve as a 'passport' for the goods. Export and import restrictions, including licence requirements, must still be observed under the Carnet system. The maximum period of validity of Carnets is one year, but they can cover a number of journeys.

Insurance documents

Arrange freight insurance through a broker with a thorough knowledge of exporting. The insurance policy should cover goods for at least their full value (110% is common), should carry all details of quantity and route, and should provide for time extensions and trans-shipments where necessary.

A Certificate of Insurance is issued by the insurance company or underwriters to certify that insurance has been arranged for the goods being exported. It should detail the degree of protection, and list the policy number and all relevant details, for example, dates, destination, transport method, route, description of the cargo, and the value for which it is insured.

Electronic Data Interchange is increasingly important to the international exchange of commercial information. It greatly reduces the time taken for document exchange and increases accuracy by eliminating transcription errors. EDI systems use conventions and standards of formatting for correct data delivery. International standards have been devised so that various documents can be exchanged between companies, for example, invoices and orders. Their precise layout makes them simpler to use for trading partners in different countries without a common language.

EDI involves a computer with a modem and communications software (to provide data translation) at either end of a telephone line. Many businesses use a Value Added Network supplier (VAN) to handle connections and forward documents. To use EDI, the exporter should set up a Trade Interchange Agreement with the customer(s). This replaces the terms and conditions of trade which normally appear on the back of a purchase order. HM Customs operates a system for exporters which allows paperless export declarations to be made.

The Internet can also be used as a means of sending documentation. Benefits include speed, accuracy (supported by database files), and the ability to send to a large number of recipients using one system. Dis-

advantages include problems of providing adequate security, and dealing with global orders without knowing the integrity of the person doing the ordering.

WHAT TO AVOID
Not getting it right first time
Make sure your documentation is correctly completed first time; delays caused by missing or incorrect paperwork can seriously affect cash flow. Mistakes can also lead to customs fines or increased duty.

Not getting the right advice
Take as much advice as possible when dealing with paperwork. Talk to SITPRO, an export counsellor, the Chamber of Commerce, the agent or distributor, and so on, to ensure that you are fully prepared.

RECOMMENDED LINKS
British International Freight Association:
www.bifa.org
British Exporters Association (BExA):
www.bexa.co.uk
The Export Control Organisation Helpline:
www.dti.gov.uk/export.control
Department of Culture, Media and Sport:
www.culture.gov.uk
The Institute of Export:
www.export.org.uk
International Chamber of Commerce:
www.iccwbo.org
Simpler Trade Procedures Board (SITPRO):
www.sitpro.org.uk

SEE ALSO
Exporting (p. 514)
Exporting for the First Time (p. 343)

Importing for the First Time

GETTING STARTED

Importing is the process of bringing goods from one country into another. The main reasons for importing are either to obtain goods or materials from a source which is the cheapest available or of the highest quality for a given price, or to obtain raw materials, components, or finished goods that are not available in this country.

This actionlist explains why you might consider importing, how to go about it, and some of the common pitfalls you should be aware of. If your business is unfamiliar with import procedures, it is a good idea to employ a clearing agent who will deal with procedures on the business's behalf.

FAQS

How might I find sources of supply?

One way is to respond to advertisements placed by would-be suppliers, for example in the trade press or on the Internet. If a supplier is required for particular items, advertise in the appropriate overseas publications and via your business's website. Research possible sources thoroughly, and make a personal visit to each supplier on your shortlist.

There are numerous directories of products and services, of which the best known is *Kompass*. Available in book form or on CD-ROM in almost 70 countries, including all the main trading nations, this publication can be found in most main libraries and Chambers of Commerce. If direct access to information on suppliers in a particular country proves problematic, the country's embassy in the United Kingdom may be able to help. There may also be a joint Chamber of Commerce that encourages trade between the United Kingdom and the country of interest.

Sometimes, an individual or organisation overseas can be appointed to act as an agent and manage deals with suppliers on your behalf. However, payment of a fee or commission will usually be required, unless the individual or organisation works on an export programme run by the foreign government.

MAKING IT HAPPEN

Arranging to import

The simplest way to import is to do it indirectly, which means that someone else handles the importation process, and goods are simply purchased from them. These importers can be wholesalers or import merchants; commission agents or distributors working for the overseas manufacturer; or a UK subsidiary of the overseas business. Indirect importing can be less risky as it usually involves buying from a UK-registered business covered by UK company law, and payment is usually in sterling. It usually costs more than direct importing, however.

Direct importing is when the business is in personal contact with the overseas suppliers. It gives the business more control over the process, and may even prove to be more profitable. However, it will be necessary to find the right overseas suppliers and to handle negotiations, regulations, and paperwork personally. Regulations covering imports from the specific countries of interest can be obtained from HM Revenue & Customs and the Department of Trade and Industry's Import Licensing Branch.

Potential pitfalls of importing

An importer often holds the linguistic advantage over a buyer, and language can be a significant barrier. Specify that any correspondence, particularly quotations and contracts, must be in English. Making initial contact overseas will be easier if the manager or an employee of the business can speak the other language.

The physical distance in moving goods increases the risk of delays and means that client-customer servicing is more expensive. These risks need to be built into planning, especially if the business is run on a just-in-time basis. The total cost of the goods bought has the potential to be much higher than the price agreed for the actual items. Additional costs may include packing, transport, insurance, and customs duty. The business will therefore need to ensure that allowances have been made for such costs in budget calculations, or that they are included in the total contract price that will be paid.

It is essential to consider which currency is to be used in the transaction. A foreign supplier is often much more comfortable dealing in their own currency and may be able to quote a more competitive price. However, you will need to pay for the exchange, and money may be lost if the exchange rate fluctuates between placing the order and making the payment. If the transaction is in pounds sterling it will be easier to ascertain how much will be paid, but the supplier may ask a higher price for the privilege. The further into the future the transaction is, the greater the uncertainty, and the more it is likely to cost. If orders are likely to be large and frequent, then buying in the foreign currency may be preferable, hedging any risk by agreeing a forward exchange contract with a bank.

The single European currency (the euro), introduced on 1 January 1999, affects UK businesses wishing to import goods. Current European Union member countries that have joined are: Austria, Belgium, Finland, France, Germany, Ireland, Italy, Luxembourg, Netherlands, Portugal, and Spain, collectively known as the euro zone. As of January 1999, businesses in these countries became entitled to trade with each other without any exchange rate risk. In January 2001 Greece also joined the single currency. If a UK business is obliged to deal in euros, then exchange rate risk could be an important issue to consider.

Import quotations and orders

State your requirements clearly and consistently when requesting quotations, so that responses can be easily compared.

Ensure that you specify the quantity, expected order date, and expected payment terms (for example, form of payment, currency, and payment date). Be clear about details such as specific packaging, labelling, and transport requirements (including terms of, and responsibility for, arranging delivery). State your requirements for goods to meet specific quality, technical, or safety standards, and the requirements that are related to the business's legal obligations (these will be of particular importance). It is important to agree under which country's legislation any trading contract is made.

The more professional the request looks, the more willing a company will be to do business. The name and title of the person to whom responses should be sent, and also the business's full address, with phone and fax numbers and e-mail addresses, should be provided.

Agreeing payment terms can be difficult until business creditworthiness has been proven. Signify good intentions by giving the supplier the name of the business's bank and inviting them to ask for a reference (the bank must be informed about this first). There are a number of ways to pay, ranging from cash in advance to cash on delivery. Two of the safest methods for the business and the supplier are letters of credit and bills of exchange. The bank will be able to give advice regarding the details.

Once a supplier has been chosen, the order placed should include the same details as the quotation, with any agreed amendments. It is also important to specify any conditions of purchase. To avoid contract disputes, the supplier must agree to all of the terms of the order, in writing.

Import controls

Import sanctions, quotas, and other controls can be imposed in the United Kingdom, which is also subject to European Union restrictions, or alternatively may be put in place by the export regulations of the supplier's country. Importers should check with the supplier to find out if an export licence from the supplier's country will be required. The main government departments involved with import licensing include the Department of Trade and Industry's Import Licensing Branch; the Health and Safety Executive; and the Department for Environment, Food, and Rural Affairs. The range of goods subject to controls is extensive, and your business should check with its regulatory body.

HM Revenue & Customs collects duty and VAT, and can also provide details of what is expected regarding an importer's responsibilities. For example, the Harmonised System is an internationally understood way of coding imports so they can be recognised in trade statistics, and for the charging of duty. The full code number should be agreed and quoted on all documents by both importer and supplier.

Transport and delivery when importing

Terms of delivery may be encountered in abbreviated form and come from an internationally recognised list, known as 'Incoterms'. In some cases the definitions of the terms may vary by country, so you should seek advice from the local Chamber of Commerce.

The terms of delivery should always be agreed in quotations and orders. They determine what the price includes, where delivery of the goods takes place, and where possession passes from the exporter to the importer. These points are important because they will affect decisions such as final cost and insurance responsibility. The choice of transport used will depend upon the type of goods, and the quantity, urgency, and cost. The route options of air, sea, road, or rail all have advantages and disadvantages. For some goods it may also be possible to use postal services.

In many cases, when importing for the first time it is a good idea to use the services of a freight forwarding company. They usually have agents overseas and can therefore arrange most aspects of overseas transportation and insurance.

WHAT TO AVOID
Not understanding the business from an exporter's point of view

As an importer, your business may be requested by its overseas contacts to trace goods or services in the United Kingdom and then export them. A willingness to fulfil such reciprocal requests will help to build a good working relationship and will also result in an improved knowledge of the supplier.

Not taking all costs into account

If price is a factor, businesses should carefully consider whether importing works out cheaper, especially in cases where payment of duty, transport costs, agent's commission, and so on, are required. Other factors, such as reliability of supply, may also be an issue.

If the business is re-exporting imports to outside the European Union, it may qualify for Inward Processing Relief. HM Revenue & Customs can be contacted for further information.

Not inspecting goods that are received

It is essential that any goods received are inspected promptly and thoroughly, in case it is necessary to reject them or make an insurance claim.

RECOMMENDED LINKS

British International Freight Association (BIFA):
www.bifa.org
Euro Information (The Official Treasury Euro Resource):
www.euro.gov.uk
HM Revenue & Customs:
www.hmrc.gov.uk
Kompass:
www.kompass.com

SEE ALSO
Exporting (p. 514)
Importing (p. 518)

WORKING ONLINE

Setting Up a Basic Website

GETTING STARTED

A website is a way of informing customers and other groups such as suppliers, journalists, or employees about your company. A basic website involves delivering essential information that is easy to read and well laid out. In website design, simplicity is always best. A website must also be actively promoted to make people aware of its existence. When approaching website design, ask yourself the following important questions:

- Who are the people that I want to communicate with (your target market)?
- How am I going to structure my information so it is easy to navigate and read?
- How am I going to let people know that my website exists?
- How am I going to keep my website updated and keep people informed of new content?

FAQS

How much information should I include on a website?

Provide the information that your visitors are likely to read. Don't fill your website with irrelevant and/or repetitive information as it will clutter your site and make the important information hard to find.

How often should I change website content?

You should change your content whenever you have something new and important to say, and whenever content already on the site is out of date. Ideally you should try to publish fresh content every week.

Can I transfer printed copy to the website?

Printed copy can be used as a starting point for web copy, but the structure and length would probably be unsuitable. People like to read short, punchy copy on the Web, so snappy headings and summaries are important. For a website to be truly effective, you must also use links (known as 'hypertext') so that people can click through for further information if they need it.

MAKING IT HAPPEN

Know who you want to reach

Before you do anything, decide who you want to reach. Prioritise your information for your most important audiences. Ask yourself the following questions:

- Do I want to reach new customers? In new markets?
- What can I say on my website that will turn a potential customer into an actual (and valuable) one?
- Do I want to offer support for existing customers?
- Do I want to provide information to attract new staff?

Keep it simple

Website design is about the design and delivery of information, not about graphic design. Only a small proportion of Internet users have access to broadband, so it is best to avoid fancy graphics and moving images. They slow down a site and frustrate visitors looking for information. Good website design has simple layout and rich content that is well organised. The best, most successful websites in the world (Yahoo, Microsoft, Amazon, eBay) don't employ fancy gimmicks; neither should you. Keep it simple. Maximise the content and minimise the presentation.

Structure your information well

When people come to your website, they want to find information quickly. They have come for a purpose and they are probably impatient and sceptical. It is therefore essential to make your website as accessible and easy to navigate as possible.

A well-structured website needs good links that allow the visitor to navigate to other sections of the site. Without these links, a page becomes a dead end.

Include important website sections and links

You should have at least some of the following sections on your website. Links to these sections should be provided in a set of essential links placed prominently on every page of the website.

Home page

The home page is the first page on your website and the most important, as it is usually the first page visitors see. From a linking point of view, the home page is referred to as 'Home'. It should always be the first link in your set of essential links. The home page itself should be full of punchy, attention-grabbing headings and summaries that quickly inform the visitor of, for example, what you do, what you have to sell, or what special offers you have. The Microsoft home page (**www.microsoft.com**) is a great example of using a home page well.

What's New

This section contains information on important news, events, and press releases. Always keep this section updated, and make sure that you date each entry. You should plan to add an entry for this section at least once a week, but remember to remove old items too.

About

This section should contain essential information about your business or organisation. If the section contains a lot of information it should be broken down into manageable subsections. 'About' information includes the following:

- mission: a short description of the organisation and what it seeks to achieve
- key strengths: key products, market position, manufacturing, skills, distribution
- company background
- management team: pictures and short biographies of key members of the management team
- financial information: annual results
- contact and location details: this should link to the Contact section on your website

Products

This is the core part of your website, containing the things you have to sell. It should contain a brief overview of products and services and links to detailed information on specific products or services, containing:

- product/services description
- product applications
- business case and ROI (return on investment): how using your product can make and/or save money
- specifications
- purchase and delivery details
- frequently asked questions (FAQs)
- pricing (be sure to specify currency)
- product reviews
- where you sell to (specify the countries or regions you do or do not sell to)

Purchase

This is an essential link if you have a facility that allows people to buy direct from your website. Ideally you should also create a small graphic to be displayed prominently, particularly on the home page, informing customers that they can purchase your products online.

Customers

People want to know who your customers are. Include a list of your key customers and a selection of quotes and case studies.

Partners

If you have a number of partners and joint ventures, you should have a section describing them, explaining how they allow you to deliver a better service.

Contact

This section should contain all your essential contact information including:

- e-mail address
- postal address and map of location
- telephone and fax numbers

Search

If your website has more than 50 pages, you need a search facility to enable visitors to find information. Aim to have a search box on every single page of your website, preferably near the top.

Offer an e-mail newsletter

Every website should offer an e-mail newsletter. If visitors give their e-mail address on their first visit, you can send them a regular weekly or monthly e-mail newsletter to tell them what's new.

Use metadata

Every web page should have a title. Where appropriate, you should create 'metadata' for your content. This is a method of describing your content and it should include: classification (type of information), page title and headings, summary, date of publication, author name, and keywords that appear in the text. Search engines use this metadata to index your website properly, so that visitors can find quickly what they are looking for.

Make sure you have proper footer information

The bottom of every page should have footer information containing:

- a list of the essential links for the website
- essential contact details: main address, telephone and fax numbers, e-mail address
- the copyright notice
- your privacy policy

Remember to promote your website

Promotional strategies include:

- registering with the major search engines (Alta Vista, Google, Yahoo), as well as search engines specific to your industry or sector
- making sure that your website and e-mail address are on all your promotional literature

Decide whether to do it yourself or get a design company

If you are a competent computer user, you may well be able to do most of the work yourself, using packages such as Microsoft FrontPage or Macromedia's Dreamweaver, but you may require a graphic designer to help you with design issues.

WHAT TO AVOID
Being too clever

Some sites try too hard to entertain without providing hard information. Animation, multimedia, video clips, and other tricks can obscure important data. Many visitors are deterred immediately by a home page that features animation.

Poor classification, navigation, and search

Good classification, navigation, and search are essential for a successful website. Customers expect easy access to the information they want. If they can't find it easily on your site, they will go somewhere else. Structure is critical because it helps people find their way around.

Content that is difficult to read

Many websites try to impress by using lots of colour, but the easiest text to read is black on a white background. Keep paragraphs, line lengths, and documents short.

RECOMMENDED LINKS

Builder.com, a detailed source of information on design:
www.builder.com
Webmonkey:
http://webmonkey.wired.com/ webmonkey

SEE ALSO

Computers, Information Technology, and E-commerce (p. 503)
Coping with Computer Viruses (p. 363)
Writing Well for the Web (p. 371)

Outsourcing Your Website

GETTING STARTED

As your business grows, you may need to upgrade your website to a larger and more sophisticated one. Running a large website is a complex operation that requires substantial IT architecture and support. This can take the focus of your business away from its core business of selling, marketing, and supporting your products and services. It will also tie up any technical staff on your team. Outsourcing involves hiring third party professionals to manage and run your website's operations for an ongoing fee.

When approaching outsourcing, remember to:

- develop a proper strategy; outsourcing needs a serious approach
- ensure that a comprehensive contract is in place, and that there are proper metrics and management structures
- make sure that you choose a robust, well-funded outsourcing vendor with a good track record for service and support

FAQS

What are the key factors that drive outsourcing?

- The need to focus on core business activities rather than on building up a large IT function.
- Lack of sufficiently skilled staff to run complex web operations.
- Flexibility: a quality outsource vendor can respond more quickly to rapid changes in customer demand.

MAKING IT HAPPEN

Develop an outsourcing strategy

When considering the outsourcing of Web functions, think about exactly why you want to outsource. Is it:

- to reduce costs?
- to give greater flexibility?
- because you can't find the right IT skills?
- to guarantee a more reliable service?
- to focus better on your core business?
- to keep your IT department as small as possible?
- to reduce staffing levels?

You should have a clear idea of your vision and objectives long before you start discussions with vendors.

Be prepared

Deciding on an outsourcer is a complex and time-consuming process, so you must think very carefully about what you want to achieve and why. When developing your strategy, it is best not to be too open with outsourcing vendors. They will naturally want to sell you what they have, and may try to shape your thinking in a way that is not appropriate. It is better initially to go to a quality independent consultant who will help you think through all the issues.

When you finally engage with your short-list of outsourcing vendors, they will have many detailed questions on how your operations are currently run. If you cannot answer these questions you will slow the whole process down, and will encourage the vendor to put forward a less fully and clearly defined contract than if it had had all the required information.

Choose a robust, well-funded outsourcer

Choose a company that has a good reputation, is well funded, and has a good track record. When choosing an outsourcing partner, ask the following questions:

- How stable and well funded is it?
- Has it got a satisfied customer base?
- Has it successfully dealt before with the same needs as mine?

Make certain that you receive the right service and support

The more you outsource, the more dependent you become on your outsourcer, so it is vital that your chosen vendor can be relied upon to deliver comprehensive service and support.

Remember that choosing an outsourcing vendor takes time

Outsourcing is a major strategic move involving much research and negotiation, so do not impose tight deadlines on yourself.

Ensure that a comprehensive contract is in place

An outsourcing contract should be precise, and should describe exactly what is to be delivered. It should state penalties for non-delivery. Legal expertise should be brought in early in the process, ideally when the RFP is being developed, so that everyone understands the legal implications of everything that is being asked for and promised. However, the IT environment is constantly changing, and the contract must recognise this. Quality contracts are designed to facilitate later change and renegotiation.

Avoid long-term contracts. Vendors will argue that, because they have to bear a high up-front cost, you should sign a five- to ten-year contract with them. This does not make sense in a rapidly changing IT and e-commerce world; a two-year contract is a more reasonable option.

Determine how this relationship will be managed and measured

You must develop a set of metrics to measure how the outsourcer is meeting the objectives set by the contract. By doing this regularly, and addressing issues as they arise, major disputes can be avoided.

Outsourcing is as much about managing the day-to-day relationship between you and the outsource vendor as it is about managing the technology. While a contract is important, prevention, by management that keeps a regular track of what is expected and what has been delivered, is better than cure.

Have a corporate technology strategy

You are outsourcing your technology, not your technology strategy, and will always need skilled in-house resources to help you plan your direction from a technological point of view. Your outsourcer cannot do this; if they do, their recommendations will reflect their own strategy rather than yours.

Remember that outsourcing is outsourcing

You can't have the same level of control over the day-to-day running of your IT infrastructure after you outsource it, but some businesses forget that and try to achieve such control. This is counterproductive. You chose your outsourcer because—you hope—they do the job better and more efficiently than you do.

Consider the security issues

Outsourcing creates an increased security risk. You must establish that the outsource vendor will adhere to your security policy, and that all work done integrates proper security procedures. Ask yourself:

- What is the outsourcer's security policy?
- What are its data back-up and disaster recovery procedures?
- How is your data safeguarded from its other customers?
- How is your data safeguarded from its own employees?
- How is it insured in relation to security breaches?

WHAT TO AVOID

Outsource vendors who promise too much

Outsource vendors have been known to over-promise and under-deliver.

Getting rid entirely of the internal IT web operation

Some internal IT resource is necessary to take a more strategic view of the web operation in order to plan its future evolution.

Going for the lowest price

Going for the lowest price rarely works out well in the long term. Service and support are critical elements in outsourcing, and the outsourcer that offers the lowest price is also, generally speaking, the one who will offer the least support.

Not being able to deliver the right information

To deliver an outsourcing service, the vendor requires very detailed information on your current IT and web setup. If you can't provide this information, you slow the whole process down, which results in imperfect solutions.

Badly framed contracts

Long-term contracts are too often developed on the basis of short-term financial goals, such as cost cutting. What invariably happens is that the contract is unsuitable and renegotiation is required.

RECOMMENDED LINKS

Business 2.0:
www.business2.com
Outsourcing Center:
www.outsourcing-center.com
Firmbuilder.com:
www.firmbuilder.com/home.asp

SEE ALSO

Computers, Information Technology, and E-commerce (p. 503)

Keeping on Top of E-mail

GETTING STARTED

E-mail is an incredibly powerful communications tool. Used properly, it is a boon for businesses of all sizes: it helps companies work more efficiently and to communicate more actively with customers. E-mail is fast and cost-effective but on the downside, it's often treated in an overly casual manner. Like every other business tool, the use of e-mail needs to be managed carefully and this seem overwhelming if you don't have that much experience of the online world. This actionlist sets out to give you some pointers, though, so bear in mind the following:

- Because e-mail is such an easy form of communication it is often misused, thus leading to e-mail overload.
- If your business has a website, it's important to create and monitor a policy for responding to e-mails so that you can keep on top of them all.
- Writing good e-mails is a skill that is too often absent in e-mail communication, but it can be learned.

MAKING IT HAPPEN

Manage e-mail overload

E-mail has revolutionised the way business is done today, but so many e-mails are sent that there is a danger that important messages may be swamped. An almost unimaginable number of e-mails are sent every year: it's estimated that 36 billion were sent every *day* in 2005. To prevent your business from succumbing to e-mail overload, you need to establish standards on how e-mail is sent and replied to. Training may well be required in order to make sure that you (and your staff, if you have any) understand and implement best practice in e-mail management.

Manage e-mails on a website

If you have a website, put your contact details on a prominent part of the site. E-mail is key part of these contact details, so give plenty of thought to this aspect. For example, think about how many e-mail addresses you'll need: will each department have its own special e-mail address, for example, sales@mycompany.com; support@mycompany.com? If you have staff to help you deal with e-mails, decide who e-mails should go to in the normal scheme of things and who can step in to help out if that person is on holiday or ill. If your company is large enough, you might want to think about whether managers should be

cc'd on all incoming e-mails. And how will e-mail communication be tracked in general?

Set some standards for how you and your team reply to external messages. Studies indicate that many businesses are unprofessional at responding to e-mail communications, and those that would never dream of leaving a phone to ring unanswered behave in a lackadaisical manner when it comes to replying to e-mail, so work out a time limit for replying to received messages, stick to it, and monitor it. You may also decide to have an automatic reply message for all your addresses; this will inform the sender that the e-mail has been received, and that a response will be given within X hours.

Write and reply to e-mails

When you're writing or replying to an e-mail, bear the following points in mind.

- Respond quickly, but only respond—or write in the first place—when you have something worthwhile to say. If you can't answer someone's question straightaway, send a short acknowledgment message that explains the situation and when you think you'll be able to reply fully.
- Make sure the subject line is appropriate and reflects the content of your message. Even if you know the person you're writing to well, avoid using 'Hello' as the subject

line in a *business* e-mail. It really grates with some people and they may not read your message at all.

- If you are replying to an e-mail, change the subject line as appropriate.
- Although the writing style for e-mails is—in general—casual, it should not be over-casual. Don't try to be too friendly. Always strive to be polite. It is good manners to address the person you are communicating with, and to sign/type your name at the end.
- Remember why you're writing to the other person—on a work-related matter—and match your tone accordingly. Obviously it's good to be friendly, especially with people you work with often, but don't let things slip and always, always be polite. It is good manners to address the person you are communicating with, and to sign/type your name at the end.
- Check your spelling; e-mails that are filled with spelling or grammatical errors won't show you in your best light. The popularity of text messages and text message speak is beginning to creep over into e-mail. While most people will understand what you mean if you send them a message along the lines of 'C U at 10' or 'mtg off', it's best not to include this type of abbreviation in messages to external clients or contacts. Use full correct spelling, even if this takes a little longer.
- Take care not to write e-mails in capital letters. This is viewed as online 'shouting' and can really annoy people.
- Some e-mail packages allow you to highlight the level of priority, but if you do use this facility, don't abuse it. It's easy to mark every e-mail as urgent or as highly important in the hope that it'll receive attention, but if you do it too often, it'll have a 'crying wolf' effect: people will start to disregard messages that you mark as urgent, even if one of them actually is. Use the facility carefully (and honestly) and you'll get the results you need.
- Keep e-mails short. Get to the point. Long e-mails put people off.
- In longer e-mails, bullet-pointed or numbered lists can help break up the text.

- Don't bombard contacts with attachments unless they're essential.
- Even if someone has been rude to you in their message, never reply to them while you're angry. Count to at least 10 before replying and even better, go and do something else for a while and then come back to the message. Take time to check that you've actually read the message properly; if you're very busy or under a lot of pressure, you may have overlooked a key word or phrase which changes the whole tone of the message. Write a dignified reply and save it as a draft, leave it for a few minutes and then read it again before you send it. Remember, even though e-mail is a very fast form of communication, it's still a rather distant one and it is very easy for misunderstandings to occur.
- Be careful what you write. Don't write anything in an e-mail that you can't defend in a court of law.
- Never, ever send spam e-mails. If you have a mailing list of customers or clients, say, and you'd like to contact them all about a new service or product you're offering, you may *only* do this if they have agreed to accept this type of e-mail from you.

Practise good housekeeping

Set aside some time to regularly prune your inbox of e-mails that you don't need to keep. E-mails can take up a lot of space on your computer system, especially if they come with large attachments, so look through them every day and delete those that you no longer need. Attachments can be saved elsewhere on your computer so that you still have the information they contain somewhere. Certain e-mail packages give you the option of automatically clearing your 'deleted items' folder every time you close down, a good way of making sure that messages aren't building up there too.

WHAT TO AVOID
You let your standards drop

E-mail is an instant medium, so it's easy to create a message quickly without considering the impact on the recipient. Although abbreviations, acronyms, minimal punctuation, and unchecked spelling save time in the short term, poor standards can damage a company's reputation.

Your messages are hard to read

E-mails are normally read on a computer screen, so any information must be concise and clearly laid out. Use upper and lower case letters and a legible typeface for clarity and avoid using capital letters too much. If you have a long message, guide the recipient by using headings for different topics.

SEE ALSO
Computers, Information Technology, and E-commerce (p. 503)
Coping with Computer Viruses (p. 363)
Using E-mail Marketing Effectively (p. 374)

Coping with Computer Viruses

GETTING STARTED

Computer viruses are a growing threat on the Internet, and if your business operates online they are something you need to bear in mind as they cost companies billions of pounds globally every year. This is genuinely a massive global problem: in January 2005, it was estimated that 15% of all e-mails sent were virus messages. In addition, it is now possible to get a computer virus by visiting a website or simply by opening an e-mail. To combat computer viruses:

- ensure that you have the very latest antivirus software and that you scan your entire computer regularly
- ensure that you have the very latest software security patches for your computer
- immediately delete e-mails that you are in any way suspicious of
- don't download anything from the Internet except from reputable websites
- back up your data regularly

MAKING IT HAPPEN
Understand computer viruses, Trojan horses, and worms

In its simplest form, a computer virus attaches itself to computer files, and then seeks to replicate itself. Viruses can infect all sorts of files, from program and system files to Word documents and HTML files. The Internet enables viruses to spread with extraordinary speed.

What is known as a 'Trojan horse' pretends to serve a useful function, such as a screen saver. However, as soon as it is run, it carries out its true purpose, which can be anything from using the computer as a host to infect other computers, to wiping the entire hard disk of the computer. Never download software over the Internet unless you are sure of its authenticity.

A computer worm does not try to damage the files it infects. Its objective is rather to replicate itself as quickly and as often as possible. Computer worms are a major drain on the Internet because they clog up bandwidth.

Remember that prevention is much better than cure

Viruses can be extremely difficult to get rid of. You may think you have cleaned them out with your antivirus software, but they may well have inserted hidden code in your operating system that is almost impossible to detect. It is, therefore, essential to stop viruses from getting into your computer in the first place. You do this by:

- making sure that you have the very latest antivirus software; popular antivirus software types include McAfee and Norton
- joining an e-mail list that will inform you of new virus attacks. As soon as you hear of them, check your vendor for the latest updates.
- scanning your entire computer for viruses at least once a week
- always making sure that you have the very latest security patches for your computer software. Viruses are always at their most potent in the first hours and days after their release, so it is vital to implement software patches as soon as they become available.
- if you use recent releases of Microsoft Windows, make sure you regularly check www.microsoft.com/security for news and updates. Microsoft also has a service that will check your computer for security weaknesses. The link can be found at: www.microsoft.com/technet/mpsa/start.asp
- only downloading software from reputable websites
- deleting e-mails you are in any way suspicious of

Act immediately if you become infected

Deal with the threat immediately. Never wait, as the longer the virus is on your computer the more files it can infect. Some viruses open up your computer system to potential hacking. There is no guaranteed way to know that your system does not contain some malicious code that will be used at a future date, even when the offending virus has been deleted. If a virus of this type has indeed infected your system, and if you want to be absolutely safe, reformat your hard disk and reinstall all your software.

Cope with virus hoaxes

The Internet is full of virus hoaxes that waste time. If you get an e-mail about a new virus, go to the website of your antivirus software provider, and check if the warning is real. In order to judge whether it's a hoax, ask yourself the following questions:

- does the message come from a reputable source?
- does it ask you to e-mail it on to anyone you know? If it does, it's probably a hoax.
- does it have a reputable link for more information?

Whatever you do, don't start forwarding on e-mails about viruses before you've found out whether they're real or not. In most cases, e-mails of this type are hoaxes, but you're likely to cause panic among your regular correspondents, especially those who aren't particularly experienced with the online world.

RECOMMENDED LINKS

McAfee antivirus software:
www.mcafee.com
Norton antivirus software:
www.norton.com

SEE ALSO

Understanding the Key Principles of Internet Marketing

GETTING STARTED

If you work online, you need to think about Internet marketing and what it can do for your business. Internet marketing is about giving, rather than getting, attention. An adjunct to traditional marketing, it supports and enhances the overall marketing message by providing comprehensive information that answers consumers' questions about a particular product or service. Internet marketing also exploits the networking capabilities of the Web by leveraging online community activities, linking, affiliate marketing, viral marketing, e-mail marketing, and loyalty programmes. When approaching Internet marketing, keep the following in mind:

- when visitors come to a website they are already aware of the brand. They want information.
- use Internet technology to understand the needs of your customers, so that you can offer them just the right information and products.
- remember that the Internet empowers the consumer. A dissatisfied consumer can use the networking capabilities of the Internet to undermine your brand.

FAQS

What sort of products and services is Internet marketing best suited to?

Internet marketing is best suited to:

- products and services that require a lot of information to sell. For example, travel and books are ideal for the Internet. Travel is a very information-intensive product. People want times, prices, and information about the destination. When buying books, they are strongly influenced by reviews, opinions of other readers, tables of contents, and sample chapters.
- products and services that people feel strongly about, such as books, music, and films. Fans network with other fans in online communities to discuss their favourite artists. Much of the huge success of *The Blair Witch Project* was credited to fans getting together on the Internet and promoting it through enthusiastic reviews and dialogue.
- products and services that are bought by the Internet demographic. Although the Internet demographic has broadened, it is still generally the domain of the well educated and better off. Those working in technology and academia are very well represented.

What about online advertising? Does it work?

As a pure branding tool, online advertising does not have the same impact as television or glossy media, because of bandwidth restrictions. Studies indicate that most consumers avoid interactive ads because they simply take too much time to download.

However, the real power of online advertising is not from a mass marketing point of view but, rather, its ability to reach niche markets and target just the right consumer with just the right product. Advertising success is claimed by opt-in e-mail-based marketing, where consumers request information on a particular product or service. In online advertising, the scattershot approach is out and laser point focus is in.

MAKING IT HAPPEN
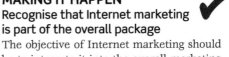
Recognise that Internet marketing is part of the overall package

The objective of Internet marketing should be to integrate it into the overall marketing strategy, where it supports and is supported by offline marketing activities. However, that is not to say Internet marketing doesn't have its own unique characteristics. Internet marketing is not about a big idea, some compelling graphics, and a killer catch-phrase. Offline marketing brings consumers to the website with such approaches. Their interest has been aroused. They have questions. Internet marketing answers those questions by having comprehensive information on offer. Remember, if people have read the brochure offline, they're not coming to the website to read it again.

Understand the consumer better

Effective Internet marketing focuses on getting to know the consumer better. The objective here is to understand consumers' exact needs so that exactly the right products and services can be offered to them at exactly the right time and in exactly the right way. The strength of the Internet is also its weakness, though. While people want information, they also suffer from massive information overload. The Internet marketer who can cut through the overload and bring to time-starved consumers the information they need is much more likely to succeed. Find websites and e-mail databases that attract the exact type of consumer you wish to target. Analyse statistics generated as a result of consumers visiting your website and react appropriately to key trends that these statistics throw up. With more sophisticated websites, you can customise consumers' experiences through personalisation systems, whereby a unique and finely targeted set of information and products is presented to each individual visitor.

Back it up with e-mail marketing

Since the Web was launched, perceptive marketers have been stressing that every website should have an e-mail marketing strategy. Consider that consumers must actively decide to go to a website, but with e-mail they join a database in which they can be regularly informed of products, services, and offers that the organisation has. The key to e-mail marketing success is getting people who want the information to join a database in which they will receive regular e-mail alerts and newsletters. Of course, the information they receive needs to be of a type and quality that they signed up to get.

Tap into the networking ability of the Internet

The Internet is a community and it offers a tremendously powerful means for people and organisations to network. Linking is one of the simplest yet most effective Internet marketing devices there is. It underpins affiliate marketing efforts by websites such as Amazon.com. Linking is like embedded word of mouth. If another website links to you, it is essentially recommending you to its own visitors. Viral marketing is a network effect, whereby groups of consumers create a buzz about a product or service by e-mailing friends and/or creating their own websites. Consumers gain a power through Internet networking that they traditionally did not have. There are hundreds if not thousands of websites and activist groups set up by disgruntled consumers with the sole objective of attacking particular organisations.

Make advertising and promotion highly focused

A website, because it is not a physical store, faces a constant challenge to achieve and maintain awareness among its target market. Traditional offline marketing, such as press advertising or direct mail, plays a key role here, but so too do specific online marketing strategies. Registration with a commercial search engine is an obvious one. This is not some simple, one-off task but an ongoing activity because the rules by which search engines classify sites are constantly changing. Banner ads can be effective, if properly targeted. Banner ad design needs to apply the unique characteristics of the medium, and not simply apply traditional advertising principles. A specialist agency can advise on suitable creative approaches. Getting other websites to link can be very effective, but this is a slow process, the rewards of which are delivered over time. E-mail signature files can promote a website effectively.

Remember that affiliate marketing and loyalty programmes can deliver

There is no better example of the success of affiliate marketing than Amazon. com. Literally hundreds of thousands of websites offer books and other products to their visitors using Amazon's affiliate programme. It's a win-win situation. The website in question offers an extra service that is easy to establish and delivers a certain amount of revenue. The affiliate sponsor opens up a new channel every time another website hooks into them. However, like all marketing techniques, it's not some magic formula. It needs to be thought through properly and applied professionally.

Loyalty programmes can work on the Internet, though they have been over-hyped. Key elements in the management of loyalty programmes are the use of customer databases and the tracking of customer purchasing behaviour. The Internet facilitates such activities, and can thus be a medium through which loyalty programmes can be run. Getting the incentive structure right is critical to the success of loyalty programmes.

Use online communities to build loyalty

Using chat, discussion boards, and e-mail mailing lists to bring people together to discuss issues of interest can enhance brand loyalty. It can also be a source of unique and cost-effective content. However, it doesn't work in all situations, and online communities that are not properly managed can quickly lose momentum.

Remember that some old marketing tricks still apply

Discounts, competitions, and free offers work as well online as they do offline. While perhaps too much has been offered free on the Internet in order to build business, properly used, these traditional marketing techniques can be effective on websites.

WHAT TO AVOID
Being flashy

Although the Internet has been around since 1996, it is amazing how many market-

ers still think it's TV on a computer screen. On the Web, visitors don't really care about the graphics; they just want the information. Splash screens, audio, video and Macromedia Flash animations should be kept to an absolute minimum.

Not building and leveraging a customer database

Bringing people to a website without strongly encouraging them to join some sort of a database is a serious mistake. Studies indicate that many consumers will visit a website once, rarely if ever to return. It's vital to get them into a database so that ongoing communication can be set up.

Focusing on volume of visitors rather than quality targeting

In the early years of the Web there was a frantic rush to build visitor traffic to a website, without any real focus on issues such as revenue per visitor, numbers who joined databases. Acquisition costs for visitors were high, and as the large number of visitors did not translate into valuable customers, the business model soon collapsed for many websites.

Focusing purely on purchase activity on a website

There is a need to understand how a website contributes to the overall purchasing process. For example, a great many people visit car websites before they make a purchase, but very few will actually make the purchase online. The key is to forget about measuring by crude visitor volume numbers and focus on the quality of the targeting, along with the influence that the website and e-mail communications have on purchase behaviour.

RECOMMENDED LINKS

Adventive e-mail mailing lists:
www.adventive.com
Web marketing information centre:
www.wilsonweb.com/webmarket

Promoting Your Website Effectively

GETTING STARTED

Launching a website is like opening up a shop at the North Pole or in the Sahara Desert. Nobody will know that you are there unless you promote yourself! Website promotion is not some one-off event that occurs at launch. It is an ongoing activity that demands a keen understanding of promotional techniques that are unique to the Web. It also requires full integration into offline marketing and promotional activities. When approaching website promotion, consider the following:

- it requires a range of promotional strategies, both online and offline
- it's an ongoing activity
- it should be fully integrated into the overall promotional and marketing strategy

FAQS

Why is website promotion of such importance?

In the property business people talk about 'location, location, location'. Well, a website doesn't really have a location. It's not on a high street where thousands of people walk by every day. Without such physical visibility, a website has a major problem attracting consumers. That is one reason why a clicks-and-mortar strategy (combining physical stores with an Internet presence) is deemed so essential for the success of a website. In a physical store, and in its related marketing and promotional activity, consumers can be exposed to the benefits of the website constantly.

What is banner advertising and does it promote a website well?

Banner advertising is the use of rectangular advertisements or logos across the width of page on an Internet site. Businesses often place advertisements of this type on a third party's site to attract users to visit their own.

The jury is still out on the effectiveness of banner advertising. However, prices for banner advertising have dropped significantly in recent years and there is certainly value to be had. It's really down to the target market you are after and whether that accurately matches the profile of visitors coming to a particular website. Online advertising systems allow for a level of targeting and measurement that is impossible in much offline media. So, if you can get to

the right target market at the right price, then the equation makes sense.

Does online advertising and promotion have to cost a lot of money?

No. Online ads have dropped significantly in price and, with proper investigation, very good value can be had. Online promotion requires dedication, but a few hours spent every week can deliver real results in the longer term.

MAKING IT HAPPEN
Get linked

Linking is one of the most powerful means of promoting a website. A link from another website is essentially embedded word of mouth, a recommendation from that site to its visitors also to visit you. The Web is huge, with millions of websites, many of them of poor quality. People who use the Internet have become very sceptical and conservative in their behaviour. Building credibility is thus of key importance to online success. There is no better way to build such credibility than to have hundreds—ideally thousands—of other websites linking to you.

Google, perhaps the Web's most popular search engine, achieved popularity because its search results were seen as more relevant than those of other search engines. The way it achieved better results was by analysing a website and seeing how many external websites had linked to it. The more links the website had, the higher in the results Google placed it. Thus, if you want your website to feature prominently with Google, the more links you can get the better.

But linking is not simply about getting placed higher in search engine results. Think of each link as another 'road' to your website; another way that the visitor can get to you. Getting links is not easy. It involves finding websites that attract your target market and convincing them to include a link to you. Usually, they will not do this unless you have valuable content that could be of interest to their customers. Another approach is to pay for a link, either through monthly fees or through what is called 'click-through payments'—you pay for every visit that results from a particular link.

Get registered with search engines

Because so many people use commercial search engines, it's extremely important that your website is properly registered. Keep the following in mind:

- there are hundreds of search engines and directories but only a handful that really matter. These include: Yahoo, Google, Alta Vista, Microsoft Network, Excite, Lycos and Ask Jeeves.
- there may well be specialist search engines and directories for your particular industry. You should register with them.
- all search engines used to be free to register with, but this is no longer the case for an increasing number. You need to consider if the fee is worth it.
- an increasing number of search engines sell special placements in their search results. You can choose a keyword and when that keyword is input by a searcher, a short, informative promotion for your website will appear.
- search engines need to be monitored regularly, as they can change the rules by which search results are presented. A set of keywords needs to be drawn up and the search engine regularly searched using these keywords. If you find your website is dropping down the results page, you may need to re-register. Also, if you launch a new product or service, you should consider registering that.
- don't register popular keywords with a

website just for the sake of increased visitors. It achieves very little, and some search engines will remove websites that continuously abuse search registration processes.

Use banner and other online advertising

As stated above, banner advertising doesn't work for everyone, but it may work for your business. It's particularly useful where a new website, product, or service is being launched. Banner ads can be paid for either on a cost-per-thousand (CPM) basis or per click-through, where the seller gets paid wherever a visitors clicks on an ad. Online ads should be a call to action, with the key objective being to get the person to click on the ad. There are a variety of online advertising options:

- banner advertisements. These ads can go across the top or bottom of the page or down the side, like wallpaper.
- interstitials. These are ads that appear before the actual web page loads. They certainly get the visitors' attention but can be very frustrating.
- pop-under ads. These ads launch in a separate browser window and have been controversial.

Consider e-mail as a form of advertising

E-mail can be a very effective form of advertising, particularly when the advertiser is reaching a targeted list that has opted in to receive information on particular products or services. The thing to watch out for in e-mail advertising is spam. Spam is mass-distributed e-mail that is unsolicited by the receiver. People are increasingly annoyed at receiving spam, and anti-spam legislation has been enacted or is pending in many countries. It's not simply about whether spam is legal or not—but it is certainly unethical, and no reputable organisation should use such an approach.

Remember e-mail signature files

An e-mail signature is the text at the bottom of an e-mail that contains information about the sender. It is also possible to place a short, two-line ad there (e-mail signatures should not be longer than five lines). E-mail signature promotion was used very effectively when Andersen Consulting changed its name to Accenture. For a period after the name change, every time one of Accenture's 60,000 employees sent an e-mail, there was a short e-mail signature ad notifying the receiver of the change of name.

Integrate with offline marketing and promotion

Every single piece of offline literature should contain the website address and, where appropriate, an e-mail address. This includes: all stationery (letterheads, business cards, compliment slips, receipts, invoices); all product packaging; training and support manuals; all ads that are placed in print, radio, or television. If the organisation has physical stores, then promotional material should be placed prominently within these stores informing visitors of the website. When planning new offline promotional and marketing activities, you should seek ways to get consumers to go to the website. For example, the website could be the place where the consumer enters a competition.

Include competitions and free giveaways

Consumers are as likely to react positively to quality web-based competitions and special promotions as they do to such tactics in the offline world. Competitions and special offers give the website a sense of vibrancy. A key objective of such promotions should be to get consumers to join databases, used in the future to inform people of other special offers and relevant information.

Use your home page

A key objective of a home page is to promote important content, products, and services situated deeper in the website. That's the job of sharp, punchy headings and summaries, supported on occasion by small graphics. The Microsoft website (**www.microsoft. com**) is a perfect example of how to use a home page to promote key events, special offers, product launches, upgrades, and so on.

WHAT TO AVOID
Seeking quantity of visitors over quality

In the early days of the Web there was a mad rush—fuelled by venture capital—to drive as many visitors as possible to websites. A stream of new brands emerged, each one seeking to out-do the next with ad spend. There is still a tendency to consider quantity over quality when it comes to building visitor numbers to a website. This is a serious and expensive mistake.

Focusing purely on search engines

Search engines are important, but they should still be only a part of an online promotional strategy. Also, abuse of search engines by bombarding them with popular keywords and other visitor-generating techniques merely serves to bulk up visitor figures. It does little or nothing for your business's bottom line.

Lack of integration with offline marketing

Organisations miss vital and cost-effective ways of promoting their websites by not fully utilising offline resources.

Lack of ongoing commitment

Too many websites have been launched enthusiastically, only to be left to wither in the wilderness of cyberspace. To be successful, promotion must be an ongoing activity.

RECOMMENDED LINK
Google:
www.google.com

SEE ALSO
Applying a Viral Marketing Approach on the Internet (p. 377)
Computers, Information Technology, and E-commerce (p. 503)
Delivering the Benefits of Affiliate Marketing on the Web (p. 379)
Understanding the Key Principles of Internet Marketing (p. 365)
Using E-mail Marketing Effectively (p. 374)

Writing Well for the Web

GETTING STARTED

People read online material differently than they do standard printed material, and you need to bear this in mind when you're putting together content that will appear online. Surprisingly, very few websites take the time to lay out their content in a way that will maximise its readability. Don't forget that it is more difficult to read on a screen than from paper so you must write and lay out your content in a more simple, straightforward manner than you would in print. If you want to make sure that your content has the best chance of being read, focus on:

- shorter sentences, shorter paragraphs and shorter documents
- plentiful use of short, punchy, and descriptive headings and summaries
- larger font sizes and sans serif fonts, because they are easier to read
- straightforward, factual prose

FAQS

In what way do people read differently on the Web?

Rather than reading every sentence fully, when people read online they scan, moving quickly across text, always looking in a hurry for the content they need. They are very fact-oriented. People don't read on the Web for pleasure—they read to do business, to be educated, to find out something—so they like to read content that gets to the point quickly.

People like reading short documents with links to more detailed information as appropriate. If a document is long, and people really have no choice but to read it, a significant number of them will print it out. In general, however, long documents tend to go unread.

Why do so many people regard web content as poor quality?

People don't trust the content they read on the Web because they come across so many websites with poor publishing standards. The Web gives everyone access to the tools of publishing, but giving someone a word processor does not make them a good writer.

Too many websites lack proper editing standards. They also translate documents that were prepared for print directly to the Web; this may save money in the short term, but if people don't read the content, it is pointless. Some websites deliberately try to

mislead people with their content. All this gives a poor impression to people who use the Web.

Is writing for the Web a difficult skill to learn?

It is not easy to learn how to write well, no matter what the medium is. However, writing for the Web is about concentrating on the facts. You don't need flowery prose; instead, you must be able to communicate the really important information in as few words as possible. This is not an easy thing to do, but with practice most people can master the basics.

MAKING IT HAPPEN

Recognise that if you're not read, you're dead

The connection between writing and reading is one that is not always considered: a surprising number of organisations create vast quantities of content without asking some obvious questions:

- Is anyone interested in reading this content?
- Is it written in a way that is understandable and easy to read?
- How are we going to let people know that we have just published this content?

Realise that less really is more

Writing is rarely about quantity, but it should always be about quality. It is easier to write 5,000 words of waffle than 500 words that are succinct, but 500 words is exactly what is needed on the Web; less is definitely more.

Editing is essential

One of the primary functions of editing is to get a long draft into shape. As George Orwell said: 'If it is possible to cut a word, always cut it'. We all have pet phrases that we love to put into sentences whenever we can. They may sound good to the writer, but very often add nothing to the meaning of what is being communicated. The Web is about functional writing; get to the point as quickly as you can and then stop.

Keep it short

When writing for the Web:

- documents should rarely be longer than 1,000 words: 500 to 700 is a good length to aim for
- paragraphs should be between 40 and 50 words
- try not to let your sentences go over 20 words

Write for the reader, not your ego

Always keep your audience in mind when you're writing. Are you writing for a sales rep, a technician, support staff, customers, or investors? Will they understand what you are writing about? Don't write to please yourself—write to please your reader and be clear and precise.

Focus on the headings

Headings are important on the Web for two central reasons. First, because people scan online, the first thing they often do is to look for headings; if the heading doesn't attract their attention, then they probably won't read any further. Second, people use search engines a lot, and the most prominent things in a page of search results are the headings. The heading really has to sell the web page and convince the person to click for more information.

Writing headings well is an art, but here are a few rules that will help you get the basics right:

- keep them short. A heading should not be longer than five to eight words.
- make your point clear. For example, 'Nasdaq crashes to record low' is more informative than 'Apocalypse Now for investors!'.
- use strong, direct language. Don't be sensational, but at the same time don't be vague, and don't hedge.
- don't deceive the reader, for example by using 'Microsoft' in a heading just because you think people will then be more likely to read it. Remember, the job of the heading is to tell the reader succinctly what is in the document.

Use subheadings

In longer documents it is always a good idea to use subheadings, as they break up the text into the more readable chunks that online readers like. Use subheadings every five to seven paragraphs.

Summarise the who, what, where and when

Next to the heading, the summary is the most important piece of text. It should be descriptive, not wandering or indirect. Tell the reader what the document is about, and who, where and when the information relates to.

Get down to write

'No man but a blockhead ever wrote. . .except for money', according to Samuel Johnson. Sound advice. Writing is not easy but someone has to do it. The first rule of writing is reading: if you are asked to write a technical paper, read how other people write them. Read how they are written on your own website, on competitors' websites, in industry journals. Find a style that works well and copy it; use its techniques and approach to structure. Whatever you do, don't plagiarise and put your own name on someone else's words, but never feel ashamed of finding good-quality writing and learning from it.

Learn how to edit

Even if you have an editor, you still want to send him or her a well-written draft. Here are a few steps to follow.

- Get a first draft written and save it.
- Leave it for a while—have a cup of tea—then print it out, or make the font size larger so that the text stands out more.
- Read it as if someone else wrote it. Be severe. Is it written in a way that the reader can easily understand? What is the writer trying to say here? Is this sentence or paragraph necessary? Has the writer covered all the essential facts?
- First drafts are often too long. When preparing the second draft, cut ruthlessly, maybe by as much as half.
- Use your word count carefully. When you are asked to write something, always ask how many words are required. If you are not given a word count then decide on one yourself. Keep it as low as possible.

Explore collaborative writing

Computers and the Internet make collaborative writing far easier, and as a result it is becoming an increasingly popular approach to writing content. Collaborative writing works well if:

- the writers spend time working through the objectives of the writing exercise, and reach agreement on such necessary matters as the style, tone, and length of the piece
- there is a lot of content to be written that can benefit from the input of multiple disciplines
- people can be given defined segments of content to write, and/or the different skills of different people can be used, for example when one person understands the subject well, while another is a good writer
- there are professional processes in place to facilitate collaboration
- the writers know and respect each other

WHAT TO AVOID
Not focusing on the needs of the reader
A surprising number of websites fail to think about who their reader is, simply adding content for its own sake. If you ignore the needs of your reader, then your reader will ignore you.

Putting non-web formats onto the Web
Translating a 40-page Word document into HTML is a simple task; persuading someone to read it is another job entirely. Have you ever tried reading an Adobe PDF file on a screen? It's a painful experience. How many of your customers have read that Power-Point presentation you translated into HTML?

Putting every piece of content you can find on the Web
The Web is not a dumping ground for content. You might have 50,000 documents, with only 5,000 suitable for your website. Publishing the other 45,000 simply wastes your readers' time—not something you want to do.

Poor editing
It is almost impossible to create quality content without sending it through a professional editorial process. No matter how good the writer, his or her content will always benefit by being checked over by an editor.

Long, rambling documents
If, after reading the heading and summary, the average web reader hasn't understood what exactly you are trying to communicate to them, then chances are they will click the Back button. Readers on the web have become ruthless about their time.

RECOMMENDED LINK
Clickz Writing for the Web:
www.clickz.com

SEE ALSO
Computers, Information Technology, and E-commerce (p. 503)
Setting Up a Basic Website (p. 354)

Using E-mail Marketing Effectively

GETTING STARTED

E-mail should be an essential part of any Internet marketing strategy. If you have someone's e-mail address, you can send them information directly. It's absolutely *crucial*, though, that the recipient has agreed to receive the information you want to send. Remember that:

- e-mail is a relatively cheap, but powerful communications tool—you can send thousands of e-mail newsletters in a simple, cost-effective way
- e-mail allows you to keep in regular contact with customers and to build up a rapport with them
- never send unsolicited e-mails (spam). E-mail should only deliver worthwhile information.

FAQS

How often should you contact customers by e-mail?

E-mail is a fast, simple, and cost-effective form of communication, so it is tempting to use it at every opportunity. Unless the information you send is valuable, though, you run the risk of annoying your customers and turning them off—exactly the opposite of what you're aiming for.

Should newsletters be free or chargeable?

It depends on the focus of your business. If you are publishing information, then it is hard to see how a business model can be developed that is advertising only. However, if you are using the information you send to help sell some other product or service, it is highly unlikely that anyone will be willing to pay for it.

What is spam?

Spam is mass-distributed, unsolicited e-mail. Spam is a major problem on the Internet today in that it is easy to buy a database of millions of e-mail addresses and send out unsolicited e-mails to them. If you want to be seen as a reputable business, you should avoid sending spam. Legislation is pending in a number of countries to make sending spam illegal.

What do the terms 'opt-in' and 'double opt-in' mean?

An opt-in approach is where someone actively decides to give you their e-mail address so that you can send them e-mail. However, the emerging convention is double opt-in. What happens here is that when a person receives a request to subscribe to an e-mail address, they reply to that address for verification that the request did in fact come from there. This ensures that the e-mail address was not maliciously set up by a third party.

Is it better to buy software or can it be rented?

Very often it is better to rent. There are a number of organisations that offer professional e-mail management services. To get a list of such companies, go to **http://directory.google.com/Top/Computers/Internet/E-mail/Mailing_Lists/Hosted_Services**.

MAKING IT HAPPEN

Isolate the information need

The first step in any e-mail strategy is to isolate the information need of your target market. What sort of information would they find useful? Would they like information on new products and special offers? Would they like information on trends within your industry? What sort of information would make them want to give you their e-mail address?

Define your publication scope and schedule

Once you have defined an information need, you must make clear what the scope of your e-mail publication is. What exactly will the person get if they subscribe? Unless you are delivering very time-sensitive information, a weekly publication is usually sufficient.

Make the subscription process prominent on your website

Getting people to subscribe is vital to the success of your e-mail strategy. There should therefore be a prominent subscription box on your website encouraging people to subscribe. Also, include subscription details in every mailing that you send out. Don't ask too many questions in the subscription process.

Many successful e-mail newsletter providers only ask for the e-mail address of the subscriber. That makes it a very easy and quick process for the potential subscriber. You can always ask for more information later on, when you have established a stronger relationship with the subscriber. As a rule, the more valuable the information is to the potential subscriber, the more information you can ask of them.

Make the unsubscription process as easy as possible

It is equally important to ensure that the unsubscription process is easy to use. People can get frustrated and angry if they find it difficult to unsubscribe from a service, and some might think you have started spamming them.

If you're offering a paid-for subscription service, offer a free 'teaser' subscription

If you plan to offer a commercial service where you charge people to subscribe, then it is a good idea to offer a free e-mail that contains brief summaries of what is included in the commercial offering. It may also be an idea to offer a free trial period, so that the subscriber can get an understanding of what you have to offer.

Decide whether you want a plain text or HTML version of your e-mail

There are two basic options for the format

you can use when delivering an e-mail to your subscriber base: plain text and HTML. Plain text is just like a normal e-mail, and is the simplest and easiest to produce. HTML is like sending a web page in an e-mail. It will deliver a lot more impact and colour, but it is more expensive to produce, and a number of older e-mail systems find it hard to read HTML. If you do decide to use an HTML e-mail approach, it's a good idea to offer a plain text version as well or a significant number of people may be unable to subscribe to your service.

For plain text e-mail layout keep the line length of text between 65 and 70 characters to avoid breaking lines, which make the layout look very ugly, and keep paragraphs nice and short—five to six lines is optimum. Use capitals for headings. Because plain text e-mails do not allow the use of bold or font sizing, capitalising is the only way to give emphasis. Use a non-proportional font such as Courier, because it remains constant regardless of the e-mail package being used.

Keep the e-mail short and punchy

Think of what you are doing as delivering a publication. You're trying to get people to read something that will make them want to act—to buy your product or use your service, for example. The scarcest commodity today is people's time. Nobody will read an e-mail that goes on and on, so focus on having punchy headings and short summaries. Avoid having articles that are longer than 500–600 words. The entire e-mail should not contain more than 1,500 words, unless you have a dedicated audience that you know is willing to read longer pieces. So keep things short, and always have some sort of call to action.

Have a strong subject line

The subject line is what subscribers see first when they download their e-mail. Because people are so busy they often scan the subject line and, if it's not interesting, delete the e-mail. However, if you are sending out a regular publication you may wish to include the title of the publication and date in the subject line. In the body of the e-mail itself, it's helpful to have a table of contents near the top that lets the reader know what to expect from the rest of the e-mail.

Use hypertext and e-mail addresses

It's a good idea to use a hypertext to link back to your website, in order to encourage the subscriber to get more information, purchase your product, and so on. However, when writing out a hyperlink (URL) always use the full URL. For example, don't use 'www.mycompany.com'; instead, use 'http://www.mycompany.com'. The reason is that some older e-mail packages will not automatically turn the URL into a link unless you include the full URL. Also, if you have a URL that is more than 65 characters long, put it in angle brackets (< >). Otherwise, a number of e-mail packages will break the URL onto two lines and make it unusable. If you are including an e-mail address, put in a 'mailto:' before the e-mail address, as this will turn it into a link to the subscriber's e-mail package. For example: 'mailto:tom@ mycompany.com'.

Include the essential things every e-mail mailing should have

Every e-mail you send out should contain the subject line (title) and date, subscription and unsubscription information, copyright and privacy policies (or links to these on the website), e-mail contact details (telephone and address may also be included), links back to the website, and brief information on the publication schedule and scope.

WHAT TO AVOID
Using a 'bait and switch' approach
Be very clear to the potential subscriber about what exactly they are subscribing to. If you specialise in special offers, e-mail and tell them so. Don't pretend that you're going to send valuable updates on a particular industry, and then just send special offers.

Not meeting a real information need

Ask yourself the question: why would anyone want to read this? Too many e-mail mailings are full of useless, repetitive, or out-of-date information.

Not keeping to a publication schedule

If you say you will deliver an e-mail every Wednesday, do it. Being late risks losing credibility and subscribers.

Not managing the subscription and unsubscription process professionally

Make it difficult for someone to subscribe and they just won't bother. By the same token, if you make it difficult for people to unsubscribe they'll become irate, and with good reason.

Spamming people

Never subscribe people against their will or without them knowing. Sending unsolicited e-mail is a 'get rich quick' strategy. It will damage your long-term reputation.

RECOMMENDED LINK
Clickz e-mail marketing section:
www.clickz.com/em_mkt

SEE ALSO
Applying a Viral Marketing Approach on the Internet (p. 377)
Computers, Information Technology, and E-commerce (p. 503)
Promoting Your Website Effectively (p. 368)

Applying a Viral Marketing Approach on the Internet

GETTING STARTED

Viral marketing is really another name for word of mouth on the Internet environment. Viral marketing can work in mysterious ways, but what is clear is that the Internet is a medium that offers significant potential for such strategy. Yahoo and Google did little or no advertising in their early years—people told other people they were great resources. News about music-swapping services such as Napster, and the independent film *The Blair Witch Project*, grew like wildfire within universities. Viral marketing works well when:

- the product is new and genuinely different, and is something opinion leaders want to be associated with
- the benefits are real—people are telling their friends; they are putting their reputations on the line
- the product is relevant to a large number of people, and it is relatively easy to communicate the benefits

MAKING IT HAPPEN

Consider incentives

Some viral marketing campaigns use an incentive-based approach. This involves rewarding people if they inform their friends and a percentage of these friends purchase the product or fill out a questionnaire, for example. It's very important to have a 'cap' on the number of people that the first person is asked to inform, though. For example, ask contributors to tell no more than five people about your product or service. If the process is open-ended then it's people are more likely to send out thousands of spam e-mails to people they don't know in order to increase their rewards. Spam is the bane of the online world, and one thing you definitely don't want to encourage, even inadvertently.

Create useful information that will be quoted and passed on

People see the Internet as an information resource. A powerful way of building a brand is to publish information that you allow people to quote and redistribute. There is no better way to enhance your reputation than for someone to pass your newsletter on to a friend, recommending that they should read it. The objective is that you be seen as an expert on a particular sub-ject that is directly related to a product or service you offer. To encourage this type of process, create an 'e-mail-to-a-friend' function on your website, which allows someone easily to e-mail information on something they have just read.

Recognise that linking is viral marketing

Linking is another form of word-of-mouth. It's one thing for someone to send an e-mail praising your product or information, but the effect is much better and longer-lasting if that person publishes a positive review on their website and links back to you.

Remember that viral marketing works well when there is something free

People love to tell their friends when there is some great new service that is free. The Hotmail free e-mail service and the Geocities free website service grew quickly with little or no marketing spend. The appeal of what is free may be losing some of its lustre as the Internet matures, but it is still a powerful driver of behaviour.

Emulate the Hotmail approach

Hotmail was a pioneer of viral marketing. Its success was not simply based on the fact that it was a free service. It embedded viral marketing into the product itself. Every time someone using Hotmail sent an e-mail, at the bottom of the e-mail was the compelling message: 'Get your private, free e-mail at http://www.hotmail.com'. With Hotmail and other communications services such as ICQ, the very use of the product became a vehicle for marketing and promotion.

Think about integrating other approaches

Depending on your type of business, you might want to investigate the option of marketing virally via text messages as well as the Internet. For example, let's say your business provides information about entertainment options in your local area. You could encourage visitors to your website to register their mobile phone numbers with you so that you can keep them up-to-date with special offers, new information, and so on via text message. This would be particularly popular in an area with a high student population. However, you must be *scrupulous* about the information you send out via text message—don't, for example, send out 'jokey' messages that may be misconstrued in any way by the recipient: in 2004, the games company CE Europe attracted a great deal of negative press when it marketed a 'Resident Evil' computer game by a text message that told users that their phone had been infected by a virus. Remember that you must *not* send unsolicited text

messages and you must remove numbers immediately from your list if anyone complains (someone else may have registered their number, for example).

Be wary of inappropriate viral marketing

Done inappropriately, viral marketing can be seen as pyramid selling, chain-letter selling and/or spam. Every e-mail sent needs to make clear that the business is not involved in spamming or other unethical practices or you'll become tarred with the same brush. If you do attract adverse attention from an irate recipient, remain calm and respond to the complainant with an apology written in a professional manner.

RECOMMENDED LINK
Business2.0:
www.business2.com/webguide

SEE ALSO

Delivering the Benefits of Affiliate Marketing on the Web

GETTING STARTED

Affiliate marketing is about paying for performance. In short, it is a type of marketing in which one company induces others to place banners and buttons on their websites in return for a commission on purchases made by their customers. Amazon.com is the pioneer of affiliate marketing. It allows other websites to publish information of their own choices of books. When people click through to Amazon and buy these books, the website in question gets a commission. Affiliate marketing can open up new channels to market for the affiliate sponsor, and be a source of extra revenue for the affiliate website. When investigating affiliate marketing, remember that:

- affiliate marketing is more suited to products than services
- you'll need to work hard with your affiliates if you want it all to work
- a well-designed compensation package will be critical to success

MAKING IT HAPPEN

Work out if your business is suited to affiliate marketing

Keep the following in mind:

- There needs to be a substantial number of websites that are attracting your target market. These websites need to show a willingness to join an affiliate programme. You might be selling medical supplies but that doesn't mean that hospital websites will become affiliates.
- Affiliate marketing is better suited to products than to services. It is much harder to track whether another website sent you visitors who, after prolonged negotiation, decide to pay you for your services.
- Is the market already saturated with affiliate programmes? It would be difficult to set up an affiliate programme today that offered commission on book sales.

Have a strong value proposition

As with all good ideas, there are a huge number of companies offering affiliate programmes. How is your programme going to attract new members? The level of compensation/commission you will offer will be important. However, on its own it will rarely be enough. You will need to work hard with your members by organising regular competitions, special offers, and other incentives that do make for an attractive value proposition both for your affiliate members and the end customer.

Keep in regular touch with your affiliates

Keeping in regular communication with your affiliates is essential in order to build their enthusiasm and trust. You should plan for an e-mail affiliate newsletter. Your affiliate members are your partners, and unless you treat them as such by working closely with them, they will drift away.

Agree a compensation approach

Critical to the success of your programme will be how the affiliate is compensated. There are a number of compensation approaches:

- You might pay commission only; for smaller-price items such as books and music, commission is a popular option.
- For more expensive items such as cars, compensation may be based on paying for qualified leads.
- If brand building is also an important objective, then you might also offer compensation every time a visitor clicks through from an affiliate.

When making payments you will need to decide how often you do it. Every month? Every quarter? A problem you may face with partners is that some of them will have achieved very little revenue for a particular period, and it will not be cost-effective to send them a cheque. So you need to inform partners that there is a certain threshold before payment is made, and that commission earned in one period, if below the threshold, will be added to the commission for the next period. You will need an affiliate agreement that will cover these and other relevant issues.

Innovate, analyse, test, and adapt

There is a need to innovate constantly so as to find the best approach. Affiliate software delivers substantial data and this needs to be carefully analysed. New initiatives need to be properly tested and you need to be willing to keep adapting and refining your offer until you find something that works for both you and your affiliates.

Decide whether to outsource or buy software

Organisations can have the choice of outsourcing much of the running of the affiliate programme or purchasing software and designing it in-house. It is better to outsource, as it allows you to focus on what you do best—selling and marketing your products and services.

RECOMMENDED LINKS

Affiliate Marketing Resource Centre:
www.affiliatemarketing.co.uk
Associate Programs:
www.associateprograms.com

SEE ALSO

Applying a Viral Marketing Approach on the Internet (p. 377)
Computers, Information Technology, and E-commerce (p. 503)
Promoting Your Website Effectively (p. 368)
Understanding the Key Principles of Internet Marketing (p. 365)
Using E-mail Marketing Effectively (p. 374)

Getting the Best from E-marketplaces

GETTING STARTED

An e-marketplace is an Internet-based environment that brings together business-to-business buyers and sellers so that they can trade together more efficiently. Used properly, e-marketplaces can make for more efficient purchasing processes, saving time and money for everyone involved. If you're thinking about moving into an e-marketplace, remember that:

- an e-marketplace gives the smaller company access to many more sales opportunities and allows it to compete on equal terms with larger companies.
- the technology is still relatively new, as are many of the companies involved. Caution is necessary before any major decisions are made.
- there are different types of e-marketplaces and you need to decide which is right for you.
- e-marketplaces should not simply focus on getting the lowest price. Collaboration and the supply of quality information are key benefits they can deliver.

FAQS

What are the key benefits of becoming involved in an e-marketplace?

Reduced sales costs, greater flexibility, saved time, better information, and better collaboration.

What are the key drawbacks of e-marketplaces?

The key drawbacks are inertia and resistance to change among key players, costs in changing procurement processes, the cost of applications and set-up, the cost of integration with internal systems, and transaction/subscription fees.

What types of e-marketplaces are there?

There are three distinct types of e-marketplace:

Independent: These are public e-marketplace environments that seek to attract buyers and sellers to trade together. Many simply didn't attract a critical mass of buyers and sellers and folded quickly. Such marketplaces have found most success in commodity-based industries, where there are buyers and sellers.

Consortium-based: These are set up on an industry-wide basis, typically when a number of key buyers in a particular industry get together. They often drive an industry-wide

move to achieve common standards for the transfer of information.

Private: These are set up by a particular organisation to manage its purchasing alone. The organisation retains full control, though related technology costs can be significant.

MAKING IT HAPPEN
Remember that there's more to it than buying and selling

The early e-marketplaces were little more than auction environments. However, as they've evolved, they have sought to help businesses trade more efficiently with partners. This has involved optimising communication and collaboration; improved time to market as information flows more quickly between parties involved; and better stock control, through better market feedback.

Consider joining an independent e-marketplace

The advantages of joining an independent e-marketplace are:

- you can find new trading partners that you might otherwise not have been aware of
- it's useful if you need to reduce inventory
- it can work well when marketing commodity products
- independents should embrace open infrastructure standards, making them easier to

plug into than private e-marketplaces, which may use more proprietary technology.

The disadvantages are:

■ a volatile environment, with many independents going out of business
■ they are not really suitable for developing long-term trading relationships
■ confidentiality and security can be an issue
■ many suppliers see such marketplaces as a way to drive down prices and are wary about getting involved. This limits the buying options.

Consider joining a consortium-based e-marketplace

The advantages are:

■ less expensive than establishing a private e-marketplace. Charges are usually in the form of subscription fees and/or commission.
■ more choice of buyers and sellers
■ cheaper prices, though this isn't always the case
■ enhanced ability to work on industry-wide issues such as achieving common data standards

The disadvantages are:

■ you are setting up a trading environment with your competitors
■ less control than with a private e-marketplace
■ it won't generally integrate as well into backend technology and processes as a private e-marketplace
■ it's more open and thus more generic. If buying/selling relationships are key to your competitive edge, then a consortium-based e-marketplace will not be a huge benefit.
■ governments may view this type of e-marketplace as cartels or monopolies, depending on the members and their power within the overall marketplace

Bear in mind that you don't have to stick with one type of e-marketplace

Depending on the complexity of your needs, you may decide to use a number of e-marketplaces. For example, you might use a consortium-based one for most of your needs, but, when you have unusual demands, use an independent to give yourself greater choice. A trading partner you meet in an independent e-marketplace may end up migrating into your private e-marketplace.

Recognise that confidentiality is key

One of the major worries regarding involvement in either independent or consortium-based e-marketplace is confidentiality. Over time, a picture will be built up of how an organisation trades; this is important information, which could be very valuable to competitors. It's essential that proper security procedures are in place.

Consider content management

Content management is an important part of an e-marketplace environment. The system will need to deal with requests for proposals (RFPs), quotations, product diagrams and specifications, pricing and delivery information, and so on. It will need to be able to archive everything in an easily accessible way, and to deal with version control so users can receive the most up-to-date information.

Train and educate your staff

E-marketplaces invariably introduce new ways of doing things. There may be resistance within the business and this will require ongoing education and evangelism. Training will be required for the staff who are expected to operate the e-marketplace.

Seller beware

Sellers have been very cautious about getting involved in e-marketplaces because of their initial tendency to focus primarily on price. Some e-marketplaces have encouraged reverse auctions, whereby sellers bid against each other to sell to a particular customer. However, the right e-marketplace can have benefits for a seller, opening up new markets and customers, and providing a way of reducing excess stock.

Consider general issues

■ What is the procedure if you want to develop a one-to-one relationship with a trading partner you meet within an e-marketplace?

■ Will the e-marketplace have any role to play in shipping and logistics?

■ What is expected of you as a participant? How, for example, do you deliver content and updates?

■ What integration work is involved? And if it doesn't fully integrate, what are the costs involved in new processes?

■ How are payments to be made?

■ How are the request for proposal (RFP) and quotation processes handled? Does the e-marketplace offer software that makes these processes more efficient?

■ Is there a certification process in place to ensure that you are dealing with reputable entities?

WHAT TO AVOID

Forgetting about corporate inertia

The expectation by e-marketplace providers that businesses would suddenly change their buying and selling habits upon the arrival of new technology was a serious mistake. Relationships and habits build up over years, and change only slowly in most situations.

Ignoring the fact that there's more to buying and selling than price

Product quality, support, and personal relationships are still key in business-to-business situations. E-marketplaces that simply focused on pitting seller against seller found that that approach simply didn't work.

Delays in getting the e-marketplace up and running

E-marketplaces are a lot more complex than was originally predicted. The more partners involved, the more difficult it becomes to synchronise the information and business processes between each entity. Delays in making some of the best-known e-marketplaces fully functional have hurt the image of the industry.

Failing to provide a robust payments process

Many e-marketplaces lack a process whereby the participants can immediately settle the whole transaction. The fact that some of the trade must then be completed offline means that both offline and online processes need to be maintained, reducing efficiencies and cost savings.

RECOMMENDED LINK

B2business.net:
www.b2business.net

SEE ALSO

Computers, Information Technology, and E-commerce (p. 503)

Getting the Best from Loyalty Programmes on the Web

GETTING STARTED

Loyalty programmes reward customers who spend more and/or stay longer with a business. Like much else about the Web, loyalty programmes were a gigantic trend that crashed pretty severely. However, much of what went wrong does not reflect an inherent fault in the loyalty model itself, but rather in the vastly overhyped expectations of what loyalty programmes can deliver. When considering using loyalty programmes on the Web, keep the following in mind:

- you should implement loyalty programmes on the Web only after you have your e-commerce fundamentals solidly in place.
- loyalty programmes are long-term projects: it can be disastrous to start a loyalty programme and then stop it within six months.
- getting the level of incentive right is critical to success—too much and your profits will be hurt; too little and you won't attract members.

MAKING IT HAPPEN

Make sure your e-commerce fundamentals are in place first

Top of the list for consumers are service, comprehensive information, appropriate returns policies, and good support. Unless these fundamentals are fully addressed, consumers will see loyalty points only as gimmicks.

Remember that loyalty programmes are long-term projects

A critical issue with regard to loyalty programmes is that, by their very nature, they have to be there for the long term. Loyalty programmes ask two key things of consumers: to collect points that will be redeemed at some future date; and to give their loyalty. There is no better way to antagonise a consumer than to start a loyalty programme and then six months later—as the member has collected half the points required for that coveted flight—to stop the programme. Don't start a loyalty programme unless you're in it for the long haul.

Find out what makes your customer loyal

If you don't know what makes your customers loyal then you cannot develop a programme that will enhance their loyalty. It is also critical to focus on making your most profitable customers more loyal.

Choose the right type of loyalty programme

The following is a selection of loyalty programme approaches:

- points systems—a very popular approach that gives points to customers based on what they purchase
- premium customer programmes—customers who spend certain amounts of money and are repeat purchasers of a product or service gain special status. This may involve them receiving special service offers, discounts, exclusive offers, gifts, and so on. The important thing here is to make the customers feel special—make them feel that they are getting things that those who are not part of the programme don't get.
- buyers' clubs—when a certain number of consumers get together to buy a particular product, they will be offered a special volume discount

Get the switching cost right

If you offer too much in your loyalty programme then your margins will be squeezed, and you will be running to stand still from a profitability point of view. If your incentives are too low then the switching cost for your customer will remain low, and the very purpose of the loyalty programme will have been negated. It would seem that the problem with a lot of loyalty programmes set up in the early days of trading on the Web was that, fuelled by venture capital, major incentives were offered in the hope of attracting huge numbers of members.

Create a loyalty path for the customer

Customers can take loyalty programmes very seriously. Some customers see it as an important achievement that they have a 'Gold Card', or are seen as a 'Premium Customer'. There needs to be a clear loyalty path to tap into this sort of loyalty psychology. The customers need to see that the more they spend and the longer they stay with you, the more rewards and better treatment they will get.

Keep the customer informed

Customers need to be able to check up on their status easily—to see, for example, how many points they have currently accumulated. Keep in touch. Send loyalty club members a regular bulletin that creates a continuing buzz about the loyalty programme, announcing competition winners, new competitions, special offers, and so on.

RECOMMENDED LINK
Business 2.0:
www.business2.com/b2/webguide

SEE ALSO
Building Loyalty Through Online Communities (p. 386)
Computers, Information Technology, and E-commerce (p. 503)

Building Loyalty Through Online Communities

GETTING STARTED

Online communities are seen first and foremost as a social phenomenon, but they are very useful for businesses of all sizes. They allow consumers to engage with one another and with your business through use of interactive tools such as e-mail, discussion boards, and chat software. (Broader and more social online communities are not the topic of this actionlist.) They are a means by which you can take the pulse of consumers to find out what they are thinking, and to generate unique content. As a stand-alone business, online communities have been found to be weak: they work best when they are supporting the need for the business to get ongoing feedback. Online communities:

- allow the consumer an ongoing voice, thus facilitating greater feedback
- require moderation and care if they are not to fizzle out, or turn negative
- offer different options for interaction that reflect the varying ways in which people like to communicate

MAKING IT HAPPEN

Keep it moderated

Online communities rarely work if you simply install some discussion board software on a website and walk away. The discussion will either quickly dry up, or else drift off to topics that have nothing to do with the company and may well be libellous or illegal. This is the last thing you need, so the key to success here is to moderate the quality of your online community. Moderators need to combine editorial and chairperson-type skills. They need to be knowledgeable about the subjects being discussed, be enthusiastic, and encourage debate and quality discussion. They need to have an understanding of legal (particularly libel and copyright) issues, and should be able to deal with negative situations where members become overly virulent. Most of all, they need to care and want to make the community work for everybody involved.

Set up e-mail mailing lists

E-mail mailing lists are an excellent way to discuss complex topics over a longer period of time. Members can be drawn from anywhere in the world and come together to share information and experience on a particular theme or subject area. The success of an e-mail mailing list is down to the quality of the contributions and moderation. Done right, it is a powerful way of transferring knowledge. An e-mail mailing list works as follows:

- A moderator establishes a list with mailing list software (this can be bought or rented; renting is usually the best option).
- The theme and focus of the list is published, and people join up, using a website form and/or e-mail address.
- The moderator invites contributions and these are duly published by e-mail.
- Subscribers react to the initial publication with their opinions and feedback; a selection of these reactions then gets published in the next e-mail sent out.
- If successful, a feedback and opinion loop is created, with new topics of discussion being introduced as older topics have received sufficient discussion.

Set up discussion boards

Discussion boards (also known as newsgroups, discussion groups, or bulletin boards) are areas on a website that allow people to contribute opinions, ideas, and announcements. They tend to be more general in nature than e-mail mailing lists, and are more suited to casual, one-off interactions. People require less commitment to participate in such boards. They can generally review a discussion topic without subscribing, although they do have to subscribe if they want to contribute something themselves. Moderation is not as essential here, although it is important to watch out for the emergence of 'off-topic' subjects—contributions that are unnecessarily negative and perhaps libellous—and copyright infringement.

A prime example of the success of the discussion board approach is how the Amazon sites around the world use it to allow consumers to publish book reviews. Discussion board software is relatively cheap and easy to install.

Set up online chat

Online chat is real-time, text-based communication. Online chat can be effective when:

- there is a specific event occurring that is of interest to people
- an expert can be made available to talk about a subject or product

To be productive, online chat needs to be well moderated. It is really only suited to small groups of people (2 to 20) at any one time. Online chat software is relatively cheap and easy to install.

RECOMMENDED LINK
Business2.0:
www.business2.com

SEE ALSO
Computers, Information Technology, and E-commerce (p. 503)
Getting the Best from Loyalty Programmes on the Web (p. 384)

SELLING ONLINE

Establishing an Enterprise Portal

GETTING STARTED

If your business has grown and you employ a number of staff, you may want to investigate enterprise portals. Put very simply, these are websites that assemble a wide range of content and services for staff. Some of this content is published by the organisation itself, and some will be acquired from third-party publishers. The principle is to bring together all the key information that staff require to do a better job. When considering developing an enterprise portal, keep the following in mind:

- the word 'portal' means different things to different people: to some, it's a souped-up intranet, to others it's a nascent e-marketplace: others will see it as part of a customer relationship management strategy
- enterprise portals, while great in theory, are complex to develop and expensive to manage
- an enterprise portal can easily fall into the trap of trying to provide all the information staff could possibly need and providing none of it very well

MAKING IT HAPPEN

Exploit the extra potential

In many ways, an enterprise portal (sometimes referred to as an enterprise information portal) is a fancy name for an intranet. The key difference is that an enterprise portal manages not just internal content, but also external content that may be useful to staff. Such external information could include, for example, specialised news feeds, or access to industry research reports.

Learn from the public portals

On the Web everyone is a publisher, but that doesn't mean that everyone is a good publisher or that people will want to read what they publish. Very few public portals have survived, mainly because they have not been able to build a viable business case.

Another portal sector that has seen great change is the much-vaunted 'vortal'. A vortal, or vertical portal, provides information that is organised around a vertical market sector, such as pharmaceuticals or plastics. Vortals and e-marketplaces have a lot in common, and in many markets may be one and the same thing. Most of these vortals, if they haven't evolved into e-marketplaces, are probably no longer in business.

The lessons that need to be learned from public portals and industry vortals include:

- people are very conservative in the way they consume content. The majority of people go to a few trusted brands
- running portals is expensive; many have not survived because they did not have a proper business model

Don't get complacent about having a captive audience

The enterprise portal would seem to have a captive audience—employees. But it's not as simple as that. Staff who use an enterprise portal demand high publishing standards. High publishing standards are expensive to maintain, and many enterprise portals are dying because they don't have enough quality content, the content is not being kept up to date, and the whole environment is not properly organised and structured. What many organisations are discovering, to their cost, is that providing all this related information is wonderful in theory, but expensive and difficult to manage in practice.

Know your employees' content needs

Ask the following questions:

- How are employees' information needs being met at present?
- Are any of these needs not being satisfied properly?
- Can I fill this gap cost-effectively?
- Will my staff trust me to fill this gap?
- Where's the return on investment?

Related information is all well and good, but the key question must be: where is the return on investment? If a member of staff can just as easily get this related information somewhere else, why duplicate the effort? Unfortunately, organisations rarely take the time to examine which content drives the business forward, and which has little effect. But having a website is being a publisher, and if you don't understand the impact of your content, you don't understand the principles of publishing.

RECOMMENDED LINK
Business2.0:
www.business2.com

SEE ALSO
Computers, Information Technology, and E-commerce (p. 503)

Managing Payments Online

GETTING STARTED

If your business sells its products or services online, it's absolutely essential you're your online payment system works well, and works safely. The system must be easy to use, as consumers dislike having to go through long, cumbersome processes to purchase products, but it must also be as secure as possible; it's estimated that fraud costs an online business three times as much as an offline one. Remember that:

- consumers may be wary of giving credit card details and other personal information online. Your first step must be to gain their trust.
- fraud and chargebacks are critical issues that can seriously affect an online business
- there is a wide range of online payment services available, so shop around to make sure you get the best one for you

FAQS

What is the most common form of payment on the Internet?

For consumer commerce it is the credit card, via 'customer-not-present' transactions. For most business-to-business transactions, payment is usually made offline. New forms of payment are emerging all the time, such as prepaid accounts and payments via mobile phone.

What are the key issues facing online payments?

- Fraud is a critical concern that must be addressed comprehensively to limit its very negative impact on businesses and customers alike.
- There is no cross-border integration of payment systems.
- People develop payment habits, and are reluctant to change them.
- Can traditional payment methods adapt to the new environment, or is a brand new payment system required?
- There is still no comprehensive hard data on how people pay online.

What is a payment culture?

Within any particular country, and sometimes within states or regions of a country, there are distinct approaches to payment, depending on:

- the range of payment options available locally
- local payment habits
- local/national payment regulations

MAKING IT HAPPEN
Understand your marketplace

Depending on the country, or the region/state within a country, people pay for things in different ways. Different countries also have different payment processing approaches and legal obligations. All of these variations are referred to as 'payment cultures'.

Understand the types of payment option available

There are a range of payment options that a website can use, including:

- credit card payment
- debit card payments
- credit transfer
- electronic cheques
- direct debit
- smart cards
- prepaid schemes
- loyalty scheme points-based approaches
- person-to-person payments
- mobile phone schemes

The approach you choose will depend on your target market. For example, if a website targets young people, who often have no credit cards, a prepaid scheme can work well. A particular website may use a variety of payment approaches, depending on its needs, but the ability to process all the major credit and debit cards is almost always essential.

Check the characteristics of an online payment system

An online payment system should have these key characteristics:

- efficiency and ease of use: a central advantage of doing business online is that it saves time and cuts costs
- robustness and reliability: because payment is such a critical function, payment systems have to be fully reliable. They cannot be 'out of action' for any length of time
- authentication: much online fraud is caused by the absence of proper authentication
- integration: a payment system must be able to integrate properly with relevant internal information systems, so that, for example, a record of the payment can be added to the account details
- insurance: facilities such as escrow services must be available to ensure that the seller gets the money and the buyer gets the goods

Select an online payment service

Finding the most suitable type of online payment service will depend on the volume of business you intend doing and the margins you make on each sale. There is a wide choice of payment services, so it is important to shop around to find the best one. However, whatever service you choose must be able to verify the credit card, process the transaction, and deposit the money in your account.

Key factors to consider include set-up fees, ongoing charges, and software and hardware expenses. Most banks offer some form of online payment service, and can be a good choice. If you don't use a bank, do make absolutely sure that you're dealing with reputable organisations. Those that advertise extremely low charges usually have expensive hidden extras.

Offer a choice of credit card payment methods

There are two distinct methods by which credit or debit card payments are made for Internet purchases: payment directly online, and payment by phoning or faxing credit card details. The first method is by far the most popular, but it is advisable to offer both options to potential consumers.

When implementing an online credit card system, a comprehensive security system using a secure server with encryption technology is essential. It is equally important to have comprehensive security procedures for the storage of the information. A database containing confidential information on thousands of individuals is far more attractive to a criminal than acquiring a single credit card number.

Keep the process simple and fast

Whatever the payment system you choose, make sure to keep the process as simple and fast as possible. Studies have indicated that many consumers abandon the online purchase process, often because it is too long and difficult to understand. Streamlining the purchasing process is extremely important where repeat business is concerned. Amazon.com, for example, has implemented a patented '1-Click' purchase process for repeat customers, avoiding a lot of form filling.

Consider business-to-business (B2B) payment options

While there is a wide range of effective business-to-consumer online payment options, payment for B2B transactions is generally made offline. One reason for this is that the amounts of money involved are usually large. However, one of the key reasons businesses embrace online B2B and join e-marketplaces is to reduce costs and to make transactions more efficient. Not being able to complete the payment online adds cost and inconvenience. A range of systems is available for B2B payment online; they focus on ensuring security and authenticity, and some also offer digital signature facilities.

Think about offering online escrow services

Online escrow services offer to hold payments while the buyer examines the products purchased. If the buyer is satisfied with the products, they then authorise the payment. An online escrow service incurs extra cost because a fee is charged, but it may be worthwhile if it is essential to give the buyer as much confidence as possible.

The system operates by giving the escrow service a tracking number for the delivery. You must agree the time period allowed to the buyer for examination of the merchandise; you must also establish who pays the carriage fees if the product is returned.

Remember that fraud and chargebacks are major issues

Some studies estimate that e-tailers are losing as much as 5% of their margin to fraud—a rate three times higher than for businesses operating offline. For e-tailers on small margins this is a very serious issue. There are many different types of fraud, but a particularly common online form is identity theft, where fraudsters acquire confidential information on an individual and use it to purchase products. Clearly, e-tailers must take great care in this area, otherwise their profits will be eaten away. Fraud detection software is available and should be used.

Chargebacks (disputed payments) are also a major concern. In 2001, MasterCard claimed that, while online purchases represented 4% of total retail transactions, they accounted for 40% of all chargebacks. Credit card companies have initiated chargeback limits for e-tailers, and penalties are imposed for those who exceed them.

Understand how payment systems work

This is how the process works:
- customers visit your site anytime, during or outside normal business hours
- they view products and brief descriptions
- they select products and put them into an electronic shopping basket
- customers are offered payment options, ideally in their own currency
- online payment is handled securely, probably by a specialist payment processor
- payment is approved and confirmed to you and the customer
- purchases are delivered to the customer

Choose the right system

An effective payment system allows your customers to buy online and allows you to manage the process efficiently. A complete payment system includes all the facilities to display products, accept payments, and manage your business. You can also choose systems that can be integrated with existing product display and business management systems. The system should allow you to:
- display products that customers can buy from your website
- calculate any taxes due
- calculate shipping or delivery charges
- provide a quick, simple ordering mechanism
- provide a secure customer payment mechanism
- accept payment by credit card, debit card, and cheque
- handle transactions from customers with approved accounts
- handle payment for small and large purchases
- accept payment in local currencies from all the countries where you have customers
- accept payments in multiple currencies
- protect your customers and your business against fraud
- handle customer refunds
- receive settlement from the payment processor
- automate stock control
- simplify administration and accounting
- expand in line with growth of business
- minimise the cost of handling transactions

Select a payment processor

You can set up your own payment processing facilities, but if you only handle a small number of transactions or if your transaction requirements are complex this may not be practical. Payment processors can provide you with an established proven system that can grow in line with your business and services of this type are offered by banks and independent specialists.

Using an external provider offers you a number of advantages: there is no need for capital investment from you; there are no hardware, software, and support requirements; high levels of security for your business and your customers are provided; there is a reliable operation, round the clock; and services can expand in line with your business.

Apply for a payment account

Many businesses, particularly smaller and medium size operations, can be put off by the complexity of the application process but bear in mind that some suppliers have simpler processes than others. For commercial and security reasons, no company can cut out initial checks but some suppliers have gone out of their way to make the application process as simple as possible. The process varies in a number of areas:

- some independents can make their own internal risk assessment without referring to banks
- you may or may not have to provide a detailed trading history
- the proportion of successful applications varies by supplier—independents generally accept a higher proportion of applicants than banks

Make sure you complete the application forms fully and return all essential documentation, including a customer agreement, direct debit mandate, bank details, and balance sheet.

Offer a clear payment page

Simplifying payment is an important part of the online shopping experience. A clear, easy-to-use order form allows customers to place their orders quickly. The form should include:

- customer details
- delivery requirements
- product details
- quantity
- price
- delivery charges
- total cost
- payment option
- account details, if appropriate

- mechanism to submit the order
- acknowledgment of the order and payment approval

Check the operation of the payment page and ensure that any changes made to the page layout reflect customer experience and feedback. Also make sure that the page is easy to navigate and simple to complete.

WHAT TO AVOID
Not understanding payment cultures

While credit cards may be very common in the United States, they are not as widely used in Europe. Different countries have different payment habits and payment legislation. Not understanding these is a serious obstacle to online business.

Not securing peace of mind for the consumer

Consumers are very concerned that their credit card numbers will be stolen on the Internet. They are equally concerned that confidential information that they give to a website will not be properly protected. Websites that fail to show clearly the steps taken to protect customer information are likely to lose potential business.

Underestimating fraud

Fraud is a pressing issue on the Internet, and can have a serious impact on profit margins.

RECOMMENDED LINKS
Epaynews.com:
www.epaynews.com
E-payment Systems Observatory:
www.e-pso.info

SEE ALSO
Computers, Information Technology, and E-commerce (p. 503)
Making Your Website Secure (p. 396)
Understanding Legal Issues in E-commerce (p. 402)

Making Your Website Secure

GETTING STARTED

Internet security is a critically important issue. The Internet is, by definition, a network; networks are open, and are thus vulnerable to attack. A poor Internet security policy can result in a substantial loss of productivity and a drop in consumer confidence. When developing such a security policy, keep the following in mind:

- be continuously vigilant: the perfect Internet security system will be out of date the next day
- combine software and human expertise: security software can only do so much; it must be combined with human expertise and experience
- secure internally as well as externally; many security breaches come from inside the business

FAQS

What are examples of best practice in Internet security?

Consider the following as best practice:

- have an Internet security policy
- if your system has been compromised, seek immediate independent expert help
- for complete safety after an attack, the best course of action is to reformat the hard disk
- strip your computer system down to its bare essentials. The more features, options, and software your system has, the more open it is to attack. This is particularly true for Internet-related software and functions
- for personal computers, be very careful about always-on connections provided by many broadband suppliers. An always-on connection to the Internet is always open to probing and attack by a hacker
- do not download software from the Internet unless you are totally confident that it is from a reputable source

Are cookies a security threat?

Cookies collect information on how you browse the Web, and are a relatively low security risk. However, cookies can encourage lazy security practices, since they remember user-names and passwords.

Can you get a virus by opening an e-mail?

Yes. It used to be impossible to be infected by a computer virus transmitted by e-mail unless you opened the e-mail attachment. However, more recent viruses simply required the opening of the e-mail itself. Be very careful about unexpected e-mails from unfamiliar sources. If in doubt, delete these e-mails without opening.

MAKING IT HAPPEN

Develop an Internet security policy

Keep the following in mind when developing your Internet security policy:

- many security breaches are internal. The fewer people with access to the inner workings of the system, therefore, the better. Those who are allowed access must be recorded and given specific access rights. Immediately delete revoked and inactive users, or users who have left the business
- put in place a rigorous procedure for granting and revoking rights of access
- streamline hardware and software: a complex system is more open to attack. In your server software, for example, strip away as many of the optional features as possible
- have a password policy. Do not allow simple or obvious passwords. Make sure passwords are changed regularly
- have procedures for data backup and disaster recovery
- have procedures for responding to security breaches
- be vigilant. The Internet security threat is constantly changing, and constant vigilance is the best security.
- have your security policy audited by an

external professional organisation, and have them on call should a major breach occur

Consider the benefits of firewalls

A firewall is software that polices the space between your computer system and the outside world. The design and management of firewalls has become more complex since the advent of the Web because of the vast increase in activity between computers and the Internet. If the firewall is too stringent, it slows everything down and prevents people from carrying out certain legitimate activities; if it is too lax, however, it opens the computer up to attack.

Deal with viruses

Computer viruses are becoming more sophisticated and widespread. In January 2005, it was estimated that e-mails containing viruses amounted to 15% of all messages sent. Quite clearly, then, it's essential to have anti-virus software and to keep it up to date. It is equally vital to upgrade your computer with the latest software security patches. For Microsoft software, more information on such patches is available at **www.microsoft.com/security**.

Deal with hackers

A hacker's main objective is to gain unauthorised access to another computer. This is done by probing for vulnerabilities on the computer, perhaps the result of flaws in the computer software and/or poor security procedures. The Web is more open than a stand-alone computer, so many hackers now focus on web-based applications. Many of these applications are still relatively new and have not developed robust security measures. Security breaches can range from the hacker changing the pricing in a shopping cart to the theft of credit card numbers. The only way to deal with hackers is to implement rigorous security procedures and to monitor activity on the network constantly.

React rapidly to a security breach

After a security breach there are two basic objectives. First, find out what happened so that you can stop it happening again. Second, find out who did it so that you can prosecute or otherwise deal with them. It is very difficult to prosecute a security breach without hard evidence, and very easy to contaminate or destroy such evidence. In dealing with security breaches, make sure that:

- you get professional advice, particularly if it is the first time your security has been breached
- you protect all log information tracking activity on the system
- the information collected is technically accurate
- information is collected from various sources to develop an overall picture of what happened
- no information is tampered with or modified

In monitoring for security breaches:
- check access and error log files for suspicious activity
- be alert for unusual system commands
- be alert for repeated attempts to enter a password

Guard against denial of service attacks

Denial of service attacks do not seek to break into a computer system, but rather to crash a website by deluging it with phoney traffic. They are difficult to defend against, and have been directed at some of the best-known websites, such as CNN and eBay. Firewalls can be designed to block repeated traffic from a particular source.

Make sure you have a secure web server

A web server is potentially an open door into your network: if someone can break into your server, they are closer to breaking into your entire computer system. Before you set up a web server you must ensure that you understand and deal effectively with the various security issues. By definition, web servers interface with the World Wide Web and its potential hazards. They are large, complex software programs that embrace open architecture and that have often been developed at great speed.

From an e-commerce perspective, a secure server is an essential prerequisite. A secure server uses encryption when transferring or receiving data from the Web. Without a secure server, credit card information, for example, could be easily targeted by a hacker. A secure server will encrypt this information, turning it into special code that will then be decrypted only when it is safely within the server environment.

Equally important is what happens to the confidential information once it has reached the server environment. Once the information has been acted on, it should be stored in encrypted form. In the case of sensitive information, such as credit card details, it should be deleted.

Restrict access to your website

You can restrict access to part or all of your website in a number of ways. The most common is by implementing a user-name and password system. However, you can also restrict access by IP (Internet) address, so that only people connecting from a certain address or domain can access information. Perhaps the most powerful approach is to use public key cryptography, whereby only the person with the assigned cryptography key can request and read the information.

Consider the security implications of outsourcing

Outsourcing creates an increased security risk. You must establish that the outsource vendor will adhere to your security policy, and that all work done adheres to proper security procedures. Specific questions that you need to ask your outsourcing vendor include:

- What is its security policy?
- What are its data backup and disaster-recovery procedures?
- How is your data safeguarded from that of other customers?
- How is your data safeguarded from the vendor's own employees?

- How is it insured with regard to security breaches?

WHAT TO AVOID
Not being continually vigilant

There is no such thing as a perfect security system. Without constant vigilance, computer systems become an open invitation for hackers and viruses. An essential part of such vigilance is having the very latest security patches and antivirus software installed.

Thinking that you won't get a virus

Viruses are becoming increasingly common. If you haven't had one so far, either you are tremendously lucky or you have excellent antivirus procedures.

Thinking that you are anonymous on the Internet

In general, you are not. When you visit a website, you will provide some or all of the following information:

- IP address
- time of access
- user-name (if a user-name and password are used)
- the URL requested
- the URL you were at just before you visited the website
- the amount of data you downloaded
- the browser and operating system you are using
- your e-mail address

RECOMMENDED LINK
CERT Internet Security Center:
www.cert.org

SEE ALSO
Computers, Information Technology, and E-commerce (p. 503)
Coping with Computer Viruses (p. 363)
Managing Payments Online (p. 392)

Collecting Consumer Data on the Internet

GETTING STARTED

If your business has a website, you'll find that Internet technologies offer a wealth of ways in which information on consumers can be gathered. Such information can either be collected directly as a result of consumers providing details, or indirectly by analysing consumers' behaviour while on a website. If you decide to gather information on consumers this way, keep the following in mind:

- privacy is a central concern of people who use the Internet, and they are becoming increasingly wary of websites that seek personal information
- the benefit to the consumer needs to be made clear. Consumers are much more willing to offer personal information when a clear benefit to them can be articulated
- it is one thing to gather information on consumers but another to analyse it properly and use it productively

FAQS

Why has privacy become such a burning issue on the Internet?

The Internet has lacked a common and comprehensive legal infrastructure and this has led to an unfortunate situation in which basic consumer rights have been exploited. Websites have gathered information on visitors in a surreptitious manner. Personal data has been sold on to third parties without making the consumer aware. This behaviour has resulted in a consumer backlash.

What are the key benefits of collecting consumer data?

Getting to know consumers better means that you have a better chance of offering them products and services that are more in tune with their needs. This is a key competitive advantage in an information-driven economy. With more and more products becoming increasingly similar in their physical makeup, competitive advantage is achieved through finding out exactly what the consumer wants and meeting those needs precisely.

Why is it so important to collect information on how a website is performing?

A website is not like a bricks-and-mortar shop in which a manager can walk around and observe what is happening. If there are always long queues at the checkout, and people are leaving the store because of these queues, this will quickly become obvious. People may be dropping out in the middle of a purchase process on a website, but unless proper data is coming through and being analysed, no one will know. The number of people visiting the website may be dropping off. How will this be known without proper data? Websites, like offline stores, need to monitor their performance continuously and adapt where appropriate. Without proper data and thorough data analysis this cannot be done.

MAKING IT HAPPEN

Use website logs to analyse consumer behaviour

Website logs (server logs) track activity on a website. For an average website, such log software is simple to install and can be purchased fairly cheaply, though for larger websites it is more complex and expensive. It is strongly advisable to use log software, as it delivers vital information on website performance.

Unless the website is hooked into a personalisation system, website logs are not able to identify who exactly has visited the website. Instead, such logs collect general website activity information. Such information includes:

- total number of visits to the website during a defined period of time

- visitor frequency. Information on the number of people who visited only once during the period (unique visitors), and those who have visited more than once.
- page impressions/views. Information on the total numbers of complete web pages visited during the period. This is a key measure for advertisers.
- hits. One of the most abused statistics on the Internet, and a totally unreliable measure of website visitor activity. Every web page is made up of a number of components—graphics, text, programming elements. Some pages may have anything from 10 to 20 components. Each of these components is counted as a 'hit'. Therefore, the total number of hits is generally very high and bears little or no relation to the actual visitor activity.
- most frequently visited pages

Website logs can deliver a mind-numbing array of data. This will seem very exciting when you first install the software but can become tedious to wade through every day. It's thus important to isolate what are the key measures required to deliver a better picture of how the website is performing.

Use cookie software to track consumers

Cookies are small files that are sent to reside in consumers' browsers in order to track those consumers the next time they visit the website. Cookies are an important component in personalisation. A typical example of the use of cookies can be seen when people have subscribed to a service on a website. Cookies allow the website to remember the user-name and password information, so that they don't have to keep filling it out every time they revisit. This is clearly a benefit for most people. However, cookies have been abused, collecting information on people without their knowing. When using cookies, clearly explain to people why they are being used and how they benefit them.

Be cautious about using Web bugs that track website usage

An alternative technology to cookies is what has become known as web bugs. Web bugs are not detectable by standard browsers, although there is software that can be downloaded to detect them. Web bugs have been controversial because they are often used in a surreptitious manner. Their very design reflects a desire not to let the person know that they are being tracked. Web bugs are adding fuel to the belief that people's privacy rights are being constantly abused on the Internet.

Collect information through the use of website forms

Website forms are used to collect information from a consumer in a structured manner. The following are guidelines to follow when designing a form:

- keep the forms as short as possible. If you make the form too long, consumers will simply not fill it out, or will skip over large sections of it.
- if forms have to be long, break them up. However, inform the person clearly of how many sections there are in the form.
- clearly mark mandatory fields. In every form there will be fields, such as e-mail addresses, that must be filled out. The convention is to mark the text associated with these fields in red and/or to place a red asterisk beside the field. At the top of the form, a clear statement needs to be made relating to the mandatory fields.
- don't demand information a consumer can't give. Offer an alternative, for example: 'If you don't have a mobile phone number, please write "None".'
- ask opinion-type questions first. Where the objective of the form is to collect opinion-type information, start off with these questions. People tend to be more open to giving opinion rather than personal information.
- isolate errors that are made. Everyone makes mistakes, particularly when they are filling out long forms. Never say, 'There's an error in your form. Go back and fill it out correctly'. Rather say, 'It seems you have not filled out your e-mail address. Please fill it out here'. Alternatively, you could highlight the field that needs to be completed in another colour, which will flag it up quickly for the user.

- make sure the fields aren't too small. Don't, for example, give people a tiny field when you want their street address, which may be quite long.
- make sure it's accessible to all. Offer an alternative approach for people with disabilities to complete the information requested; these disabilities can range from issues such as colour blindness to physical impairment. Minimum accessibility standards are increasingly required by law.
- test regularly. You can't just test your forms once before you launch and then keep your fingers crossed. Forms break. Test them regularly as part of your standard website maintenance and take action as appropriate.

Follow best practice in consumer data collection

People have become rightly uneasy about the abuse of personal information on the Web. To assuage fears and create a win-win situation with online customers, put into practice the following:

- clearly inform people why the information is being collected and what purposes it will be used for
- never use this information in a way that was not originally intended
- allow the consumer to find out what information has been collected on them
- allow them to delete any or all of this information if they desire
- publish a comprehensive privacy statement in a prominent position on the website

Protect consumer data

Hackers—people who break into computer systems—love to target consumer databases. The reason is that these databases may contain credit card information (it is not advisable to store credit card numbers on a website). More usually, hackers know that publicising the theft of consumer databases will be hugely damaging and embarrassing to the organisation. It is therefore vital that any consumer data collected is properly protected and backed up.

Take care when collecting consumer data on children

The rules for collecting consumer data on children are quite naturally a lot stricter than for adults. While the law is evolving, numerous companies have been fined for collecting too much information on children who visit their websites. It's not enough simply to check your national legislation on this issue. The Web is international and your websites should adhere to international standards when it comes to children's privacy rights.

WHAT TO AVOID
Surreptitiously collecting data

People have become very wary about their privacy on the Internet. Too many websites have collected data on consumers without them knowing. This may produce short-term benefit but has led to an inevitable backlash.

Collecting too much data

Software today can deliver seas of data, and websites with large numbers of visitors can easily get flooded. Not focusing on what is the really important data to collect is a common problem. It's important to remember that analysing data takes time, and that if tangible benefits are not delivered then it will be wasted time.

Not protecting consumer data properly

There are numerous high-profile cases in which hackers broke into websites and exposed confidential consumer data. Make sure that your consumer data is properly protected.

RECOMMENDED LINKS
Information Commissioner's Office:
www.informationcommissioner.gov.uk
Web Accessibility Initiative:
www.w3.org/WAI

SEE ALSO
Computers, Information Technology, and E-commerce (p. 503)

Understanding Legal Issues in E-commerce

GETTING STARTED

In any e-business strategy, it is important to address comprehensively the key legal issues. At a basic level, these are matters such as copyright and libel; at a more advanced level, such things as unique restrictions pertaining to the sale of your product within particular jurisdictions need to be dealt with. When addressing legal issues on the Web, keep the following in mind:

- Prevention is better than cure. Establishing a sound legal structure early on is much easier than trying to firefight legal problems as they occur.
- Legal systems are getting a grip on the Internet. More and more laws are being passed that deal with doing business online.
- While you can't deal with the unique legal aspects of every jurisdiction, you still need to isolate the key jurisdictions for your online business and make sure you adhere to their relevant laws.

FAQS

Why should you address legal issues from the start?

Because it's important to guard against unpleasant consequences if you get legal things wrong, or just ignore them. Some early e-commerce businesses adopted the latter approach, believing that cyberspace was a kind of laissez-faire utopia beyond the reach of terrestrial governments.

Is it not the case that many laws do not apply online?

Nobody believes that fallacy any more. This is fortunate, because courts and governments around the world have shown no hesitation about claiming jurisdiction over online activity—in some cases, even when the website in question is hosted on another continent. They have applied civil sanctions (such as injunctions and damages) and also criminal penalties (fines and even imprisonment) in certain instances.

Is there a pragmatic approach to dealing with legal issues online?

Yes. The practical approach is to get legal advice on three specific types of territory for your website:

- the country (or countries) in which your web operations are principally based, which will often, but not always, be where the site is hosted

- the countries that are the primary target market of the website
- any other countries which may claim authority over the website, and the breach of whose laws might cause unpleasant consequences. The United States is by far the best example of this: its legal regime has a dauntingly long reach

MAKING IT HAPPEN
Understand the different kinds of website

While there are many different types of website, they can broadly be divided into those with the following attributes:

- shop window websites, which provide information about a company and its products, but without encouraging any significant visitor interaction—rather like an online company brochure
- contributed content websites, which allow visitors to contribute content, such as information about their identity, or postings on message boards
- full e-commerce websites, through which visitors can purchase goods or services, either physical products which are delivered offline, or digitised material which is available for download

Recognise shop window website issues

Even shop window websites have legal issues to address. They comprise various types of digitised content, such as graphics, text, images, music and coding, that raise issues which apply to all forms of website.

Website owners must assume that all such content is protected: either by copyright—which, in effect, disallows its inclusion in another website without the copyright owner's permission; or, in some cases, by moral rights—which require the author to be attributed, and that the work should not be significantly modified without the owner's permission.

These clearances can take the form of a licence or an assignment of copyright from the relevant rights holder, which might be a third-party website designer, photographer, journalist, or (in the more complicated case of music) two or more rights-holding organisations.

In addition, you must ensure that content on your website satisfies other requirements, including:

- Using the registered trade marks of a third party as part of your website's metadata will generally constitute trade mark infringement. Even a straightforward reference on a website to a third party's trade mark can constitute an infringement.
- Hypertext linking, particularly by means of deep linking or framing, to third-party websites without the consent of those websites should be avoided.
- Misleading price indications, for example where online prices have not been updated, can incur penalties.
- Incorrect product descriptions, where inaccurate statements are made as to the quantity, size, fitness for purpose or performance of goods, can also cause repercussions.
- Unfair comparative advertising, such as comparisons between goods or services that are not intended for the same purpose, must be avoided.

As well as guarding against infringement of third parties' rights, it is important for owners to include wording in the terms and conditions of their websites which protects their own copyright and other rights. Usually this is done by means of terms which appear directly on the home page or, more commonly, are linked to/from the home page, as well as at the bottom of every other page on the website.

Appreciate contributed content website issues

Websites that encourage visitors to interact are exposed to several additional forms of legal risk. One of the most basic means of facilitating visitor interaction is a discussion board or chat room. Such environments can pose legal problems, as they are often unchecked and allow visitors to post information without any apparent restriction. You need to recognise that you can find yourself liable, either as a civil matter (where a third party's rights have been infringed) or, more extremely, under the criminal law, unless steps are taken to control material which appears on your website.

Some of the most obvious problems here include:

- defamatory statements
- infringement of copyright material
- obscene, blasphemous, threatening, racially discriminatory, and other legally objectionable material

To avoid liability for such material, you need to establish one or more of the following safeguards:

- proactive moderation of material before it appears on the website
- a documented 'notice and take down' procedure, under which infringing content is removed from the website as soon as it has been notified
- regular reviewing of material which has been posted, and removal of any which appears problematic

These issues all need to be addressed in your website's terms and conditions, so that visitors (and potential third-party complainants) are aware of the steps taken to prevent infringement. Many prudent owners also require visitors to register with the website before they can post messages. This allows the owner to contact the visitor if a problematic posting is made by the visitor, and, in certain circumstances, to provide that visitor's personal and contact information to a wronged third party, or to a law enforcement authority.

Account for full e-commerce website issues

Clearly, there is a wide variety of goods and services which are capable of being traded through a website. Further, the seller can be either the website owner or a third party trading through the website, as in an online auction service.

It is impossible to cover here all the issues which the various kinds of products can raise. Many have specific regulations which have been imposed by governments for social, ethical and fiscal reasons. Examples of these include:

- sale of alcohol
- sale of medicines, particularly prescription-only medicines
- financial services
- betting, gaming and lotteries
- auctions, particularly in various European countries

Depending on the jurisdiction and type of product being sold, a website may need to adhere to regulations such as:

- provision of clear information to consumers before the conclusion of a contract, including: the identity of the supplier; the main characteristics of what's being sold; payment and delivery arrangements; and the principal terms and conditions of the contract between seller and purchaser
- a minimum period during which a consumer may withdraw from the contract for any reason, and reject whatever has been purchased

Whatever you sell through your e-commerce website, it is important that you form a legally binding contract with the purchaser. For example, you might ensure that such a contract is formed by requiring the visitor to scroll through your terms and conditions and click on an 'I accept' button before a transaction is completed.

WHAT TO AVOID
Doing nothing because you think it's just too complicated

It is certainly true that there is a dizzying array of legal issues to ponder when trading over the Web. However, that's not an excuse for doing nothing. There is a basic minimum that can and should be addressed. The key is to understand the legal issues that, if not addressed properly, can have a major impact on your business.

Assuming that the long arm of the law does not reach online

This is a false assumption. Yes, it is often more difficult successfully to prosecute an organisation that is trading over the Web. However, that does not mean that governments and legal systems are ignoring those who they feel are breaking their laws, just because they happen to be on the Web.

Failing to deal with copyright and libel issues quickly

If a third party accuses you of libel or copyright infringement, it is imperative that you deal with it urgently. In many courts of law, the longer the libel remains published on the website, the greater the penalties.

RECOMMENDED LINKS
LLRX.com:
www.llrx.com
British and Irish Legal Information Institute:
www.bailii.org

SEE ALSO
Computers, Information Technology, and E-commerce (p. 503)
Managing Payments Online (p. 392)

MANAGING YOURSELF
AND OTHERS

Managing Your Time

GETTING STARTED

Time is a man-made concept. Animals do not understand the idea. They live *in* time; they are in the moment; the present is all that counts. Remembering this can be useful in the business world: being able to focus on the present is often an effective way of getting through laborious tasks and not worrying about the past or future.

In business, time is money. The paradox is that as technology has become more widespread (with the promise that it will increase productivity) and more easily accessible, it has made working life a lot more complicated: some managers assume fewer staff are needed to complete the work. The only realistic way out of this conundrum is to make better use of time.

FAQS

How can I be a better time manager?

Wanting to be good at time management is half the battle, but you need to be aware of the choices you have to make. These relate to your overall life balance and the values you hold.

As a first step, look at what you need to do and why. If some requests are outside your area of responsibility or expertise, work with your partner(s) and team (if you have one) to clarify the boundaries. Delegate as much as you can. Although this might seem difficult in a small business environment, it's a really useful skill to develop and it will benefit the business as whole—things will get done rather than sit on your desk.

You'll also need to be more realistic about your strengths and capabilities. Set realistic deadlines and build in some slack in the schedule to give yourself the best possible chance of meeting deadlines.

I run a very efficient team. One of my team members seems incredibly disorganised. What can I do?

Good managers often need to work with individual team members to help them to understand what is expected. Set realistic goals and give them adequate time and resources to complete the work. If at all possible, ask them to look at their performance objectively and identify patterns of behaviour that contribute to being disorganised. Often time management requires a change in habits that have been built up over a long time and the best way to make

this happen is to build awareness, chart a clear route, and reward success.

I've recently invested in a hand-held organiser but find I am still using a diary as well. How can I get away from using redundant systems?

If you're serious about using an electronic organiser, you'll need to plan the time it will take to learn the new technology and transfer your information. Ask for a tutorial from someone who has made the leap already and then, over a period of a month, wean yourself off the dual system by cutting out the diary. You'll soon find the computerised method more versatile and convenient than anything you have used in the past. Remember to back up your data regularly to avoid losing vital information due to battery or power failures, though, as this can be distressingly common.

MAKING IT HAPPEN

Conduct a 'time audit'

A 'time audit' is a useful exercise for anyone keen to improve time management skills. What is the balance between the demands placed upon you at work and those that define your private life? Does this balance satisfy you, or do you find yourself sacrificing one element for another? One key to good time management is being aware of the wider world in which you live and the interrelationships between its component parts. Another key is prioritising—if in fact there is not enough time to satisfy all competing demands—and then choosing how you apportion your time.

Take a large sheet of paper and write your name in the centre. Around this, write all the demands of your life. Include work hours, commuting, socialising, eating, sleeping, household duties, and family commitments. Remember that taking time for family and friends, exercise, hobbies, holidays, and just plain fun is important. Mark the number of hours that you dedicate to each of these areas throughout the day, month, or year. For example, in a normal day you may have: work (8), commuting (2), picking up children from school (0.5), and so on. This will give you a (literal!) representation of your life in terms of the choices and tradeoffs you're making in those areas that are important to you.

Ask yourself, is this how I want to live my life? You may decide to sacrifice some important areas in the short term, but be aware of what might happen when a particular phase of your life comes to an end. For example, how will you manage if you get married or divorced; when children grow up and leave home; if your business takes off and starts to demand much more of your time; if you have an accident or long-term illness; when you retire?

Evaluate what action needs to be taken

Take a highlighter and mark those areas on your chart that need attention. If, for instance, you are spending too much time at work, you need to rethink carefully your work goals and decide how to achieve a better, more effective balance.

For example, you may find that you can win more time by working from home, if your type of business suits it and your family will respect the necessary home-work boundaries. You'll probably find that there are other ways to prune hours from the day that are otherwise wasted. For instance, if you like to play sport or keep fit, consider finding a club near work where you can go early in the morning, instead of having to fit this in during the evening.

Look for patterns in the way you use your time. You may find that you are constantly in meetings that run late or that you pick up a lot of work that is not really profitable, or not what you really want to do because you are not assertive enough in saying no. If you don't have enough time and your own behaviour is contributing to the shortage, change your patterns of behaviour.

Learn to use the right tools

Time-management tools and techniques are only as useful as the time you invest in using them. Some commercially available tools and techniques include:

- handheld organisers, also known as personal digital assistants (PDAs)
- organisers, both computer-based programs and paper diaries or schedulers
- 'to do' lists
- prioritising work according to its importance, and focusing only on the essential
- shared diaries—team, secretarial, professional groups

If you are a person more accustomed to focusing on 'the moment' rather than the 'big picture', it may be a good idea to learn to stand back and look at time as a continuum, in terms of past, present, and future. Doing so gives you a sense or order, structure, and perspective.

If too much work is the issue, look at your workload, prioritise, and refer back to how it fits your job description. Decide, perhaps in consultation with partners, which of your tasks add value to the business and its potential, and which would be better delegated to others.

WHAT TO AVOID
Buying a new gadget but still relying on old time-management tools

If you're going to buy a new device to help you plan your time better, you need to plan the time to learn to use it competently! Don't buy something and try to pick it up as you go along as this will make you very frustrated *and* inefficient.

Expecting too much of yourself and become disenchanted

Change is difficult and often requires a new set of skills. The principles of time man-

Some dos and don'ts of time management

Do	**Don't**
Undertake a 'time audit'	Spend time on unnecessary activities or those that do not serve your purpose
Be honest about how long things take	
Build in time for reflecting and learning	Try to undertake the impossible
Build in time for yourself	Blame others for your disorganisation
Delegate wherever you can	Get hung up on process
Anticipate the pressure of commitments that you make	Make commitments that you can't meet
	Expect others to make up for what you can't do
Communicate with others where you have time conflicts	Give up
Plan ahead	

agement sound completely logical and straightforward, but in fact we lead extremely complex lives, and these simple principles are hard to put into practice. Don't overwhelm yourself by trying to change everything at once. Instead, establish a series of small, clear goals, and achieve them one by one.

Not being prepared to break bad habits, and not asking for help

Old habits do die hard, and one of the hardest to break is the way we structure and use our time. Everyone knows people who are always late or always early, those who jump right onto tasks or are terrible procrastinators, those who are stressed-out workaholics or who always seem miraculously refreshed and relaxed. The choices we make in managing our time are connected to the way we view ourselves and the world: making different choices affects our sense of identity and our relationships. Take it slowly, look to family, friends, and work colleagues for support in making these changes, and don't rule out taking workshops or looking for a consultant to help you.

RECOMMENDED LINK
Mindtools.com, Time Management tab:
www.mindtools.com

SEE ALSO
Delegate without Guilt (p. 412)
Managing Pressure (p. 409)

Managing Pressure

GETTING STARTED

Pressure is increasingly a way of life for managers and executives, and when you are running or growing a small business, you may feel as if you have to soak up the stress that in larger organisations would be shared among a larger team. This actionlist sets out to help you to identify different types of pressure and find ways to cope with them.

FAQS

My business partner thrives on pressure and expects me to do the same, but I work more effectively in a less intense environment. How can we work well together?

This is a common problem. If you can find a way to work together, however, your differing styles can actually complement each other. Try to broach this issue with your partner, and put together a plan of action.

I work well under pressure and have no problem with it, but it is now affecting my relationships with others who don't. What do I do?

Although pressure often gives us the boost we need to get a job done well and on time, it can, however, become such a habit that we don't realise it's a constant presence in our workplace. While people can become very focused in such an environment, they may also begin to neglect other parts of their lives such as their relationships with friends and family, or even their health. In the long term, pressure is not a desirable permanent fixture in working life.

How do I maximise the benefits and minimise the downside of pressure?

Pressure can improve our performance, but sometimes it can be at the detriment of other factors such as relationships. Under pressure people often become highly task-orientated and focus on the immediate areas. Other people become very short-term orientated. Observe your own behaviour, seek feedback, and evaluate whether you believe there is an issue or not. The earlier you recognise it, the easier it is to ensure that the negative impact of pressure is alleviated.

MAKING IT HAPPEN

Work towards a work/life balance ✔

Managing pressure is about achieving some sort of balance in your life and activities. It is usually in the workplace that we are most susceptible to pressure, but be aware that pressure sometimes stems from home or the social environment. Pressure can make us do or say things that, on reflection, we wish we hadn't. Where possible, try to make sure that work is not the central focus of your life. For example, take advantage of your allotted number of holidays, take exercise regularly, and maintain your relationships with friends and family. Having hobbies and interests that help you to 'turn off' is also very useful. When you run your own business, it's that much harder as you're the sole focus of the stress. If you're in a partnership, though, do talk to your partner about how he or she is feeling and explore ways you could change the way you work for the better.

Recognise the symptoms of pressure

Symptoms of pressure fall into four main categories:

- **physical**—headaches, sweats, panic attacks, raised blood pressure, sickness, sleeplessness, palpitations
- **physiological**—over-production of adrenalin, leading to tension, aggression, feelings of stress in the so-called 'fight or flight' syndrome
- **emotional**—depression, having feelings of inadequacy, loss of confidence, detachment, denial
- **behavioural**—focus on short-term tasks, loss of temper, dismissive behaviour, self-centredness, irritability, impatience with others

Know the causes and types of pressure

There are numerous causes of pressure in the workplace today, many of which are linked. Some of the most obvious are:

- insufficient resources—not enough time, funds, or staff to get the job done properly
- insufficient *appropriate* resources—skills gaps in certain areas
- unreasonable demands on your time—customers expecting you constantly to be at their beck and call
- improper staffing or staff direction—failure to understand what different people are capable of
- insufficient training
- poor planning
- promising to do too much too quickly

There are also many *types* of pressure. The most common is time pressure—too much to do and too little time to do it in. However, there are plenty of coping strategies to help manage it. For example:

- Anticipate where the pressure may come from.
- Plan and resource what needs to be delivered and when.
- Prioritise actions to ensure that things are done efficiently.
- Communicate progress to other stakeholders in the task and manage expectations. For example, if a task will take longer to complete than originally thought, be upfront. The sooner you alert people to potential problems, the sooner you can work together to plan for contingencies.
- Understand how others respond to pressure and work with them.

While this may not alleviate time pressure by actually extending your deadline, it will allow you to feel more in control.

Where time pressure continues to be an issue, it may indicate that you need to re-evaluate your role and its demands and resources. Are you delegating enough? Have you prioritised your actions? Are you promising to do too much too quickly?

Find a solution

Solutions fall into two areas:

- organisational—structure, planning
- personal—intellectual, behavioural, physical

Organisational solutions

Pressure can exist because of the nature of a job or of how the role fits in with the rest of the business. In the small company environment, responsibilities may not be as clearly defined as in a larger concern as everyone is more likely to pitch in together to get things done. To cut down on the pressure you're under, it will be worth looking dispassionately at your job and seeing if you can put some boundaries in place. If you have members of staff working with you, help them develop their skills by delegating to them, and make sure you're all managing your time and prioritising well. All of this will reduce pressure.

In addition, better planning, with the ability to anticipate pressure points, can help ensure that resources are in the right place at the right time. Sometimes pressure is unavoidable, but certainly more bearable if it is for short periods of time.

Personal solutions

On a personal level, we may put ourselves under pressure when we lose confidence in our ability. Having a good self-awareness and understanding of our real skills is important. Building and supporting confidence is also invaluable.

Be aware of how you respond to pressure. Some symptoms you display may be positive and motivating, others not, so know your balance and how others respond. At the same time, you need to also be aware of how pressure affects others: don't assume that they'll react in the same way as you do, as no two people respond to it in the same way.

Physically there are things we can do to help manage pressure. Exercise is good from a health viewpoint, and often gets rid of a lot of pent-up stress. Even stretching in your chair, going for a quick walk, or talking to a friend or confidante are good remedies for relieving pressure. Try to take a break through regular holidays, even if you think you can't afford the time. Starting up a business will soak up a lot of your energy reserves and you'll need to replenish them. If you have family or friends that you've been neglecting, a holiday is a good time to catch up with them.

Try to remember that you're not alone and that there are others in your life who want you to succeed and will help you *if you let them*. Having a sense of humour can help, as can remembering to step back from a situation. It is important to tackle the underlying causes of pressure if you can, rather than just dealing with the symptoms. Above all, remember that you're not alone. Don't hesitate to confide in a friend or colleague or seek counselling if you need help.

WHAT TO AVOID
Thinking you can do it all alone
People sometimes take on too much, thinking that they can cope without additional support. Perhaps you think you are saving your business money by covering a number of responsibilities—but in reality you could be wasting money in missed opportunities or inefficiency. Often, when we are under pressure, the one thing we become incapable of doing well is delegating work appropriately. Better communication and prioritising objectives are therefore essential. Working on identifying better resource management, prioritising the work load, building in time/slack, anticipating pressure points, and monitoring progress are all important elements when dealing with pressure.

Never saying 'no'
Perhaps you're one of those people who are capable of sustaining high levels of activity over a long period of time, and it has become expected that you always perform at that pitch. The solution is about being assertive and saying no when the pressure is too great. Like a car, you can't stay in fifth gear all the time; you have to vary your speed and occasionally have a 'pit stop'.

Succumbing to a 'long hours culture'
Sometimes people assume that the longer they work, the better, and that longer hours equals great productivity. It's just not true. When you are your own boss, there'll be times when you've so much to do you think you should stay up all night to finish the tasks at hand, but try not to do this if you can. Anything you write, create, or produce when you're half-asleep will probably have to be done again anyway. Try instead to adjust the way you think. Shift your focus from the hours that you work and concentrate instead on the achievement of your goals or tasks.

Taking it out on others
Pressure is no respecter of boundaries. Stress in one area of your life will eventually affect all other parts of it too. Be aware of how these pressures may affect your work performance and try not to transfer them to those who are not part of the problem. Work on the causes and not the symptoms. Compartmentalisation will only work in the short term.

RECOMMENDED LINKS
About.com site:
http://stress.about.com
Mindtools.com:
www.mindtools.com/smpage.html
UK National Work-Stress Network:
www.workstress.net

SEE ALSO
Delegate without Guilt (p. 412)
Managing Your Time (p. 406)

Delegating without Guilt

GETTING STARTED

If you have a team working for you, you need to get to grips with delegation. It's a key skill to develop. Delegation isn't about giving tasks to others because you can't be bothered to do them yourself—it *is* about getting a particular job done, clearly, but it's also about encouraging people to learn new skills and reach their potential, all of which helps a business to grow.

Many of us like being in control of everything and find it hard to let go of things we know we can do well ourselves. However, if we want to be successful managers—and preserve our own sanity—that's exactly what we must do.

FAQS

Why do people find it difficult to delegate?

There are many reasons why you may find it difficult to delegate. Often, it seems quicker to perform the task yourself rather than bother to explain it to somebody else and then correct his or her mistakes. You might worry that the person will make a bit of a hash of it and it'll take a long time to put right the mistakes they make. On the other hand, you may feel threatened by the competence of a person who is quick on the uptake and does well. There is a fear that the employee may take over the role of being the person the rest of the staff goes to with their problems. They may even find something wrong with the way *you* do things.

If you lack confidence, you may find it hard to give instructions and you'll put off delegating. If you do delegate, and problems arise because the employee fails to do what you've asked him or her to do, you may doubt your own ability to confront the person about his or her actions. If staff have been given increased responsibilities and have done well, you may not be confident of being able to reward them sufficiently. Conversely, you might be reluctant to delegate tasks that you think are too tedious.

Finally, you may realise that delegation is necessary, but you don't know where to start, or how to go about it. You need some kind of method to follow. The following paragraphs will help put you on the right track.

How can delegation help me?

Delegation offers many benefits. Done well, it will allow you to concentrate on the things you do best and also give you the time and space to tackle more interesting and challenging tasks in the future. You'll be less likely to put off making key decisions and you'll be much more effective. Your staff will benefit too; everyone needs new challenges, and by delegating to them, you'll be able to test their ability in a range of areas and increase their contribution to the business. Staff can take quick decisions themselves and they'll develop a better understanding of the details concerned. Done well, delegation should improve the overall productivity of employees.

It's all too tempting to withdraw into 'essential' tasks and not develop relations with your team. The bottom line is that it's wasteful for senior staff to be given big salaries for doing low-value work, and passing tasks down the line is essential if other people are to develop. Not knowing how to do this is recognised as one of the biggest obstacles to small business growth. By delegating, you'll have much more time to do your own job properly.

Delegation doesn't make things easier (there will always be other challenges), but it does make things more efficient and effective. Essentially, it represents a more interactive way of working with a team of people, and it involves instruction, training, and development. The results will be well worth the time and effort you invest in doing it properly.

When should I delegate?

Delegation is fundamental to successful management—look for opportunities to do it. If you have too much work to do, or if you don't have enough time to devote to important tasks, delegate. When it's clear that certain staff need to develop, particularly new employees, or when an employee clearly has the skills needed to perform a specific task, delegate.

What tasks should I delegate?

Begin with any routine administrative tasks that take up too much of your time. There are likely to be many small everyday jobs which you've always done—you may even enjoy doing them (for example, sending faxes)—but they're not a good use of your time. Review these small jobs and delegate as many of them as you can. Being your company's point of contact for a particular person or organisation, which is important but can be time consuming, is also an excellent task to delegate.

On a larger scale, delegate projects that it makes sense for one person to handle; this will be a good test of how the person manages and co-ordinates the project. Give the person something he or she has every chance of completing successfully, rather than an impossible task at which others have failed and which may well prove a negative experience for the person concerned. Also delegate tasks for which a particular employee has developed a special aptitude.

Who should I delegate to?

Make sure you understand the person you're delegating to. He or she must have the skills and ability—or at least the potential—to develop into the role and must be someone you can trust. It's a good idea to test out the employee with small tasks that will help show what he or she can do. Also make sure that the employee is available for the assignment—don't put too much pressure on your most effective workers. Spread out the tasks you delegate among as many people as possible: two or more people

could even share a task if it's particularly complicated.

MAKING IT HAPPEN

Be positive

Think positively: you have the right to delegate and, frankly, you must delegate. You won't get it 100% right the first time, but you'll improve with experience. Be as decisive as you can and if you need to improve your assertiveness skills, consider attending a course or reading one of the many books on the subject. A positive approach will also give your employees confidence in themselves, and they need to feel that you believe in them.

If you expect efficiency from the person you delegate to, organise yourself first. If there's no overall plan of what's going on, it'll be hard to identify, schedule, and evaluate the work being delegated. Prepare before seeing the person (but don't use this as a ploy to delay!). Assess the task and decide how much responsibility the person will have. Assess the person's progress regularly and make notes.

Discuss the task to be delegated

When you meet the person or people you're delegating to, discuss the tasks and the problems in depth, and explain fully what's expected of them. It's crucial to give people precise objectives, but encourage them to seek these out themselves by letting them ask you questions and participate in setting the parameters. They need to understand why they're doing the task, and where it fits into the scheme of things. Ask them how they'll go about the task, then discuss their plan and the support they might need.

Set targets and offer support if necessary

Targets should be set and deadlines scheduled into diaries. Summarise what has been agreed, and take notes about what the person is required to do so everyone is clear. If he or she is given a lot of creative scope and is being tested out, you may decide to be deliberately vague, but if the task is urgent and critical, you must be specific.

How much support you offer and give will very much depend on the person and your relationship with them. In the early stages you might want to work with him or her and to share certain tasks, but you'll be able to back off more as your understanding of the person's abilities increases. Encourage people to come back to you if they have any problems—while it's important to have time alone, you should be accessible if anyone has a problem or the situation changes. If someone needs to check something with you, try to get it back to him or her quickly. Don't interfere or criticise if things are going according to plan.

Monitoring progress is vital—it's very easy to forget all about the task until the completion date, but in the meantime, all sorts of things could have gone wrong. When planning, time should be built in to review progress. If more problems were expected to arise and nothing has been heard, check with the employee that all is well. Schedule routine meetings with the person and be flexible enough to changes deadlines and objectives as the situation changes.

How did it go?

When a task is complete, give praise and review how things went. If an employee's responsibilities are increased, make sure he or she receives fair rewards for it. On the other hand, there may be limits on what can be offered, so don't offer rewards you can't deliver. Also bear in mind that development can carry its own rewards. Such career development issues can be discussed with the employee in appraisals, and the results of delegated tasks noted for this purpose. If the person has failed to deliver, discuss it with them, find out what went wrong, and aim to resolve problems in the future.

WHAT TO AVOID
You expecting employees to do things like you do

Managers often criticise the way things are done because it isn't the way they would have done it themselves. Remember that people prefer working in different ways and concentrate on the results rather than the methods used to obtain them.

You don't give people a chance

If you're giving someone something new to do, you must be patient. It'll take time for employees to develop new skills, but it's time that will pay off in the end. Have faith in the people around you.

You delegate responsibility without authority

It's unfair to expect results from someone with one hand tied behind his or her back. If you're going to delegate responsibilities, make sure that those involved know this, and confer the necessary authority upon the person you're delegating to.

RECOMMENDED LINKS
businessballs.com:
www.businessballs.com/delegation.htm
iVillage.co.uk:
www.ivillage.co.uk/workcareer/survive/ opolitics/articles/ 0,,156475_157030,00.html
jobserve.com
www.jobserve.com/news/ NewsStory.asp?SID=2009
Mind Tools:
www.mindtools.com/tmdelegt.html

SEE ALSO
Developing Leadership Skills (p. 444)
Managing Pressure (p. 409)
Small and Growing Businesses (p. 486)

Staff Planning

GETTING STARTED

As your business grows, it will naturally require more people to carry out the work and new skills will be required to handle a wider range of business activities and developing technology. You'll need to have new employees in place in good time to meet increased demand, and you should provide opportunities to develop, train, and promote existing staff. Future salary and training costs need to be built into the cash-flow forecast and financial plan. It is important to foresee these requirements and to plan accordingly.

This actionlist looks at the main issues that a small business needs to address as it plans for its staffing requirements.

FAQS

What is the best way to approach staff planning?

A number of statistical methods have been developed to help businesses to analyse, predict, and plan future staffing requirements. Each business is different, so there is no single answer to how best to plan. In basic terms, though, you'll need to forecast sales and plan future production levels, estimate the amount and type of work that will be required, identify who can do this work and how training and recruitment can fill the gaps, and then implement the plan and review its success.

Link staff planning to the wider strategic planning process. Your staffing plan should develop from the long-term forecast for the development of sales and the required increase in working capacity that this represents. The various types of work must be identified and quantified so that you can then work out costs. You'll need to plan for the long term (for example, five years), the year ahead (relating to the annual budget), and possibly month by month to show how change may be phased in during the year ahead (coinciding with the cash-flow forecast). All this should feed back into your main strategic plan for business development.

▶ MAKING IT HAPPEN

Estimate future work requirements

In addition to estimates for future levels of output, you need information about how work is done, who does it, and what the

options are for making changes. The first step is to analyse jobs by clarifying the main job elements and determining how much work is required to carry them out.

Don't make too many assumptions about what people do and how they do it. Your staff are more in touch than you are with how things are really done, so make sure you ask them and take on board what they say. For example, what looks like a small job may take much longer than you think; another task may be so boring that it seriously threatens effectiveness and job satisfaction. While a scientific 'work study' can be useful, informal discussion and team meetings are often much more effective.

Next, you need to estimate how workloads will increase. From sales forecasts you can work out the required level of production from month to month. These estimates then need to be shown in terms of staffing levels. The number of workers required will often increase in proportion to the volume of work, for example, double the work (usually) requires double the workers. In some cases the workload might be helped by further training or the introduction of different working methods. Nevertheless, it is often helpful to create estimates based on the amount of work required to produce one unit of production (sometimes known as the Workload Method). The work required to produce one unit is split into its constituent parts. Each part is given a time value. These can then be multiplied by the number of units required, giving the total amount of work of each type. For example:

Types of work	Time/unit	@180/month	@200/month
Assembly	1.0	180hrs (24 days)	200hrs (26.6 days)
Testing	0.4	72hrs (9.6 days)	80hrs (10.6 days)
Packaging	0.2	36hrs (4.8 days)	40hrs (5.3 days)

Fluctuations in demand are important in many industries. In some cases you may need to employ some people on a casual basis in order to meet peak demand. Some industries work to annualised hours whereby an employee will work a set number of hours per year but with a staggered working pattern.

This may mean that the majority of their hours are in the summer months (for example) but their wages are evenly spread throughout the year. This removes problems of overtime payments for the business and removes the need to be continually training casual workers. It may also help to switch resources or to build up stock in order to even out these fluctuations. On the whole, most organisations will not want extra stock on the premises because of storage and increased insurance costs, fire risks, lack of space and so on.

Analyse the workforce
It can be helpful to profile the people you employ by summarising and collating information about individuals into a single quick-reference document. For example, you could look at what each person does, areas of competence, qualifications, and development options. If these can be presented on a single sheet it can help you identify the various options for development. Include also the basic information in your staff audit, such as salary and length of service.

You can also profile your workforce as a whole, by identifying some key measures for the way it has been developing. For example, you could look at staff turnover (number leaving divided by total workforce) and growth (number of staff year on year). Other measures might include supervision (number of staff per supervisor/manager) and promotion (number of managers from the workforce compared to the number of managers recruited from outside). You could also consider the annual recruitment cost (include the time required to interview and coach new staff), annual training costs, and productivity (turnover divided by number of staff).

Also consider the average time that employees stay with the company, and staff stability (this can be measured by a staff stability index, which looks at staff with long service and provides an indication of those with tendency to stay with the organisation and those who decide to leave).

Staff planning is not an exact science. Comparative information may be available through your trade association. Key measures are mainly useful to help you understand the present situation, to set targets, and to measure success. There may be limits to what can be achieved (for example, in your competitive environment, promotion opportunities may be limited for junior staff or salary development may be very difficult to implement).

Relate tasks to individuals
Adjusting individual work roles can become very complicated. Where a large team is working on a variety of projects, changing one factor can have an impact upon everyone else. You need a simple way to look at who does what, and then to look at what happens if you change who does what, and how this will develop over a period of time. A computer spreadsheet is especially useful for this, enabling you to reconsider values without having to recalculate totals every time.

One approach is to create a matrix that sets individuals against specific work areas. For example, calculating on an average of 18 working days (allowing for sickness and holiday) per full-time employee per month, the diagram shows how work (shown in days) is split between a number of employees, for an estimated level of activity in each area.

Types of work	Amount	Ali	Jim	Aisha	Helen	Justin	Omar
Sales and Admin	18	3	12	3			
Research	47		4	15	16	6	6
Edit/Proofing	28		2		2	12	12
DTP	15	15					
Total Days	108	18	18	18	18	18	18

An overview chart for the year ahead is a useful budgeting tool. A month-by-month chart showing fluctuations in production requirements will help you to plan for change in good time to meet your future commitments.

Consider staff development issues

Staff planning provides an opportunity to put into action your plans for developing individuals. Your personnel policy document should be a useful framework to help you take decisions that will affect individual employees.

Job design and job satisfaction are two important areas to consider. As the business and the individuals employed by it change and develop, so new jobs need to be defined. Make sure that roles are job descriptions are clearly defined, and that there's some variety built in to the jobs as well. Look for activities that complement each other and suit the skills and experience of the people concerned.

When it comes to management development, be open minded about what people can achieve. Don't assume that some people aren't up to taking on new responsibilities, or conversely, that others will jump at them. To provide scope for staff to develop, aim to take new people on at the most junior level, while promoting existing staff into new positions of responsibility when more senior vacancies arise.

If changes to your business or range of products means that new skills are need among your team, think about whether existing staff could be trained to meet them. The cost of training should be offset against the benefits of being able to use someone familiar with the business and who (unlike a new recruit) is not an unknown quantity. Training is a benefit to staff and is also a motivator.

Also think about pay increases. If pay is improved ad hoc, you may risk not being able to provide fair long-term benefits across the board. A *clear* pay structure, though, will help long-term financial planning. If you want to keep your experienced staff, you'll have to compete with the going industry rate; lower pay may keep your prices competitive, but you won't be able to hold onto the best staff available. Investigate standard rates of pay and create salary bands related to skill and responsibility.

Be realistic about lead times

Do remember that it takes new staff time to settle in. Even the most competent people take time to learn about the job and to gain the trust of their colleagues. If you do need to recruit, the lead times can be long. You may need to start the whole process as much as six months in advance of the time when the person's full workload will be required. Recruitment can take up a lot of a manager's workload, so also bear this in mind when you do your forward planning.

WHAT TO AVOID
Not thinking about your own staff first
Remember to talk to your staff first about how jobs, individuals, and teams can be developed and improved. Aim to develop and retain your existing workforce before thinking of recruitment from outside.

RECOMMENDED LINKS
Chartered Institute of Personnel and Development:
www.cipd.co.uk

SEE ALSO
Conducting Interviews and Making Job Offers (p. 423)

Focus On: Finding and Keeping Top Talent
Philip Sadler

GETTING STARTED

Just as businesses have changed dramatically in nature over the last 20 years, so have people's attitudes to their employers—and the attitudes of the most talented people are no exception. Furthermore, knowledge is more important than ever before and a major source of competitive advantage. Attracting, finding, and retaining talented people is therefore vital for success. Not only are people the most decisive and expensive resource, they also determine the success of every activity within the business.

This actionlist explains how to find and keep the best people—a challenge that involves:

- understanding the characteristics of talent-intensive businesses.
- choosing the best ways to attract, recruit and retain the most talented people.
- building the right work environment and culture.

FAQS

What are the characteristics of talent-intensive businesses?

Businesses that are rich in talented can be spotted in the following ways.

- Their principal assets (that is, their talented people) do not appear on the balance sheet (although they are, or should be, the main determinants of the company's market valuation).
- These key assets are mobile. They can, despite contracts of service, simply walk away.
- Talent-intensive businesses rely particularly on creativity and imagination.
- The success criteria for talent-intensive organisations stretch far beyond the accountants' bottom line. For example, winning an award for innovation may weigh far more than profit or cash-flow.

MAKING IT HAPPEN
Find the best people

Don't assume that finding top talent will be expensive or lengthy: it need not be, even for the most senior appointments. If you have a vacancy, first of all ask your current team to see if they know anyone who might be a good candidate. Because they understand you, the role, and the business, they are best placed to find a good candidate. There may be other people in your company's network that could also suggest a candidate: shareholders, suppliers, customers, and professional advisers may all be able to recommend good people.

Make sure you allow enough time to make the right appointment, and to ensure that others meet the preferred candidate. Time pressures and isolation are two key factors that can lead managers to make appointments that are flawed.

Choose the best way to recruit

The recruitment activity itself can be separated into two quite distinct processes. The first is attracting people whose talent has already been established and recognised elsewhere. This can be called the 'transplanting' type of recruiting, equivalent to digging up and repositioning a mature tree or shrub in the quest for an instant garden.

The second process is the 'seed bed' or 'nursery' approach, recruiting young people straight from school or university, nurturing or developing their emerging talents and bringing them to fruition. This is clearly a longer-term approach and can be a bit risky. For example, you may give too much weight to academic qualifications. Less risky, however, is the process of finding talent among existing employees. Assuming they've been in employment for some time, a well-designed appraisal and a development procedure can be a good way of finding promising candidates.

Keep the best people

Remember that keeping top talent is as much about the people, the job, and the business as it is about the specific individual. Ask yourself at regular intervals the following key questions:

- who are my key people?
- what makes them exceptional?
- how are they feeling? Positive (for example, stimulated, challenged, valued) or negative (under pressure, concerned, struggling to perform at their best)?
- are their working environment and terms and conditions of employment competitive?
- do they know how much I value them?
- what are their aspirations and are they realistic? If so, what am I doing to support them? Do they know I'm doing this?

Finally, it is worth remembering that whether you are trying to find or to keep someone, pay remains important for most people, if not for its own sake, then for the sense of recognition that it brings to the individual.

Build a culture that retains talent

As mentioned above, when it comes to retaining talent within your business, the need for an adequate rewards package goes without saying. What makes the real difference in keeping talented employees loyal, however, is the extent to which the company provides them with a working environment favourable to creativity, self-expression, and the exercise of initiative. Small business have an advantage over larger organisations here, as bigger companies are hierarchical, bureaucratic, and conformist in order to achieve efficiency and uniformity, yet it is just these characteristics that turn off highly creative people.

The chief characteristics of a culture that nurtures talent are:

- effective teams
- authority residing in expertise and competence rather than rank or status

- talented people respecting and recognising the contribution of the colleagues who support them
- respected leadership—talented people are critical people who do not follow blindly, and know when the emperor has no clothes
- freedom, autonomy, space, and flexibility
- openness and trust
- encouragement of risk-taking

WHAT TO AVOID
Thinking that money is everything

Companies often make the mistake of assuming that cash is the most important factor in attracting or retaining someone, which often puts small businesses at a disadvantage. An outstanding performer in any field is unlikely to move from one business to another if it involves a drop in pay, but there are other factors to consider. In the case of highly talented people, for example, a key influence on the decision whether or not to move jobs is the reputation the recruiting business has in its particular field. Is it at the leading edge? Does it set the pace for its industry? Does the individual feel flattered by being approached? Reputation building, therefore, is a key element in recruiting strategy.

Failing to distinguish between recruiting and finding talent

The distinction between recruiting talent and finding it is important; sometimes an business looks outside for new talent when the potential for outstanding performance already exists unnoticed among the existing team.

RECOMMENDED LINK
Leaders Direct:
www.leadersdirect.com

SEE ALSO
Assessing Your Entrepreneurial Profile: Do You Have What It Takes? (p. 6)

Understanding Key Elements of Employment Law

GETTING STARTED

When your business employs people, it must comply with a number of legal requirements. Many of these are there to protect the rights of your employees, while others relate to aspects such as employees' tax, National Insurance, working time, and health and safety.

Employment legislation is changing all the time and 2003 and 2005 were particularly busy years for new legislation. It is important that you keep up to date with what is going on in the field of employment law to ensure your employees are treated fairly and to avoid potentially costly employment tribunals. This actionlist contains a brief guide to the most important recent developments, and tells you where you can go for help and advice.

FAQS

Where can I get advice on employment law?

There are many sources of help and advice you can access, the most important of which are listed below.

Department of Trade and Industry— TIGER website: the DTI's Employment Relations Directorate has developed a website devoted to certain aspects of employment law. TIGER stands for Tailored Interactive Guidance on Employment Rights. Currently the site has sections on the national minimum wage, maternity rights, paternity rights, adoption rights, and flexible working rights. All of these areas have seen massive changes in related legislation since 2003 and the site provides comprehensive guidance on all the changes.

Department of Trade and Industry— Employment Relations Directorate: The Employment Relations Directorate is actually responsible for producing employment legislation. It produces guidance on all employment legislation, which can be ordered through DTI Publications or can be downloaded free from the Directorate's website. The website also has a 'Hot Topics' page which gives details of the latest legislation and potential legislation which is being consulted on or currently going through parliament. The DTI does not provide information on individual cases.

Advisory, Conciliation and Arbitration Service (Acas): Acas works to prevent and resolve employment disputes, conciliates in actual or potential complaints to employment tribunals, provides information and advice, and promotes good practice. Acas has several offices throughout the United Kingdom which can be contacted for advice. There is also a central telephone helpline (on 0845 747 4747) which can deal with inquiries on employment legislation. Acas has its own publications service which provides a wide range of free and priced publications covering several aspects of employment law, for example, recruitment and selection, discipline and grievance procedures, and handling redundancy. Many of these are available for download free from the Acas website.

Commission for Racial Equality: The Commission provides advice and assistance on equal opportunities policy and practice to many organisations and businesses, large and small. The Commission has produced an 'Employment Code of Practice' and provides information on how to ensure that job advertisements comply with the Race Relations Act 1976. The Commission has a number of offices throughout the United Kingdom and general inquiries can be made to its head office on telephone number (020) 7939 0000.

Equal Opportunities Commission: The Commission is the expert body on equality between women and men in the United Kingdom. It provides information on implementing equal opportunities policies in the workplace and compliance with sex discrimination laws. The Commission has offices in England, Wales, and Scotland, and its website provides a wide range of free information and publications which can be downloaded.

Disability Rights Commission: The Disability Rights Commission (DRC) has been set up to provide information and advice to disabled people, employers, and service providers about their rights and duties under the Disability Discrimination Act 1995 (DDA). The DRC's comprehensive website provides practical guidance about the best ways to ensure that disabled people are treated fairly, and the Commission can also provide advice on recruiting disabled people and providing equal treatment in the workplace. The DRC can be contacted via a national helpline (0845 762 2633) or through its website.

Other sources of help and advice: Your solicitor will be able to keep you updated on changes in employment law. In addition, advice can be obtained from your local Business Link, Small Business Gateway, Business Eye, or Invest Northern Ireland office.

MAKING IT HAPPEN
There were a large number of changes in employment law during 2003 and more in 2005. Here is a summary of the major changes.

Working time—young workers
Under the Working Time (Amendment) Regulations 2002, from 6 April 2003, workers aged between the minimum school leaving age and 18 must not work longer than 40 hours per week and 8 hours per day. These hours cannot be averaged out and there is no opt-out. Young workers may work longer hours where this is necessary either to maintain continuity of service or production, or in response to a surge in demand for a service or product—*provided* that there is no adult available to perform the task, and the employer ensures that the training needs of the young worker are not adversely affected.

Flexible working
Under the Employment Act 2002, from 6 April 2003, parents with children aged under six or disabled children aged under 18 will have the right to request a flexible working pattern, and their employers will have a duty to consider their applications seriously. The right enables parents to request to work flexibly. It does not provide an automatic right to work flexibly, as there will always be circumstances when the employer is unable to accommodate the employee's desired work pattern. The employee has a responsibility to think carefully about his or her desired working pattern when making an application, and the employer is required to follow a specific procedure to ensure requests are considered seriously.

Parental rights
From 6 April 2003, several new rights were provided regarding maternity, paternity, and adoption leave.

Maternity leave: The length of ordinary maternity leave has been extended to 26 weeks. In addition, a woman can take up to 26 weeks additional maternity leave. A woman who intends to return to work at the end of her full maternity leave entitlement is no longer required to give any further notification to her employer. Statutory maternity pay has increased to £106 per week.

Paternity leave: Providing an employee meets certain conditions, he is able to take one or two weeks paid paternity leave following the birth of his child. Employees must inform their employer of their intention to take paternity leave by the end of the 15th week before the baby is expected. They are entitled to £106 statutory paternity pay per week.

Adoption leave: Adopters are entitled to up to 26 weeks ordinary adoption leave, followed immediately by up to 26 weeks additional adoption leave—a total of up to 52 weeks leave. Adopters are required to inform their employer of their intention to take adoption leave within seven days of being notified by their adoption agency that they have been matched with a child for adoption. They are entitled to £106 per week statutory adoption pay during ordinary adoption leave.

Equal pay

The equal pay questionnaire, which came into effect on 6 April 2003 under the Equal Pay (Questions and Replies) Order 2003, is intended to help employees who believe they may not have received equal pay, to request key information from their employers to establish whether this is the case and, if so, the reasons why. The point of the questionnaire is to help establish whether an individual is receiving less pay and whether the employer agrees that the people being compared are doing equal work. The information should help to establish key facts early on and make it easier to resolve any disputes in the workplace.

WHAT TO AVOID

Assuming you know everything about employment law

If you are not aware of changes in employment law you can not comply with them. If you fail to comply, you are at risk of being taken to an employment tribunal by a disgruntled employee and could be liable for large fines if you are found in breach of the law.

RECOMMENDED LINKS

Advisory, Conciliation and Arbitration Service (Acas):
www.acas.org.uk
Business Eye (Wales):
www.businesseye.org.uk
Business Gateway (Scotland):
www.bgateway
Business Link (England):
www.businesslink.gov.uk
Commission for Racial Equality:
www.cre.gov.uk
Disability Rights Commission:
www.drc-gb.org
DTI—Tailored Interactive Guide on Employment Rights:
www.tiger.gov.uk
DTI Employment Relations Directorate:
www.dti.gov.uk/er
DTI Publications:
www.dti.gov.uk/publications
Equal Opportunities Commission:
www.eoc.org.uk
Invest Northern Ireland:
www.investni.com

SEE ALSO

Employment Law (p. 508)
Staff Planning (p. 415)

Conducting Interviews and Making Job Offers

GETTING STARTED

There are two main purposes to any job interview: the first is to find out whether the candidate is suitable for the job, and the second is to provide the candidate with information about the job and the business. To make sure the right person is appointed, it's very important that the interviewer gives all candidates the same opportunities to give the best presentation of themselves. Candidates should be free to demonstrate their suitability and to ask questions about the business and the job. To make the process worthwhile for everyone concerned, interviewers must know exactly what they're looking for in terms of the 'ideal candidate' and must be ready to spend time putting together useful questions that will help find him or her. This actionlist gives advice on preparation for the interview, interview technique, and how to move things long once the interview is over.

FAQS

What information should be provided before the interview?

Before the interview, give the prospective interviewees clear instructions on how to get to your place of work and also tell them who they should ask for when they arrive. Also tell them what they should bring with them (such as pens, paper, or a calculator), roughly how long the interview is likely to last, and whether they will be reimbursed for travel expenses. If you are going to give them a test (for example, a short proof-reading test if you are hoping to recruit an editor), it's polite to let the candidates know first.

Who should carry out the interview?

As a small business owner, you may be the only manager and therefore the sole interviewer. If you do work with others, though, you might like to ask a colleague to join you so that you get another opinion on each candidate. If the interviewee will be working for someone other than you, involve the candidate's prospective line manager or supervisor as much as possible. If possible, you might also want to involve someone in the business who has specialist technical knowledge related to the job vacancy.

How long should the interview take?

There are no hard and fast rules and obvi-ously how long you talk to someone depends on how well you get on with them, but generally interviews last between 30 and 60 minutes, including time for the candidate to ask questions of the interviewer. Schedule a break of about 20 minutes between interviews to give you time to make notes on the last interview and briefly prepare for the next. Interviewing is a tiring process, so don't schedule more than four or five interviews in a day and avoid doing them back to back if you can.

MAKING IT HAPPEN

Prepare for the interview

Decide what questions you are going to ask, basing them on the selection criteria for the job. Include general questions on the candidate's experience and skills, as well as questions which probe more directly into how well they are suited to the job description. You should also prepare questions specific to each candidate, such as queries about gaps in their curriculum vitae, or any issues that are not clear on their application forms. Take the time to read over their applications thoroughly.

As well as preparing questions, you also need to give some thought to where the interviews are to be conducted. Find a place where there will be no interruptions and make sure that you've made any adjustments needed to accommodate an interviewee who has indicated a disability.

Conduct the interview

The first thing to do is welcome the candidate and introduce yourself, and any other interviewers who may be present. Follow this by giving a brief outline of how the interview will be structured, and also some background about the organisation and the job.

Start the interview with easy 'getting to know you' questions, which will help put the candidate at his or her ease. These questions can also be used to build up to more probing, in-depth questions. Ask about the candidate's skills and experience first. When you have covered these, move on to why the candidate thinks they are suitable for the job, and what his or her ambitions and expectations are.

While you are conducting the interview, observe the candidate's behaviour as well as what she or he says. This is often a good indication of his or her general level of confidence, as non-verbal behaviour is usually a subconscious use of the body to telegraph meaning. It goes without saying that you shouldn't jump to conclusions and make snap judgments, but watch the interviewees' reactions to a range of questions and see how they react under pressure.

Towards the end of the interview, ask the candidate whether they have any questions. It is a good way to find out how much homework about the business the candidate has done, and whether he or she is really interested in the job. Also ask them if they can briefly summarise for you what *they* understand the job to be—this will help you to check that they have grasped the outline you've given them and that you have explained it unambiguously. Finally, remember to thank the candidate for coming to meet you and explain to them what the likely next steps are (for example, if there are likely to be second interviews) and when they should expect to hear from you.

Think about questioning techniques

Try to ask open-ended questions that can't be answered by just saying 'yes' or 'no'.

When you want more information, make sure you probe for specific answers. If a candidate seems to be avoiding a topic, use follow-up questions to try to fill in the blanks. Encourage candidates to expand on descriptions of their skills, and to demonstrate how they relate to the requirements of the job. Use questions that will encourage the candidate to sell him or herself to you. For example, you could ask questions such as, 'Why should I hire you?', and, 'Why do you want to work here?'

It is often a good idea to ask situational or hypothetical questions. These involve the interviewer describing a situation or case related to the business; the interviewee then has to propose a solution to handle the situation. This is a useful way to test problem-solving and reasoning ability. For example, you might ask the interviewee, 'Your boss tells you to do a certain task. Shortly afterwards a colleague says they need your help for a high-priority project. What do you do?'

Remember to keep your tone mild and non-judgmental, particularly when asking difficult questions. Keep to a logical sequence of questions so that the candidate does not become confused. Make sure that you allow pauses in the conversation, to give the candidate time to think. It might be difficult, especially if a candidate is struggling with a particularly tricky question, but try not to interrupt—give each candidate the opportunity to get his or her point across.

Assess the interviewee

It's essential that you give yourself time after the interview to make notes on anything said that is directly relevant to your decision. Do this as soon as you can so that the conversation is still fresh in your mind. If you've prepared properly before the interview, you'll already have decided on key selection criteria; the final decision should be based on how closely each candidate matched the person specification for that particular job. You may find that a marking system, which gives a score to each candidate for each of the areas highlighted in the job specification, makes it easier for you to make your decision.

Keep an open mind

Depending on the type of job you're recruiting for (see below), try not to jump to conclusions about your applicants' suitability for the role. Many companies these days are making a real effort to contribute to their local community by trying to break down barriers in the workplace and employing people with disabilities. If you are interested in growing your team in this way, there are good sources of help available to you. Disability employment advisers are on-hand at many Jobcentres, and you could also investigate the Access to Work programme, the Job Introduction Scheme, or Workstep. All of these schemes offer a variety of help, sometimes including grants, to employers and potential employees with a disability.

Follow up after the interview

If you've narrowed down your field of candidates to two or three people, now is the time to invite them back to second interview. Once you've you've finally selected the person you want to recruit, let him or her know as soon as possible, preferably by telephone as there is always the possibility that he or she will have other interviews to attend. Discuss salary (or other benefits) with the successful candidate at this point and address any queries he or she has thought of since you last met.

If the candidate accepts, follow up your conversation with a letter formally confirming the job offer and containing details of start dates and basic terms and conditions. If the selection has been narrowed down to two or three people, they can then be asked to come back for a second interview. Finally, write to unsuccessful candidates informing them of the outcome of the interview as soon as the decision has been made. Some candidates may request feedback on their interview, so be prepared to answer their queries (you might like to arrange another time to telephone them so that you have your notes in front of you).

Draw up an employment contract

You may want to add extra weight to the confirmation letter mentioned above by drawing up an employment contract—understandably, employees want some protection from being dismissed at will, and without an employment contract, they may feel that they're at the whim of employers who don't need legal, concrete reasons for terminating them. From an employer's point of view, without a contract of employment, those you recruit aren't necessarily bound to allegiance or secrecy, and could defect to a competitor company without you having any legal recourse. Having a contract might also discourage less than honourable people from applying, knowing that your recruitment and employment practices would probably turn up something about their past and the baggage they bring with them.

If you are putting together a contract for the first time, here is a list of key elements to include. If you are thinking of overhauling your recruitment procedure and are thinking of rewriting contracts for future employees, the list may include things that have been missing in the past, or that might help avoid future conflicts:

- name of employee and the company
- name of the job and job description
- dates (starting and ending if the contract is for a limited duration)
- condition of employment (for example, probationary period) and place(s) of work
- the salary or rate of pay, plus details about its calculation and when paid
- company benefits (health and medical, holiday entitlements, sick leave, bonuses, retirement, and so on)
- terms and conditions of employment—place, hours, flexi-time, and so on
- options for termination and notices required
- process for filing a grievance and recourse for appealing disciplinary action
- confidentiality, non-disclosure, and non-compete clauses (so that essential information cannot be taken to any new jobs that the employee takes up in the future)
- ownership rights to property and product (intellectual and real) developed while employed

WHAT TO AVOID
Asking unlawful questions
Legally, there are many questions that you must not ask because they are considered to be discriminatory, and therefore unlawful. Three of the more obvious ways in which your questions could be seen in this light are described below:

- **Sex discrimination.** Obviously everyone should avoid making sexists comments, but you must also avoid questions such as 'Are you planning to start a family?'. If you refuse to employ someone because they say that they are, you are being discriminatory, and the candidate can lodge a complaint against you.
- **Racial discrimination.** Similarly, you must not discriminate on grounds of race. This covers both ethnic background and country of origin. Do not ask candidates if they have any religious affiliations.
- **Disability discrimination.** If the candidate discloses a disability, you cannot use it as a reason not to employ him or her unless it is justified. For example, while somebody who is visually impaired would not be able to take up employment as a driver, he or she could take up a variety of roles in an office setting with the right equipment. If it will only take small adjustments for a disabled person to do a job and that person is the best-qualified candidate, then you have to make the adjustments. Any questions relating to disability have to be carefully worded and must centre on how you can enable the candidate to do the job with the disability, rather than on why the disability would exclude the candidate.

New legislation is scheduled to come into effect in October 2006 relating to age discrimination. It will outlaw unjustified age discrimination in vocational training and employment and also affect retirement ages and the rights of those due to retire.

Making unjustified assumptions
It's very easy for stereotyped assumptions to creep into the interview process. In particular, you should beware of rejecting candidates on the grounds of a 'gut feeling', or the idea that they would not 'fit in'. Employment tribunals are increasingly suspicious of such comments, as they are seen to be based on discriminatory assumptions, and may lead to complaints and legal challenges.

Causing the candidate to believe they have been offered the job
It's very important that you avoid making statements during the interview that could be alleged to create a contract of employment. It's easy to find yourself saying 'you' when you are describing what the successful candidate would be doing in his or her job (for example, 'You would be liaising with partners on a variety of projects.'). Try to avoid this as much as you can, and use more general terms such as 'the post-holder'. You should also avoid making excessive assurances about job security. Courts have, on occasion, held that promises made by the prospective employer during interviews created contracts of employment.

RECOMMENDED LINKS
Chartered Institute of Personnel and Development (CIPD):
www.cipd.co.uk
Commission for Racial Equality:
www.cre.gov.uk
Disability Rights Commission:
www.drc-gb.org
Equal Opportunities Commission:
www.eoc.org.uk

SEE ALSO
Employee benefits/Compensation (p. 507)

Running a Payroll System

GETTING STARTED
As soon as your business starts to employ people (including company directors), you will need to set up and manage a payroll system. This will allow you to make the correct deductions from staff wages or salaries, make the necessary payments to HM Revenue & Customs (HMRC) on time, and maintain an orderly system of pay-related records.

This actionlist explains the requirements for administering staff wages, including the deduction of tax and National Insurance (NI) contributions. At first glance, the process might look rather complicated, but actually it is quite simple, if a little time-consuming.

FAQS
What must I deduct from employees' pay?
The deductions you are required to make from your employees' pay are usually for income tax, and for National Insurance contributions under the Pay As You Earn scheme (PAYE). You then pay these deductions to HMRC in the month (or quarter, if you qualify as a PAYE small employer) after the staff have been paid.

You may also deduct pension contributions, and you may pay tax credits to your staff through the payroll. You are also expected to administer Statutory Sick Pay (SSP), Statutory Maternity Pay (SMP), and the Student Loan Deductions Scheme, if any of these apply to an employee.

How do I calculate net pay?
Many businesses use computerised payroll systems, but if your business only has a few employees, you may want to do the calculations manually. Even if you use a computer, it will be helpful to understand the principle of how to calculate pay and tax. HMRC provides forms and tables that simplify the calculations. There are four basic steps you need to follow.
- Add up the gross pay. This comprises the amount that you intend to pay your employee, together with any additional payments such as Statutory Sick Pay and Statutory Maternity Pay.
- Calculate the tax and National Insurance contributions. HMRC forms make this process straightforward.
- Add tax credits, or deduct student loan payments if applicable.

- Prepare a payslip for each employee, pay the employee, and send the deductions to HMRC.

At the end of each year, you will need to give each employee a summary of their pay and deductions for the year and send copies to HMRC, together with a reconciled statement of gross pay, deductions, and amounts sent to HMRC during the year.

How much tax must I deduct?
Explaining how to calculate an employee's tax is probably best done by using an example. If an employee earns £12,000 a year (gross), they will be entitled to a certain amount of tax-free income, normally the single person's allowance of £4,895. They will then pay tax of 10% on the first £2,090 of taxable pay, 22% on further taxable income up to £32,400, and 40% on the balance. The calculation is as follows:

Gross income	£12,000
Tax-free allowance	£4,895
Taxable pay	£7,105
Tax payable on first £2,090	£209
(10% of £2,090)	
Tax payable up to £32,400	£1,103
(22% of £5,015)	
Total tax	£1,312
Net pay	£10,688

Staff will normally be paid monthly, fortnightly, or weekly. Deductions can either be calculated based on the annual amount (as a computer does) or you can use the tables provided by HMRC.

How much National Insurance must I deduct?

Both employers and employees make National Insurance contributions. Except for some special cases, the amount depends solely on the level of the employee's salary, not on their personal circumstances (as in the case of income tax). The amount to be deducted can be easily determined from the tables provided by HMRC.

MAKING IT HAPPEN
Written pay statements

You must provide a written pay statement (payslip) to every employee when you pay them, setting out how their pay has been calculated. It must show gross pay, the amount of any deductions and the purpose for which they are made, and take-home pay. The table below shows an example of a pay statement.

Statutory sick pay

Employers have to pay Statutory Sick Pay (SSP) to employees who satisfy certain conditions and who have been sick for at least four consecutive days (including weekends and bank holidays). Statutory Sick Pay is paid to the business by deduction from National Insurance contributions. For the employee, it is treated as earnings. It is subject to tax and National Insurance contributions from the employee and employer.

There are various rules that need to be followed for periods of incapacity for work and qualifying days. The first three 'qualifying days' are known as waiting days and do not qualify for Statutory Sick Pay. There is now one standard rate of pay for Statutory

Sick Pay. For the financial year 2005/06, an eligible employee is entitled to £68.20 per week up to a maximum of 28 weeks in one spell of absence, but you should note that spells of at least four days with eight weeks or less between them are counted as one spell.

The employer must keep proper records to justify any claims. There is no prescribed form, although HM Revenue & Customs can provide form SSP2 to be used. The employer must record the dates of each reported incapacity, details of agreed qualifying days, Statutory Sick Pay paid, and dates when Statutory Sick Pay was not paid, with reasons.

The business may qualify for the Percentage Threshold Scheme, designed to reimburse employers who have a high percentage of workers off sick at any one time. If, in the tax month (which runs from the sixth of one month to the fifth of the following month), your Statutory Sick Pay is more than 13% of the total gross Class 1 National Insurance contributions liability, you can claim back the difference.

You may decide to pay sick employees a higher amount than the Statutory Sick Pay, for example, full salary for a month, and dropping after that. This is not compulsory and is not subject to the payment and reimbursement provisions outlined above.

Statutory Maternity, Paternity and Adoption Pay

Employers have to pay Statutory Maternity Pay (SMP), which works in much the same way as Statutory Sick Pay. The employer pays it to the employee for up to 26 weeks;

Employee		Number		Employer	
Jane Smith		***		Smith and Sons	
Payments		**Deductions**		**To Date**	
Gross:	£1,000.00	PAYE:	£109.93		£1,000.00
		NI:	£66.15	TAX:	£109.93
				NI:	£65.19
Total:	£1,000.00	Total:	£174.52	**NET PAY:**	**£825.78**
PAY DATE:		TAX CODE: 489L		PAY DATE:	
TAX PERIOD: 1		NI No: NZ-**-**-**-*		25/01/06	

most of this can be reclaimed from the government by way of deductions from National Insurance contributions. The employer can (but is not obliged to) add to this amount, although only the statutory element is recoverable. Female employees absent from work to have a baby are usually eligible to claim Statutory Maternity Pay. Statutory Maternity Pay is paid at 90% of weekly earnings for the first six weeks, then £106 per week for the next 20 weeks (or, if the employee earns less than £106 per week, 90% of average weekly earnings).

You can reclaim 92% of Statutory Maternity Pay contributions, although firms qualifying for Small Employers' Relief (SER) can claim back 100%, plus a further 5% of Statutory Maternity Pay paid to cover employers' National Insurance contributions. HMRC should be contacted for details of eligibility.

New fathers are entitled to take one or two consecutive weeks of paternity leave after their child is born, and most are entitled to Statutory Paternity Pay (SPP). Adoptive parents are entitled to take up to 26 weeks' ordinary adoption leave (paid) and again, most are entitled to Statutory Adoption Pay (SAP). The rate of pay for both categories of parent is the same as that standard rate of SMP: currently £106 per week or 90% of average weekly earnings if this is less than £106.

Tax credits

Lower paid staff might be entitled to the Child Tax Credit and the Working Tax Credit (these replaced the Working Families Tax Credit, Disabled Person's Tax Credit, and Children's Tax Credit in April 2003). You are required to add the tax credit amount (as notified by HMRC) to the employee's net pay. Tax credits are offset against the combined total of PAYE tax, National Insurance contributions, and student loan deductions

paid to HM Revenue & Customs. If credits exceed the total deductions, you may apply to HMRC for funding.

WHAT TO AVOID
Not doing your homework

Make sure you find out exactly what is required of you. HM Revenue & Customs has a good website with a great deal of information and all the current rates. It also publishes a number of guides which you may find helpful: *CA30 Statutory Sick Pay Manual for Employers*, and the *Employer's Annual Pack (Covering National Insurance, PAYE, SSP, etc)*. These can be ordered via the Employers' Orderline (0845 764 6646). The HM Revenue & Customs also runs three helplines: for the newly self-employed (0845 915 4515); for new employers (0845 607 0143); and for employers (0845 714 3143).

Not getting the right advice

It is important to run a payroll system correctly, so make sure you get the proper advice. PAYE and National Insurance calculations are usually easy to work out. However, if you are having difficulties, seek advice from an HM Revenue & Customs helpline, your local enterprise agency, or your accountant. If employees want to understand more about their entitlements, the Department of Work and Pensions has a website with information that will help. Website addresses are given below.

RECOMMENDED LINKS
Department of Work and Pensions:
www.dwp.gov.uk
HM Revenue & Customs:
www.hmrc.gov.uk

SEE ALSO
Employee benefits/Compensation (p. 507)

Complying with the National Minimum Wage Act 1998

GETTING STARTED

All businesses in the United Kingdom must comply with the National Minimum Wage Act 1998, which requires them to pay workers aged 18 or over at least the national minimum wage. This actionlist gives the current national minimum wage rate, explains who it applies to, and lists the exceptions. It also describes which elements of workers' pay are included in the minimum wage, and stresses the importance of keeping relevant records.

FAQS

How much is the national minimum wage?

As from October 2005, the minimum hourly rate for adult workers aged 22 or over is £5.05 before deductions. The minimum 'development rate', for 18 to 21 year olds and those on accredited training courses, is £4.25 per hour. The minimum wage has increased annually since its introduction in 1999, and this may continue if economic conditions remain favourable.

Who does the national minimum wage apply to?

All workers aged 18 or over, working in the United Kingdom, are entitled to the national minimum wage (subject to certain exemptions given below). No employer is exempt from paying the national minimum wage, whatever the size of their business. All types of workers are covered (whether full- or part-time), including casuals, temporary workers supplied through employment agencies, sub-contractors, trainees (with certain exceptions), and homeworkers.

Any employer refusing to pay a worker the minimum wage will be committing a criminal offence and can be fined. Fines can be up to £5,000 and employers may be ordered to make back-payment to employees. Employers must keep sufficient records to prove that they have paid their employees the minimum wage. The legislation applies equally across the United Kingdom (but not in the Channel Islands or the Isle of Man).

Workers aged 22 or over, on accredited

training courses, can be paid the development rate for only the first six months of a new job with a new employer. The employer must have agreed in writing to provide 26 days of accredited training before the end of the first six months of employment. After this period they must be paid the standard rate. Accredited training includes training for National Vocational Qualifications, Scottish Vocational Qualifications, and General National Vocational Qualifications; verified in-house training; and vocational training undertaken as part of the New Deal programme for 18 to 25 year olds.

Who is exempt from the national minimum wage?

Workers under 18 do not need to be paid the national minimum wage. Apprentices and Modern Apprentices under the age of 19 do not qualify for the national minimum wage, nor do apprentices under 26 who are in the first 12 months of their apprenticeship. Further exclusions include people working and living as part of a family, such as au pairs, friends, neighbours, and family who help out with household chores. Also exempt are non-employed trainees on government-funded training schemes, students working as part of sandwich courses, and teacher trainees placed in schools for work experience as part of their course. Homeless people who take part in a scheme for which they are provided with shelter in return for doing some form of work are exempt; so are voluntary workers who work for a charity, voluntary organisation, charity shop, school, hospital, or similar body, who receive any reasonable expenses or benefits in kind, or are placed by a charity or similar body with another charity and receive money for subsistence. All the people listed above can legally be paid less than the minimum wage.

How many hours must a person work to qualify?

There is no minimum period that a person must work before they qualify. The minimum wage is payable for the time when a worker is required to be at work or available for work. This includes time spent training and travelling for the purposes of the job (this does not include commuting to and from work).

As an employer, you must pay an average hourly rate of no less than the minimum wage appropriate to the worker. This is true for all types of workers, including those paid by output rather than time. Check with the DTI to make sure you are paying different workers the right rates, as these rates can change. Piece workers, for instance, must be paid 120% of the minimum wage, as of April 2005. It is the employer's responsibility to ensure that a worker is paid the national minimum wage over the period of time they work, regardless of how pay is calculated.

What makes up the minimum wage?

Elements that count towards the minimum wage include tips collected by an employer for employees and paid through the payroll, incentive payments, and bonuses. Elements that do not count towards the minimum wage include tips paid directly to workers by customers, and any loans, advances, pension payments, redundancy payments, awards by a court, or awards under staff suggestion schemes. Benefits in kind, such as meals or luncheon vouchers, and premium payments for overtime or shift work, are not included. Neither are allowances that are not consolidated into pay (for example, regional allowances), or the use of a company car and petrol.

Some elements may be deducted without reducing the amount paid to an employee for the purposes of the minimum wage.

These include penalties imposed upon an employee for misconduct, where the employer is permitted to make the deduction under the terms of the contract. Also included are the repayment of any loans, advance of wages, or purchase of shares, and repayments of any accidental overpayment of wages. Payments made by an employee to the employer for goods or services purchased may be deducted, as may the cost of accommodation provided by the employer, up to a limit. The cost of items related to the worker's employment (for example, uniforms and tools) can also be deducted. It is a good idea to get advice on these deductions, as they can be extremely complicated.

MAKING IT HAPPEN
Keep good records

As an employer, you must keep records to prove that your workers have received at least the minimum wage. The legislation does not define exactly what records should be kept as this will vary from employer to employer. Examples include general records kept for tax and National Insurance purposes, as these will usually detail how much the employee has been paid, and over what period.

If any queries arise about minimum wage payments, it is up to the employer to prove they have paid the minimum. It is not the employee's responsibility to prove that he or she has not been paid it. Records must be kept for a minimum of three years after the relevant pay reference period. The records must be produced on request, whether this request is by the worker, HM Revenue & Customs (HMRC), employment tribunal, or civil court. Under most circumstances, an employer has 14 days to produce the records following a request from the worker. Failure to do so may result in a penalty.

Understand employee rights concerning the minimum wage

The worker has three main rights. First, if a worker has reasonable grounds to believe that he or she has not been paid the national minimum wage, they have the right to see and copy the employer's records relating to them. They must make a written request to the employer who has to provide the records within 14 days. Second, employees can not be dismissed just because they have become eligible for a higher rate of pay under the minimum wage legislation. Where an employer fails to comply with the legislation, workers may enforce their rights by complaining to an enforcement agency; this agency may be HM Revenue & Customs, an employment tribunal, or a civil court. If this happens, the employee making the complaint must continue to be treated the same as all other employees. Third, a worker cannot agree to accept less than the minimum wage if they are entitled to it.

Know how the minimum wage is enforced

HM Revenue & Customs (HMRC) has overall responsibility for enforcing the national minimum wage. It has the power to serve enforcement and penalty notices, and to carry out visits to employers' premises to determine that the minimum hourly rate has been paid.

The Low Pay Commission (LPC) was established to recommend the coverage and initial level of the national minimum wage. In 2004 the LPC submitted a report recommending a number of changes concerning the development rate, compliance and enforcement, and future increases in the national minimum wage rate.

WHAT TO AVOID
Not keeping employees informed
You should display details of the national minimum wage prominently in your workplace so that your employees know their rights.

Refusing or neglecting to pay
Refusing or wilfully neglecting to pay the national minimum wage is a criminal offence and is punishable by a fine of up to £5,000.

Not getting the right advice
The Department of Trade and Industry's TIGER website (address given below) provides advice on how to calculate wages in compliance with the national minimum wage. The National Minimum Wage Helpline publishes two guides, *A Detailed Guide to the National Minimum Wage* and *National Minimum Wage—A Short Guide for Employers*, which may be helpful. It also has a number of telephone lines: 0845 600 0678 for inquiries, 0845 845 0360 for information and publications, and 0845 602 4027 for information in large print, in Braille, and on audio cassette.

RECOMMENDED LINKS
Department of Trade and Industry (DTI):
www.tiger.gov.uk
Low Pay Commission (LPC):
www.lowpay.gov.uk

SEE ALSO
Employee benefits/Compensation
  (p. 507)
Employment Law (p. 508)

Setting up Job Shares

GETTING STARTED

Job sharing is an increasingly popular option for working parents or carers. It's an arrangement in which two employees share the responsibility of one full-time position with the salary, paid leave, pension rights, and fringe benefits divided between them, according to the time each works. This actionlist looks at some of the advantages and disadvantages of job sharing, and provides a brief guide to setting up a job-sharing scheme.

FAQS

What are the advantages of job sharing?

Job sharing enables employees to retain the responsibility and status of full-time work while being able to work shorter, and often more flexible, hours. Job sharers are usually better paid, more highly skilled, and have better prospects for promotion than most part-time workers.

Job sharing benefits the employer too. Job sharing schemes can help you to retain skilled and experienced staff who are unable or don't want to work full-time but do not wish to leave their present job. It can also help to reduce absenteeism, as each job sharer has a greater amount of free time to organise other commitments and domestic responsibilities. As job sharers work fewer hours, they may also be take off less time for stress-related disorders.

Job sharing can ensure greater continuity of work. When one job-share partner is off sick or on holiday, at least one half of the job is still being done, and it may be possible to organise the job-share agreement so that both partners can be present at peak times. Job sharing also enables employers to get the best of two people's skills and experience for the price of one. Job sharers can organise their workload to take advantage of respective strengths and weaknesses, so that each person's capabilities are used to the full.

What are the disadvantages of job sharing?

Job sharing usually increases administrative costs. However, recruitment will often be for one worker to make up the job share (as

you'll normally have one person on your team already), and if two workers are employed at once, costs such as advertising, induction, and so on can be combined for the two.

Poor communication can be a problem, and it may be difficult to call meetings. Address this by making sure that both job sharers are kept properly informed of all developments, and, if possible, incorporate an overlap period, even if it's just a few hours a week, so that sharers can discuss their work. Ask both sharers to keep good records of what they do, have done, and are expecting to do so that everyone is clear and work isn't duplicated.

The job share may make extra work for managers in terms of allocating work, co-ordinating the work of the sharers, and communicating requirements. This will vary with the type of job and the way your business is structured. The division of responsibilities of the post will also need careful consideration, but time used in planning will be well spent.

MAKING IT HAPPEN

Start a scheme

Before you implement a job-share scheme, make sure that everyone in your business understands, approves of, and accepts the principles of job sharing, especially those who will have contact with the job sharers. Be aware of prejudices against part-time workers, who may be regarded as less committed to the company. Other considerations that you need to bear in mind are discussed in more detail below.

Create a job description

A detailed job description, clearly defining the duties and responsibilities of the post, will make it easier to divide responsibilities according to requirements. Many clerical posts can be split by hours, providing continuous coverage. Management and professional posts can be split by client, referral, project, and areas of expertise. Some jobs may have quite autonomous responsibilities, for example, different client caseloads, whereas others may require both of the job-share partners to contribute to the same project. In that case, if the job involves making important decisions, it will be necessary to decide if one partner's decisions must be upheld by the other.

Working hours

Job shares can be split in a variety of ways. Common patterns of work include split days, with one employee working in the morning and one in the afternoon; split weeks, where one employee works one half of the week and one the other; alternate weeks; or no fixed schedule, which is a less formal arrangement. Work out which pattern will suit the requirements of the job and the employees involved. Jobs may not always be split equally; one sharer may want to work fewer hours than the other. Bear in mind, however, that if one sharer only has very few hours, it may be difficult to replace that person if he or she leaves.

Overlap periods

Most job shares incorporate an overlap period for sharers to discuss developments and communicate problems. The length and frequency of the overlap periods will depend on the pattern of hours worked and the splitting of responsibilities; job sharers in a secretarial post may only need five minutes a day to discuss unfinished work, whereas partners who share a job as environmental consultants will obviously need more time to discuss clients and workloads.

Workspace

Job sharers will often share the same working area. However, if there are significant periods of overlap, it may be necessary to provide extra accommodation.

Training and induction

If possible, job sharers should attend induction training together. This will help to develop a working relationship and ensure that both receive the same training. Further training can either be undertaken individually, according to areas of expertise and interest, or together, in areas of shared training needs.

Management and supervision

Job-share posts will require more management time, with an emphasis on good verbal and written communication. Meetings could be alternated between job sharers, and every third meeting could be with both in attendance.

Promotion

It is usual to allow those who job share to apply for promotion on equal terms with full-time employees. Some organisations only consider the sharers together, and either appoint or reject them both; others will consider them individually as well as together, and appoint the best person for the job.

Holidays

Job sharers usually receive the same amount of holiday as full-time workers, but they are paid in proportion to the number of hours worked. For example, where a job-share partner works the equivalent of half a full-time job, working five half-days a week, he or she may be allowed to take 25 days holiday, the same as other employees, but only 12.5 of those will be paid holiday. Public holidays may cause some difficulties, as they usually fall on a Monday and therefore mostly within one job-share partner's working period. Public holidays are usually split into hours and divided between partners, with the time taken elsewhere by one partner.

Pension Schemes

Pensions are usually paid pro rata, depending on the number of hours worked by each individual.

Recruiting job sharers

Decide which jobs will be open to job sharing and how they will be advertised. In many cases these will be internal applications, and it will be important to decide whether or not those wishing to job share must identify a partner before applying. Consider whether separate application forms are required from each partner, whether they have to justify why they want to job share and demonstrate how they are compatible to do so on the application form, and whether they will be interviewed together, or separately, or both. Decide how applications from job sharers without a partner should be treated. Careful selection is necessary when recruiting two people for a job share. Their qualifications, experience, and skills should be compatible, and they should appear capable of forming a close working relationship. You must also consider whether you will make the position a full-time job, if you are only able to recruit one partner.

Employment rights

Job shares usually consist of two people sharing the workload normally assigned to one person. This usually involves a weekly workload spread over between 15 and 20 hours. The workers have the same rights as full-time employees according to the Employment Rights Act 1996. The rights of job sharers have been further extended by the introduction of the Part-time Workers (Prevention of Less Favourable Treatment) Regulations 2000 which came into force in July 2000. Under these Regulations, job sharers receive the same hourly rate as full-time workers, and the same hourly rate of overtime as comparable full-time workers, once they have worked more than the normal full-time hours. The regulations also cover the rights of employees not to be excluded from training simply because they work part time, and to have the same entitlements to annual leave and maternity/parental leave on a pro rata basis as their full-time colleagues. They should also have equal access to pension schemes. If an employee feels they have been less favourably treated, they can request a written statement for this from their employer, who must respond within 21 days. The new regulations should encourage more people to consider working part time as their circumstances change.

What to do if one partner leaves

If one job-share partner leaves, the procedure adopted by many organisations is to offer the job on a full-time basis to the remaining partner. If he or she does not accept the offer of full-time employment, the next step is to advertise the post as a job share, detailing the number of hours available. If no suitable replacement is found within a reasonable length of time (this time period varies considerably between organisations but is usually between three and six months), the remaining partner may be offered a part-time post or be redeployed elsewhere, if possible.

WHAT TO AVOID
Not keeping people informed
Inform all employees and management about the principles behind job sharing, and how it differs from part-time work, before a job-sharing scheme is implemented.

Not getting the right partners
How well a job share works depends on the people involved, so extra care will need to be taken with recruitment and selection procedures. It is important that both partners are able to communicate and interact well with each other, as well as with other employees, managers, and outside contacts.

RECOMMENDED LINKS
Department for Work and Pensions:
www.dwp.gov.uk
iVillage.co.uk:
www.ivillage.co.uk/workcareer/worklife
New Ways to Work:
www.new-ways.co.uk
Recruitment and Employment
  Confederation:
www.rec.uk.com

SEE ALSO
Employment Law (p. 508)

Employing People with Disabilities

GETTING STARTED

As an employer, you have a general duty not to discriminate against any employee. The Disability Discrimination Act 1995 (DDA) specifically prohibits discrimination on the basis of disability, whatever the size of your business.

This actionlist explains what is expected of employers when they interview and employ a disabled person. It describes the legal requirements and also suggests ways to improve the employment environment to accommodate disabled staff so they are not disadvantaged.

FAQS

What is a disability?

The Act defines a person with a disability as someone with a physical or mental impairment that has a substantial or long-term adverse affect on their ability to carry out normal day-to-day activities. In June 2005, new legislation widened the definition of the term 'disabled' to include those affected by cancer, HIV, or multiple sclerosis.

What are my legal obligations?

The Act requires employers to consider the ability of the person and to make reasonable adjustments in working arrangements or to the physical features of the premises. You need to take fair steps to prevent these arrangements or features placing the disabled person at a disadvantage. These will vary from situation to situation. You will need to consider how effective the adjustments will be in helping the disabled person, whether they are practical to implement, how much they will cost, and whether you can you afford them. You will also need to check whether there is any financial assistance available to help you make the adjustments.

How do these rules apply in Northern Ireland?

The Disability Discrimination Act applies in the same way in Northern Ireland as it does in the rest of the United Kingdom, but there is a separate Northern Ireland Code of Practice for eliminating discrimination against disabled people (available from the Stationery Office).

In Northern Ireland, the Disablement Advisory Service provides services and programmes for disabled people equivalent to the Jobcentre Plus in England, Scotland, and Wales. Disability Employment Advisers are known as Disablement Employment Advisers.

MAKING IT HAPPEN

Prevent discrimination when recruiting

If you're using advertisements to recruit new staff, it's good practice to welcome applications from people with disabilities. Provide information about the job in an accessible format such as large print (which people with learning disabilities or sight difficulties will find easier to read) or with illustrations. If you place your advert with the Disability Employment Adviser at the Jobcentre or Jobcentre Plus, you can guarantee that disabled people will see it. You can also mail your vacancy bulletins to local specialist agencies and offer job-share vacancies to allow applicants flexible working arrangements.

Some people with learning disabilities can fill in an application form themselves; others will need help from a supporter. Consider allowing candidates to submit an application in different formats, such as by telephone, audio-tape, or e-mail. It's good practice to include a question on the application form to ask applicants if they would have any special requirements at an interview.

Make your workplace friendlier to disabled staff

If any physical feature of your premises, or any arrangements made by you, causes a substantial disadvantage to a disabled person compared with non-disabled people, you have to take reasonable steps to address this. Physical features include things like a building's design or construction, access to a building, fixtures, fittings, furnishings, equipment, or materials. For example, the design of a workplace may make it difficult for someone with a hearing impairment to hear.

The Act gives a number of examples of steps that you may have to take. You may have to make adjustments to premises, such as providing a wheelchair ramp, or allocate some of the disabled person's duties to another employee. Another step might be to transfer the person to fill an existing vacancy, or to assign the person to a different place of work. Other examples include altering the person's working hours, or allowing him or her to be absent during working hours for rehabilitation, assessment, or treatment. You may be required to arrange for training for the person, to acquire or modify equipment, or to provide a reader, interpreter, or extra supervision.

Avoid discrimination against disabled people

Take care that your actions, or lack of them, do not lead to what is known as 'constructive dismissal', a situation in which a disabled employee's job is made too difficult for them to continue. Your employee can then take legal action if you did not make reasonable adjustments to enable them to do their job.

If an employee complains of, or shows signs of, physical pain, such as back pain caused by lifting, or stress related to work, it's best to talk to him or her about it and see if anything can be done to remedy the situation. Record all interviews of this kind, even if the employee says that it's not a problem.

Adopting good practice can help minimise or avoid the risk of costly litigation. There is a Code of Practice on the employment provisions of the Act. Good practice is about looking beyond the disability to what the person can actually do, sometimes with a bit of adjustment to the workplace or working practices.

Find out about support for employers of disabled staff

Effective and practicable adjustments for disabled people often involve little cost or disruption. However, if you think you may not be able to afford the necessary changes, the Government Access to Work scheme might assist. This is a grant for any extra costs incurred by an employer resulting from the disability of an employee. It gives financial support for a variety of areas, such as aids and adaptations.

The funding available depends on the employment status of the disabled person at the time of the application. For disabled people already employed, you can receive a maximum of 80% of the costs of special equipment or adaptations costing between £300 and £10,000, and 100% of costs over £10,000. It can cover 100% of approved costs for unemployed disabled people taking up employment, for disabled people who have been in work for less than six weeks, and for disabled people who are self employed.

Other support agencies and initiatives include Jobcentre Plus (part of the Department for Work and Pensions), which can advise on benefits and employment. The Jobcentre Plus service has set up Employer Direct customer service centres with one central number to help you find candidates to fill vacancies. There is also New Deal, the Government's flagship initiative to move socially excluded people into work. There are several New Deal programmes aimed at helping individuals improve their employability and find work. If you offer jobs to people with disabilities you also receive practical support and help from New Deal personal advisers, including advice on their eligibility for additional funding through the Access to Work scheme. Disability Employment Advisers can advise about the New Deal programmes available to employers, and your nearest Job Centre can help you contact them.

The Job Introduction Scheme (JIS) provides a weekly grant towards the cost of employing a disabled person for a trial period. You usually receive a grant of £75 a week over a trial period of six weeks (although it can be extended for up to 13 weeks). The job can be full or part time, but must be expected to last for at least six months after the JIS grant ends. You must apply for JIS before the person begins paid work.

WHAT TO AVOID
Not getting the right advice
The Job Introduction Scheme (JIS) can help you if you're thinking of recruiting someone with a disability. You can discuss any practical concerns to do with taking on someone with a disability with a Disability Employment Adviser (DEA). They will then decide whether JIS can help you. Further information can be found in your local Jobcentre Plus office or Jobcentre.

Not demonstrating your commitment to equal opportunities
Show that you have a commitment to equal opportunities. Mention disability explicitly in any equal opportunities policy and reassure any disabled applicants that their needs will be met. Make sure all your staff implement such policies.

RECOMMENDED LINKS
Department of Trade and Industry:
www.dti.gov.uk
The Stationery Office:
www.tso.co.uk
Disability Service Team (part of
   Jobcentres):
www.jobcentreplus.co.uk
Disability Rights Commission:
www.drc-gb.org
Department for Work and Pensions:
www.dwp.gov.uk
Employers' Forum on Disability:
www.employers-forum.co.uk
Employers' Forum on Disability (Northern
   Ireland):
www.efdni.org

SEE ALSO
Employment Law (p. 508)

Benefiting from Apprenticeships

GETTING STARTED

Apprenticeships were introduced in 1995 (when they were called 'modern apprenticeships', as they still are in some areas of the United Kingdom) and are designed to provide support for businesses recruiting and training 16 to 24-year-olds. As part of its youth guarantee policy, the government gives priority to those between the ages of 16 and 18.

The responsibility for modern apprenticeships falls on the following training organisations: in England, Learning and Skills Councils; in Wales, Education and Learning Wales; in Scotland, by Scottish Enterprise and Highlands and Islands Enterprise Companies; in Northern Ireland, the Department for Employment and Learning.

FAQS
How does apprenticeship work?

There are two levels of apprenticeship: Foundation and Advanced. Foundation modern apprenticeships result in the attainment of National Vocational Qualification (NVQ) Level 2. The Advanced modern apprenticeship is based on the attainment of the minimum of a National Vocational Qualification Level 3, and the development of key skills such as communication, information technology, team working, and problem solving. Many of the advanced level apprenticeships now also include study for a technical certificate relevant to the apprentice's specific vocation.

The length of apprenticeships can vary, and depends very much on the young person in question and the type of career they are working towards. Some apprenticeships can take up to five years, while others can take from twelve to twenty four months. Applicants are usually expected to have at least five GCSEs at grade C or above. They must be at least 16 and be able to complete their training programme by their 25th birthday.

Apprenticeships are available in over 80 industry and business sectors, including engineering, construction, information technology, business administration, catering, accountancy, retailing, hairdressing, and hospitality.

What are the benefits of this scheme for employers?

Recruiting modern apprentices may help you find and train people to have exactly the skills you need to build your business and to remain competitive within your chosen industry. You can also enrol people who work for you already on to the scheme, which will assist in their development and may also help you retain the skills your business can call on. You'll receive financial assistance for funding the scheme too—see below for more information.

What are my obligations as an employer to the modern apprentice?

At the start of an apprenticeship, the employer, the apprentice, and the Learning and Skills Council (or equivalent) sign a 'pledge'. The employer agrees to provide training and experience to industry-recognised standards; the apprentice agrees to be hard working and loyal.

A training schedule is drawn up. This will specify the skills the apprentice needs to develop, how and where the training is to be delivered, and the qualifications that will be attained. The skills identified can be general (such as communications and numeracy) or specific (such as learning a foreign language). Employers tend to work closely with the Learning and Skills Council to develop the training programme.

MAKING IT HAPPEN
Recruit modern apprentices

Apprentices are recruited using a variety of methods, usually through colleges, Learning and Skills Councils (or equivalent), or the Careers Service, all of which might provide support in the recruitment process. Other methods include newspaper advertising and word of mouth.

Apprentices can be selected using various guidelines for the business sector, as well as personal criteria. An apprenticeship programme may be run without recruiting new staff, as long as the business has employees under the age of 24.

Fund modern apprenticeships
Apprentices are usually employed by an organisation. In rare cases where employment is not possible, the apprentice will be linked to one or more employers and paid an allowance. Arrangements regarding wages and/or allowances will be made between the parties concerned.

The Department for Education and Skills (DfES) provides the funds for the apprenticeships. They are channelled through the Learning and Skills Councils (or equivalent), which will agree funding levels with individual employers according to local arrangements. Employers will normally have to meet the cost of wages, and may also be asked to contribute towards training costs.

Remember to note that the national minimum wage does not need to be paid to apprentices who are under the age of 18. People who start apprenticeships aged 16 or 17 and continue until they are 18 will not need to be paid the national minimum wage until they are 19.

WHAT TO AVOID
Not thinking ahead
Remember that you need to plan staffing to meet future as well as current business needs, so that you don't get caught on the hop. Also bear in mind that you need to include the cost of training in your budgets.

Not getting the right advice
If employing under-18s, it is important to check if your local authority has any relevant by-laws and guidelines.

The range of modern apprenticeships is being expanded to cover more business and industry sectors. Trade associations and the training organisations mentioned in the introduction can provide details of apprenticeships relevant to your business.

RECOMMENDED LINKS
Department for Education and Skills (DfES):
www.dfes.gov.uk
Department for Employment and Learning (Northern Ireland):
www.delni.gov.uk
Education and Learning Wales:
www.elwa.org.uk
Learning and Skills Council:
www.apprenticeships.org.uk
Scottish Enterprise:
www.scottish-enterprise.com

SEE ALSO
Employment Law (p. 508)

Understanding the Working Time Regulations 1998

GETTING STARTED

The Working Time Regulations were introduced to lay down the minimum health and safety requirements for the organisation of working time. They implement a European Council Directive on the Organisation of Working Time (which is commonly referred to as the Working Time Directive). The Regulations also implement parts of the European Community Young Workers Directive, which specifically contain sections defining young workers. This actionlist explains how you are affected by these regulations.

FAQS

What types of business are affected by the Working Time Regulations?

The Working Time Regulations 1998 apply to all sectors, both public and private. Industries which are excluded include air, rail, road, sea, inland waterway and lake transport, sea fishing, and the activities of doctors in training, the armed forces, and police force. The self-employed are also excluded.

When did the Working Time Regulations come into force?

The Working Time Regulations came into force on 1 October 1998. The regulations were amended in 1999 to add in further provisions that apply to workers whose working time is partly measured, predetermined, or determined by the worker, and partly not. The regulations were also amended on 5 October 2001 to include the entitlement of four weeks' annual leave for all workers.

Who enforces the Working Time Regulations?

The responsibility for enforcing the regulations lies with different bodies. The Health and Safety Executive is responsible, for example, for administering the 48-hour limit and health assessments for night workers in sectors including factories, fairgrounds, farms, and building sites. Local authorities have responsibility for retailing, offices, hotels and catering, sports, leisure, and consumer services. Employment tribunals cover problems relating to employee rights, for example, leave and rest breaks. They

also provide workers with the opportunity to present complaints, any breach of the regulations, and related cases of unfair dismissal. The Health and Safety Executive has the power to ensure that an employer complies with the regulations. If you fail to do so, you could be faced with a fine or imprisonment.

What is the purpose of the Working Time Regulations?

The regulations are intended to provide protection to the most vulnerable employees, and to lay down the minimum health and safety requirements for the organisation of working time. They also offer flexibility for an employer and worker to make arrangements that suit them both. They establish guidelines for minimum periods of daily and weekly rest, annual leave, breaks, and maximum weekly working time. This helps to ensure an alert work force which may reduce the risk of an accident occurring or a mistake being made. They also cover aspects of night work, shift work, and overall patterns of work.

What do the terms used in the Working Time Regulations mean?

The term 'workers' covers those with a contract of employment, plus a wider group who undertake work under other forms of contract, for example, agency and temporary workers, and freelancers. However, it does not cover the self-employed. 'Young workers' refers to workers who have reached school-leaving age but who are not yet over 18 years old.

The term 'working time' in relation to a worker refers to any period during which he or she is working, at the employer's disposal, and carrying out his or her activities and duties. In relation to young workers, it also includes any time spent doing in-house training or work experience, for example, on a National Traineeship or New Deal scheme.

The term 'rest period' is any period of time that is not classed as working time.

'Night time' is a period of not less than seven hours, which must include the hours between midnight and 5am. Under the regulations, this is defined (in absence of other industry agreements) as the period between 11pm and 6am. A 'night worker' is any worker who works at least three hours of their daily working time as part of night time. It also applies to those who are likely to work a certain proportion of annual working time during night time.

The term 'shift work' applies to the organisation of work according to shift patterns where workers need to work at different times over a period of days or weeks. A 'shift worker' is any worker who is employed to do shift work.

MAKING IT HAPPEN
Realise opt-out agreements are voluntary

As an employer, you are obliged to take all reasonable steps to ensure that workers are not required to work more than an average of 48 hours per week. The exception to this is when a worker has signed an opt-out, which allows him or her to work longer than the 48-hour limit. Signing an opt-out agreement must be voluntary on the part of the worker. The opt-out agreement needs to be in writing and signed by the worker. There is no need for it to be renewed. Workers have the right to cancel the opt-out agreement when they want. However, they are obliged to give you a minimum of seven days' notice, or as long as three months, if appropriate. Do note that the European Union is attempting to abolish the opt-out clause and it is not known how long the United Kingdom will be allowed to keep it.

Know working time limits

You must be familiar with what counts as working time and what does not. It will also be useful to have an understanding of how average weekly working time is calculated. The Department of Trade and Industry's publication *Your Guide to the Working Time Regulations* may be useful for you and you can download it from their website (address below)

Remember night workers

It is important that you comply with the regulations if you employ workers who can be classified as night workers. Employers should be aware of how many hours night workers normally work, and how they may be able to reduce the hours of work of those night workers who normally work more than eight hours in any 24-hour period. It is essential to give special consideration if a night worker does work involving special hazards, or involving heavy physical or mental exertion.

Night workers are entitled to a free health assessment before they commence work and at regular intervals following employment—although workers are not obliged to have a health assessment. A health assessment comprises two parts: a questionnaire and a medical examination, which is only necessary if the worker's fitness for night work is in question. Seek help from a qualified health professional when drawing up and assessing the questionnaire. Those suffering from problems related directly to working at night should be transferred to day work where possible. The suitability of certain vulnerable groups of people for night work, especially new or expectant mothers and young workers, should be given special consideration.

Give time off and rest breaks

Check how working time has been arranged in your organisation, and that workers are able to take the time off they are entitled to. Employers need to be familiar with the special provisions that apply to young workers. You are also obliged to check whether there are any exceptions that apply to workers taking time off.

You should also be informed about who is entitled to annual leave. Each worker (including part-time) is now entitled to four weeks' paid annual leave. Annual leave may not be replaced by remuneration in lieu, except where the employment contract is terminated. There is no statutory right to bank holidays, and as such, the annual leave requirement includes them. Employers have the right to stipulate rules for when annual leave should be taken, for example, over the Christmas period.

Employees must be able to take the rest breaks that they are entitled to. You need to be familiar with the different rest break periods that apply to young workers. As an employer, you are also obliged to check whether there are any exceptions that apply to workers taking rest periods. It is possible for employers and workers to agree to vary their entitlement to rest periods, with the workers receiving 'compensatory rest'. This is a period of rest that is identical in length to the period of rest that the worker has missed.

Keep records

You are obliged to keep records to show that you have complied with the working time limit per week within your organisation. It is the responsibility of each employer to decide what records need to be kept to fulfil this obligation. Existing records, which are currently employed for other purposes, may be used, or alternatively, you may choose to compile and maintain new records. It is important to keep up-to-date records of workers who have signed an opt-out agreement to work more than 48 hours a week. Records of regular health assessments of night workers also need to be kept. Records must be kept for two years. Keeping records of rest breaks, days off, and annual leave is not required.

Be aware of exemptions from the regulations

Certain professions, for example, managing executives, family workers, or those in office at religious ceremonies and religious communities, cannot completely comply with the regulations due to the nature of their job. These are people whose time cannot be measured and can only be determined by the workers themselves. They are exempt from the provisions in the regulations relating to weekly working time, night work, rest periods, and breaks.

Further situations that cannot fully comply include: workers whose place of employment and place of residence are distant from each other; security and surveillance activities that require permanent presence; activities involving continuity of service or production, for example, hospitals, residential institutions, dock and airport workers, media, ambulance, fire and civil protection services; and activities in which there is a potential surge of activity, for example, agriculture, tourism, and postal services. Workers in these situations must be provided with periods of compensatory rest.

WHAT TO AVOID
Not seeking the right advice
Consult a solicitor or legal adviser if you have any queries about how the business may be affected. You can also contact the Health and Safety Executive and the Advisory Conciliation and Arbitration Service for further information—local offices are listed in the phone book.

Not keeping staff informed
Members of staff who are affected by the changes should be identified and all staff provided with a brief outline of the new regulations.

RECOMMENDED LINKS
Advisory Conciliation and Arbitration
  Service (Acas):
www.acas.org.uk
Department of Trade and Industry:
www.dti.gov.uk/er/work_time_regs
Employment Tribunals Service:
www.employmenttribunals.gov.uk
Health and Safety Executive (HSE):
www.hse.gov.uk

SEE ALSO
Employment Law (p. 508)

Developing Leadership Skills

GETTING STARTED

There are many myths about leaders—'leaders are born and not made' being a prime example. Owner-managers of small businesses might not necessarily have been in a leadership role before they started their company, and while some people are naturally better suited to leadership roles than others, the good news is that the necessary skills *can* be learned.

FAQS

Now that my business is growing I've been on a leadership course and understand the theory of being a good leader. How do I put this into practice?

Being an owner-manager will give you plenty of opportunities to put your new skills to the test, but remember that leadership capability does not emerge overnight; it takes time and practice, so don't expect too much of yourself too soon. Why not make a start, though, by leading a new project, where you can test out the skills you've acquired? Make sure you plan carefully for resources and support. Taking this first step will give you the opportunity to test out your responses to this new situation. In turn, you'll then be able to evaluate what has worked and what hasn't, helping you plan what to do or avoid doing next time.

I seem to command an audience easily when I make presentations, but will I make a good leader?

Commanding an audience is a great skill and many leaders have it, but it's not the sole requirement. Leaders also need to be problem-solvers and have originality and flair, confidence and self-knowledge, strong interpersonal skills, the ability to listen, visioning capability, good organisational skills, and so on. Your ability as a speaker suggests that you're articulate and self-confident. If you possess the other qualities too, you are well on the way to being the leader your business needs.

styles. Think of three shepherds. The first opens the gate and walks through, allowing the flock to follow—this shepherd **leads from the front**. Another stands behind the sheep and pushes or guides them through, demonstrating a **supportive leadership style**. The third moves from front to back and sometimes to the middle of the flock, demonstrating an **interactive leadership style**. For leaders to exist, there must be followers, and the needs of followers change depending on the context. Knowing how to apply different leadership styles can help you respond equally effectively in many different kinds of situations.

Another school of thought recognises four leadership styles: directive, process, creative, and facilitative, each one related to a personality trait. So, being more relaxed doesn't necessarily mean you can't be a leader. You simply have natural tendencies for a certain type of leadership. And you may be able to learn other styles—more dominant, intuitive, or structured—as you become more confident and practised in leadership. Try to work with your preferred style until you are comfortable enough to branch out.

Evidently, certain styles are suited to particular situations. A structured leader, for example, is likely to succeed in a situation where process is important, for example, in running an operation. The relaxed or facilitative leader may be one who manages a professional group of people. Dominant leaders may be needed in businesses where there is a real drive for change.

MAKING IT HAPPEN

Understand the different facets of leadership

There are different types of leadership

Get some training

If your budget permits, a leadership course will help you gain a fuller understanding of what leadership is, and, by extension, how it will work for your business. Courses usually range from business theory to developing strategy to and understanding business risk.

Having well-developed commercial awareness and a good business education will not only give you confidence, but will also help command respect from others in the organisation.

Build self-awareness

Your leadership style is the means by which you communicate. The more self-aware you are, the more effectively it will work for you. This means knowing:

- what you are like
- what your preferences are
- what your goals are
- how other people perceive you and your goals
- how you are motivated to achieve them

Numerous tests and questionnaires can be used to help you explore your personality and preferences; they are widely available from books, the web, consultancies, and other sources. Surveys are also useful. Business schools have valuable data on expected leadership behaviours. You can combine information from all these sources to establish a benchmark for yourself.

Apply leadership skills

Leadership opportunities are often thrust upon us unexpectedly, but in a small business environment you'll come across them more frequently. As in most situations, your best bet is to start with an analysis of the situation. Decide what is needed, and how you can best achieve it.

Some leadership positions require you to set the objectives for others to follow. In these situations, scheduling, consultation, and team building are essential to success. Leaders often need to work as intermediaries between two groups—those wanting the results (boards, investors, etc.), and those who will deliver the results. In this case you need to establish good communication channels with both parties. Try to pick teams that have a good balance between competent managers and energetic, loyal

team members. Teams need consistent, positive energy levels to sustain momentum. Thus choosing a team by the mix of talent required, rather than based on friendships or politics, is critical.

If you are trying out new systems or approaches, do surround yourself with the right people, create a framework for support, and document the process so you can later evaluate what you have done.

WHAT TO AVOID
Mirroring other leaders too closely

People new to leadership roles may try to copy a leader they respect, because the person provides an easy model. This can create a false impression of what you are really like, or, worse, make you look foolish for trying to mimic a style incompatible with your own personality. Leadership behaviours come from within. Understand what it is you respect in the other leader and think about how you can best display that attribute. If it doesn't work, don't be afraid to try a new approach.

Not working at it

Many people hope that they have natural leadership skills, and accept leadership positions without proper training or mental adjustment. This sink-or-swim approach works sometimes, but not always! Building up leadership skills, increasing awareness of yourself, and evaluating what you do have much more potential for success. It will also give you more room to make mistakes without losing credibility.

RECOMMENDED LINKS
Emerald:
www.managementfirst.com/experts/ leadership.htm
Entrepreneur.com:
www.entrepreneur.com (management tab)
The Leadership Trust:
www.leadership.co.uk

SEE ALSO
Delegating without Guilt (p. 412)

Focus On: Win-win Appraisals
Patrick Forsyth

GETTING STARTED

As your business grows and you become responsible for managing other people, it's likely that you will need to conduct performance appraisals. These face-to-face discussions (ideally undertaken annually) are an opportunity for an employee's work to be discussed and reviewed, and should aim to improve motivation and performance during the coming year. Unfortunately, many managers dislike conducting appraisals and worse, many employees rate their appraisals as worthless—or something even less flattering. In reality, appraisals are a major opportunity for both managers and staff.

This actionlist will review:

- why appraisals are necessary and what the benefits are to managers and staff. Primarily, they ensure and improve future performance.
- how effective appraisals should be planned and undertaken to maximise their positive impact while avoiding negative pitfalls.
- the impact of appraisals on the long-term success of an organisation. Appraisals provide considerable opportunity for improving on-going operations, effective management, and catalysing change.

FAQS

What are the reasons for performance appraisals?

There are many positive reasons why appraisals are necessary. They give managers an opportunity to review individuals' past performance, plan their future work and role, and set and agree specific individual goals for the future. Making time to hold a meeting with the person to be appraised also allows for on-the-spot coaching which in turn can identify development needs and set up development activity.

In addition, appraisals can:

- allow the exchange of feedback
- reinforce or extend the reporting relationship
- act as a catalyst for delegating work
- focus on longer-term career progression
- underpin or increase motivation

It's also worth bearing in mind that there is a close relationship between appraisals and employment legislation (for example, lack of appraisal may make it impossible to terminate someone's employment).

Overall the underlying intention is to improve future performance. The good appraisal presupposes that even the best performance can be improved, and seeks to increase the likelihood of future plans being brought to fruition.

How should the appraisal be organised?

For a well-organised appraisal, you need to:

- allow enough time. Few appraisals will be accomplished properly in less than an hour; some may last two or three hours or more—and will still be time usefully spent.
- allow no disturbances. Pausing to take even one telephone call sends out the wrong signals.
- create a suitable environment. Appraisals should be held somewhere private, comfortable, perhaps less formal than across a desk, yet suitably business-like.
- put the individual at ease. Remember that, even with good communication beforehand, appraisals may be viewed as somewhat traumatic. Anything that can be done to counter this is useful.

MAKING IT HAPPEN
Prepare throughout the year

Unsurprisingly, the key to effective appraisals is preparation by both parties. The manager must:

- spend sufficient time with staff during the year.
- communicate clearly and thoroughly the purpose and form of the appraisal so that people know what to expect. Employees should understand the need for appraisal, its importance, the specific objectives it addresses, and how both parties can get the best from it.
- prepare throughout the year, keeping clear records. Keeping an appraisal collection file means you don't have to rely on memory. In this, you should note matters that can usefully be raised at appraisals, making notes and filing copies of documents that will assist the process.

The person being appraised should keep running records and should plan in detail the kind of meeting he or she intends to have.

Successful appraisal is the culmination of a year's worth of thinking. Recalling every detail of an employee's working year is difficult, but you can only appraise properly by being informed.

Relevant background information needs checking: for example, the appraisee's job description (which may need amendment after the appraisal), specific past objectives, possible changes to the job, its responsibilities, or circumstances, and the records of any previous appraisals.

Prepare and plan carefully

- Prepare written notification. As well as confirming mutually convenient timing, this should recap the purpose of the appraisal and highlight background information. Distribute copies of any documents or forms you intend to use or refer to during the meeting.
- Study the person's file, making sure that you have all the information you need about what was supposed to happen during the year and what actually did happen. Make notes of points needing discussion and ensure that you can navigate the documents easily as the meeting progresses.
- Review agreed standards and identify any that are no longer relevant or that need to be changed.

- Draft a provisional assessment. Brief notes can provide a starting point, prompt the agenda, and link to the system. Don't prejudge the discussion or make decisions prematurely.
- Assess your initial thoughts. Check your rationale, asking yourself the question 'why?' as you note each thing down. If no clear answer comes, more research may be necessary.
- Consider specific areas of the appraisal. It may be clear that some training is necessary, for example. Again without prejudging, it may be useful to check out what might be suitable so that you have ready suggestions at the meeting.
- Think ahead. Remember that the most important part of the discussion will be about the future. You may need to plan particular projects and tasks, taking both development and operational considerations into account.
- Consult with others. Speak to those who work or deal with the person to get a complete picture.
- Be clear about the link with a pay review. Many managers feel this should be kept for a separate occasion, as otherwise it can be difficult to stop people from thinking all that matters is the potential increase.

Handle the appraisal effectively

Before you go any further, make completely sure that everybody being appraised understands the need for appraisal, its importance, its objectives, and its mutual benefits. When the appraisal starts:

- explain the agenda and how things will be handled. Remember to ask what the employee's priorities are.
- act to direct the proceedings. Do not, however, ride roughshod over the other person.
- ask questions. Open questions prompt and focus discussion.
- listen. The meeting is primarily an opportunity for the person being appraised to communicate. In a well-conducted appraisal, he or she should do most of the talking; the manager's job is to make that happen.
- keep primarily to agreed performance factors. Don't indulge in amateur psychology

or attempt to measure personality factors—it's how someone actually does their job that's important here.

■ use the system. Stick to an agenda or follow an appraisal form to guide the meeting; working through the form systematically will ensure most of what needs to happen does.

■ encourage discussion. Consider the employee's personal strengths and weaknesses, successes and failures, and their implications for the future. Concentrate the appraisal process on future performance, and don't confuse it with discussion of remuneration.

■ set out action plans. Agree those that can be decided there and then (who will do what, when); note those needing more deliberation in terms of when and how action will be taken. Deal with each factor separately, for example, by devoting time to development action.

■ conclude on a positive note. Always thank the person for the role he or she has played and for the past year's work. Link this to any subsequent documentation.

■ follow up appraisals promptly, sending all necessary written material to the person and flagging any opportunity for further discussion.

WHAT TO AVOID
You treat appraisals as an end, rather than a means to an end

Appraisals achieve most when placed in a long-term context and linked to ongoing operations. Bear in mind:

■ the ongoing management relationship: an effective appraisal should make all management processes through the year easier.

■ the link with training and development: consultation, counselling, mentoring, and informal discussions are all just as important extensions of appraisal as formal training.

■ motivation: appraisals must themselves be motivational, and what stems from them must help someone remain motivated going forward.

You dwell too much on the past
This shouldn't really account for more than 60% of the discussion at most; you also need to discuss future activities, priorities, development needs, and objectives.

You're too directive or too critical
Successful appraisals are dynamic, positive discussions, not a witch-hunt or a chance to heap blame and ignominy on someone. (If you do need to tackle a problem, do it when the problem arises, and don't just store it up for the appraisal!)

Your comments and feedback aren't clear enough
You must be clear, honest, and open in your comments. The more you hedge, the more chance there is that misunderstandings will creep in.

You fail to follow up after the meeting
There is one key action here: to complete all documentation and confirmations that are necessary promptly after the meeting. Send copies to the person appraised, flagging any opportunity for further discussion. If your business is big enough to have a personnel department, send a copy there too.

RECOMMENDED LINKS
AllBusiness:
www.allbusiness.com
businessballs.com
**www.businessballs.com/
   performanceappraisals.htm**
Performance Management & Appraisal
   Help Center:
www.performance-appraisals.org

Focus On: Mentoring
Max Landsberg

GETTING STARTED

Mentoring suits smaller organisations especially well. It can build productively on the small-world environment in which 'everybody knows everybody else' to enhance professional skills and relationships. It can also make up for a potential lack of advanced HR systems—systems the smaller firm might be unable to afford.

- Mentoring is crucial to developing employees and retaining them.
- Mentors give advice on a spectrum of topics, ranging from specific skills to broader issues of career direction.
- Mentees gain advice, access to established networks, and broader personal and professional perspectives.
- Though mentoring happens naturally to some degree, it can be boosted by programmes which match seasoned employees to colleagues who are new either to the business or to their role. These programmes are designed to have a measurable impact.

This actionlist offers advice on how to get the best from a mentoring relationship, whether you a mentor hoping to keep a valued member of staff, or a mentee aiming to build your role in a small business.

FAQS

What is mentoring?

Mentoring is the process by which wisdom and experience is shared between two people, one of whom (the mentor) is typically senior to the other (the mentee). The advice that the mentor conveys to the mentee supports development of the mentee's skills, career, and networks.

Most of us have probably acquired our mentors more by luck than through planning, but with the erosion of traditional career ladders and the increasingly organic and unstructured composition of the modern firm (especially small firms), individuals and companies alike are seeing ever greater merits to this once informal relationship.

What is the scope of a mentoring relationship?

In a business setting a mentoring relationship focuses on skills, career, and personal development. At the start of their relationship, neither the mentor nor the mentee can anticipate all the issues that they'll end up discussing. Nevertheless, both parties should be aware of the topics which they might usefully discuss, or which might emerge

anyway. These topics fall into two broad categories: helping the mentee to achieve learning and career goals, and building the mentee's confidence and self-awareness.

Career issues typically include:

- whether the mentee's career vision and goals seem relevant and viable
- how to 'decode' the business's feedback to the mentee, for example, from an annual appraisal or from a promotion received or missed
- what experience and expertise to acquire in the short and long term
- where to find role models with whom the mentee can identify
- how the mentee should best interact with his or her manager
- whether to accept an internal (or external) job offer
- how best to promote a initiative within the business that the mentee has conceived
- how to react to unacceptable behaviour experienced by the mentee, for example, apparent bias, favouritism, or harassment
- how to deal with the effects of a personal or family problem

Issues of **Confidence and self-awareness** issues may include:

- how the mentee can make a frank review of his or her own strengths and weaknesses
- whether feedback received by the mentee about his or her personal style is accurate or not
- how to overcome apparent career setbacks, or feelings of isolation or depression

Despite this great breadth of role, mentoring relationships do have limits. If you are a mentor, remember to:

- focus on advice rather than 'rescue'
- *not* build a nepotistic relationship in which you try to exert undue influence in favour of your mentee
- direct the mentee to a professional counsellor if needed

MAKING IT HAPPEN
Understand different types of mentoring

There are four main types of mentoring which an individual may seek, or which a business may wish to promote. Note that these four models are not mutually exclusive, and also that most people have more than one mentor, each of whom may play complementary roles.

Informal or **'natural'** mentoring happens when a more experienced person decides to take a less experienced person under his or her wing, often to give career advice. Such relationships tend to form spontaneously and are usually based on a similarity of interests, expertise, or personal history. These relationships tend to grow and flourish and often continue after one or both the people leave the business.

Situational mentoring is the providing of advice for a specific circumstance, such as when the mentee has to implement a new computer system, or set up a new office. Although these relationships are often short-term, they can develop into a longer term mentoring connection.

Positional mentoring occurs when the mentor is the manager of the mentee. All good managers mentor their team members to some extent, but there are natural constraints to the effectiveness of this approach. Firstly, the mentee may find it difficult to raise issues of switching jobs or roles.

Secondly, the mentor will not provide an impartial view of their relationship as superior and junior. Thirdly, the manager may be accused of favouritism, if one of his or her mentees advances more rapidly than others.

Formal mentoring programmes emerged during the 1990s in an attempt to gain the advantages of natural mentoring while recognising the limitations of positional mentoring. They are discussed in more detail below.

Understand the benefits for all parties

Mentees are the most obvious beneficiaries of mentoring—they receive advice, guidance, access to contacts and networks, reassurance, and a broader perspective on their careers. Mentors also benefit, however. They typically strengthen their interpersonal skills, find insights into the workings of their business and teams, and have the satisfaction of seeing others grow. Finally, businesses benefit through better recruitment, induction, and retention of staff; better communication across all areas of the business, faster learning within the company, and a stronger overall culture.

Excel as a mentor

As a mentor, you will sometimes need to be a coach, sometimes a motivator, or guide, counsellor, role model, or provider of contacts. To excel in these different roles, you will need to:

- help the mentee to focus his or her efforts, and to clarify goals
- prompt the mentee to develop effective strategies, and act as Devil's advocate to challenge them
- help the mentee to identify appropriate resources, contacts, and role models
- share knowledge and wisdom based on your own experiences
- act personally as a source of inspiration and motivation, while maintaining confidentiality

To accomplish this, ask penetrating questions that help the mentee distinguish 'real' issues from apparent ones; accept the mentee unconditionally, asking 'how' or 'what' rather than 'why'; listen actively to the mentee's feelings as well as to the words; and volunteer your observations where appropriate. Having said that, don't aim to become a personal 'fixer' of your mentee's problems. Instead, help your mentee learn how to develop problem-solving skills which will feed into his or her overall development.

Excel as a mentee

If you are being mentored by someone else, be open, take initiatives, and show your consideration for your mentor's time.

In terms of openness, be open about your objectives and aspirations, but also be open to feedback or other observations made by your mentor. If your mentor finds that any frank comments are met with defensiveness, the relationship will soon wither.

In taking initiative, be proactive in meeting with your mentor, and in relating to him or her: arrive at your meetings fully prepared and with clear objectives, and take the lead in suggesting new ways of viewing your issues. Actively follow up on any ideas generated in the meetings, and let your mentor know of progress you make.

Finally, show consideration for the mentor's investment of time. This involves: identifying what the mentor wants to derive from the relationship; accommodating the mentor's schedule when arranging meetings; and providing feedback, praise, and thanks in an appropriate way.

Get the best from mentoring programmes

Larger businesses increasingly use formal programmes to encourage mentoring and to reap its benefits. Compared with natural mentoring (see above), formal mentoring tends to be based on more specific objectives. It also aims at more measurable impact (e.g., employee retention); runs for a more limited period; typically involves discussions of more prescribed structure; and is based on pairing that is balanced more in favour of the mentee.

Such programmes require focus, and

typically aim to support employees who are new to the business, new to a role, or who are part of a group that is in some way specialised or disadvantaged. Efforts to provide mentoring for *all* employees in a business rarely succeed, if those efforts are based purely on formal programmes. The broader objective of 'mentoring for all' is best tackled as part of a wider programme of cultural change, which should also examines how the company's day-to-day business is conducted.

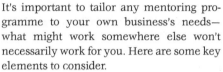

WHAT TO AVOID
Not building the right programme for your business

It's important to tailor any mentoring programme to your own business's needs—what might work somewhere else won't necessarily work for you. Here are some key elements to consider.

- decide whether to adopt a formal programme, or one that includes some element of natural mentoring
- have simple criteria for people's eligibility to be mentees and mentors, and for the maximum number of mentees per mentor
- agree whether mentees choose mentors (recommended), or vice versa; establish a matching process that is seen as fair by everyone
- explain the ground rules clearly, for example, a commitment to a duration of one year, the ability to terminate the relationship at any time with no blame, and complete confidentiality
- provide training for mentors and mentees, and set out the expected benefits
- plan how you will check whether the programme is working. Monitor it periodically. reward, praise or thank the mentors
- do not over-design the program: make it clear to potential mentees that the quality of mentoring they receive will in large measure depend on their own ability to attract mentors

RECOMMENDED LINK
www.itstime.com/oct99.htm offers up-to-date resources and links.

Focus On: Building Great Teams
Meredith Belbin

GETTING STARTED

The problem about the word 'teamwork' is that it has become too popular and has therefore lost its meaning. A person thought to be good at teamwork is all too often someone who fits into a group and keeps out of trouble. Complying with majority decisions and being willing to do anything that's required is seen as being ideal behaviour, but if everyone behaved like that, a team just wouldn't work effectively—a flock of sheep may hang together well, but their only accomplishment is to eat grass.

Teams and team-based working have developed into the normal way of structuring organisations and undertaking tasks, yet managing teams is a difficult aspect of leadership and is usually developed through experience. Every leader has his or her own style, and when developing a high performing team this needs to combine with an understanding of:

- the benefits of team-building—what it can achieve and what the leader should be striving for
- team roles and dynamics—how teams work and achieve their greatest success
- the key stages of team development—what they are and how to support the team in each stage
- the features of a successful team and team leader
- how to avoid potential problems and pitfalls

FAQS

What makes a good team leader?

Leadership, in broad strokes, is the capacity to establish direction and motivate others towards working for a common aim. Successful teamwork depends on the team leader's ability to make sure all team members know their common aim and what they each need to do to achieve it.

Naturally, all teams are different and have their own dynamic, and all leaders develop their own style for forming, developing, and leading them, but there are some general characteristics of a good team leader. For a team to work, it's essential that all members are committed, so leaders must be supportive, enthusiastic, and motivating people to work with. They must organise and communicate well in order to co-ordinate team efforts both *within* the team and with others *outside* the team. During difficult or stressful times, team leaders need to be approachable, good listeners who can offer feedback and advice.

What are the features of a good team?

It goes without saying that successful teams are ones in which people don't waste time trying to achieve success at the expense of others. Instead, they work at understanding each other, and communicate honestly and openly. They're committed to the team's success and are respectful and supportive of each other, always sharing information and experience.

Conflict is unavoidable in most work situations, but a good team will work through it and reach an understanding by generating new ideas. A good team also acknowledges the role of the leader and understands when he or she needs to act and make a decision (in an emergency, for example, or if there is a major problem or disagreement).

MAKING IT HAPPEN
Focus on the work

For anyone interested in productive teamwork, it's often better to start with the work rather than the team. First of all, think about whether the job in hand really does need a team to tackle it. Some types of work, such as repetitive or unskilled tasks and, at the other extreme, specialist activities, are best performed by loners. Rounding up such people and making them members of a team risks producing a double disadvantage: their personal productivity falls and their privacy is invaded. While it's currently popular to strive for such an 'all inclusive' approach in the workplace and some people argue that isolated workers need a social dimension to their work, there are often few benefits to forcing this set-up on someone. Introverts need work suitable for introverts, while extroverts need work appropriate to extroverts.

Enable the team to succeed

The team approach for organising work depends on empowerment, that is, making sure that each person is allowed to perform to the best of his or her abilities. This relies on trust, the confidence that a manager places on the qualities and calibre of the employees. It also depends on how well members of a group have developed an understanding of each other's strengths and weaknesses. That's why, if your budget allows, training in teamwork is so important and why it helps to understand the language of team roles.

Reward teams at the right time

All teams need to be assessed, but how should this be done so that it's positive and constructive? One way is to set objectives for teams and judge how well these have been met. This view is popular in the 'top-down' school of management, where, as the name would suggest, senior managers make all the decisions and these are then passed down through the ranks to employees. In larger organisations, this approach is given added impetus by performance-related bonuses.

The argument put forward is that teams need fixed incentives to perform well, an assumption linked with the converse view that without such an incentive the team will not perform satisfactorily. However, it's

possible for this approach to backfire. Success in meeting given criteria depends partly on circumstances and contingencies, and may not be commensurate with effort or skill. Objectives may be too easy to reach or too difficult. In the end, people may focus more on the shortcomings of the incentive than on the sense and purpose of their work. Retrospective awards for good team performance (that is, awards given once the project is complete) are better received than prospective rewards for teams given set targets.

Stick to the essentials of effective teamworking

Again, start with the work and think about whether it really calls for a team at all. If you do decide that a team is the best way to tackle a task, work out who will be doing what; also, decide at the beginning which remaining responsibilities can be assigned to individuals, and make them subject to personal accountability.

If possible, train your team so that it plays to the best strengths of its individual players. Make sure each person is allowed to develop ownership, pride, and maximum commitment to the team's responsibilities. One way you can do this as team leader is by delegating effectively (see pp. 412–414). Finally, understand what motivates the team—what gives it its momentum?

WHAT TO AVOID ✗
You misunderstand people

While it's obviously crucial that you understand the nature of the work being undertaken, you also need to be aware of the skills, experience and approach of those doing the work. Taking account of people's strengths and motivations can certainly help to build or break teams.

You fail to understand teams and what they need to succeed

Don't become too glib about the terminology—'team' and 'teamwork' too easily become meaningless words, so check their significance. Remember to spend time on evaluating whether you really need a team to complete a given task before you embark on a team exercise, and if you do go ahead bear in mind that not everyone flourishes in a team—some people will need more support than others.

If you're the team leader, remember that you have to allow team members the freedom to do what their role entails—empower them. Give them all the information they need and set boundaries to make sure that things happen.

RECOMMENDED LINKS

Belbin:
www.belbin.com
businessballs.com:
**www.businessballs.com/
teambuilding.htm**

Handling Resignations

GETTING STARTED

Although it is disappointing to lose key people, especially in a small business environment where some of your employees will have been with you from the start, resignations give companies a chance to plan ahead and recruit people who will assist in the growth of the business. They provide the opportunity to take a fresh look at what is working and what is not, and whether or not changes need to be made.

From the employees' standpoint, resignations allow people to move on in their careers, learn new skills, and take on new responsibilities. An individual leaving a company is not necessarily withdrawing his or her loyalty or influence over its future direction. Indeed, past employees may well be instrumental in instigating joint projects or ventures that will change the fortunes of the business at which they once worked.

FAQS

My second in command has just handed in her resignation. How can I convey this information to the rest of the team without risking a drop in morale?

You might find that calling the team together, along with the person who has resigned, allows an open discussion to take place in which you can address both the resignation and its implications. By showing your concern about their feelings and asking for input, you'll be involving your team and giving them a sense of control. It will also give you an opportunity to discuss any structural or resource issues that may arise from the departure.

I run a team of specialists who are hard to replace, and as soon as one left the others started to follow. What can I do to prevent talent from haemorrhaging out of the business?

This indicates one or more things: perhaps terms and conditions for their employment are more favourable elsewhere, or perhaps conditions in your business have deteriorated substantially without you noticing. If you hold an exit interview with those who leave, though, you may pick up on the reason for their exodus and start being able to do something about structuring a solution. Talk to your remaining staff and get them to contribute to the discussion on improving conditions. This may also be a time to look at your succession plans for the company.

Are you preparing others for these specialist roles, and what are the routes to them? Can you do something to clear the path for succession?

A member of my team wishes to leave full-time employment and become a contractor to the business on a project basis. Is this a good idea?

Increasingly, businesses are using contract employees to suit many different circumstances. Doing so allows more flexible working arrangements, and also reduces the direct cost of employment. In many instances, contract employees are responsible for the cost of their own office space off premises as well as funding their own benefits such as health insurance, pensions, taxes, and so on. However, contract employees will often charge more for their services (usually at an hourly rate) than they were paid as an employee. The key issues are costs and benefits. Another part of the equation is how you manage the situation with others in the team, so that there is no ambiguity about how work is to be done and who has responsibility.

I was handed a resignation by someone whom I was happy to see leave. However, he then changed his mind and asked to stay. How do I handle this?

If you feel strongly that your business would be better off without this person, you're within your rights as the supervisor to deny his request. If your business is big enough to have someone other than you in a management position and you think the reluctant resignee might be suited for a job elsewhere in your company, you could advise him to discuss the matter with the appropriate manager. It's not unusual for people to panic when leaving a role they know well, so this may just be pre-leaving nerves rather than anything more serious.

MAKING IT HAPPEN
Be prepared

Most small and growing businesses value a stable workforce, but it's inevitable that a certain percentage of the workforce will move on each year, picking up skills and experience in your company and taking them elsewhere. Whatever position the employee leaves, you need to handle his or her departure well and professionally. These people will speak of your business after they leave, and they can help build, or destroy, its reputation in the marketplace.

Acknowledge the intention to leave

Verbal notice may be acceptable, but it's usual for a resignation to be submitted in writing. This kick-starts the process of removing the employee from the payroll and the final account and allocation of benefits may begin.

Confirm the leaving date

Notice periods vary according to the role/job and the seniority level of the departing employee. You may find that the person who is leaving wants to negotiate an early departure, so this will have to be considered alongside their role demands and the volume of work pending. If work priorities allow, you may be willing to sanction this.

Handover

Depending on the nature of the work that the departing employee was engaged in, there will need to be a programme to ensure the smooth handover of projects and responsibilities. This could be a simple plan developed jointly by the employee and his or her manager, or it may involve a wider group of people who will be affected by the resignation.

Increasingly, businesses—especially cash-strapped ones—use 'natural attrition' to reduce their workforce. This means that departing employees are not replaced and their responsibilities allocated to other members of the team. Remember that a good handover programme will take some time. Allow for time to brief colleagues, tie up administrative loose ends, and perhaps instigate some training in areas where special skills are required.

If the person who is leaving has a network of business relationships crucial to your business—key clients or customers, for example—these will also need attention. Meetings between the client and the new person on your team, perhaps with the departing employee also present, will it make it more likely that things will carry on as normal. If the person leaving developed personal relationships with key clients or suppliers, though, this can be a difficult time. The client and former employee may wish to remain in touch with one another. Loyalty to an individual instead of to an organisation means that such departures leave the company vulnerable to loss of business, especially if the former employee then becomes your competitor in the marketplace.

Conduct an exit interview

As discussed above, exit interviews are a good idea if you want to find out why someone is leaving your company and what his or her experience of it has been. In larger organisations, exit interviews are normally conducted with a member of the human resources team but if you manage all your business's staff, you'd be the best person to chair it. During the interview, the person leaving should be encouraged to discuss all aspects of the role/job that they are vacating, their reasons for leaving, and any issues that contributed to that decision.

The exit interview should be a positive experience, although it's likely that some grievances may be aired. If this is the case, don't get defensive and do listen to what the person has to say. Sometimes, things that haven't been said before this point will be relevant for those remaining at the company. Obviously, grievances can vary, but if you're hearing the same thing repeatedly at exit interviews, it's clearly a need to change something within the business to make it a better place to work.

Remember other considerations

There may be circumstances when the employee will be asked to leave immediately upon resignation—for example, when the employee has access to confidential information and is leaving to join a competitor. It may also occur where there is a risk of disruption or sabotage, where the health of the employee may not be good, or where work has dried up. In these cases, it is usual to pay the salary equivalent in lieu of notice.

Leaving a job—even under the best of circumstances—is not always comfortable, so handling someone's departure sensitively makes the experience easier. Of course, there will be those who are desperate to move on and who share their excitement freely, but in most instances, it's customary to host a farewell event of some kind and give a gift to show appreciation for the work done.

WHAT TO AVOID
Taking it personally

Taking a resignation personally can lead to distress on both the employee's and employer's side. People decide to leave for a wide variety of reasons; it is not necessarily an act of betrayal. Try and be open to hearing the reasons behind the decision and explore the options, if there are any. Don't be aggressive.

Ignoring the implications of the resignation

Don't ignore the fact that one of your team is leaving. Ignoring the prospect of someone's departure can leave you vulnerable. Everyone involved needs to pitch in to make sure that the leaving causes as little disruption as possible, so try bringing those affected by the departure together to create a smooth transition.

Showing that you're pleased he or she is going

No matter how unlikable, annoying, disruptive, or incompetent the employee has been, try not to show your delight that he or she is leaving: it's disrespectful to the departing employee and demoralising for those who remain. Be professional at all times, from the moment you receive the resignation throughout the exit process, and leave your ego to one side.

RECOMMENDED LINK
I-resign.com:
www.i-resign.com/uk/resignationkit/ exit_interview.asp

SEE ALSO
Staff Planning (p. 415)

RETREATING WITH DIGNITY

Deciding to Move On

GETTING STARTED

Some entrepreneurs are extremely good at getting new ventures under way. They like the thrill of inventing a new product or developing a new service, and enjoy finding the initial customers who will make the business a success. They may be inspirational leaders who can motivate their team to achieve great things.

They may, though, be less good at managing a business that is growing slowly, or perhaps not growing at all. They may be less good, too, at keeping on top of the administrative and regulatory requirements of managing a business, or managing people. Other people, however, are very good at setting and implementing strategic objectives; at recruiting, managing, and getting the best out of people; and at managing administrative detail. If you feel that you fit into just one of these category or the other, don't worry; successful businesses need both!

FAQS

What choices do I have?

Some entrepreneurs—often known as serial entrepreneurs—recognise that they match the first description above and aim to move on once they have launched a new business and got it established. There are two ways of moving on: in some cases, the entrepreneur will simply sell the business and use the proceeds to launch the next venture; in other cases, the entrepreneur will aim to bring in professional managers to manage and develop the business. This is the approach that Richard Branson takes, for example.

What happens if I decide to sell the business?

You simply look for someone who is willing to buy the business at a price that is satisfactory and transfer to them the shares (if it is a company) or the assets, including the intellectual property, and the goodwill. You then have no more to do with the business. You will need to take particular care over the intellectual property rights if you think that you may want to use them in the future – for example, for developing further products – so it would be sensible to consult your solicitor early in the process.

What happens if I bring in a manager?

If you decide that you would rather continue to own the business, then you'll want to bring in a professional manager. You'll

probably still want to set the strategic direction, particularly if you expect the company to be part of a group of complementary businesses, but you'll also need to make sure that you give your manager the freedom to develop and grow the business. If they feel that you're looking over their shoulder all the time, the likelihood is that they won't stay long. You'll need to take care over the recruitment process to make certain that the person you recruit is a capable manager and can quickly command the respect and loyalty of your staff—otherwise they may leave.

MAKING IT HAPPEN
Sell your business

Selling your business is relatively straightforward—you can choose to sell a business to your employees, to your partners or company shareholders, or to outsiders—but it may take six months or more to complete.

You should seek advice from professionals such as a business adviser, solicitor, accountant, or valuer. Companies House can also advise on the processes required by law for dissolving a company. You'll need to:

- prepare your business for sale
- collate all the relevant information and documentation, including a sales memorandum
- place a value on its assets
- deal with issues such as taxation

If your business package is well prepared

and you continue to trade during the sale process, you're much more likely to gain a good price. You'll need to identify and contact potential buyers, for example by advertising in trade publications or the local press, or engaging the services of an estate agent or a business transfer agent. After negotiations have taken place, a Sale and Purchase Agreement which sets out the contractual terms of the sale will be signed, closely followed by the exchange of contracts. You may want to consider building other safeguards and checks into the process.

Recruit a manager

Recruiting a manager is no different to recruiting any other member of staff—except that you'll need to take extra care. You're looking for someone to whom you'll be entrusting the future wellbeing of your business. Even if you're involved in setting the strategic direction, you should give your manager free rein to manage the business on a day-to-day level. As with recruiting other staff, you'll need to prepare a detailed job description and a detailed person specification. However, you should remember that the reason you're recruiting a manager is because you think that you're weak in some aspects of management. There is a danger, therefore, that you'll recruit someone with similar skills and experience to your own, simply because you can relate to that more easily. If you can afford it, you might want to bring in an expert adviser to assist you with writing the person specification, and possibly with the whole recruitment exercise, as they will be able to take a more objective stance and help you find someone with the rights skills.

Keep your eye on the ball

It can be very easy, having decided that you need to hand over the management, to move on to the next opportunity before you've recruited the person that you need. You want to hand over a business to your new manager in the best possible shape so that he or she can build on your previous success. If you really need to move quickly, then look at bringing in an interim manager. This can be an expensive option, but if taking someone on in this role allows you to exploit another opportunity, it'll be worthwhile and will allow you to take a little bit longer to recruit a permanent manager.

Offer the right rewards

It's impossible to set in stone recommendations for the type of pay that a manager is likely to want—clearly it depends on the individual, your business, and what you're hoping they'll achieve. Do bear in mind that if you recruit someone who is entrepreneurial and who expects to develop the business, he or she will probably want a stake in the enterprise. It will almost certainly be necessary to allow the person to buy some shares; some managers may expect to be given shares to tempt them to come in the first place. Many are likely to want part of their remuneration package to come in the form of share options, so that they'll be handsomely rewarded if they do really well.

Move to a board structure

Even if your business is incorporated, it's possible that you've never really run it through a board, but have simply managed everything yourself. Bringing in a manager may also be a good point at which to think about imposing a more formal board structure on the business. Senior managers can be appointed as directors, if they're not already so. You may decide that your best role is as chairman, which keeps you involved, but not on a day-to-day basis. And you may also use the opportunity to bring in a non-executive director or two.

WHAT TO AVOID
Reacting rashly to a potential opportunity

Don't wait until you spot your next potential money-making opportunity before deciding that you need to recruit a manager. If you think that this is the route for you, then start planning early so that you can move quickly when that opportunity presents itself. Indeed, if you're certain that you want to bring in a manager, don't wait at all. Do it as soon as the business can afford it, which will free you up to search for the next opportunity.

Rushing the process

It's important to take your time over the appointment. If you get it wrong, it could be catastrophic for your business. Be sure of exactly the right person you need to take your business on to the next level and don't waste all the effort and care you've lavished on the business thus far.

Failing to take independent advice

Independent advice from someone who knows you and your business will help you draw up the right personal specification for a manager. The same person may also be able to help you appoint the most suitable person by making a detached judgement on the qualities of the people you have selected as candidates. It's always good to have a second opinion.

RECOMMENDED LINKS

BDO Stoy Hayward guide to selling your business:
www.bdo.co.uk
Business Eye (Wales):
www.businesseye.org.uk
Business Link (England):
www.businesslink.gov.uk
Business Gateway (Scotland):
www.bgateway.com
Invest Northern Ireland:
www.investni.com

Succession Planning

GETTING STARTED

If you're planning to retire in the near future or you want to hand over the reins of running your business for other reasons, it's important to plan carefully for your succession. This will help you to protect the value of your business if you decide to sell it or pass it on to a member of your family. As the owner-manager of a business that you may have founded and built up over time, you're likely to have kept close control over most, if not all, of the major functions. This will have left the business highly dependent on your personality, skills, and decision-making. Therefore, to make sure that the transition to a new owner is a smooth one, you need to prepare a succession plan that will enable you to depart from the business at a time that suits your purposes without disrupting its operations.

FAQS

What choices over succession do I have?

If you leave yourself with plenty of time to plan your succession, you could think about the following options:

- selling the business
- handing over control to a family member
- grooming one of your existing management team as successor
- appointing a professional manager from outside to take over the running of the business

One of the essential things about succession planning is to allow as much time as possible to think through and decide on the best option. Ideally, the process should be planned out over a couple of years, rather than being made hurriedly a few months before you leave. If you're able to identify a possible successor, the longer you give this person to understand the way the business operates and the responsibilities they must assume, the better the eventual outcome could be.

What should a succession plan involve?

The plan describes and clarifies the succession process and should be developed as part of the overall strategy for your business. It will detail how you'll choose your successor and the role you'll have, if any, after you hand over control. The plan may outline, for example, how the future leader of your business will go about managing its operations, and the structure and responsibilities of the team that will be involved. If you

don't sell the business outright, you could think about giving up your role in all the day-to-day decisions and responsibilities, while still acting as a 'consultant' when major strategic choices need to be made or when the new management believes that your advice would be beneficial. Having this type of role could be reassuring to your successor in the early stages of taking over control. Another thing you could consider would be to act as an ambassador for the company, as it would benefit from your links with customers or suppliers.

What should I consider in identifying a successor?

When you begin drawing up your succession plan, describe your functions and responsibilities and the kind of qualities required of the person who will take over from you. This involves listing the skills, interests, and abilities that your successor should possess. Bear in mind that the future leader of your business may need different skills and attributes to your own as the business has moved on, so a strong entrepreneurial drive, for instance, may be less important than managerial and administrative expertise. You can then draw up a list of possible candidates and a summary of their experience, qualifications, and career history. This will be easier, of course, if a potential successor is already on your staff or is a family member, but be as objective as possible about the details you compile.

MAKING IT HAPPEN
Prepare your succession plan

It's crucial that, before you put your succession plan in writing, you discuss your intentions and the changes you envisage with as many as possible of the people who'll be affected. By consulting with employees and, where appropriate, members of your family, you'll reassure them about the steps you're planning to take. Once the plan is complete, put it in writing to reduce the possibility of misunderstandings, and to make sure that everyone involved is clear about what is going to happen to the business and where they fit in. Tell everyone concerned about the main points of the plan so that the succession process gets off to the right start.

Come up with a timetable

A detailed timetable for the transition process is vital. Set targets for the training of your successor (if appropriate) and your planned date of departure. Unexpected events such as the resignation of a key member of staff, and unanticipated changes such as the appearance of new competitors or the loss of a major customer, may occur if you're planning a lengthy transition period, so remember to build in a degree of flexibility to the timetable.

Get some advice and support

Depending on the nature of your business, succession planning could prove complex and hazardous if you're uncertain about the right steps to take or you make the wrong decisions. It's worthwhile, then, to seek advice and support from people who have experience of succession planning, such as business consultants. Your accountant or solicitor may also be able to identify aspects of the process that you may have overlooked. Others you could turn to include business colleagues or friends who have been through the same process themselves, as they may be able to give you valuable insights and ideas. Finally, if you have members of staff, think about setting up a team to help you develop your succession plan and monitor its implementation—they will appreciate feeling involved and it may allay any fears they could have about your departure.

Choose the successor

In addition to the list of skills, qualities, and experience that you should have compiled on the candidates for succession, when it comes to evaluating them and making a choice there are some other attributes you should look out for. For example:

- How committed are they to the business?
- Can they develop it further?
- Do they have the leadership qualities and interpersonal skills needed to motivate others?
- Can they operate independently and in an appropriate manner?

Perhaps the best choice of successor may be obvious, such as a son or daughter, or one of your management team who has a thorough understanding of the business. If you choose to pass on the baton to a family member, allow enough time for him or her to get any training necessary. This could include you passing on some of the finer points about the way the business runs, as well as making personal introductions to important customers and contacts. Make sure they have the right motivations—you might not have been in it for the money and the money alone, but are they?—and aspirations. Also remember that they should be able to relate well to your employees and not provoke rivalries or ill feelings.

Sometimes, it's in the best interests of your business for you to recruit a successor from outside. A professional manager, with an appropriate track record and experience, may be much better qualified to take your business forward than family members, however close to them you may be.

WHAT TO AVOID
Reacting to a crisis

Don't wait until a crisis strikes your business before you decide to search for a successor. The kind of crisis that usually precipitates this sort of move is ill health or a sudden change in the market that requires radical changes in the way a business is run. It's much better to decide on a succession plan while your business is stable and profitable, as this will allow you a to choose from a full range of options rather than be forced into a hasty decision you could regret.

Rushing to the wrong decision

Keep an open mind about your succession options. You may be anxious to retain your business within your family, but handing it over to your son or daughter could be a big mistake. Do they really want the pressures and responsibilities involved? Do they have what it takes to run a successful business? Would a loyal, long-serving member of staff feel seriously snubbed by your choice? The best course is to leave as much time as possible to make the right decisions, giving yourself plenty of opportunities to consult your employees and business colleagues to get good ideas and suggestions.

Failing to take independent advice

If you've taken a very hands-on approach to the running of your business and imposed your personality on it, you're likely to be too close to the situation to take objective decisions and see the best way forward. Independent advice from someone who knows your business and market well—looking at the issues involved from a distance—will help you identify the pitfalls and bad decisions to avoid. The same person may also be able to identify the right person to succeed you by making a detached judgement on the qualities of the people you have selected as candidates for succession.

Hanging on too long

You may believe you're indispensable to your business and be tempted to hang on for too long. This is one of the worst things you can do. Don't leave your decision too late and when you *do* decide to go, don't interfere in what your successor is doing unless things are really spiralling out of control or your successor specifically asks you for help. Letting go is really hard, but if you plan your succession properly you should feel confident about your choice.

RECOMMENDED LINKS

BDO Stoy Hayward guide to selling your business:
www.bdo.co.uk
Business Eye (Wales):
www.businesseye.org.uk
Business Link (England):
www.businesslink.gov.uk
Business Gateway (Scotland):
www.bgateway.com
Invest Northern Ireland:
www.investni.com

Deciding Whether to Sell Your Business

GETTING STARTED

The reasons behind selling your business will determine how you approach the task, and will also affect your expectations of the transaction. If you are selling so that you can retire, for instance, you could sell at any time over a number of years to get the best offer available. Selling due to ill health may require a quicker sale, but if the business is in a good state it need not be immediate. If the business is in financial crisis, a low selling price may be necessary for a quick sale before you lose too much money. A forced sale may also be due to changed market circumstances or technological changes. As well as business-related reasons for sale (such as diversification, receivership, or bankruptcy), you may also have personal reasons for wanting to sell up, such as a death in the family, or the breakdown of a partnership.

FAQS

When is the best time to sell?

Ideally, you should sell your business after a number of consecutive profit-making years, so that prospective buyers can be sure that the business is a viable concern and that they can make realistic estimates of future earnings. The selling value of your business will tend to be based largely on what the purchaser expects to earn in the few years immediately after acquiring the business. Depending on the sector you are in, and the expectations of investors in that sector, the purchaser will want to be sure that the business delivers a minimum rate of return so that they can recover the purchase price within a number of years.

If the business is not yet profitable, or has been through an unprofitable patch, consider building it up for a few years before putting it on the market. This is often the only way of retrieving some value from your business for all the investment you have made in product development, market recognition, customer loyalty, and sweat equity. Without some hard evidence of profit-making history or potential, you could find it difficult to put a realistic sale value on your business.

What are the alternatives to selling?

If you are selling because of financial problems, consider whether the prospects for the business really are so bad. Have you considered the options? For example, could a manager or partner be taken on to help you

cope, or to address the main problems? Could particularly troublesome aspects of the operation be minimised?

It is important to compare realistically the costs of selling up with the costs of keeping going. What is the most likely outcome from the sale, for instance, and will this be a financial solution? Look at alternatives like:

- selling assets (such as land and machinery) and then leasing them back to the business to improve cash flow
- taking on a partner who will contribute capital and take on some responsibilities
- scaling down operations to focus on the most profitable work

Should I sell all or part of the business?

Raising cash is often the motivation behind the sale of a business. But selling your whole business is a big step, and will often prevent you from building on your experience in that sector (you will usually be required to sign a 'restraint of trade' agreement preventing you from competing with your old business for a number of years). This may undermine your own position, and make it difficult to develop your career the way that you would like. One way around this is to sell only part of your business to raise some capital, and use this to strengthen the portion that you keep.

MAKING IT HAPPEN

Prepare the business for sale

There are a few aspects of the business that you can usefully focus on in preparation for a sale—the most important of which are listed below.

- **Reduce discretionary expenditure.** This is expenditure not necessary to keep the business going. You don't necessarily have to eliminate discretionary expenditure, just highlight it to potential buyers. Common areas of discretionary expenditure include travel and entertainment, and running expensive company cars.
- **Reduce costs.** Other expenditure can also be reduced, but it is important not to cut back in vital areas. Buyers will often look for consistent expenditure trends. A sudden reduction in expenditure will be very noticeable and potentially negate the positive effects you were hoping it would have on potential buyers.
- **Maintain your property and assets well.** If you have leasehold property, security of tenure and rent reviews should be obtained. Keep machinery in good condition, using maintenance contracts if necessary.
- **Improve your working capital position.** For instance, reduce excess stock levels and make better use of creditors.
- **Keep employees informed.** The strength of many businesses hinges on the skill and experience of certain key workers. The sale may unsettle them, so keep them informed and secure their loyalty (it might be necessary to consider incentives).
- **Make sure you have the loyalty of key customers and suppliers.** This can often be done with long-term contracts, as buyers will be keen to ensure continuity of supply. If the business operates under licence, it is important that you ensure the licence is transferable to potential buyers.

Work out a price

Valuing a small business can be difficult, as normally there is no publicly trading share price that can be simply multiplied by the number of shares issued. Working out the value will involve the hard figures such as assets, liabilities, historical earnings, and cash flow, as well as more subjective figures such as projected earnings, know-how, quality of management, and goodwill. External factors also need to be considered, such as current market conditions and industry popularity. Ultimately, however, what a business is worth comes down to what both parties agree it is worth. Get some expert help to make sure that you get the best price possible.

Check the legal status

The legal status of the business for sale is very important to bear in mind, mainly because it defines exactly who owns the various assets to be sold. If you operate as a sole trader, you own all the assets of the business and it is up to you if, and how, they are sold. Similarly, partners will own their share of the assets, and any sale must be agreed according to the provisions of the partnership agreement. A limited company is a separate legal entity from its owners. In this case, selling the business may simply be a matter of selling shares in the business, or the shares might be retained while the equipment, premises, and goodwill are sold.

WHAT TO AVOID
Waiting too long

Perhaps the worst time to sell a business is once it is deep in debt. If you are forced into a sale, the chances are that you will not get a reasonable price—even if your business is still potentially profitable. By taking on debts, and perhaps even a loss-making enterprise, a purchaser is also taking on the substantial financial risk that the business will not respond to remedial action. The purchaser will therefore want to reduce this risk by paying a lower purchase price and keeping cash in reserve to fund possible future losses. For your part, you need to plan as far ahead as possible to anticipate what trading conditions might be like at the time you wish you sell. It is easier to demand a premium price when business is growing; that way, a purchaser is more likely to acknowledge some 'blue-sky' value and pay for it.

Setting an unrealistic asking price

When working out your asking price, don't get carried away by the theoretical prospects of your business. While there may well be potential for a new investor to exploit, this must be weighed against the hard realities of what is possible within your business and within your particular market. The financial history of your business will be the foundation on which valuations are based, so build your arguments on that.

Getting stuck in protracted negotiations

Keep your negotiations about selling as short as possible. If you can, set yourself some deadlines for certain key decisions about who to sell to, under what terms, and at what price. This will avoid the danger of letting the selling process drag on for too long. There is inevitably going to be a feeling of insecurity among staff and customers, so it is best for all parties to conclude a deal as quickly as possible. Bear in mind that a successful sale might not be agreed, in which case everyone is expected to return to business as usual; this is often difficult after months of uncertainty.

RECOMMENDED LINKS

Daltons Business (a useful selling guide): **www.daltonsbusiness.com/ sellguide.asp**
Deloitte and Touche (online guide to selling your business): **www.deloitte.com**

SEE ALSO

Bankruptcy and Business Failure (p. 497)
Finding Potential Buyers for Your Business (p. 475)
Management Buyouts (p. 522)
Understanding the Legal Ramifications of Winding Up a Business (p. 481)
Venture Capital (p. 553)

Knowing When and How to Liquidate a Business

GETTING STARTED

If your business is experiencing financial difficulties and there is an imminent likelihood of insolvency, you may decide to cease trading to avoid adding to the debt. You have a legal duty to stop trading when there is no chance of your business recovering and paying back its debts.

To make a reasonable judgment about this, you need to have up-to-date information about your finances and the immediate prospects. Your business accounts need to be current, and you need to be able to take into account the commercial effect of future contracts. You also need to have an accurate account of your business assets, as these would be off set against debts if you decided to wind up the enterprise.

FAQS

Where can I get advice about winding up a business?

There are many sources of professional help available, and it is crucial that you seek the right advice in order to achieve the best possible outcome for your business, your customers, and your staff:

- **Solicitors**—Sourcing and listening to good legal advice is vital during this type of business process. A solicitor will also be required to draft legal documents relating to the dissolution of the business.
- **Accountants**—Your accountant will provide essential advice on financial planning and tax aspects of the dissolving or sale of your business. An accountant should be consulted as early in the proceedings as possible. He or she will also be able to help when drawing up the business package for prospective buyers.
- **Insolvency practitioners**—These specialists will advise you on the implications of insolvency for your business, and how to embark on a winding-up process.
- **Companies House**—This government agency can advise on the processes of dissolving a company. It also produces a wide variety of business booklets on key aspects of company law, which are available both in hard copy and in a PDF downloadable format online.
- **Business advisers**—Your business adviser will provide a range of commercial informa-

tion and assistance on all aspects of the decision to cease trading. Seeking the advice of an impartial adviser often helps keep the processes in perspective and can present an objective outside view at what can be a very difficult time for a business.

MAKING IT HAPPEN
Check whether you are solvent

Do a detailed analysis of your business's financial position, asking yourself a series of questions—it's important to be realistic about the answers. Is the business able to pay its debts at or near the time they are due? Are the assets of the business worth more than the liabilities? (Make sure you consider the liabilities you are likely to incur in the future, and also any liabilities that you may incur unexpectedly.) If the business were liquidated now, could it meet all its liabilities in full? (Remember to include the cost of debt collection and liquidation.)

Dissolving a limited company

The best route is a members' voluntary liquidation (MVL) which allows a solvent company's members to pay off its creditors and wind up the company. A majority of the directors must make a statutory declaration of solvency not more than five weeks before the passing of the winding-up resolution. The declaration must contain a statement that the directors are confident that the company will be able to pay all debts within a period of not more than 12 months from the date of winding up, and a statement of company assets and liabilities, which should be as up to date as possible.

Shareholders in private limited companies are in effect part-owners of the business. If you are a director of a company, you have a duty to be honest with your shareholders and not to mislead them. If the company is to be wound up and creditors paid, the principle of limited liability means that shareholders are only liable for company debts up to the value of their shares.

Dissolving a partnership

As a partnership has no separate legal identity, it may be dissolved by an agreement between partners or by notice of dissolution given by one partner to the others. The partnership agreement may provide for dissolution after a specified period of time, or on other set terms.

Once an agreement has been reached, dissolution may proceed in the normal way—usually handled by the partners themselves. Partnership accounts are prepared and the dissolution will be advertised. All clients must be given notice that the business has been wound up—issuing of this notice represents the end of the partners' authority to bind the firm.

The mutual responsibilities of partners in the event of dissolution of their business should be set down in the partnership agreement. It is important to note, however, that when a partnership is wound up, any premiums (fees which may have been paid by new partners on joining) are usually treated as priority debts.

Duties of a director

As a result of the Insolvency Act 1986 and the Company Directors Disqualification Act 1986, it is important for directors of a company to be able to demonstrate that they acted properly in the event of the company becoming insolvent. Both of these acts have been amended by the Insolvency Act 2000, insofar as it strengthens the rules covering the disqualification of unfit directors.

Regular board meetings should be held,

all decisions properly documented, and the minutes circulated to all of the directors. Under the Insolvency Act 1986, the directors may be held personally liable for a company's debts where that company has gone into insolvent liquidation, and if at some time before liquidation the directors knew, or ought to have concluded, that there was no reasonable prospect of the company avoiding liquidation. This is the civil offence of 'wrongful trading'. Resigning as a director in advance of insolvency if it might have been expected will not absolve responsibility—although if a director lodges written disapproval of the business continuing to trade wrongfully it can be taken into account during any legal proceedings resulting from wrongful trading.

A director will not be liable if it can be shown that every step was taken that ought to have been to minimise the loss to the creditors. Directors should therefore ensure that they are always aware of the company's trading position and financial status, and should minute the discussions at meetings, and the consideration they give to the company's future prospects.

Directors have unlimited liability for fraud or negligence. However, it is possible, and slowly increasing in popularity, for directors to take out some insurance cover to protect themselves against liability to the company, shareholders, and third parties. Directors' insurance cover is a relatively new trend, with some prohibitive costs involved, so professional advice should be sought before taking up this option.

Responsibilities to employees when winding up a business

Debts which a business owes to employees for wages or services rendered during the four months prior to its insolvency, and all accrued holiday pay (up to a total of £800) are designated as 'preferential' debts and should be settled before any other claims.

If immediate payment is not forthcoming, employees have the right to apply direct to the Secretary of State for payment of a designated portion of what is owed from the National Insurance Fund.

It is important during winding up or liquidation that employees are kept informed of what is happening so that you can try to retain as much loyalty as possible while the process is being worked through. Employees working in the finance or accounting area are particularly important during this phase, due to their knowledge of the business accounting procedures, financial filing and archiving systems, and so on.

WHAT TO AVOID
Not drawing up a detailed partnership agreement
When a business partnership is formed, it is vital to draw up an agreement which is a legally binding document. The agreement will set out the procedures to be followed during liquidation or winding up.

Not keeping employees informed about the state of the business
It is important to keep employees informed of what is going on and to try to give them as much notice as possible of any changes, especially if they risk redundancy as a result of any decision. This will enable them to look for other work if necessary.

RECOMMENDED LINKS
Companies Registry (Northern Ireland): **www.detini.gov.uk**
Insolvency Service: **www.insolvency.gov.uk/index.htm**
Registrar of Companies: **www.companieshouse.gov.uk**

SEE ALSO
Bankruptcy and Business Failure (p. 497)
Management Buyouts (p. 522)
Venture Capital (p. 553)

Knowing the Value of Your Business

GETTING STARTED

Knowing the value of your business is very important if you are considering selling it or looking for external investment into your venture. Ultimately, the value of a business comes down to what both parties agree it is worth. A company which has shares listed on the Stock Exchange has a clear value in the number of shares in the company, multiplied by their value set by the Exchange. The share value in a small business, however, is harder to calculate and must take into account such elements as assets, liabilities, profitability, customer base, goodwill, and trading history.

This actionlist provides some general 'rules of thumb' on how to value your business, or how to check that it has been properly valued by someone else.

FAQS

Who should value the business?

If you're using a business broker, it will be down to them to value your business. However, it would still be wise to value the business yourself so that you can relate to the price that the broker has specified. For whatever price they place on your business, you should establish how they arrived at this figure so that you can be completely sure that the price is fair.

Likewise, if you use an accountant to value your business, you should still value the business yourself so that you are satisfied that they have given a reasonable and fair value. After all, who knows your business better than you do?

It may be that you decide to value the business alone, without the assistance of professionals; however, their input could add valuable credibility to your arguments when it comes to negotiating a final price and terms with prospective buyers.

How is a business valued?

Valuation is not an exact science. It is difficult to set the value of a business at a single figure, as so many factors should be taken into account. Hard figures such as assets, liabilities, historical earnings, and cash flow must be accounted for, but more subjective figures such as projected earnings, know-how, quality of management, and goodwill should also be used. External factors should be considered, such as current market conditions and industry popularity. What you

estimate to be the value of your business and its final selling price may differ widely depending on the circumstances surrounding the sale or investment into the business. Is the buyer keen to buy quickly? Is there more than one investor/buyer interested? What form will the payment or investment take? What is the level of risk involved for the buyer or investor? How urgently do you want to sell?

Do you need to compare your business with similar businesses?

Before proceeding with the valuation, you should compare the financial results of your business with those of similar organisations within the same industry. This will help you determine whether there should be a premium added or discount given over the value of comparable businesses. Financial comparisons should be made using several measures including: sales growth; gross margin; earnings before tax as a percentage of sales; return on assets; current ratio, and debt-to-net-worth ratio. What is the growth rate of the business compared to the industry as a whole? Is the business gaining or losing market share?

MAKING IT HAPPEN

Value the business

The final valuation figure will depend on the technique adopted. There are effectively three methods of valuing a business—net assets, multiple of earnings, and standard formulae.

Calculate net assets

Valuing a business by calculating its net assets is the most easily understood method, and the one most commonly used for small businesses. The net assets (the net worth of the business) are shown on the balance sheet. If everything was sold at the value recorded on the balance sheet, the amount of money realised would be equal to the net assets. Sometimes buyers are reluctant to pay much more than net asset value, as it is very difficult to make a suitable allowance for intangible assets such as goodwill. The value of other intangibles can also be considered, such as ownership of patents, trade marks, and copyrights; the value of long-term contracts, licence agreements, and so on.

The net-assets figure may need to be adjusted to reflect the true worth of the assets. Buildings, for example, may be worth more than shown on the balance sheet. Equipment, especially computers, may be worth far less. You may need to enter into negotiations about how assets will be valued, but take into account replacement value and realisable value.

Calculate the earnings multiple

The earnings multiple calculation for valuing a business is based on the price/earnings ratio (P/E ratio). The P/E ratio is the price of one share to the earnings (that is, the net profit after tax) attributable to that share. The P/E ratio gives an indication of how much investors are prepared to pay to buy the shares.

If, for example, a company has earnings per share (EPS) of 18.5p and one share costs £5 then it has a P/E ratio of 27 (500 divided by 18.5). You can apply this to any business. Take the net profit, apply a suitable multiplier, and that gives you the value of the business. Try selecting a suitable multiplier by looking at the P/E ratios for quoted companies, usually printed in the financial sections of newspapers. However, you will need to apply a discount to take account of the smaller size, the greater risk, and the difficulty for investors wishing to sell shares

in private limited companies. Typically, you should apply a discount of 30–40%, though if your profit is less than £1 million, the discount should probably be at least 50%.

For example, you have achieved earnings of £100,000 per annum over a number of years and can show that this trend is likely to continue. If, in your business sector, the average P/E ratio is 12, you then need to apply a discount of 50%, which then gives a multiplier of 6. This implies that the business is worth £600,000. You should remember to exclude non-recurring expenditure (such as one-off purchases) when you calculate the earnings for a particular year.

Understand standard formulae

Standard methods of valuing a business have become established in some industry sectors. For example, the valuation of a milk round depends on the average daily delivery; and insurance brokers often multiply their gross commission one to two times to work out the value of their business. There may be an accepted formula applied in your business sector, and it may be worth investigating this further before committing yourself to any valuation process.

Divide the shares

Valuing the business only gives you a starting point. If you are looking for an external investor, you then have to negotiate the proportion of shares that might be exchanged for a certain amount of finance. The owners of a business will have invested their own finance—though this should, in effect, be reflected in the valuation. They will also have invested considerable time and effort to build up the business to the point where they are seeking additional equity. This, too, should be recognised and rewarded.

One way of doing this is to add a notional amount to the net asset valuation to represent the 'sweat equity'—that is, the hard work and effort already applied to build the business up to its current position but which is not reflected in the valuation of the business. If, for example, a business has a net asset valuation of £50,000, a further £50,000 might be added as sweat equity. An investor providing an additional £50,000 would then receive 33% of the shares.

Understand the buyer's valuation

The value that you place on your business, whichever method you choose, is very unlikely to be the price that you receive: it merely forms the starting point for negotiations. You should therefore add a little to the price, say 5–10%, as you can always expect the buyer to try to negotiate a lower price, even if they feel they have found a bargain.

The buyer will not value the business until they have seen the business inside and out. After this, they will probably involve their accountant or broker to help reach a realistic value for your business. It's likely that they will use a different valuation method to the one you have used, as quite often buyers will find a value that compensates for the expected return they hope to receive by investing in the business.

Buyers will always have a keen eye on the future performance and profitability of your business. You should therefore prepare to be offered an amount that reflects how profitable your business is expected to be in the future.

In basic terms, you have to acknowledge one important rule of valuation: a business is only worth what someone is willing to pay for it.

WHAT TO AVOID
Having unrealistic valuations

You are aiming for an achievable valuation—one on which both parties can agree—so you need to be realistic. If you're using the P/E ratio as the basis of your valuation, make sure you select a realistic ratio and discount it by an amount which is appropriate for the size of your business.

Getting the wrong advice

The first common mistake is hiring the wrong adviser. For example, many sellers decide to hire a solicitor but will often be attracted to the first contact they find and consequently overlook the more qualified and experienced people. This can lead to the wrong decisions and advice being made at crucial moments in the selling process. The same scenario can be applied to business brokers and accountants.

RECOMMENDED LINKS
Business Eye (Wales):
www.businesseye.org.uk
Business Link (England):
www.businesslink.gov.uk
Invest Northern Ireland:
www.investni.com
Business Gateway (Scotland):
www.bgateway.com

SEE ALSO
Bankruptcy and Business Failure (p. 497)
Management Buyouts (p. 522)
Venture Capital (p. 553)

Finding Potential Buyers for Your Business

GETTING STARTED

If you've decided to sell your business, potential buyers could come from a number of sources including competitors, suppliers, customers, and new market entrants. While you might want to reach as many potential buyers as possible, you will probably want to keep your dealings confidential until you decide to inform employees, suppliers, and customers.

For many small businesses, networking is one of the most effective ways of communicating with parties who may be interested in buying you out. However, if you need to be more pro-active about the process, and do not have the time to pursue it yourself, you could employ the services of a business broker (see below for more information). A broker will actively seek out interested parties, either directly or through networking with other business brokers. Your broker could also advise and support you through the negotiation and sale of your business. To advertise your business yourself, the most effective media are newspapers, magazines (both in your sector and specialist publications advertising businesses for sale) and the Internet. The Internet is fast becoming one of the most popular ways to advertise a business for sale, its main advantage being that it can reach a wide and global audience quickly. Although not the best source of advertisements for all businesses (for example, those with a very defined, local appeal), it's highly recommended for small businesses with a wider appeal.

FAQS

What is a sales memorandum and why use one?

A sales memorandum is a detailed description of your business that you can provide to prospective purchasers. It outlines the history, products and services, assets, and market and financial performance of your business. It needs to include your reason for selling and your asking price. The memorandum should also include a detailed business plan for the next few years, and the likely outcomes of that plan. The aim of the memorandum is to inspire interest from prospective buyers, as well as to anticipate some of the questions that they may want answered.

What could a business broker do for me?

A business broker will research the market for prospective purchasers of your business. She or he will work with you to establish a list of businesses or individuals who might be interested in finding out more about your business. Your broker will arrange the signing of confidentiality agreements, and hold preliminary discussions with some or all of the interested parties. He or she will then process the responses and advise you on which options are worth pursuing, leaving you with more time to get on with running the business.

How do I keep the process confidential?

When you advertise your business in a newspaper or magazine, or on the Internet, do not mention your business name. Simply describe the sector you are in, your turnover and your asking price, as well as your regional location (but do not give the exact town or city). Give the interested parties a PO Box number or an e-mail address to reply to. Before you provide any information to an interested party, get a confidentiality letter or agreement signed by the interested party (this usually only relates to information that is not publicly available). You can then release a sales memorandum with a request for a response on a given date.

What is a qualifying buyer?

When you consider the replies to your advertisements, you need to sort out those expressions of interest that are serious from those that will only waste your time. Draw up a list of qualifying buyers, and limit your distribution of sales memoranda to this group only.

MAKING IT HAPPEN
Spend time preparing the business for the sale

Spending some time preparing the business for sale can enhance the price. Issues to consider include: reducing discretionary expenditure (for example travel and entertainment); reducing business costs without cutting back on vital areas (buyers will look for consistent spending patterns and sales figures); making sure that any property and equipment is well maintained; and reducing excess stock levels to improve the level of working capital.

Decide what type of buyer you want

If you want cash from a deal, it may rule out buyers below a certain size. If you're looking for a friendly purchaser who will safeguard future employment of staff and management, there is little point talking to known 'asset strippers', that is, those who set out to acquire a company and sell its assets for a profit without regard for the acquired company's future business success.

In conjunction with your professional advisers, you should put together a list of possible buyers. You may well hold market information about prospective trade buyers, but do not rule out prospective new entrants to the sector. Non-executive directors, or specialist professional advisers, should have the ability to identify 'non-trade' buyers who may be prepared to pay a premium to enter your market.

Keep your target list to manageable proportions. If you have to advertise, the time drags on and you end up sending out the wrong signals to the industry as well as attracting time-wasters.

Prepare a sales memorandum

It is advisable to prepare your sales memorandum with an adviser or accountant, or with the business broker who is helping you sell your business. You could consider preparing a summary of the main points of interest as well as a more comprehensive document. The former can be sent out to all parties that express an interest in your business. The latter should only be sent to those parties who then request more information.

Select qualifying buyers

Look for buyers who want to add to their own business portfolios; these are generally the most likely to put in a serious offer. They will often be players already in your sector, so they will understand how your business would contribute to their own. They will also have a good idea of the financial benefits they could derive. It is important that you try to establish whether the interested party has the finance necessary to purchase your business. Otherwise, this might become a problem as your negotiations proceed.

Send out confidentiality letters

Once you have identified those parties that you believe to be serious about buying your business, you need to send confidentiality letters to them. Make sure that the letters are professionally drafted. They will need to be signed and returned before you send out the sales memoranda. It is a good idea to give a deadline of about a fortnight. This will also help you establish which parties are prepared to give priority to the matter.

Send out sales memoranda

This can be done in two phases. The first phase involves sending out a summary. Distribution of the full sales memoranda should then be limited to those parties who have read the summary and have requested a full document. This indicates that they are genuinely interested in finding out more.

WHAT TO AVOID
Releasing too much information to competitors

One of the dangers of putting your business up for sale is that it presents your competitors with an opportunity to gain access to sensitive financial information. In this respect, it is useful to have the input of a business broker. Your broker can advise you on whether your competitors' interest is genuine or not, and will also maintain your anonymity right up to the stage of narrowing down to a few genuinely interested parties. You will need carefully to balance the need for interested parties to see your financial history with the possible commercial advantage that a competitor could gain from this information.

Spending too much time with time-wasters

There are bound to be a number of responses to your advertisements which simply do not warrant following up. It is important that you identify these as early as possible, as you will probably need to spend a considerable amount of time with each of the interested parties in the near future. You should only pursue expressions of interest from parties that look like serious businesses with enough finance to make a reasonable offer. Carrying out a credit check, or sourcing a company report, can provide useful insights into your potential buyers.

RECOMMENDED LINKS

Businesses for sale:
www.daltonsbusiness.com
Companies for Sale:
www.companiesforsale.uk.com
UK Business Base:
www.ukbusinessbase.com

SEE ALSO

Bankruptcy and Business Failure (p. 497)
Deciding Whether to Sell Your Business (p. 466)
Management Buyouts (p. 522)
Venture Capital (p. 553)

Selling Shares

GETTING STARTED

People sell shares in their companies for a variety of reasons. They may be hoping to raise additional finance, or alternatively could be hoping to dispose of the company by selling all or most of the shares. Shares can be sold to business angels, venture capitalists, individuals, and other businesses—the motive for buying shares may well be different depending on who buys them, and purchasers' expectations of dividends and exit routes will also differ.

This actionlist provides a rough guide to the main points you need to take into account when considering whether to sell shares.

FAQS

What are shares?

Shares in a company represent a proportion of the ownership of that company. Initially, shares are exchanged for cash and that cash is then available to the business. This pot of cash is known as the 'equity capital' or as the 'share capital'. Shares can be sold by the owner of a company, though in a small, unquoted, business, there are regulations governing the way in which the shares can be sold.

Can a company sell shares at any time?

Companies set an authorised amount of share capital in their Memorandum of Association (MOA), that is, the total number of shares that the company is permitted to sell. The authorised share capital can be raised at any time by the shareholders, and the company can then sell the additional shares. Unquoted companies normally include a 'pre-emption' clause in their Articles of Association (AOA) requiring that any additional shares are first offered to existing shareholders before being offered to other potential new investors.

Are there different types of shares?

Companies can create different classes of shares. The main, voting shares are known as 'ordinary shares'. Companies also often create 'preference shares' in order to raise equity capital. In the event of a company being wound up, the preference shares are considered for repayment before the ordinary shares.

Preference shares usually attract a fixed dividend (provided, of course, there is enough profit to cover the dividend). Sometimes these shares are cumulative—if the dividend is missed one year, it is carried forward until such time as there is sufficient profit to pay it. Dividends on ordinary shares cannot be paid until the dividend on the preference shares is paid. Preference shares are usually redeemable, meaning that the company can buy them back and cancel them, if it so desires. Usually they are repaid at par (that is, for the amount for which they were bought), but the repayment amount can be varied. The values for redemption are normally set out in the company's AOA.

What is internal rate of return?

You may have heard talk of equity investors expecting high levels of return—typically 35–40% internal rate of return. That return does not come solely from dividends, but includes the return achieved when the shares are eventually sold. The total rate of return, from income and capital growth, on an annualised basis, is known as the internal rate of return.

What is private equity?

Private equity is simply the term used for finance from venture capitalists, seed funds, and business angels in exchange for a share of the business.

What is an exit route?

The term 'exit route' is used to describe the way that a business angel or venture capitalist exits from an investment. In general, there are just three routes: flotation of the company; a buy back from the founders of the business; or a trade sale. In practice, early investors may also exit by selling shares to a bigger investor. For example, a business angel might exit when a venture capitalist decides to invest and provides an exit route for business angel by buying his or her shares.

What is an IPO?
An initial public offering (IPO) is the term used if you sell shares to the public through a stock exchange, such as OFEX (which specialises in small and medium-sized enterprises) or the Alternative Investment Market (AIM), which trades in shares of small or emerging companies that are not eligible for listing on the London Stock Exchange.

MAKING IT HAPPEN
Sell a business
In order to sell your business you will need to make sure that you have up-to-date accounts, and be willing to spend time talking to prospective purchasers. If your objective is to sell your business, say, because you want to retire, or want the money to start a new venture, then in most cases your best bet will be to use a business transfer agent, who will help you advertise the business and seek prospective buyers. It is worthwhile, though, mentioning your intention to sell your business to local accountants and business support organisations, as they may well have clients who would be interested in buying.

You may want to stay in the business, or buyers may wish you to stay, at least for a period, so think about whether this is of interest. Some buyers may want to structure a deal over two or even three financial years; this improves their cash flow and maintains a period of stability and continuity in the business, but may also help your tax position. Some buyers may want an earn-out, whereby at least part of the price is dependent on future profit levels—so it is important to be realistic about future prospects.

Raise equity for investment
If your objective is to raise money to reinvest in the business, then you need to do much more work. You need to consider what makes the business attractive to an equity investor—do you have proprietary intellectual capital; do you have the potential for high returns; is there an attractive exit route; and, perhaps most important of all, do you have the management team in place to make it all happen? If the answer to these questions is 'yes', then you need to prepare a detailed business plan setting out the business's prospects for the next three to five years. You need to demonstrate, too, that you have the determination and commitment to succeed.

Find an investor
The hardest part is finding potential investors. The best starting point is to talk to your local business support organisation. The advisers there will be able to help you prepare your business plan, but will also be able to give advice on approaching business angels and venture capitalists.

WHAT TO AVOID
Exaggerating the figures
Be realistic in valuing your business—but also make an allowance for the sweat equity that you have put into your business.

Not spending enough time on your proposals
Venture capitalists reject hundreds of plans for every one in which they invest—so you need to work hard to capture their attention and persuade them that your business should be the one to receive their money. Regard this as a marketing exercise. You need to grab their attention—and then you need to build on that by making a solid case for investment.

Being overly optimistic
Don't over-estimate your chances of success; be realistic about the size of the market and about how long it will take you to win customers.

RECOMMENDED LINKS
British Business Angel Association:
www.bbaa.org.uk
British Venture Capital Association:
www.bvca.co.uk
European Business Angel Network:
www.eban.org

Venture Capital Report:
www.vcr1978.com

SEE ALSO
Bankruptcy and Business Failure (p. 497)
Management Buyouts (p. 522)
Venture Capital (p. 553)

Understanding the Legal Ramifications of Winding Up a Business

GETTING STARTED

Winding up or liquidation is the process of gathering in the assets of a business, to settle the corporate debts. Once this process is completed, the business is then dissolved. It is important to take advice about whether this is the best route for your business. If it is insolvent with serious debts, there may be no choice—creditors can petition for its liquidation. Where the operation is solvent, however, or you as the owner confidently expect to be able to pay off debts, then the potential options for voluntary dissolution should be explored. This actionlist deals with some of the key issues.

FAQS

How is a partnership wound up?

As a partnership has no separate legal identity, it may be dissolved by an agreement between the partners, or by notice of dissolution given by one partner to the others. The partnership agreement may provide for dissolution after a specified period of time, or on other set terms.

Once an agreement to dissolve the business has been reached, dissolution may proceed in the normal way—usually handled by the partners themselves. Partnership accounts are prepared and the dissolution will be advertised. All clients must be given notice that the business has been wound up—issuing of this notice represents the end of the partners' authority to agree to contracts and transactions with clients.

How is a private limited company wound up?

Liquidation is a legal process resulting in a company ceasing to exist. It involves distributing a company's assets to pay off its creditors' debts. The company's assets are placed in the hands of an insolvency practitioner (a licensed person who specialises in insolvency, authorised by a professional body or the Secretary of State). Following liquidation, the company is wound up. A company may be wound up either voluntarily by its shareholders, or through the courts by creditor petitioning.

MAKING IT HAPPEN

Be aware of the legal implications when a partnership is wound up

The law on partnership insolvency comes from the Insolvency Act 1986, the Insolvency Rules 1986, the Insolvency Act 1994, the Insolvency Act 2000, and the Insolvent Partnerships Order 1994 (as amended). Insolvency, under the 1986 Act, means being unable to pay, provide security, or come to an acceptable arrangement for the payment of a debt of £750 or more, within three weeks of a formal demand for payment.

Where a business is insolvent and partners cannot pay its debts, it may be treated as an unregistered company and wound up (usually in the County Court), under the terms of the Insolvency Act 1986. Under the principle of unlimited liability, however, once all partnership assets have been exhausted in the payment of creditors, each partner can be made bankrupt and creditors may lodge petitions against the partners' individual estates. Wealthier partners may find that partnership creditors will pursue their assets before those of their co-partners.

When joint bankruptcy orders are made against partners, an official receiver immediately becomes trustee of the partners' separate estates and trustee of the partnership. The partnership is then wound up—that is, assets will be gathered in and used to settle business debts, and the partnership dissolved.

Appraise the assets of the partnership

Unlike sole traders, whose personal and business assets are counted together for the purposes of creditors in bankruptcy, in a partnership, separate accounts must be kept of the joint (partnership) estate, and of each partner's individual estate. Once a partnership is dissolved, separate statements of affairs for joint and individual estates must be lodged with the court.

It is an offence to have disposed of valuable assets within five years before the bankruptcy, either by giving them away or selling them cheaply to relatives or friends, unless it can be proved that the disposal was an innocent transaction.

Bank accounts will be frozen at the point of bankruptcy, and the trustees will sell assets as they think fit. A spouse who has a joint interest in property will normally be protected for a year, but after this period, the court puts the interests of the creditors first.

Pay creditors

Through unlimited liability, a situation may arise where two sets of creditors are chasing payment of debts from partners—creditors owed money by the business, and personal creditors of individual partners. In this case the partnership assets pay off partnership debts, and partners' individual estates are used to pay off their personal debts. Any surplus in the joint estate then goes to the partners' estates in proportion to their share in the partnership, while any surplus from partners' estates goes to the joint estate to pay off partnership debts.

Certain 'secured creditors' may have direct claims on specific assets which will be satisfied first of all. Other creditors may be designated as 'preferred', 'ordinary', or 'deferred', being paid according to their status.

A shortfall in the partnership estate may be 'proved for' (claimed) in the individual estate equally with the individual creditors' claims.

Understand the legal implications when a private limited company is wound up

The main legislation covering company insolvency comes from the Insolvency Act 1986 (as amended). The Insolvency Rules 1986 will also apply, as will the Insolvency Regulations 1994.

Consider voluntary liquidation

If a company is facing serious financial trouble, its members/directors may decide that liquidation is the only option for the business. Two types of voluntary liquidation exist:

1. Members' voluntary liquidation (MVL) may be initiated by solvent companies, that is when a company has sufficient assets to meet all its debts. The directors of the company sign a declaration of solvency, which must include a statement that they will be able to pay off all creditors within 12 months following commencement of liquidation. The declaration must also include an up-to-date account of all the company's assets and liabilities. Members must hold a meeting to pass a resolution to wind up the company voluntarily and to appoint a liquidator who will handle the affairs of the company and distribute assets to pay off creditors.

2. Creditors' voluntary liquidation (CVL) occurs when shareholders vote for a voluntary liquidation, despite the majority of directors having not made a solvency declaration. Unlike an MVL, the company may already be insolvent. In order to vote for a voluntary liquidation, shareholders must hold a general company meeting and pass a voluntary winding-up resolution stating that they cannot continue to trade due to their liabilities. A creditor meeting must also be held to inform them of the company's financial position. Creditors are given the opportunity to nominate somebody to act as liquidator, and their decision will generally take priority over that of any nominations made by the company.

Consider compulsory liquidation

Compulsory liquidation occurs when a court orders a company into liquidation. This normally happens following a winding-up petition from a creditor, or group of creditors (who must be owed at least £750).

However, the company itself or its directors may also file a winding-up petition. Following a court order, an official receiver will be appointed as liquidator by the court to handle the winding up of the company and investigate the possible causes of the liquidation.

Remember employees' rights when a business is wound up

An employer may owe debts to employees for wages, salary, or accrued holiday pay. If it is solvent when it ceases trading, employees may also be entitled to redundancy payments. Where insolvency leads to winding up, up to £800 of the sum owed to an employee for the previous four months can be designated as 'preferential' debts, to be settled before the claims of ordinary creditors. The remainder is designated as ordinary debts.

WHAT TO AVOID
Not drawing up a deed of partnership when setting up

When forming a partnership, a deed of partnership should be drawn up. It should specify arrangements to be followed in insolvency. Otherwise the partnership is subject to the relevant provisions of the Partnership Act 1890, which may not best suit the needs of the business.

Providing the wrong information

The court and any insolvency practitioners should be provided with all the information they require—omissions or false statements can result in criminal proceedings.

RECOMMENDED LINKS
Companies House:
www.companieshouse.gov.uk
Companies Registry (Northern Ireland):
www.detini.gov.uk
Insolvency Service:
www.insolvency.gov.uk/index.htm

SEE ALSO
Bankruptcy and Business Failure (p. 497)
Deciding Whether to Sell Your Business (p. 466)
Management Buyouts (p. 522)
Venture Capital (p. 553)

ESSENTIAL
INFORMATION
DIRECTORY

Small and Growing Businesses

BOOKS AND DIRECTORIES

Beating the Odds in Small Business
Tom Culley
London: Simon & Schuster, 1998
320pp ISBN: 0684841835
This book is a survival manual for new businesses, and systematically explains and analyses every key 'survival priority', upon which the sustainability of a new business is dependent in the critical first years. The author shows how the odds can be turned in your favour by avoiding the distractions of chasing easy success in order to get rich quick, and instead focusing only on the harsh realities of the business jungle.

Business Development: A Guide to Small Business Strategy
David Butler
Oxford: Butterworth-Heinemann, 2001
192pp ISBN: 0750652470
This book aims to help owner-managers of small businesses draw up a plan for the long-term future. The subjects covered include: reviewing performance, resource implications, sales and marketing strategy, market expansion, staffing, and financial performance. The standards for business development established by the Small Firms Enterprise Development Institute (SFEDI) are appended.

The Business Valuation Book: Proven Strategies for Measuring a Company's Value
Scott Gabehart, Richard Brinkley
New York: AMACOM, 2002
352pp ISBN: 0814406424
Accurately valuing a business can be a daunting task for many businesspeople, but this book illustrates how the basic principles of business valuation are straightforward. Following the ARM (Adjusted cash flow, Rules of thumb, Market comparables) approach, the reader is led through the principles of: Establishing an asking price and selling terms; planning and settling tax issues; obtaining financing; establishing risk management levels, and implementing an Employee Stock Ownership Plan (ESOP). The pack contains a CD-ROM full of practical tools.

Capitalizing on Success
Neil Coade
London: Thomson Learning, 2000
240pp (Smart Strategies Series)
ISBN: 1861527659
This book takes a practical approach to the process of business development. After discussing the stages of business growth, it considers the challenges that face emerging businesses and may prevent them from reaching their potential. As means of meeting those challenges, it stresses the importance of effective leadership, good management practice, and creative people able to move the business forward.

The E-Myth Revisited: Why Most Small Businesses Still Don't Work and What You Can Do About Yours 2nd ed
Michael E. Gerber
London: HarperCollins, 2005
288pp ISBN: 0060766611
First published in 1986, this best-selling book provides information and guidance on starting and maintaining a small business or franchise. 'E-myth' stands for 'entrepreneurial myth' and refers to Gerber's belief that entrepreneurs do not necessarily make good business people. The book shows the reader how to simplify the systems involved in running a business, and instead create an incredibly organised and regimented plan, so that the systems can more or less run themselves, freeing the entrepreneur's mind to focus on long-term strategy.

Enterprise and Small Business: Principles, Practice and Policy
Sara Carter, Dylan Jones-Evans
Harlow: Financial Times Prentice Hall, 2000
528pp ISBN: 0201398524

This book provides a comprehensive introduction to small businesses, covering the environment in which they operate, the nature of entrepreneurship, and the techniques of practical management. Its authors draw on the work of leading academics in the United Kingdom and Europe and cover the latest thinking and research in the field.

Entrepreneur's Ultimate Start-up Directory
James Stephenson
Irvine, California: Entrepreneur Media, Inc, 2002
432pp ISBN: 1891984330
This book offers an extensive listing of business ideas, covering more than 1,300 potential start-ups across over 30 industries. It covers new and traditional business areas, including working from home and working via the Internet. Each entry is rated according to the following criteria: ease of start-up; estimated cost and potential income; possibility of exploiting the idea online; skills required; whether the start-up could be run part-time; and licensing/franchising opportunities.

Financial Management for the Small Business: A Practical Guide 5th ed
Colin Barrow
London: Kogan Page, 2001
256pp (Business Enterprise Series)
ISBN: 0749435003
The author provides practical advice on proper financial planning and control for the small business. The three main sections cover key financial statements, financial analysis tools, and business plans and budgeting. A list of further reading and sources of information is included.

Finding Your Perfect Work: The New Career Guide for Making a Living, Creating a Life
Paul Edwards, Sarah Edwards
New York: Penguin Putnam, Inc, 2003
480pp ISBN: 1585422169
This book is aimed at those in the crucial first phase of setting up a business: assessing yourself. Considering what you really want to do and get from your own business is explored in depth here, and the book contains worksheets to help the reader pinpoint their own strengths, weaknesses, and goals.

Go It Alone: The Streetwise Secrets of Success
Geoff Burch
Oxford: Capstone, 2003
336pp ISBN: 1841124702
An easy-to-read, practical guide to those thinking of starting their own business, packed with anecdotal advice. The author's very original and humorous approach helps get across his wealth of experience in entrepreneurship and sales.

Growing Business Handbook: Inspiration and Advice from Successful Entrepreneurs and Fast-growing UK Companies 7th ed
Richard Willsher, Adam Jolly, eds
London: Kogan Page, 2004
400pp ISBN: 0749442220
Designed to help businesses with an established market position, this handbook presents a range of practical strategies for managing growth. The contributors, who come from a variety of backgrounds, provide advice in areas including funding options, competition, managing the risks, making the most of IT, external relations, and competitive purchasing.

ISO 9001 2000 for Small Businesses 2nd ed
Ray Tricker
Oxford: Butterworth-Heinemann, 2001
464pp ISBN: 0750648821
This book explains the requirements of the new ISO9000 2000 standard and looks at how smaller companies can benefit from it and set up their own quality management systems. Background information on ISO9000 and the importance of quality control and quality assurance is provided.

Limited Company Guide
London: Law Pack, 2000
96pp ISBN: 1902646584

This guide aims to explain how to set up your own limited company. Valid in England, Scotland, and Wales, it describes the essential procedures and incorporates examples of forms from Companies House, Articles and Memoranda of Association, and directors' resolutions.

The Loyalty Effect: The Hidden Force Behind Growth, Profits, and Lasting Value
Frederick F. Reichheld
Boston, Massachusetts: Harvard Business School Press, 2001
352pp ISBN: 1578516870
Loyalty is not dead, and this book explains why, demonstrating the power of loyalty-based management as a profitable alternative to a constant flux of employees, investors and customers.

Managing Difficult People: A Survival Guide for Handling Any Employee
Marilyn Pincus
Avon, Massachusetts: Adams Media Corporation, 2004
224pp ISBN: 1593371861
While you may have a marvellous business idea, you may not be the world's most confident manager, and as your business grows, that's something you'll need to work on. If you work with someone with a challenging personality, this book will help you find practical ways of dealing with them so that you can both get on with your job. Offering practical help on how to get a tricky situation back on track, this book profiles several different types of awkward colleagues, including: The Bully, The Complainer, The Procrastinator, the Know-it-All; and The Silent Type.

New Venture Adventure: Succeed with Professional Business Planning
Ueli Looser, Bruno Schlapfer eds
London: Texere Publishing, 2001
224pp ISBN: 1587990032
This manual, written by consultants from McKinsey, offers professional advice on starting up a business. The book opens with an overview of the stages a typical start-up

company will go through and a consideration of what constitutes on attractive business idea. The main focus is on the preparation of a professional business plan and an example of a business plan is provided. The book also covers the questions of how to value a start-up business and how to raise equity.

The Next Level: Essential Strategies for Achieving Breakthrough Growth
James B. Wood
Cambridge, Massachusetts: Perseus Books Group, 2000
224pp ISBN: 0738201596
An accessible guide to planning and managing the stages of company growth, *The Next Level* centres around the use of powerful, field-tested diagnostic tool, the Inc Growth Strategy Analysis. James Wood carefully shows entrepreneurs and established business leaders alike how to analyse their organisation's growth potential, identify the key constraints to future growth, and put into practice the strategies that will enable them to arrive at new levels of expansion and profit generation.

The On-Purpose Business: Doing More of What You Do Best More Profitably
Kevin W. McCarthy
Colorado Springs, Colorado: Navpress Publishing Group, 2002
192pp ISBN: 1576833216
Written in a story format and with a spiritual backdrop, this book examines the principles of management and introduces the 'On-Purpose' model, which focuses on all areas where each individual joins, belongs, and contributes to an organisation.

Outsmarting Goliath: How to Achieve Equal Footing with Companies That Are Bigger, Richer, Older and Better Known
Debra Koontz Traverso
London: Kogan Page, 2000
224pp ISBN: 0749432985
The author presents practical advice on how to help small businesses present a professional image, produce high-quality

marketing materials, and win contracts that may seem out of reach for a small company. The book also outlines innovative ways to enhance company profile.

Setting Up a Limited Company 2nd ed
Mark Fairweather, Rosy Border
London: The Stationery Office, 2004
160pp (Pocket Lawyer)
ISBN: 1859418570
This is a practical guide to the procedures for setting up a limited company in the United Kingdom. The text covers: considering the options; roles and responsibilities and completing the required forms. Sample letters, minutes, resolutions, and articles of association are included in the text and on floppy disk. Listings of frequently asked questions and useful contacts are also provided.

Setting Up and Running a Limited Company: A Comprehensive Guide to Forming and Operating a Company as a Director and Shareholder 4th ed
Robert Browning
Oxford: How To Books, 2003
192pp ISBN: 1857038665
This guide is aimed at anyone thinking of establishing a limited company and addresses statutory requirements as well as advising on best practice. The book includes information on: the responsibilities of shareholders and directors; setting up your business; preparing financial records; sourcing venture capital; and retreating gracefully if things don't go to plan.

Small Time Operator: How to Start Your Own Business, Keep Your Books, Pay Your Taxes, and Stay Out of Trouble 7th ed
Bernard B. Kamoroff
Willits, California: Bell Springs Publishing, 2004
208pp ISBN: 0917510224
Kamoroff presents the reader with the essentials of building a business, from obtaining initial permits and licenses, to seeking financing, locating the right business area, establishing an accounts and book-keeping system, and taking on new staff. Continually updated, Kamoroff is conscious of reflecting the very latest thinking in tax and business management.

Spare Room Tycoon: Succeeding Independently—The 70 Lessons of Sane Self-Employment
James Chan
London: Nicholas Brealey Publishing, 2000
224pp ISBN: 1857882474
Written by a entrepreneur with over 20 years' experience of working from home, this book is aimed at anyone thinking of setting up a home-based business. It offers support and tips on how to avoid isolation and to spread the word about your business. The book focuses on 'soft' skills, such as work/life balance, building confidence, and coping with the emotional demands of being your own boss and offers reassuring anecdotal advice.

Starting Your Own Business: The Bestselling Guide to Planning and Building a Successful Enterprise 4th ed
Jim Green
Oxford: How To Books, 2005
304pp ISBN: 1845280709
This practical guide examines the steps that need to be taken before starting a business. These include preparing a business plan, raising finance, and developing marketing strategies. The role of the Internet is also considered. The book includes a directory of sources of advice and information.

The Startup Garden: How Growing a Business Grows You
Tom Ehrenfeld
Maidenhead: McGraw-Hill, 2001
288pp ISBN: 0071368248
Ehrenfeld identifies a current trend toward entrepreneurship, and in this book he shows his readers how they can construct their own perfect job. *The Startup Garden* takes the reader through the processes involved in starting a company and shows how this is matched to the reader's hopes and dreams, demonstrating the link between your personal life and your business drives.

Understanding and Negotiating Business Contracts: Master the Small Print and Get a Better Deal
Jonathan Rush
Oxford: How To Books, 2002
176pp ISBN: 1857037987
This book offers clear, easy-to-read guidance for small businesses on the basics of drawing up contracts. The chapters are structured along the lines of a contract and avoid complex terms and jargon.

Understanding the Small Family Business
Denise Fletcher ed
London: Routledge, 2002
224pp ISBN: 0415250536
This book offers an overview of current research in the small family business sector with the main focus on the relationship between work and family and the tensions and contradictions that can arise. The contributions are organised in three sections relating to rationality discourse, resource-based discourse and critical discourse.

What No One Ever Tells You about Starting Your Own Business: Real Life Start-up Advice from 101 Successful Entrepreneurs
Jan Norman
Chicago, Illinois: Upstart Publishing, 2004
256pp ISBN: 0793185963
Drawing on the experience of, and mistakes made by, 100 businesspeople, this book contains helpful and practical advice on how to start your own business without headaches.

Your First Business Plan: A Simple Question and Answer Format Designed to Help You Write Your Own Plan 4th ed
Joseph Covello, Brian Hazelgren
Naperville, Illinois: Sourcebooks, 2002
160pp ISBN: 1402200021
This popular book contains practical advice on writing an impressive business plan, including useful information on the constituent parts of a business.

WEBSITES
BBC Business Basics - Small Business
http://news.bbc.co.uk/1/hi/in_depth/ business/2003/small_business/ default.stm
The small business section of the BBC's main business pages offers articles clarifying the key issues and answering practical questions related to the running of a small business. These short Q&A articles are divided up into subject areas, inlcluding marketing, finance, and management. Many of the articles provide links to other related areas on the BBC website, such as Working Lunch (the award-winning daily business, personal finance, and consumer news programme), or other organisations on the Web where further information can be found.

Benchmark Index
www.benchmarkindex.com
Affiliated to Business Link, this website offers help and advice on benchmarking to businesses, advisors, and networks. It aims to help businesses understand their current position and effectively plan for the future.

BizMove.com
www.bizmove.com
This US-based site features the Small Business Knowledge Base, a range of free information resources for small businesses.

Business Europe
www.businesseurope.com
This site offers advice, information, and news for all small businesses based in the United Kingdom. It is packed with features. The site provides access to a extensive range of practical guides to challenges in the areas of start-up/exit, finance, technology, people, e-commerce, sales and marketing, import/ export, and operations. A detailed directory enables users to search for suppliers by name, location, and industry type, and businesses may also register to appear in the directory themselves. There is also a forum in which users may ask questions of experts or register to answer others' questions if they have an area of expertise.

Business Eye (Wales)
www.businesseye.org.uk
Launched in September 2003, Business Eye (Wales) replaces Business Connect as a free information service for all businesses in Wales. The service is managed by the Welsh Development Agency and has more than 25 offices throughout Wales. Business Eye does not business support or grants itself but instead aims to 'signpost' users towards the best sources of help for their particular needs. The website offers a gateway to numerous resources for Welsh entrepreneurs, including links to useful sites across more than 20 key topics, a business forum, business news, information on courses and training, a support directory, and contact details of the local branches in North, Mid-, West, and South-East Wales.

Business Gateway (Scotland)
www.bgateway.com
Aimed at both start-ups and existing businesses in Scotland, Business Gateway (Scotland) operates in partnership with Scottish Enterprise, the Scottish Executive, and Scottish local authorities. There are local offices ('Gateways') in 13 regions across Scotland, but the website offers a range of help and advice to the reader, including a business information service, start-up and high growth start-up services, and a business growth service.

Business Link
www.businesslink.gov.uk
The UK Small Business Service runs this site to provide advice for small business owners and anyone thinking of setting up a small business in England. The site is packed with helpful information and easily navigable Business Link offers a telephone support line on 0845 600 9006 and can also has a network of 45 operators across the country which puts you in touch with an advisor.

Business Owner's Toolkit
www.toolkit.cch.com
This site is packed with information for budding small business owners. Offering a series of brief guides to key aspects of starting up your own company, the site also features a selection of downloadable document templates, official government forms, and spreadsheet templates.

Community Interest Companies (CICs)
www.dti.gov.uk/cics
Between March and June 2003, the Department for Trade and Industry consulted on a new legal framework for both companies and charities ('Enterprise for Communities—Proposals for a CIC'). The results, available on the DTI website, would be of particular interest to those planning on starting a business with social, ethical, or environmental aims.

Department for Trade and Industry
www.dti.gov.uk/bss
This site contains links to all relevant UK government departments and also offers a variety of helpful information, including as taxation advice, sources of finance and legal requirements, and more generally useful 'best practice' guides for small businesses from the Small Business Service.

Environment Agency
www.environment-agency.gov.uk/netregs/
This government website aims to help small businesses get to grips easily with the environmental legislation with which they are legally obliged to comply.

Formationshouse.com
www.formationshouse.com
This online company-formation service that guides you through the process of forming and registering a limited company.

Inc.com
www.inc.com
Inc.com is the online version of the magazine *Inc*. The website provides information, products, services, and online tools—accumulated from a variety of sources—for many business or management tasks. This information has also been organised into categories to help the user find quickly what they need.

Invest in Northern Ireland
www.investni.com
This site offers practical advice on how to establish a business in Northern Ireland. It has an excellent section of source of further information made up of weblinks to key organisations and industries in the area. The site is colourful, well designed and features key facts about Northern Ireland.

Jordans Limited UK
www.jordans.co.uk
An online company-formation service that also offers additional services such as search functions and debt recovery.

Redwoods Dowling Kerr
www.dowlingkerr.com
An agency that deals in businesses for sale, from retailers to nurseries. This site offers free access to lists of businesses as well as additional fee-based services, such as finding a business that meets your specification.

Scottishbusinesswomen.com
www.scottishbusinesswomen.com
Part of the Scottish Enterprise Network initiative, this website is aimed at women in Scotland who either run their own business or who are thinking about establishing one. It offers support and advice on how to grow and develop existing businesses and also offers practical help and valuable sources of information for start-ups.

smallbusinessadvice.org.uk
www.smallbusinessadvice.org.uk
Smallbusinessadvice.org.uk is a free and independent source of information and advice for entrepreneurs, owner managers, and the self employed, starting or running a business with fewer than 10 staff and based in England. The website operates a business enquiry service which links users to over 200 accredited business advisers. It also offers online guides to various aspects of business planning, a resource centre,

e-business advice, discussion boards, and help for students.

Smallbusiness.co.uk
www.smallbusiness.co.uk
Sponsored by Vodafone, this website offers extensive help on variety of key small business issues. The site is divided into seven main areas (including starting up, finance, people, technology, legal, and property) that are then subdivided into more detailed sections.

Small Business Research Portal
www.smallbusinessportal.co.uk
Intended for academics, policy makers, and support agencies, the portal provides a collection of links to small business sites under categories that include news, publications, research, institutes, and conferences.

UK Company Registration
www.uk-company-registration.co.uk
Another site which helps users set up companies on-line. The site is easy to navigate and has a helpful list of frequently asked questions.

UK National Work-stress Network
www.workstress.net
An informative site that aims to educate users about the causes of work-stress and various ways of coping with it. While the site does not offer stress counselling, it does feature helpful sources of, and links to, sources of further information and support.

ORGANISATIONS
British Chambers of Commerce
65 Petty France, London, SW1H 9EU
T: +44 (0) 20 7654 5800
F: +44 (0) 20 7654 5819
E: info@britishchambers.org.uk
www.chamberonline.co.uk
This is an umbrella body for a national network of locally-based chambers of commerce serving local businesses. The Chambers provide advice on importing and import services to member companies.

Federation of Small Businesses
Sir Frank Whittle Way, Blackpool Business Park, Blackpool, Lancashire, FY4 2FE
T: +44 (0) 1253 336 000
F: +44 (0) 1253 348 046
E: membership@fsb.org.uk
www.fsb.org.uk
The FSB, which has 160,000 members in the United Kingdom, represents the interests of small businesses with up to 200 employees. It organises an annual conference, publishes a bimonthly magazine, *First Voice*, and lobbies on policy issues, while its local branches provide networking and research facilities in addition to general support services for members.

Forum of Private Business
Ruskin Chambers, Drury Lane, Knutsford, Cheshire, WA16 6HA
T: +44 (0) 1565 634 467
F: +44 (0) 870 241 9570
E: info@fpb.org
www.fpb.co.uk
The FPB aims to influence laws and policies affecting private businesses in the United Kingdom and provide support for its members.

Institute of Business Advisers
Response House, Queen Street North, Chesterfield, S41 9AB
T: +44 (0) 1246 453 322
F: +44 (0) 1246 453 300
E: info@iba.org.uk
www.iba.org.uk
The IBA is a non-profit-making organisation which aims to help small firms throughout the United Kingdom and Ireland. It has over 2,000 members who provide advice, training, and counselling for clients so that their businesses become more effective and thus more profitable.

National Federation of Enterprise Agencies
12 Stephenson Court, Fraser Road, Priory Business Park, Bedford, MK44 3WH, United Kingdom
T: +44 (0)1234 831623
E: enquiries@nfea.com

www.nfea.com
The NFEA is a network of independent, non-profit local enterprise agencies for the support of small and growing businesses, especially startups and micro-businesses. The organisation aims to identify the needs of such businesses, encourage the government and others to provide the conditions for them to flourish, and provide a forum for members to share best practice. The British Volunteer Mentor Programme is an initiative of the NFEA.

The Prince's Trust
18 Park Square East, London, NW1 4LH
T: +44 (0) 800 842 842
F: +44 (0) 20 7543 1200
E: info@princes-trust.org.uk
www.princes-trust.org.uk
The Prince's Trust was established by the Prince of Wales in 1976 to help young people realise their full potential. Aimed at those aged between 14–30 (or 14–25 in Scotland), the Trust offers support and financial assistance across a range of core programmes including business start-ups. Since 1983, the Trust has helped over 60,000 businesses and its business programme currently offers: a low-interest loan of up to £4,000 for a sole trader or £5,000 for a partnership; a test marketing grant of up to £250; advice lines and seminars; and access to a volunteer business mentor.

Small Business Bureau
Curzon House, Church Road, Windlesham, Surrey, GU20 6BH
T: +44 (0) 1276 452 010
F: +44 (0) 1276 451 602
E: info@sbb.org.uk
www.smallbusinessbureau.org.uk
The Small Business Bureau was founded in 1976 to promote the interests of small businesses in the United Kingdom. Its activities include an annual conference and a magazine, *Small Business News*, which is published three times a year. The organisation has also set up Women into Business to encourage more women to choose business and business ownership as a career.

Small Business Service

Kingsgate House,
66–74 Victoria Street,
London, SW1E 6SW
T: +44 (0)207 215 5000
E: gatewayenquiries@sbs.gsi.gov.uk
www.sbs.gov.uk
The SBS provides advice and consultancy
services to small businesses in the United
Kingdom. It is a network of about 150 locally
based organisations sponsored by the
Department of Trade and Industry. Further
details can be obtained from the website
(**www.dti.org.uk**) and also from
www.businesslink.gov.uk.

Small Firms Enterprise Development Initiative

SFEDI Ltd, Suite 101, Dunston Innovation
Centre, Dunston Road, Chesterfield,
Derbyshire, S41 8NG
T: +44 (0)8456 381 333
F: +44 (0)8456 381 333
E: info@sfedi.co.uk
www.sfedi.co.uk
The SFEDI has been appointed by the UK
government to identify standards of best
practice for small businesses and to work
with providers of small-business training,
education, and advice to raise standards of
support.

SEE ALSO
Entrepreneurs (p. 511)

Accounting

BOOKS AND DIRECTORIES

Accounting in a Nutshell: Finance for the Non Specialist

Janet Walker
London: CIMA Publishing, 2001
170pp ISBN: 1859714951
This introductory text is designed for non-
specialist managers and students who need
an understanding of the basic principles of
financial and management accounting. The
topics covered include accounting
statements, profit and loss accounts, cost
analysis, and budget planning and control.

The Best Small Business Accounts Book (Blue Version)

Peter Hingston and Stuart Ramsden
Hereford: Hingston Publishing Co., 2004
64pp ISBN: 090655523X
There are three versions of this book, all
designed for the UK tax system. This blue
version, which has a monthly layout, is ideal
for non-VAT registered credit-based
businesses. Updated since its initial
publication in 1991, this book allows the
small business owner to keep the accounts
in one compact book. It provides full

instructions and worked examples to help
the user to book-keep correctly and
effectively, including 16 columns to analyse
cheques and an easy-to-do monthly bank
statement check.

The Best Small Business Accounts Book (Yellow Version)

Peter Hingston
Hereford: Hingston Publishing Co., 2004
64pp ISBN: 0906555221
There are three versions of this book, all
designed for the UK tax system. This yellow
version, which has a week-to-page layout, is
ideal for non-VAT registered cash
businesses. Initially published in 1991, this
book enables the small business owner to
keep complete accounts in one compact
book, offering detailed instructions and
worked examples along the way.

Book-keeping & Accounting for the Small Business: How to Keep the Books and Maintain Financial Control Over Your Business 7th ed

Peter Taylor
Oxford: How To Books, 2003
192pp ISBN: 1857038789

Aimed at both students and anyone running or responsible for the accounts of a small business, this guide offers structured advice on the essentials of book-keeping.

CIMA Dictionary of Finance and Accounting

London: A & C Black, 2003
352pp ISBN: 0747566895
With the stamp of approval of the Chartered Institute of Management Accountants, this is an authoritative and reliable finance and accounting dictionary. It is a useful reference for both practitioners and students of all areas of business.

Cost and Effect

Robert S. Kaplan, Robin Cooper
Boston, Massachusetts: Harvard Business School Press, 1997
357pp ISBN: 0875847889
This book demonstrates how the principles of activity-based costing and other advanced cost management techniques can drive business performance. It includes examples from a variety of leading companies worldwide.

Excel 2003 for Dummies

Greg Harvey
Chichester: John Wiley & Sons Ltd, 2003
408pp ISBN: 0764537563
This book gives the reader key advice and help on how to get to grips with this useful computer package. It covers the basics of setting up a worksheet to creating formulas, charts, graphs, and spreadsheets so that all your essential business information can be safely and effectively stored.

How to Read a Financial Report 6th ed

John A. Tracey
Chichester: John Wiley & Sons Ltd, 2004
216pp ISBN: 0471478679
Tracey provides guidance on interpreting company accounts (with relation to US practice), with particular reference to the three essential parts of every financial report—the balance sheet, the income statement, and the cash-flow statement. His explanations are illustrated with many examples.

Intermediate Accounting 11th ed

Donald E. Keiso, Jerry J. Weygandt, Terry D. Warfield
Chichester: John Wiley & Sons Ltd, 2003
776pp ISBN: 0471426393
The book covers the conceptual framework underlying financial accounting, financial reporting standards and statements, and more complex topics and transactions that are encountered in today's business environment. Specific guidance is provided for numerous topics including accounting for cash and receivables, inventory, intangible assets, current and long-term liabilities, income taxes, leases, shareholders' equity, and revenue recognition.

The Meaning of Company Accounts 8th ed

Walter Reid, D.R. Myddleton
Aldershot: Gower Publishing, 2005
310pp ISBN: 0566086603
The authors aim to help people using company accounts to gain a firm grasp of what they mean and to understand how they relate to business activities. Managers without formal accounting or financial training should find the book useful. It will also provide a basic introduction to company accounts for those taking formal accounting or business studies courses.

Teach Yourself Book Keeping

Andrew G. Piper, Andrew Lymer
London: Hodder Arnold, 2003
356pp (Teach Yourself)
ISBN: 0340859423
This book aims to demystify the area of book keeping, essential for small business owners and managers. Offering plenty of examples to help explain key terms and concepts, the book covers the double-entry system, the processes of recording purchases, and different types of transactions. Profit and loss accounts and balance sheets are also explained. The book also includes helpful completed exam pages with worked examples.

Teach Yourself Small Business Accounting
Mike Truman
London: Hodder Arnold, 2003
176pp (Teach Yourself)
ISBN: 0340859415
This practical guide is for the small business owner with no aptitude for figures or interest in book keeping or accountancy. It provides jargon-free step-by-step instructions, using the examples of real businesses, how to record each transaction, as well as advice on pricing goods and services. It also offers an alternative, easier, and less time-consuming system to that of double-entry book-keeping.

Test Your Financial Awareness
John Hodgson, Liz O'Neill
London: Hodder & Stoughton, 2000
93pp (Test Yourself Series)
ISBN: 0340782870
If you are responsible for the way in which assets are utilised, sales revenues earned, or expenses incurred, then this book is intended to sharpen and consolidate your financial skills. The authors provide an introduction to basic financial awareness, help you assess your understanding with a before-and-after test, explain how to calculate key financial measures, and discuss how to make better business decisions based on financial input.

Unlocking Company Reports and Accounts
Wendy McKenzie
Harlow: Financial Times Pitman, 1998
400pp ISBN: 0273632507
McKenzie provides a key to understanding company reports and accounts from first principles, explaining every point through the use of worked examples. She takes extracts from published accounts, including those of overseas companies, to illustrate accounting presentation, and enables the reader to understand and analyse a company's accounts and so build a comprehensive picture of its financial state.

WEBSITES
Accounting Web
www.accountingweb.co.uk
This site is an extensive UK-based online resource. It contains material from a number of providers intended for accountancy and finance professionals. It has received an award as the New Media Business Website of the Year.

ORGANISATIONS
Association of Accounting Technicians (AAT)
154 Clerkenwell Road, London, EC1R 5AD
T: +44 (0) 20 7415 7500
F: +44 (0) 20 7837 6970
E: aat@aat.org.uk
www.aat.co.uk
The AAT awards qualifications in accounting at NVQ levels 2, 3, and 4. An accounting technician is qualified to a slightly lower level than a fully qualified accountant.

Association of Chartered Certified Accountants (ACCA)
2 Central Park Quay, 89 Hydepark Street, Glasgow, G3 8BW
T: +44 (0) 141 582 2000
F: +44 (0) 141 582 2222
E: info@accaglobal.com
www.acca.co.uk
The Association is a professional and examining body in accountancy, recognised under the Companies Act 1989 by the UK Department of Trade and Industry.

Chartered Institute of Management Accountants (CIMA)
26 Chapter Street, London, SW1P 4NP
T: + 44 (0) 20 8849 2251
www.cimaglobal.com
CIMA is the leading UK professional organisation for management accountants but it also has a global reach: it represents more than 85,000 students and 65,000 members in more than 150 countries.

Chartered Institute of Public Finance and Accountancy (CIPFA)
3 Robert Street, London, WC2N 6RL
T: +44 (0) 20 7543 5600
F: +44 (0) 20 7543 5700
E: joan.lavery@cipfa.org
www.cipfa.org
CIPFA is a professional accountancy body whose main aim is to train managers to understand public finance and manage public money. Its members are drawn from both the public and private sectors. In addition to providing membership services, running courses, and awarding certification, it organises conferences and produces publications.

Institute of Chartered Accountants in England and Wales (ICAEW)
Chartered Accountants' Hall, PO Box 433, Moorgate Place, London, EC2P 2BJ
T: +44 (0) 20 7920 8100
F: +44 (0) 20 7920 0547
www.icaew.co.uk

This, the largest professional accountancy organisation in Europe with over 120,000 members, is responsible for educating and training chartered accountants and maintaining standards of professional conduct among its members.

Institute of Chartered Accountants of Scotland (ICAS)
CA House, 21 Haymarket Yards, Edinburgh, Scotland, EH12 5BH
T: +44 (0) 131 347 0100
F: +44 (0) 131 347 0105
E: enquiries@icas.org.uk
www.icas.org.uk
The ICAS is the leading professional accounting body in Scotland, and the oldest professional body of accountants in the world.

SEE ALSO
Budgeting (p. 499)
Reading a Balance Sheet (p. 165)
Taxation (p. 551)

Bankruptcy and Business Failure

BOOKS AND DIRECTORIES
Introduction to Corporate and Personal Insolvency Law
Fiona Tolmie
London: Sweet & Maxwell, 1998
429pp ISBN: 0421598506
This introductory text covers personal and corporate insolvency in the United Kingdom. It summarises the relevant legislation and explains how it works in practice. Key policy issues and areas where the law may be changed in the future are also highlighted.

Managing Your Solvency: A Guide to Insolvency and the Financial Viability of your Organisation
Michael Norton, ed
London: Directory of Social Change, 1994
154pp ISBN: 1873860285
This guide provides technical and practical information on the problems of insolvency for charities and voluntary organisations. The following topics are covered: the meaning and consequences of insolvency; the accountant's perspective; insolvency and trustee liability; fundraising to avoid crisis; reserves and working capital; and protecting assets and activities. The question of how to create successful financial and organisational structures is also considered.

WEBSITES
Business Bankruptcy Info
**www.creditworthy.com/topics/
bankruptcy.html**
This website, hosted by Creditworthy Co.,
provides links to business bankruptcy
information covering the United States,
Canada, and United Kingdom. It includes
information on, and links to, US bankruptcy
courts, an overview of the US Bankruptcy
Code, and statistics and research on
bankruptcy filings.

InsolvencyAsia
www.insolvencyasia.com
This site, based in Hong Kong, provides
insolvency-related news together with
information on bankruptcy legislation and
listings of consultants, associations, and
regulatory authorities in Asian countries.

Insolvency Services
www.insolvency.gov.uk
This government-sponsored site provides
practical information and advice on
personal and corporate insolvency in the
United Kingdom, including statistics and a
database of insolvency practitioners.

InterNet Bankruptcy Library
www.bankrupt.com
This site, sponsored by the Bankruptcy
Creditors' Service and the Beard Group, is
aimed particularly at creditors. It includes a
news archive, a database of bankruptcy
professionals, information on legal rules in
US states, and details of publications, as well
as providing access to discussion groups.

ORGANISATIONS
Insolvency Practitioners Association
52–54 Gracechurch Street, London, EC3V
0EH
T: +44 (0) 20 7623 5108
F: +44 (0) 20 7623 5127
E: secretariat@insolvency-
practitioners.org.uk
www.insolvency-practitioners.org.uk
The IPA, founded in 1961, is a professional
organisation for insolvency practitioners. Its
main objectives are to promote training and
education in insolvency administration and
to maintain the standards of performance
and conduct of those working in the field.

R3, The Association of Business Recovery Professionals
8th Floor, 120 Aldersgate Street, London,
EC1A 4JQ
T: +44 (0) 20 7566 4200
F: +44 (0) 20 7566 4224
E: association@r3.org.uk
www.r3.org.uk
R3 (Rescue, Recovery, Renewal), founded in
1990 and formerly known as the Society of
Practitioners of Insolvency, is a professional
organisation for insolvency practitioners
and turnaround managers which places a
growing emphasis on reconstruction,
turnaround management, and corporate
recovery. Its activities include courses,
conferences, and producing publications—
including the quarterly journal *Recovery*.

SEE ALSO
Accounting (p. 494)

Budgeting

BOOKS AND DIRECTORIES

Beyond Budgeting: How Managers Can Break Free from the Annual Performance Trap
Jeremy Hope, Robin Fraser
Boston, Massachusetts: Harvard Business School Press, 2003
272pp ISBN: 1578518660
An enlightening read for all managers, not just finance specialists, this book posits that traditional budgeting processes are unproductive. Recognising the fact that many executives are forced to spend their time 'making the numbers work' rather than making the most of their company's potential, the book offers an alternative way forward. Case studies and findings from the 'Beyond Budgeting Roundtable' are also included.

Budgeting Basics and Beyond: A Complete Step-by-Step Guide for Nonfinancial Managers 2nd ed
Jae K. Shim and Joel G. Siegel
Englewood Cliffs, New Jersey: Prentice Hall Trade, 2005
416pp ISBN: 0471725021
A guide to effective budgeting, taking the reader through every step from preparing and presenting budgets to handling budgeting difficulties. Extra features include case studies, illustrations and checklists, together with suggestions for getting the most out of accounting software packages and spreadsheet applications.

Budgeting for Non-Financial Managers: How to Master and Maintain Effective Budgets
Iain Maitland
Harlow: Financial Times Prentice Hall, 1999
204pp (Smarter Solutions Series)
ISBN: 0273644947
This book takes you through each stage of the budgeting process, explaining all you need to know about it. From understanding the procedures for making budgets and forecasts to developing realistic contingency plans, it shows how to turn your budgeting strategy into a valuable management tool. It also contains a wide range of model forecasts, forms, and budgets, and comes complete with checklists and case studies.

Cash Flows and Budgeting Made Easy: How to Set and Monitor Financial Targets in Any Organization 4th ed
Peter Taylor
Oxford: How To Books, 2002
160pp ISBN: 1857038037
This practical guide aims to cover the whole budgeting process, and contains information on planning financial requirements, forecasting, VAT, managing cash flows, and using IT to help make your financial life easier.

Costing, Pricing and Credit Control: How to Improve Profitability and How to Get Paid Promptly 2nd ed
Keith Kirkland, Stuart Howard
London: Kogan Page, 1998
189pp (Simple and Practical Series)
ISBN: 0749429305
The book aims to provide a sound understanding of how to work out the cost of a product or service, fix the right price for it, work out the break-even point, handle price discounting, deal with loss-making activities, formulate a credit control strategy, control debt, and recover bad debt through the courts.

Get to Grips with Budgets: How to Take the Stress Out of Working with Numbers
London: A & C Black, 2005
96pp (Steps to Success)
ISBN: 074757734X
Aimed at anyone who has to work with numbers but who feels uncomfortable with them, this book is a practical and down to earth guide to budgeting. Featuring a special jargon-busting section, it covers a wide range of key issues including drawing up and managing budgets, keeping on top of costs, solving cash-flow problems, and

interpreting balance sheets and profit and
loss accounts.

Managing by the Numbers
Chuck Kremer, Ron Rizzuto, John Case
*Cambridge, Massachusetts: Perseus Books
Group, 2000*
224pp ISBN: 0738202568
This is a handy and practical guide to
reading and using balance sheets, income
statements, and cash flow statements to
drive business growth and profitability.

Mastering Spreadsheet Budgets and Forecasts: How to Save Time and Gain Control of Your Business
Malcolm Secrett
Harlow: Financial Times Prentice Hall, 1999
260pp (Smarter Solutions Series)
ISBN: 0273644912
This step-by-step, jargon-free guide
demonstrates the advantages and potential
of using spreadsheets to prepare and
present budgets and forecasts. It includes
examples of budgets and forecasts, followed
through completely from beginning to end.

WEBSITES
Accounting Web
www.accountingweb.co.uk
This site is an extensive UK-based online
resource. It contains material from a
number of providers intended for
accountancy and finance professionals. It
has received an award as the New Media
Business Website of the Year.

Credit to Cash
www.credit-to-cash.com
This UK portal provides a wide range of
financial information and advice,
specifically on credit management and
policy, debt recovery, cash-flow control, and
other issues of interest to small businesses.

The Dyer Partnership
www.netaccountants.com
The site provides a wide range of
information on UK tax and accounting
matters and other business issues of interest
to owners and managers of UK businesses.

ORGANISATIONS
Association of Chartered Certified Accountants
2 Central Park Quay, 89 Hydepark Street,
Glasgow, G3 8BW
T: +44 (0) 141 582 2000
F: +44 (0) 141 582 2222
E: info@accaglobal.com
www.acca.co.uk
The Association is a professional and
examining body in accountancy, recognised
under the Companies Act 1989 by the UK
Department of Trade and Industry.

Chartered Institute of Management Accountants (CIMA)
26 Chapter Street, London, SW1P 4NP
T: + 44 (0) 20 8849 2251
www.cimaglobal.com
CIMA is the leading UK professional
organisation for management accountants.

Institute of Chartered Accountants in England and Wales
Chartered Accountants' Hall, PO Box 433,
Moorgate Place, London, EC2P 2BJ
T: +44 (0) 20 7920 8100
F: +44 (0) 20 7920 0547
E: dsbds@icaew.co.uk
www.icaew.co.uk
This, the largest professional accountancy
organisation in Europe with over 120,000
members, is responsible for educating and
training Chartered Accountants and
maintaining standards of professional
conduct among its members.

Institute of Chartered Accountants of Scotland
CA House, 21 Haymarket Yards, Edinburgh,
Scotland, EH12 5BH
T: +44 (0) 131 347 0100
F: +44 (0) 131 347 0105
E: enquiries@icas.org.uk
www.icas.org.uk
The ICAS is the leading professional
accounting body in Scotland, and the oldest
professional body of accountants in the
world.

Institute of Credit Management

The Water Mill, Station Road,
South Luffenham, Oakham, Leicestershire,
LE15 8NB
T: +44 (0) 1780 722 900
F: +44 (0) 1780 721 333
E: info@icm.org.uk
www.icm.org.uk
The Institute of Credit Management (ICM)
is the largest organisation of credit
professionals in Europe, and the focal point
in the United Kingdom for all matters
relating to credit management and its
ancillary functions. The ICM sets
professional standards and tests and
assesses those who wish to gain its
professional qualification. It also provides
advice to government and other national
bodies.

Institute of Financial Accountants

Burford House, 44 London Road, Sevenoaks,
Kent, TN13 1AS
T: +44 (0) 1732 458 080
F: +44 (0) 1732 455 848
E: mail@ifa.org.uk
www.ifa.org.uk
The Institute of Financial Accountants,
established in 1916, is the largest
professional body of its type in the world. It
represents members and students in more
than 80 countries around the world and
provides a qualification and continuing
professional development for those who
want to become financial accountants. It
also sets both technical and ethical
standards within the profession.

SEE ALSO
Accounting (p. 494)
Controlling a Budget (p. 120)
Controlling Costs (p. 123)
Drawing Up a Budget (p. 126)

Business Plans and Planning

BOOKS AND DIRECTORIES
The Business Plan Workbook
4th ed
Colin Barrow, Paul Barrow,
Robert Brown
London: Kogan Page, 2005
384pp ISBN: 0749443464
The processes and procedures required to
write a business plan are brought together in
this workbook, and are illustrated with
examples from actual business plans. The
seven-phase approach focuses on: the
business history and position to date;
market research; competitive business
strategies; operations; forecasting results;
business controls; and writing up and
presenting your business plan. Appendices
give market research information sources
and sources of finance for new and small
businesses.

The Definitive Business Plan: The Fast Track to Intelligent Business Planning for Executives and Entrepreneurs 2nd ed
Richard Stutley
Harlow: Financial Times Prentice Hall, 2005
288pp ISBN: 1405822171
This text is written for both the newcomer
and the experienced planner. It provides a
concise guide to the business planning
process, and focuses attention on strategic
planning and strategic and operational
controls. The practical aspects of
constructing various types of business plan
are explained in some detail.

How to Prepare a Business Plan: Planning for Successful Start-up and Expansion
Edward Blackwell
London: Kogan Page, 2002
190pp (Sunday Times)
ISBN: 0749437472

A highly-recommended title that takes the owner/manager through the process of developing a business plan for start-up or expansion. This book covers financial forecasting and planning and gives useful case studies of businesses preparing and following business plans.

The Successful Business Plan: Secrets and Strategies 4th ed
Rhonda M. Abrams
Palo Alto, California: Running R Media, 2003
409pp ISBN: 0966963563
This book is designed to help readers create a business plan that will attract the funding they need to get started. It presents insights from some 200 business owners, venture capitalists, and CEOs, but, in addition, contains worksheets and sample business plans, provides tools to help in number-crunching, and offers guidance on the length of an ideal plan and the way it should be worded and formatted.

Successful Business Plans in a Week 2nd ed
Iain Maitland
London: Hodder & Stoughton, 1998
93pp (Business in a Week Series)
ISBN: 034071199X
This step-by-step guide to the process of compiling and writing a business plan explains how to identify goals, make preparatory notes, compile the financial and commercial sections, and present the plan.

WEBSITES
Business Plan Guide
www.business-plans.co.uk
This site, sponsored by Miller Consultancy,

provides information on business planning resources. It includes books, links to websites, articles, and an e-mail newsletter.

Business Plans
www.bplans.com
This site, created by Palo Alto Software, offers planning advice for small businesses and a substantial range of sample plans, which subscribers to bplans' software can download and edit. It also includes a resource centre with links to other websites, as well as an 'ask the experts' section.

More Business
www.morebusiness.com
This site has a lengthy business and marketing plans section and provides some useful sample business plans.

Venture Associates
www.venturea.com/business.htm
Produced by an investment banking and management consulting firm, the site provides freely available information on various aspects of business planning. It also includes a useful business plan outline.

Venture Capital Resource Library
www.vfinance.com
This site provides a business plan template, general articles, and texts of SEC and UCC rules and regulations, as well as leads to sources of venture capital. It is particularly useful for those with business commitments in the United States.

SEE ALSO
Budgeting (p. 499)
Small and Growing Businesses (p. 486)

Computers, Information Technology, and E-commerce

BOOKS AND DIRECTORIES

Absolute Beginner's Guide to Computer Basics 3rd ed
Michael Miller
Indianapolis, Indiana: Que, 2005
480pp (Absolute Beginner's Guide)
ISBN: 0789734303
This book sets out to equip readers with the knowledge they need to set up and learn more about their PC. It includes advice on maintenance, adding new hardware and devices, using the Internet, shopping online, and buying and selling on eBay. Readers' basic skills are developed and these can then be applied in more specialist or business-related areas.

The Beginner's Guide to Computers and the Internet
Susan Holden, Matthew Francis
Chichester: Summersdale Publishers, 2004
416pp ISBN: 1840243961
This is a guide to the basics of using computers. Avoiding technical jargon, the book explains key terms and concepts and shows a range of time-saving shortcuts for those unfamiliar with computers. E-mail and the Internet are also covered.

E-Business for the Small Business
John G Fisher
London: Kogan Page, 2001
192pp (Business Enterprise Guide)
ISBN: 0749434791
E-business presents many new opportunities for businesses of all sizes. This guide takes owner-managers through the necessary steps for building a successful and sustainable e-business. It deals with: finding the funds; getting the right equipment; setting up a website; legal issues; online marketing and advertising; business-to-business opportunities; and developing an e-business plan.

E-commerce Law for Business Managers
Charles Chatterjee
Canterbury: Financial World Publishing , 2002
338pp ISBN: 0852975643
Aimed specifically at smaller businesses, this is a reference guide to the legal issues of launching a commercial internet site. Some of those issues include: e-commerce security; corporate identity; service provision; intellectual property rights; domain names; and email marketing. Many well established businesses have been caught out by the requirements of the Data Protection Act, and so this book seeks to help readers to understand the legal status of electronic money, signatures, privacy, and consumer rights. It provides this advice in a clear, practical, and user-friendly format, so that all types of manager can gain an understanding of key UK legislation and EU directives.

IT Investment: Making a Business Case
Dan Remenyi
Oxford: Butterworth-Heinemann, 1999
210pp (Computer Weekly Professional Series)
ISBN: 0750645040
The author presents clear arguments for preparing an IT business case and includes model questionnaires and forms that managers can use in preparing a case of their own. He stresses in particular the importance of demonstrating the improvements an IT project can make to business processes, practice, and efficiency, and introduces a five-factor model which ties the project into an organisation's corporate strategy.

Learning to Succeed in Business with Information Technology
Tim Lane, David Snow, Peter Labrow
Manchester: NCC Education, 2000
192pp ISBN: 1902343328
Aimed at managers within industry, this book addresses the reasons why it is

important to invest in the IT skills of the workforce. Changes within the workforce, business attitudes to IT education, IT certification and accreditation, and methods of learning are examined in detail. The authors also make recommendations regarding best practice in IT skills training in organisations and for the IT training industry.

Learning Web Design 2nd ed
Jennifer Niederst
Farnham: O'Reilly UK, 2003
496pp ISBN: 0596004842
Aimed at those new to Web design, this book is a comprehensive introduction to the fundamentals. The book is accessible in both tone and lay-out and is split into four sections: an overview of the Web design process; an introduction to HTML, the coding that makes up the background of Web pages; a guide to Web graphics; and advice on design. Jargon-free and full of practical tips, this book is ideal for beginners.

The Really, Really, Really Easy Step-by-step Computer Book: For Absolute Beginners of All Ages
Robynn Hofmeyr, Gavin Hoole
Cape Town, South Africa: Struik Publishers, 2001
80pp ISBN: 1868726827
As the title would suggest, this illustrated book is aimed at the absolute beginner. It offers step-by-step advice and information on a variety of essential skills, including choosing the right PC for you, getting to know your machine, creating and saving documents, and using e-mail.

The Rough Guide to the Internet 10th ed
Peter Buckley, Duncan Clark
London: Rough Guides, 2004
576pp ISBN: 1843533383
One of the most popular guides to the Internet for beginners, this book explains how to get to grips with the online world. It gives information on how to search, shop, browse, play, and communciate online as well as on how to create a Web page. Fully updated, some of the book's new features include a glossary to define complex terms when they first appear in the text, information boxes to anticipate common mistakes, and a variety of exercises so that readers can test their newly-gained skills. This book will be a boon to all new or unpractised Internet users.

Small Business Websites That Work: Get Online to Grow Your Company
Sean McManus
Harlow: Prentice Hall, 2001
240pp ISBN: 0273654861
A guide to help you get to grips with the essentials of website design and management. This book will be particularly helpful if you are outsourcing your website and need to learn not only how to brief people effectively so that you save time and money, but also how the basic technology behind the Web.

WEBSITES
Beginners.co.uk
www.beginners.co.uk
This website offers advice for both absolute beginners and those with some IT knowledge. The site offers a range of free tutorials and online training courses to help those who would like to gain or expand their IT knowledge for work or personal use, and also offers packages of courses that may be purchased. The site is easy to navigate even for Internet novices.

@Brint.com
www.brint.com
This extensive portal and community network for e-business, information, technology, and knowledge management contains news, articles, book reviews, and links to relevant websites in the featured areas.

CMC Information Sources
www.december.com/cmc/info
This site, which focuses on computer-mediated communications, offers a set of

links to essential websites concerned with computer training, applications, technology, and culture.

E-commerce focus
www.ecomfocus.com
This site offers useful guidance on e-commerce and its importance for businesses and also provides a list of contacts for further information. Click on the 'E-commerce' tab.

Which? Online
www.which.net
A subscription website, *Which?* Online offers access via the Internet to the wide range of information contained in the range of *Which?* magazines, including *Computing Which?*. The site offers a tour and a 30-day free trial. Subscribers gain access to thousands of reports contained in the print versions of all *Which?* magazines, searchable guides, and interactive features.

PC Magazine online
www.pcmag.co.uk
This easily navigable site offers a range of helpful services to the user. These include an 'e-shopper' facility which allows you to compare specifications and prices on IT products and a forum whereby users can pose questions to the magazine's editors. There are also a series of information centres on news, products, downloads, advice, and careers as well as subsections on

e-business, communications, business hardware, business software, security, personal computing, and gaming.

ORGANISATIONS
British Computer Society
1 Sanford Street, Swindon, SN1 1HJ
T: +44 (0) 1793 417 417
F: +44 (0) 1793 480 270
E: bcshq@hq.bcs.org.uk
www.bcs.org.uk
Founded in 1957, the British Computer Society is a professional and learned society with members from both the United Kingdom and overseas. It aims to provide a voice for the IT industry in discussions with the UK government. In addition, it offers both its own qualifications and others accredited by the Engineering Council that can lead to Chartered Engineer status.

National Computing Centre Limited
Oxford House, Oxford Road, Manchester, M1 7ED
T: +44 (0) 161 242 2121
F: +44 (0) 161 242 2499
E: info@ncc.co.uk
www.ncc.co.uk
Founded in 1966, the National Computing Centre is an international, membership-based organisation that aims to promote the effective use of IT and computers. Its areas of particular interest include systems design, computer security, communications, and training.

Direct Marketing

BOOKS AND DIRECTORIES
2,239 Tested Secrets for Direct Marketing Success
Denny Hatch, Don Jackson
Maidenhead: McGraw-Hill, 1999
368pp ISBN: 0844203491
Divided in topic sections for easy reference, this book is an excellent source of direct marketing advice drawn from the experience of experts.

Commonsense Direct Marketing 4th ed
Drayton Bird
London: Kogan Page, 2000
392pp ISBN: 0749431210
This is a practical textbook, introducing direct marketing, that is packed with international case studies and demonstrations of successful strategies. It covers the following topics: the role of the marketing department; how to acquire and

keep customers; how to achieve objectives and evaluate results; what you should sell; how to position products effectively; how to choose an agency and how to do without one; and the Internet, the direct marketer's newest and potentially most effective tool.

Direct and Database Marketing

Graeme McCorkell
London: Institute of Direct Marketing/Kogan Page, 1997
315pp ISBN: 0749419601
The best UK introduction to direct marketing, this book was written to be read from cover to cover and contains some good small business examples. This text is also useful to dip into for examples of how direct marketing campaigns are measured and evaluated. Case studies and illuminating examples are included.

Direct Marketing: Strategy, Planning, Execution 4th ed

Edward L. Nash
Maidenhead: McGraw-Hill, 2000
600pp ISBN: 0071352872
This updated edition is a classic in the direct marketing industry. The author, a direct marketing company executive, presents a thorough overview of all aspects of direct marketing, including strategic planning, media-specific marketing techniques, the economics of direct marketing, and direct marketing considerations for Internet and global marketing.

Enterprise One-to-One: Tools for Competing in the Interactive Age

Don Peppers, Martha Rogers
London: Currency/Doubleday, 1999
464pp ISBN: 038548755X
Written by the champions of customer relationship marketing, this is a best-selling guide to using new technology in your quest to get ahead, and stay ahead, of the field.

Making It Personal: How to Profit from Personalization without Invading Privacy

Bruce Kasanoff, Don Peppers, Martha Rogers
Cambridge, Massachusetts: Perseus Books Group, 2001
240pp ISBN: 0738205362
This book is a study of how the forthcoming growth in the use of personal information will affect the corporate world. Using research carried out in real-life, the author investigates the contradiction that can exist between increasing profits through personal interaction and not invading privacy.

Successful Direct Marketing Methods 7th ed

Bob Stone, Ron Jacobs
Maidenhead: McGraw-Hill, 2001
608pp ISBN: 0658001450
This updated edition provides a classic guide to direct marketing, combining new media with traditional marketing strategies to provide effective direct marketing to consumers. The content includes identifying and meeting consumers' needs, business to business marketing, and e-commerce techniques, such as powerful branding strategies for Internet sites.

WEBSITES
The Direct Marketing Association
www.the-dma.org
The Direct Marketing Association is a trade association serving the needs of direct marketing users and suppliers. Its website provides comprehensive information on direct marketing. This includes: conferences and seminars; professional development; industry guidelines; directories of direct marketers listed by name and type of service; a job bank; privacy information; research; and legislative issues.

Royal Mail
www.royalmail.com
The Direct Mail section of this website offers information on principles of best practice in that area, as well as lots of useful help on

creating, planning, and budgeting a campaign.

ORGANISATIONS
Direct Marketing Association UK
DMA House, 70 Margaret Street, London, W1W 8SS
T: +44 (0) 20 7291 3300
F: +44 (0) 20 7323 4426
E: info@dma.org.uk
www.dma.org.uk
Founded in 1992, the Direct Marketing Association (UK) is Europe's largest trade association in this sector. Committed to the promotion of best practice and the raising of industry standards, the DMA (UK) aims to raise the stature of the direct-marketing industry and to give the consumer trust and confidence in direct marketing.

Federation of European Direct Marketing
Tervurenlaan, Avenue de Tervuren 439, Brussels, B-1150, Belgium
T: +32 2779 42 68
F: +32 2779 42 69
E: info@fedma.org
www.fedma.org
A membership organisation for national direct-marketing associations, FEDMA aims to promote, protect, and provide information about the European direct-marketing industry.

Information Commissioner's Office
Wycliffe House, Water Lane, Wilmslow, Cheshire, SK9 5AF
T: +44 (0) 1625 545 745
F: +44 (0) 1625 524 510
E: mail@ico.gsi.gov.uk
www.informationcommissioner.gov.uk
The Information Commissioner is responsible for enforcing the eight principles of good practice regarding the processing of personal data in the United Kingdom as set out in the Data Protection Act 1998 and the Freedom of Information Act 2000.

Institute of Direct Marketing
1 Park Road, Teddington, Middlesex, TW11 0AR
T: +44 (0) 20 8977 5705
F: +44 (0) 20 8943 2535
E: enquiries@theidm.com
www.theidm.co.uk
Founded in 1987, the IDM describes itself as 'Europe's leading professional development body for direct, data, and digital marketing'. The Institute has trained more than 67,000 marketing practitioners.

SEE ALSO
Marketing Management (p. 522)

Employee Benefits/Compensation

BOOKS AND DIRECTORIES
The Executive Handbook on Compensation: Linking Strategic Rewards to Business Performance
Charles H. Fay, et al
London: Free Press, 2001
896pp ISBN: 0684842335
This book is written for managers at all levels of experience and provides detailed information regarding employee compensation. The authors commissioned international compensation professionals to create this guide on linking employee compensation to performance. Topics include merging compensation and business goals, and designing effective and competitive compensation packages.

Flexible Benefits
Industrial Society
London: Audit Commission, 2000
64pp (Managing Best Practice 75)
This booklet presents the results of a survey of flexible benefits schemes carried out among UK human resource managers in June 2000. Topics covered include: how common flexible benefits are; how costs are calculated and controlled; and the

drawbacks of flexible benefits schemes. Case studies of Cable and Wireless, Cadbury, PriceWaterhouseCoopers, and the Spring Group are used, and consultancy advice and sources of further information are also provided.

The HR Book: Human Resources Management for Small Business
Lin Grensing Prophal
Naperville, Illinois: Sourcebooks, 1999
280pp ISBN: 1551802414
This book is a 'complete guide' to human resource management for the small business. Although written from a US perspective, its message is useful for small businesses all over the world.

WEBSITES
BenefitsLink.com
www.benefitslink.com
This large US site is aimed at employers and provides news, compliance information, a question and answer service, links to articles, a bookshop, and a database of speakers.

Employee Benefit News
www.benefitnews.com
This US-focused site provides news and analysis of benefits issues and an e-mail newsletter. Registration is required.

Employee Benefits Interactive
www.employeebenefits.co.uk
The site includes a knowledge bank of articles from *Employee Benefits* magazine and a comprehensive range of useful information, including a contact directory. To access some of the details, you must register.

Employee Benefits Survey
www.bls.gov/ncs/ebs
This site provides access to data from the US Bureau of Labor Statistics Employee Benefits Survey in PDF format.

SEE ALSO
Employment Law (p. 508)

Employment Law

BOOKS AND DIRECTORIES
Butterworths Employment Law Handbook 13th ed
Peter Wallington, ed
London: Butterworths, 2005
2000pp ISBN: 1405704535
Published annually, this is a comprehensive reference source of statutory and non-statutory material relating to employment law in the United Kingdom. This latest edition takes into account the amendments to the Employment Relations Act 2004, Employment Tribunal Regulations, new ACAS Code of Practice on Disciplinary and Grievance Procedure, two new Disability Rights Commission Codes of Practice, the ACAS Arbitration Scheme (Flexible Working) Regulations, new Regulations on Information and Consultation, the new

Claim and Response forms for tribunal claims, plus guidance notes on completing them.

Collective Labour Law
Gillian Morris, Timothy J. Archer
Oxford: Hart Publishing, 2000
623pp ISBN: 1841131776
A masterly book on collective labour law which is suitable both for specialists and for those with no detailed prior knowledge. Trade union and worker rights and obligations are covered along with coverage of the law relating to industrial action. The book takes full account of the Human Rights Act and of European law. Appendices include comprehensive information to assist further research.

Contracts of Employment: Law, Practice and Precedents
Michael Duggan
Welwyn: EMIS Professional Publishing, 2001
424pp ISBN: 1858112397
As well as providing samples of complete employment contracts, this book provides hundreds of clauses for special situations with commentary to explain points to be considered and the reasons behind the suggested wording. It comes with a CD-ROM in an innovative format (PCs only) which makes it easy to compile complete contracts to suit various situations.

Essentials of Employment Law 8th ed
David Lewis, Malcolm Sargeant
London: Chartered Institute of Personnel and Development (CIPD), 2004
312pp ISBN: 1843980010
Lewis and Sargeant have put together a comprehensible introduction to the main statutory and common-law rules in the United Kingdom that govern such challenging issues as contracts of employment, discrimination, and union rights. Other areas covered include the sources and institutions of employment law, the national minimum wage, working time regulations, parental and maternity rights, dismissal and redundancy, health and safety, data protection, trade union recognition, and sex, race, disability, and age discrimination.

Maternity Rights 2nd ed
Chartered Institute of Personnel and Development
London: Chartered Institute of Personnel and Development (CIPD), 2000
43pp (Legal Essentials Series)
ISBN: 0852928750
The issue of maternity rights affects every workplace and is the area of employment law that HR departments most frequently encounter. This new and updated edition of *Maternity Rights* includes recent case law, a new section on frequently asked questions, a sample maternity policy, and a sample parental leave policy. It takes full account of the changes introduced by both the Employment Relations Act 1999 and the Maternity and Parental Leave Regulations 1999.

Tolley's Employment Handbook 19th ed
Croydon: LexisNexis, 2005
648pp ISBN: 0754528812
This handbook seeks to explain the legislation in its context, along with the common law and EC law on employment matters. It is intended to serve as a comprehensive handbook on employment law.

Welfare Benefits and Tax Credits Handbook 2nd ed
Carolyn George, Simon Osborne ed
London: Audit Commission, 2005
1784pp ISBN: 1901698750
This book is excellent value for money, offering comprehensive information on all means-tested and non-means-tested benefits. It has been fully updated and revised to incorporate information on the wide-ranging changes to the UK benefits system launched in April 2003 and the latest information on tax credits, pension credit and work-focused interviews.

WEBSITES
British Employment Law
www.emplaw.co.uk
This site offers information and services to those seeking advice on employment law as well as professionals. The site offers both free and subscription areas: as part of the free area, users may access information on current regulations, while subscribers can access the links. There is also a map showing the location and contact details of employment law specialists throughout the United Kingdom. Users may register for a free monthly e-mail which brings them up to date with new initiatives.

Butterworths
www.lexisnexis.co.uk
Butterworths, part of the Reed Elsevier group, is one of the leading and longest

established legal publishers in the UK. Their online subscription services include two employment law sites, based respectively on their *Tolley's Handbook* and on a combination of *Harvey*, their definitive five volume loose-leaf service, and their IRLR and All England law reports. The search engine on the Butterworths site is particularly good.

CompactLaw
www.compactlaw.co.uk
The CompactLaw document centre provides an extensive range of free factsheets, articles on recent aspects of employment law, and an employment law question-and-answer section.

emplaw.co.uk
www.emplaw.co.uk
This site offers information and services to those seeking advice on employment law as well as professionals. A free area gives information on current regulations and a series of links is available to subscribers. There is also a map showing the location and contact details of employment law specialists throughout the United Kingdom. Users may register for a free monthly e-mail which brings them up to date with new initiatives.

Incomes Data Services
www.incomesdata.co.uk/brief/law.htm
The site offers news, reports, and guidance on a wide range of employment law issues. There is some free information; otherwise you are directed to the extensive range of IDS published products.

OneClick HR
www.oneclickhr.com
A truly comprehensive site on all matters concerned with HR management and personnel issues which includes a useful employment legislation section. The site offers a wide range of services, including specimen letters and forms (some of which are free) for use in situations from recruitment to dismissal. There is also a free weekly email update service.

Sweet & Maxwell
www.sweetandmaxwell.co.uk/online/index.html
Sweet & Maxwell offer various online subscriber services, including daily case reports from the New Law online service, printed case report booklets (monthly) and journal (fortnightly) at discount prices, email alerts

UK Department of Trade and Industry
www.dti.gov.uk/er
This government site contains a wealth of useful information on a wide range of issues affecting people at work. There are links to sections on employment relations, including a series of employment rights factsheets (www.dti.gov.uk/er/regs.htm), and tailored interactive guidance on employment rights. The main site covers recent consultations and press notices. The other part of the DTI website relevant to employment law is at www.dti.gov.uk/employment.

ORGANISATIONS
Advisory Conciliation and Arbitration Service (ACAS)
Euston Tower, 286 Euston Road, London, NW1 3JJ
T: + 44 (0) 20 7396 0022
www.acas.org.uk
ACAS is a nationwide organisation (with its head office in London) of employment relations experts. It has been working with employers, employees, trade unions and other representatives for more than 25 years. The organisation has a network of telephone helplines giving free help and information, and the Advisory Service works with hundreds of companies every year to develop a joint approach to problem-solving. Most cases going to an employment tribunal are first of all referred to ACAS to see if there is a less damaging and expensive way of sorting the problem out. The organisation also runs workshops and seminars around the country, targeting small businesses without specialist personnel sections.

Chartered Institute of Personnel and Development (CIPD)

151 The Broadway, Wimbledon, London, SW19 1JQ
T: +44 (0) 20 8612 6200
F: +44 (0) 20 8612 6201
www.cipd.co.uk
Formed in 1995 from the amalgamation of the Institute of Personnel Management and the Institute of Training and Development,

the CIPD is a professional body for personnel and training professionals which aims to promote good practice in the management and development of people—a company's core strength.

SEE ALSO
Employee Benefits/Compensation (p. 507)

Entrepreneurs

BOOKS AND DIRECTORIES
Against the Odds: An Autobiography 2nd ed
James Dyson
London: Texere Publishing, 2003
400pp ISBN: 1587991705
The story of man and machine, this book charts the path to the shops of James Dyson's innovative vacuum cleaner.

Anyone Can Do It
Sahar Hashemi, Bobby Hashemi
Oxford: Capstone, 2004
224pp ISBN: 1841125792
Written by the brother and sister team behind the successful Coffee Republic chain, this book offers the reader '57 real-life laws on entrepreneurship'. An accessible and inspirational read, the book is a truthful, no-holds-barred description of getting a great idea off the ground.

Boo Hoo: A Dot-com Story
Ernst Malmsten, Erik Portanger, Charles Drazin
London: Random House Business Books, 2002
416pp ISBN: 0099418371
A cautionary tale of life at the height of the dot-com boom, this book details the rise and fall of boo.com, an online fashion site. While only portraying one side of the story, this is an entertaining tale that, if nothing else,

reminds the reader of the importance of backing up fantastic-sounding plans with action and funds.

Fostering Entrepreneurship
Organisation for Economic Co-operation and Development
Paris, France: The Brookings Institution, 1999
286pp ISBN: 9264161392
This book explains the importance of entrepreneurship and its benefits in terms of job creation and economic growth. It looks at ways of removing impediments and developing the conditions that enable entrepreneurs to flourish. A second section provides country-by-country information on the entrepreneurial climate, and summarises the lessons that can be learned from their experience.

Generation Entrepreneur
Stuart Crainer, Des Dearlove
London: Financial Times Business, 2000
266pp ISBN: 0273649205
This title looks at the future of business in the hands of 'Generation X'. This inspirational book suggests that entrepreneurship is now a 'lifestyle choice' for young people wise in the ways of e-commerce, but there are lessons here for more traditional businesses.

Good to Great: Why Some Companies Make the Leap and Others Don't

Jim Collins
London: Random House Business Books, 2001
324pp ISBN: 0712676090
Written by one of the world's bestselling business writers and based on an extensive research of over 1,000 businesses, this book focuses on eleven of the world's leading corporations and analyses their successes. Concluding that an excellent corporate culture is on the way forward, this book offers advice and useful tactics for all aspiring business builders.

How I Made It: 40 Successful Entrepreneurs Reveal All

Rachel Bridge
London: Kogan Page, 2004
192pp ISBN: 0749443111
This book features the inspiring stories behind 40 successful businesses. Adapted from interviews conducted by the author in her columns in the *Sunday Times*, each piece focuses on the early life, career, and motivation behind each business person's achievements. Those profiled include Rosemary Conley, Prue Leith, and Mark Ellingham (founder of the Rough Guides series).

The HP Way

David Packard
London: HarperCollins, 1996
224pp ISBN: 0887308171
In this book, Packard charts the emergence of his technology business: Hewlett Packard. He attributes the company's success to the unique outlook of the firm, 'The HP Way', which promotes a combination of openness, honesty, and flexibility. The book should interest both entrepreneurs and technologists alike, in demonstrating the growth of a major contemporary technology company.

Inside Intel: Andy Grove and the Rise of the World's Most Powerful Chip Company

Tim Jackson
New York: Plume Books, 1998
432pp ISBN: 0452276438
Most of today's computers operate using Intel chips, and this book provides an account of how the company under CEO Andrew Grove rose to such global dominance. In using both public and private documents and a number of selected interviews, *Financial Times* columnist Tim Jackson charts the story of Intel from its conception to the present day.

Marketing and Entrepreneurship in SMEs: An Innovative Approach

David Carson, Stanley Cromie, Pauric McGowan, Jimmy Hill
Harlow: Prentice Hall, 1996
296pp ISBN: 0131509705
Combining entrepreneurial theory and research with marketing knowledge to give a new perspective on the small business, this book is useful as both a reference book and as a support to general business education.

Matsushita Leadership: Lessons From the 20th Century's Most Remarkable Entrepreneur

John P. Kotter
London: Simon & Schuster, 1997
320pp ISBN: 068483460X
This book chronicles the life of Japanese entrepreneur Konosuke Matsushita, founder of the Matsushita Electric Corporation and Panasonic. It pays particular attention to his visionary management and leadership style, and highlights his views on the social responsibility of business.

The MouseDriver Chronicles

John Lusk, Kyle Harrison
Cambridge, Massachusetts: Perseus Books Group, 2003
272pp ISBN: 0738208019
Lusk and Harrison, MBA graduates, narrate their experiences of starting their own

company, and the problems they encountered along the way. Their product was the MouseDriver, a computer mouse fashioned as a golf club head, which experienced mixed fortunes in a volatile technology market. Lusk and Harrison describe the events leading up to the product's conception, and how they managed to support it in a continually changing market place.

Winning: The Ultimate Business How-to Book

Jack Welch, Suzy Welch
London: HarperCollins, 2005
384pp ISBN: 0007197691
Written by a giant of 20th century business in the United States, *Winning* is Jack Welch's boot camp (in print form) for aspiring entrepreneurs. Aimed at people who, in Welch's own words are 'in the trenches', the book is divided into three key sections: working within an organisation, dealing with competitors, and handling work/life balance.

WEBSITES
Entrepreneur.com
www.entrepreneur.com
This is a magazine site sponsored by Entrepreneur Media, Inc., offering a comprehensive range of practical information for owners of small businesses. The information includes a search engine, databases, blogs, and links to free business tools.

Entrepreneurial Edge
www.lowe.org
The Michigan-based Edward Lowe Foundation provides information and resources for entrepreneurs including news and relevant articles.

EntreWorld
www.entreworld.org
This is a collection of resources for entrepreneurs provided by the Kauffman Center for Entrepreneurial Leadership in Kansas City. Three sections focus on starting, growing, and finding support for a

business. The site includes articles, a glossary, practical advice, an e-mail newsletter, an events calendar, and a bookshop.

eWeb
http://eweb.slu.edu/eweb.htm
This website is provided by Saint Louis University, and provides information on entrepreneurial education programmes, organisations, research centres, and assistance for entrepreneurs, including advice on business planning.

Global Entrepreneurship Institute
www.gcase.org
The site sponsored by this non-profit, non-governmental organisation provides open source material for entrepreneurs and managers of small businesses, and includes articles, book lists, and useful links.

ORGANISATIONS
National Federation of Enterprise Agencies
12 Stephenson Court, Fraser Road, Priory Business Park, Bedford, Bedfordshire, MK44 3WH
T: +44 (0) 1234 831 623
F: +44 (0) 1234 831 625
E: enquiries@nfea.com
www.nfea.com
The NFEA is a network of independent, non-profit local enterprise agencies for the support of small and growing businesses, especially startups and micro-businesses. The organisation aims to identify the needs of such businesses, encourage the government and others to provide the conditions for them to flourish, and provide a forum for members to share best practice. The British Volunteer Mentor Programme is an initiative of the NFEA.

Small Firms Enterprise Development Initiative
SFEDI Ltd, Suite 101, Dunston Innovation Centre, Dunston Road, Chesterfield, Derbyshire, S41 8NG

T: +44 (0)8456 381 333
F: + 44 (0)8456 381 333
E: info@sfedi.co.uk
www.sfedi.co.uk
The SFEDI has been appointed by the UK
government to identify standards of best
practice for small businesses and to work
with providers of small-business training,
education, and advice to raise standards of
support.

UK Business Incubation
Faraday Wharf, Aston Science Park,
Birmingham, B7 4BB
T: +44 (0) 121 250 3538
F: +44 (0) 121 250 3542
E: info@ukbi.co.uk
www.ukbi.co.uk
UKBI is a public/private sector initiative set
up by the Department of Trade and Industry
and HM Treasury to provide information
and support for the incubator industry in
the United Kingdom. The organisation runs
the incubation network in the UK, lobbies
on behalf of the industry, produces

publications, and provides consultancy and
networking opportunities.

Young Enterprise UK
Peterley House, Peterley Road, Oxford,
Oxfordshire, OX4 2TZ
T: +44 (0) 1865 776 845
F: +44 (0) 1865 775 671
E: info@young-enterprise.org.uk
www.young-enterprise.org.uk
Young Enterprise is a national educational
charity founded in 1963 to develop links
between schools and industry, and to
encourage young people to learn and
succeed through involvement in enterprise.
Programmes organised by Young Enterprise
involve thousands of young people and
volunteer advisors from local and national
businesses. The programmes include the
Company Programme, Team Enterprise,
and the Entrepreneurship Masterclass.

SEE ALSO
Small and Growing Businesses (p. 486)
Venture Capital (p. 553)

Exporting

BOOKS AND DIRECTORIES
**Building an Import/Export Business
3rd ed**
Kenneth D. Weiss
Chichester: John Wiley & Sons Ltd, 2002
320pp ISBN: 0471202495
This is a user-friendly guide to starting and
building a successful import or export
business. It gives guidance on potential
areas of concern, such as operational
procedures, trade agreements, and
marketing techniques. It also provides
practical advice on how best to tap into the
lucrative global markets. It includes
bibliographical references and an index.

The Export Handbook
Harry Twells, ed
London: Kogan Page, 1998
368pp ISBN: 0749421576
Published jointly with the British Chambers

of Commerce, this handbook provides an
easy-to-use guide to export procedures and
documentation. It also includes a directory
of suppliers of export services.

**Global Jumpstart: The Complete
Resource for Expanding Small and
Midsized Businesses**
Ruth Stanat, Chris West
*Cambridge, Massachusetts: Perseus Books
Group, 2000*
198pp ISBN: 073820160X
This book is a useful resource guide for
companies of the size mentioned in the title
who have reached any stage of the
expansion process. It provides in-depth
analysis of business opportunities around
the world, while also giving a valuable
insight into the pitfalls in international
markets for small companies.

Principles of Management in Export
James Conlan
Oxford: Blackwell Business, 1994
325pp (Principles of Export Guidebooks)
ISBN: 0631191941
Using the syllabus of the Institute of Export as a basis, the author shows how all areas of export practice can be integrated. The emphasis is on profitable export management, covering the core topics of running and structuring an export business, and including all the necessary techniques and measuring and benchmarking systems for assessing profitability, setting strategic goals, and creating quantifiable reporting and control systems.

WEBSITES
British Chambers of Commerce
www.chamberonline.co.uk
The site offers an extensive range of services to member companies covering all aspects of exporting. It also provides links to all local chambers, which together represent more than 100,000 businesses in the United Kingdom.

Business Link
www.businesslink.gov.uk
This comprehensive online government service provides an extensive range of general information for small businesses, as well as details of the services available through the network of 150 local Business Links. The latter provide face-to-face advice on exporting and importing for small businesses.

HM Revenue & Customs
www.hmrc.gov.uk
Established in 2005, HM Revenue & Customs combines the roles formerly adopted by the Inland Revenue and HM Customs and Excise. HMRC is responsible for collecting taxes of all types, including VAT, tax credits, National Insurance, and excise duties. Its website offers advice for individuals, businesses and corporations, and employers.

Market Access Database
http://mkaccdb.eu.int/mkaccdb2/indexPubli.htm
The Market Access Database is provided by the DG Trade, European Commission. Certain parts of the site are open only to people having an ISP connection located in Europe but the section on trade barriers is open to all Internet users. The site contains details about trade barriers by market sector and country, import formalities by country and import duties by product code and by country.

Thomas Global Register
www.tgrnet.com
Formerly the American Export Register, this comprehensive web-based directory run by Thomas Publishing gives details of some 700,000 manufacturers and distributors across 28 countries, divided into 11,000 product and service classifications.

UK Trade & Investment
www.uktradeinvest.gov.uk
The UKIT site provides information and advice for UK businesses wishing to realise their potential internationally. Users may register to receive free regular updates and to browse the online help guide. The site also caters for overseas businesses planning to locate in the United Kingdom.

ORGANISATIONS
British Chambers of Commerce
65 Petty France, London, SW1H 9EU
T: +44 (0) 20 7654 5800
F: +44 (0) 20 7654 5819
E: info@britishchambers.org.uk
www.chamberonline.co.uk
This is an umbrella body for a national network of locally-based chambers of commerce serving local businesses and providing advice on importing and import services to member companies.

Institute of Export
Export House, Minerva Business Park,
Lynch Wood, Peterborough,
Cambridgeshire, PE2 6FT

T: +44 (0) 1733 404 400
F: +44 (0) 1733 404 444
E: institute@export.org.uk
www.export.org.uk
This professional membership body aims to raise standards in international trade management and export practice. It offers training programmes and other education to members.

World Trade and International Trade Rules
Bay 4141, 1 Victoria Street, London, SW1E 0ET

T: +44 (0) 20 7215 5000
E: dti.enquiries@dti.gsi.gov.uk
www.dti.gov.uk/ewt/import.htm
The Department of Trade and Industry is responsible for UK trade policy at international, European, and national levels, and for harmonising customs tariff levels with European Union member states. It is also responsible, in conjunction with several other government departments, for policy on all UK export and import prohibitions and restrictions.

SEE ALSO
Importing (p. 518)

Franchising

BOOKS AND DIRECTORIES
Buying a Franchise
Phil Stone
Oxford: How To Books, 2000
63pp ISBN: 1857036182
This concise book offers advice on the various pros and cons of buying a franchise and suggests key points to consider. It covers: the basic concept of franchising; selecting the right franchise for you; evaluating a franchise; cost considerations; and what to do once the purchase is complete.

Franchise Bible: How to Buy a Franchise or Franchise Your Own Business 5th ed
Erwin J. Keup
Central Point, Oregon: PSI Research, 2004
288pp ISBN: 1932156623
This practical guide to franchising includes sample documents and checklists aimed at helping newcomers to this form of business by providing discussion of the kinds of agreements involved, the advantages and disadvantages of franchising, how to rate potential opportunities, and how to decide if this is the right road to success for them.

Franchising for Dummies
Michael Seid, Dave Thomas
New York: Hungry Minds, 2000
378pp ISBN: 0764551604
A simple-to-follow but detailed guide to entering the world of franchises, this volume presents the basics, ranging from initial research, selecting locations, training employees, and running and developing the business. One of the authors is the late Dave Thomas, founder of the ultra-successful *Wendy's International*; the other is a consultant with more than 20 years of hands-on experience. Their book provides practical advice on the major issues facing those who decide to follow this route to self-employment.

The Guide to Franchising 7th ed
Martin Mendelsohn
London: Cassell, 2004
416pp ISBN: 1844801624
The author introduces franchising by describing its history and development and deals with fundamental questions such as: why franchise your business?; why take up a franchise?; and what can be franchised?

He also provides essential information on the legal aspects of the franchise contract. Profiles of the British Franchise Association and the Franchise Consultants Association are included.

Tips and Traps When Buying a Franchise 2nd ed
Mary E. Tomzack
Oakland, California: Source Book Publications, 1999
236pp ISBN: 1887137122
The second, revised edition of this guide provides those new to franchising with information on the right questions to ask at the outset, how to find the right location, where to get loans, how to find and train employees, and the ins and outs of buying equipment. It contains war stories and success secrets from a wide variety of franchisees.

WEBSITES
British Franchise Association
www.british-franchise.org
The British Franchise Association's site offers a comprehensive range of advice and information on all aspects of franchising from the perspectives of both franchisors and franchisees. It also provides useful links to other relevant sites.

Entrepreneur
www.entrepreneur.com
This site is a good source of information for those interested in going into business for themselves, with an informative page on franchising as well as pages covering management and marketing.

Franchising.org
www.franchising.org
This is a useful US site with links to many other franchise organisations. Articles, advice, and information are also provided.

Franinfo
www.franinfo.com
This site provides an overview of franchising, as well as advice and guidance.

It contains two self-tests to determine whether you are suited to being a franchisee and what type of franchise would suit you best.

International Franchising
www.franchiseintl.com
This is a guide to international franchising and offers news, articles, and a bookshope among its resources. There is also a list of the top 100 franchises in the United States, split across three key sectors: food, retail, and service.

Nolo-Law for All
www.nolo.com
This is a good source of legal information, some of which is specifically related to franchising.

ORGANISATIONS
British Franchise Association
Thames View, Newtown Road, Henley-on-Thames, Oxfordshire, RG9 1HG
T: +44 (0) 1491 578 050
F: +44 (0) 1491 573 517
E: mailroom@british-franchise.org.uk
www.british-franchise.org
The BFA was formed in 1977 to promote high standards of practice in franchising; member companies adhere to a code of ethics drawn up by the Association. It also provides a comprehensive range of information to both member and nonmember organisations through its extensive website and publications. It is affiliated to the World Franchise Council and the European Franchise Federation.

European Franchise Federation
Avenue Louise 179/15, Brussels, 10750, Belgium
T: +32 2 520 16 07
F: +32 2 520 17 35
E: info@eff-franchise.com
www.eff-franchise.com

The Federation is an international non-profit organisation, founded in 1972, that aims to promote franchising in Europe and the interests of the national franchise associations or federations that make up its membership.

SEE ALSO
Franchising Your Business (p. 327)
Small and Growing Businesses (p. 486)

Importing

BOOKS AND DIRECTORIES
Building an Import/Export Business 3rd ed
Kenneth D. Weiss
Chichester: John Wiley & Sons Ltd, 2002
320pp ISBN: 0471202495
This is a user-friendly guide to starting and building a successful import or export business. It gives guidance on potential areas of concern, such as operational procedures, trade agreements, and marketing techniques. It also provides practical advice on how best to tap into the lucrative global markets. It includes bibliographical references and an index.

Import/Export: How to Get Started in International Trade 3rd ed
Carl Nelson
Maidenhead: McGraw-Hill, 2000
340pp ISBN: 0071358714
This book is aimed at those wanting to make a start in international trade. Fully revised and including a section on e-commerce, it sets out to guide beginners through the myriad challenges of importing and exporting.

WEBSITES
Business Link
www.businesslink.gov.uk
This comprehensive online government service provides an extensive range of general information for small businesses, as well as details of the services available through the network of 150 local Business Links. The latter provide face-to-face advice on exporting and importing for small businesses.

Kelly's Directory
www.kellys.co.uk
This online searchable database lists over two million manufacturers and service organisations and ten million products. Users may enter key terms into the search box or use the alphabetical listings given.

Kompass
www.kompass.com
This online searchable database lists some 1.9 million companies in about 70 countries, under 53,000 product headings. The databases for individual countries may also be purchased in printed format. CDs are also available.

Market Access Database
http://mkaccdb.eu.int/mkaccdb2/indexPubli.htm
The Market Access Database is provided by the DG Trade, European Commission. Certain parts of the site are open only to people having an ISP connection located in Europe but the section on trade barriers is open to all Internet users. The site contains details about trade barriers by market sector and country, import formalities by country and import duties by product code and by country.

Thomas Global Register
www.tgrnet.com
Formerly the American Export Register, this comprehensive web-based directory run by Thomas Publishing gives details of some 700,000 manufacturers and distributors across 28 countries, divided into 11,000 product and service classifications.

ORGANISATIONS
British Chambers of Commerce
65 Petty France, London, SW1H 9EU
T: +44 (0) 20 7654 5800
F: +44 (0) 20 7654 5819
E: info@britishchambers.org.uk
www.chamberonline.co.uk
This is an umbrella body for a national
network of locally-based chambers of
commerce serving local businesses and
providing advice on importing and import
services to member companies.

Department of Trade and Industry (DTI)
Trade Policy, Albany House,
1 Victoria Street, London, SW1H 0ET
T: +44 (0) 20 7215 4557
F: +44 (0) 20 7215 4556
E: dti.enquiries@dti.gsi.gov.uk
www.dti.gov.uk
The Department of Trade and Industry is
responsible for UK trade policy at
international, European, and national
levels, and for harmonising customs tariff
levels with European Union member states.
It is also responsible, in conjunction with
several other government departments, for
policy on all UK export and import
prohibitions and restrictions.

HM Revenue & Customs
New King's Beam House, 22 Upper Ground,
London, SE1 9PJ
T: +44 (0) 845 010 9000
www.hmce.gov.uk
Her Majesty's Revenue & Customs is the
department responsible for administering
and collecting all import duties as detailed
in the Customs Tariffs. It also has specific
responsibility for enforcing all prohibitions
and restrictions on the export (and import)
of certain classes of goods.

Simpler Trade Procedures Board (SITPRO)
Oxford House, 8th Floor, 76 Oxford Street,
London, W1D 1BS
T: +44 (0) 20 7467 7280
F: +44 (0) 20 7467 7295
E: info@sitpro.org.uk
www.sitpro.org.uk
SITPRO is dedicated to giving practical help
to UK exporters and importers. In addition
the site offers ElecTra toolkits for paperless
international trade and have prepared a
WebElecTra system.

SEE ALSO
Exporting (p. 514)

Intellectual Property

BOOKS AND DIRECTORIES

Copyright in a Week
Graham Cornish
London: Hodder & Stoughton, 2002
96pp (in a Week Series)
ISBN: 0340849444
This introductory text will help you understand what copyright is, why it is important to respect it, and how you can make use of copyright law in business, management, and everyday life.

Essentials of Intellectual Property
Alexander I. Poltorak, Paul J. Lerner
Chichester: John Wiley & Sons Ltd, 2002
260pp ISBN: 0471209422
Poltorak and Lerner have compiled a concise and useful primer for professionals who need answers fast and novices who would like to learn more about this subject. The book goes from the basics of the intellectual property field to copyright laws to strategies and technologies that are in place today.

How to Prepare a UK Patent Application
Patent Office
Newport, 1999
28pp
This pamphlet provides a layman's guide to the preparation of an application for a UK patent. Guidance on the subsequent procedures is also given.

Patent It Yourself 11th ed
David Pressman
Berkeley, California: Nolo Press, 2005
512pp ISBN: 1413301800
As an experienced patent attorney and former patent examiner of the US Patent and Trademark Office (PTO), David Pressman has developed a very useful guide containing all the instructions and forms necessary to patent an invention in the United States. The book offers comprehensive and up-to-date advice for obtaining a high quality patent and presents the information in a user- friendly, jargon-free, and well-illustrated way.

Protecting Your #1 Asset: Creating Fortunes from Your Ideas: An Intellectual Property Handbook
Michael A. Lechter
London: Abacus, 2003
320pp ISBN: 0446678317
Placing its emphasis on protecting intellectual property (IP), this book makes the case for understanding developments in this arena. It covers topics including identifying and benefiting from IP assets, using IP assets to build barriers to competition, licensing IP assets, and using IP assets to raise capital.

Registering a Trade Mark
Patent Office
Newport, 1999
24pp
This publication is intended as a guide to the procedures for registering a trade mark in the United Kingdom.

WEBSITES

Copyright and Fair Use: Stanford University Libraries
http://fairuse.stanford.edu
The site provides a quick search facility and overview of copyright law, with links to Internet resources, current legislation, cases, judicial opinions, regulations, treaties, and conventions.

Copyright Clearance Center
www.copyright.com
Copyright Clearance Center, Inc, the largest licenser of text reproduction rights in the world, was formed in 1978 to facilitate compliance with US copyright law. It provides licensing systems for the reproduction and distribution of copyrighted materials in print and electronic formats throughout the world.

The Copyright Licensing Agency
www.cla.co.uk
The Agency is the United Kingdom's reproduction rights organisation—the UK equivalent of the US Copyright Clearance Center.

Franklin Pierce Law Center
www.fplc.edu
Sponsored by a law school, the site offers an extensive list of articles relating to intellectual property.

Intellectual Property
www.intellectual-property.gov.uk
This site gives information and advice on patents, trademarks, design, and copyright with links to the relevant government departments. It also addresses key questions on protection, permissions, and enforcing rights.

International Intellectual Property Alliance
www.iipa.com
Sponsored by a private-sector coalition formed to protect US copyrighted material around the world, the site offers articles on a variety of IP topics and country-specific copyright information.

UK Patent Office
www.patent.gov.uk
The website of the UK government department responsible for intellectual property—copyright, patents, designs, and trade marks—has a section of links to government, academic, and general IP sites.

United States Copyright Office
www.loc.gov/copyright
The US Copyright Office is located in the Library of Congress. The site has a section for FAQs and another for requests relating to the Freedom of Information Act, besides material on copyright legislation and an international section with links to the WIPO.

United States Patent and Trademark Office
www.uspto.gov
The PTO promotes industrial and technological progress in the United States and strengthens the national economy by administering the laws relating to patents and trademarks, and advising the US government on patent, trademark, and copyright protection, and on trade-related aspects of intellectual property.

World Intellectual Property Organization
www.wipo.org
WIPO is a Geneva-based specialised agency of the United Nations whose mandate is to promote the protection of intellectual property worldwide. Counting 182 countries among its member states, WIPO administers 23 treaties in the field of intellectual property. The first general group of treaties defines internationally agreed basic standards of intellectual property in each of the member states.

Management Buyouts

BOOKS AND DIRECTORIES
The Art of M&A: A Merger Acquisition Buyout Guide 3rd ed
Stanley Foster Reed, Alexandra Reed Lajoux
Maidenhead: McGraw-Hill, 1999
1008pp ISBN: 0070526605
Presented in a question-and-answer format, this book looks at over 1,000 aspects of mergers, acquisitions, and buy-outs. Questions covered range from locating a suitable target to closing and post-merger integration. The book gives real-world insights through synopses of dozens of landmark cases and includes sample forms and checklists.

Buyout: The Insider's Guide to Buying Your Own Company
Rick Rickersten, et al
New York: AMACOM, 2001
304pp ISBN: 0814406262
This book gives you the tools and strategies you need to lead a successful management buy-out. It includes everything from how to select the company you want to buy, through due diligence issues and finding equity partners, to running the company when you succeed in your buy-out.

WEBSITES
Are You Management Buyout Material?
www.cfo.com/Article?article=2117
Management buy-outs are not for everyone. It takes the right team with appropriate backing. This checklist can help you determine whether you have what it takes to be successful.

Survey of the Economic and Social Impact of Management Buyouts and Buyins in Europe
www.pwcglobal.com/fr/pwc_pdf/ pwc_economic_impact_of_buyouts.pdf
This site contains the full text of a report based on a pan-European survey conducted by the Centre for Management Buy-Out Research (CMBOR) on behalf of the European Private Equity and Venture Capital Association.

ORGANISATIONS
Centre for Management Buyout Research
Nottingham University Business School, Jubilee Campus, Wollaton Road, Nottingham, Nottinghamshire, NG8 1BB
T: +44 (0) 115 951 5493
F: +44 (0) 115 951 5204
E: margaret.burdett@nottingham.ac.uk
www.nottingham.ac.uk/business/ Cmbor
The CMBOR was founded by Barclays Private Equity Limited and Deloitte & Touche at the Nottingham University Business School in March 1986 to monitor and analyse management buy-outs in a comprehensive and objective way. A database of MBOs in the United Kingdom and Europe has been developed, and quarterly reviews and research papers are published.

SEE ALSO
Venture Capital (p. 553)

Marketing Management

BOOKS AND DIRECTORIES
The 22 Immutable Laws of Marketing: Violate Them at Your Own Risk!
Al Ries, Jack Trout
London: HarperCollins, 1994
160pp ISBN: 1861976100
Designed by marketing strategists for marketing strategists, this perenially popular illustrated book contains 22 practical rules aimed at promoting readers' success in global marketing of products and services.

101 Ways to Market Your Business
Andrew Griffiths
Crow's Nest, New South Wales:
Allen & Unwin, 2001
272pp ISBN: 1865083860
Packed full of practical yet simple
marketing ideas for business owners, this
book will be a huge help to anyone thinking
of setting up or running a small business.
With suggestions of ways to attract new
customers—and keep them—and how to
develop a strong corporate image, the book
also features quick marketing strategies that
take less than 30 minutes. The book steers
clear of theory and concentrates instead on
easy-to-follow advice that should reap
rewards.

The Anatomy of Buzz: How to Create Word-of-Mouth Marketing
Emanuel Rosen
London: HarperCollins, 2002
320pp ISBN: 0385496680
Rosen discusses the benefits of 'word-of-
mouth' marketing, and explores the
capacity of large companies to exploit this
strategy.

Direct and Database Marketing
Graeme McCorkell
*London: Institute of Direct Marketing/Kogan
Page, 1997*
315pp ISBN: 0749419601
The best UK introduction to direct
marketing, this book was written to be read
from cover to cover and contains some good
small business examples. This text is also
useful to dip into for examples of how direct
marketing campaigns are measured and
evaluated.

The End of Marketing As We Know It
Sergio Zyman
London: HarperCollins, 2000
272pp ISBN: 0887309836
In this title, the author argues that for
marketing to be truly efficient, it must sell
the product and not merely focus on
advertising image. The book contains
several stories concerning campaigns at
Coca-Cola, where Zyman was chief
marketing officer.

Getting Business to Come to You 2nd ed
Paul Edwards, Sarah Edwards, Laura
Clampitt Douglas
New York: JP Tarcher, 1998
688pp ISBN: 087477845X
A popular book aimed at helping businesses
expand their customer base. Although
written from a US perspective, the tips and
examples offered work well wherever your
business is located.

Gonzo Marketing: Winning through Worst Practices
Christopher Locke
London: Perseus Books Group, 2002
256pp ISBN: 0738207691
This book is a knuckle-whitening ride to the
place where social criticism, biting satire,
and serious commerce meet. . .and where
the outdated ideals of mass marketing and
broadcast media are being left in the dust.
As master of ceremonies at the wake for
traditional one-size-fits-all marketing, Locke
has assembled a unique guest list, from
Geoffrey Chaucer to Hunter S. Thompson,
to guide us through the revolution that is
rocking business today, as people connect
on the Web to form powerful micromarkets.
These networked communities, based on
candor, trust, passion, and a general disdain
for anything that smacks of corporate
smugness, reflect much deeper trends in
our culture, which Locke illuminates with
his characteristic wit.

Inside the Tornado 2nd ed
Geoffrey A. Moore
London: HarperCollins, 2004
272pp (HarperBusiness Essentials)
ISBN: 0060745819
This book addresses the ever-changing face
of market-focused business, aiming to
highlight the importance of adapting to keep
up with competitors. Moore uses examples
from inside the industry to discuss a range
of managerial strategies, and how they can
be usefully applied in today's marketing
world.

It's Not About Size: Bigger Brands for Smaller Business
Paul Dickinson
London: Virgin Books, 2001
208pp (Virgin Business Guides)
ISBN: 0753505932
This book aims to address comprehensively the issue of branding and its importance for small businesses. It covers a range of key challenges, including finding out what is best for your customers, which media will get your message across best, how to use advertising to differentiate yourself from your competitors, and how to increase profits through canny branding.

Kotler on Marketing: How to Create, Win, and Dominate Markets
Philip Kotler
London: Free Press, 2001
272pp ISBN: 0684860473
In this title, Kotler discusses his ideas on how marketing programs should be approached by executives. The book is divided into several sections addressing strategy, tactics, administrative issues, and transformational marketing. The latter is a term that the author uses to describe the effect of new technology, such as the Internet and cable TV, on marketing practice.

Marketing Plans That Work 2nd ed
Malcolm H.B. McDonald, Warren J. Keegan
Oxford: Butterworth-Heinemann, 2001
264pp ISBN: 0750673079
With discussions of new product development, market extension and diversification strategies and a step-by-step planning system, this book offers a comprehensive guide to preparing a strategic marketing program.

Marketing Warfare
Al Ries, Jack Trout
Maidenhead: McGraw-Hill, 1997
224pp ISBN: 0070527261
A 'military' approach to the world of marketing—Ries and Trout aim to teach marketers tough strategies, both defensive and offensive, to deal with the competition.

The Market Planning Guide: Creating a Plan to Successfully Market Your Business, Product, or Service 6th ed
David H. Bangs
Chicago, Illinois: Dearborn Trade Publishing, 2002
256pp ISBN: 0793159717
This book provides the tools for developing an effective marketing strategy for every size of business. This is a user-friendly workbook which helps readers master the basics before applying marketing principles to the marketing plans of actual companies.

Permission Marketing: Turning Strangers into Friends, and Friends into Customers
Seth Godin, Don Peppers
New York: Free Press, 2002
255pp ISBN: 0743221427
In this title, the authors claim that traditional forms of advertising such as magazines and radio are no longer sufficient in themselves. They assert that what is most important is to find a way of luring the customer into giving some of their time, and then creating a lasting relationship with them. The book backs up this theory concerning permission marketing by discussing the techniques of some of the companies who use it.

Rand McNally 2005 Commercial Atlas and Marketing Guide 136th ed
Chicago, Illinois: Rand McNally & Co., 2005
ISBN: 0528934651
Containing population, economic, and geographic data for more than 124,000 US places, and large-scale maps that are detailed and thoroughly indexed for easy cross-referencing, this 'big book' should be the first point of reference for up-to-date business planning data. The many raw data listings include: 2000 census information and Year 2007 projections; latest estimations on population for the US states, counties, cities, MSAs, and trading areas; information on income, buying power, and sales; and corporate economic profiles.

Real Time: Preparing for the Age of the Never Satisfied Customer
Regis McKenna
Boston, Massachusetts: Harvard Business School Press, 1999
224pp ISBN: 0875847943
In this book, McKenna addresses the issue of what customers expect from the modern world. In order to fulfil customer expectations, he argues, companies must be prepared to adapt to the increasingly rapid modes of global communication (e-mail, fax, etc.). McKenna aims to clarify the abstract notion of collecting and using 'real time', with the view that this can lead to greater organisational success and consumer satisfaction.

Relationship Marketing: Successful Strategies for the Age of the Customer
Regis McKenna
Harlow: Addison-Wesley, 1993
242pp ISBN: 0201622408
McKenna focuses on the importance of building strong bonds in the marketing world, in order to gain success and become dominant in the marketplace. He provides industry examples to help outline ways of achieving market ownership.

Selling the Invisible
Harry Beckwith
London: Texere Publishing, 2001
272pp ISBN: 1587990660
Selling the Invisible is aimed at marketers who work to promote a service ('the invisible') rather than a tangible product. The book contains a large range of practical suggestions and ideas, addressing some new developments in marketing, and discussing how an organisation can use them to best effect.

Successful Direct Marketing Methods 7th ed
Bob Stone, Ron Jacobs
Maidenhead: McGraw-Hill, 2001
608pp ISBN: 0658001450
This newly updated edition provides a classic guide to direct marketing, combining new media with traditional marketing strategies to provide effective direct marketing to consumers. The content includes identifying and meeting consumers' needs, business to business marketing, and e-commerce techniques, such as branding strategies for Internet sites.

Successful Marketing for the Small Business 5th ed
Dave Patten
London: Kogan Page, 2001
272pp (Business Enterprise Guides)
ISBN: 0749435240
An updated edition of this popular book, which aims to show how organisations can benefit from tackling marketing effectively. Aimed at those thinking of starting a business or those running one already, this book is full of practical advice on a range of key issues including advertising, market research, promotion, launches, and exporting.

The Tipping Point: How Little Things Can Make a Big Difference
Malcolm Gladwell
London: Abacus, 2002
288pp ISBN: 0349113467
Although no standard marketing textbook, this extremely popular book may help many a marketer understand more about how and why some products or services take off while others languish in the doldrums. Tying together multiple strands of social history, business, and psychology, it offers an engaging insight into mass behaviours.

WEBSITES
American Marketing Association
www.marketingpower.com
The American Marketing Association (AMA) is an international professional organisation for people involved in the practice, study, and teaching of marketing. As well as setting industry standards, the AMA seeks to help marketers by providing them with information, products, and services, many of which are available online, including a career centre, best practice articles, a marketer's toolkit, and newsletter. Registration is free.

Guerrilla Marketing
www.gmarketing.com
This is the online home of the very
successful 'Guerrilla Marketing' series of
books. Users may subscribe to a free weekly
newsletter offering marketing tips.

SEE ALSO
Direct Marketing (p. 505)
Market Research and Competitor
    Intelligence (p. 526)
Public Relations (p. 541)
Selling and Salesmanship (p. 546)

Market Research and Competitor Intelligence

BOOKS AND DIRECTORIES
Managing Frontiers in Competitive Intelligence
Craig S. Fleisher, David Blenkhorn
Westport, Connecticut: Quorum Books, 2000
328pp ISBN: 1567203841
This book is a nice balance of the theoretical
and the practical aspects of Competitive
Intelligence (CI). While describing the best
practices in the industry, the authors
present the steps necessary to counter CI.
They provide information on how to
improve your intelligence collection
process, methods, and tools. Significantly,
they tie CI back to the needs of the business
and point out its interface with finance,
research and development, and product
development.

Marketing Research 8th ed
David A. Aaker, V. Kumar, George S. Day
Chichester: John Wiley & Sons Ltd, 2003
800pp ISBN: 047123057X
This text adopts a 'macro-micro-macro'
approach towards marketing research and
its uses within organisations. The authors
initially explore the uses and place of
marketing research in managerial decision
making, as well as the industry itself (briefly
examining both suppliers and users) at
macro-level. The authors also examine the
processes of marketing research in more
depth, including industry examples to fulfil
the micro phase of the text. Provides
coverage of the most recent research
techniques.

Marketing Research for Managers 3rd ed
Sunny Crouch, Matt Housden
Oxford: Butterworth-Heinemann, 2003
352pp ISBN: 0750654538
This is one of the leading UK texts for
managers seeking to understand market
research. Rather than proffering over-
detailed explanations of how to undertake
research, this book explains enough for
managers to be able to commission
worthwhile research from professionals.

Market Research Matters: Tools and Techniques for Aligning Your Business
Robert Duboff, Jim Spaeth
Chichester: John Wiley & Sons Ltd, 2000
320pp ISBN: 0471360058
The authors explain the value of market
research and forecasting techniques to
successful business strategies. They
describe the tools and techniques that
enable analysts to anticipate marketplace
shifts and the methods of using them.
Among other topics, they discuss customer
loyalty, brand management, competition,
distribution channels, employee
performance and loyalty, and the Internet.
Diagnostic material to allow readers to
assess the progress of their business in each
area is also included.

The Market Research Toolbox: A Concise Guide for Beginners 2nd ed
Edward F. McQuarrie
London: Sage Publications, 2005
224pp ISBN: 1412913195
Aimed at giving a basic understanding of
market research tools, this book looks at

market research in the context of making a business decision. Beginning with an explanation of market research, the author goes on to describe how each of the six traditional market research techniques works, along with its costs, uses, and tips for success. Also examined are the nontraditional methods that have evolved in recent years.

Millennium Intelligence: Understanding and Conducting Competitive Intelligence in the Digital Age
Jerry P. Miller
Medford, New Jersey: Information Today, 2000
240pp ISBN: 0910965285
Miller assembled a thinktank of practising experts in Competitive Intelligence (CI). Together they lay out the reasons for conducting a planned and thought out CI programme for your company. Their book details the skills required, the tools and methods available for gathering and analysing the information, and the reasons and methods to do so in an ethical and legal manner.

Proven Strategies in Competitive Intelligence: Lessons from the Trenches
John E. Prescott, Stephen H. Miller, eds
Chichester: John Wiley & Sons Ltd, 2001
288pp ISBN: 0471401781
The editors have assembled a collection of articles that identify and explore proven practicable approaches to competitive intelligence that can be applied across a variety of business areas. Once the concept of competitive intelligence has been introduced and its legal and ethical boundaries have been explored, further contributions from leading executives and market leaders highlight the best techniques that can be used to outwit and outperform current, emerging, and potential competitors.

The WarRoom Guide to Competitive Intelligence
Steven M. Shaker, Mark P. Gembicki
Maidenhead: McGraw-Hill, 1998
240pp ISBN: 007058057X

This book is written for managers who want to use information more intelligently, with a view to improving corporate strategies. The authors advise business leaders on gathering and analysing information in order to become more competitive within the industry. Explores ways of creating a 'WarRoom' within an individual organisation in which to collate information for future use.

WEBSITES
ECNext
www.ecnext.com
This is a site offering online access to a database of business and market intelligence from global publishers.

Esomar Glossary
www.esomar.org
This glossary of market research terms seeks to explain frequently used marketing research terms in language that someone new to the industry can easily understand.

Euromonitor International
www.euromonitor.com
In-depth strategic analysis and up-to-date market statistics and market reports are all available to purchase online from this site.

Key Note Market Information Centre
www.keynote.co.uk
This site is run by suppliers of market research reports, which are available for purchase, and provides free executive summaries.

Market Research.com
www.marketresearch.com
Collecting reports from all over the world, marketresearch.com is one of the largest sources of published research on the Web. Reports can be bought and managed with a personal account, and the site has other features, such as an e-mail update service.

@ResearchInfo.com
www.researchinfo.com
This site is a remarkable collection of information on the market research

industry. It includes the Market Research Roundtable, a directory of research companies, software reviews, and market research calculators.

ORGANISATIONS
Association of European Market Research Institutes
26 Granard Avenue, London, SW15 6HJ
T: +44 (0)20 8780 3343
F: +44 (0) 20 7246 6893
E: info@aemri.org
www.aemri.org
The Association is a representative organisation for market research institutes in Europe and other parts of the world.

British Market Research Association
Devonshire House, 60 Goswell Road, London, EC1M 7AD
T: +44 (0) 20 7566 3636
F: +44 (0) 20 7689 6220

E: admin@bmra.org.uk
www.bmra.org.uk
The BMRA aims to represent and promote the professional and commercial interests of its members, to increase the professionalism of market research, and to promote confidence in the market research industry generally.

Market Research Society
15 Northburgh Street, London, EC1V 0JR
T: +44 (0) 20 7490 4911
F: +44 (0) 20 7490 0608
E: info@mrs.org.uk
www.mrs.org.uk
The MRS sets and enforces the ethical standards to be observed by research practitioners. Its framework of qualifications and membership grades reflects the education, knowledge, and competence required for the effective conduct of market research.

Negotiation

BOOKS AND DIRECTORIES
Business Negotiation: A Practical Workbook
Paul T. Steele, Tom Beasor
Aldershot: Gower Publishing, 1999
270pp ISBN: 0566080729
This practical textbook provides a step-by-step guide to acquiring key negotiating skills and the techniques for using them successfully as well as identifying the key topics in negotiation. Each chapter includes a checklist of the key points made and exercises for applying what has been learned.

Difficult Conversations
Douglas Stone, Bruce Patton, Sheila Heen
New York: Penguin Putnam, Inc, 2000
272pp ISBN: 014028852X
This book aims to help readers to become calm and assertive in difficult situations (such as asking for a pay rise, or experiencing problems with colleagues). In discussing the different emotions and

requirements that arise from such conversations, the book aims to pinpoint ways of managing them more effectively.

Essentials of Negotiation 3rd ed
Roy J. Lewicki, David M. Saunders, John W. Minton
Maidenhead: McGraw-Hill, 2003
272pp ISBN: 0071232540
This book looks at the psychology of bargaining and negotiation and the dynamics involved in conflict and its resolution. It provides an in-depth discussion of aspects of negotiation such as communication, strategy and tactics, dealing with breakdowns in negotiations, social context, ethics, third party roles, and power.

Getting Past No: Negotiating Your Way from Confrontation to Cooperation
William Ury
London: Random House Business Books, 1992
176pp ISBN: 0712655239

This book provides a step-by-step method for negotiation that aims to ensure that satisfactory agreement is reached with even the most intransigent people. It contains advice, hints, and tips, useful strategies and plenty of real examples.

Getting to Yes 2nd ed
Roger Fisher, William Ury, Bruce Patton
London: Arrow, 2003
224pp ISBN: 1844131467
By working around four main principles of effective negotiation and discussing some of the difficulties that can arise, the authors show the reader how to pursue his or her own interests while keeping adversaries happy at the same time. A few principles will guide the reader no matter what the other side does, or whatever what tricks they may resort to.

Negotiate Successfully: How to Get Your Way and Find Win-win Solutions
London: A & C Black, 2004
96pp (Steps to Success)
ISBN: 0747572097
A short, action-packed guide to the world of negotiating. This book offers advice on negotiation basics and planning tips as well as how to negotiate over the phone or via e-mail. There are also special sections on coping with difficult negotiations and negotiating with people from other cultures.

Negotiating Skills
Tim Hindle
London: Dorling Kindersley, 1998
72pp (Essential Managers)
ISBN: 0751305316
A helpful introduction to the art of negotiation, including information on how to prepare your argument, brief a team, maintain good relations, and close a deal. The book is full of practical advice on how to achieve the best result.

The Negotiation Toolkit: How to Get Exactly What You Want in Any Business or Personal Situation
Roger J. Volkema
New York: AMACOM, 1999
208pp ISBN: 081448008X

This book offers a guide to negations aimed at helping people build the skills and self-confidence to become good negotiators. It explores the golden rule of negotiation, explains when not to negotiate, discusses the issue of tough negotiators and how to deal with them, describes the tactics, skills, and behaviours of star negotiators, looks at cross-cultural negotiations, and provides ways to measure your own skills.

The Power of Nice: How to Negotiate So Everyone Wins—Especially You!
Ronald M. Shapiro, Mark A. Jankowski, James Dale
Chichester: John Wiley & Sons Ltd, 2001
304pp ISBN: 0471080721
This book is based on Shapiro's belief that negotiation works best if two negotiators can build a common bond between them. In exploring this theory, Shapiro offers advice on various types of negotiation, and on creating effective proposals.

Thinking on Your Feet in Negotiations: Rapid Response Tactics
Jane Hodgson
Harlow: Prentice Hall, 1999
252pp ISBN: 0273644998
This is a manager's guide to the latest techniques for developing negotiation skills, thinking creatively in situations which need a quick response, building a good rapport with colleagues and clients, dealing effectively with conflicts, and solving problems.

When I Say No, I Feel Guilty
Manuel J. Smith
New York: Bantam Books, 1985
352pp ISBN: 0553263900
This best-selling book offers a range of strategies to help people feel comfortable when they assert their needs at work and at home. It also offers advice on how to combat manipulation and emotional game-playing by others.

WEBSITES

Interneg—For and About Negotiation
http://interneg.org/interneg/links/
learning.html
This site is a directory of resources for the negotiation field with links to numerous other sites covering areas from training and teaching materials to games to programmes and seminars.

Mediate.com
www.mediate.com
This site provides articles and news on mediation, conflict resolution, and arbitration. It also includes information about training, events, organisations, and academic courses in this field.

SEE ALSO
Pricing (p. 536)

New Product Development

BOOKS AND DIRECTORIES

Marketing the Unknown: Developing Market Strategies for Technical Innovations
Paul Millier
Chichester: John Wiley & Sons Ltd, 1999
256pp ISBN: 0471986216
How do you make a product successful? This is one of the basic questions that this practical book sets out to answer. It also discusses what is the best process to follow, and how you choose or transform markets so as to ensure a successful launch. It paves the way for marketing, for R and D, and for project managers in industrial organisations to launch and market innovations successfully in a very competitive field, and outlines strategies for further development.

Product Juggernauts: How Companies Mobilize to Generate a Stream of Market Winners
Jean-Philippe Deschamps, P. Ranganath Nayak
Boston, Massachusetts: Harvard Business School Press, 1995
480pp ISBN: 0875843417
The authors cite stories from real companies around the world to illustrate guidelines for determining the products customers want and designing the products they want to buy. Examples used to demonstrate the importance of company-wide focus on product include (among others) Ford, Canon, and Toshiba. Using these case studies, the authors demonstrate how organisations can achieve high market performance and improve their current strategies.

Product Leadership: Pathways to Profitable Innovation 2nd ed
Robert G. Cooper
Cambridge, Massachusetts: Perseus Books Group, 2005
304pp ISBN: 046501433X
Over a third of new products fail at launch, and many never gain a profitable return. So how do companies like 3M, Merck, and Procter & Gamble continually lead the way with exceptional new products? Cooper reveals the winners' secrets, and offers valuable advice on implementing and overseeing new product processes and strategies, managing product portfolios, determining which products to develop, and fostering ingenuity to outperform the competition.

The Product Manager's Handbook 2nd ed
Linda Gorchels
Maidenhead: McGraw-Hill/NTC, 2000
304pp ISBN: 0658001353
This book focuses on skills acquisition, making it suitable for new product managers or people interested in moving into that line of work. The text is written as an overview and introduction to the skill set necessary for product managers, but segments of the book are also devoted to product development and launch.

Successful Product Development: Speeding from Opportunity to Profit

Milton D. Rosenau, Jr
Chichester: John Wiley & Sons Ltd, 1999
160pp ISBN: 047131532X
This book sets out the process of product development from beginning to end, starting with the formation of ideas and moving through design and engineering to the finished product. It is intended for all practitioners involved with any aspect of developing new products and services.

World-Class New Product Development: Benchmarking Best Practices of Agile Manufacturers

Dan Dimancescu, Kemp Dwenger
New York: AMACOM, 1995
276pp ISBN: 0814403115
Recounting the findings of research, benchmarking, and working with international companies, this book shows how 'corporate champions' manage robust product development operations and presents a system to enable other organisations to do the same. It covers the implementation of a holistic management style, effective cross-functional teaming, rigorous product reviews, systematic capture of the demands of customers, the involvement of suppliers, and the market driven R & D continuum. All its points are illustrated by examples.

WEBSITES

American Productivity and Quality Center
www.apqc.org
This site features articles on training, conferences, case studies, presentations, executive summaries and more. This organisation makes available several white papers on product development. The APQC is essentially a group working towards corporate organisational improvement. They sponsor conferences on product development as well as providing resources online.

Department of Trade and Industry: New production development guidelines
www.dti.gov.uk/ccp/topics1/guide/ gps2005guide.pdf
As of October 2005, new rules have come into effect that may affect you if you are a retailer or a manufacturer. These regulations are laid out in this site and they relate to the safety of new or second-hand goods sold on to customers. They aim to cut down on any potential risk to customers by ensuring that they are informed fully about any safety issues before they make a purchase.

Experts on New Product Development
www.expertson.com/New_Product_ Development/ new_product_development.html
The resources on which information is available from this site include new product development associations, new product development centres, directories, newsgroups, mailing lists, new product development publications, and new product development reference tools.

Global New Products Database
www.gnpd.com
This site can be used to access a comprehensive database that monitors worldwide product innovation in the consumer packaged-goods market, offering coverage of new product activity for both competitor monitoring and product idea generation. Users must register to gain access to the database, but registration is free.

Product Development and Management Association
www.pdma.org
This site is everyone's first stop when trolling the Internet for information on product development. It features articles, a job bank, conference listings, a bookshop, and more.

SEE ALSO
Product and Brand Management (p. 537)

Outsourcing

WEBSITES
Network Outsourcing Association
www.noa.co.uk
This site provides access to recent articles
by members and details of Association
events. It also has a members-only section.

Outsourcing Center
www.outsourcing-center.com
This website provides comprehensive
information and links regarding
outsourcing. Its content includes industry-
specific outsourcing information, research,
outsourcing processes, and an online
journal. It also provides material on
suppliers and legal issues.

The Outsourcing Institute
www.outsourcing.com
The Outsourcing Institute is a professional
association providing information and
networking resources related to
outsourcing. Its website offers information
on the outsourcing process, including
needs assessment and the selection of
service providers. It also has information
targeted at buyers and sellers of
outsourcing services. Registration is
required for some information; online
membership is free.

The Outsourcing Management Zone
www.theoutsourcerzone.com
This site is aimed at both outsourcing
professionals and those new to the concept.
It provides numerous articles, a directory,
information on outsourcing, and also
explains how and why outsourcing can
affect your business.

Outsourcing Research Center
www.cio.com/forums/outsourcing
The site provides online access to recent
articles and gives details of forthcoming
events.

TechWeb Business Technology Network
www.techweb.com
This site focuses on recent news and articles
on IT outsourcing, plus links to events in its
'Tech Calendar'.

Virtual Corporations and Outsourcing
www.brint.com
A selection of articles on outsourcing can be
sourced from this site.

ORGANISATIONS
Network Outsourcing Association
Martyn Hart, Chair
Keswick House, 207 Anerley Road, London,
SE20 8ER
T: +44 (0) 20 8778 9449
F: +44 (0) 20 8778 8402
E: admin@noa.co.uk
www.noa.co.uk
The Association is an independent body,
formed in the early 1990s, that acts as a
forum for the business technology
outsourcing community. Its membership is
made up of UK and overseas companies
with experience in outsourcing, and
suppliers and consultants who support the
industry.

Packaging

BOOKS AND DIRECTORIES
The Marketer's Guide to Successful Package Design
Herbert M. Meyers, Murray J. Lubliner
Maidenhead: McGraw-Hill/NTC, 1998
320pp ISBN: 0844234389
A guide for product marketers, this book explores the elements of marketing and design that can lead to successful packaging results. The authors' approach to the subject is analytical, including discussions on the research and planning involved in launching a new design.

Packaging Design—Design Brief to Finished Product
Conway Lloyd Morgan, Russell Sellers, eds
Hove: Rotovision, 1997
160pp ISBN: 2880462622
A model design brief is used throughout the text in a structured and systematic way, as the reader is guided through the whole production process from the design brief to the finished article. The contributors discuss real products and brands and also give advice on the briefing, planning, and execution of packaging design.

The Packaging Designer's Book of Patterns 2nd ed
Laszlo Roth, George L. Wybenga
Chichester: John Wiley & Sons Ltd, 2000
608pp ISBN: 0471385042
This book features over 500 patterns for paper packaging. Folding cartons, trays, tubes, sleeves, wraps, folders, corrugated containers, rigid paper boxes, and point-of-purchase displays are featured and ready for application on 100% recyclable paper products. An interesting history of papermaking is included in the introduction.

Packaging: The Facts
Jim McDermott, Anne Emblem
Stamford: The Packaging Society, 2000
128pp ISBN: 0946467048
Although primarily aimed at schools and colleges, this book is also an excellent general introduction for those new to packaging. It covers all aspects, explaining the packaging process in detail and discussing the materials involved from glass to shrink-and-stretch wrapping. It also deals with the economics, marketing, and environmental issues of packaging.

Trade Secrets of Great Design Packaging 2nd ed
Stafford Cliff
Gloucester, Massachusetts: Rockport, 2002
224pp ISBN: 1564968723
This international collection of 50 outstanding packaging designs covers a broad selection of products and approaches. Each of the designs is individually profiled, outlining the challenges and problems each designer faced with the particular product. The case studies document the packaging design process and include discussion of new materials and methods of construction.

WEBSITES
Environmental Packaging International
www.enviro-pac.com
Sponsored by a consultancy firm specialising in compliance with state and international environmental packaging and product laws, the site provides a list of services, industry news, and links to other sites.

Packaging Business
www.packagingbusiness.com
Sponsored by a private company in the packaging industry, the site offers industry news, discussions, classifieds, job fair information, and links to other sites.

Packaging Digest
www.packagingdigest.com
This site contains articles from current and past issues of *Packaging Digest*, together with other information resources including news and reports of developments in packaging

materials, machinery, technology, and market trends from around the world.

Packaging Network
www.packagingnetwork.com
This site is primarily a marketplace that also provides news, access to a library, a discussion forum, trade publications, and a job search. Site visitors may buy, sell, and advertise online. A free e-newsletter is also available.

Packaging Strategies
www.packstrat.com
This site provides a newsletter, articles, news, a product guide, and a calendar of events.

Packaging World
www.packworld.com
This online packaging magazine from the United States has databases of topical articles on machinery, products, companies, design, materials, and regulations, along with information about jobs, events, and associations connected with the packaging industry.

ORGANISATIONS
Institute of Packaging
Willoughby House, Broad Street, Stamford, Lincolnshire, PE9 1PB
T: +44 (0)1780 759200
F: +44 (0)1780 759220
E: iop@pi2.org.uk
www.pi2.org.uk
The aim of the Institute is to advance public education in, and improve the technology of, packaging in all its aspects, in particular by promoting the education and training of persons engaged or interested in packaging as an occupation.

The Packaging Federation
Vigilant House, 120 Wilton Road, London, SW1V 1JZ
T: +44 (0) 20 7808 7217
F: +44 (0) 20 7808 7218
E: enquiries@packagingfedn.co.uk
www.packagingfedn.co.uk
The Federation is a trade organisation representing all the material streams within the industry. Its aims are to improve significantly the way in which the industry is perceived and to protect the interests of packaging manufacturers through properly managed lobbying and public relations programmes.

Presentation/Speaking

BOOKS AND DIRECTORIES
Effective Presentation: How To Create and Deliver a Winning Presentation 2nd ed
Antony Jay, Ros Jay
London: Financial Times Management, 2004
144pp ISBN: 0273688030
Drawing on their own experience and on tips from experts and trainers in presentation and communication skills, the authors offer a step-by-step guide to planning, designing, and delivering successful presentations. They give advice on scheduling and staging the presentation, choosing appropriate visual aids, and engaging the audience.

Effective Presentation Skills: A Practical Guide for Better Speaking 3rd ed
Steve Mandel
Menlo Park, California: Crisp Publications, 2000
96pp ISBN: 1560525266
This basic overview of presentations offers advice on topics including skill assessment, presentation planning, visual aids, teleconferencing and videoconferencing, the presentation environment, and dealing with hostile questions. It contains an especially useful section for nervous presenters on dealing with anxiety and projecting confidence.

Give Great Presentations: How to Speak Confidently and Make Your Point
London: A & C Black, 2005
96pp (Steps to Success)
ISBN: 0747577358
Full of advice on how to prepare and deliver a knock-out speech, this practical book is ideal for anyone who suffers from pre-presentation nerves. Opening with essential sections on how to prepare and structure a good presentation, the book also tackles coping with nerves, boosting your message with your body language, creating online or virtual presenations, and coping with worst-case scenarios.

Knockout Presentations: How to Deliver Your Message with Power, Punch, and Pizzazz
Diane Diresta
Madison, Wisconsin: Chandler House, 1998
304pp ISBN: 1886284253
This experienced coach presents a clear and precise method of approaching public speaking. Her suggestions are easy to implement, and many readers have found this book an invaluable reference tool.

Point, Click and Wow! A Quick Guide to Brilliant Laptop Presentations 2nd ed
Claudyne Wilder, Jennifer Rotondo
San Francisco, California: Jossey-Bass Wiley, 2002
240pp ISBN: 0787956694
Aimed at business people of all levels, this book offers a practical guide to using technology in effective presentations. The authors explore how to balance on-screen activity and human interaction, how to deal with software and hardware issues, and how, when, and where to practise. The book includes checklists and illustrations.

Say It with Presentations: How to Design and Deliver Successful Business Presentations
Gene Zelazny
Maidenhead: McGraw-Hill, 1999
160pp ISBN: 0071354077
Intended as a simple overview of presentations, this book is targeted mainly

at beginners but could also offer some tips to experienced presenters. The topics it covers include defining the purpose of the presentation, keeping the audience in mind, designing charts, and using humour. Its main focus is on how to deliver presentations with confidence and conviction.

Talking Shop: Over 5,000 Business Quotes to Help You Through Your Working Day
London: A & C Black, 2003
432pp ISBN: 0747572151
This comprehensive and easy-to-use resource contains over 5,000 inspirational quotations from over 1,500 influential business figures and commentators around the world. Ordered by subject, with detailed author information and source references, this book will help you find what you want to say, and tell you who said it first.

WEBSITES
Advanced Public Speaking Institute
www.public-speaking.org
This site offers free advice and articles on all aspects of public speaking, including performance and storytelling techniques, how to develop a topic, the use of props and handouts, humour, tricks, gimmicks, and stage fright.

Art of Speaking in Public
www.angelfire.com
This site offers a collection of over 60 rapid read tips for effective public speaking and effective performance in classes, presentations, conferences, seminars, events, and discussions.

PowerPointers
www.powerpointers.com
This site has many articles on making and creating effective presentations. Areas of interest include communicating effectively, building and planning a presentation, and communicating about your speciality.

Presentations.com
www.presentations.com
The online counterpart to *Presentations* magazine, the site offers news, articles, information on upcoming conferences and events, technological information, and resources.

ORGANISATIONS
The Speakers Trust
19 Waterer Rise, Wallington, Surrey, SM6 9DN
T: +44 (0) 20 8669 2300
www.speakerstrust.org.uk
The Trust promotes the work of speakers' clubs across the United Kingdom, with a view to making them better known and understood and increasing their membership. It offers support to existing clubs by organising competitions, sponsoring new members, providing funds, and producing educational materials.

Pricing

BOOKS AND DIRECTORIES
The Strategy and Tactics of Pricing: A Guide to Profitable Decision Making 3rd ed
Thomas T. Nagle, Reed K. Holden
Harlow: Prentice Hall, 2002
400pp ISBN: 013026248X
This is a complete guide that integrates pricing with overall managerial goals. It utilises mini-case studies to illustrate success stories and examples of pricing failures. The elements of strategic pricing are explained. Other topics included are competition, segmentation of buyers, pricing and marketing mix, the psychology of pricing, and the ethical and legal aspects of pricing. Step-by-step procedures for problem analysis and strategy are provided.

WEBSITES
Professional Pricing Society
www.pricingsociety.com
Sponsored by a professional society dedicated to pricing management, the site offers forums, mailing list archives, products for purchase, Webinars, and a bookstore for related books. Membership services are also available, as is a free newsletter.

Strategic Pricing Group
www.strategicpricinggroup.com
Sponsored by a consultancy firm that specialises in strategic pricing, this site provides articles, recommended reading, a calendar of events, and information on educational services and consulting.

ORGANISATIONS
Chartered Institute of Marketing (CIM)
Moor Hall, Cookham, Maidenhead, Berkshire, SL6 9QH
T: +44 (0) 1628 427 500
F: +44 (0) 1628 427 499
E: marketing@cim.co.uk
www.cim.co.uk
The CIM is the main organisation for professional marketers in the United Kingdom. It runs courses, holds examinations, produces publications, and offers information services covering all aspects of marketing.

SEE ALSO
Marketing Management (p. 522)
Packaging (p. 533)

Product and Brand Management

BOOKS AND DIRECTORIES
The 22 Immutable Laws of Branding
Al Ries, Laura Ries
London, Profile Books, 2000
192pp ISBN: 1861976054
In this title, the authors argue that branding is the basis of a strong marketing programme. If it is not possible to create a strong brand, then nothing a company does, including advertising campaigns and public relations events, will help. The book looks at both successful brands and those that have failed, providing coherent explanations of the various factors involved.

Brand It Like Beckham: Building a Brand with Balls
Andy Milligan
London: Cyan Books, 2005
192pp ISBN: 1904879292
Part of the growing 'Brand It Like. . .' series, this book explains how success in one arena (in this case, sport) can translate into commercial pulling power in many other areas. Explaining the key concepts behind building an international brand, this book is an entertaining take on the nature of celebrity, image, and marketing.

Brand Warfare: 10 Rules for Building the Killer Brand
David F. D'Alessandro, Michele Owens
Maidenhead: McGraw-Hill, 2001
192pp ISBN: 0071362932
This book considers ways in which companies often mishandle their brands. The authors offer advice, based on their own experience and on company examples, to those wishing to build a successful brand in any market.

Building Strong Brands
David A. Aaker
San Francisco, California: Jossey-Bass Wiley, 2002
384pp ISBN: 0743232135

Aaker discusses the varying elements of a brand, and emphasises the need for managers to be aware of the importance of strong brands in today's marketplace. In discussing various large corporations (such as McDonald's and Kodak), Aaker demonstrates the process of managing a hugely successful brand. The author also explores ways of retaining a certain brand while under some pressure to alter it. A reference tool for anybody involved in brand management.

Differentiate or Die: Survival in Our Era of Killer Competition
Jack Trout, Steve Rivkin
Chichester: John Wiley & Sons Ltd, 2001
240pp ISBN: 0471028924
This title is a useful guide on how to make ones product differ from those of everyone else and lists several ways to achieve this. These include being the first person to do something, being the latest person to do a version of something, and becoming the first choice of a certain type of consumer group.

Product Strategy and Management
Michael Baker, Susan Hart
Harlow: Prentice Hall, 1998
528pp ISBN: 0130653683
This textbook is aimed at students and provides a broad introduction to the concepts and techniques of product strategy and management. It explores the theoretical foundations, new product strategy, product management, and product elimination.

Smart Things to Know about Brands and Branding
John Mariotti
Oxford: Capstone, 1999
240pp (Smart Series)
ISBN: 1841120391
Mariotti's purpose in this book is to give managers advice on creating a brand, understanding brand values, growing a

brand, becoming a smart brand manager, measuring success, and championing their organisation's brand.

What Makes Winning Brands Different: The Hidden Method behind the World's Most Successful Brands
Andreas Buchholz, Wolfram Wordemann
Chichester: John Wiley & Sons Ltd, 2000
240pp ISBN: 0471720259
The authors analyse the results of a research study of over 1,000 winning brands in order to establish a blueprint for brand growth and development. They argue that brands can achieve outstanding growth by adhering to specific laws or 'growth codes', of which they identify 27. Putting these 'codes' into effect is explored through case studies and best practice examples.

WEBSITES
Allaboutbranding.com
http://www.allaboutbranding.com/
This site has multiple articles concerned with branding's role in the marketplace and what it takes to create and maintain a brand name. Site features include an 'Analyze Your Brand' test, free e-mail updates, quotes, definitions of useful terms, and sections that accurately cover the field.

brandchannel.com
www.brandchannel.com
This site, produced by Interbrand, provides for an online exchange about branding. It contains a debate area, features, papers, and details of books and training.

BrandingAsia.com
www.brandingasia.com
This site focuses on branding issues in Asia, and includes brand news, tips, case studies, articles, and a discussion board. A free monthly e-mail newsletter is available.

Building Brands – Unlocking Your Potential
www.buildingbrands.com
This site contains both free content, with articles, definitions, and did-you-knows, to premium services, which include training, web seminars, student mentoring, and executive coaching.

Knowledge Roundtable
www.knowledge-roundtable.com
This membership-based service aims to connect people around the world and provide information to aid product development and collaboration. Members may gain access to news, networking opportunities, an ask the expert facility, an audio conferences.

KnowThis.com
www.knowthis.com
This section of the Virtual Library contains articles and links to resources for successful product management, branding, and packaging.

SEE ALSO
Marketing Management (p. 522)
New Product Development (p. 530)

Project Management

BOOKS AND DIRECTORIES
The Accidental Project Manager: Surviving the Transition from Techie to Manager
Patricia Ensworth
Chichester: John Wiley & Sons Ltd, 2001
272pp ISBN: 047141011X
When projects fail it is often because the person in charge has no idea how to manage projects. This no-nonsense guide provides basic project management information including project planning, the roles of team members, the tools of the trade, and project control metrics. It also supplies templates, checklists, and sample forms for the beginner to use.

Effective Project Management 3rd ed
Robert Wysocki, et al
Chichester: John Wiley & Sons Ltd, 2003
512pp ISBN: 0471432210
This book and CD-ROM package provides
novices with a complete introduction to the
principles of project management, and
offers experienced project managers an
opportunity to fine-tune their skills. It
describes the management tools and
techniques you need to stay on schedule
and within budget without compromising
quality. It adheres to the Project
Management Institute's curriculum outline
(PMBOK), and follows the necessary course
requirements for professional certification.
The CD-ROM provides a simulated
environment in which to apply the
principles, tools, and techniques described
in the book.

A Guide to the Project Management Body of Knowledge 3rd ed
Project Management Institute
*Newtown Square, Pennsylvania: Project
Management Institute, 2004*
384pp ISBN: 193069945X
This book is the basic Project Management
reference and the accepted standard for the
profession. It details the nine knowledge
areas and 39 processes essential to a project
management model that will work in any
industry. By establishing a standard, the
guide also provides a common language for
talking about project management. It is a
key resource for those seeking Project
Management Professional (PMP)
certification.

Project
Ros Jay
Harlow: Prentice Hall, 2000
96pp (Fast Thinking)
ISBN: 0273653113
This book aims to help people cut through
the muddle of panic that often sets in during
the working day and to become more
efficient. It offers helpful advice on what to
do, say, and plan for when you have a
pressing deadline and an objective to meet.

Project Management for Dummies
Stanley Portny
Chichester: John Wiley & Sons Ltd, 2000
288pp ISBN: 076455283X
Highly recommended by professional
project managers, this book explains what
project management is and then goes on to
offer advice on how best to do it. It includes
information on scheduling, assembling
teams, and assessing resources.

Project Management: The Managerial Process 3rd ed
Clifford Gray
Maidenhead: Irwin/McGraw-Hill, 2005
576pp ISBN: 0073126993
This book presents a balanced view of the
technical and socio/cultural dimensions of
managing projects. It is suitable for a course
in project management, and for individuals
seeking a project management handbook.
The text is application-oriented for
managing any type of project, and includes
advice on discovering the strategic role of
projects in contemporary organisations,
prioritising, planning and scheduling
projects, and orchestrating the complex
network of relationships. It includes a CD-
ROM, bibliographical references, and an
index.

The Project Manager's MBA: How to Translate Project Decisions into Business Success
Dennis J. Cohen, Robert J. Graham
*San Francisco, California: Jossey-Bass Wiley,
2000*
*336pp (Jossey-Bass Business and Management
Series)*
ISBN: 0787952567
This text aims to provide an introduction to
the business basics that every project
manager needs to understand. These
include value creation, accounting and
finance strategy, and marketing. These
concepts are related to the decisions project
managers face every day. The aim is to
develop the skills of project managers so
that they can meet both their technical and
their business objectives.

Project Planning, Scheduling, and Control 3rd ed

James P. Lewis
Maidenhead: McGraw-Hill, 2000
352pp ISBN: 0071360506
This book offers an applications-oriented, non-theoretical understanding of the flexibility required in day-to-day management situations, and provides guidelines that apply to every phase of steering a project to its successful conclusion. This third edition has been updated to include easy-to-follow steps for managing multiple projects, effective risk management strategies, and an innovative blueprint for developing a workable project methodology.

Project Skills

Sam Elbeik, Mark Thomas
Oxford: Butterworth-Heinemann, 1998
196pp (New Skills Portfolio Series)
ISBN: 0750639784
The authors provide a practical and accessible guide to managing projects of all sizes and across all industries. Presented as an action-focused training guide, the book explains real-world project management and introduces the key skills and techniques needed in the six stages of managing a project.

The Project Workout 3rd ed

Robert Buttrick
Harlow: Financial Times Prentice Hall, 2005
512pp ISBN: 0273681818
A best-selling guide to project management, this book provides an illustrated approach to the practical theory behind best practice in the field. The package includes a CD-ROM to allow interactive practice.

Successful Project Management in a Week 3rd ed

Mark Brown
London: Hodder & Stoughton, 2002
96pp (Business in a Week Series)
ISBN: 0340849371
The book explains the basic principles of project management for the benefit of anyone new to the technique and describes the practical steps involved in managing a project. It focuses on understanding the nature of projects, on setting up, planning, and controlling projects, and on the role and personal qualities of a project manager.

WEBSITES

AllPM.com – The Project Manager's Homepage

www.allpm.com
This site offers free membership which allows users access to a forum, event calendar, articles and tips, and a project management template library.

Association for Project Management

www.apm.org.uk
The site offers visitors details of news, events, qualifications, services, and publications in the field of project management. It also has information on member benefits and links to related organisations, and provides short reading lists. Its resources section includes a glossary and bookshop.

PMFORUM

www.pmforum.org
This information dissemination and exchange forum includes a portal to information, resources, and working groups associated with project manager accreditation, certification, education, research, and standards. It also contains listings of software, consulting services, and training resources, plus a calendar of events.

Project Management

www.projectmagazine.com
This Web site is actually a 'magazine' that's free to anyone. With meaningful articles, book reviews, software reviews, and access to a free newsletter, this is an audience-oriented resource for the project manager.

Project Management Institute

www.pmi.org
The Project Management Institute (PMI) has over 100,000 members worldwide and is the leading non-profit professional association in this field. The site offers

information on member services, including careers and awards programmes, a bookshop, links to other project management organisations, and information on project management standards. It also provides opportunities for organisations to contribute to a corporate council, and lists PMI seminars.

Project Management Library
www.mapnp.org/library/plan_dec/project/project.htm
Part of the Management Assistance Program for Nonprofits, this site's resources include a project management overview, information on team building and group leadership, general resources, and on-line discussion groups.

ORGANISATIONS
Association for Project Management
Thornton House, 150 West Wycombe Road, High Wycombe, Buckinghamshire, HP12 3AE
T: +44 (0) 1494 440 090
F: +44 (0) 1494 528 937
E: info@apm.org.uk
www.apm.org.uk
A professional body founded in 1970, the APM aims to be the UK national authority on project management. It promotes project management skills and training, and develops standards and certification for project managers. Services are delivered through joint ventures or through its members. The association is affiliated to the International Project Management Association.

Public Relations

BOOKS AND DIRECTORIES
Effective Writing Skills for Public Relations 3rd ed
John Foster
London: Kogan Page, 2005
272pp (PR in Practice)
ISBN: 0749443812
This book is a practical guide to writing style for students and PR practitioners. It looks at grammar, developing a house style, headlines and captions, press releases, and speeches and public speaking.

Face the Media: The Complete Guide to Getting Publicity and Handling Media Opportunities 2nd ed
Judith Byrne
Oxford: How To Books, 2002
144pp ISBN: 1857037979
This guide offers advice on how to make contacts in the media and generate and sustain interest in your or your business. Issues covered include: securing an interview; talking to journalists; improving confidence; developing 'soundbites'; and crisis management.

Free Publicity for Your Business in a Week
Guy Clapperton
London: Hodder & Stoughton, 2002
96pp (In a Week)
ISBN: 0340858273
This book is aimed at cash-strapped small business owners and managers who need to make a splash. It covers a range of issues including how to handle the press, writing effective press releases, responding to feedback, and crisis management if things do not go to plan.

Guerrilla PR Wired: Waging a Successful Publicity Campaign Online, Offline, and Everywhere In Between
Michael Levine
Maidenhead: McGraw-Hill, 2003
288pp ISBN: 0071382321
This book re-examines the very popular principles of 'Guerrilla PR' (introduced in the author's book *Guerrilla PR*, HarperCollins, 1993), the technique for creating cost-effective publicity, for the age of the World Wide Web. The book explains

how the key tenets have changed with developments in technology, and introduces new tactics for conveying online messages. Readers will learn how the pros use the web efficiently for publicity, how to focus on a target to get superior results and how to avoid all the pitfalls that lie in wait for the web PR novice. The book also features a wide variety of empirical examples.

Planning and Managing a Public Relations Campaign 2nd ed
Anne Gregory
London: Kogan Page, 2001
160pp ISBN: 0749429917
Gregory presents a step-by-step guide to the stages of a PR campaign, covering all the important aspects, and including instructional case studies and a ten-point action plan.

Public Relations: A Practical Guide to the Basics 2nd ed
Philip Henslowe
London: Kogan Page, 2003
160pp (PR in Practice)
ISBN: 0749440724
This is an introduction to the basic principles of public relations. It is an easy-to-read, effective reference guide that provides an overview of the main areas, and is suitable for people who are not PR experts, but who need to do some public relations work.

The Public Relations Handbook 2nd ed
Alison Theaker
London: Routledge, 2004
384pp ISBN: 0415317932
A detailed introduction to the theory and practice of public relations is provided by this comprehensive handbook. It looks at all aspects of the subject, including training and entry into the profession, ethical issues, the use of new technology, and contains case studies.

Public Relations Kit for Dummies
Eric Yaverbaum, Robert Bly
New York: Hungry Minds, 2000
352pp ISBN: 0764552775

Part of a series offering concise, practical information on a variety of topics, this book addresses what all business owners and managers need to know about effective public relations. Presented in an easy to understand style, this title offers specific strategies and eminently practical techniques for public relations, along with information on using new technologies, such as the Internet, in PR campaigns. Also included is a CD-ROM with lists of PR firms and media contacts.

Public Relations: Strategies and Tactics 8th ed
Dennis L. Wilcox, Glen T. Cameron
Harlow: Longman, 2005
640pp ISBN: 0205450725
This book presents a comprehensive outline of the principles, concepts, and methods of public relations. This latest edition focuses specifically on global issues, use of the Internet and other new technologies, and ethical issues in public relations. The text differs from similar texts in the field through the inclusion of a series of up-to-date case studies.

Risk Issues and Crisis Management: A Casebook of Best Practice 3rd ed
Michael Regester, Judy Larkin
London: Institute of Public Relations, 2005
192pp (PR in Practice)
ISBN: 0749423935
This book deals with the successful handling of crisis situations so that damage and disruption are minimised. Case studies and models are included and illustrate how complex crises have been handled in practice, both successfully and unsuccessfully.

WEBSITES
Managing Public Relations
www.workz.com/content/
view_content.html?section_id=465
This website serves as a resource for small business owners. It offers comprehensive information on public relations techniques, including guides for creating an effective PR plan, giving your company a PR makeover, and avoiding bad PR.

PR Place
www.prplace.com
This site contains a listing of Internet
resources on public relations. The
categories it covers include organisations in
PR, publications, news sources, and
databases.

Public Relations Resources
www.publicrelationsresources.com
The mission of this site is to provide regular
informative articles on how to promote
events, people, and businesses. It includes
free articles, news headlines, and a list of
links.

ORGANISATIONS
Chartered Institute of Public Relations
The Old Trading House, 15 Northburgh
Street, London, EC1V 0PR
T: +44 (0) 20 253 5151
F: +44 (0) 20 490 0588
E: info@ipr.org.uk
www.ipr.org.uk

The CIPR is a UK professional body for
those working in the area of public relations.
The biggest PR institute in Europe, it has
more than 8,000 members.

**Public Relations Consultants
Association**
Willow House, Willow Place, Victoria,
London, SW1P 1JH
T: +44 (0) 20 7233 6026
F: +44 (0) 20 7828 4797
E: flora@prca.org.uk
www.prca.org.uk
The PRCA, set up in 1969, is a trade
association with 140 members, these being
consultancies of all sizes working in PR in
the United Kingdom. It provides
representation for the industry to
government and the media, and such
services as PRJobseek, training, and
financial management. It also runs
seminars, conferences, and research
projects.

Recruitment and Selection

BOOKS AND DIRECTORIES
**45 Effective Ways for Hiring Smart! How
to Predict Winners & Losers in the
Incredibly Expensive People-reading
Game 2nd ed**
Pierre Mornell
Berkeley, California: Ten Speed Press, 2003
240pp ISBN: 1580085148
This is a practical guide to help employers
cut through the complexities of recruitment,
and select the best candidate for a particular
job. As the title suggests, this text presents
45 techniques designed to take the measure
of potential recruits, emphasising behaviour
not words.

**101 Hiring Mistakes Employers
Make. . .and How to Avoid Them**
Richard Fein
Manassas Park, Virginia: Impact Publications,
1999
128pp ISBN: 157023129X
This book is an analytical study of
interviewing techniques, based on material
from genuine interviews. It aims to outline
some of the main recruiting errors that can
eventually burden an organisation with an
unsatisfactory employee. The author aims
to help minimise 'hiring mistakes' and
increase the employer's understanding of
interview questioning.

Finding and Keeping the Right People: How to Recruit Motivated Employees

Jon Billsberry
Harlow: Prentice Hall, 1999
240pp (Smarter Solutions series)
ISBN: 0273644815
Aiming to give managers and recruiters a practical perspective on recruitment and selection, this book stresses the need to pay continuous attention to the business purpose of the exercise and integrate it into the process. The text also deals with attracting and assessing applicants, making decisions about terms and conditions, and retaining employees once they have been recruited.

A Manager's Guide to Hiring the Best Person for Every Job

DeAnne Rosenberg
Chichester: John Wiley & Sons Ltd, 2000
320pp ISBN: 0471380741
This book on recruitment and selection interviewing is written in simple language and gives detailed help with structuring the dialogue and questioning in interviews in such a way as to retain control and focus on the job requirements involved. A matrix designed by the author for identifying trade-offs among competing candidates is included.

Recruit & Retain the Best

John McCarter, Ray Schreyer
Manassas Park, Virginia: Impact Publications, 2000
128pp ISBN: 1570231346
The authors claim that, to remain competitive, you must create a talent-powered company. Their solution begins with recruiting new employees based on competencies from education or previous employment. They discuss innovative recruiting tools, like the Internet and employee referral programmes. However, the focus of this book is on the retention of the top employees. The last third of the book addresses ways to make your company a place where the best want to stay.

Recruiting, Interviewing, Selecting, and Orienting New Employees 3rd ed

Diane Arthur
New York: AMACOM, 1998
400pp ISBN: 0814404014
This book is designed to give comprehensive guidance through the four stages of the employment process to HR specialists and others whose work involves recruitment and selection. Besides describing methods and techniques applicable to the basic task of hiring new employees, this revised edition takes in new material dealing with areas such as additional interviewing approaches, workplace diversity, the retention of new staff, and online recruitment.

Recruiting within the Law

Patricia Leighton, Giles Proctor
London: Chartered Institute of Personnel and Development (CIPD), 2001
80pp (Legal Essentials Series)
ISBN: 0852929579
In this booklet the legal framework of UK and European legislation relating to recruitment is described by experts. Written in layman's language and aimed at human resources specialists and others involved in recruitment, the text first deals with frequently asked questions, then identifies and considers the key legal rules that currently apply to recruitment, employment offers, health screening, references, and employment contracting.

Recruitment Strategies

Market Tracking International Ltd
London: Haymarket Publishing
416pp
This expensive, late 1990s report, aimed at senior strategists, is based on a wide-ranging survey of recruitment strategies in UK companies. It examines change factors and trends, and covers areas including government initiatives and legislation, recruitment methods, the use of agencies or consultants, selection procedures, and training and development incentives.

The Selection Interview
Penny Hackett
London: Chartered Institute of Personnel and Development (CIPD), 1998
96pp (Management Shapers Series)
ISBN: 0852927568
First published in 1995, this short, clear, and easily understood book gives advice to help managers recruit more effectively through focused, well-planned, and skilled selection interviewing. It includes information on drawing up job descriptions, setting up the interview, different interview strategies and styles, questioning and listening skills, the evaluation of interview results, and decision-making leading to selection.

Smart Hiring: The Complete Guide to Finding and Hiring the Best Employees 3rd ed
Robert W. Wendover
Naperville, Illinois: Sourcebooks, 2002
240pp ISBN: 140220003X
This book offers practical advice to employers on improving their employee-selection skills. Examining various topics such as recruiting errors, telephone interviews, and the assessment of a potential employee, Wendover's approach is pragmatic. Also included in the book are step-by-step guides to job advertising and analysing CVs.

Writing Job Descriptions
Alan Fowler
London: Chartered Institute of Personnel and Development (CIPD), 2000
80pp (Management Shapers Series)
ISBN: 0852928661
This booklet aims to give managers and HR professionals a focused introduction to writing clear, accurate job descriptions for effective recruitment and selection. Help is included on defining essential job constituents, legal issues, defining reporting relationships, dealing with unspecified duties, and job dimensions. The use of job descriptions for job evaluation is covered, and key points are summarised.

WEBSITES
Benefits News.com
www.benefitnews.com
This US-based resource for benefits professionals is free, but requires registration to access some of its services. Its contents include a weekly e-newsletter, *Benefitnews Connect*, links, discussion groups, and information on events, products, and service.

Monster.co.uk
www.monster.co.uk
This site is part of Monster.com, a global online careers network, aiming to connect companies and qualified individuals. It offers member-employers various services, including job postings, CV screening, a CV database, and CV routing. Job seekers can use it to access vacancies, and take advantage of features and services such as CV management, a job-search agent, and a careers network.

Recruiters Network
www.recruitersnetwork.com
Recruiters Network is a free association for HR professionals, recruiters, and hiring managers. Its goal is to provide leading resources and information on the recruiting and Internet recruiting industry. Members receive a monthly newsletter, access to a resource directory, and links to related blogs.

Recruiters Online Network
www.recruitersonline.com
Recruiters Online Network is a global community of recruiters, headhunters, and staffing firms. It features separate sections for job seekers to post CVs and search for jobs, for recruiters to post jobs and search CV databases, and for employers to find talent or a recruiting firm.

ORGANISATIONS
Chartered Institute of Personnel and Development (CIPD)
151 The Broadway, London, SW19 1JQ

T: +44 (0) 20 8612 6200
F: +44 (0) 20 8612 6201
www.cipd.co.uk
The CIPD is a professional body for personnel and human resources management specialists. It offers qualifications and developmental support in these fields, and also makes publications, courses, and information available to members. It treats performance appraisal and performance management as one of its central areas of concern within the wider field of personnel management.

Recruitment and Employment Confederation
36–38 Mortimer Street, London, W1W 7RG
T: +44 (0) 20 7462 3260
F: +44 (0) 20 7255 2878
E: info@rec.co.uk
www.rec.uk.com
The Confederation is an organisation for recruitment and employment agencies and consultancies operating in most fields of employment. Its activities include conferences, meetings, research, and the provision of information.

Selling and Salesmanship

BOOKS AND DIRECTORIES
Clients Forever: How Your Clients Can Build Your Business For You
Doug Carter, Jenni Green
Maidenhead: McGraw-Hill, 2003
256pp ISBN: 007140256X
This book shows you how to build your business through solid, long-term relationships with your favourite kind of clients. It provides the know-how and confidence to focus your efforts on the people you most enjoy working with, generate better results with less effort, build relationships with clients, and develop an approach that accentuates your personal strengths.

Coaching Champions: How to Get the Absolute Best Out of Your Salespeople
Frank Salisbury, Cariona Nearym, Karl O'Connor
Dublin: Oak Tree Press, 2001
272pp ISBN: 1860762034
This book sets out to provide all sales managers from executive level to first-line managers with the tools and techniques to develop their sales people into star performers. Using the POWER coaching method, the authors show that coaching is a much more powerful tool than mere training and that remarkable results are possible if used properly. Performance

coaching is, according to them, the ideal tool for turning ordinary salespeople into champions.

Fast Forward MBA in Selling: Become a Self-motivated Profit Center—and Prosper
Joy Baldridge
Chichester: John Wiley & Sons Ltd, 2000
224pp ISBN: 0471348546
This book is a comprehensive guide to becoming a successful salesperson. It explores a wide range of topics, including setting the standards for success, self-motivation, time management, getting and staying connected, preparation, technology, and successful sales calls.

Global Account Management: Creating Value
H. David Hennessey, Jean-Pierre Jeannet
Chichester: John Wiley & Sons Ltd, 2003
272pp ISBN: 0470848928
The globalisation of many industries, it is suggested, has created a unique opportunity to interact with a client on a co-ordinated global basis. The handling of large global customers requires special expertise, systems, and organisational alignment. This book examines the key aspects of the practice of global account management and of developing and managing global

customers and illustrates these with case studies.

How to Become a Rainmaker: The Rules for Getting and Keeping Customers and Clients
Jeffrey J. Fox
London: Vermilion, 2001
176pp ISBN: 0091876540
This book is written to assist in identifying, attracting and keeping customers. It identifies Rainmakers (people who bring revenue into organisations), who may be CEOs, owners, partners, sales representatives, or fundraisers. Jeffrey J. Fox explains how the reader can become a Rainmaker, enabling him/her to attract more customers and rise above the competition in any company.

Improving Customer Satisfaction, Loyalty, and Profit: An Integrated Measurement and Management System
Michael D. Johnson, Anders Gustafsson
San Francisco, California: Jossey-Bass Wiley, 2000
240pp ISBN: 0787953105
By outlining in detail five key areas, this book offers ways to improve customer loyalty. By outlining key measures of customer satisfaction and giving suggestions for marketing strategy and product development, the book enables a more cohesive measurement and management system.

Key Account Management: A Complete Action Kit of Tools and Techniques for Achieving Profitable Key Supplier Status 3rd ed
Peter Cheverton
London: Kogan Page, 2004
368pp ISBN: 0749441690
This comprehensive textbook takes a broad perspective on key account management (KAM), starting from the premise that it is not just to do with selling but with developing profitable relationships between customers and suppliers. Peter Cheverton starts by defining KAM and explains how to

understand the customer's perspective, put in place the organisational systems and processes required, identify key accounts, develop management strategies, and meet customer needs. Advice on developing key account plans and keeping track of progress and examples of good and bad practice are provided throughout.

Key Account Management and Planning: The Comprehension Handbook for Managing Your Company's Most Important Strategic Asset
Noel Capon
London: Free Press, 2001
480pp ISBN: 074321188X
With a greater level of competition and increased costs of selling, the nature of the selling process has changed. Using research, real-life stories of successes and failures, and clarifying figures, the author presents his four-part 'congruence model' of key account management. He explains: how to select the key account portfolio; how to manage key accounts; how to recruit, select, train, reward and retain key account managers, and how to formulate and execute key account strategies.

Key Account Management: Learning from Supplier and Customer Perspectives
Malcolm McDonald, Beth Rogers
London: Butterworth-Heinemann, 1998
208pp ISBN: 075063278X
Key account management, it is suggested, is rapidly becoming more important as purchasing power is increasingly concentrated in the hands of fewer, larger buyers. This text, based on research by Cranfield School of Management, presents a new framework for understanding the development of key account relationships. It explains the processes of identifying and targeting key accounts, key account planning, the role and skills of key account managers, and the positioning of key account activity. The book also considers the future of key account management.

Knock Your Socks Off Selling

Jeffrey Gitomer, Ron Zemke
New York: AMACOM, 1999
160pp ISBN: 0814470300
An overview of sales techniques from basic selling to developing relationships, the book is appropriate for salespeople at every level. Placing an emphasis on making a partnership out of the buyer/seller relationship, the book discusses networking, generating leads, making presentations, and following through.

Marketing and Selling Professional Services: Practical Approaches to Practice Development 3rd ed

Patrick Forsyth
London: Kogan Page, 2003
320pp ISBN: 0749440902
This book is intended to help professionals of all kinds to develop successful strategies for marketing what are essentially intangible services. The author starts by explaining the importance and role of marketing in professional service businesses and goes on to explore a range of practical issues including: marketing planning, promotional mix, advertising, and postal promotion. The second section deals with professional personal selling and covers persuasive writing and communication, and systematic client development.

Sales Management: Concepts and Cases 8th ed

Douglas J. Dalrymple, William L. Cron, Thomas E. DeCarlo
Chichester: John Wiley & Sons Ltd, 2003
624pp ISBN: 047123060X
This book includes theoretical discussions and case studies covering all aspects of sales management. The topics dealt with in its various sections are: strategic planning and budgeting; personal selling; territory management; estimating potentials and forecasting sales; recruiting and selecting personnel; sales training; leadership; motivating salespeople; compensating salespeople; and evaluating performance.

Selling Dreams: How to Make Any Product Irresistible

Gian Luigi Longinotti-Buitoni
London: Simon & Schuster, 1999
336pp ISBN: 0684850192
The author, who is president and CEO of Ferrari North America, describes how companies can market their products and services by connecting with the imagination and aspirations of their customers. The principles of 'dreamketing', or selling dreams, are outlined as they relate to the most unlikely products.

Selling in a Week 3rd ed

Christine Harvey
London: Hodder & Stoughton, 2002
96pp (Business in a Week)
ISBN: 0340849827
This is an introductory guide to both the skills and systems of selling. It covers organisational preparation, gaining product expertise, finding emotional motives, a three-part objection process, prospect action systems, overcoming roadblocks and price objections, and self-motivation.

The Seven Keys to Managing Strategic Accounts

Sallie Sherman, Joseph Sperry, Samuel Reese
Maidenhead: McGraw-Hill, 2003
256pp ISBN: 0071417524
Offering market-proven strategies for generating competitive advantage by identifying and looking after your best customers, this book provides decision-makers with a strategy for profitably managing their largest and most critical accounts.

SPIN Selling

Neil Rackham
Aldershot: Gower Publishing, 1995
272pp ISBN: 0566076896
Practical, easy-to-use and understand information on how to make selling easier for the salesperson. Based on extensive research, its direct and helpful advice may also be helpful in all other work situations.

The SPIN Selling Fieldbook: Practical Tools, Methods, Exercises and Resources
Neil Rackham
Maidenhead: McGraw-Hill, 1996
208pp ISBN: 0070522359
Full of case studies and practical information, this book shows the reader how to put into practice the help and advice given in *SPIN Selling.*

Successful Sales Management: How to Make Your Team the Best
Grant Stewart
Harlow: Prentice Hall, 1999
192pp (Smarter Solutions Series)
ISBN: 0273644882
This is a practical guide for managers on how to manage the sales function. Its contents cover: the sales manager's job; motivation; management style; standards of performance; planning and control; recruitment and selection; sales meetings; and sales audits.

Tough Calls: Selling Strategies to Win Over Your Most Difficult Customers
Josh Gordon
New York: AMACOM, 1997
224pp ISBN: 0814479251
Focusing on the challenges of difficult customers, the book outlines 20 different 'tough sells' and strategies to counteract them. It provides advice on what to do and what not to do with customers who, for example, are incompetent, do not have buying authority, will not see you, buy elsewhere because of company politics, or like what you say but still don't buy.

The Ultimate Sales Letter: Boost Your Sales with Powerful Sales Letters 2nd ed
Dan S. Kennedy, Daniel Kennedy
Avon, Massachusetts: Adams Media Corporation, 2000
224pp ISBN: 1580622577
This text provides clear examples that assist in writing focused sales letters that target specific customer bases. Tips and features include: creating powerful headlines,

improving readability, when to use bullet points, which font to use, and which demographics to target. All this is performed within 28 structured steps, and should interest sales reps, business owners, and advertising people.

WEBSITES
BestOfSales.com
www.bestofsales.com
A list of links to sales resources on the Internet is given on this site.

Just Sell
www.justsell.com
This site offers a selection of useful sales checklists and evaluation tools for sales professionals. Users must register to access the information, but registration is free.

Saleslinks.com
www.saleslinks.com/links
Run by Mentor Associates, this site is aimed at anyone who is engaged in selling for a living. It includes links to sales resources on the Internet, arranged in categories.

Salesmanship
www.dmoz.org/Business/Marketing_and_Advertising/
Maintained as part of the Open Directory Project, this site contains a large list of other websites, each with a brief description, relating to all aspects of salesmanship.

Sales Rep Central
www.salesrepcentral.com
A portal for sales professionals, the site contains news, articles, a community message board, jobs, sales leads, and travel services.

SalesVault
www.salesvault.com
This site is aimed at professional sales people. It also includes articles, news, and advice and also advertises courses that users may wish to take up for a fee.

Selling Power
www.sellingpower.com
The online counterpart to *Selling Power* magazine, the site offers archived issues of the magazine, electronic newsletters on several sales-related topics, and advice on motivation and management. Much of the information on the site can be viewed by non-members, but to access other areas you will need to register. Registration is free.

ORGANISATIONS
Direct Selling Association UK
29 Floral Street, London, WC2E 9DP
T: +44 (0) 20 7497 1234
F: +44 (0) 20 7497 3144
E: info@dsa.org.uk
www.dsa.org.uk
The DSA aims to promote the understanding of direct selling as a distribution channel. Its benefits are potentially huge, as the site cites figures which claim that direct selling is worth more than £1.6 billion each year. The DSA's website has four major categories: protecting the consumer, direct selling today, information on the Association, and 'A Business of Your Own', which gives information on how direct selling can be helpful to start-up businesses.

Institute of Professional Sales
Moor Hall, Cookham, Maidenhead, Berkshire, SL6 9QH
T: +44 (0) 1628 427 370
F: +44 (0) 1628 427 369
www.cim.co.uk
The Institute shares the same facilities, values, and objectives as the Chartered Institute of Marketing. Its vision is to raise the profile of sales professionals, gain recognition for them, and promote their interests, as well as to offer training, develop best practice, promote sales qualifications, and provide networking opportunities.

Institute of Sales and Marketing Management
Harrier Court, Lower Woodside, Bedfordshire , LU1 4DQ
T: +44 (0)1582 840 001
F: +44 (0)1582 849 142
www.ismm.co.uk
Established in 1966, the ISMM is a professional body for salespeople in the United Kingdom. It promotes standards of excellence in the industry and provides qualifications and training. Its members are individuals at all levels from students to sales directors. The organisation holds a conference in Birmingham every October.

Institute of Sales Promotion
Arena House, 66–68 Pentonville Road, London, N1 9HS
T: +44 (0) 20 7837 5340
F: +44 (0) 20 7837 5326
E: enquiries@isp.org.uk
www.isp.org.uk
The Institute of Sales Promotion was set up in 1979. It offers education, training, legal advice, and networking opportunities for members.

Society of Sales and Marketing
40 Archdale Road, East Dulwich, London, SE22 9HJ
T: +44 (0) 20 8693 0555
F: +44 (0)709 234 2170
E: info@ssam.co.uk
www.ssam.co.uk
This professional body was established in 1980. It exists to encourage the study of selling and sales management, marketing principles and practice, retail management, and international trade. It provides professional status for salespeople and accredits educational programmes.

SEE ALSO
Marketing Management (p. 522)

Taxation

BOOKS AND DIRECTORIES

Tolley's Tax Guide 2005/06
Rita Burrows, Arnold Homer
London: LexisNexis Butterworths Tolley, 2005
ISBN: 0754528707
Useful for both tax professionals and those who assess themselves, this book presents all the latest tax legislation accessibly. It covers the entire range of UK taxes and also features roughly 150 worked examples as well as useful checklists and planning tools. Tables of 2005–06 tax rates and allowances and summaries of recent changes are also included.

Zurich Tax Handbook 2005/2006
Tony Foreman ed
Harlow: Prentice Hall, 2005
720pp ISBN: 027370592X
This comprehensive guide to the tax system in the United Kingdom offers practical advice to the individual on managing his or her tax affairs, including self-assessment and completion of the Tax Return, dealing with HM Revenue & Customs, stakeholder pensions, and employee share schemes.

WEBSITES
Chartered Institute of Taxation
www.tax.org.uk
This site includes CIOT press releases, technical articles and research papers and letters of engagement. It also has useful external links to equivalent tax organisations in other countries.

HM Revenue & Customs
www.hmrc.gov.uk
This content-rich site features news and information on tax and national insurance matters in the United Kingdom. There are specific sections for individuals, established businesses, start-up businesses, employers, practitioners, non-UK residents, and charities.

HM Revenue & Customs UK Trade Info
www.uktradeinfo.com/
This site, which is linked to HM Revenue & Customs, offers users advice on many aspects of UK and international trade, including an extensive range of codes and guides, an information centre, and useful data section.

HM Revenue & Customs: Starting Up in Business
www.hmrc.gov.uk/startingup/ index.htm
This section of the main Revenue & Customs website sets out to help small-business people identify key areas of compliance in the areas of tax and National Insurance. An easy-to-use series of frequently asked questions and links takes users to the areas of most interest to them. The site also highlights other important legal areas that are not within the Revenue's own remit, but which also need to be considered, and provides a helpful series of links.

Institute for Fiscal Studies
www.ifs.org.uk
The site of the Institute of Fiscal Studies details their conferences and publications with the full text of some working papers and articles. It has a useful 'Fiscal Facts' section giving tax rates going back to 1973.

Tax and Accounting Sites Directory
www.taxsites.com
This site provides an international gateway to country specific tax and accounting resources on the Web. It has a US bias.

UK Taxation Directory
www.uktax.demon.co.uk
This site is a gateway to UK tax websites which provide material of potential interest to tax professionals and others seeking online information on UK tax matters.

ORGANISATIONS
Association of Taxation Technicians (AAT)
12 Upper Belgrave Street, London, SW1X 8BB
T: +44 (0) 20 7235 9381
F: +44 (0) 20 7235 4571
E: info@att.org.uk
www.att.org.uk
Established in 1989, the Association of Taxation Technicians provides a qualification for individuals undertaking tax compliance work, namely the preparation of tax returns for corporate and individual taxpayers.

Chartered Institute of Taxation
12 Upper Belgrave Street, London, SW1X 8BB
T: +44 (0) 20 7235 9381
F: +44 (0) 20 7235 2562
E: post@ciot.org.uk
www.tax.org.uk
As the senior professional body in the United Kingdom concerned solely with all aspects of taxation, the Chartered Institute of Taxation aims to advance public education in, and promote the study of, the administration and practice of taxation. It has nearly 12,000 members encompassing the professions and many occupations in industry, commerce, the public sector, and the taxation authorities. Membership is by examination and members have the practising title of 'Chartered Tax Adviser'.

Institute for Fiscal Studies
7 Ridgemount Street, London, WC1E 7AE
T: +44 (0) 20 7291 4800
F: +44 (0) 20 7323 4780
E: mailbox@ifs.org.uk
www.ifs.org.uk
The IFS aims to promote and disseminate the economic implications of tax and fiscal policy in Britain and elsewhere. It has a significant influence on policy through its analyses and publishes a quarterly journal, *Fiscal Studies*.

Institute of Chartered Accountants in England and Wales
Chartered Accountants' Hall,
PO Box 433, Moorgate Place, London, EC2P 2BJ
T: +44 (0) 20 7920 8100
F: +44 (0) 20 7920 0547
www.icaew.co.uk
This, the largest professional accountancy organisation in Europe with over 120,000 members, is responsible for educating and training chartered accountants and maintaining standards of professional conduct among its members.

Institute of Chartered Accountants of Scotland
CA House, 21 Haymarket Yards, Edinburgh, Scotland, EH12 5BH
T: +44 (0) 131 347 0100
F: +44 (0) 131 347 0105
E: enquiries@icas.org.uk
www.icas.org.uk
The ICAS is the leading professional accounting body in Scotland, and the oldest professional body of accountants in the world.

SEE ALSO
Accounting (p. 494)
Budgeting (p. 499)

Venture Capital

BOOKS AND DIRECTORIES
The VC Way: Investment Secrets from the Wizards of Venture Capital
Jeffrey Zygmont
Cambridge, Massachusetts: Perseus Books Group, 2002
240pp ISBN: 0738205923
This text offers a behind-the-scenes perspective of the venture capital market, revealing to investors how to strategise and invest in successful companies before their profits are certain. Zygmont also offers the reader a brief tutorial in creating a portfolio of holdings that may increase in value, as Apple and Yahoo did.

Venture Capital and Private Equity: A Casebook 3rd ed
Josh Lerner, et al
Chichester: John Wiley & Sons Ltd, 2003
576pp ISBN: 0471230693
The book explains in detail the venture capital and private equity markets. Divided into four sections, the book covers the fundraising process required to start a venture capital fund, investment selection, and the relationship between the venture capitalist and entrepreneur, the various exit strategies available, and some key issues unique to the private equity market.

Venture Capital Funding: A Practical Guide to Raising Finance
Stephen Bloomfield
London: Kogan Page, 2005
272pp ISBN: 0749442913
Written in an informal and jargon-free style, this book offers step-by-step advice on how to attract venture capital funding for your business. To make the process seem less daunting, the process is broken down into a number of manageable sections.

Venture Capital Investing: The Complete Handbook for Investing in Private Businesses for Outstanding Profits 2nd ed
David Gladstone, Laura Gladstone
Harlow: Prentice Hall, 2003
304pp ISBN: 013101885X
This classic serves as a primer on venture capital investing. It outlines the key considerations for investing private capital, including an analysis of management, compensation, marketing and sales, financial statements and projections, and the production process. From due diligence and deal negotiation to the exit strategy, the author suggests a logical, step-by-step process that is filled with insights and actual examples from his experience as a venture capitalist. While most books are focused on how an entrepreneur can raise venture capital, this book provides an in-depth look at what it takes to be a successful investor in small private businesses.

Where to Go When the Bank Says No: Alternatives for Financing Your Business
David R. Evanson
Princeton, New Jersey: Bloomberg, 1998
304pp (Bloomberg Small Business Series)
ISBN: 1576600173
Practical advice for small or new businesses on raising capital is provided here by an expert in the field. He discusses the pros and cons of alternative options such as equity capital, initial public offerings (IPOs), and venture capital, and gives guidance on valuing a business and drawing up business plans and financial reports. A resources guide with contact details of organisations in the field is also included.

WEBSITES
PriceWaterhouseCoopers Moneytree Survey
www.pwcmoneytree.com
This survey, sponsored by the accounting

firm of PriceWaterhouseCoopers, provides a comprehensive list of venture capital investing in the United States by industry, stage of funding, geography, and type of financing on a quarterly basis. The report tracks venture capital firm investments and the enterprises receiving capital by region and industry.

vcapital
www.vcfodder.com
This is is an action-packed site for entrepreneurs with a distinct editorial voice. It features an 'Dr VC' feature, whereby users can ask for specific advice and encourages users to e-mail in their own stories of success and failure also.

Venture Economics
www.ventureeconomics.com
News, statistics, product information, and a glossary of terms are to be found on this site, provided by a publisher of journals and research on the venture capital industry worldwide.

ORGANISATIONS
British Business Angels Network
52–54 Southwark Street, London, SE1 1UN
T: +44 (0) 20 7089 2305
F: +44 (0) 20 7089 2301
E: liz@bbaa.org.uk
www.bbaa.org.uk
NBAN is a non-profit company sponsored by financial institutions and the Department of Trade and Industry in the United Kingdom. It provides a service linking businesses seeking equity finance with investors seeking opportunities through a network of associates across the country. A monthly bulletin of opportunities is sent to all registered investors. An online service, BestMatch, is also provided.

British Venture Capital Association
Essex House, 12–13 Essex Street, London, WC2R 3AA
T: +44 (0) 20 7025 2590
F: +44 (0) 20 7025 2951
E: bvca@bvca.co.uk
www.bvca.co.uk
The BVCA was founded in 1983 and is the representative body for the UK venture capital industry. It promotes private equity and venture capital for the benefit of entrepreneurs, investors, practitioners, and the economy as a whole. Its members are venture capital companies and professional firms involved in advising on venture capital transactions. Its wide variety of activities include training, workshops, lobbying, and research, and it produces publications.

European Private Equity and Venture Capital Association (EVCA)
Minervastraat 4, Zaventem, 1930, Belgium
T: +32 2 715 00 20
F: +32 2 725 07 04
E: evca@evca.com
www.evca.com
EVCA was founded in 1983 and now has over 850 members. Its aim is to promote and facilitate the development of the European venture capital industry through lobbying and initiatives such as conferences, training, and networking opportunities. The organisation was involved in the creation of EASD (European Association of Security Dealers) and the EASDAQ pan-European capital market.

SEE ALSO
Entrepreneurs (p. 511)

Index